International
RUGBY
Encyclopedia

Andrew de Klerk, with his almost pathological passion for rugby football, was born in 1979, and grew up in the small educational town of Grahamstown in the Eastern Cape province of South Africa where Saturday-morning rugby matches were enthusiastically attended and vociferously supported by the locals. He was educated at St Andrew's College, Graeme College and Rhodes University in Grahamstown where he obtained a BSc (Hons) in geology. His job as an environmental geologist takes him all over the world, which affords him some unique opportunities between flights to check out international rugby matches, stadia, museums, players and administrators, in his never-ending quest for the minutest detail of a perhaps long-forgotten test match. Andrew is an avid bird-watcher and loves the bush (he once spent a year as a game ranger at Mala Mala near the Kruger National Park). He takes a great interest in most ball sports and regularly plays tennis and squash. He is a member of the Geological Society of South Africa, is married, has a son, and lives in Johannesburg.

For my wife Liz and our son William,
without whom none of this would have happened

www.internationalrugby.co.za

First edition, first impression
Published in 2009 by 30° South Publishers (Pty) Ltd.
28, Ninth Street, Newlands
Johannesburg 2092, South Africa
www.30degreessouth.co.za
info@30degreessouth.co.za

Copyright © Andrew de Klerk, 2009

Design and origination by 30° South Publishers (Pty) Ltd.
Printed and bound by Pinetown Printers, Durban

ISBN 978-1920143-34-3

International
RUGBY
Encyclopedia

Andrew de Klerk

CONTENTS

Chapter Nine
Stadia

Author's notes

This book brings to the everyday rugby fan the whole story and a complete statistical compendium of international rugby since the beginning of the game's history. In-depth focus is given to each of the tier-one nations – Argentina, Australia, England, France, Ireland, Italy, New Zealand, Scotland, South Africa and Wales, with chapters on the famous combined international sides of the British & Irish Lions and Pacific Islanders, plus dedicated chapters to those tier-two and -three nations which have appeared in at least one Rugby World Cup (RWC). In 1987, the International Rugby Football Board (IRFB) staged the first RWC in New Zealand, co-hosted with Australia. Today, more than twenty years on and several World Cup tournaments later, the game of rugby union has evolved to become a very different sport. By staging a Rugby World Cup tournament, the IRFB, now the IRB, ensured that the game has become a more globally recognised sport and, indeed, many people's knowledge and interest in the game of rugby is limited to the RWC. With this in mind, this book aims to introduce to the reader rugby prior to and between RWCs.

The definition of what constitutes an international test match differ from rugby board to board. Nevertheless, *International Rugby Encyclopedia* outlines each and every test match involving all the tier-one nations since the first 'test match' was played between Scotland and England in 1871. Detailed chapters are devoted to each of these great rugby nations. Other sections focus on the history of the game since its earliest origins, international tournaments, internationally renowned rugby grounds, famous players and the scintillating matches, fascinating rugby facts and trivia, and international records. But records are there to be broken. All statistics and records in this book have been verified up to the end of the 2009 British and Irish Lions tour of South Africa (4 July 2009). However, with the book at the printers during the 2009 Tri-Nations, yet more records are currently being broken, which will be reflected in next year's edition. With the game becoming a more complete global sport over the last two decades and the gap slowly beginning to close between the top- and bottom-tier nations, future editions of this book will likely include more detailed sections on emerging nations such Fiji, Georgia, Portugal and others, with sevens and women's rugby also on the agenda. Watch this space!

A book of this nature does not come together without the collaborative efforts of a wide variety of people and organisations who have assisted in degrees, all crucial, in collating and presenting the story of international rugby through this encyclopedia. I would like to acknowledge the gracious help received from the staff of the following rugby institutions. My deepest thanks, in no special order, go to: Alan Evans of the Barbarians Football Club; Andrea Cimbrico and Yannick Skender of the Federazione Italiana Rugby; Andrés Domínguez of the Federación Española de Rugby; Ben Koteka of the Cook Islands Rugby Union; Bill McMurtrie, Jennifer Craig and Isobel Irvine of the Scottish Rugby Union; Bronwyn Wood and Sophie Erskine of the Australian Rugby Union; Kate Hutchison, Brian Finn and Charlotte Wilson of the New Zealand Rugby Union; Willow Murray and Tracey Hadnett of the Irish Rugby Football Union; Chris Fell and Stan Whitehead of the Cambridge University Rugby Union Football Club; Don Whidden, former manager of the Canadian Rugby Team; Dragan Pavlović of the Serbian Rugby Union; Inger Marie Godvin the Dansk Rugby Union; Jeremy Duxbury of Sports Communications Fiji Ltd.; John Gallard of the South African Rugby Museum; Klaus Moermann of Deutscher Rugby-Verband; Michael Rower and Lindsay Simmons of the Twickenham Rugby Museum; Marcos Servente of the Unión Argentina de Rugby; Peter Sealey of the Sussex Rugby Football Union; Sally Wright of the Oxford University Rugby Football Club; Stephen Berg of the New Zealand Rugby Museum; Sue Goodenough of the Middlesex County Rugby Football Union; Trevor Arnold of Rugby Canada; Andy Colquhoun of SA Rugby; Gwyn Dolphin and Natalie Mock of the Welsh Rugby Union and Jane Barron of the Rugby Football Union.

Others who have assisted me, not directly affiliated to a rugby union, who also deserve my special thanks, include: Frédéric Humbert, enthusiastic editor, owner and author of www.rugby-pioneers.com, who assisted me in sourcing pictures of bygone eras; Simon Hawkesley, editor, owner and author of www.richardlindon.com, who granted permission to use his unique rugby pictures at no cost; Dion Fowler of Sedley Place, London who assisted me in simplifying the design and schematic layout of a rugby field; François Ferreira, my good friend, who went out of his way to assist and provided some unique ideas from layout through to marketing while camping in Mali, meeting with me in London or exploring Serbia; the staff of the Rhodes University Library in Grahamstown, South Africa; Scott Allen, a close friend who so generously provided me with access to his personal collection of photos; Adrian van de Vyver for his great photos; Vicky Stillwell and Martin Hood for their legal advice and Craig McNaught of Gravity Media (www.gravitymedia.net.za) who freely provided his time and professional services to create the centrepiece webpage for the book at www.internationalrugby.co.za.

Photographer Thys Lombard: a huge debt of gratitude is due to you for your eleventh-hour photo-rescue mission. Thys can be contacted at thys@tokara.co.za. Another eleventh-hour photo saviour was Jacques of sarugby.org.uk who kindly stepped in to fill some of the gaps.

A massive thank-you must go to the the 30° South Publishing team. Were it not for the forethought of Chris and Kerrin Cocks this publication would not be what it is today. Their guidance, vision, patience and energy has had a profound effect on me and how this book has evolved. Through them I have learned a great deal for which I am extremely grateful. To Aulette Goliath, also at 30° South, for her exhaustive proof-reading, often with a magnifying glass scanning for wayward semicolons. To the rest of the publishing team, including overseas distributors, agents and friends – Grant 'Grunter' Robertson, Owen Early, Steve Crump and Hugh and Diana Bomford – a huge thanks for their support, enthusiasm and liaison efforts. Also to Mark Ronan whose years of experience as an editor and proof-reader have shaped the book into what it has become.

Last but not least, grateful thanks to my family who have all been involved in this project, one way or another, over the last eighteen years. To my mother Vivian who has always provided a guiding academic hand while writing and who so patiently proof-read the entire manuscript. To my father Billy who stirred my passion for the game and who took my brother Christopher and me as young kids to every one of the few high-profile rugby games that came to Port Elizabeth – you have no idea how much of an impact this had on me: watching countless rugby matches with you and Chris are fond memories and I look forward to many more. To my sister Jennifer who so proudly and vociferously plugged the manuscript-turned-book to anyone who cared to listen. To Gerry and Lizzie for adopting my passion for the game and opening so many rugby doors for me in the United Kingdom: without your home, resources and utter willingness to help, much of this would never have happened.

And finally, to my wife Liz who deserves the biggest thanks of all. Words cannot express my gratitude for the way you love me and my passion for the game. Your resolute patience, tireless encouragement and determination to make this dream come true has left an indelible mark on my life that cannot be explained other than through the way in which I love you. Thank you.

Andrew de Klerk
Johannesburg
August 2009
www.internationalrugby.co.za

◆◆◆◆◆

The rules are simple:
Pick up the ball and carry it to the other end of the field
The journey there is what makes rugby GREAT

The Barbarians: Back: W. Sugden, A. Rotherham, P.H. Hancock, C.A. Hooper, C.M. Wells, W.H. Manfield, P. Maud, R. Budworth. Middle: D.W. Evans, F.H.R. Alderson, W.P. Carpmael, S.M.J. Woods. Front: A. Allport, F.T. Aston, T.A.F. Crow, T. Parker, T.W.P. Storey. *Photo*: Commons.wikimedia.org/creative commons license

A rugby match being played on The Close at Rugby School c.1870, as published in *Harper's Weekly*.
Image: Frédéric Humbert/www.flickr.com/photos/rugby_pioneers/creative commons license

Abbreviations

ACT	Australian Capital Territories
ANC	African National Congress
ARFU	Australian Rugby Football Union
ARU	Australian Rugby Union
CBE	Commander of the Order of The British Empire
CRFU	Canadian Rugby Football Union
CRU	Canadian Rugby Union
CVO	Commander of The Royal Victorian Order
DCNZM	Distinguished Companion of The New Zealand Order of Merit
DRSU	Durban Rugby Sub Union
ELVs	Experimental Law Variations
EPRFU	Eastern Province Rugby Football Union
FA	Football Association
FFR	Fédération Française de Rugby (French Rugby Federation)
FIFA	Fédération Internationale de Football Association
FIRA	Fédération Internationale de Rugby Amateur (Federation of International Amateur Rugby)
FRR	Federaţia Română de Rugby (Romanian Rugby Federation)
GAA	Gaelic Athletic Association
GWRFU	Griqualand West Rugby Football Union
IB	International Board
IFU	Irish Football Union
IOC	International Olympic Committee
IOCC	International Olympic Committee Congress
IRA	Irish Republican Army
IRB	International Rugby Board
IRFB	International Rugby Football Board
IRFU	Irish Rugby Football Union
KNZM	Knight Companion of The New Zealand Order of Merit
MBA	Master of Business Administration
MBE	Member of The British Empire
MNZM	Member of The New Zealand Order of Merit
NSW	New South Wales
NZ	New Zealand
NZRFU	New Zealand Rugby Football Union
NZRU	New Zealand Rugby Union
NRU	Natal Rugby Union
OBE	Order of The British Empire
ONZ	Order of New Zealand
ONZM	Officer of The New Zealand Order of Merit
QRL	Queensland Rugby League
QRU	Queensland Rugby Union
RAF	Royal Air Force
RBS	Royal Bank of Scotland
RFC	Rugby Football Club
RFU	Rugby Football Union
RU	Rugby Union
RWC	Rugby World Cup
SA	South Africa
SAA	South African Airways
SAARB	South African African Rugby Board
SACOS	South African Council on Sport
SANZAR	South African, New Zealand, Australian Rugby Union
SARA	South African Rugby Association
SARB	South African Rugby Board
SARF	South African Rugby Federation
SARFU	South African Rugby Football Union
SARU	South African Rugby Union
SCG	Sydney Cricket Ground
SFU	Scottish Football Union
SRFU	Scottish Rugby Football Union
SRU	Scottish Rugby Union
SWA	South West Africa
TMO	Television Match Official
TRFU	Transvaal Rugby Football Union; Tongan Rugby Football Union
WPRFU	Western Province Rugby Football Union
UAR	Unión Argentina de Rugby
URU	Uruguay Rugby Union
WRFU	Welsh Rugby Football Union
WRU	Welsh Rugby Union

Chapter One
The history of rugby

Early days

It is possible to trace the origins of this famous game back by almost 2,000 years to an age when 'sports' similar to both modern-day soccer and rugby existed. Centuries before William Webb Ellis first picked up the ball and ran with it at Rugby School, there are records of ancient Romans garrisoned in Scotland playing a sport called *harpastum*, which involved two teams who ran, passed and threw a small round ball with the aim of crossing the opponents' line at the far end of a rectangular field.

In the Middle Ages, village games revolved around a stuffed animal stomach, often with huge crowds of players taking part, wrestling, shoving and kicking in their objective to get the 'ball' from one side of a village to the other. Few rules, it would seem, existed and any number of players could join in. Such games were traditionally played in the Border towns of Scotland, where two villages would compete, often taking hours to finish. Records of these medieval games have been preserved through the ages and from these it is clear that the authorities of the era did not approve of such antics and regarded them as a public nuisance, with violence, vandalism and looting often perpetrated by the heaving masses of players (has much changed?). Records from 1424 indicate that due to the chaos and disorder that characterised this form of 15th-century football, England, Scotland and France all passed laws banning the 'sport'. Among the reasons cited for the prohibition were injuries caused to players, interrupted Sunday worship and because the games distracted men from the important practice of archery – vital to the defence of the country before the invention of gunpowder. Despite being outlawed, sport nevertheless survived simply because men enjoyed playing the sport.

It was in the nineteenth century that football began to transform into a more 'orderly affair' within the English public schools as a recreation for boys when not studying. Matches were internal contests and all boys attending the school were expected to play in teams randomly composed of boys of all ages and statures. This was the spirit of *mens sana in corpore sano* (a healthy mind in a healthy body) – which embodied the British public-school ethos. With no formal rules for football, the organisation, structure and rules required for a particular match were decided upon either prior to, or even during the game, with no supervision by the schoolmasters and no referee. When the boys moved on from school to university or a career, many wanted to continue playing the sport. A sporting periodical catering for the upper and middle classes of the time explains why: 'Surely nothing could be better than football in October, an otherwise dull time of the year for all except hunting men.'

Within this public-school context, the legend of the birth of rugby emanates from Rugby School in the English Midlands. In 1823, there were relatively few senior boys at Rugby School and one seemingly rather unpopular boy took advantage of the situation to put his mark on the game of football played at the time. He quite simply cheated – and was big enough to get away with it. His name was William Webb Ellis and he did the unthinkable by picking up the football and running with it to score a goal. The sole existing source of this famous story is a certain Mr Matthew Bloxam (a local antiquarian and former Rugby pupil), who, in October 1876, wrote to *The Meteor* – the Rugby School magazine – that he had learned from an unnamed source that the transition from a kicking game to a handling game had '. . . originated with a town boy, or foundationer, of the name of Ellis, William Webb Ellis'. A commemorative plaque outside Rugby School today records William Webb Ellis's actions in a rather positive light, considering the likely events that actually took place:

> 'William Webb Ellis, who with a fine disregard for the rules of football as played in his time, first took the ball in his arms and ran with it, thus originating the distinctive feature of the rugby game.'

Despite these records, no one actually knows for certain if this story involving William Webb Ellis's school-game misdemeanour is in fact true. It first came to be told later in the nineteenth century, when former pupils of Rugby School tried researching the origins of the game. By then few of Webb Ellis's classmates were still alive and Webb Ellis himself had died in 1872 and been buried in Menton, southern France. The myth of the William Webb Ellis story was first used to promote the game of rugby union at the end of the nineteenth century when the game was under pressure from the breakaway rugby league. But what is a known fact is that by 1845,

The statue portraying William Webb Ellis running with ball in hand, in front of Rugby School, England. *Photo*: Andrew de Klerk

Right: The William Webb Ellis plaque at The Close at Rugby School, commemorating his 'fine disregards for the rules of football'. *Photo*: Andrew de Klerk

THIS STONE COMMEMORATES THE EXPLOIT OF **WILLIAM WEBB ELLIS** WHO WITH A FINE DISREGARD FOR THE RULES OF FOOTBALL AS PLAYED IN HIS TIME FIRST TOOK THE BALL IN HIS ARMS AND RAN WITH IT THUS ORIGINATING THE DISTINCTIVE FEATURE OF THE RUGBY GAME. A D 1823

running with the ball in hand was accepted in the first written set of laws produced by the pupils of Rugby School. These rules stipulated that running with the ball was only allowed provided the ball had been caught from a kick or while bouncing; it was illegal to pick up a rolling or stationary ball. One can only surmise the chaos resulting from such an interpretable rule. By the time this first set of rules had been written, the game of rugby had begun to spread across the country, promoted by Rugby School pupils and masters.

The first attempt at forming a rugby club was when a certain Arthur Pell attempted to establish one at Cambridge University in 1839. His attempts did not succeed because would-be members, who had played the game according to different sets of rules at their various schools, could not agree on an accepted set of rules and for this very reason the idea was abandoned. Shortly after this initial setback, however, rugby clubs overcame this technical obstacle and slowly began to spring up. In 1843, the Guy's Hospital club in London was the first to be formed. The next was founded 11 years later in 1854 when the Dublin University Rugby Football Club was formed, which is today the official rugby club of Trinity College in Dublin. With a limited number of clubs, the first matches were internal, contested by teams from among a club's membership. During the second half of the nineteenth century, with the British Empire at its height, rugby spread across the globe with the help of the old boys of Rugby School and others who knew the game – often members of the Queen's forces. In these early days, the game was referred to as 'that game played at Rugby' or 'Rugby's game'. Later it was simplified to 'rugby'.

The first rugby match played in South Africa took place in 1862 between Civilians and Military. In Australia the first recorded match was between Sydney Football Club and Sydney University in 1865. Farther south, the first match to be played in New Zealand was in 1870 between the Nelson Football Club and Nelson College. By this time, rugby had become increasingly popular in the United Kingdom and Ireland and the first international match was played between Scotland and England in 1871.

From this point, it is difficult to summarise the growth of the game, as its popularity grew exponentially. Soon after the first international 'test' in 1871, the other home rugby unions of Wales and Ireland, made their international debuts, while the first overseas tour took place when New South Wales toured New Zealand in 1882. The first overseas international tour took place between South Africa and the British Isles in 1891 and by 1906, all the traditional top eight nations had played international rugby – the last being France. The first established international competition was called the Home Nations Championship (sometimes referred to as the Four Nations Tournament), involving England, Scotland, Wales and Ireland, which had its debut in 1883. It was later expanded to become the Five Nations when France joined in 1910 and is today known as the RBS Six Nations Tournament after Italy joined in 2000. Much emphasis was placed on tours in these early days – especially by southern-hemisphere nations. Due to the notoriously hard-nosed attitude of the IRFB, it was not until 1987 that the first Rugby World Cup (RWC) was staged and, with the advent of professionalism, the first Tri-Nations Tournament was contested in 1996 between South Africa, New Zealand and Australia.

How the game evolved

In its infant years, rugby bore little resemblance to the game we know today and was perhaps more like a game of soccer – a player running with the ball would have been a rare sight, even less so passing the ball from hand to hand. Teams were made up of 20 players who ran as a tightly grouped mass, kicking the ball forward toward the opposition line. Large masses of up to 30 players would form a scrum – the principal feature of the game – which could last for several minutes as they kicked the ball forward through the scrum while attempting to heave forward. The remaining ten players essentially formed the then primitive backline. In these scrums, players were encouraged to kick the opposition's shins in an attempt to force them out of the way – a practice known as 'hacking', which was eventually banned in 1871 along with the tactic of 'hacking over' (the action of tripping a running player, which would today earn you a yellow card). One can only begin to imagine with horror the plethora of injuries incurred from such tactics. With these bans the early rugby traditionalists had already started complaining that the game was becoming too soft. (What would they say about today's rugby rules?) Each team had a set of halfbacks around the fringe of this massive maul of players who snapped up any loose balls, as well as some deeper three-quarters and fullbacks whose sole aim it was to field deep balls, kick and tackle. Passing in these early days was looked down upon and booed by the crowd as it was deemed a cowardly move.

In 1875, in the annual varsity match between Oxford and Cambridge, the numbers in each team were reduced to 15 for the first time. It became apparent that fewer players would make for a more skilful, open and entertaining game, but it was not until 1877 that the first 15-a-side international was held, when England played Ireland in London and it was only in 1892 that it became written into rugby law that all teams should have 15 players. Fewer players in the team meant fewer players in a scrum, resulting in an organised structure in the scrum and players began pushing with the head down instead of in the old upright position. Scottish clubs began to put more emphasis on providing the backs with greater possession and encouraged passing between players, thereby creating a more open game, a tactic that was slowly adopted by other clubs and unions.

Teams were split into forwards and backs, originally with six backs (made up of two halfbacks, three three-quarters and one fullback) and nine forwards who had little structure, simply packing down into a scrum in an order depending on who arrived at the scrum position first, following the rule, 'first up, first down'. Wales can lay claim to being the first nation to play with the formation of seven backs and eight forwards at Cardiff Club in 1884. This system was generally accepted across the United Kingdom during the 1890s and by the beginning of the twentieth century rehearsed backline moves were commonly used. It was not until 1905, however, that specialist forward positions were conceptualised – initially by Guy's Hospital Club, whose numbers were then made up predominantly of burly South Africans living in London. To get the most out of these heavy forwards and ensure forward domination in a match, the club allotted forwards to specific positions in the scrum depending on a player's bulk. Hookers and back rows were the first to be specialised and by the 1960s, the front row had evolved into specialist positions where size was no longer the only aspect that mattered – scrumming technique and strength proving the critical scrummaging criteria. The scrum structure of 3-2-3 was used until the 1920s, when the South

African's first began using the 3-4-1 formation which is still used today. However, New Zealand remained steadfast and refused to adopt this structure until they were forced to do so following the 1930 British Lions tour to New Zealand, when it was written into law that the front row had to be composed of three players. The excuse used by New Zealand following their 1937 home-series defeat to South Africa was that this 'significantly affected' their competitiveness in the scrum, as they preferred to operate with a seven-man scrum which had two front-row forwards. In this instance the eighth remaining forward acted as a 'rover' at the back who essentially played between the eighthman and the scrumhalf and whose role was to harass the opposition scrumhalf at scrum time.

Throughout these formative years, however, rugby remained a sport that centred around the ability to kick the ball to gain territory, with games often becoming tedious affairs. Indeed, in the 1963 Wales vs Scotland international in Edinburgh, an undeniably dour match was played. With the focus on tactical kicking, a record 111 lineouts were notched up! In an attempt to limit the kicking and keep the ball more in play, the rule of kicking the ball directly into touch was altered in 1970 to allow this to occur only when kicking from behind the 22-metre line (the 25-yard line at the time). This rule has further evolved since the 1970 rule, whereby players were initially allowed to run backward over the 22-metre line to kick the ball out. Under today's rules a player has to field the ball directly from behind the 22-metre line. The rule was again altered with the Experimental Law Variations (ELVs) adopted in the 2008 Super 14 tournament (written into the IRB, International Rugby Board, laws in 2009), which further limits a player's ability to kick the ball directly out – he may only do this when receiving the ball in his own 22 from the opposition. This has allowed the fullback to become more involved in attacking play and less tied up in fielding kicks. These changes have successfully resulted in a more entertaining game, with the ball being kicked less and consequently more emphasis placed on passing and running skills.

Development of the scoring system

In the early game, the purpose of crossing the opposing side's (try) line was solely to win an attempt at kicking a goal over the posts. If the attempted goal was missed, no score was awarded – not even for crossing the opponent's line. This was known as a 'try at goal', hence the contracted term, 'try', to describe the action of grounding the ball behind the opponent's goal line. The try at goal was a place kick and not a drop kick. Inevitably, however, given the monumental effort involved in attempting to cross the opponent's line, which added nothing to the score – and was in vain if the goal was missed – this method of scoring displeased and frustrated many involved in the game. The scoring system of rugby has evolved considerably over the game's history, with the first standard points system being adopted in 1886 when the IRFB first devised the scheme. Prior to this, scoring had varied from union to union and even from club to club. The following is a summarised timeline of the history of scoring in rugby union:

- 1838 to 1839: 'running in' (a try in modern terminology) becomes an accepted term and feature of the Rugby School game.
- June 1871: the first English Rugby Football Union (RFU) scoring laws state that 'a match shall be decided by a majority of goals only'.
- March 1875: the first points-scoring system was rejected by the RFU, as was a proposal that three tries should be equivalent to one goal.
- November 1875: the first emphasis was given to the

Did you know: Why is it called a try? During the very early years of rugby, a try was called a 'touch-down', 'try-at-goal' or 'rouge'. It later came to be known as a try because during these early days, the sole aim was to be able to attempt to kick between the posts at goal and thereby score points. In the event of a team touching the ball down over the opponent's line they were then awarded a 'try' at kicking a goal.

Did you know: In the early days, the goalposts had no crossbar and one simply had to kick the ball through the posts at any height to score a goal. However, there was no rule on how many 'goalies' a team was allowed and more often than not the entire team would crowd in front of the goals, making goal-scoring nigh impossible. So to make scoring easier, posts were extended to 18 feet with a crossbar installed at ten feet and players had to kick the ball over the crossbar to score a goal.

Did you know: The tallest rugby posts in the world are at Wednesbury Rugby Club's ground in the West Midlands, England, measuring 38.26 metres in height – a full 35.26m above the minimum IRB-specified height of 3m!

importance of scoring a try when it was decreed: 'A match shall be decided by a majority of goals, but if the number of goals is equal or no goals kicked, by a majority of tries. When a goal has been kicked from a try only the goal is scored.' (RFU, 1875)

- In 1881 and 1882, the RFU rejected proposals for a points-based scoring system.
- By 1886, a model favoured at Cheltenham College in Gloucestershire, England, was adopted by the RFU, which stated:

> 'A match shall be decided by a majority of points, a goal shall equal three points, and a try one point. If the number of points be equal, or no goal kicked or try obtained, the match shall be drawn. Where a goal is kicked from a try the goal only is scored.'

- In the period from 1875 to 1890, chaos in the scoring system existed as individual countries each developed their own points-scoring systems. Some of these systems even gave the attacking team a point or half a point when they forced the defending team to touch down behind their own line. Bringing unity to the scoring system was one of the major tasks of the International Rugby Football Board (IRFB) when England joined in 1890. This was a slow and difficult task.
- Penalty kicks did not exist, as players were expected to play in a sporting spirit. In the event of a game being stopped due to illegality then it would simply resume with a scrummage. Penalties were first introduced for deliberate infringements in 1882, but goals could not be kicked from them. This changed shortly after.
- In October 1886, the RFU introduced scoring by points, adopting the Cheltenham College system.
- In October 1888, a 'fair catch' or 'mark' was introduced – essentially a second type of goal of less value. This new law stated: 'A goal shall equal three points, with the exception of a goal kicked from a kick awarded by way of penalty, which shall equal two points, and a try one point.'
- By September 1891, the IRFB finally became responsible for the scoring system which they had devised and had been agreed upon by all. It read as follows: 'A match shall be decided by a majority of points. A try shall equal two points, a penalty goal three points, a goal from a try (the try not also to count) five points. Any other goal shall equal four points. If the number of points is equal or no goal is kicked or try obtained, the match shall be drawn.'
- March 1893: the RFU and WRU raised the value of a try from two to three points, with the value of the conversion changed from three to two, meaning that the value of a converted try remained five points, but importantly, for the first time, more value was assigned to scoring a try. The IRFB adopted this scheme the following year.
- March 1905: the option of scoring a field goal was abolished. A field goal was scored when the ball was kicked between the posts during open play. 'A try equals three points. A goal from a try (in which case the try shall not count) equals five points. A dropped goal (except from a mark or penalty kick) equals four points. A goal from a mark or penalty kick equals three points.'
- March 1948: the value of a dropped goal was reduced to three points.
- 1971: the value of a try was increased to four points, placing more emphasis on try-scoring.
- 1977: the option of scoring a goal from a mark was abolished and the free-kick clause introduced.
- 1992: the value of the try was increased to five points to emphasise the importance of scoring a try and to promote a more entertaining brand of rugby. In addition, several rugby tournaments around the world adopted the bonus- or log-point system to promote try-scoring. This was first introduced during the 1996 Super 12 tournament where an additional log point was awarded to any side that scored four tries or more in a match. The RWC has since adopted this system.

An accurate and complete timeline of rugby union's scoring system from the beginning of the game is difficult to compile, bearing in mind that each home union originally had its own laws and scoring systems. However, during this time the RFU laws and scoring systems were generally adopted – summarised in the table below. Only from 1891 was the IRFB's scoring system for internationals used, and this was not formally adopted for non-international games until 1930. In the table the points for a try/conversion are shown as cumulative. Strictly speaking, separate points for a goal after a try was scored was not introduced by the IRFB until 1979. Prior to this, a goal (conversion) from a try overrode any points awarded for the try itself. Effectively, this meant that before the 1979 ruling, if a try was scored three/four were awarded, but if a goal was converted from this try then five/six points were awarded for the goal and the three/four points from the try were nullified. Confusing?

Points for different scoring methods					
Northern-hemisphere season	Try	Conversion	Penalty	Drop goal	Goal from a mark
1886–87 to 1887–88	1	2	-	3	-
1888–89 to 1890–91	1	2	2	3	-
1891–92 to 1892–93	2	3	3	4	4
1893–94 to 1904–05	3	2	3	4	4
1905–06 to 1947–48	3	2	3	4	3
1948–49 to 1970–71	3	2	3	3	3
1971–72 to 1977–78	4	2	3	3	3
1977–78 to 1991–92	4	2	3	3	-
1992–93 to present day	5	2	3	3	-

Did you know: In 1875 scoring regulations were so harsh in New Zealand that if a defending team were to 'touch down' behind their own line, the attacking team would be awarded a 'force-down', which was valued at half a point. Otago beat Auckland under this system by a scoreline of 9½ –½.

The first laws

At Rugby School games were played on a large field, known as The Close where, today, the plaque commemorating Webb Ellis's antics is erected. It was here that the boys would gather, discuss the rules of the game they had just played and decide what changes needed to be made. This eventually led to the first set of written rules for rugby union. Interestingly, early laws of the game at Rugby School during the 1820s initially forbade the handling of the ball on the field of play unless the ball was in the air, in which case it could be caught, upon which the catcher and all other players had to stand still. The catcher could then retreat from where he had caught the ball and either kick it wherever he wished or place it on the ground and attempt to kick a goal. It was not permitted, however, to run with the ball, and until the catcher had passed the spot from where he had originally caught the ball no one could move. This rule slowly changed and the catcher was allowed to run with the ball toward the opponent's goal line and by the 1840s, this had become the norm.

Most public schools of the time, however, played some sort of kicking game, following their own house rules which were influenced by the size of the field and the number of students available to play. Teams could be enormous and often with uneven numbers, with accounts existing of 60 playing against 200. Early rules were few and variable and it was often hard to tell the difference between players and spectators, with little emphasis on making games fair or sides equal. In 1839, Albert Pell, an old boy of Rugby School, organised a series of 'football' matches at Cambridge University, but all who competed played by the rules of their old schools. Needless to say, this caused huge confusion so, to compromise, a set of rules was produced by which everyone could play. This was the first attempt in rugby's history to form one set of rules, which would eventually lead to the publication of the Cambridge Rules. In 1841, running with the ball was formally accepted by Rugby School and players could run forward before kicking the ball (an action previously deemed as cheating). Once running forward became the norm, so tackling or 'hacking' became acceptable.

On 25 August 1845, three senior pupils from Rugby School – William Delafield Arnold, W.W. Shirley and Frederick Hutchins – none of whom were older than 17, were tasked with writing the first set of rules for the game. Three days later, they submitted a total of 37 rules, which were passed by the school and the first rules ever written for any form of football were printed. In 1862, a revised edition of the laws was released by Rugby School. Some of the basic fundamentals of these laws still apply to today's modern game. For example:

FLOREAT RUGBEIA.

H. J. LINDON,

FOOTBALL MANUFACTURER,

(Successor to the late R. Lindon,)

6, LAWRENCE SHERIFFE STREET, RUGBY,

INVENTOR OF THE

TRUE RUGBY BALL,

ALSO

INFLATOR FOR THE SAME,

Which has caused the Game to become so universal.

Makers, in succession, for the last 40 years,

OF THE

BIG-SIDE MATCH BALLS

For RUGBY SCHOOL.

A TRIAL SOLICITED.

An advertisement placed in the 1890 IRFB Rules Book for Lindon's rugby balls which clearly indicates Lindon's involvement in the invention of the ball.
Photo: Simon Hawkesley, www.richardlindon.com

'A player is offside when the ball has been kicked, or thrown, or knocked on, or is being run with by any one on his own side behind him. A player entering a scrummage on the wrong side is off his side . . . though it is lawful to hold any player in a maul, this holding does not include attempts to throttle, or strangle, which are totally opposed to all the principles of the game.'

In 1863, the Cambridge Rules, as they are known and first agreed upon in 1839, were published, and essentially represented an amalgamation of the various forms of football played across the country. The core element of the Cambridge Rules, which makes rugby distinctive and which of course still applies today, is that the ball can only be passed backward – a rule which distinguishes American football from rugby (to which it owes its origins – American football was formed in 1906 when the backward-pass rule was dropped).

Over the next century, the laws of rugby were tweaked and changed, with the result that, with time, the game has gradually become faster and more entertaining. Scores have also become higher. In recent times, much effort has also been devoted to making the game cleaner, to remove the thuggery which has become so synonymous with rugby. The system of yellow and red cards, as used in soccer, was adopted to impose bans on players found guilty of deliberate dirty play, which also facilitated better control of the game. Yellow and red cards were first used in association football at the 1970 World Cup in Mexico and the same system was adopted in rugby union in 2000 – a player shown a yellow card is suspended from the game for ten minutes, while the red card is shown for an offence that merits a permanent send-off. Prior to 2000, a player shown a yellow card could remain on the field (as in soccer).

With the increasing importance of television and the development of technology, a television match official (TMO) was first utilised in an international during the two-test series between South Africa and England in 2000. The TMO's role is to ensure that decisions involving try scoring that are difficult to adjudicate by the referee are made through the use of a third party. The TMO has the option of watching several replays of the action from different camera angles before giving a decision to the on-field referee. Surprisingly, despite all the slow-motion replays, the TMO's decision can still be incorrect.

The ELVs were adopted in the 2008 southern-hemisphere season. Once again, these were designed to encourage a faster, more entertaining game, for example by awarding a free kick instead of a penalty kick in many cases. In addition, the use of the TMO was experimentally extended in South Africa's 2008 Currie Cup provincial tournament to include referrals for acts of foul play or other infringements not picked up by the referee. It must be conceded that this experiment was a failure and became a farce: matches were extended by up to 30 minutes and ludicrous referrals were demanded of the TMO from several phases back in play. As André Watson (head of South Africa's refereeing association) stated, the game does not need expert TMOs and average on-field referees.

Most recently, in 2008 an experiment known as the white card was tested in the final of a domestic tournament in South Africa. Each captain was granted one white card per half which he could use to lawfully query a referee's decision, which would then be referred to the TMO for assessment. The white-card experiment proved successful and perhaps deserves a permanent place in the game. But it certainly needs some refining before being brought to the professional circuit.

> **Did you know:** 'Half time'. On 16 November 1867, Rugby School played its first 'foreign' match, a 20-a-side affair against A.C. Harrison Esq.'s on The Close at Rugby School. It was a match played in blustery conditions with a strong southwesterly wind blowing across the length of the field. Due to the strength of the wind it was agreed between the two captains to change ends after 30 minutes to allow each team an equal share of the wind. Half-time was thus born, with the players taking a brief rest before changing ends.

Referees

During the early years of rugby, referees were not part of a match, with the rules and decisions made by the captains of the competing teams. The captains would discuss and agree upon a set of rules prior to a match and would together rule on any contentious issues that occurred during the match. However, the two captains were often unable to agree on an issue and so two umpires were introduced, whose role was solely to decide these issues of contention. Inevitably these umpires were unable to agree upon issues themselves and they were often accused of bias. To solve this problem, a referee was introduced to decide upon those issues that the two captains could not resolve and which the two umpires could not agree upon. This confusing system of policing was quickly resolved when the referee was finally given the sole right to make his own decisions from the outset, with the original two umpires relegated to become line umpires. Subsequently, their name was changed, first to 'touch judge' and today as 'assistant referee'.

At the time of the first international in 1871, two umpires controlled the game, with a referee only being introduced in 1876. The referee was gradually granted full authority over internationals during the period from 1891 to 1906. Referees first used whistles in 1885 and umpires were given sticks, which were later replaced with flags. The first neutral referee was appointed for the England–Scotland international in 1882, which ironically coincided with the first-ever away win – Scotland beat England in Manchester. Neutral referees were common from this date on in the Home Nations Championship and Five Nations Tournament, but were unheard of in the southern hemisphere, mainly because of travel constraints. Complaints of biased refereeing by the touring side were lodged during virtually every tour in the southern hemisphere. Take the example of South Africa's tour to Australia in 1965 when Australian referees, Kevin Crowe and Craig Ferguson, notoriously officiated in the most biased display of refereeing ever seen. It was not until June 1975, when Scot Norman Sanson refereed South Africa–France in Bloemfontein, that the first neutral referee officiated in an international in the southern hemisphere. Neutral referees of internationals are now an accepted norm. Jonathan Kaplan of South Africa broke the trend, however, in August 2007 when he was appointed to referee the international between South Africa and Namibia in Cape Town.

All Black loose forward Cyril Brownlie becomes the first player to be sent off in an international. Welsh referee Albert Freethy gives him his marching orders early in the 1925 international against England at Twickenham. Despite being reduced to 14 men New Zealand went on to win the match 17-11.
Photo: New Zealand Rugby Museum

The ball

The first footballs used in the early days of rugby and football alike were pigs' bladders inflated by human lung power and knotted at the end to form a pear-shaped balloon. This delicate ball, however, was prone to burst as it was ruggedly kicked about and so a leather casing was introduced to protect it, which replicated the pear shape of the bladder. These early balls were neither round (like soccer balls) nor spheroidal (like modern rugby balls). Until the 1860s, both rugby and soccer were played with these pear-shaped balls whose size depended on the size of the bladder. The rugby ball as we know it today owes its origins to Richard Lindon, who grew up in the town of Rugby during the early 1800s. He invented the inflatable bladder and a brass handpump specially designed to inflate it. As a young boy, Lindon was an apprentice to the shoemaker William Gilbert at his workshop next door to his father's business and would later transfer the skills that he learned from Gilbert into history. Lindon took over his father's business, also a shoemaker, and developed it into making balls for the boys of Rugby School – a burgeoning business at the time. Inflating the bladders, unsurprisingly, was an unsought-after job, as it had to be performed while the bladder was still fresh and soft and in a 'very smelly green state' (http://www.rugbyfootballhistory.com). Amazingly, it was Lindon's wife who inflated the balls herself – a hazardous career, as this part of a diseased pig could transmit infection to the inflator. And indeed, when Mrs Lindon had blown up one too many bladders, she contracted a lung disease that ultimately led to her death.

Richard Lindon, the man who designed and invented the original rugby ball for Rugby School, displays a brace of four-panelled Big-side Match 'Buttonless Balls', 1880. Lindon revolutionised the industry when he invented the inflatable bladder and brass handpump.
Photo: Simon Hawkesley, www.richardlindon.com

By the 1850s, both William Gilbert and Richard Lindon were the main suppliers of pigs' bladders and leather-clad balls. With the death of his wife, Lindon sought a safer alternative to pigs' bladders, resulting in a change of the manufacture of rugby balls. In 1862, he overtook Gilbert as the leading supplier by introducing India rubber inner tubes. This pliable rubber ball could be made to any required shape. The rubber inner tube was inflated with a brass handpump, which had started out as a simple brass syringe. With this invention, Rugby School requested that their balls be distinguishable from other schools' balls and opted for an 'exaggerated egg', or oval shape, to distinguish their hand-and-foot game from soccer. Lindon created a ball that could take and retain this shape. For the first time, a template for the leather-casing panels was designed and the balls replicated to exacting standards. So it is Richard Lindon, maker of 'Rugby School's Big-Side Match Balls', was the founding father of the original oval rugby ball. In 1892, the RFU endorsed Lindon's oval-shaped ball as compulsory, with the following dimensions written into law:

- Length: 11 to 11¼ inches
- Circumference (end on): 30 to 31 inches
- Circumference (in width): 25½ to 26 inches
- Weight: 12 to 13 ounces
- Hand-sewn with not less than eight stitches to the inch

These dimensions evolved over time, resulting in the ball becoming more oblong. In 2004, the IRB Rugby Laws stipulated the following:

- The ball must be oval and made of four panels
- Length in line: 280–300mm
- Circumference (end to end): 740–770mm
- Circumference (in width): 580–620mm
- Material: leather or suitable synthetic material, which may be treated to make it water-resistant and easier to grip
- Weight: 410–460g
- Air pressure at start of play: 65.71–68.75 kilopascals, or 0.67–0.70 kilograms per square centimetre, or 9.5–10.0 lbs per square inch

Sadly for Richard Lindon, he never patented his ball, bladder or pump. Instead it was the man next door for whom he had once worked as a young boy in the 1840s, William Gilbert, who went on to have his name written into rugby history. It is thanks to the efforts of

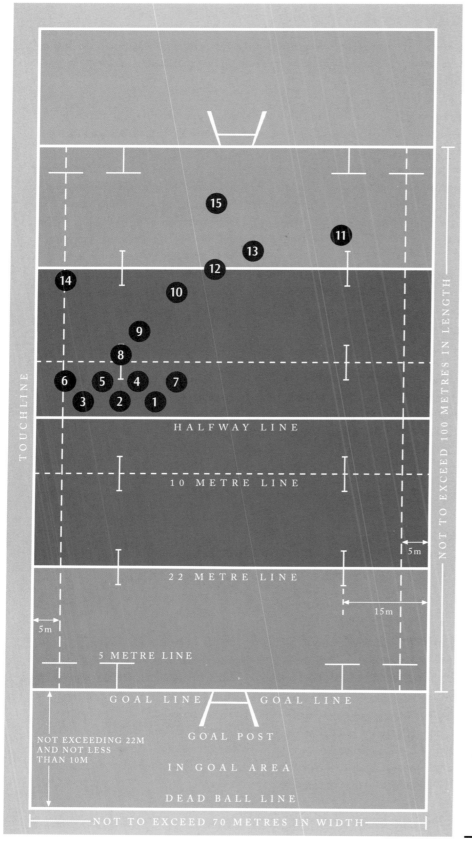

IRB field dimensions and team positions

1. Loosehead prop
2. Hooker
3. Tighthead prop
4. Loosehead lock
5. Tighthead lock
6. Blindside flank
7. Openside flank
8. Eighthman
9. Scrumhalf
10. Flyhalf
11. Left wing
12. Inside centre
13. Outside centre
14. Right wing
15. Fullback

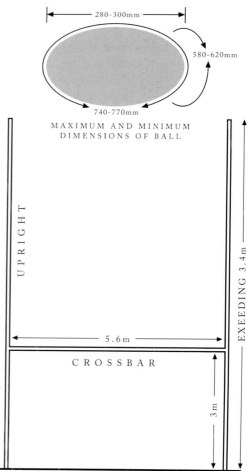

280-300mm

580-620mm

740-770mm

MAXIMUM AND MINIMUM
DIMENSIONS OF BALL

UPRIGHT

EXEEDING 3.4m

5.6m

CROSSBAR

3 m

Gilbert's great-nephew, James John Gilbert (the last Gilbert to run the company) that the family tradition made the name Gilbert synonymous with rugby and rugby balls today. He personally checked and stamped each and every match ball and made great efforts in getting the Gilbert ball exported to New Zealand, South Africa and Australia.

However, without an international agreement on the dimensions of the ball, each nation had its own preference on the design. Australia and New Zealand favoured the pointed shape and South Africa the eight-panel ball which offered better grip. In the United Kingdom and Ireland the four-panel ball was favoured. The Gilbert match ball predominantly remained the ball of choice through the early years of the game, but with the new synthetic balls being favoured from the 1970s, Gilbert struggled to compete and eventually sold the business in 1978. Nonetheless, several subsequent owners of the Gilbert Company managed to compete with new technologies and have developed a new ball for every RWC since 1995. In 2002, Grays of Cambridge bought Gilbert and returned it to its original headquarters in Rugby – although Gilbert is no longer an independent company, the name is maintained by Grays as a strong, traditional brand. Since the 2003 RWC, all major rugby-playing nations have given their allegiance to Gilbert's balls, including New Zealand, the last to do so, but they did lay informal complaints about the ball during practice sessions at the 2007 RWC. Questions were raised after star kickers, such as Daniel Carter, Stirling Mortlock and Jonny Wilkinson, missed numerous kicks at goal. However, it was found the ball was no different to any other previously used, and it was concluded that 'any perceived difference reported can only be explained by incorrect inflation and natural wear and tear' (http://www.rugbyfootballhistory.com/ball.htm). The ball has become flatter in shape as the game has evolved. By the 1970s, the traditional leather-encased ball had been replaced with synthetic waterproof casings – although this was not completely accepted until 1997, when France finally ceased using leather balls in internationals.

Player positions

Nomenclature for player positions differs across the world and has changed through the ages. The diagram on the previous page shows the positions as they occur on a rugby field. Player numbers 1–8 are known as the forwards (sometimes referred to as the pack); players 1–5 are further known as the tight five (or front five); players 1–3 are the front row; 6–8 are the loose forwards (or back row) and 9–15 are the backs. New Zealand, Britain and Ireland quite often use the older-fashioned variations as below:

Standard IRB	Variations
lock	second row
flank	flanker, wing forward, breakaway
scrumhalf	halfback, inside half
flyhalf	outside half, out half, stand-off, five-eighth, first five-eighth, first five
inside centre	second five-eighth
outside centre	centre three-quarter
wing	winger, wing three-quarter

Professionalism

On 26 August 1995, on the completion of the third RWC and after many years of revision to the amateur regulations of the game, the IRFB concluded that the only way to keep control of rugby was to declare the game 'open'. The commercial success of the 1995 RWC in South Africa ensured that the game finally bowed to the inevitable and turned professional, with no restrictions on payments or benefits to those connected to rugby union. The game's traditionalists resisted this as far as they could, claiming the game would be destroyed by the introduction of money. The reality was that this had been the case for at least the preceding ten years, with players receiving underhand payments and favours in return for playing the game. The hypocrisy and deceit in rugby over the previous decade was becoming ludicrous and it was time to bring commercialisation into the open and make it acceptable. The fears of the pro-amateur traditionalists have proved unfounded. Indeed, the international game has gone from strength to strength and each RWC and Lions tour to the southern hemisphere has become bigger and more successful than the previous.

Chapter Two
International rugby tournaments

Six Nations Championship

History

The Six Nations Championship has had a rich and sometimes turbulent history and remains one of the great festivals of sport to this day. The Six Nations retains an aura similar to that of the Lions tours and RWCs. Of all the international rugby tournaments played across the world, the Six Nations Championship is the oldest; today contested by England, Ireland, Scotland, Wales, France and Italy. Its name has changed over the years as teams have joined and left the championship. It was previously known as the Five Nations Championship (France being the fifth nation when they joined in 1910) and before that it was known as the Home Nations Championship. The following is a timeline of the Six Nations:

- 1883–1909   Home Nations Championship
- 1910–1931   Five Nations Championship (upon France joining)
- 1932–1939   Home Nations Championship (following France's expulsion)
- 1940–1999   Five Nations Championship (upon France rejoining)
- 2000 to present   Six Nations Championship (upon Italy joining)

There was no formal name for the championship in its early years. In fact, amateur rugby purists insist that such a thing as the Five Nations Championship has never existed and claim that it was merely a coincidence that these five nations had played rugby friendlies against one another for over a hundred years and that there has never been any formal tournament format – a bizarre suggestion! Other titles for the early form of the championship included the Four Nations Championship, the Triple Crown Championship or simply the International Championship.

The Five Nations Championship never had a winner's trophy to play for, as it was not really regarded as an official tournament, since each team played for the honour of simply winning these 'friendlies'. The idea of awarding a trophy to the winning team was first mooted by the Earl of Westmorland and in 1993, a trophy was first awarded to the victorious team, France – the same year that the points-difference scheme was introduced to help split shared titles. The RBS (Royal Bank of Scotland) Six Nations trophy was designed by James Brent-Ward of the London silversmith firm, William Comyns. It is made of sterling silver with 15 side panels representing the 15 members of the team and with three handles to represent the three officials involved in a match. Within the mahogany base of the trophy is a concealed drawer which contains six finials, each a replication of the six national team emblems. The reigning champion's finial sits proudly at the top of the trophy. The capacity of the trophy is equivalent to five bottles of champagne – one for each of the original five nations and it has been designed with a lip on the rim to make for easy drinking. In fact the inside of the trophy was originally silver, but it became so tarnished from champagne that it has since been lined with 22-carat gold to protect it.

The notion that no formal tournament ever existed was reflected in the way fixtures were scheduled. In today's Six Nations three matches are played every weekend or every other weekend – normally two on a Saturday and one on a Sunday – from early February through to late March according to a roster. But this system has only been in place since the 1974 championship. Prior to this, each fixture had a traditional date on which it was played – for example the Scotland–France international was always the first game of the season in early January, while the England–Scotland international was always played on the third Saturday of March. Such a scheduling system had a profound effect on the quality of rugby played in these matches, considering the weather and ground conditions encountered during these different months. For instance, the England–Wales and Scotland–France matches were always played in early January, usually in pouring rain and on poorly drained, muddy pitches. It comes as no surprise then to hear that these matches were more often than not low-scoring and error-ridden, while the Wales–France internationals, which were always played in late March or early April on spring days, inevitably produced a higher quality of rugby, higher scores and were more entertaining. Today, the effect of the weather is not as marked, thanks to better pitch drainage and, in the case of the Millennium Stadium, a retractable roof that can be closed during inclement weather.

Format

The format of the Six Nations Championship is quite simple, with each team playing each other once in the tournament, with home-field advantage alternating from one year to the next. Two points are awarded for a win, one for a draw and none for a loss. There have been calls in recent years to adopt the bonus-point system, as used in the Tri-Nations tournament and the RWC, whereby teams losing by seven points or less, or which score four tries or more in a match are awarded a bonus point. This call has been ignored by the home union traditionalists (those who don't wish to change the game in any respect and, if they could, would keep it amateur). And so it remains that only wins and draws are accredited with points. Prior to 1993, teams tied on log points upon the completion of the championship shared the title and in 1973, the remarkable feat of all five competing nations sharing the trophy occurred when each of the five competing nations won two games apiece – the only ever Five Nations five-way tie.

Following this, ties were broken by taking into consideration points differences, so teams with a better points difference would win the tournament. This was formulated to ensure there was an outright winner every year, a principle which became all the more important in the professional era, but which is frowned upon by traditionalists. It is a somewhat unfair method of log separation and one that still requires some refining, as the system does not take into account weather conditions: on a clear, sunny day more points will normally be scored than in wet, windy conditions. In 2007, the importance of points difference was clear for all to see. Going into the final round, four teams had a mathematical chance of winning the championship. France just pipped Ireland to the title after an injury-time TMO decision gave France the critical scoreline of 46–19 to better Ireland's points difference by just three points. In the event of points differences being tied then positions are determined by the highest amount of tries scored.

France makes it five nations, then four . . . and five again

With France becoming a more competitive rugby nation in the early part of the twentieth century, they competed in an international against a home union for the first time on 22 March 1906, going down 8–35 to England in Paris. The France–England international became an annual fixture from this date on, followed by internationals against Wales (1908), Ireland (1909) and Scotland (1910). It was also in 1910 that France played their first complete set of fixtures and with this the Five Nations Championship was born.

Once France was incorporated into the Five Nations Championship, French rugby developed at such a pace that the existing rugby organisation could not cope with managing the game. French players were at a premium, and the wealthier French clubs had no alternative but to offer cash inducements to keep their top players. The four home unions became increasingly alarmed at these commercial developments and sent repeated warnings to the FFR, which fell on deaf ears. By the end of the 1931 season, the IRFB had had enough and sent the following infamous letter to the FFR:

> 'Owing to the unsatisfactory condition of the game of Rugby Football as practised and played in France, neither our Union, nor the clubs or unions under our jurisdiction, will fulfil or arrange fixtures with France, or French clubs, at home or away, after the end of this season until we are satisfied that the control and conduct of the game have been placed on a satisfactory basis in all essentials.'

And so it was that France was banned from the Five Nations in 1932 and did not play again in the championship until 1947. During this period, the Five Nations Championship simply reverted to the old Home Nations Championship and went on as usual, with the four home unions once again competing solely for the Triple Crown.

During World War II no international rugby was played between any of the home unions and France and by 1945, France had been forgiven for their 'professional' running of the game. They would have been admitted back into the championship prior to the outbreak of the war, but this was not to be and instead a further six years were added to their banishment because of the war. Then in 1951, just four years later, and again in 1952, the French were accused of the same offence that had led to their ban two decades previously. The French promised to drop their club championship and eventually the matter was forgotten. Many believe the rationale was the home unions – and the rest of the rugby world – were too afraid to lose the superb ball-handling skills of the French backs from the international game once again.

From here, the championship went ahead without incident until the 1972 season, when the Irish home fixtures were not completed owing to the threats of terrorist attacks in Northern Ireland. Each nation has dominated the championship at some stage, with Scotland holding the title of being the last-ever champions of the Five Nations. This victory occurred after England dramatically lost to Wales by a single point at Wembley, having led the entire game and literally having had one hand on the Grand Slam Five Nations title until Scott Gibbs scored the winning try for Wales. This was the last international of the Five Nations and the trophy was presented to Scottish captain, Gary Armstrong in suit and tie, at Murrayfield the following day.

Italy makes it six

During the late 1990s, there was growing pressure from the global rugby community on the IRB to acknowledge the constantly improving strength of Italian rugby and include them in the Five Nations Championship. Following the 1994 Italian tour to Australia, where the Italians very nearly upset the then world champions in their own backyard, losing two tests 20–23 and 7–20 respectively, the Italians notched up some noteworthy victories (and many narrow losses) over the traditional rugby powerhouses – particularly over the home unions. In Treviso in 1995, the Italians defeated the Irish for the first time by 22–12, a feat they repeated two years later in 1997, this time in Dublin, by 37–29. That same year, the Italians racked up arguably the greatest victory in their history, with a 40–32 defeat of the Grand Slam champions, France, away from home in Grenoble, a result they repeated by comprehensively defeating the Irish later that year by 37–22. In 1998, Italy recorded their first victory against Scotland by 25–21 and a narrow loss to England in an RWC qualifying fixture by 15–23 in Huddersfield. In between these matches, Italy suffered several narrow losses to the Welsh and Irish – games that might have gone their way had it not been for some iffy refereeing decisions. With these results in the bag prior to the 1999 RWC, the IRB announced that Italy would join the Five Nations Championship the following year, expanding it to the Six Nations Championship as we know it today. But things did not go well for the Italians, who suffered record losses against South Africa (0–101), then against New Zealand during the World Cup (3–101), against England (7–67) and a further demoralising loss to Tonga by 25–28.

Italy's initiation into the Six Nations Championship was similar to that of France, who struggled initially to win any matches when they were introduced into the Five Nations Championship. By 2009, ten seasons after joining the Six Nations, the Italians have managed just a single away victory when they beat Scotland in Edinburgh by 37–17. To date they have just five home victories in total – against Scotland in 2000, 2004 and 2008 and Wales in 2003 and 2007. However, Italy's first-ever match in the championship against reigning champions, Scotland, resulted in a victory.

Interruptions

There have been very few interruptions in the Six Nation Championship. During the early years of the Home Nations Championship, however, few tournaments were fully completed, often because of arguments between unions over various matters, including laws, refereeing and allegations of professionalism . In 1886, England refused to join the International Board, newly formed by Wales, Scotland and Ireland and were refused international fixtures from 1888 to 1889 until they agreed to join in 1890. In addition, the 1897 tournament was not completed due to a squabble among the home unions about professionalism in Wales. Amateur management of the growing game in the 1880s saw continued spats over fixture dates between unions and resulted in the 1883 and 1885 seasons not being completed. In 1914, the championship was not competed after Scotland refused to play against France following a hotly disputed refereeing decision from the previous year's international, which led to sour relations between the two nations for many years. Additional interruptions occurred to those fixtures preceding and after the World War years (1915–1919 and 1940–1946). In 1972, the Welsh and the Scots refused to tour Ireland due to political and religious unrest in the country after terrorist threats were directed at the two teams.

In 1996, the RFU signed a deal with British Sky Broadcasting, resulting in English home games being exclusively shown on Sky. This caused a great deal of anger among the other competing unions and England was threatened with expulsion from the tournament, with emergency plans put in place to replace them with Italy. The broadcasting deal never went ahead and consequently the rights to show the Five Nations matches in Britain stayed with the BBC. However, the 1997 season was very nearly cancelled due to this spat, with England threatening to replace their Five Nations fixtures with regular annual games against South Africa and New Zealand instead. In 2001, fixtures were once more delayed in Ireland due to the outbreak of foot-and-mouth disease in Europe, pushing the usual February/March fixtures to September – a rescheduling programme that England used to blame their failure to achieve a Grand Slam after losing their final fixture to Ireland in September. According to England, had they played Ireland during the normal season they would have triumphed, taking into consideration the form they had displayed at the time. However, they still managed to win the championship.

Eras of domination

One of the great distinctions of the Six Nations Championship is the fact that these annual fixtures (or friendlies) have occurred for more than 125 years, allowing each nation to have dominated one another at some time. To break these trends of domination, there have been occasional upsets – on average, one per championship. The most recent was when Wales defeated the 2007 Rugby World Cup finalists, England, at Twickenham in 2008 for the first time in 20 years, after being 6–16 down at half-time – this after having lost 5–62 at the same venue just six months earlier.

England dominated the tournament in its early years from 1883 to 1892, from before World War I until 1928, during a brief stint in the 1950s, then again in the 1990s and during the early part of the new millennium. Scotland was to dominate from 1886 to 1891, through the first decade of the twentieth century, in the mid-1920s and briefly in the mid-to-late 1980s and in 1990. Wales took charge famously from 1900 to 1911, in the mid-1950s and again in the mid-1970s. Since then, pickings have been lean. However, Grand Slam triumphs in 2005 and 2008 hint at further Welsh domination. Ireland had a brief stint of domination from 1894 to 1899, most notably in the late 1940s, again during the mid-1980s and most recently when they won Triple Crowns in 2004, 2006 and 2007 and a magnificent Grand Slam in 2009. France made a slow start to tournament dominance (they lost 17 championship games on the trot from 1911 to 1920), but featured strongly for the first time in the late 1950s, through the 1960s and ever since, as they have won at least one Grand Slam every decade since the 1960s. Italy have found the going tough, but are showing signs of improving against their illustrious neighbours – especially in 2007 when they won two championship games in a season for the first time.

Home-ground advantage has proved to be crucial – especially in its early years, thanks in no small part to many home victories being accredited to biased home referees. Nearly all Triple Crown and Grand Slam successes come at home, with only Wales (2005) and Ireland (2009) achieving a Grand Slam with more away games than home. A home stadium has become something of a fortress for home nations, with away teams finding it exceedingly difficult to win away. Scotland has won just four times out of 44 attempts at Twickenham, Ireland never won against France at the Parc des Princes in the latter part of the twentieth century, England could not win at Cardiff's National Stadium from 1965 to 1989, Wales had no victories at Twickenham from 1988 to 2008 and neither did Scotland in Cardiff from 1964 to 1980.

The Triple Crown

In the 1882–1883 season England became the first nation to achieve the feat of a Triple Crown. This title is awarded to the home union that defeats all other three home unions in a season. Until 2006, there was no trophy as such – just a fiercely sought-after title. Today, this title comes in the form of a silver dish. However, it was not until 1899 that the term 'Triple Crown' was first coined to describe the success of the Irish that year. Scotland won their first Triple Crown in 1891, Wales in 1893 and Ireland in 1894. The Four Nations Championship, the Home International Championship and the Triple Crown Championship were unofficial names for this early form of the tournament, but the simple reason behind the existence and success of this early championship was the close geographical proximity of the four home unions. As a result, it was possible to play annual fixtures against one another quite easily (on a home-and-away rotation basis). Venues were often determined in the early days by the route taken by the travelling team, with early games between Ireland and Scotland played in Belfast and games between Ireland and Wales played in Swansea, thanks to the convenience of these cities to the two competing nations. Ireland are the current Triple Crown champions following their 2009 Grand Slam.

The Grand Slam

With France joining the championship in 1910, each country now played to win the elusive Grand Slam – the feat of winning all four championship matches in a single season and remaining unbeaten. However, the term 'Grand Slam' did not exist in the early years of the tournament, although the teams were obviously fully aware that they had won all of their matches in the championship. The phrase only become popular in the mid-twentieth century. The term is thought to have been coined by *The Times* rugby journalists in 1957 to celebrate the fact that England won all of their Five Nations internationals that year. In the event of a home union side winning the Grand Slam they would automatically also win the Triple Crown, but a Triple Crown could still be won even if a Grand Slam were not achieved (for example losing to France or Italy), as Ireland did in 2006. Therefore, France and Italy cannot win the Triple Crown, but they can win the Grand Slam. Yet despite France joining the Five Nations Championship, fixtures against them were regarded by the home unions as supplementary and unnecessary to the real business of winning the Triple Crown. The first nation to achieve a Grand Slam in the Five Nations Championship was Wales in 1911, although they did remain unbeaten in all four of their fixtures in 1908 and 1909 prior to France officially joining the Five Nations Championship and have been accredited with the feat, as such. England soon followed suit, winning their first Grand Slam in 1913, Scotland in 1925, Ireland in 1948 and France in 1968. Italy has yet to achieve the feat – the closest they came was in 2007 when they won two of their five fixtures.

France became the first nation to win a Grand Slam in the Six Nations Championship in 2002 and Wales achieved the impressive feat of not only winning a Grand Slam in 2005, but also became the first team in the tournament's history to achieve this by playing more away games (three) than home games (two). They again achieved Grand Slam status in 2008 but were toppled by Ireland who registered only their second Grand Slam in 2009.

Other competitions

In addition to the Grand Slam and the Triple Crown, several other individual titles and competitions take place under the umbrella of the main Six Nations tournament. These include the Calcutta Cup (Scotland vs England), Centenary Quaich (Scotland vs Ireland), Giuseppe Garibaldi Trophy (France vs Italy) and the Millennium Trophy (England vs Ireland).

Unique to the Six Nations is the title of Wooden Spoon winners – an accolade that every team desperately tries to avoid. This is awarded to the team which finishes bottom of the table in the Six Nations Championship. The so-called wooden spoon does not actually exist. Its origins go back to the Cambridge University graduates who went on to play in the championship and simply carried this nineteenth-century Cambridge tradition with them. The Cambridge mathematics department awarded the 'wooden spoon' title to the student who got the lowest mark in the class but still managed to achieve a pass. As such, the Cambridge graduates who went on to feature in the Five Nations from 1909 onward wanted to preserve this tradition by awarding the wooden spoon to the nation finishing last in the Five Nations. This tradition developed into the Wooden Spoon Society, a charity organisation formed in 1983 after a group of English supporters were commiserating England's award of the Wooden Spoon that year. Currently, the Wooden Spoon Society is the official charity of both the English and Irish Rugby Football Unions and has distributed over £12 million to charity.

Records

The statistics presented in this section include those matches played during the Home Nations Championship, the Five Nations Championship and the Six Nations Championship.

English centre Charles Hooper passes in the tackle to his centre partner Samuel Morfitt to score a magnificent length-of-the-field try against Wales in Birkenhead in 1894, a match ultimately won 24-3 by England. *Image*: Frédéric Humbert/www.flickr.com/photos/rugby_pioneers/creative commons license

Championship titles

Tournament	Year	Overall winner(s)	Triple Crown	Grand Slam
Home Nations	1883	England	England	
	1884	England	England	
	1885	Not completed		
	1886	Scotland England		
	1887	Scotland		
	1888	Not completed		
	1889	Not completed		
	1890	England Scotland		
	1891	Scotland	Scotland	
	1892	England	England	
	1893	Wales	Wales	
	1894	Ireland	Ireland	
	1895	Scotland	Scotland	
	1896	Ireland		
	1897	Not completed		
	1898	Not completed		
	1899	Ireland	Ireland	
	1900	Wales	Wales	
	1901	Scotland	Scotland	
	1902	Wales	Wales	
	1903	Scotland	Scotland	
	1904	Scotland		
	1905	Wales	Wales	
	1906	Ireland Wales		
	1907	Scotland	Scotland	
	1908	Wales	Wales	Wales
	1909	Wales	Wales	Wales
Five Nations	1910	England		
	1911	Wales	Wales	Wales
	1912	England Ireland		
	1913	England	England	England

Tournament	Year	Overall winner(s)	Triple Crown	Grand Slam
Five Nations	1914	England	England	England
	World War I			
	1920	England Scotland Wales		
	1921	England	England	England
	1922	Wales		
	1923	England	England	England
	1924	England	England	England
	1925	Scotland	Scotland	Scotland
	1926	Scotland Ireland		
	1927	Scotland Ireland		
	1928	England	England	England
	1929	Scotland		
	1930	England		
	1931	Wales		
Home Nations	1932	England Wales Ireland		
	1933	Scotland	Scotland	
	1934	England	England	
	1935	Ireland		
	1936	Wales		
	1937	England	England	
	1938	Scotland	Scotland	
	1939	England Wales Ireland		
	World War II			
Five Nations	1947	Wales England		
	1948	Ireland	Ireland	Ireland
	1949	Ireland	Ireland	
	1950	Wales	Wales	Wales
	1951	Ireland		
	1952	Wales	Wales	Wales
	1953	England		

Tournament	Year	Overall winner(s)	Triple Crown	Grand Slam
Five Nations	1954	England France Wales	England	
	1955	France Wales		
	1956	Wales		
	1957	England	England	England
	1958	England		
	1959	France		
	1960	England France	England	
	1961	France		
	1962	France		
	1963	England		
	1964	Scotland Wales		
	1965	Wales	Wales	
	1966	Wales		
	1967	France		
	1968	France		France
	1969	Wales	Wales	
	1970	France Wales		
	1971	Wales	Wales	Wales
	1972	Not completed		
	1973	England France Wales Ireland Scotland		
	1974	Ireland		
	1975	Wales		
	1976	Wales	Wales	Wales
	1977	France	Wales	France
	1978	Wales	Wales	Wales

Tournament	Year	Overall winner(s)	Triple Crown	Grand Slam
Five Nations	1979	Wales	Wales	
	1980	England	England	England
	1981	France		France
	1982	Ireland	Ireland	
	1983	France Ireland		
	1984	Scotland	Scotland	Scotland
	1985	Ireland	Ireland	
	1986	France Scotland		
	1987	France		France
	1988	Wales France	Wales	
	1989	France		
	1990	Scotland	Scotland	Scotland
	1991	England	England	England
	1992	England	England	England
	1993	France		
	1994	Wales		
	1995	England	England	England
	1996	England	England	
	1997	France	England	France
	1998	France	England	France
	1999	Scotland		
Six Nations	2000	England		
	2001	England		
	2002	France	England	France
	2003	England	England	England
	2004	France	Ireland	France
	2005	Wales	Wales	Wales
	2006	France	Ireland	
	2007	France	Ireland	
	2008	Wales	Wales	Wales
	2009	Ireland	Ireland	Ireland

Summary

Nation	Completed tournaments	Outright championship titles	Shared championship titles	Grand Slams	Triple Crowns
England	109	25	10	12	23
Wales	109	24	11	10	19
Scotland	109	14	8	3	10
Ireland	109	11	8	2	10
France	78	16	7	8	n/a
Italy	10	-	-	-	n/a

Player career records

Most points by a player in a Five/Six Nations career

No.	Player	Country	Period	Tests	Points			
					T	C	P	DG
499	Ronan O'Gara	Ireland	2000–2009	46	9	71	99	5
479	Jonny Wilkinson	England	1998–2008	33	4	81	90	9
406	Neil Jenkins	Wales	1991–2002	41	5	41	93	7
382	Stephen Jones	Wales	2000–2009	41	4	58	79	3
361	Chris Paterson	Scotland	2000–2009	48	7	31	87	1
288	Gavin Hastings	Scotland	1986–1995	36	4	20	77	-
270	David Humphreys	Ireland	1996–2005	34	3	27	62	5
232	Paul Grayson	England	1996–2004	17	2	30	48	6
207	Michael Kiernan	Ireland	1982–1991	35	3	21	46	5
201	Andy Irvine	Scotland	1973–1982	39	10	19	41	-

Most caps in a Five/Six Nations career

Player	Caps	Country	Period
Mike Gibson	56	Ireland	1964–1979
Jason Leonard	54	England	1991–2004
Willie-John McBride	53	Ireland	1962–1975
Philippe Sella	50	France	1983–1995
Rory Underwood	50	England	1984–1996
Fabien Pelous	49	France	1996–2006
Fergus Slattery	49	Ireland	1970–1984
John Hayes	49	Ireland	2000–2009
Chris Paterson	48	Scotland	2000–2009
Martyn Williams	47	Wales	1998–2009

Most tries by a player in a Five/Six Nations career

No.	Player	Country	Tests	Period
24	Ian Smith	Scotland	31	1924–1933
21	Brian O'Driscoll	Ireland	45	2000–2009
18	Gareth Edwards	Wales	45	1967–1978
18	Cyril Lowe	England	24	1913–1923
18	Rory Underwood	England	50	1984–1996
17	Shane Williams	Wales	32	2000–2009
16	Ben Cohen	England	29	2000–2006
16	Gerald Davies	Wales	38	1967–1978
16	Ken Jones	Wales	41	1947–1957
16	Willie Llewellyn	Wales	19	1899–1905

Most drop goals by a player in a Five/Six Nations career

No.	Player	Country	Tests	Period
9	Jonny Wilkinson	England	33	1998–2008
9	Rob Andrew	England	40	1985–1997
9	Jean-Patrick Lescarboura	France	14	1982–1988

Most conversions in a Five/Six Nations career

No.	Player	Country	Tests	Period
81	Jonny Wilkinson	England	33	1998–2008
71	Ronan O'Gara	Ireland	46	2000–2009
58	Stephen Jones	Wales	41	2000–2009
41	Neil Jenkins	Wales	41	1991–2002
32	Jack Bancroft	Wales	32	1909–1914

Most penalties in a Five/Six Nations career

No.	Player	Country	Tests	Period
99	Ronan O'Gara	Ireland	46	2000–2009
93	Neil Jenkins	Wales	41	1991–2002
90	Jonny Wilkinson	England	33	1998–2008
87	Chris Paterson	Scotland	48	2000–2009
77	Gavin Hastings	Scotland	36	1986–1995

Player tournament records

Most points by a player in a Five/Six Nations tournament

No.	Player	Country	Tests	Tournament	Points			
					T	C	P	D
89	Jonny Wilkinson	England	5	2001	1	24	12	-
82	Ronan O'Gara	Ireland	5	2007	4	10	14	-
80	Gerald Merceron	France	5	2002	1	9	18	1
78	Jonny Wilkinson	England	5	2000	-	12	18	-
77	Jonny Wilkinson	England	5	2003	-	13	12	5
76	Ronan O'Gara	Ireland	5	2006	1	10	17	-
75	Jonny Wilkinson	England	5	2002	2	19	8	1
74	Neil Jenkins	Wales	4	2001	1	9	12	5
73	David Humphreys	Ireland	5	2003	2	6	16	1
67	Jonathan Webb	England	4	1992	3	11	11	-

Most tries by a player in a Five/Six Nations tournament

No.	Player	Country	Tests	Tournament
8	Ian Smith	Scotland	4	1925
8	Cyril Lowe	England	4	1914
7	Willie Stewart	Scotland	3	1913
6	Vincent Coates	England	4	1913
6	Howard Catchside	England	4	1924
6	Johnnie Wallace	Scotland	4	1925
6	Maurice Richards	Wales	4	1969
6	Will Greenwood	England	5	2001
6	Shane Williams	Wales	5	2008

Most conversions in a Five/Six Nations tournament

No.	Player	Country	Tests	Tournament
24	Jonny Wilkinson	England	5	2001
19	Jonny Wilkinson	England	5	2002
14	Paul Grayson	England	4	1998
13	Jonny Wilkinson	England	5	2003
12	Jonny Wilkinson	England	5	2000
12	Stephen Jones	Wales	5	2005

Most drop goals by a player in a Five/Six Nations tournament

No.	Player	Country	Tests	Tournament
5	Jonny Wilkinson	England	5	2003
5	Neil Jenkins	Wales	4	2001
5	Diego Dominguez	Italy	5	2000
5	Guy Camberabero	France	3	1967
4	Guy Laporte	France	3	1981
4	Jean-Patrick Lescarboura	France	4	1984
4	Jonathan Davies	Wales	4	1988

Most penalties in a Five/Six Nations Tournament

No.	Player	Country	Tests	Tournament
18	Gérald Merceron	France	5	2002
18	Jonny Wilkinson	England	5	2000
18	Simon Hodgkinson	England	4	1991
17	Paul Grayson	England	4	1996
17	Ronan O'Gara	Ireland	5	2006

Match records

Most points by a player in a Five/Six Nations test by a player

No.	Player	Points				Country	Versus	Result	Venue	Date
		T	C	P	DG					
35	Jonny Wilkinson	1	9	4	-	England	Italy	80–23	Twickenham, London	17/02/2001
30	Ronan O'Gara	-	6	6	-	Ireland	Italy	60–13	Lansdowne Road, Dublin	04/03/2000
30	Jonny Wilkinson	1	5	4	1	England	Wales	50–10	Twickenham, London	23/03/2002
29	Diego Dominguez	-	1	6	3	Italy	Scotland	34–20	Stadio Flaminio, Rome	05/02/2000
28	Neil Jenkins	1	4	3	2	Wales	France	43–35	Stade de France, Paris	17/03/2001
27	Neil Jenkins	-	3	7	-	Wales	Italy	47–16	Millennium Stadium, Cardiff	200019/02/
27	Jonny Wilkinson	1	2	5	1	England	Scotland	42–20	Twickenham, London	03/02/2007
26	David Humphreys	1	3	5	-	Ireland	Scotland	36–6	Murrayfield, Edinburgh	16/02/2003

Most tries by a player in a Five/Six Nations test by a player

No.	Player	Country	Versus	Result	Venue	Date
5	George Lindsay	Scotland	Wales	20–0	Raeburn Place, Edinburgh	26/02/1887
4	Maurice Richards	Wales	England	30–9	National Stadium, Cardiff	12/04/1969
4	Ian Smith	Scotland	Wales	24–14	St Helen's, Swansea	07/02/1925
4	Ian Smith	Scotland	France	25–4	Inverleith, Edinburgh	25/01/1925
4	Ronnie Poulton	England	France	39–13	Stade Colombes, Paris	13/04/1914
4	William Stewart	Scotland	Ireland	29–14	Inverleith, Edinburgh	22/02/1913
4	Willie Llewellyn	Wales	England	26–3	St Helen's, Swansea	07/01/1899

Most drop goals by a player in a Five/Six Nations test by a player

No.	Player	Country	Versus	Result	Venue	Date
3	Neil Jenkins	Wales	Scotland	28–28	Murrayfield, Edinburgh	17/02/2001
3	Diego Dominguez	Italy	Scotland	34–20	Stadio Flaminio, Rome	05/02/2000
3	Jean-Patrick Lescarboura	France	England	9–9	Twickenham, London	02/02/1985
3	Pierre Albaladejo	France	Ireland	23–6	Stade Olympique Yves-du-Manoir, Paris	09/04/1960

Most conversions by a player in a Five/Six Nations test by a player

No.	Player	Country	Versus	Result	Venue	Date
9	Jonny Wilkinson	England	Italy	80–23	Twickenham, London	17/02/2001
8	Jack Bancroft	Wales	France	49–14	St Helen's, Swansea	01/01/1910
7	Paul Grayson	England	Wales	60–26	Twickenham, London	21/02/1998

				Most penalties by a player in a Five/Six Nations test		
No.	Player	Country	Versus	Result	Venue	Date
7	Chris Paterson	Scotland	Wales	21–9	Murrayfield, Edinburgh	210/02/007
7	Gérald Merceron	France	Italy	33–12	Stade de France, Paris	02/02/2002
7	Neil Jenkins	Wales	Italy	47–16	Millennium Stadium, Cardiff	19/02/2000
7	Jonny Wilkinson	England	France	21–10	Twickenham, London	20/03/1999
7	Rob Andrew	England	Scotland	24–12	Twickenham, London	18/03/1995
7	Simon Hodgkinson	England	Wales	25–6	National Stadium, Cardiff	19/01/1991

		Most points by a team in a Six Nations test						
No.	Result	Points				Country	Versus	Venue	Date
		T	C	P	DG				
80	80–23	10	9	4	-	England	Italy	Twickenham, London	17/02/2001
60	60–13	6	6	6	-	Ireland	Italy	Lansdowne Road, Dublin	04/03/2000
60	60–26	8	7	2	-	England	Wales	Twickenham, London	21/02/1998
59	59–12	8	5	2	1	England	Italy	Stadio Olympio, Rome	18/03/2000
56	56–13	7	6	3	-	France	Italy	Stadio Flaminio, Rome	19/03/2005
54	54–10	6	3	6	-	Ireland	Wales	Lansdowne Road, Dublin	03/02/2002
53	53–27	7	6	2	-	France	Italy	Stadio Flaminio, Rome	23/03/2003
51	51–24	8	4	1	-	Ireland	Italy	Stadio Flaminio, Rome	17/03/2007
51	51–0	7	5	2	-	France	Wales	Wembley, London	05/04/1998
51	51–16	7	5	2	-	France	Scotland	Murrayfield, Edinburgh	21/02/1998
50	50–9	7	3	3	-	England	Italy	Stadio Flaminio, Rome	15/02/2004
50	50–10	5	5	4	1	England	Wales	Twickenham, London	23/03/2002
50	50–18	6	4	4	-	England	Ireland	Twickenham, London	05/02/2000
50	50–8	7	3	3	-	France	Italy	Stadio Flaminio, Rome	21/03/2009

The art of scoring a Grand Slam of tries

As tough as it is for a team to record a Grand Slam season, it is even rarer to witness a player accomplishing the achievement of scoring a try in every single match in a championship. This has been achieved by just six players in the championship's 127-year history: Howard Carston Catcheside, Johnny Wallace, Patrick Esteve, Philippe Sella, Gregor Townsend and Philippe Bernat-Salles (*see* below). In addition, Australian flyhalf Mark Ella accomplished the task on the 1984 Australian tour to the British Isles, thereby becoming the only player from the southern hemisphere ever to score against each of the home nations in successive tests on the same tour.

Player	Championship	Country
Howard Carston Catcheside	1924	England
Johnny Wallace	1925	Scotland
Patrick Esteve	1983	France
Philippe Sella	1986	France
Gregor Townsend	1999	Scotland
Philippe Bernat-Salles	2001	France

Above left: The 1898 English side, captained by Fred Byrne (ball in hand), to play against Ireland in that year's Home Nations Championship. The match was won 9-6 by the Irish at Richmond Athletic Ground. Photo: Frédéric Humbert/www.flickr.com/photos/rugby_pioneers/creative commons license

Above right: The 1893 England side that took on Scotland in the Calcutta Cup, a match won 8-0 by Scotland in Leeds.
Photo: Frédéric Humbert/www.flickr.com/photos/rugby_pioneers/creative commons license

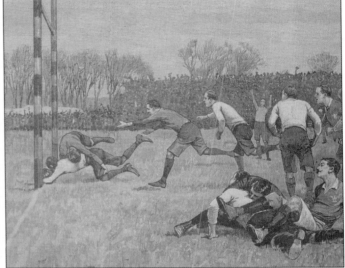

Above left: Team photograph of the victorious 1895 Scottish side that successfully defended the Calcutta Cup against England in Richmond. Captained by Robert MacMillan (ball in hand) the Scots won the match by 6-3.
Photo: Frédéric Humbert/www.flickr.com/photos/rugby_pioneers/creative commons license

Above: An unidentified English player scores one of four English tries against Wales during the 1892 Home Nations Championship match against Wales in Blackheath, won 17-0 by England. Image: Frédéric Humbert/www.flickr.com/photos/rugby_pioneers/creative commons license

Left: The 1892 English Triple Crown champions who conceded not a single point during their campaign. Photo: Frédéric Humbert/www.flickr.com/photos/rugby_pioneers/creative commons license

Top: England captain Frederick Alderson powers forward against Scotland during the 1892 Calcutta Cup fixture at Raeburn Place in Edinburgh, a match won 5-0 by England. *Image*: Frédéric Humbert/www.flickr.com/photos/rugby_pioneers/creative commons license

Above left: The 1895 Welsh side that came third in that year's Home Nations Championship and which was captained by great centre Arthur Gould (seated third from right). *Photo*: Frédéric Humbert/www.flickr.com/photos/rugby_pioneers/creative commons license

Above right: The 1896 Irish Home Nations champions who drew 0-0 with Scotland in Dublin, captained by Samuel Lee (with ball). *Photo*: Frédéric Humbert/www.flickr.com/photos/rugby_pioneers/creative commons license

Left: The 1911 Grand Slam Welsh side captained by William Trew that beat England by 15-11 in Swansea. *Photo*: Frédéric Humbert/www.flickr.com/photos/rugby_pioneers/creative commons license

Below: England scramble to secure loose ball against Scotland at Inverleith in Edinburgh during the 1902 Calcutta Cup clash won 6-3 by England. *Photo*: Frédéric Humbert/www.flickr.com/photos/rugby_pioneers/creative commons license

Bottom: An England winger is tackled on the touch line during the 1904 Calcutta Cup match versus Scotland at Inverleith, a match won 6-3 by Scotland. *Photo*: Frédéric Humbert/www.flickr.com/photos/rugby_pioneers/creative commons license

Lineout action from the 1914 Five Nations test between France and England in Paris, a match won 39-13 by England.
Photo: Frédéric Humbert/www.flickr.com/photos/rugby_pioneers/creative commons license

France and England scramble to secure a loose ball during the 1930 Five Nations international won 11-5 by England at Twickenham. *Photo*: Frédéric Humbert/www. flickr.com/photos/rugby_pioneers/creative commons license

England and France battle for the ball in a lineout during the 1930 Five Nations test match, a match won 11-5 by England at Twickenham in London.
Photo: Frédéric Humbert/www.flickr.com/photos/rugby_pioneers/creative commons license

Above: Team photograph of the first-ever French side to compete in the Five Nations, against Wales on 1 January 1910. It was not to be a memorable occasion for the French as they lost by a record scoreline of 14-49 at St Helen's in Swansea. *Photo*: Frédéric Humbert/www.flickr.com/photos/rugby_pioneers/creative commons license

Right: Cyril Lowe of England in action against France during the 1920 Five Nations fixture. To this day, Lowe shares the Five/Six Nations record of eight tries in a single tournament with Ian Smith of Scotland. *Photo*: Frédéric Humbert/www.flickr.com/photos/rugby_pioneers/creative commons license

Below: Prop forward Jean Sebedio scores France's only try of their ill-fated 1913 Five Nations clash versus Scotland, a match won 21-3 by Scotland in Paris. The match finished in such poor spirits that the two sides refused to honour the clash the following year. *Photo*: Frédéric Humbert/www.flickr.com/photos/rugby_pioneers/creative commons license

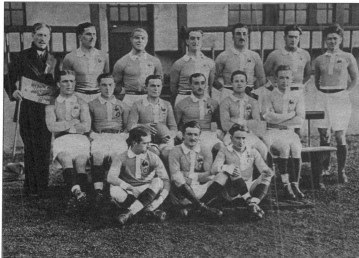

Left: The 1921 French side that secured France's first-ever away victory when they beat Scotland by 3-0 at Inverleith in Edinburgh during the Five Nations. *Photo*: Frédéric Humbert/www.flickr.com/photos/rugby_pioneers/creative commons license

Centre left: Action photograph between France and England during the 1910 Five Nations clash in Paris, a match won 11-3 by England. *Photo*: Frédéric Humbert/www.flickr.com/photos/rugby_pioneers/creative commons license

Below right: The French backline hot on attack during the 1911 Five Nations fixture against Wales in Paris, won 15-0 by Wales who went on to become Grand Slam champions. *Photo*: Frédéric Humbert/www.flickr.com/photos/rugby_pioneers/creative commons license

Bottom: The 1931 Five Nations fixture between Scotland and France at Murrayfield, Edinburgh: a tight match won 6-4 by Scotland. *Photo*: Frédéric Humbert/www.flickr.com/photos/rugby_pioneers/creative commons license

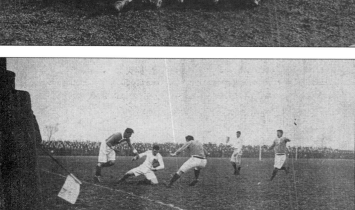

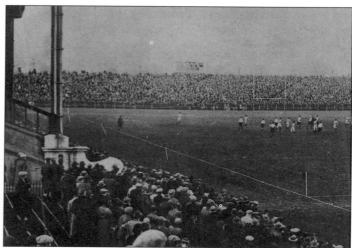

Top left: The 1937 English Triple Crown champions, captained by fullback Harold Owen-Smith, who beat Wales 4-3 at Twickenham, London.
Photo: Frédéric Humbert/www.flickr.com/photos/rugby_pioneers/creative commons license

Top right: Scotland's first-ever Grand Slam side, the 1925 team that beat England at Murrayfield by 14-11 to secure the prestigious title. *Photo*: Frédéric Humbert/www.flickr.com/photos/rugby_pioneers/creative commons license

Centre left: Irish flyhalf and player of the century Jacky Kyle kicks past Welshman Roy John during their 1951 Five Nations fixture. Despite a typically brilliant Kyle try Ireland were only able to secure a 3-3 draw in Cardiff.
Photo: Frédéric Humbert/www.flickr.com/photos/rugby_pioneers/creative commons license

Above: Italian scrumhalf Alessandro Troncon prepares to feed an attacking Italian scrum during their 2007 Six Nations international against Ireland on a sunny Rome day at the Stadio Flaminio. This high-scoring international was won 51-24 by Ireland. *Photo*: Federazione Italiana Rugby

Left: Muddy action from the 1914 Five Nations clash between France and Ireland in Paris, a match won 8-6 by Ireland. *Photo*: Frédéric Humbert/www.flickr.com/photos/rugby_pioneers/creative commons license

Pool 1 - final standings							
Country	P	W	L	D	F	A	P
Australia	3	3	-	-	108	41	6
England	3	2	1	-	100	32	4
USA	3	1	2	-	39	99	2
Japan	3	-	3	-	48	123	0

Pool 2 - final standings							
Country	P	W	L	D	F	A	P
Wales	3	3	-	-	82	31	6
Ireland	3	2	1	-	84	41	4
Canada	3	1	2	-	65	90	2
Tonga	3	-	3	-	29	98	0

Pool 3 - final standings							
Country	P	W	L	D	F	A	P
New Zealand	3	3	-	-	190	34	6
Fiji	3	1	2	-	56	101	2
Argentina	3	1	2	-	49	90	2
Italy	3	1	2	-	40	110	2

Pool 4 - final standings							
Country	P	W	L	D	F	A	P
France	3	2	-	1	145	44	5
Scotland	3	2	-	1	135	69	5
Romania	3	1	2	-	61	130	2
Zimbabwe	3	-	3	-	53	151	0

Quarter-finals

The quarter-finals of the first RWC were a disappointing set of matches, which failed to produce rugby of a high quality and which were fairly one-sided events. New Zealand comfortably defeated a game Scottish side, thanks mainly to the boot of ace flyhalf, Grant Fox; France saw off the challenge from the Fijians at Eden Park in Auckland in a match marred by foul play; while the Australians defeated Ireland in the most entertaining of the four weekend quarter-finals. The last of the quarter-finals was the most anticipated of the lot, between the two old foes, England and Wales. However, the match was a dismal, scrappy affair, with Wales eventually winning, to end England's woeful campaign.

Quarter-final 1 (winner pool 3 vs runner-up pool 4)
6 June, Lancaster Park, Christchurch
New Zealand   30   T: A Whetton, Gallagher; C: Fox (2); PG: Fox (6)
Scotland   3   PG: G Hastings

Quarter-final 2 (winner pool 1 vs runner-up pool 2)
7 June, Concord Oval, Sydney
Australia   33   T: Burke (2), Smith, McIntyre; C: Lynagh (4); PG: Lynagh (3)
Ireland   15   T: McNeill, Kiernan; C: Kiernan (2); PG: Kiernan

Quarter-final 3 (winner pool 4 vs runner-up pool 3)
7 June, Eden Park, Auckland
France   31   T: Lorieux, Lagisquet, Rodriguez (2); C: Laporte (3); PG: Laporte (2); DG: Laporte
Fiji   16   T: Qoro, Damu; C: Koroduadua; PG: Koroduadua (2)

Quarter-final 4 (winner pool 2 vs runner-up pool 1)
8 June, Ballymore, Brisbane
Wales   16   T: Roberts, Jones, Devereux; C: Thorburn (2)
England   3   PG: Webb

Semi-finals

Semi-final 1 (winner quarter-final 2 vs winner quarter-final 3)

13 June, Concord Oval, Sydney

Australia	24	T: Campese, Codey; C: Lynagh (2); PG: Lynagh (3); DG: Lynagh
France	30	T: Lorieux, Sella, Blanco, Lagisquet; C: Camberabero (4); PG: Camberabero (2)

This was undoubtedly the match of the tournament, but unfortunately it was played before a disappointingly small crowd at the new Concord Oval venue in Sydney. It was a semi-final that did not produce a single try until the 40th minute, but it finished with six by the end. It was a classic, but a heartbreaker for the home team and their supporters. This was a match that either side could have won, with Australian flyhalf, Michael Lynagh, twice missing crucial kicks at goal to put the Australians further in front. The lead changed hands throughout the game and at one stage, the French trailed 0–9. Remarkably, with time up, the scores were locked at 24–all, only for the French to score one of the great tries in international rugby history and one of the most exciting in RWC history. In a move that ran from one end of the field to the other, the exhausted Australian side were unable to stop the legendary French fullback Serge Blanco from diving into the corner and eluding the desperate attempts of Australian hooker, Tom Lawton. Didier Camberabero kicked a remarkable conversion from the touchline and the French were, surprisingly, in the first RWC final.

Semi-final 2 (winner quarter-final 1 vs winner quarter-final 4)

14 June, Ballymore, Brisbane

New Zealand	49	T: Shelford (2), Kirwan (2), Drake, Brooke-Cowden, Stanley, A Whetton; C: Fox (7); PG: Fox
Wales	6	T: Devereux; C: Thorburn

Prior to this encounter, the Welsh had not beaten the All Blacks since 1953 and it seemed unlikely that they would manage a victory at the neutral venue of Ballymore. The match was a far cry from the previous semi-final and will not only be remembered for its one-sided scoreline, but also for its dirty nature, with Welsh lock, Huw Richards, being given his marching orders towards the end of the match after managing to get up woozily from a Wayne 'Buck' Shelford punch that had nearly knocked him out. Wales had not managed their squad system very well through the tournament and as a result of injuries were missing a few of their top forwards for the all-important encounter. But it is unlikely that their best players would have made any difference to the outcome, as this was a great All Blacks side that were unlikely to be knocked out at this stage in the competition. New Zealand were the eventual winners by eight tries to one and the Welsh were branded with the unfortunate nickname of 'The 49ers'.

Third and fourth play-off (loser semi-final 1 vs loser semi-final 2)

18 June, International Stadium, Rotorua

Australia	21	T: Burke, Grigg; C: Lynagh (2); PG: Lynagh (2); DG: Lynagh
Wales	22	T: Roberts, P Moriarty, Hadley; C: Thorburn (2); PG: Thorburn (2)

1987 Rugby World Cup final (winner semi-final 1 vs winner semi-final 2)

20 June, Eden Park, Auckland

New Zealand	29	T: Jones, Kirk, Kirwan; C: Fox; PG: Fox (4); DG: Fox
France	9	T: Berbizier; C: Camberabero; PG: Camberabero

The first RWC final was contested between New Zealand and France in Auckland, New Zealand. The New Zealanders were strong favourites, having scored a total of 40 tries through the competition, with just three scored against them until the final. But France was in an excellent position to claim the title as their own. They were the Five Nations Grand Slam champions of that year, had beaten the All Blacks convincingly in their previous encounter in Nantes the year before and had downed the Australians in a thrilling semi-final in Sydney the week before. The final turned out to be a fairly disappointing encounter and was described as boring and stereotyped. Yet the New Zealanders cannot be blamed for employing safety-first tactics in a match where there was so much at stake. French captain

Daniel Dubroca was unable to inspire his men to the levels of their semi-final, and All Blacks flyhalf Grant Fox kicked 17 points, with the first try being scored by All Blacks flanker Michael Jones from a blocked drop-goal attempt. The next try was a breakaway effort by skipper David Kirk, then another by their brilliant winger John Kirwan who dived in at the corner, with French centre Philippe Sella trying in vain to stop him. With the score at 29–3, the French managed a late consolation try through their scrumhalf Pierre Berbizier, to finish the match as runners-up with a scoreline of 29–9. Although the final did not turn out to be the most exciting encounter many had hoped it would be, it did produce the most tries ever to be scored in an RWC final – a total of four. And so it was that New Zealand efficiently and deservedly won the 1987 RWC. They scored a total of 298 points (43 tries) to 52 (four tries) against: no one could argue that they did not deserve the title – although the banned South Africans will always claim that they had a case. And so captain David Kirk became the first player to raise the coveted William Webb Ellis Trophy and to this day remains the only New Zealand captain to have held it. No twentieth-century team has since won an RWC in such an emphatic style as New Zealand.

The tournament had its problems – mistakes which future tournament organisers were to learn from. In the pool matches, the best teams met one another in the first round, which devalued the remainder of the pool matches. Emerging nations tended to field weaker teams against the stronger nations so as to save their best players for clashes with other minnows and to ensure themselves a quarter-final berth. Competing nations all came to realise the importance of a well-managed squad system, as injuries decimated many of the squads. Only New Zealand made sensible use of their resources, hence it was not surprising that they became the eventual champions.

1991 Rugby World Cup
(co-hosted by England, Ireland, Scotland, Wales and France)

The second RWC was hosted by the four home unions – England, Scotland, Wales and Ireland – as well as France. Despite the lessons learned from the 1987 RWC, which illustrated that having the tournament hosted by more than one nation was a difficult exercise, the 1991 RWC was split between five. This ensured that all five unions benefited financially by hosting world cup matches, with each receiving home support. This had the consequence of diffusing the tournament hype and atmosphere across distance. Sharing the tournament among five rugby nations and three different legal codes remains the most complicated hosting arrangement for the RWC to date and is unlikely to be repeated. Interestingly, it is often erroneously assumed that England were the sole hosts, given the fact that the opening game and final were played in London. For the first time, a qualification route was followed, whereby the eight 1987 quarter-finalists (who qualified automatically) were joined by the eight qualifying teams. The opening match of the tournament was between the official tournament hosts, England, and defending champions, New Zealand, who won a tough encounter 18–12, with Michael Jones becoming the first man to score the opening try in two RWCs. The tournament was considered more successful than that of 1987, with the lesser nations competing gamely against the established nations. Western Samoa famously dumped Wales out of the tournament when they beat the Welsh at Cardiff Arms Park by 16–13. (The inevitable jokes after the clash claimed that Wales were lucky not to be playing the whole of Samoa!) Interestingly, Canada pushed France close to defeat and gave New Zealand a tough encounter in the quarter-final.

1991 RWC pools

Pool 1	
Country	Previous best finish
New Zealand	Champions '87
England	Quarter-finalists '87
Italy	Contestants '87
United States	Contestants '87

Pool 2	
Country	Previous best finish
Scotland	Quarter-finalists '87
Ireland	Quarter-finalists '87
Japan	Contestants '87
Zimbabwe	Contestants '87

Pool 3	
Country	Previous best finish
Australia	4th Place '87
Wales	3rd Place '87
Argentina	Contestants '87
Western Samoa	Debutant

Pool 4	
Country	Previous best finish
France	Runners-up '87
Fiji	Quarter-finalists '87
Romania	Contestants '87
Canada	Contestants '87

Pool results

3 October, Twickenham, London (Pool 1)
England 12 PG: Webb (3); DG: Andrew
New Zealand 18 T: M Jones; C: Fox; PG: Fox (4)

4 October, Stradey Park, Llanelli (Pool 3)
Australia 32 T: Campese (2), Horan (2), Kearns; C: Lynagh (3); PG: Lynagh (2)
Argentina 19 T: Teran (2); C: del Castillo; PG: del Castillo; DG: Arbizu (2)

4 October, Parc Sauclieres, Beziers (Pool 4)
France 30 T: Saint-André, Roumat, Lafond, penalty try; C: Camberabero; PG: Camberabero (4)
Romania 3 PG: Nichitean

5 October, Cross Green, Otley (Pool 1)
Italy 30 T: Barba, Francescato, Vaccari, Gaetaniello; C: Dominguez (4); PG: Dominguez (2)
United States 9 T: Swords; C: Williams; PG: Williams

5 October, Stade Jean Sauger, Bayonne (Pool 4)
Canada 13 T: Stewart; PG: Rees (3)
Fiji 3 DG: Serevi

5 October, Murrayfield, Edinburgh (Pool 2)
Scotland 47 T: S Hastings, Stanger, Chalmers, penalty try, White, Tukalo, G Hastings; C: G Hastings (5); PG: G Hastings (2), Chalmers
Japan 9 T: Hosokawa; C: Hosokawa; DG: Hosokawa

6 October, Lansdowne Road, Dublin (Pool 2)
Ireland 55 T: Robinson (4), Curtis, Popplewell (2), Geoghegan; C: Keyes (4); PG: Keyes (5)
Zimbabwe 11 T: Dawson, Schultz; PG: Ferreira

6 October, Cardiff Arms Park, Cardiff (Pool 3)
Wales 13 T: Emyr, I Evans; C: Ring; PG: Ring
Western Samoa 16 T: Vaega, Viafale; C: Vaea; PG: Vaea (2)

8 October, Stade Lesdiguieres, Grenoble (Pool 4)
France 33 T: Lafond (3), Sella (2), Camberabero; C: Camberabero (3); PG: Camberabero
Fiji 9 T: Naruma; C: Koroduadua; PG: Koroduadua

8 October, Kingsholm, Gloucester (Pool 1)
New Zealand 46 T: Wright (3), Timu, Earl, Purvis, Tuigamala, Innes; C: Preston (4); PG: Preston (2)
United States 6 PG: Williams (2)

8 October, Twickenham, London (Pool 1)
England 36 T: Guscott (2), Webb, Underwood; C: Webb (4); PG: Webb (4)
Italy 6 T: Cuttitta; C: Dominguez

9 October, Murrayfield, Edinburgh (Pool 2)
Scotland 51 T: Tukalo (3), Turnbull, Stanger, S Hastings, Weir, White; C: Dods (5); PG: Dods (2); DG: Wyllie
Zimbabwe 12 T: Garvey (2); C: Currin (2)

9 October, Stade Ernest-Wallon, Toulouse (Pool 4)
Canada 19 T: McKinnon, Ennis; C: Wyatt; PG: Wyatt (2); DG: Rees
Romania 11 T: Lungu, Sasu; PG: Nichitean

9 October, Pontypool Park, Pontypool (Pool 3)
Australia 9 PG: Lynagh (3)
Western Samoa 3 PG: Vaea

9 October, Lansdowne Road, Dublin (Pool 2)
Ireland 32 T: Mannion (2), O'Hara, Staples; C: Keyes (2); PG: Keyes (4)
Japan 16 T: Hayashi, Kajihara, Yoshida; C: Yoshida (2)

9 October, Cardiff Arms Park, Cardiff (Pool 3)
Wales 16 T: Arnold; PG: Ring (3), Rayer
Argentina 7 T: Simon; PG: del Castillo

11 October, Twickenham, London (Pool 1)
England 37 T: Underwood (2), Carling, Skinner, Heslop; C: Hodgkinson (4); PG: Hodgkinson (3)
United States 9 T: Nelson; C: Williams; PG: Williams

12 October, Cardiff Arms Park, Cardiff (Pool 3)
Wales   3   PG: Ring
Australia   38   T: Roebuck (2), Slattery, Campese, Horan, Lynagh; C: Lynagh (4); PG: Lynagh (2)

12 October, Parc Municipal des Sports, Brive (Pool 4)
Romania   17   T: Ion, Dumitras, Sasu; C: Racean; PG: Nichitean
Fiji   15   T: Turuva (2); C: Rabaka (2); DG: Turuva

12 October, Murrayfield, Edinburgh (Pool 2)
Scotland   24   T: Shiel, Armstrong; C: G Hastings (2); PG: G Hastings (3); DG: Chalmers
Ireland   15   PG: Keyes (4); DG: Keyes

13 October, Sardis Road, Pontypridd (Pool 3)
Western Samoa   35   T: Tagaola (2), Lima (2), Bunce, Bachop; C: Vaea (4); PG: Vaea
Argentina   12   T: Teran; C: Arbizu; PG: Arbizu, Laborde

13 October, Welford Road, Leicester (Pool 1)
New Zealand   31   T: Z Brooke, Tuigamala, Hewitt, Innes; C: Fox (3); PG: Fox (3)
Italy   21   T: Cuttitta, Bonomi; C: Troiani (2); PG: Troiani (3)

13 October, Stade Municipal, Agen (Pool 4)
France   19   T: Lafond, Saint-André; C: Camberabero; PG: Lacroix (2), Camberabero
Canada   13   T: Wyatt; PG: Rees, Wyatt; DG: Rees

14 October, Ravenhill, Belfast (Pool 2)
Japan   52   T: Yoshida (2), Mashuho (2), Kutsuki (2), Horikoshi, Luaiufi, Matsuo, Hosokawa; C: Hosokawa (6)
Zimbabwe   8   T: Tsimba, Nguruye

Pool 1 - final standings							
Country	P	W	L	D	F	A	P
New Zealand	3	3	-	-	95	39	9
England	3	2	1	-	85	33	7
Italy	3	1	2	-	57	76	5
USA	3	-	3	-	24	113	3

Pool 2 - final standings							
Country	P	W	L	D	F	A	P
Scotland	3	3	-	-	122	36	9
Ireland	3	2	1	-	102	51	7
Japan	3	1	2	-	77	87	5
Zimbabwe	3	-	3	-	31	158	3

Pool 3 - final standings							
Country	P	W	L	D	F	A	P
Australia	3	3	-	-	79	25	9
Western Samoa	3	2	1	-	54	34	7
Wales	3	1	2	-	32	61	5
Argentina	3	-	3	-	38	83	3

Pool 4 - final standings							
Country	P	W	L	D	F	A	P
France	3	3	-	-	82	25	9
Canada	3	2	1	-	45	33	7
Romania	3	1	2	-	31	64	5
Fiji	3	-	3	-	27	63	3

Quarter-finals

The quarter-finals were all tightly contested affairs, with Scotland perhaps playing their match of the tournament when they defeated the tough and physical Western Samoa by 28–6. New Zealand saw off Canada in the rain, and England had the unenviable task of beating a fired-up French side in Paris. In a dirty and physical game, England stood up to the challenge with a monumental performance from their pack and won by 19–10, thereby ending the career of the great Serge Blanco, who was to retire at the end of France's tournament campaign. In Dublin, Ireland–Australia arguably produced the match of the tournament, with the Irish on cloud nine after the whole of Lansdowne Road had cheered on flanker Gordon Hamilton, who outpaced David Campese to score what seemed the winning try, superbly converted by Ralph Keyes. With just three minutes remaining, it seemed unlikely Australia could win, but stand-in captain, Michael Lynagh, was to score a last-second, match-winning try to beat the Irish by 19–18. Poor Ireland! A deafening silence fell across Lansdowne Road. Ireland was out and Australia met New Zealand at the same venue a week later in the semi-finals.

Quarter-final 1 (winner pool 2 vs runner-up pool 3)
19 October, Murrayfield, Edinburgh

Scotland	28	T: Jeffrey (2), Stanger; C: G Hastings (2); PG: G Hastings (4)
Western Samoa	6	PG: Vaea (2)

Quarter-final 2 (winner pool 4 vs runner-up pool 1)
19 October, Parc des Princes, Paris

France	10	T: Lafond; PG: Lacroix (2)
England	19	T: R Underwood, Carling; C: Webb; PG: Webb (3)

Quarter-final 3 (winner pool 1 vs runner-up pool 4)
20 October, Stade du Nord, Lille

New Zealand	29	T: Timu (2), Z Brooke, Kirwan, McCahill; C: Fox (3); PG: Fox
Canada	13	T: Charron, Tynan; C: Wyatt; PG: Wyatt

Quarter-final 4 (winner pool 3 vs runner-up pool 2)
20 October, Lansdowne Road, Dublin

Ireland	18	T: Hamilton; C: Keyes; PG: Keyes (3); DG: Keyes
Australia	19	T: Campese (2), Lynagh; C: Lynagh (2); PG: Lynagh

Semi-finals

Semi-final 1 (winner quarter-final 1 vs winner quarter-final 2)
26 October, Murrayfield, Edinburgh

Scotland	6	PG: G Hastings (2)
England	9	PG: Webb (2); DG: Andrew

Two of rugby's oldest rivals, England and Scotland, met in the first semi-final of the 1991 RWC. England was determined to triumph at Murrayfield, having lost the previous year in the 1990 Grand Slam showdown. It proved to be a tense forward-dominated encounter. Towards the end of the second half, the two teams were deadlocked at six points all, with Scotland being awarded a penalty directly in front of the posts within the 22. It was a certain three points to put the Scots in the lead as the ever-reliable Gavin Hastings stepped up to take the kick. But, to the shock and horror of the Murrayfield crowd, Hastings sent the kick wide and English spirits soared. They soon drove forward, getting Rob Andrew into a position to slot the winning drop goal. It was heartbreaking for Scotland with the pressure of playing in an RWC symbolised up by Gavin Hastings's miss. England were on their way to their first final.

Semi-final 2 (winner quarter-final 3 vs winner quarter-final 4)
27 October, Lansdowne Road, Dublin

Australia	16	T: Campese, Horan; C: Lynagh; PG: Lynagh (2)
New Zealand	6	PG: Fox (2)

Like the first semi-final, this was also a clash between two archrivals. As defending champions and with convincing performances throughout the tournament, New Zealand were strong favourites to win, but it was Australia who took a memorable 16–6 win, with the Lansdowne Road crowd strongly behind them. It is a match that will be remembered for the magic of David Campese, who took the game to the New Zealanders in a magical display of attacking rugby. Campese had a pivotal hand in both the game's tries, scoring the first himself when he turned his opposite winger John Kirwan inside out to score in the left corner. The second was scored by centre Tim Horan, after Campese had seized upon a bouncing Michael Lynagh kick, weaved between defenders and then threw a blind pass over his shoulder, allowing Horan to scuttle through close to the posts. Australia never looked like losing and at the final whistle, the defending champions had been knocked out with Australia to appear in their first final.

Third and fourth play-off (loser semi-final 1 vs loser semi-final 2)

30 October, Cardiff Arms Park, Cardiff

| New Zealand | 13 | T: Little; PG: Preston (3) |
| Scotland | 6 | PG: G Hastings (2) |

1991 Rugby World Cup final (winner semi-final 1 vs winner semi-final 2)

2 November, Twickenham, London

| England | 6 | PG: Webb (2) |
| Australia | 12 | T: Daly; C: Lynagh; PG: Lynagh (2) |

On 2 November 1991, the centrepiece of the 1991 Rugby World Cup unfolded at Twickenham before Her Majesty the Queen. The home team had made the final against all odds, after having lost to New Zealand, resulting in a more difficult qualification route, with a quarter-final in Paris against France and a semi-final in Edinburgh against Scotland. (The Scottish team actually came to watch the final at the stadium donned in Australian supporters' gear.) Having gone through the tournament unbeaten and having convincingly disposed of New Zealand in the semi-final, Australia found themselves favourites to win the trophy – a feat made all the easier when, remarkably, England decided to change their successful forward-orientated game plan to more of a running game. Australia took an early lead with a penalty. The only try was scored when prop forward Tony Daly crashed over from a lineout near the try line. It was not until the second half that England scored their first points with a Jonathan Webb penalty. Michael Lynagh countered this with a penalty of his own soon after, taking the score to 12–3. Then came the most controversial incident of the match when, through a series of phases, England worked the ball left toward their flying winger Rory Underwood, who had a clear overlap and path to the try line. With the ball in mid-flight to him, David Campese dived in, slapping the ball away – a deliberate knock-on, for which a penalty was awarded by referee Derek Bevan. But did it warrant a penalty try? Would Underwood have outstripped the Australian cover defence? There was no certainty and the penalty was the correct decision. Jonathan Webb converted the penalty, the last score of the match. Had the incident occurred in today's form of the game, Campese would probably have been shown a yellow card, but he remained on the field and Australia won their first Rugby World Cup 12–6. It was a bitter-sweet moment for the Queen when captain Nick Farr-Jones received the trophy from her and Australia deservedly became the 1991 world champions.

1995 Rugby World Cup
(hosted by South Africa)

With political change occurring in South Africa in 1990 following the release of Nelson Mandela, the Springboks were readmitted to world rugby in 1992. The Rainbow Nation (as Archbishop Emeritus Desmond Tutu so aptly named South Africa) had been granted the rights to host the third Rugby World Cup and with such rugby personalities as captain François Pienaar and team manager, Morné du Plessis, the tournament was a key event to help bring together the once-divided nation.

The qualifying process for the tournament was the biggest yet as 43 countries vied for the eight available spots. Wales, traditionally one of the world's finest rugby nations, found themselves in the embarrassing position of having to qualify (having not made the 1991 quarter-finals), playing against minnow European rugby nations such as Spain and Portugal. The big surprise in the qualifying stages was Côte d'Ivoire who beat off the challenges of Namibia, Zimbabwe and Morocco for the second African spot. Since returning to international rugby, South Africa had struggled to compete, but under the guidance of new coach Kitch Christie, there was hope in the Rainbow Nation that they could indeed triumph.

The opening match of the tournament was a tantalising clash between defending champions Australia, and tournament debutants and hosts South Africa, in Cape Town. President Nelson Mandela officially opened the tournament and South Africa took on the favourites Australia, who had been undefeated the previous season. A try from Pieter Hendriks and a full house from Joel Stransky ensured a famous 27–18 victory for South Africa. The tournament had begun with a bang – Australia's 'operation repeat' was becoming 'operation defeat'. Results from the pool stages were as expected, with France pipping Scotland for the all-important top spot in pool D, and England narrowly seeing off Italy and Argentina to top pool B. New Zealand unveiled a legend in the making, with 19-year-old Jonah Lomu helping New Zealand crush Ireland and Wales, with length-of-the-field tries. Japan were thrashed by a cricket score of 145–17.

Following his performances in the tournament, Lomu was to become the sensation of this World Cup and one of the first global rugby superstars. There were other highlights in the pool stages, as Côte d'Ivoire scored their first World Cup points with 18 against France, while Japan pushed Ireland all the way in their 28–50 loss – the defeat thanks in no small part to having two penalty tries awarded against them. There were also low points: Max Brito of Côte d'Ivoire was paralysed after he broke his neck in a ruck during the Côte d'Ivoire–Tonga encounter in Rustenburg, and three players were sent off after the notorious 'Battle of the Boet', when South Africa defeated Canada 20–0 in a dirty match. All three rejects – South Africa's James Dalton and Canadian prop Rod Snow and skipper Gareth Rees – were subsequently banned, while South Africa's Pieter Hendriks was cited and banned, allowing Chester Williams (South Africa's first non-white Springbok since readmission) to enter the fray – much to the delight of the home fans.

1995 RWC pools

Pool A	
Country	Previous best finish
Australia	Champions '91
South Africa	Debutant
Canada	Quarter-finalists '91
Romania	Contestants all world cups

Pool B	
Country	Previous best finish
England	Runners-up '91
Western Samoa	Quarter-finalists '91
Argentina	Contestants all world cups
Italy	Contestants all worl cups

Pool C	
Country	Previous best finish
New Zealand	Champions '87
Ireland	Quarter-finalists '87, '91
Wales	3rd place '87
Japan	Contestants all world cups

Pool D	
Country	Previous best finish
France	Runners-up '87
Scotland	4th place '91
Tonga	Contestants '87
Côte d'Ivoire	Debutant

Pool results

25 May Newlands, Cape Town (Pool A)
South Africa 27 T: Hendriks, Stransky; C: Stransky; PG: Stransky (4); DG: Stransky
Australia 18 T: Lynagh, Kearns; C: Lynagh; PG: Lynagh (2)

26 May, Boet Erasmus Stadium, Port Elizabeth (Pool A)
Canada 34 T: Charron, McKenzie, Snow; C: Rees (2); PG: Rees (5)
Romania 3 PG: Ivancuic

26 May, Loftus Versfeld, Pretoria (Pool D)
France 38 T: Lacroix (2), Hueber, Saint-André; C: Lacroix (3); PG: Lacroix (3); DG: Delaigue
Tonga 10 T: T Va'enuku; C: Tu'ipulotu; PG: Tu'ipulotu

26 May, Olympia Park, Rustenburg (Pool D)
Scotland 89 T: Hastings (4), Logan (2), Walton (2), Burnell, Wright, Chalmers, Stanger, Shiel; C: Hastings (9); PG: Hastings (2)
Côte d'Ivoire 0

27 May, Basil Kenyon Stadium, East London (Pool B)
Western Samoa 42 T: Lima (2), Harder (2), Kellett, Tatupu; C: Kellett (3); PG: Kellett (2)
Italy 18 T: Vaccari, Cuttitta; C: Dominguez; PG: Dominguez; DG: Dominguez

27 May, Free State Stadium, Bloemfontein (Pool C)
Wales 57 T: Thomas (3), I Evans (2), Moore, Taylor; C: Jenkins (5); PG: Jenkins (4)
Japan 10 T: Oto (2)

27 May, Kings Park, Durban (Pool B)
England 24 PG: Andrew (6); DG: Andrew (2)
Argentina 18 T: Noriega, Arbizu; C: Arbizu; PG: Arbizu (2)

27 May, Ellis Park, Johannesburg (Pool C)
New Zealand 43 T: Lomu (2), Kronfeld, Bunce, Osborne; C: Mehrtens (3); PG: Mehrtens (4)
Ireland 19 T: Halpin, McBride, Corkery; C: Elwood (2)

29 May, Newlands, Cape Town (Pool A)
South Africa 21 T: Richter (2); C: Johnson; PG: Johnson (3)
Romania 8 T: Guranescu; PG: Ivanciuc

30 May, Olympia Park, Rustenburg (Pool D)
France 54 T: Lacroix (2), Benazzi, Accoceberry, Viars, Costes, Techoueyres, Saint-Andre; C: Lacroix (2), Deylaud (2); PG: Lacroix (2)
Côte d'Ivoire 18 T: Camara, Soulama; C: Kouassi; PG: Kouassi (2)

30 May, Loftus Versfeld, Pretoria (Pool D)
Scotland 41 T: G Hastings, Peters, S Hastings; C: G Hastings; PG: G Hastings (8)
Tonga 5 T: Fenukitau

30 May, Basil Kenyon Stadium, East London (Pool B)
Western Samoa 32 T: Lam, Leaupepe, Harder; C: Kellett; PG: Kellett (5)
Argentina 26 T: Crexwell, Arbizu; C: Cilley (2); PG: Cilley (4)

31 May, Boet Erasmus Stadium, Port Elizabeth (Pool A)
Australia 27 T: Tabua, Roff, Lynagh; C: Lynagh (3); PG: Lynagh (2)
Canada 11 T: Charron; PG: Rees (2)

31 May, Free State Stadium, Bloemfontein (Pool C)
Ireland 50 T: Corkery, Francis, Geoghegan, Halvey, Hogan, penalty try (2); C: Burke (6); PG: Burke
Japan 28 T: Latu, Izawa, Hirao, Takura; C: Yoshida (4)

31 May, Kings Park, Durban (Pool B)
England 27 T: A Underwood, R Underwood; C: Andrew; PG: Andrew (5)
Italy 20 T: Cuttitta, Vaccari; C: Dominguez (2); PG: Dominguez (2)

31 May, Ellis Park, Johannesburg (Pool C)
New Zealand 34 T: Little, Ellis, Kronfeld; C: Mehrtens (2); PG: Mehrtens (4); DG: Mehrtens
Wales 9 PG: Jenkins (2); DG: Jenkins

3 June, Danie Craven Stadium, Stellenbosch (Pool A)
Australia 42 T: Roff (2), Foley, Burke, Smith, Wilson; C: Burke (2), Eales (4)
Romania 3 DG: Ivanciuc

3 June, Olympia Park, Rustenburg (Pool D)
Tonga 29 T: 'Otai, Tu'ipulotu, Latukefu; C: Tu'ipulotu (3); PG: Tu'ipulotu
Côte d'Ivoire 11 T: Okou; PG: Dali (2)

3 June, Boet Erasmus Stadium, Port Elizabeth (Pool A)
South Africa 20 T: Richter (2); C: Stransky (2); PG: Stransky (2)
Canada 0

3 June, Loftus Versfeld, Pretoria (Pool D)
France 22 T: N'Tamack; C: Lacroix; PG: Lacroix (5)
Scotland 19 T: Wainwright; C: G Hastings; PG: G Hastings (4)

4 June, Basil Kenyon Stadium, East London (Pool B)
Italy 31 T: Vaccari, Gerosa, Dominguez; C: Dominguez (2); PG: Dominguez (4)
Argentina 25 T: Corral, Martin, Cilley; C: Cilley (2); PG: Cilley (2)

4 June, Free State Stadium, Bloemfontein (Pool C)
New Zealand 145 T: Ellis (6), Wilson (3), Rush (3), R Brooke (2), Loe, Osborne (2), Ieremia, Dowd, Henderson, Culhane; C: Culhane (20)
Japan 17 T: Kajihara (2); C: Hirose (2); PG: Hirose

4 June, Kings Park, Durban (Pool B)
England 44 T: R Underwood (2), Back, penalty try; C: Callard (3); PG: Callard (5); DG: Catt
Samoa 22 T: Sini (2), Umaga; C: Fa'amasino (2); PG: Fa'amasino

4 June, Ellis Park, Johannesburg (Pool C)
Ireland 24 T: McBride, Halvey, Popplewell; C: Elwood (3); PG: Elwood
Wales 23 T: Humphreys, Taylor; C: Jenkins (2); PG: Jenkins (2); DG: A Davies

Pool A - final standings							
Country	P	W	L	D	F	A	P
South Africa	3	3	-	-	68	26	9
Australia	3	2	1	-	87	41	7
Canada	3	1	2	-	45	50	5
Romania	3	-	3	-	14	97	3

Pool B - final standings							
Country	P	W	L	D	F	A	P
England	3	3	-	-	95	60	9
Western Samoa	3	2	1	-	96	88	7
Italy	3	1	2	-	69	94	5
Argentina	3	-	3	-	69	87	3

Pool C - final standings							
Country	P	W	L	D	F	A	P
New Zealand	3	3	-	-	222	45	9
Ireland	3	2	1	-	93	94	7
Wales	3	1	2	-	89	68	5
Japan	3	-	3	-	55	252	3

Pool D - final standings							
Country	P	W	L	D	F	A	P
France	3	3	-	-	114	47	9
Scotland	3	2	1	-	149	27	7
Tonga	3	1	2	-	44	90	5
Côte d'Ivoire	3	-	3	-	29	172	3

Quarter-finals

Quarter-final fixtures saw Western Samoa feature in their second consecutive quarter-final, with Wales again bowing out in the pool stages after losing the crucial pool fixture against Ireland 23–24. France outplayed Ireland in Durban, but the scoreline flattered France somewhat, as Emile N'Tamack sneaked a late intercept try which, along with Thierry Lacroix's eight penalty goals, France won 36–12 and sent Ireland home. In the South Africa–Western Samoa encounter, Chester Williams set the World Cup alight in his first appearance by scoring a then South African record of four tries in an international. It was a brutal match, one in which referee, Jim Fleming of Scotland, failed to take control, resulting in some fierce, illegal Samoan tackling, with fullback André Joubert having his hand broken by an obscenely high Mike Umaga tackle. South Africa triumphed by 42–14 and Western Samoa waved goodbye to their second world cup. The following day in Pretoria, Scotland were comprehensively outplayed by New Zealand and in particular by Jonah Lomu. It was an emotional farewell for Scotland's Gavin Hastings – he retired following the defeat. The pick of the quarter-finals was the rematch of the 1991 Rugby World Cup final between England and Australia. The two teams had not met since the 1991 encounter. Each team scored a single try and the lead changed hands several times as veteran flyhalfs, Lynagh and Andrew, matched penalty for penalty throughout the encounter. Deep into injury time, with scores locked at 22–22, England won a lineout inside the Australian half. The forwards drove up and from the 10-metre line Rob Andrew dropped the match-winning goal to send the defending champions home.

Quarter-final 1 (winner pool D vs runner-up pool C)
10 June, Kings Park, Durban

France	36	T: Saint-André, N'Tamack; C: Lacroix; PG: Lacroix (8)
Ireland	12	PG: Elwood (4)

Quarter-final 2 (winner pool A vs runner-up pool B)
10 June, Ellis Park, Johannesburg

South Africa	42	T: Williams (4), Andrews, Rossouw; C: Johnson (3); PG: Johnson (2)
Western Samoa	14	T: Falaniko, Nu'uali'itia; C: Fa'amasino (2)

Quarter-final 3 (winner pool C vs runner-up pool D)
11 June, Loftus Versfeld, Pretoria

New Zealand	48	T: Little (2), Lomu, Mehrtens, Bunce, Fitzpatrick; C: Mehrtens (6); PG: Mehrtens (2)
Scotland	30	T: Weir (2), S Hastings; C: G Hastings (3); PG: G Hastings (3)

Quarter-final 4 (winner pool B vs runner-up pool A)

11 June, Newlands, Cape Town

| England | 25 | T: A Underwood; C: Andrew; PG: Andrew (5); DG: Andrew |
| Australia | 22 | T: Smith; C: Lynagh; PG: Lynagh (5) |

Semi-finals

Semi-final 1 (winner quarter-final 1 vs winner quarter-final 2)

17 June, Kings Park, Durban

| South Africa | 19 | T: Kruger; C: Stransky; PG: Stransky (4) |
| France | 15 | PG: Lacroix (5) |

Rain in sunny, hot, tropical Durban is rare in June – so they said! On 17 June 1995, the rain fell and didn't stop. It flooded the Kings Park pitch so that the game had to be postponed for 90 minutes in an effort to clear the field of the water, with the ground staff literally sweeping the water off with brooms. There was the distinct possibility that the game would have to be abandoned in the interests of the players' safety. With no reserve day scheduled for such an event, France would have been declared winners due to South Africa's worse disciplinary record, after the sending off of James Dalton in the Canadian match. The whole of South Africa watched anxiously as the rain continued to fall, but to the delight of the home nation, referee Derek Bevan eventually declared the field fit for play and the two teams made their way out. It was never going to be a classic due to the weather conditions, and midway through the first half the rain returned with force, worsening the playing conditions and bringing fears of players possibly drowning, trapped at the bottom of lengthy rucks. Under the circumstances, referee Bevan had to stop the rucks quickly and scrums became the main feature of the game. South Africa managed to score the only try of the match when flanker Ruben Kruger was shoved over in a maul in the first half and Joel Stransky and Thierry Lacroix exchanged penalties right until the end. With time nearly up and the French pressing, their flyhalf Christophe Deylaud put in a challenging up-and-under. Fullback Joubert, playing with a broken hand, failed to gather and French flanker Abdelatif Benazzi latched onto it and dived toward the try line for what many thought would be the match-winning score. However, incredibly winger James Small was on hand to stop Benazzi just inches short of the line and South Africa went on to win. The Rainbow Nation erupted: they were in the final–against all odds.

Semi-final 2 (winner quarter-final 3 vs winner quarter-final 4)

18 June, Newlands, Cape Town

| New Zealand | 45 | T: Lomu (4), Kronfeld, Bachop; C: Mehrtens (3); PG: Mehrtens; DG: Mehrtens, Z Brooke |
| England | 29 | T: Underwood (2), Carling (2); C: Andrew (3); PG: Andrew |

England faced the unenviable task of taking on New Zealand and their new sensation Jonah Lomu, who had been in unstoppable form throughout the tournament. A packed Newlands witnessed one of the finest rugby performances in RWC history as New Zealand destroyed England, with the result clear before the end of the first half. It took Lomu just over a minute to get on the score sheet when he brushed aside Tony Underwood and Will Carling and famously ran directly over Mike Catt to score. He went on to score four tries in the match, with commentator Keith Quinn aptly putting it as 'the greatest quartet of tries you will ever see'. The game was taken away from England after 20 minutes, and to make matters worse, a young Andrew Mehrtens was in sublime form, slotting touchline conversions. To add insult to injury, the All Blacks' eighthman, Zinzan Brooke, scored one of the most audacious-ever drop goals from near the halfway line and on the run. A late flurry of tries by captain Will Carling and winger Rory Underwood in the second half ensured England were not humiliated by the scoreline and who indeed outscored New Zealand in the second half. But too little too late.

Third and fourth play-off (loser semi-final 1 vs loser semi-final 2)

22 June, Loftus Versfeld, Pretoria

| France | 19 | T: Roumat, N'Tamack; PG: Lacroix (3) |
| England | 9 | PG: Andrew (3) |

1995 Rugby World Cup final (winner semi-final 1 vs winner semi-final 2)

24 June, Ellis Park, Johannesburg

South Africa	15	PG: Stransky (3); DG: Stransky (2)
New Zealand	12	PG: Mehrtens (3); DG: Mehrtens

June 24 1995 is a date that will forever go down in the annals of not only South African rugby, but also the political history of South Africa and, for once, for all the right reasons. On this day, rugby drew the entire Rainbow Nation together as the country celebrated and cheered as one, with images of blacks and whites dancing together in the streets portrayed in the media. Ellis Park was packed to the brim to witness South Africa's greatest rugby moment and arguably the greatest Rugby World Cup final Against all odds, François Pienaar's Springboks defeated the All Blacks who were massive favourites to win, after having convincingly defeated all their opponents throughout the tournament. It is not a final that will be remembered for its running rugby and glittering tries – rather one of big hits and tight defence where inches gained was a battle won. A South African Airways plane set the mood when it flew low over the stadium with the words 'Good luck, Bokke' painted on the underside of the wings. President Nelson Mandela appeared on the field, wearing the Springbok jersey, to meet the two sides. The scene was set.

New Zealand claimed an early lead after Mehrtens slotted a penalty, but after all the hype that had surrounded Jonah Lomu, South Africa was ready and he was to have little impact on the game. South Africa did not miss a single tackle on the big man, with Joost van der Westhuizen, James Small and Japie Mulder standing out in defence against Lomu. At half-time, the Boks led 9–6, but by full time it was locked at 9–9 after Mehrtens had missed a crucial, potentially match-winning drop goal from in front of the posts in the final minute. And so, for the first time in Rugby World Cup history, a match went into extra time, with South Africa knowing full well that if, after extra time, scores were still locked, New Zealand would win the title, thanks to South Africa's worse disciplinary record. After half-time of extra time scores were still tied – this time at 12–12, but by the end of the second half of extra time Joel Stransky had etched his name in rugby history. With seven minutes remaining, Stransky slotted the greatest kick of his life from a set-piece scrum to put South Africa ahead, sending the nation into delirium. South Africa held out for the most important victory in its history and Nelson Mandela, donned in the number 6 Springbok jersey, presented the cup to his captain and number 6, François Pienaar, thereby allowing South Africa to celebrate together as a multiracial society for the first time in its history. Pienaar credited his team's success to the support of each and every one of the 43 million South Africans. New Zealand were obviously devastated and a few days later, claimed that a waitress, whom they knew only by the name of Suzie, had food-poisoned them. This had allegedly laid them low just hours before the game, severely affecting their performance – so much so that their coach Laurie Mains said that he thought it was a miracle they scored any points at all. The claim was never proved and it is South Africa who shall forever remain the 1995 Rugby World Cup champions.

1999 Rugby World Cup
(co-hosted by Wales, England, Scotland, Ireland and France)

The fanatical rugby nation Wales hosted the fourth Rugby World Cup, which was co-hosted by England, Scotland, Ireland and France – a move many thought to be ill-advised after the poor spirit of the 1991 tournament, which had created so many logistical errors and split the atmosphere across the five different nations. For Wales, who had failed to reach the quarter-finals for the previous two tournaments, this was an opportunity to emulate or go one further than their 1987 predecessors under the guidance of their new coach, Graham Henry.

It was the first time in the tournament's history that 20 nations were to compete for the coveted trophy, and the event was strangely structured by the IRB into five pools of four teams, rather than the obvious four pools of five teams. This created the problem of choosing eight quarter-finalists from five pools, resolved by introducing an extra set of midweek games – the quarter-final playoffs. This extra set of games would be a disadvantage, as it added an extra tough fixture just days before the quarter-final weekend for those sides finishing second in their pools, while the other sides who topped their respective pools would have a full week's rest, giving them a distinct advantage. There were debuts for Namibia, Uruguay and Spain and the tournament was kicked off with a scrappy affair played between hosts, Wales, and Argentina, with Wales winning a tight encounter by 23–18. The pool games produced a high quality of rugby, with upsets by smaller nations occurring more regularly than before. Samoa once again defeated Wales in Cardiff, this time with an impressive scoreline of 38–31. The only good thing to come out of this game from a Welsh perspective was that it resulted in Neil Jenkins becoming the first man in international rugby to surpass 1,000 points. Memorable moments from the pool stages included Keith Wood becoming the first hooker to score four tries in an international when Ireland beat the United States; Tonga's last-second, match-winning drop goal against Italy and Jonah Lomu's scintillating 50-metre run to gain a try against England, ensuring that New Zealand topped their pool. Disappointments came from Italy, who were to join the Five Nations the following year, and failed to win a game, in the process losing by over a hundred points against New Zealand.

1999 RWC pools

Pool A	
Country	Previous best finish
South Africa	Champions '95
Scotland	4th Place '91
Uruguay	Debutant
Spain	Debutant

Pool B	
Country	Previous best finish
New Zealand	Champions '87
England	Runners-up '91
Italy	Contestants all world cups
Tonga	Contestants '87, '95

Pool C	
Country	Previous best finish
France	Runners-up '87
Fiji	Quarter-finalists '87
Canada	Quarter-finalists '91
Namibia	Debutant

Pool D	
Country	Previous best finish
Wales	3rd Place '87
Samoa	Quarter-finalists '91, '95
Argentina	Contestants all world cups
Japan	Contestants all world cups

Pool E	
Country	Previous best finish
Australia	Champions '91
Ireland	Quarter-finalists '87, '91, '95
United States	Contestants '87, '91
Romania	Contestants all world cups

Pool results

1 October, Millennium Stadium, Cardiff (Pool D)
Wales   23   T: Taylor, Charvis; C: Jenkins (2); PG: Jenkins (3)
Argentina 18   PG: Quesada (6)

1 October, Stade Méditerranée, Beziers (Pool C)
Fiji   67   T: Lasagavibau (2), Satala (2), Tikomaimakogai, Mocelutu, Tawake, Smith, Rauluni; C: Serevi (8); PG: Serevi (2)
Namibia 18   T: Senekal, Jacob; C: van Dyk; PG: van Dyk (2)

2 October, Stade Méditerranée, Beziers (Pool C)
France   33   T: Dourthe, Magne, Castaignede, N'Tamack; C: Dourthe (2); PG: Dourthe (3)
Canada   20   T: Williams; C: Rees, Ross; PG: Rees, Ross

2 October, Netherdale, Galashiels (Pool A)
Uruguay 27   T: Ormaechea, Cardoso, penalty try, Menchaca; C: Sciarra, D Aguirre; PG: D Aguirre
Spain   15   PG: Kovalenco (5)

2 October, Twickenham, London (Pool B)
England 67   T: Dawson, Hill, de Glanville, Perry, Wilkinson, Back, Luger, Corry; C: Wilkinson (6); PG: Wilkinson (5)
Italy   7   T: Dominguez; C: Dominguez

2 October, Lansdowne Road, Dublin (Pool E)
Ireland   53   T: Wood (4), Bishop, O'Driscoll, penalty try; C: Humphreys (4), Elwood (2); PG: Humphreys (2)
United States   8   T: Dalzell; PG: Dalzell

3 October, Racecourse Ground, Wrexham (Pool D)
Samoa   43   T: Lima (2), Leaega, A So'oialo (2); C: Leaega (3); PG: Leaega (4)
Japan   9   PG: Hirose (3)

3 October, Ashton Gate, Bristol (Pool B)
New Zealand   45   T: Lomu (2), Kronfeld, Maxwell, Kellaher; C: Mehrtens (4); PG: Mehrtens (4)
Tonga   9   PG: Taumalolo (3)

3 October, Murrayfield, Edinburgh (Pool A)
Scotland   29   T: Tait, M Leslie; C: Logan (2); PG: Logan (4); DG: Townsend
South Africa   46   T: van der Westhuizen, le Roux, Kayser, Fleck, B Venter, A Venter; C: de Beer (5); PG: de Beer (2)

3 October, Ravenhill, Belfast (Pool E)
Australia   57   T: Kefu (3), Roff (2), Little, Horan, Paul, Burke; C: Burke (5), Eales
Romania   9   PG: Mitu (3)

8 October, Murrayfield, Edinburgh (Pool A)
Scotland   43   T: Leslie, Armstrong, Simpson, Metcalfe, Russell, Townsend; C: Logan (5); PG: Logan
Uruguay   12   PG: Aguirre (3), Sciarra

8 October, Stade Lescure, Bordeaux (Pool C)
France   47   T: Mola (3), Mignoni, Bernat-Salles, N'Tamack; C: Dourthe (3), Lamaison; PG: Dourthe (3)
Namibia   13   T: A Samuelson; C: van Dyk; PG: van Dyk (2)

9 October, Stade Lescure, Bordeaux (Pool C)
Fiji   38   T: Satala (2), Vunibaka, penalty try; C: Little (3); PG: Little (3); DG: Little
Canada   22   T: James; C: Rees; PG: Rees (4); DG: Rees

9 October, Millennium Stadium, Cardiff (Pool D)
Wales   64   T: Taylor (2), Bateman, penalty try, Howley, Gibbs, Howarth, Llewellyn, Thomas; C: Jenkins (8); PG: Jenkins
Japan   15   T: Ohata, Tuidraki; C: Hirose; PG: Hirose

9 October, Twickenham, London (Pool B)
England   16   T: de Glanville; C: Wilkinson; PG: Wilkinson (3)
New Zealand   30   T: Wilson, Lomu, Kelleher; C: Mehrtens (3); PG: Mehrtens (3)

9 October, Lansdowne Road, Dublin (Pool E)
Romania   27   T: Solomie (2), Petrache (2); C: Mitu (2); PG: Mitu
United States   25   T: Lyle, Hightower, Shuman; C: Dalzell (2); PG: Dalzell (2)

10 October, Stradey Park, Llanelli (Pool D)
Argentina   32   T: Allub; PG: Quesada (8); DG: Quesada
Samoa   16   T: Paramore; C: Leaega; PG: Leaega (3)

10 October, Lansdowne Road, Dublin (Pool E)
Ireland   3   PG: Humphreys
Australia   23   T: Horan, Tune; C: Burke (2); PG: Burke (2), Eales

10 October, Murrayfield, Edinburgh (Pool A)
South Africa   47   T: Vos (2), Leonard, Swanepoel, Muller, Skinstad, penalty try; C: de Beer (6)
Spain   3   PG: Velasco

10 October, Welford Road, Leicester (Pool B)
Tonga   28   T: Taufahema, S Tuipulotu, Fatani; C: S Tuipulotu (2); PG: S Tuipulotu (2); DG: S Tuipulotu
Italy   25   T: Moscardi; C: Dominguez; PG: Dominguez (6)

14 October, McAlpine Stadium, Huddersfield (Pool B)
New Zealand   101   T: Wilson (3), Lomu (2), Osborne (2), Brown, Mika, Randell, Robertson, Gibson, Cullen, Hammett; C: Brown (11);
                       PG: Brown (3)
Italy   3   PG: Dominguez

14 October, Millennium Stadium, Cardiff (Pool D)
Wales   31   T: penalty try (2), Thomas; C: Jenkins (2); PG: Jenkins (4)
Samoa   38   T: Bachop (2), Falaniko, Lam, Leaega; C: Leaega (5); PG: Leaega

14 October, Thomond Park, Limerick (Pool E)
Australia 55 T: Staniforth (2), Larkham, Foley, Burke, Strauss, Latham, Whitaker; C: Burke (5), Roff; PG: Burke
United States 19 T: Grobler; C: Dalzell; PG: Dalzell (3); DG: Niu

14 October, Stade Municipal, Toulouse (Pool C)
Canada 72 T: Nichols (2), Snow (2), Stanley (2), Williams, Charron, Ross; C: Rees (9); PG: Rees (3)
Namibia 11 T: Hough; PG: van Dyk (2)

15 October, Twickenham, London (Pool B)
England 101 T: Greenwood (2), Healey (2), Luger (2), Perry, Greening (2), Guscott (2), Dawson, Hill; C: Grayson (12); PG: Grayson (4)
Tonga 10 T: Tiueti; C: S Tu'ipulotu; PG: S Tu'ipulotu

15 October, Hampden Park, Glasgow (Pool A)
South Africa 39 T: van den Berg (2), Kayser, Fleck, van der Westhuizen; C: de Beer (4); PG: de Beer (2)
Uruguay 3 PG: Aguirre

15 October, Lansdowne Road, Dublin (Pool D)
Ireland 44 T: O'Shea (2), O'Cuinneagain, Ward, Tierney; C: Elwood (5); PG: Elwood (2); DG: O'Driscoll
Romania 14 T: Sauan; PG: Mitu (3)

16 October, Stade Municipal, Toulouse (Pool C)
France 28 T: Julliet, penalty try, Dominici; C: Dourthe (2); PG: Dourthe (2), Lamaison
Fiji 19 T: Uluinayo; C: Little; PG: Little (4)

16 October, Murrayfield, Edinburgh (Pool A)
Scotland 48 T: Mather (2), penalty try, Hodge, Murray, McLaren; C: Hodge (5); PG: Hodge
Spain 0

16 October, Millennium Stadium, Cardiff (Pool D)
Argentina 33 T: Pichot, Albanese; C: F Contepomi; PG: Quesada (8)
Japan 12 PG: Hirose

Pool A - final standings							
Country	P	W	L	D	F	A	P
South Africa	3	3	-	-	132	35	9
Scotland	3	2	1	-	120	58	7
Uruguay	3	1	2	-	42	97	5
Spain	3	-	3	-	18	122	3

Pool B - final standings							
Country	P	W	L	D	F	A	P
New Zealand	3	3	-	-	176	28	9
England	3	2	1	-	184	47	7
Tonga	3	1	2	-	47	171	5
Italy	3	-	3	-	35	196	3

Pool C - final standings							
Country	P	W	L	D	F	A	P
France	3	3	-	-	108	52	9
Fiji	3	2	1	-	124	68	7
Canada	3	1	2	-	114	82	5
Namibia	3	-	3	-	42	186	3

Pool D - final standings							
Country	P	W	L	D	F	A	P
Wales	3	2	1	-	118	71	7
Samoa	3	2	1	-	97	72	7
Argentina	3	2	1	-	83	51	7
Japan	3	-	3	-	36	140	3

Pool E - final standings							
Country	P	W	L	D	F	A	P
Australia	3	3	-	-	135	31	9
Ireland	3	2	1	-	100	45	7
Romania	3	1	2	-	50	126	5
United States	3	-	3	-	52	135	3

Quarter-final play-offs

The second-placed teams from all five pools (England, Scotland, Ireland, Samoa and Fiji) plus the best third-placed finisher (Argentina) qualified for this midweek fixture to compete for a place in the weekend quarter-finals. A strong, fast Fijian outfit gave England a tough challenge during this vital midweek encounter, with the scoreline somewhat flattering the English, thanks to seven accurate Wilkinson penalty goals, as they eventually outplayed the Fijians by four tries to three. In Edinburgh, Scotland downed an extremely powerful Samoan side on a wet and cold afternoon, while later on that same day, Argentina, recorded one of the great upsets of world cup rugby when they deservedly beat Ireland in a thrilling encounter in Lens. Gonzalo Quesada and David Humphreys exchanged penalty after penalty until late into the game and, with time running out, a wonderful Argentinian backline move put winger Diego Albanese in for the only try of the match and sent Ireland out of the tournament without making the quarter-finals, for the first time.

Quarter-final play-off 1 (runner-up pool B vs runner-up pool C)

20 October, Twickenham, London

| England | 45 | T: Luger, Back, Beal, Greening; C: Wilkinson, Dawson; PG: Wilkinson (7) |
| Fiji | 24 | T: Satala, Tikomaimakogia, Nakauta; C: Little (3); PG: Little |

Quarter-final play-off 2 (runner-up pool A vs runner-up pool D)

20 October, Murrayfield, Edinburgh

| Scotland | 35 | T: penalty try, Leslie, C Murray; C: Logan; PG: Logan (5); DG: Townsend |
| Samoa | 20 | T: Setiti, Lima; C: Leaege (2); PG: Leaege (2) |

Quarter-final play-off 3 (runner-up pool E vs best third-placed finish)

20 October, Stade Felix Bollaert, Lens

| Argentina | 28 | T: Albanese; C: Quesada; PG: Quesada (7) |
| Ireland | 24 | PG: Humphreys (7); DG: Humphreys |

Quarter-finals

There was great expectation throughout Wales, despite their pool-stage loss to Samoa, that their side, as hosts, could defeat the Australians to reach their first semi-final since 1987. Unfortunately, it was not to be, as the Australians proved too powerful for the Welsh with a brace of tries by scrumhalf George Gregan, and one by winger, Ben Tune, that saw Australia triumph 24–9 in Cardiff, ending the Welsh campaign. It was a heartbreaking end to a disappointing tournament for the Welsh. For the Australians it was the next step forward to setting aside the disappointment of the 1995 tournament and regaining the trophy they had won in 1991.

Across the English Channel in Paris, England prepared to do battle with South Africa at the mighty Stade de France, a match that will always be remembered for the world-record kicking of Springbok flyhalf Jannie de Beer. It was an extremely tight affair until half-time, when, with the English leading 12–9, South African captain Joost van der Westhuizen was awarded a dubious try in the corner. South Africa went into the break 16–12 up. In the second half, Jannie de Beer came to the fore and sunk the English with a kicking display never before seen in rugby history. In just 40 minutes, de Beer kicked five magnificent drop goals from five attempts to smash the previous record of three in a match held by various players. He effectively took the game away from the English. This flawless kicking display and a further try by winger Pieter Rossouw, saw off the English by 44–21. It was a bitterly disappointing world cup campaign for England, in which they managed to beat only Italy, Tonga and Fiji.

The following day, Dublin saw Argentina enter the game confidently, as France had not yet proved themselves, having struggled to overcome Fiji and Canada. Argentina played some brilliant rugby, but were just not good enough against the French back three, who scored all five of France's tries. Nevertheless, it was a very successful World Cup for the Argentinians, as they reached their first-ever quarter-final and could look forward to the next World Cup. The French were to reach their third World Cup semi-final.

In Edinburgh, a heavily favoured All Blacks side battled their way through the foul Edinburgh weather to down a very competitive Scotland. The mighty New Zealand back three, Lomu, Umaga and Wilson, scored all the New Zealand tries as the All Blacks continued their seemingly unstoppable march to World Cup glory.

Quarter-final 1 (winner pool D vs winner pool E)

23 October, Millennium Stadium, Cardiff

| Wales | 9 | PG: Jenkins (3) |
| Australia | 24 | T: Gregan (2), Tune; C: Burke (3); PG: Burke |

Quarter-final 2 (winner pool A vs winner quarter-final play-off 1)

24 October, Stade de France, Paris

| South Africa | 44 | T: van der Westhuizen, Rossouw; C: de Beer (2); PG: de Beer (5); DG: de Beer (5) |
| England | 21 | PG: Grayson (6), Wilkinson |

Quarter-final 3 (winner pool C vs winner quarter-final play-off 3)

24 October, Lansdowne Road, Dublin

| France | 47 | T: Garbajosa (2), N'Tamack, Bernat-Salles (2); C: Lamaison (5); PG: Lamaison (4) |
| Argentina | 26 | T: Pichot, Arbizu; C: Quesada (2); PG: Quesada (3), Contepomi |

Quarter-final 4 (winner pool B vs winner quarter-final play-off 2)

24 October, Murrayfield, Edinburgh

| Scotland | 18 | T: Pountney, C Murray; C: Logan; PG: Logan; DG: Townsend |
| New Zealand | 30 | T: Umaga (2), Wilson, Lomu; C: Mehrtens (2); PG: Mehrtens (2) |

Semi-finals

Semi-final 1 (winner quarter-final 1 vs winner quarter-final 2)

30 October, Twickenham, London

| Australia | 27 | PG: Burke (8); DG: Larkham |
| South Africa | 21 | PG: de Beer (6); DG: de Beer |

A clash of the defending champions versus the 1991 champions offered an enticing encounter with no firm favourite – both had won their quarter-finals convincingly and both had beaten each other during that year's Tri-Nations. Unfortunately, the British weather did not play its part, as the London rain swept across Twickenham for the entire duration of the game. Not a single try was scored with defence as the name of the game, although both sides did get close to scoring a try through their respective centres, Tim Horan and Robbie Fleck. It was a nail-biting encounter, with kickers Matt Burke and Jannie de Beer exchanging penalties through the match. De Beer, attempted to repeat his drop-goal antics from the weekend before, but only one attempt proved successful. The Australians led 12–6 at half-time and with full time up on the clock and the Australians leading 18–15, replacement Owen Finegan was penalised by Welsh referee Derek Bevan. From wide out, Jannie de Beer was given the unenviable task of converting the penalty to tie the scores and put the game into extra time. And he did. For the second time in World Cup history, a match went into 20 minutes' extra time. An early penalty by Jannie de Beer gave South Africa a 21–18 lead, but they were not to score again. Matt Burke evened the scores soon after and it was then that Wallaby flyhalf, Stephen Larkham, kicked the greatest kick of his career – a 50-metre drop that took the game away from the Springboks. A fantastic semi-final came to an end, with the South Africans unable to defend their 1995 title, while the Australians were to play in their second World Cup final.

Semi-final 2 (winner quarter-final 3 vs winner quarter-final 4)

31 October, Twickenham, London

| France | 43 | T: Lamaison, Dominici, Dourthe, Bernat-Salles; C: Lamaison (4); PG: Lamaison (3); DG: Lamaison (2) |
| New Zealand | 31 | T: Lomu (2), Wilson; C: Mehrtens (2); PG: Mehrtens (4) |

This was arguably the greatest upset in Rugby World Cup history. New Zealand were massive favourites and were expected not only to win, but win well, particularly considering how they had defeated the French by 50 points earlier in the year. Jonah Lomu was in sublime form, smashing his way forward to two early tries. But the French did not sit back. With the All Blacks leading 24–15, French flyhalf Christophe Lamaison, playing an outstanding match, scored France's first try. This inspired the French to one of the greatest displays of running rugby ever seen. For the remainder of the match, the French completely outplayed the New Zealanders who seemed to have rested on their laurels, certain of victory as they looked ahead to 'their' final against archrivals, Australia. A splendid breakaway try by winger Christophe Dominici was followed by a Richard Dourthe touchdown, and the All Blacks were suddenly 34–24 down. This was not to be the end of the mauling, with speedy French winger Philippe Bernat-Salles, chasing an Olivier Magne hack ahead to beat All Blacks fullback Jeff Wilson for a try under the posts. In what seemed like the blink of an eye, the French were suddenly leading a shell-shocked New Zealand outfit by 43–24, with time just about up. A late try by Jeff Wilson gave the scoreline an element of respectability for New Zealand, but the French had achieved their greatest moment in Rugby World Cup history – and in true French style. A bitterly disappointed New Zealand side walked off the Twickenham turf beside a euphoric French team, who were to play in their second World Cup final, while the All Blacks were left to play in their second semi-finals losers' play-off match.

Third and fourth play-off (loser semi-final 1 vs loser semi-final 2)
4 November, Millennium Stadium, Cardiff

South Africa	22	T: Paulse; C: Honiball; PG: Honiball (3); DG: Montgomery (2)
New Zealand	18	PG: Mehrtens (6)

1999 Rugby World Cup final (winner semi-final 1 vs winner semi-final 2)
4 November, Millennium Stadium, Cardiff

Australia	35	T: Tune, Finegan; C: Burke (2); PG: Burke (7)
France	12	PG: Lamaison (4)

This was a World Cup final played between two teams who many believed would never reach the final. However, it was certainly played between two teams who thoroughly deserved to be there. Unfortunately, a packed Millennium Stadium in Cardiff bore witness to the most disappointing World Cup final in history – one in which Australian captain John Eales threatened South African referee André Watson that he would walk his team off the field because of the dirty antics employed by the French. Australia led 12–6 at half-time, with all points coming by way of penalties. Australia were lucky not to have conceded a try in the first half when Abdelatif Benazzi touched down in the corner, only to have the try (correctly) disallowed due to a foot in touch.

In the second half the French reverted to their dirty tactics, which involved, among other things, biting, scratching, kicking and eye-gouging. Referee Watson gave French captain Raphael Ibanez a final warning on the matter. The Australians proved too powerful in the second half, with the French unable to produce the magic they had shown a week earlier against New Zealand. A slick backline move saw Wallaby winger Ben Tune crash over in the corner, putting the game was out of reach for the French. A flawless kicking display by fullback Matt Burke and a magnificent solo effort by replacement lock forward Owen Finegan saw the Wallabies win by 35–12. The Australians became the first side in World Cup history to win the title twice – both triumphs achieved in the United Kingdom. The Australians deservedly won the tournament, having conceded just a single try throughout their campaign – against the United States.

2003 Rugby World Cup
(hosted by Australia)
Defending champions Australia were granted the rights to host the fifth Rugby World Cup. The tournament was again contested by 20 nations, but after the strange structure of the 1999 tournament involving a quarter-final play-off stage, the more sensible option of grouping five teams in four pools was adopted, with the top two teams from each pool advancing to the next stage. For the first time in the tournament, a bonus-point scheme was adopted during the pool stages (as used in the Super 14 and Tri-Nations tournaments), whereby an extra log bonus point was granted to those teams scoring four or more tries in a match or to those which lost by seven points or fewer. The pool matches produced some of the highest-quality rugby ever witnessed at such a stage in the tournament, although the inevitable cricket scorelines were still amassed, with fledglings comprehensively crushed by the tournament favourites. Namibia was on the receiving end of a record scoreline when Australia defeated them 142–0 and Uruguay got a hiding 13–111 from England. Such scorelines are a concern for the IRB and world rugby does not need them. However, besides these one-sided victories, many matches

were competitive to the end, as witnessed in the thrilling Fiji–United States match, when, with time up, Mike Hercus missed a touchline conversion, resulting in a 19–18 win for Fiji. The much-anticipated matches of the pool stages included the England–South Africa clash, won 25–6 by England (thus avoiding a meeting with New Zealand in the quarter-finals) and Australia–Ireland, won 17–16 by Australia. The pick of the games included Scotland–Fiji (22–20), Ireland–Argentina (16–15) and, possibly the match of the tournament, New Zealand–Wales, which New Zealand were expected to win well. Instead, after 50 minutes, they found themselves trailing the Welsh 36–37, but later rallied to win 53–37.

2003 RWC pools

Pool A	
Country	Previous best finish
Australia	Champions '91, '99
Ireland	Quarter-finalists '87, '91, '95
Argentina	Quarter-finalists '99
Namibia	Contestants '99
Romania	Contestants all world cups

Pool B	
Country	Previous best finish
France	Runners-up '87, '99
Scotland	4th Place '91
Fiji	Quarter-finalists '87
United States	Contestants '87, '91, '99
Japan	Contestants all world cups

Pool C	
Country	Previous best finish
South Africa	Champions '95
England	Runners-up '91
Samoa	Quarter-finalists '91, '95
Uruguay	Contestants '99
Georgia	Debutant

Pool D	
Country	Previous best finish
New Zealand	Champions '87
Wales	3rd place '87
Italy	Contestants all world cups
Canada	Quarter-finalists '91
Tonga	Contestants '87, '95, '99

Pool results

10 October, Telstra Stadium, Sydney (Pool A)
Australia	24	T: Sailor, Roff; C: Flatley; PG: Flatley (4)
Argentina	8	T: Corletto; PG: F Contepomi

11 October, Telstra Dome, Melbourne (Pool D)
New Zealand	70	T: Howlett (2), Spencer (2), Rokocoko (2), Thorne, Thorn, Marshall, Carter, MacDonald; C: Carter (6); PG: Spencer
Italy	7	T: Phillips; C: Peens

11 October, Central Coast Stadium, Gosford (Pool A)
Ireland	45	T: Hickie (2), Horgan, Wood, Costello; C: Humphreys (3), O'Gara; PG: Humphreys (4)
Romania	17	T: penalty try, Maftei; C: Tofan, Andrei; PG: Tofan

11 October, Suncorp Stadium, Brisbane (Pool B)
France	61	T: Jauzion (3), Dominici (2), Harinordiquoy, Ibanez; C: Michalak (4); PG: Michalak (6)
Fiji	18	T: Naevo, Caucau; C: Little; PG: Little (2)

11 October, Subiaco Oval, Perth (Pool C)
South Africa	72	T: van der Westhuizen (3), Botha (2), Bands, Greeff, Fourie, van Niekerk, Rossouw, Delport, Scholtz; C: Koen (5), Hougaard
Uruguay	6	PG: D Aguirre (2)

12 October, Telstra Dome, Melbourne (Pool D)
Wales	41	T: Parker, Cooper, M Jones, Charvis, Thomas; C: Harris (5); PG: Harris (2)
Canada	10	T: Tkachuk; C: Pritchard; DG: Ross

12 October, Dairy Farmers Stadium, Townsville (Pool B)
Scotland	32	T: Paterson (2), Grimes, Taylor, Danielli; C: Paterson, Townsend; PG: Paterson
Japan	11	T: Onozawa; PG: Hirose (2)

12 October, Subiaco Oval, Perth (Pool C)
England   84   T: Greenwood (2), Cohen (2), Robinson, Tindall, Luger, Dawson, Thompson, Dallaglio, Back, Regan; C: Wilkinson (5),
                          Grayson (4); PG: Wilkinson (2)
Georgia   6   PG: Urjukashvili, Jimsheladze

14 October, Central Coast Stadium, Gosford (Pool A)
Argentina   67   T: Gaitan (3), Bouza (2), N Fernandez-Miranda, J Fernandez-Miranda, penalty try (2), Mendez; C: Quesada (7); PG: Quesada
Namibia   14   T: Grobler, Husselman; C: Wessels (2)

15 October, Suncorp Stadium, Brisbane (Pool B)
Fiji   19   T: Naevo; C: Little; PG: Little (4)
United States   18   T: Schubert, van Zyl; C: Hercus; PG: Hercus (2)

15 October, Canberra Stadium, Canberra (Pool D)
Italy   36   T: D Dallan (2), M Dallan; C: Wakarua (3); PG: Wakarua (5)
Tonga   12   T: Payne, Tu'ifua; C: Tu'ipulotu

15 October, Subiaco Oval, Perth (Pool C)
Samoa   60   T: Fa'asavulu (2), Lima (2), Feaunati, Fa'atau, Palepoi, Tagicakibau, Lemalu, Vili; C: Va'a (3), Vili (2)
Uruguay   13   T: Lemoine, Capo; PG: Aguirre

17 October, Telstra Dome, Melbourne (Pool D)
New Zealand   68   T: Muliaina (4), Ralph (2), So'oialo (2), Meeuws, Nonu; C: Carter (9)
Canada   6   PG: Baker (2)

18 October, Suncorp Stadium, Brisbane (Pool A)
Australia   90   T: Rogers (3), Burke (2), Larkham (2), Flatley, Roff, Mortlock, Giteau, Tuqiri, Smith; C: Flatley (11); PG: Flatley
Romania   8   T: Toderasc; PG: Tofan

18 October, Dairy Farmers Stadium, Townsville (Pool B)
France   51   T: Rougerie (2), Pelous, Dominici, Crenca, Michalak; C: Michalak (5), Merceron; PG: Michalak (3)
Japan   29   T: Konia, Ohata; C: Kurihara (2); PG: Kurihara (5)

18 October, Subiaco Oval, Perth (Pool C)
England   25   T: Greenwood; C: Wilkinson; PG: Wilkinson (4); DG: Wilkinson (2)
South Africa   6   PG: Koen (2)

19 October, Canberra Stadium, Canberra (Pool D)
Wales   27   T: Cooper, M Williams; C: S Jones; PG: S Jones (4); DG: M Williams
Tonga   20   T: Hola, Kivalu, Lavaka; C: Hola; PG: Hola

19 October, Sydney Football Stadium, Sydney (Pool A)
Ireland   64   T: Quinlan (2), Horgan (2), Miller (2), Dempsey, Kelly, Hickie, Easterby; C: O'Gara (7)
Namibia   7   T: Powell; C: Wessels

19 October, Subiaco Oval (Pool C)
Samoa   46   T: Lima, Feaunati, Va'a, Tagicakibau, Sititi, So'oialo; C: Va'a (5); PG: Va'a (2)
Georgia   9   PG: Jimsheladze (2); DG: Jimsheladze

20 October, Suncorp Stadium, Brisbane (Pool B)
Scotland   39   T: Danielli (2), Kerr, Townsend, Paterson; C: Paterson (4); PG: Paterson (2)
United States   15   PG: Hercus (5)

21 October, Canberra Stadium, Canberra (Pool D)
Italy   19   T: Parisse; C: Wakarua; PG: Wakarua (4)
Canada   14   T: Fyffe; PG: Barker (3)

22 October, Sydney Football Stadium, Sydney (Pool A)
Argentina   50   T: Bouza (2), Hernandez (2), M Contepomi, Gaitan, N Fernandez-Miranda; C: J Fernandez-Miranda (4), Quesada (2);
                          PG: J Fernandez-Miranda
Romania   3   PG: Tofan

23 October, Dairy Farmers Stadium, Townsville (Pool B)
Fiji   41   T: Tuilevu (2), Ligairi (2), Vunibaka; C: Little (2); PG: Little (3), Serevi
Japan   13   T: Miller; C: Miller; PG: Miller; DG: Miller

24 October, Suncorp Stadium, Brisbane (Pool D)
New Zealand   91   T: Muliaina (2), Ralph (2), Howlett (2), Carter, Flynn, Braid, Spencer, Meeuws, penalty try, MacDonald; C: MacDonald (12), Spencer
Tonga   7   T: Hola; C: Tu'ipulotu

24 October, Sydney Football Stadium Sydney (Pool C)
South Africa   46   T: Rossouw (2), Botha, van Niekerk, Fourie, Burger, Hougaard; C: Hougaard (4); PG: Hougaard
Georgia   19   T: Dadunashvili; C: Jimsheladze; PG: Jimsheladze (3), Kvirikashvili

25 October, Adelaide Oval, Adelaide (Pool A)
Australia   142   T: Latham (5), Tuquri (3), Giteau (3), Rogers (2), Roe, Grey, Turinui (2), Lyons, Mortlock, penalty try, Paul, Burke; C: Rogers (16)
Namibia   0

25 October, Canberra Stadium, Canberra (Pool D)
Wales   27   T: M Jones, Parker, D Jones; C: Harris (3); PG: Harris (2)
Italy   15   PG: Wakarua (5)

25 October, Telstra Stadium, Sydney (Pool B)
France   51   T: Betsen, Harinordoquy, Michalak, Galthie, Brusque; C: Michalak (4); PG: Michalak (4); DG: Michalak, Brusque
Scotland   9   PG: Paterson (3)

26 October, Adelaide Oval, Adelaide (Pool A)
Ireland   16   T: Quinlan; C: Humphreys; PG: O'Gara (2), Humphreys
Argentina   15   PG: Quesada (3); DG: Quesada, Corletto

26 October, Telstra Dome, Melbourne (Pool C)
England   35   T: Back, penalty try, Balshaw, Vickery; C: Wilkinson (3); PG: Wilkinson (2); DG: Wilkinson
Samoa   22   T: Sititi; C: Va'a; PG: Va'a (5)

27 October, Central Coast Stadium, Gosford (Pool B)
United States   39   T: Khasigan, Schubert, Hercus, Eloff, van Zyl; C: Hercus (4); PG: Hercus (2)
Japan   26   T: Ohata, Kuirhara; C: Kurihara (2); PG: Kurihara (4)

28 October, Sydney Football Stadium, Sydney (Pool C)
Uruguay   24   T: Cardaso, Lamelas, Brignoni; C: D Aguirre (2), Menchaca; PG: D Aguirre
Georgia   12   PG: Kvirikashvili (3), Urjukashvili

29 October, WIN Stadium, Wollongong (Pool D)
Canada   24   T: Abrahams, Fauth; C: Pritchard; PG: Pritchard (4)
Tonga   7   T: Afeaki; C: Holah

30 October, York Park, Launceston (Pool A)
Romania   37   T: Petrichei, Sauan, Chiriac, Sirbu, Teodorescu; C: Tofan (3); PG: Tofan (2)
Namibia   7   T: Isaacs; C: Wessels

31 October, WIN Stadium, Wollongong (Pool B)
France   41   T: Liebenberg (3), Poux, Bru; C: Merceron (2); PG: Merceron (3); DG: Yachvili
United States   14   T: Schubert, Hercus; C: Hercus (2)

1 November, Sydney Football Stadium, Sydney (Pool B)
Scotland   22   T: Smith; C: Paterson; PG: Paterson (5)
Fiji   20   T: Caucaunibuca (2); C: Little (2); PG: Little (2)

1 November, Suncorp Stadium, Brisbane (Pool C)
South Africa   60   T: van Niekerk, Smith, Hougaard, Willemse, Muller, van der Westhuyzen, de Kock, Fourie; C: Hougaard (5), Koen (2); PG: Hougaard; DG: Hougaard
Samoa   10   T: Palepoi; C: Va'a; PG: Va'a

1 November, Colonial Stadium, Melbourne (Pool A)
Australia   17   T: Smith; PG: Flatley (3); DG: Gregan
Ireland   16   T: O'Driscoll; C: O'Gara; PG: O'Gara (2); DG: O'Driscoll

2 November, Suncorp Stadium, Brisbane (Pool C)
England   111   T: Lewsey (5), Balshaw (2), Catt (2), Gomarsall (2), Robinson (2), Moody, Luger, Abbott, Greenwood; C: Grayson (11), Catt (2)
Uruguay   13   T: Lemoine; C: Menchaca; PG: Menchaca (2)

2 November, Telstra Stadium, Sydney (Pool D)
New Zealand   53   T: Rokocoko (2), Howlett (2), MacDonald, Williams, Spencer, Mauger; C: MacDonald (5); PG: MacDonald
Wales   37   T: Taylor, Parker, Charvis, Williams; C: S Jones (4); PG: S Jones (3)

Pool A - final standings							
Country	P	W	L	D	F	A	P
Australia	4	4	-	-	273	32	18
Ireland	4	3	1	-	141	56	15
Argentina	4	2	2	-	140	57	11
Romania	4	1	3	-	65	192	5
Namibia	4	-	4	-	28	310	0

Pool B - final standings							
Country	P	W	L	D	F	A	P
France	4	4	-	-	204	70	20
Scotland	4	3	1	-	102	97	14
Fiji	4	2	2	-	98	114	10
United States	4	1	3	-	86	125	6
Japan	4	-	4	-	79	163	-

Pool C - final standings							
Country	P	W	L	D	F	A	P
England	4	4	-	-	255	47	19
South Africa	4	3	1	-	184	60	15
Samoa	4	2	2	-	138	117	10
Uruguay	4	1	3	-	56	255	4
Georgia	4	-	4	-	46	200	-

Pool D - final standings							
Country	P	W	L	D	F	A	P
New Zealand	4	4	-	-	282	57	20
Wales	4	3	1	-	132	98	14
Italy	4	2	2	-	77	123	8
Canada	4	1	3	-	54	135	5
Tonga	4	-	4	-	46	178	1

Quarter-finals

The All Blacks and the Springboks had met twice previously in World Cup play-offs, producing rugby of the highest quality. But this was an encounter in which South Africa failed to compete through all phases of the game and were lucky to lose to a committed New Zealand side by a margin of just 9–29. The South Africans were never really in it and following their exit, the controversial training programme of *Kamp Staaldraad* (barbed-wire camp), as instigated by coach Rudolph Straeuli, was revealed, which many believed led to South Africa's poor performances. For the first time in the RWC, Scotland and Australia met and produced a tight affair, which had scores tied at nine apiece at half-time, thanks to a Chris Paterson drop goal from 50 metres. But the Australians proved too strong in the second half, outstripping the Scottish by three tries to one. With Ireland having beaten the French earlier in the year, this fixture was billed to be *the* clash of the quarter-finals, but it was not to be, with the French playing sublime rugby to race to an unassailable 43–0 lead. A late rally by Irish centres Brian O'Driscoll and Kevin Maggs brought the scoreline back to a respectable 43–21. It was a disappointing end to the Irish campaign and saw the exit from the game of their inspirational hooker and leader, Keith Wood, who retired following the defeat. Following their performances against the Welsh earlier that year, England were expected to win comfortably in their quarter-final against Wales. However, in what turned out to be a thrilling match, the English scraped home with a somewhat flattering scoreline, thanks to the boot of Jonny Wilkinson. Stephen Jones scored the try of the tournament in the first half, but had it not been for his wayward kicking, Wales might well have triumphed. Jones did not succeed with a single attempt at goal and Wales lost despite outscoring the English by three tries to one. England's single try was a magical effort from Will Greenwood, linking with Jason Robinson who scored in the corner. This was a match the English looked back on and admitted they were genuinely lucky to win, for it was certainly more of a case of Wales losing the game rather than England winning it.

Quarter-final 1 (winner pool D vs runner-up pool C)
8 November, Telstra Dome, Melbourne
New Zealand 29 T: Mealamu, MacDonald, Rokocoko; C: MacDonald; PG: MacDonald (3); DG: Mauger
South Africa 9 PG: Hougaard (3)

Quarter-final 2 (winner pool A vs runner-up pool B)
8 November, Suncorp Stadium, Brisbane
Australia 33 T: Mortlock, Gregan, Lyons; C: Flatley (3); PG: Flatley (4)
Scotland 16 T: Russell; C: Paterson; PG: Paterson (2); DG: Paterson

Quarter-final 3 (winner pool B vs runner-up pool A)

9 November, Telstra Dome, Melbourne

| France | 43 | T: Magne, Dominici, Crenca, Harinordoquy; C: Michalak (4); PG: Michalak (5) |
| Ireland | 21 | T: O'Driscoll (2), Maggs; C: Humphreys (3) |

Quarter-final 4 (winner pool C vs runner-up pool D)

9 November, Suncorp Stadium, Brisbane

| England | 28 | T: Greenwood; C: Wilkinson; PG: Wilkinson (6); DG: Wilkinson |
| Wales | 17 | T: S Jones, M Williams, Charvis; C: Harris |

Semi-finals

Semi-final 1 (winner quarter-final 1 vs winner quarter-final 2)

14 November, Telstra Stadium, Sydney

| Australia | 22 | T: Mortlock; C: Flatley; PG: Flatley (5) |
| New Zealand | 10 | T: Thorne; C: MacDonald; PG: MacDonald |

This was an eagerly anticipated game. It was the centenary year of this famous transTasmanian clash and one which had not occurred at a Rugby World Cup since the 1991 tournament. New Zealand were strong favourites to win following their unbeaten Tri-Nations campaign earlier in the year which saw them notch up 50 points against Australia at the same venue in Sydney. New Zealand started well, pressurising the Australians for the first ten minutes deep in their 22 and were unlucky when Mils Muliaina was stopped just short of scoring in the corner. The Australian defence held out and when All Blacks flyhalf Carlos Spencer threw a long pass while on attack, Wallaby centre Stirling Mortlock intercepted and sprinted the length of the field, leaving Joe Rokocoko in his wake to score under the posts. From that moment on the Australians never seemed like losing, despite a jinxing run from Spencer to set up a brilliant try for All Blacks skipper Rueben Thorne. Poor goal kicking by Leon MacDonald and superb Australian defence resulted in the downfall of the All Blacks and once again the New Zealanders fell short of winning their first World Cup since 1987. Coach John Mitchell was fired soon after, despite losing just two internationals the entire season. It was a test that New Zealand felt they should and could have won, but one that the Australians deservedly won with a game plan based around a strong defence. Australia were on course to becoming the first nation to defend a Rugby World Cup title.

Semi-final 2 (winner quarter-final 3 vs winner quarter-final 4)

15 November, Telstra Stadium, Sydney

| England | 24 | PG: Wilkinson (5); DG: Wilkinson (3) |
| France | 7 | T: Betsen; C: Michalak |

The second semi-final was as much awaited as the first – a classic encounter between two old enemies. Coming into the tournament England were the Six Nations Grand Slam Champions, with France having held the title the year before. There was no clear favourite. Unfortunately, the Sydney weather did not behave itself as a strong rain and cold wind swept across Telstra Stadium. It soon became evident that the match would revolve around tactical kicking and accurate goal kicking – step up Jonny Wilkinson. France scored first, with a superb early touchdown by flanker Serge Betsen, putting them ahead 7–0, thanks to Michalak's conversion. The English fought back to lead 12–7 at half-time, with Jonny Wilkinson punishing the French with his unerringly accurate boot, which turned out to be the crucial difference between the two sides. Wilkinson's counterpart, young Frederick Michalak, failed miserably when it counted most, succeeding with just one attempt from five – a performance which resulted in him being dubbed 'Frederick Miss-a-lot' by the British press. In the end, the English won comfortably by 24–7, thanks to five Wilkinson penalties and three drop goals. Had Michalak been on song the encounter might have been a different affair. However, England and Wilkinson took their chances and were set to play in their second Rugby World Cup final.

Third and fourth play-off (loser semi-final 1 vs loser semi-final 2)

20 November, Telstra Stadium, Sydney

New Zealand	40	T: Jack, Howlett, Rokocoko, Thorn, Muliaina, Holah; C: Carter (4), MacDonald
France	13	T: Elhorga; C: Yachvili; PG: Yachvili; DG: Yachvili

2003 Rugby World Cup final (winner of semi-final 1 vs winner of semi-final 2)

22 November, Telstra Stadium, Sydney

England	20	T: Robinson; PG: Wilkinson (4); DG: Wilkinson
Australia	17	T: Tuqiri; PG: Flatley (4)

Prior to the 2003 international rugby season, the Australians were undefeated against the English in Australia, but by the end of the year they had lost to the English twice in their own backyard, following their 14–25 loss in Melbourne earlier that year. England were strong favourites, with referee André Watson achieving the rare feat of refereeing in two consecutive Rugby World Cup finals. On 22 November 2003, a packed Telstra Stadium watched one of the great games of rugby in a final, comparable only with the 1995 final. It will not be remembered for its amazing tries or individual flair, but instead for tight defence and an extremely tight finish. The Australians started well, following an early try by their Fijian-born winger, Lote Tuqiri, only to find themselves trailing 5–14 at half-time after a thrilling try by English winger Jason Robinson. At this stage, with the English holding a commanding lead, it seemed more and more likely that England would win and win well. But, remarkably, the game took a turn and some uncharacteristic errors by the English allowed the Australians back into the match. Elton Flatley slotted two penalty goals and with the score at 11–14, England were looking rattled. England had a chance to close the game down when a sweeping movement from one end of the field to the other saw Matt Dawson pass to lock Ben Kay who only had to catch the ball and fall over to score the winning try. Unbelievably, to the shock of the English supporters, he spilled the ball – the Australians were thrown a lifeline. With time up and the English seemingly having won, referee Watson penalised the English front row for a technical infringement and offered Elton Flatley a long-range shot to tie the scores at 14–14 and move the game into extra time. He held his nerve and for the third time in World Cup history the game went into extra time. As the rain set in for the extra phase of play, England scored first with an early Jonny Wilkinson penalty. However, the scores were again tied when, with just a single minute of extra time remaining, Elton Flatley slotted his second high-pressure penalty. With time almost up, England and Jonny Wilkinson produced what was required of champions – England drove up following the restart and from a Matt Dawson break around a scrum, Wilkinson kicked one of the most famous drop goals in Rugby World Cup history – in the same mould as those kicked by Joel Stransky, Jannie de Beer and Stephen Larkham in previous tournaments. England were leading 20–17 at the final whistle and became the first northern hemisphere side to win the William Webb Ellis Trophy. Captain Martin Johnson hoisted the trophy and England once again tasted World Cup victory – the first time since their footballing counterparts in 1966.

2007 Rugby World Cup (co-hosted by France, Wales and Scotland)

Having co-hosted Rugby World Cup matches in 1991 and 1999, France had been granted the sole rights of hosting the 2007 tournament, but it ended up being co-hosted with Wales and Scotland. As with all previous consecutive tournaments, the 2007 RWC turned out to be the most successful to date, bettering the 2003 tournament in Australia, not only when judged by the quality of rugby played but also in terms of revenue. The tournament was structured in exactly the same manner as the 2003 tournament. The bonus-point method was again adopted, following the successful use of the system four years previously. The quality of the pool games was there for all to see, with just a single scoreline in excess of 100 points being registered when New Zealand brushed aside tournament debutants Portugal by 108–13. However, the performance of the Portuguese was one of the highlights of the tournament. Although they failed to record a win, they managed to score a try against each of their opponents and very nearly toppled Romania before losing 10–14 in Bordeaux. The support of the French crowds was demonstrable, as every stadium was full for every game. The Welsh and the Scottish crowds, however, failed to show any such tournament spirit, with full stadiums seldom achieved. Upsets were certainly the mark of the pool stages. This was evident right from the first game, with Argentina shocking the hosts France, beating them 17–12 in Paris. Following this surprise package, Tonga beat Samoa, finishing the game with 13 men; Argentina comprehensively trounced Ireland 30–15 and in the game of the tournament, Fiji stunned Wales to win a thrilling encounter 38–34 to send the Welshmen home without a quarter-final berth. At the opposite end of this spectrum of upsets, South Africa and New Zealand had made their ambitions clear, each comprehensively outplaying their opponents, with New Zealand scoring an astounding 309 points with just 35 against. South Africa meanwhile embarrassed defending champions England 36–0 in a match where, had South Africa taken all their chances, they might well have scored in excess of 50.

2007 RWC pools

Pool A	
Country	Previous Best Finish
England	Champions '03
South Africa	Champions '95
Samoa	Quarter-finalists '91, '95
United States	Contestants '87, '91, '99, '03
Tonga	Contestants '87, '95, '99, '03

Pool B	
Country	Previous Best Finish
Australia	Champions '91, '99
Wales	3rd Place '87
Fiji	Quarter-finalists '87
Canada	Quarter-finalists '91
Japan	Contestants all world cups

Pool C	
Country	Previous Best Finish
New Zealand	Champions '87
Scotland	4th Place '91
Italy	Contestants all world cups
Romania	Contestants all world cups
Portugal	Debutant

Pool D	
Country	Previous Best Finish
France	Runners-up '87, '99
Ireland	Quarter-finalists '87, '91, '95, '03
Argentina	Quarter-finalists '99
Georgia	Constestants '03
Namibia	Contestants '99, '03

Pool results

7 September, Stade de France, Paris (Pool D)
France   12   PG: Skrela (4)
Argentina   17   T: Corleto; PG: F Contepomi (4)

8 September, Stade Velodrome, Marseille (Pool C)
New Zealand   76   T: Howlett (3), McCaw (2), Sivivatu (2), Collins (2), Jack, Muliaina; C: Carter (7), McAlister (2); PG: Carter
Italy   14   T: Stanojevic, Mi Bergamasco; C: Bortolussi, de Marigny

8 September, Stade Gerland, Lyon (Pool B)
Australia   91   T: Elsom (3), Latham (2), Barnes (2), Mitchell (2), Sharpe, Ashley-Cooper, Smith, Freier; C: Mortlock (7), Giteau (3); PG: Mortlock (2)
Japan   3   PG: Ono

8 September, Stade Felix Bollaert, Lens (Pool A)
England   28   T: Robinson, Barkley, Rees; C: Barkley (2); PG: Barkley (3)
United States   10   T: Moeakiola; C: Hercus; PG: Hercus

9 September, Stade de la Beaujoire, Nantes (Pool B)
Wales   42   T: S Williams (2), AW Jones, Parker, Charvis; C: S Jones (4); PG: Hook (3)
Canada   17   T: Cudmore, Culpan, Williams; C: Pritchard

9 September, Parc des Prince, Paris (Pool A)
South Africa   59   T: Habana (4), Montgomery (2), Fourie, Pietersen; C: Montgomery (5); PG: Montgomery (3)
Samoa   7   T: Williams; C: Williams

9 September, Stade Geoffroy-Guichard, Saint-Etienne (Pool C)

| Scotland | 56 | T: R Lamont (2), Lawson, Dewey, Southwell, Brown, Parks, Ford; C: Parks (4), Paterson (4) |
| Portugal | 10 | T: Carvalho; C: Pinto; PG: Pinto |

9 September, Stade Chaban-Delmas, Bordeaux (Pool D)

| Ireland | 32 | T: Easterby, Trimble (2), O'Driscoll, penalty try; C: O'Gara (2); PG: O'Gara |
| Namibia | 17 | T: Niewenhuis, van Zyl; C: Wessels (2); PG: Wessels |

11 September, Stade Gerland, Lyon (Pool B)

| Argentina | 33 | T: Borges (2), Albacete, Aramburu; C: Contepomi, Hernandez; PG: Contepomi (3) |
| Georgia | 3 | PG: Kvirikashvili |

12 September, Stade de la Mosson, Montpellier (Pool A)

| Tonga | 25 | T: Maka, Vaka, Vaki; C: Hola (2); PG: Hola (2) |
| United States | 15 | T: MacDonald, Stanfill; C: Hercus; PG: Hercus |

12 September, Stade Toulouse, Toulouse (Pool B)

| Fiji | 35 | T: Qera (2), Rabeni, Leawere; C: Little (3); PG: Little (3) |
| Japan | 31 | T: Thompson (2), Soma; C: Onishi (2); PG: Onishi (4) |

12 September, Stade Velodrome, Marseille (Pool C)

| Italy | 24 | T: Dellape, penalty try; C: Pez; PG: Pez (3), Bortolussi |
| Romania | 18 | T: Manta, Tincu; C: Dimofte; PG: Dimofte (2) |

14 September, Stade de France, Paris (Pool A)

| South Africa | 36 | T: Pietersen (2), Smith; C: Montgomery (3); PG: Montgomery (4), Steyn |
| England | 0 | |

15 September, Stade Gerland, Lyon (Pool C)

| New Zealand | 108 | T: Rokocoko (2), Mauger (2), Smith (2), Toeava, Williams, Collins, Masoe, Leonard, Evans, Ellis, Hore, MacDonald, Hayman; C: Evans (14) |
| Portugal | 13 | T: Cordeiro; C: Pinto; PG: Pinto; DG: Malheiro |

15 September, Millennium Stadium, Cardiff (Pool B)

| Wales | 20 | T: J Thomas, S Williams; C: Hook (2); PG: Hook, S Jones |
| Australia | 32 | T: Latham (2), Giteau, Mortlock; C: Mortlock (2), Giteau; PG: Mortlock; DG: Barnes |

15 September, Stade Toulouse, Toulouse (Pool D)

| Ireland | 14 | T: Best, Dempsey; C: O'Gara (2) |
| Georgia | 10 | T: Shkinin; C: Kvirikashvili; PG: Kvirikashvili |

16 September, Millennium Stadium, Cardiff (Pool B)

| Fiji | 29 | T: Ratuvou (2), Leawere, Delasau; C: Little (3); PG: Little |
| Canada | 16 | T: Smith; C: Pritchard; PG: Pritchard (3) |

16 September, Stade de la Mosson, Montpellier (Pool A)

| Tonga | 19 | T: Taione; C: Hola; PG: Hola (4) |
| Samoa | 15 | T: Williams (5) |

16 September, Stade Municipal, Toulouse (Pool D)

| France | 87 | T: Clerc (3), Nallet (2), Chabal (2), Heymans, Marty, Dusautoir, Bonnaire, Elissalde, Ibanez; C: Elissalde (11) |
| Namibia | 10 | T: Langenhoven; C: Losper; DG: Wessels |

18 September, Murrayfield, Edinburgh (Pool C)

| Scotland | 42 | T: Hogg (3), R Lamont (2), Paterson; C: Paterson (6) |
| Romania | 0 | |

19 September, Parc des Princes, Paris (Pool C)

| Italy | 31 | T: Masi (2), Bergamasco; C: Bortolussi (2); PG: Bortolussi (4) |
| Portugal | 5 | T: Penalva |

20 September, Millennium Stadium, Cardiff (Pool B)

| Wales | 72 | T: S Williams (2), M Williams (2), A Jones, Hook, James, Morgan, R Thomas, Morgan, Phillips, Cooper; C: S Jones (5), Sweeney (2); PG: S Jones |
| Japan | 18 | T: Endo, Onozawa; C: Robins; PG: Onishi (2) |

21 September, Stade de France, Paris (Pool D)

| France | 25 | T: Clerc (2); PG: Elissalde (5) |
| Ireland | 3 | DG: O'Gara |

22 September, Stade de la Beaujoire, Nantes (Pool A)
England   44   T: Sackey (2), Corry (2); C: Wilkinson (3); PG: Wilkinson (4); DG: Wilkinson (2)
Samoa   22   T: Poluleuligaga; C: Crichton; PG: Crichton (5)

22 September, Stade Velodrome, Marseille (Pool D)
Argentina   63   T: Leguizamon (2), M Contepomi, F Contepomi, Tiesi, Corleto, penalty try, Todeschini, Roncero; C: Contepomi (4),
                     Todeschini (2); PG: Contepomi (2)
Namibia   3   PG: Schreuder

22 September, Stade Felix Bollaert, Lens (Pool A)
South Africa 30   T: Pienaar, Skinstad, Smith; C: Pretorius, Montgomery; PG: Steyn, Montgomery
Tonga   25   T: Pulu, Vaki, Wufanga; C: Hola (2); PG: Hola (2)

23 September, Stade de la Mosson, Montpellier (Pool B)
Australia   55   T: Mitchell (3), Giteau (2), Ashley-Cooper, Hoiles; C: Giteau (4); PG: Giteau (3); DG: Barnes
Fiji   12   T: Ratuva, Neivua; C: Bai

23 September, Murrayfield, Edinburgh (Pool C)
New Zealand 40   T: Howlett (2), McCaw, Kelleher, Williams, Carter; C: Carter (2); PG: Carter (2)
Scotland   0

25 September, Stade Chaban Delmas, Bordeaux (Pool B)
Canada   12   T: Riordan, van der Merwe; C: Pritchard
Japan   12   T: Endo, Taira; C: Onishi

25 September, Stade Chaban Delmas, Bordeaux (Pool C)
Romania   14   T: Tincu, Corodeanu; C: Dumbrava, Calafeteanu
Portugal   10   T: Ferreira; C: Pinto; PG: Malheiro

26 September, Stade Felix Bollaert, Lens (Pool D)
Georgia   30   T: Giorgadze, Kacharava, Machkhaneli; C: Kvirikashvili (3); PG: Kvirikashvili (3)
Namibia   0

26 September, Stade Geoffroy-Guichard, Saint-Etienne (Pool A)
Samoa   25   T: Fa'atau, Thompson, A Tuilagi; C: Crichton (2); PG: Crichton (2)
United States 21   T: Ngwenya, Stanfill; C: Hercus; PG: Hercus (3)

28 September, Parc des Princes, Paris (Pool A)
England   36   T: Sackey (2), Tait, Farrell; C: Wilkinson (2); PG: Wilkinson (2); PG: Wilkinson (2)
Tonga   20   T: Hufanga, T'Pole; C: Hola (2); PG: Hola (2)

29 September, Stade Municipal, Toulouse (Pool C)
New Zealand 85   T: Rokocoko (3), Sivivatu (2), Toeava (2), Howlett, Evans, Hore, Masoe, Smith, Mauger; C: Evans (6), McAlister (4)
Romania   8   T: Tincu; PG: Viaicu

29 September, Stade Chaban Delmas, Bordeaux (Pool B)
Australia   37   T: Mitchell (2), Baxter, Freier, Latham, Smith; C: Shepherd (2); PG: Huxley
Canada   6   PG: Pritchard (2)

29 September, Stade de la Beaujoire, Nantes (Pool B)
Fiji   38   T: Delasau, Leawere, Qera, Dewes; C: Little (3); PG: Little (4)
Wales   34   T: M Jones, Popham, G Thomas, S Williams, M Williams; C: S Jones (2), Hook; PG: S Jones

29 September, Stade Geoffroy Guichard, Saint Etienne (Pool C)
Scotland   18   PG: Paterson (6)
Italy   16   T: Troncon; C: Bortolussi; PG: Bortolussi (3)

30 September, Stade Velodrome, Marseille (Pool D)
France   64   T: Dominici (2), Poitrenaud, Nyanga, Bonnaire, Bruno, Nallet, Martin, Beauxis; C: Beauxis (5); PG: Beauxis (3)
Georgia   7   T: Maisuradze; C: Urjukashvili

30 September, Parc des Princes, Paris (Pool D)
Argentina   30   T: Borges, Agulla; C: F Contepomi; PG: F Contepomi (3); DG: Hernandez (3)
Ireland   15   T: O'Driscoll, Murphy; C: O'Gara; PG: O'Gara

30 September, Stade de la Mosson, Montpellier (Pool C)
South Africa 64   T: Habana (2), Fourie (2), Burger, Steyn, Smith, van der Linde, du Preez; C: Montgomery (6), James (2); PG: Montgomery
United States 15   T: Ngwenya, Wyles; C: Hercus; PG: Hercus

Pool A - final standings							
Country	P	W	L	D	F	A	P
South Africa	4	4	-	-	189	47	19
England	4	3	1	-	108	88	14
Tonga	4	2	2	-	89	96	9
Samoa	4	1	3	-	69	143	5
United States	4	-	4	-	61	142	1

Pool B - final standings							
Country	P	W	L	D	F	A	P
Australia	4	4	-	-	215	41	20
Fiji	4	3	1	-	114	136	15
Wales	4	2	2	-	168	105	12
Japan	4	-	3	1	64	210	3
Canada	4	-	3	1	51	120	2

Pool C - final standings							
Country	P	W	L	D	F	A	P
New Zealand	4	4	-	-	309	35	20
Scotland	4	3	1	-	116	66	14
Italy	4	2	2	-	85	117	9
Romania	4	1	3	-	40	161	5
Portugal	4	-	4	-	38	209	1

Pool D - final standings							
Country	P	W	L	D	F	A	P
Argentina	4	4	-	-	143	33	18
France	4	3	1	-	188	37	15
Ireland	4	2	2	-	64	82	9
Georgia	4	1	3	-	50	111	5
Namibia	4	-	4	-	30	212	-

Quarter-finals

The quarter-finals of the 2007 Rugby World Cup will be remembered as being one of the most thrilling weekends of rugby ever. Of the four fixtures, it was almost a dead cert that the winning four would all be from the southern hemisphere. Australia were strong favourites to beat the hapless defending champions, considering England's horrific form through the tournament (which at one point very nearly saw them not progressing past the pool stages, with laboured victories over Samoa, Tonga and the USA). However, it was not to be. Wilkinson single-handedly sunk the Australians in sunny Marseille with four penalty goals and thereby ended the careers of George Gregan and a weepy Stephen Larkham.

Four hours later, in Cardiff, New Zealand and France shaped up for the second semi-final, which New Zealand were massive favourites to win – again. Their entire season had been geared to winning this tournament, but in one of the great upsets in world rugby, France again denied the Kiwis with a shock 20–18 victory, sending New Zealand home with their worst-ever tournament finishing position. The Rugby World Cup is undoubtedly New Zealand's Achilles tendon of rugby, labelled 'chokers', following their poor performances at consecutive tournaments. After 39 minutes, New Zealand led 13–0, but, remarkably, they eventually lost following one of the most hotly disputed tries in rugby history, when a clear forward pass from Yannik Jauzion to Frederick Michalak was ignored by referee Wayne Barnes, which ultimately led to the winning try by Jauzion. Barnes was later to receive death threats from disgruntled All Blacks fans.

Following the shock exits of Australia and New Zealand, new tournament favourites South Africa lined up the next day against surprise package Fiji, and were pushed all the way. It was a game South Africa were expected to win and at half-time, they duly led by 13–3, a lead which soon grew to 20–6 following a try by J.P. Pietersen. Then came the turn of the fleet-footed Fijians who for ten minutes in the second half played some of the most sublime rugby they had ever played in their history, with a magnificent solo effort from winger Vilimoni Delasau, and then a sweeping length-of-the-field movement that led to a try by Sireli Bobo. With the lead now a slender 23–20, the game was Fiji's for the taking. Lock forward Ifereimi Rawaqa crashed over for what seemed to be yet another amazing Fijian try, only for a TMO decision to rule that winger, J.P. Pietersen's magnificent tackle had in fact denied Fiji the score. South Africa rallied, with skipper John Smit leading from the front. South Africa eventually ran out comfortable winners following tries from Juan Smith and Butch James.

Later that evening, Scotland and Argentina contested for the last semi-final position, with Argentina strong favourites to appear in their first World Cup semi-final – a position they had never previously reached. It was a scrappy affair, with both sides scoring a single try, but it was the determination and spirit of the Argentinians that overcame the Scots and put the South Americans into their first-ever semi-final.

Quarter-final 1 (winner pool B vs runner-up pool A)

6 October, Stade Velodrome, Marseille

| England | 12 | PG: Wilkinson (4) |
| Australia | 10 | T: Tuqiri; C: Mortlock; PG: Mortlock |

Quarter-final 2 (winner pool C vs runner-up pool D)

6 October, Millennium Stadium, Cardiff

| France | 20 | T: Dusautoir, Jauzion; C: Beauxis, Elissalde; PG: Beauxis (2) |
| New Zealand | 18 | T: McAlister, So'oialo; C: Carter; PG: Carter (2) |

Quarter-final 3 (winner pool A vs runner-up pool B)

7 October, Stade Velodrome, Marseille

| South Africa | 37 | T: Smit, Smith, James, Pietersen, Fourie; C: Montgomery (3); PG: Montgomery, Steyn |
| Fiji | 20 | T: Delasau, Bobo; C: Bai (2); PG: Bai (2) |

Quarter-final 4 (winner pool D vs runner-up pool C)

7 October, Stade de France, Paris

| Argentina | 19 | T: Longo; C: F Contepomi; PG: F Contepomi (3); DG: Hernandez |
| Scotland | 13 | T: Cusiter; C: Paterson; PG: Paterson, Parks |

Semi-finals

Semi-final 1 (winner quarter-final 1 vs winner quarter-final 2)

13 October, Stade de France, Paris

| England | 14 | T: Lewsey; PG: Wilkinson (2); DG: Wilkinson |
| France | 9 | PG: Beauxis (3) |

For the fourth time in the Rugby World Cup, these two sides were to meet, with France strong favourites to win on home soil against the defending champions, following their incredible victory over New Zealand. England meanwhile had surprised most by reaching the semi-finals but, being the defending champions, were not going down without a fight against their arch rugby enemies. True to inconsistent form, the French were unable to repeat their Cardiff heroics as England rose to the occasion to win in Paris and end the host nation's dream of winning the tournament. It started as early as the second minute when French fullback Damien Traille misjudged a Jonny Wilkinson kick, which winger Josh Lewsey latched onto and scored in the corner. The French regained the lead and with 70 minutes up they led 9–8. However, once again, Jonny Wilkinson stamped his authority on the game with a critical penalty to regain the lead, followed by a brilliant drop goal. Amazingly, England had reached the World Cup final and their dream of becoming the first nation to defend their title was in reach.

Semi-final 2 (winner quarter-final 3 vs winner quarter-final 4)

14 October, Stade de France, Paris

| South Africa | 37 | T: Habana (2), Rossouw, du Preez; C: Montgomery (4); PG: Montgomery (3) |
| Argentina | 13 | T: M Contepomi; C: F Contepomi; PG: F Contepomi (2) |

For the first time in the tournament's history, a nation other than one of the traditional top eight qualified for the semi-finals, and Argentina thoroughly deserved it. One of the great success stories of the 2007 tournament, Argentina's rise in world rugby came to a crescendo as they beat Ireland, Scotland and hosts France, to reach the semi-finals. Their opposition had also remained unbeaten, with convincing victories running up to the semi-final. As such, South Africa found themselves as tournament favourites, with game-breakers such as Bryan Habana, Fourie du Preez, Jaque Fourie and Percy Montgomery in sublime form. The match was a bridge too far for the Argentinians and the South

Africans left the field convincing winners by 37–13, with Percy Montgomery notching up a 100-percent kicking record. Bryan Habana scored two magnificent tries, equalling Jonah Lomu's record of eight tries in a tournament, with additional tries scored by scrumhalf Fourie du Preez and eighthman Danie Rossouw. All the Pumas' points were scored by the Contepomi twins, although Manuel's try was dubious to say the least. Despite a TMO referral to Tony Spreadbury, replays clearly indicated that Contepomi had lost the ball forward in the act of grounding it. South Africa took their chances well, feeding off the Argentinian mistakes, with two of their tries coming from long-range interceptions (du Preez and Habana), one from a dropped Argentinian pass (Rossouw) and the other a piece of individual brilliance from Habana. It was a disappointing end to Argentina's tournament, but nevertheless an incredibly successful one. While South Africa were to feature in their second final, Argentina had to rise to the occasion in the hope of winning the tournament bronze medal, which they did.

Third and fourth play-off (loser semi-final 1 vs loser semi-final 2)
19 October, Parc des Princes, Paris

Argentina	34	T: F Contepomi (2), Kareilis, Aramburu, Corleto; C: F Contepomi (3); PG: F Contepomi
France	10	T: Poitrenaud; C: Beauxis; PG: Elissalde

2007 Rugby World Cup final (winner of semi-final 1 vs winner of semi-final 2)
20 October, Stade de France, Paris

South Africa	15	PG: Montgomery (4), Steyn
England	6	PG: Wilkinson (2)

This was by no means a classic, but rather a typical final and also the first World Cup final that featured just a single method of scoring – a total of seven penalties accounted for all the points scored in the match. South Africa were strong favourites, having beaten England twice by over 50 points in June and by 36–0 in the pool stages. However, this was a completely different affair and one which England genuinely thought they could win and thereby become the first nation to defend the title. The aspiration was to prove beyond England's capabilities as a determined South African side triumphed by 15–6.

After leading 9–3 at half-time, a 50-metre François Steyn penalty in the second half proved decisive, thereby ensuring that he became the youngest player to win an RWC. Irish referee Alain Rolland was given the honour of refereeing the most important match of the rugby calendar and did so very successfully when he and his refereeing team made quite possibly the toughest call ever in a World Cup final. A try by English winger Mark Cueto,was referred to TMO,Stuart Dickinson. It initially appeared as though the winger had scored a fair try but after studying numerous angles of the incident, it became apparent that the desperate diving tackle from eighthman Danie Rossouw had forced Cueto's left foot to glance the touchline milliseconds before the ball was grounded. A very tight call in an very tight final – one that was correctly made and of monumental importance, for had the try been awarded the momentum of the game would indeed have shifted.

The two penalties from Jonny Wilkinson could not compete with the penalty by François Steyn and the four by Percy Montgomery who notched up an impressive 100-percent goal-kicking success rate in both the semi-final and final. It was a fairy-tale finish for South African coach Jake White who had toiled through four tough years as South African coach and for legendary prop forward Pieter 'Os' du Randt who won his second World Cup title no fewer than 12 years after his first. This was South Africa's second World Cup title in just four attempts, giving them a 50-percent success rate. Captain John Smit hoisted the trophy for South Africa alongside President Thabo Mbeki as memories of the famous 1995 triumph with François Pienaar and Nelson Mandela flooded across the Rainbow Nation.

Did you know: Only six players have won two RWC winners' medals in their career: South Africa's Pieter 'Os' du Randt (1995 and 2007) and Australia's John Eales, Tim Horan, Jason Little, Dan Crowley and Phil Kearns, who were all part of the teams that won in 1991 and 1999.

RWC team records

Most points by a team in an RWC match

No.	Match	Tournament
145	New Zealand vs Japan	1995
142	Australia vs Namibia	2003
111	England vs Uruguay	2003
108	New Zealand vs Portugal	2007
101	New Zealand vs Italy	1999
101	England vs Tonga	1999

Most conversions by a team in an RWC match

No.	Match	Tournament
20	New Zealand vs Japan	1995
16	Australia vs Namibia	2003
14	New Zealand vs Portugal	2007
13	New Zealand vs Tonga	2003
13	England vs Uruguay	2003

Did you know: Brian Lima of Samoa is the only player to have played in five RWC tournaments – 1991, 1995, 1999, 2003 and 2007 – a record surely never to be bettered.

Most tries by a team in an RWC match

No.	Match	Tournament
22	Australia vs Namibia	2003
21	New Zealand vs Japan	1995
17	England vs Uruguay	2003
16	New Zealand vs Portugal	2007
14	New Zealand vs Italy	1999

Most penalties by a team in an RWC match

No.	Match	Tournament
8	Australia vs South Africa	1999
8	Argentina vs Samoa	1999
8	Scotland vs Tonga	1995
8	France vs Ireland	1995

Most drop goals by a team in an RWC match

No.	Match	Tournament
5	South Africa vs England	1999
3	Fiji vs Romania	1991
3	England vs France	2003
3	Argentina vs Ireland	2007

RWC player records

Most points by a player in an RWC match

No.	Player	Match	Tournament
45	Simon Culhane	New Zealand vs Japan	1995
44	Gavin Hastings	Scotland vs Côte d'Ivoire	1995
42	Mat Rogers	Australia vs Namibia	2003
36	Tony Brown	New Zealand vs Italy	1999
36	Paul Grayson	England vs Tonga	1999
34	Jannie de Beer	South Africa vs England	1999
33	Nick Evans	New Zealand vs Portugal	2007
32	Jonny Wilkinson	England vs Italy	1999

Most conversions by a player in an RWC match

No.	Player	Match	Tournament
20	Simon Culhane	New Zealand vs Japan	1995
16	Mat Rogers	Australia vs Namibia	2003
14	Nick Evans	New Zealand vs Portugal	2007
12	Paul Grayson	England vs Tonga	1999
12	Leon MacDonald	New Zealand vs Tonga	2003

Most drop goals by a player in an RWC match

No.	Player	Match	Tournament
5	Jannie de Beer	South Africa vs England	1999
3	Jonny Wilkinson	England vs France	2003
3	Juan-Martin Hernandez	Argentina vs Ireland	2007

Most tries by a player in an RWC match

No.	Player	Match	Tournament
6	Marc Ellis	New Zealand vs Japan	1995
5	Chris Latham	Australia vs Namibia	2003
5	Josh Lewsey	England vs Uruguay	2003
4	Iuean Evans	Wales vs Canada	1987
4	Craig Green	New Zealand vs Fiji	1987
4	John Gallagher	New Zealand vs Fiji	1987
4	Brian Robinson	Ireland vs Zimbabwe	1991
4	Gavin Hastings	Scotland vs Côte d'Ivoire	1995
4	Chester Williams	South Africa vs Western Samoa	1995
4	Jonah Lomu	New Zealand vs England	1995
4	Keith Wood	Ireland vs United States	1999
4	Mils Muliaina	New Zealand vs Canada	2003
4	Bryan Habana	South Africa vs Samoa	2007

Most penalties by a player in an RWC match

No.	Player	Match	Tournament
8	Matt Burke	Australia vs South Africa	1999
8	Gonzalo Quesada	Argentina vs Samoa	1999
8	Gavin Hastings	Scotland vs Tonga	1995
8	Thierry Lacroix	France vs Ireland	1995

Individual RWC tournament records

Most points by a player in an RWC tournament

No.	Player	Country	RWC
126	Grant Fox	New Zealand	1987
113	Jonny Wilkinson	England	2003
112	Thierry Lacroix	France	1995
105	Percy Montgomery	South Africa	2007
104	Gavin Hastings	Scotland	1995
103	Frederick Michalak	France	2003
102	Gonzalo Quesada	Argentina	1999
101	Matthew Burke	Australia	1999

Most tries by a player in an RWC tournament

No.	Player	Country	RWC
8	Jonah Lomu	New Zealand	1999
8	Bryan Habana	South Africa	2007
7	Marc Ellis	New Zealand	1995
7	Jonah Lomu	New Zealand	1995
7	Doug Howlett	New Zealand	2003
7	Mils Muliaina	New Zealand	2003
7	Drew Mitchell	Australia	2007

Most conversions by a player in an RWC tournament

No.	Player	Country	RWC
30	Grant Fox	New Zealand	1987
22	Percy Montgomery	South Africa	2007
20	Simon Culhane	New Zealand	1995
20	Michael Lynagh	Australia	1987
20	Leon MacDonald	New Zealand	2003
20	Nick Evans	New Zealand	2007

Most penalties by a player in an RWC tournament

No.	Player	Country	RWC
31	Gonzalo Quesada	Argentina	1999
26	Thierry Lacroix	France	1995
23	Jonny Wilkinson	England	2003
21	Grant Fox	New Zealand	1987
21	Elton Flatley	Australia	2003
20	Rob Andrew	England	1995

Most drop goals by a player in an RWC tournament

No.	Player	Country	RWC
8	Jonny Wilkinson	England	2003
6	Jannie de Beer	South Africa	1999
5	Jonny Wilkinson	England	2007
4	Juan-Martin Hernandez	Argentina	2007

Individual RWC career records

Most points by a player in RWCs

No.	Player	Country	RWC Era
249	Jonny Wilkinson	England	1999–2007
227	Gavin Hastings	Scotland	1987–1995
195	Michael Lynagh	Australia	1987–1995
170	Grant Fox	New Zealand	1987–1991
163	Andrew Mehrtens	New Zealand	1995–1999

Most conversions by a player in RWCs

No.	Player	Country	RWC Era
39	Gavin Hastings	Scotland	1987–1995
37	Grant Fox	New Zealand	1987–1991
36	Michael Lynagh	Australia	1987–1995
29	Dan Carter	New Zealand	2003–2007
27	Paul Grayson	England	1999–2003

Most tests by a player in RWCs

No.	Player	Country	RWC Era
22	Jason Leonard	England	1991–2003
20	George Gregan	Australia	1995–2007
19	Michael Catt	England	1995–2007
18	Martin Johnson	England	1995–2003
18	Brian Lima	Samoa	1991–2007
18	Raphael Ibanez	France	1999–2007

Most drop goals by a player in RWCs

No.	Player	Country	RWC Era
13	Jonny Wilkinson	England	1999–2007
6	Jannie de Beer	South Africa	1999
5	Rob Andrew	England	1987–1995
5	Gareth Rees	Canada	1987–1999
4	Juan-Martin Hernandez	Argentina	2003–2007

Most tries by a player in RWCs

No.	Player	Country	RWC Era
15	Jonah Lomu	New Zealand	1995–1999
13	Doug Howlett	New Zealand	2003–2007
11	Rory Underwood	England	1987–1995
11	Joe Rokocoko	New Zealand	2003–2007
11	Chris Latham	Australia	1999–2007

Most penalties by a player in RWCs

No.	Player	Country	RWC Era
53	Jonny Wilkinson	England	1999–2007
36	Gavin Hastings	Scotland	1987–1995
35	Gonzalo Quesada	Argentina	1999–2003
33	Michael Lynagh	Australia	1987–1995
33	Andrew Mehrtens	New Zealand	1995–1999

Top left: South Africa threaten against Fiji during the third quarterfinal of the 2007 RWC at the Stade Velodrome in Marseille, France. The match was won 37-20 by South Africa with Fiji very nearly inflicting a shock defeat upon the former World Champions. *Photo*: Scott Allen

Top right: South Africa and England take to the Stade de France in Paris for their crucial Pool A encounter during the 2007 RWC, a match in which South Africa humiliated the reigning World Champions by 36-0. *Photo*: Scott Allen

Above: South African flyhalf Butch James attacks the Scottish line with teammate and prop forward CJ van der Linde (number 3) at Murrayfield in Edinburgh. The match was a warm-up fixture for the 2007 RWC and was won 27-3 by South Africa. *Photo*: Adrian van de Vyver

Left: Action from the 2007 RWC match between South Africa and Samoa at the Parc des Princes, Paris. South African won easily by 59-7 to advance to the quarterfinals. *Photo*: Adrian van de Vyver

79

Tri-Nations

History

Given the vast distance that separates the southern-hemisphere nations and Europe, emphasis was placed on lengthy international tours to the United Kingdom during the early part of the twentieth century. Fixtures against the southern-hemisphere nations were rare for the European teams in these early years because of travel logistics. Tours were drawn-out affairs, often involving 30 or more matches over three months and were closely followed by the host nations' supporters and sports journalists. With the advent of air travel, international rugby involving the southern-hemisphere nations became more frequent and in 1987, New Zealand hosted the first RWC. It was widely agreed by the southern-hemisphere nations that the Five Nations Championship was a great rugby event and one they dearly wanted to emulate. Following the success and growth of the RWC and the evolution of the game from amateur to professional status in 1995, multimillion-pound negotiations between the South African, New Zealand and Australian unions got underway. This ultimately resulted in the formation of the South African, New Zealand, and Australian Rugby Union (SANZAR) – a consortium board formed by the rugby-governing bodies of the ARU, NZRFU and SARFU. The new union announced a ten-year deal worth £360 million, which culminated in the first Tri-Nations competition in 1996 between the three southern-hemisphere giants. The SANZAR Tri-Nations competition was in part a concerned response from the southern-hemisphere rugby unions about a major funding injection into rugby league in Australia, which might have posed a threat to the growth of the union game. The three nations signed a multimillion-dollar deal with Rupert Murdoch's News Corporation which gave News Corp exclusive television rights to screen the competition for ten years. This tournament proved to be a massive success and has gone from strength to strength since its inception.

Format

To start with, each team played each other twice – on a home-and-away basis. Since 2006, however, each team plays each other three times, except during an RWC year, in which case the tournament reverts to its original format. It is widely agreed, however, that a three-fixture format is overkill and runs the risk of devaluing the games, which used to be rare, much-anticipated encounters. In a year when each team plays each other three times, home advantage alternates on an annual basis, with teams benefiting from two home games out of three every other year. The Tri-Nations was the first international tournament to utilise the log bonus-point scheme to complement the standard log points system – a system successfully adopted in the 1996 Super 12 tournament. This bonus-point scheme rewards those teams which lose by seven points or fewer and those who manage to score four or more tries in a match, thus making it possible for a team to lose an international but still notch up two log points. This was the case in 2000 when New Zealand lost 40–46 to South Africa, but still gained two log points for their efforts. Log points are awarded as shown in the table overleaf.

The argument for Argentina

Persistent rumours of incorporating Argentina (and even the combined Pacific Islands team) into the tournament have been circulating for some time and, with the continued growth and success of Argentinian rugby, especially in the 2007 RWC, it has become tougher for the IRB to ignore this. In February 2007, the IRB began negotiations with SANZAR to admit Argentina as early as 2008, but this came to nought. What's more, South Africa is highly dissatisfied with the current format, as it necessitates the Springboks to tour for a full month away from home, while Australia and New Zealand simply fly in and out of South Africa for a week to play their games, not suffering the adverse effects of extended touring. Hence South Africa is in favour of including Argentina, as this would even things out. However, the two biggest stumbling blocks against incorporating Argentina are 1) the problem of the split in broadcasting revenue (which is currently shared equally between the three SANZAR unions), and 2) persuading the Argentina Rugby Union to accept professionalism. Rugby in Argentina is still fiercely pro-amateur: almost all their national players have to play abroad in Europe to earn money. The current TV contract between SANZAR and News Corporation expires in 2010, so the likelihood of Argentina being included in the tournament before then remains realistically low.

Did you know: In the 2003 Tri-Nations fixtures between Australia and South Africa there was a remarkable shared experience that existed between Australian captain George Gregan and South African captain Corné Kriege: both players were born in the same hospital in Lusaka, Zambia.

Year	Tournament structure	Log points system
1996–2005	Each team plays each other twice, on a home-and-away basis	4 points for a win
2006	Each team plays each other three times, with the two home tests' advantage alternating on an annual basis	2 points for a draw
2007	Each team plays each other twice, on a home-and-away basis	1 point for losing within 7 points 1 point for scoring 4 or more tries
2008	Each team plays each other three times, with the two home tests' advantage alternating on an annual basis	0 points for a loss

Eras of domination

The Tri-Nations has produced some scintillating rugby in its short existence, featuring some of the greatest games in recent rugby history. New Zealand has dominated the competition, winning nine of the 13 tournaments to date. South Africa and Australia have each won twice. South Africa is the only team to have avoided the ignominy of losing all their matches in a season, with New Zealand losing all four in 1998 and Australia in 2005. It is widely accepted that the 2000 and 2004 tournaments were the most exciting. In 2000, Australia won the title for the first time, with thrilling last-second, one-point victories over both New Zealand and South Africa. In 2004, just a single log point separated the teams, with South Africa triumphing on 11 points and New Zealand last on nine.

Trophies within the Tri-Naions

Several individual trophies are contested under the umbrella of the main Tri-Nations tournament. New Zealand and Australia compete for the Bledisloe Cup, South Africa and New Zealand for the Freedom Cup and South Africa and Australia for the Nelson Mandela Challenge Plate. Each of these trophies and titles are discussed in more detail in the international results chapters.

Records

Tournament winners		
Year	Winner	Captain
1996	New Zealand	Sean Fitzpatrick
1997	New Zealand	Sean Fitzpatrick
1998	South Africa	Gary Teichmann
1999	New Zealand	Taine Randell
2000	Australia	John Eales
2001	Australia	John Eales
2002	New Zealand	Reuben Thorne
2003	New Zealand	Reuben Thorne
2004	South Africa	John Smit
2005	New Zealand	Tana Umaga
2006	New Zealand	Richie McCaw
2007	New Zealand	Richie McCaw
2008	New Zealand	Richie McCaw

	Country	P	W	L	D	F	A	PD	LP	BP	TP
1996	New Zealand	4	4	-	-	119	60	59	16	1	17
	South Africa	4	1	3	-	70	84	-14	4	2	6
	Australia	4	1	3	-	71	116	-45	4	2	6
1997	New Zealand	4	4	-	-	159	109	50	16	2	18
	South Africa	4	1	3	-	148	144	4	4	3	7
	Australia	4	1	3	-	96	150	-54	4	2	6
1998	South Africa	4	4	-	-	80	54	26	16	1	17
	Australia	4	2	2	-	79	82	-3	8	2	10
	New Zealand	4	-	4	-	65	88	-23	-	2	2
1999	New Zealand	4	3	1	-	103	61	42	12	-	12
	Australia	4	2	2	-	84	57	27	8	2	10
	South Africa	4	1	3	-	34	103	-69	4	-	4
2000	Australia	4	3	1	-	104	86	18	12	2	14
	New Zealand	4	2	2	-	127	117	10	8	4	12
	South Africa	4	1	3	-	82	110	-28	4	2	6
2001	Australia	4	2	1	1	81	75	6	10	1	11
	New Zealand	4	2	2	-	79	70	9	8	1	9
	South Africa	4	1	2	1	52	67	-15	6	-	6
2002	New Zealand	4	3	1	-	97	65	32	12	3	15
	Australia	4	2	2	-	91	86	5	8	3	11
	South Africa	4	1	3	-	103	140	-37	4	3	7
2003	New Zealand	4	4	-	-	142	65	77	16	2	18
	Australia	4	1	3	-	89	106	-17	4	2	6
	South Africa	4	1	3	-	62	122	-60	4	-	4
2004	South Africa	4	2	2	-	110	98	12	8	3	11
	Australia	4	2	2	-	79	83	-4	8	2	10
	New Zealand	4	2	2	-	83	91	-8	8	1	9
2005	New Zealand	4	3	1	-	111	86	25	12	3	15
	South Africa	4	3	1	-	93	82	11	12	1	13
	Australia	4	-	4	-	72	108	-36	-	3	3
2006	New Zealand	6	5	1	-	179	112	67	20	3	23
	Australia	6	2	4	-	133	121	12	8	3	11
	South Africa	6	2	4	-	106	185	-79	8	1	9
2007	New Zealand	4	3	1	-	100	59	41	12	1	13
	Australia	4	2	2	-	76	80	-4	8	1	9
	South Africa	4	1	3	-	66	103	-37	4	1	5
2008	New Zealand	6	4	2	-	152	106	46	16	3	19
	Australia	6	3	3	-	119	163	-44	12	2	14
	South Africa	6	2	4	-	115	117	-2	8	2	10
2009	New Zealand										
	Australia										
	South Africa										

Key:

P: Played	A: Points against
W: Won	PD: Points difference
L: Lost	LP: Log points
D: Drawn	BP: Bonus points
F: Points for	TP: Total points

Career records

Most points by a player in a Tri-Nations career

No.	Player	Country	Tests	Tournaments	Points T	C	P	DG
328	Andrew Mehrtens	New Zealand	26	1996–2004	1	34	82	3
312	Dan Carter	New Zealand	22	2003–2008	5	37	69	2
271	Matt Burke	Australia	28	1996–2004	7	19	65	1
210	Percy Montgomery	South Africa	34	1997–2008	4	26	43	3
198	Stirling Mortlock	Australia	29	2000–2008	9	21	37	-
153	Carlos Spencer	New Zealand	13	1997–2004	3	21	32	-
121	Matt Giteau	Australia	25	2003–2008	4	19	19	2

Most tries by a player in a Tri-Nations career

No.	Player	Country	Tests	Tournaments
16	Christian Cullen	New Zealand	24	1996–2002
13	Doug Howlett	New Zealand	21	2000–2007
13	Joe Rokocoko	New Zealand	20	2003–2007
9	Justin Marshall	New Zealand	35	1996–2004
9	Stirling Mortlock	Australia	29	2000–2008
9	Lote Tuqiri	Australia	25	2003–2008

Most caps in a Tri-Nations career

Player	Caps	Country	Tournaments
George Gregan	48	Australia	1996–2007
Stephen Larkham	38	Australia	1997–2007
Justin Marshall	35	New Zealand	1996–2004
George Smith	35	Australia	2001–2008
Percy Montgomery	34	South Africa	1997–2008
Victor Matfield	30	South Africa	2001–2008
Nathan Sharpe	30	Australia	2002–2008
Phil Waugh	30	Australia	2001–2008
Greg Somerville	30	New Zealand	2000–2008

Most conversions by a player in a Tri-Nations career

No.	Player	Country	Tests	Tournaments
37	Dan Carter	New Zealand	22	2003–2008
34	Andrew Mehrtens	New Zealand	26	1996–2004
26	Percy Montgomery	South Africa	34	1997–2008
21	Stirling Mortlock	Australia	29	2000–2008
21	Carlos Spencer	New Zealand	13	1996–2003

Most penalties by a player in a Tri-Nations career

No	Player	Country	Tests	Tournaments
82	Andrew Mehrtens	New Zealand	26	1996–2004
69	Dan Carter	New Zealand	22	2003–2008
65	Matt Burke	Australia	28	1996–2004
43	Percy Montgomery	South Africa	34	1997–2008
37	Stirling Mortlock	Australia	29	2000–2008
32	Carlos Spencer	New Zealand	13	1996–2003

Most drop goals by a player in a Tri-Nations career

No.	Player	Country	Tests	Tournaments
4	André Pretorius	South Africa	12	2002–2006
3	Percy Montgomery	South Africa	26	1997–2008
3	Andrew Mehrtens	New Zealand	34	1996–2004

Tournament records

Most points by a player in a Tri-Nations tournament								
No.	Player	Country	Year	Tests	Points			
					T	C	P	DG
99	Daniel Carter	New Zealand	2006	6	1	14	21	1
84	Carlos Spencer	New Zealand	1997	4	2	13	16	-
82	Daniel Carter	New Zealand	2008	6	2	12	15	1
71	Stirling Mortlock	Australia	2000	4	4	6	13	-
69	Andrew Mehrtens	New Zealand	1996	4	-	6	19	-
68	Andrew Mehrtens	New Zealand	1999	4	1	3	19	-
64	Jannie de Beer	South Africa	1997	4	2	12	8	2
62	Daniel Carter	New Zealand	2007	4	1	6	15	-
60	Stirling Mortlock	Australia	2006	6	-	12	12	-
60	Carlos Spencer	New Zealand	2003	4	1	8	13	-

Most conversions by a player in a Tri-Nations tournament				
No.	Player	Country	Tests	Year
14	Daniel Carter	New Zealand	6	2006
13	Carlos Spencer	New Zealand	4	1997
12	Jannie de Beer	South Africa	4	1997
12	Stirling Mortlock	Australia	6	2006
12	Daniel Carter	New Zealand	6	2008
11	Matt Giteau	Australia	6	2008
10	Andrew Mehrtens	New Zealand	4	2000

Most drop goals by a player in a Tri-Nations tournament				
No.	Player	Country	Tests	Year
2	François Steyn	South Africa	2	2007
2	Percy Montgomery	South Africa	4	2005
2	André Pretorius	South Africa	4	2005
2	Andrew Mehrtens	New Zealand	4	2000
2	Jannie de Beer	South Africa	4	1997

Most tries by a player in a Tri-Nations Tournament				
No.	Player	Country	Tests	Year
7	Christian Cullen	New Zealand	4	2000
6	Joe Rokocoko	New Zealand	4	2003
5	Doug Howlett	New Zealand	4	2003
4	Christian Cullen	New Zealand	4	1997
4	Stirling Mortlock	Australia	4	2000
4	Jongi Nokwe	South Africa	2	2008

Most penalties in a Tri-Nations tournament				
No	Player	Country	Tests	Year
21	Daniel Carter	New Zealand	6	2006
19	Andrew Mehrtens	New Zealand	4	1996
19	Andrew Mehrtens	New Zealand	4	1999
16	Carlos Spencer	New Zealand	4	1997
15	Daniel Carter	New Zealand	6	2008
15	Daniel Carter	New Zealand	4	2007
14	Matthew Burke	Australia	4	2001
13	Carlos Spencer	New Zealand	4	2003
13	Braam v. Straaten	South Africa	3	2001
13	Braam v. Straaten	South Africa	4	2000
13	Stirling Mortlock	Australia	4	2000
13	Matthew Burke	Australia	4	1999

Match records

Most points by a player in a Tri-Nations test

No.	Player	Points				Country	Versus	Result	Venue	Date
		T	C	P	DG					
29	Andrew Mehrtens	-	1	9	-	New Zealand	Australia	34–15	Eden Park, Auckland	24/07/1999
26	Jannie de Beer	1	6	3	-	South Africa	Australia	61–22	Loftus Versfeld, Pretoria	23/08/1997
25	Daniel Carter	-	2	7	-	New Zealand	South Africa	35–17	Westpac Stadium, Wellington	22/07/2006
25	Carlos Spencer	1	4	4	-	New Zealand	South Africa	55–35	Eden Park, Auckland	09/08/1997
25	Joel Stansky	1	1	6	-	South Africa	Australia	25–19	Free State Stadium, Brisbane	03/08/1996
24	Matt Burke	2	1	4	-	Australia	New Zealand	24–16	Melbourne Cricket Ground	11/07/1998
23	Daniel Carter	-	1	6	1	New Zealand	South Africa	28–30	Carisbrook, Dunedin	12/07/2008
23	Daniel Carter	1	3	4	-	New Zealand	South Africa	33–6	Jade Stadium, Christchurch	14/07/2007
23	Matt Burke	-	1	7	-	Australia	New Zealand	28–7	Stadium Australia, Sydney	28/08/1999
22	Carlos Spencer	1	4	3	-	New Zealand	South Africa	52–16	Securicor Loftus, Pretoria	19/07/2003
22	Jannie de Beer	-	2	4	2	South Africa	New Zealand	32–35	Ellis Park, Johannesburg	19/07/1997
22	Andrew Mehrtens	-	2	6	-	New Zealand	Australia	25–32	Lang Park, Brisbane	27/07/1996

Most tries by a player in a Tri-Nations test

No.	Player	Country	Versus	Result	Venue	Date
4	Jongi Nokwe	South Africa	Australia	53–8	Coca-Cola Park, Johannesburg	30/08/2008
3	Doug Howlett	New Zealand	Australia	34–24	Eden Park, Auckland	03/09/2005
3	Marius Joubert	South Africa	New Zealand	40–26	Ellis Park, Johannesburg	14/08/2004
3	Joe Rokocoko	New Zealand	Australia	50–21	Telstra Stadium, Sydney	26/07/2003

Most penalties by a player in a Tri-Nations test

No.	Player	Country	Versus	Result	Venue	Date
9	Andrew Mehrtens	New Zealand	Australia	34–15	Eden Park, Auckland	24/07/1999
7	Daniel Carter	New Zealand	Australia	26–12	Eden Park, Auckland	21/07/2007
7	Daniel Carter	New Zealand	South Africa	35–17	Westpac Stadium, Wellington	22/07/2006
7	Matt Burke	Australia	New Zealand	28–7	Stadium Australia, Sydney	28/08/1999
7	Andrew Mehrtens	New Zealand	South Africa	34–18	Minolta Loftus, Pretoria	07/08/1999
6	Daniel Carter	New Zealand	South Africa	28–30	Carisbrook, Dunedin	12/07/2008
6	Braam van Straaten	South Africa	Australia	18–19	ABSA Stadium, Durban	26/08/2000
6	Joel Stransky	South Africa	Australia	25–19	Free State Stadium, Bloemfontein	02/08/1996
6	Andrew Mehrtens	New Zealand	Australia	32–25	Suncorp Stadium, Brisbane	27/07/1996

Most conversions by a player in a Tri-Nations test

No.	Player	Country	Versus	Result	Venue	Date
6	Jannie de Beer	South Africa	Australia	61–22	Loftus Versfeld, Pretoria	23/08/1997
5	Stirling Mortlock	Australia	South Africa	49–0	Suncorp Stadium, Brisbane	15/07/2006
5	Braam van Straaten	South Africa	New Zealand	46–40	Ellis Park, Johannesburg	19/08/2000
4	Daniel Carter	New Zealand	Australia	28–24	Suncorp Stadium, Brisbane	13/09/2008
4	Matt Giteau	Australia	New Zealand	34–19	ANZ Stadium, Sydney	26/07/2008
4	Daniel Carter	New Zealand	South Africa	45–26	Loftus Versfeld, Pretoria	26/08/2006
4	Carlos Spencer	New Zealand	South Africa	52–16	Securicor Loftus, Pretoria	19/07/2003
4	Werner Greeff	South Africa	Australia	33–31	Ellis Park, Johannesburg	17/08/2002
4	Andrew Mehrtens	New Zealand	South Africa	40–46	Ellis Park, Johannesburg	19/08/2000
4	Andrew Mehrtens	New Zealand	Australia	39–35	Stadium Australia, Sydney	15/07/2000
4	Carlos Spencer	New Zealand	South Africa	55–35	Eden Park, Auckland	09/08/1997

Most drop goals by a player in a Tri-Nations test by a player

No.	Player	Country	Versus	Result	Venue	Date
2	François Steyn	South Africa	Australia	22–19	Newlands, Cape Town	16/06/2007
2	Jannie de Beer	South Africa	New Zealand	32–35	Ellis Park, Johannesburg	19/07/1997

Most points by a team in a Tri-Nations test

No.	Result	T	C	P	D	Country	Versus	Venue	Date
61	61–22	8	6	3	-	South Africa	Australia	Loftus Versfeld, Pretoria	23/08/1997
55	55–35	7	4	4	-	New Zealand	South Africa	Eden Park, Auckland	09/08/1997
53	53–8	8	5	1	-	South Africa	Australia	Coca-Cola Park, Johannesburg	30/08/2008
52	52–16	7	4	3	-	New Zealand	South Africa	Securicor Loftus, Pretoria	19/07/2003
50	50–21	7	3	3	-	New Zealand	Australia	Telstra Stadium, Sydney	26/07/2003
49	49–0	6	5	2	1	Australia	South Africa	Suncorp Stadium, Brisbane	15/07/2006
46	46–40	6	5	2	-	South Africa	New Zealand	Ellis Park, Johannesburg	19/08/2000
45	45–26	5	4	4	-	New Zealand	South Africa	Loftus Versfeld, Pretoria	26/08/2006
43	43–6	6	2	3	-	New Zealand	Australia	Athletic Park, Wellington	06/07/1996
41	41–20	5	2	3	1	New Zealand	South Africa	Westpac Trust Stadium, Wellington	20/07/2002

Most consecutive test wins

No.	Period	Country	Details
8	06/07/1996–16/08/1997	New Zealand	Australia (H), South Africa (H), Australia (A), South Africa (A), South Africa (A), Australia (A), South Africa (H), Australia (H)
8	13/08/2005–26/08/2006	New Zealand	Australia (A), South Africa (H), Australia (H), Australia (H), South Africa (H), Australia (A), Australia (H), South Africa (A)
7	10/08/2002–24/07/2004	New Zealand	South Africa (A), South Africa (A), Australia (A), South Africa (H), Australia (H), Australia (H), South Africa (H)

The Olympic Games

One of the great trivia questions of rugby is: Who are the reigning Olympic rugby champions? The answer, surprisingly, is the United States. In 1900, Baron Pierre de Coubertin (often referred to as the father of the modern Olympic Games) introduced rugby to the Summer Olympics of 1900 held in Paris. De Coubertin was a great supporter of the game with strong rugby ties, having previously refereed in the French domestic championship. Only three teams entered the 1900 games: France beat Germany and Great Britain to win the gold medal. Germany was awarded the silver and Great Britain the bronze.

Rugby did not feature at the 1904 games in St Louis but in 1908, was again played at the Olympics, this time in London, with just two teams entering the games – a touring Australian side and Great Britain. Just a single match was played. Australia won the gold medal with a 32–3 victory. Rugby did not feature in the 1912 games in Stockholm, but in 1920 was again played, this time in Antwerp. Once again, just two sides entered, the United States and France, with the United States taking the gold medal with an 8–0 win over the French favourites. Rugby featured again in the 1924 Paris Olympics. Three teams competed – France, the United States and Romania. Each nation played two matches, with the final played on 18 May 1924 between France and the United States, both of whom had defeated the Romanians. The Americans outscored their hosts by five tries to one and went on to win the gold medal with a 17–3 victory. But the Americans had become unpopular with the French public throughout the games and the match finished in an uproar – the Americans were pelted with bottles and rocks, and with further shades of football hooliganism, one of their reserves was knocked flat by a walking stick belonging to a vitriolic French supporter. The Stars and Stripes anthem was jeered and on this sour note, rugby met its demise as an Olympic sport.

The United States, therefore, remain to this day the Olympic rugby champions. However, rugby was never taken very seriously at the games. The leading rugby nations rarely entered teams and those that did were hardly representative of their nation. The 1900 French side came from a Paris club side; the Germans from Eintracht Frankfurt and the British team from Moseley Wanderers RFC. In 1908, the British side was actually Cornwall and the victorious 1920 and 1924 American sides were in fact the Stanford University football team. Despite the International Olympic Committee (IOC) Congress decree in 1921 that rugby should be placed on the programme 'so that hereafter … rugby would be a positive part of the Olympic program', the sport was rejected from the 1928 games in Amsterdam on the following grounds:

- The uproar experienced at the 1924 gold-medal match between France and the United States
- The IOC was placing increasing emphasis on individual sports
- Women's athletics had swollen the number of competitors in the games, making it more difficult to manage competitor numbers
- The sport did not receive the backing needed from the British entrants

It is generally believed that rugby was lost to the Olympics because de Coubertin retired as IOC president in 1925. Despite rugby selling more tickets than the track and field events at the 1924 games, it never featured again. For the 1980 Moscow and 1988 Seoul games, attempts were made to have rugby readmitted but to no avail – although Seoul did come close. Thus only six nations have ever competed for the gold medal in rugby at the Olympic Games: France, Germany, Great Britain, Australia, the United States and Romania. Their statistics and medal tallies are shown below:

Team	Played	Won	Lost	For	Against	Gold	Silver	Bronze
United States of America	3	3	-	64	3	2 (1920, 1924)	-	-
France	5	3	2	116	53	1 (1900)	2 (1920, 1924)	-
Australia	1	1	-	32	3	1 (1908)	-	-
Great Britain	2	-	2	11	59	-	1 (1908)	1 (1900)
Germany	1	-	1	17	27	-	1 (1900)	-
Romania	2	-	2	3	98	-	-	1 (1924)

Left: Team photograph of the French rugby side at the 1924 Paris Olympic Games who finished as silver medallists. *Photo*: Frédéric Humbert/www.flickr.com/photos/rugby_pioneers/creative commons license

Centre: The celebrated United States team: the 1924 Olympic gold medallists who to this day remain the reigning Olympic rugby champions after defeating hosts France 17-3 in the final. *Photo*: Frédéric Humbert/www.flickr.com/photos/rugby_pioneers/creative commons license

Bottom: France against the United States of America at the Paris Olympics of 1924, Stade de Colombes. *Photo*: Commons/wikimedia.org/creative commons license

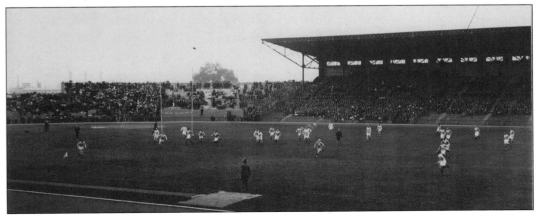

Chapter Three
Tier-one rugby nations

Tiering system

After the 1987 RWC, a tiering system was adopted by the IRFB to rank and develop rugby-playing countries internationally. Nations are ranked and tiered across three levels according to their ability, with competition structures organised by the IRB to ensure that like play like more often than not. Rugby internationals across the three tiered groups are relatively rare, with only the tier-two nations playing the tier-one nations from time to time (and rarely winning).

The RWC provides the only opportunity for tier-three nations to compete against top-tier nations if they qualify for the tournament. But these sides often lose by record margins. In an attempt to avoid such scorelines and ensure the improvement of rugby in the lower-tier nations, the IRB raises and allocates funds for the development of the game in those nations which show the most potential for promotion to the higher levels, with cross-border tournaments designed to provide the necessary quality of opposition that these sides require in order to improve. In addition, some funds are set aside for the tier-one nations to ensure that they retain their top-tier status. Below are brief definitions of the tiering system:

Tier 1 nations: Developed rugby nations made up of the 'traditional top eight' – who were the only members of the IRFB prior to the 1987 RWC – along with Italy and Argentina

Tier 2 nations: Developing rugby nations, all of which have played in at least one RWC

Tier 3 nations: Countries in which the sport is relatively new or has a very small player base from which to choose a national side. A small number of these nations have taken part in an RWC

As of April 2009, 117 nations were affiliated to the IRB. This book focuses on the traditional, top-ranked tier-one nations in most detail, currently: Argentina, Australia, England, France, Ireland, Italy, New Zealand, Scotland, South Africa and Wales. The British and Irish Lions and their historic tours are covered in Chapter 4. Other two- and three-tier rugby nations which have each qualified for at least one RWC are also covered, in Chapter 6.

Tier 1 nations (10)	Argentina, Australia, England, France, Ireland, Italy, New Zealand, Scotland, South Africa, Wales
Tier 2 nations (7)	Canada, Fiji, Japan, Romania, Samoa, Tonga, United States
Tier 3 nations (7)	Côte d'Ivoire, Georgia, Namibia, Portugal, Spain, Uruguay, Zimbabwe
Yet to play in an RWC (93)	American Samoa, Andorra, Arabian Gulf, Armenia, Austria, Azerbaijan, Bahamas, Barbados, Belgium, Bermuda, Bosnia-Herzegovina, Botswana, British Virgin Islands, Burundi, Brazil, Brunei, Bulgaria, Cambodia, Cameroon, Cayman Islands, Chile, China, Chinese Taipei, Columbia, Cook Islands, Croatia, Czech Republic, Denmark, Finland, Germany, Ghana, Guam, Guyana, Hong Kong, Hungary, India, Indonesia, Israel, Jamaica, Kazakhstan, Kenya, Korea, Kyrgyzstan, Laos, Latvia, Lithuania, Luxembourg, Madagascar, Malaysia, Mali, Malta, Mauritania, Mauritius, Mexico, Moldova, Monaco, Mongolia, Morocco, Netherlands, Nigeria, Niue, Norway, Pakistan, Papua New Guinea, Paraguay, Peru, Philippines, Poland, Russia, Rwanda, St Lucia, St Vincent and the Grenadines, Serbia, Senegal, Singapore, Slovenia, Solomon Islands, Sri Lanka, Swaziland, Sweden, Switzerland, Tahiti, Tanzania, Thailand, Togo, Trinidad and Tobago, Tunisia, Uganda, Ukraine, Uzbekistan, Vanuatu, Venezuela, Zambia

History of the International Rugby Board

At a meeting in London on 26 January 1871, representatives from 21 clubs formed the Rugby Football Union (RFU). Its remit was to manage and formalise the rules of the sport. Since the first rugby international was played in 1871, there was seldom an international that did not produce a major dispute between opposing countries over an aspect of the game's rules. In 1884, heated arguments about a try being scored in the international between Scotland and England came to such a head that the two refused to play each other the following season until the dispute had been resolved. Until 1885, England, the founder union, had made the laws of the game and claimed that, as they determined the laws, if they said it was a try, then a try it was. Scotland had disputed the try in question. This heavy-handed approach did not go down well with the Scots who then refused to play England. Such incidents needed to be avoided and so the Irish (neutrals in this incident) proposed the creation of an International Board (IB) in 1886. Ireland, Scotland and Wales duly formed the IB to regulate international matches, with the first official meeting of the board taking place on 5 December 1887, with representatives from Scotland, Wales and Ireland in attendance. England, however, stubbornly refused to join the board, determined to remain the leading voice in rugby, but later stipulated it would join if granted a greater representation on the basis that they had a greater number of clubs. They also refused to accept that the IB should be the game's recognised lawmaker and, with this, the IB decided that all member countries would not play England until the RFU agreed to join the IB. England were initially steadfast in their refusal to join, but eventually acquiesced in 1890, thereby becoming the first non-founding member to join the IB. With their membership the International Rugby Football Board (IRFB) was formed.

The IRFB published the first set of international laws that same year and henceforth all international games were played under IRFB rules. Bizarrely, each union retained its own set of domestic laws for home matches – the IRFB's authority only extending to international matches – until 1930 when England proposed, and Ireland seconded, that 'all matches should be played under the laws of the IRFB'. Since 1930, the IRFB has governed all aspects of the game worldwide. The IRFB has also had a hand in matters other than rugby-management issues. On 4 August 1914, as World War I erupted, the IRFB advised all players to join the armed forces. In total, 133 international players from the British Isles, Australia, New Zealand, South Africa, France and Romania were killed in the war following this instruction. A similar message was issued at the start of World War II, which resulted in 88 international players from the British Isles, New Zealand, Australia, South Africa, France, Germany and Romania dying.

From its first meeting in 1887 and England's membership in 1890, the IRFB gradually grew to seven unions in 1948 when Australia, New Zealand and South Africa were admitted. France joined in 1978, taking the number to eight. These first eight nations to join the IRFB are today known as the 'traditional top eight' nations in world rugby. In 1987, Argentina, Fiji, Italy, Canada, Japan, Romania, Tonga, the United States and Zimbabwe joined the IRFB. The original eight nations retained their two seats; the other countries were granted a single seat, with a host of other nations joining the IRFB the following year. After initially being based in England, today the IRB has its headquarters in Dublin. In 1997, the IRFB dropped the 'Football' ('F') from its title to become known simply as the International Rugby Board (IRB).

Argentina

Like rugby in the other southern-hemisphere nations, the sport was first introduced to Argentina by British expatriates in the late 1800s. The first recorded game of rugby in Argentina was in 1873 when Banks played City, but it was not until 1886 that the first rugby club was formed – the Buenos Aires Cricket and Rugby Club, whose members were predominantly expatriates. The first club formed by and catering for local Argentinians was founded in 1904, when the Buenos Aires University Club was constituted. In 1899, four clubs in Buenos Aires got together to agree on the governance of the fledgling game in the country. The result was the formation of the River Plate Rugby Union – the first union in Argentina to govern rugby – some 26 years after the first game had been played. This body evolved into the national rugby union and is today known as the Unión Argentina de Rugby (UAR), which became a member of the IRFB in 1987 when they were invited to participate in the first RWC. In the same year of the formation of the River Plate Rugby Union, the first Argentinian club championship was held under the union's auspices, known today as the Zona Campeonato Argentino, which involves the country's eight top teams.

In 1910, Argentina hosted their first high-profile touring side when John Raphael of England led a touring British Isles side for six matches, including a match against the Argentinian national side – Argentina's first test match, although not recognised by the British as a capped international. This touring side was billed on departure from Southampton as the English Rugby Union Team, but was correctly labelled as the Combined British Team by their Argentinian hosts upon arrival, as the squad contained three Scotsmen (the team was also referred to as a Great Britain XV). The visitors remained unbeaten, encountering limited opposition, beating Argentina 28–3 in the test match on 12 June 1910 at the GEBA stadium in Buenos Aires.

Following the success of this tour and the undeniable growth of the sport in Argentina, other teams took to touring the country with the idea that a new southern-hemisphere rugby giant was emerging in South America – an exotic touring location. In 1927, the British

Isles again visited Argentina with the hope of developing the game further and establishing another rugby powerhouse in the southern hemisphere. The tour was organised by the River Plate Rugby Union and paid for by donations and union fundraisers. It was a massive success all round. The tourists received no real opposition in the nine tour matches, scoring 295 points to just nine against and winning the test series 4–0. Despite the one-sided nature of the matches, all stadiums were filled on each occasion, with the host union garnering some handsome profits. With the success of this tour, the popularity of rugby began to spread across Argentina; consequently South Africa sent a touring Junior Springboks outfit in 1932 to test the strength of their South American counterparts. The South Africans were unbeaten and comfortably won the two-test series.

In 1936, the British Isles again returned with the hope of receiving stiffer competition. It was not to be: they easily won all their matches, including the lone test 23–0. Again caps were not awarded for the international. It was clear that the Argentinians' game was not improving, as was initially hoped, and this British tour turned out to be the last to Argentina for some time to come. Soon after the departure of the British, Argentina went on their first tour, to Chile, where they played a two-test series against their South American neighbours, winning both and thereby achieving their first test victory, on 20 September 1936, in Valparaiso, by 29–0.

International opposition in these early years was few and far between for Argentina, with test caps awarded against various combined touring sides, including matches against a combined Oxford and Cambridge Universities XV ('Oxbridge') in 1948, 1956, 1965 and 1971. In 1949, France became the first top rugby nation to play against Argentina at full international level, awarding test caps to their players during the two-test series on their tour to Argentina – both won by the French but by narrow margins. An Irish touring side arrived in 1952; it did not award caps in the two-test series, which the Irish won 1–0, with one test drawn – a result that was a clear indication of the improving quality of rugby in Argentina.

In 1951, the UAR decided to organise and host the first South American Rugby Championship as part of the Buenos Aires Pan American Games, with the intention of growing the game in South America. Chile, Uruguay and Brazil were invited to take part in the tournament, with Argentina comfortably winning all three of their matches and the title. In 1958, Argentina defended their crown as South American champions despite a wild night of partying in Santiago the day before playing Chile – a game they won 14–0. Argentina have since won this championship with ease on each occasion they have competed, regularly notching up record victories in the process. This has been a source of disappointment to the UAR, in that the game has not developed and improved across the continent as they had hoped. Indeed today, Argentina no longer competes in the tournament, given the gross disparities in the standard of rugby between them and the rest. In 1981, Uruguay won the championship, due only to the fact that Argentina did not take part that year. To avoid the inevitable cricket scorelines, Argentina 'A' now compete instead and win regularly. If one considers the 1951 Pan American Games tournament to be the first, then the 2009 tournament will be the 30th South American Rugby Championship, which is today split between a Division A and B.

In 1965, Argentina undertook their first overseas tour when they visited South Africa, playing 16 matches in all and winning 11, including the only 'test match' of the tour, played against the Junior Springboks. It was on this tour that the nickname for the Argentinian team, the Pumas, was first coined when a Rhodesian journalist for the *Rhodesia Magazine,* in an effort to assign a nickname to the touring side, mistakenly identified the embroidered animal on the tourists' jerseys as a puma rather than a jaguar. Since then, the team has always been fondly – if erroneously – referred to as *los Pumas.*

In 1966, the South African Gazelles toured Argentina for the first time – essentially a Junior Springbok B outfit – with Argentina losing both tests against the tourists by close margins. However, following a series victory over a Welsh XV in 1968, international competition for the Pumas swiftly increased and by 1970 they had recorded victories against Irish and Scottish XVs. In 1979, Argentina achieved their first test victory over an IRFB member when they defeated Australia 24–13, thanks to a superb kicking display from flyhalf legend Hugo Porta who kicked three drop goals and amassed a total of 16 points. Argentina followed this up in 1985 with their first victory over France, the same year they held the All Blacks to a thrilling draw in Buenos Aires when Hugo Porta kicked all 21 of his team's points.

It was in the 1980s that Argentinian rugby began to improve immeasurably; they were invited to take part in the inaugural RWC in 1987. Later that year, they beat Australia in a two-test series, and following a disappointing 1991 RWC, they scored their first victory against France on French turf. In 1999, Argentina advanced to the quarter-finals of the RWC, with their ace flyhalf, Gonzalo Quesada, finishing the top point scorer of the tournament, with a personal haul of 102 points.

In the new millennium, Argentina began establishing themselves as a consistent world rugby force. They won regularly against top nations, which was highlighted by their first-ever series victory over France, in 2003, and fantastic victories over France in Marseilles (2004), England at Twickenham (2006) and an amazing 25-all draw against the British and Irish Lions in Cardiff in 2005. Their form peaked at the 2007 RWC where Argentina proved everybody wrong and advanced to the semi-finals, in which they lost to eventual champions, South Africa. They ultimately finished third when they defeated France for the second time in the tournament and were subsequently officially ranked third in the world by the IRB ranking system following this success – above such teams as France, England and Australia.

With the advent of professionalism in rugby union in 1995, the UAR steadfastly refused to adopt the new dispensation and insisted on rugby remaining forever amateur in Argentina. This resulted in a large number of quality Argentinian players having to play overseas for a living – not an ideal situation, considering that growing and improving the game in a country is best done when its top players play in the national and provincial competitions. Nonetheless, players who do opt to play abroad are still eligible for national selection.

Great pressure has recently been placed on Argentina to join the premier southern-hemisphere competition – the Tri-Nations – but with little success. Since Argentina's test-series win over Wales in June 2006, it became evident that to ensure the continued success of the Pumas it was necessary to include them in regular top-flight international rugby. However, due to contractual issues it is currently impossible for Argentina to join the Tri-Nations until at least 2011. With this in mind, the then captain, Agustín Pichot, publicly requested that Argentina be considered to join and expand the present Six Nations Tournament, whereby Argentina would play their home games at neutral venues in Europe, such as Belgium or Portugal. This has yet to be realised and it is probable that Argentina will have to wait until 2011 to play in a top tournament on an annual basis. The reason cited for the delay by the IRB was current fixture congestion in the southern hemisphere and the lack of a professional structure in Argentina.

However, following Argentina's amazing third-place finish at the 2007 RWC, their cause was even more strongly justifiable, and at an IRB conference in November 2007, it was agreed that Argentina would play more annual tests against top international opponents (increased from six to nine per annum) and that between 2008 and 2012 Argentina would develop a professional structure with the ultimate goal of luring their top-flight players back to Argentina. This all to ensure that by 2012, Argentina will (according to the IRB) be 'fully integrated into the southern top-flight rugby-playing structure'.

Incredibly, following these resolutions by the IRB, the UAR unanimously voted to keep the domestic Argentinian league strictly amateur – a serious obstacle to the development and growth of the game in the country and one that will probably ensure that Argentina remains the only top-tier nation not to be involved in an annual competition.

Despite rugby remaining largely amateur in Argentina, the game is second only in popularity to soccer and is particularly popular in the greater Buenos Aires urban area and in the Tucumán Province, where rugby has a larger following than football. Argentina's continued success in rugby since the 1999 RWC has seen the game's popularity increase exponentially in the country over the last decade.

9 August 1980. The Argentinian National Selection to take on the Rest of the World in a charity match, in aid of the Beunos Aires Province flood victims as well as commemorating the capital's 400th birthday. The match, refereed by South African Stefanus Strydom, was won 36–22 by the Argentinians in an 11-try classic, with captain Hugo Porta (seated centre with ball) converting all seven Argentinian tries, scored by Mastai (2), Sansot (2), Campo, Silva and Ure. The opposition tries were scored by Fouroux, Fenkick, Slemen and Scott, with Slemen and O'Brien adding the kicking points. *Photo*: UAR

Australia

Rugby is one of the oldest sports in Australia. The game was first mentioned in local newspapers just six years after William Webb Ellis first ran with the ball. It has been suggested that New South Wales was the first centre to feature rugby outside of Great Britain, with football of various sorts being played in Australia as early as 1829. Conflicting evidence suggests either rugby union or a form of Australian Rules football was played on 25 July 1829 at the soldiers' barracks in Sydney. Later, an ex-Rugby School pupil by the name of Thomas Wills attempted to introduce his school's rules to Melbourne in 1857. He was unsuccessful and two years later, a group of Melbournites drew up their own rules, which came to be known as Victorian Rules. And so Australian Rules football (aka Aussie Rules) was born, the dominant winter sport in Victoria. The first rugby union game to be played in Victoria did not take place until 1888.

With rugby becoming the established sport in New South Wales it soon became an integral part of life in schools and universities, but not in Melbourne where Aussie Rules was dominant. The Sydney University Club was founded in 1863, the oldest rugby club in Australia and outside of the British Isles. However, most of the early rugby clubs in Australia were in fact cricket clubs, with rugby only being played during the winter months in order to keep the cricketers fit. By 1880, there were about a hundred clubs in New South Wales where rugby was played. The first New South Wales–Queensland rugby match was on 12 August 1882 at the Sydney Cricket Ground and was won 28–4 by New South Wales. With this match, one of the greatest rugby rivalries in the world was born. In 1874, the Southern Union (which changed its name to the New South Wales Rugby Union in 1892) was formed. This was followed by the formation of the Northern Union in 1883 (to become the Queensland Rugby Union in 1892). Elsewhere in Australia, however,

All Black scrumhalf Charlie Saxton (head obscured, on ground at left) scores the first of his two tries in the first test of the 1938 Bledisloe Cup series in Sydney. New Zealand won the match 24-9 and ultimately the series 3-0 to retain the cup. *Photo*: New Zealand Rugby Museum

rugby took off more slowly. The Melbourne Union (changed to the Victoria Rugby Union in 1926) was not formed until 1888.

Despite rugby's early roots in Australia, it was not until 1949 that the Australian Rugby Football Union was formed – mainly in response to a proposal from the British-dominated International Board – in order to give formal representation on the IRFB to all three of the major southern-hemisphere rugby-playing countries. Prior to this, control of the game lay exclusively with the Southern Rugby Union, while Queensland fell under the jurisdiction of the Northern Rugby Union. Because New South Wales continuously supplied the lion's share of players to the Australian national side they were, and still are, able to consistently produce a side of the highest quality and regularly record famous victories against overseas touring teams.

Australia has remained consistent in being able to compete in the game of rugby union, an amazing feat when considering the drain of resources on the game following the rise in popularity of rugby league and Australian Rules football – a game that was first played in 1858, which split from rugby union because of the rigidity of the rules governing the sport. Fortunately for Australian rugby, Queensland and New South Wales declined to join the breakaway movement. In 1882, New South Wales undertook its first overseas rugby tour to New Zealand – at the time a five-day journey by ship. Six years later in 1888, the British Isles despatched their first overseas visitors to Australia on a tour that lasted for more than a year. Sadly, the British lost their tour captain, R.L. Seddon, after he drowned in a canoeing accident. In 1899, the British Isles were again to tour Australia. This time, 18 of the tour matches were played against Australian Rules opposition. By the end of the tour, Britain had won the four-test series 3–1. Since these early days, Australian rugby has grown from the two dominant unions of New South Wales and Queensland to four, including Australian Capital Territories (ACT) based out of Canberra and the Western Force in Perth, who now compete in the Super 14 tournament.

During World War I competitive club rugby in Australia completely shut down and by 1919, only six clubs had been able to re-establish themselves – all in New South Wales. New South Wales did manage to play New Zealand both home and away during this time and completed the Waratahs tour to the United Kingdom in 1927/1928. During these years, a number of Queensland and Victorian players registered with and played for the New South Wales union as the Queensland and Victoria unions had failed to resume operations at the end of World War I: hence the only union in Australia at the time to be affiliated to was New South Wales. No rugby matches were played in Queensland until 1928, with the Queensland Rugby Union only being re-formed in 1929. For this reason matches against New South Wales during this period were not considered to be international fixtures by either New Zealand or South Africa (who toured in 1921), as the Waratahs did not reflect a fully representative Australian side selected from across the country. However, during the 1927/1928 Waratahs tour of the United Kingdom and France, all five home nations recognised these fixtures as full internationals, with Australia touring as the Waratahs. In 1986, the Australian Rugby Union (ARU) also recognised these matches as fully fledged Australian internationals, considering that the New South Wales club and team of the time were also comprised of players from Queensland and Victoria – so essentially New South Wales represented Australia's best.

However, the greatest challenge that Australian rugby faced was the issue of professionalism during the earlier part of the twentieth century. Players became aware of the breakaway that had occurred in the game in England and the resultant growth of a professional rugby league. They were niggled by the ARU's negative attitude toward assisting injured players with their medical bills from injuries incurred in the sport and in 1907 the issue came to a head when a professional New Zealand side stopped over in Australia en route to the United Kingdom. During the stopover they played three matches against the top Sydney union players and as a consequence the Australian players were (very harshly) banned for life from playing rugby by the union. As a result of this cruel ruling these players predictably broke away to play rugby league. Again in 1909, after a tour to the United Kingdom by both Australian union and league teams, the

Did you know: The first British Barbarians fixture was played against the 1947/1948 touring Australian side to the United Kingdom. It was the last game of the tour and was a hastily arranged fixture to help raise funds to ensure the tourists could pay their fares home. The match turned out to be such a success that a Barbarians match has since become an essential part of every major southern-hemisphere tour to the British Isles.

Did you know: The second Wallaby overseas touring side didn't play a single match on their tour to the United Kingdom. The team arrived in Britain in 1939 just as World War II broke out, and within a couple of weeks they were on the boat back home.

two sides, upon returning to Australia, played a series of exhibition matches against each other. This infuriated the ARU who decided to expel all those union players involved in these matches. These players were essentially left with no option but to defect to the league establishment, further boosting league rugby in Australia. The union game continued to lose players to the league with crowds and subsequent revenues inevitably following the more successful league game. With time, rugby league became the more popular code of rugby in Australia, right up to today. However, with union rugby turning professional, players have slowly begun returning to the union fold, and stars such as Lote Tuqiri and Mat Rogers have turned successful league performances into glittering union careers.

Since playing their first international on 24 June 1899, Australia have completed numerous tours to the British home unions. Their first was in 1908/1909 when they were first dubbed the Wallabies. Two internationals out of a total of 31 matches were played but the tourists will always be remembered for their poor disciplinary record, with three of their players sent off for various indiscretions during the tour. Nonetheless, the tour finished on a high note, with Australia managing a hard-fought 9–3 victory over England in a rough and tough international.

In 1927/1928, the second Australian team arrived in Britain and France and were nicknamed the Waratahs once the British press had learned that the entire touring team was made up of members from the New South Wales Union. (The waratah is a plant indigenous to New South Wales.) For the first time, a full fixture list of five internationals was played with the Aussies winning three – against Wales, Ireland and France. The tour will forever be remembered for the expansive, entertaining brand of rugby played by the Australians.

The next tour, in 1947/1948, was very successful for the Australians, who lost only one international and played a historic first match against the British Barbarians, who have gone on to become one of the most famous rugby-playing sides anywhere in the world. Following this tour, the decades from the 1950s through to the 1980s were lean times for rugby down under. Australia managed to record just 36 victories out of 118 internationals – many of which were against lowly opposition, such as Fiji, Tonga and Japan. The Lions stopped over en route to New Zealand in 1950, 1959 and 1966 for a two-test series on each occasion, winning them all. And in 1971, for the first time, they didn't even bother to arrange an international against Australia. There were some highlights in this period, however, including inflicting their first defeat on South Africa in 15 years on 5 September 1953 in Cape Town. This period of poor form came to an end in spectacular fashion when the eighth touring Australian side to the United Kingdom and Ireland recorded their first Grand Slam tour, defeating all four unions comprehensively, with Mark Ella notching up the rare achievement of scoring a try in each of the four internationals. Since then, Australia has been on the up, securing the Bledisloe Cup in 1986 and reaching the semi-final against France in the 1987 RWC.

Soon after, Australia inflicted record defeats over Wales (63–6 in 1991) and England (40–15 in 1991), before claiming their first RWC title, beating England at Twickenham 12–6 in November 1991. They reclaimed the Bledisloe Cup in 1993 and retained it the following year when a young George Gregan put in a last-second, match-saving tackle on Jeff Wilson diving over the line for the winning try. Australia went unbeaten in 1994, but were brought back down to earth the following year when South Africa beat them in the opening game of the 1995 RWC, which eventually resulted in the defending champions being knocked out in the quarter-finals. Four years later, in 1999, they reclaimed the RWC in Cardiff and the following year won their first Tri-Nations tournament, thanks to two single-point victories in consecutive matches over New Zealand and South Africa. They retained the title the following year in 2001, and in 2003 came within 30 seconds of becoming the first nation in rugby history to win back-to-back RWC titles.

By their own admission, Australia have performed poorly on the world stage since 2002, losing for the first time to Wales in 18 years in 2005 and to Ireland for the first time in 23 years. They lost every game of the 2005 Tri-Nations during a run of seven consecutive test defeats and were dumped out of the 2007 RWC in the quarter-final stage. But never discount the Aussies …

There have been many variations in the Australian team colours over the years. The first touring Wallabies in 1908/1909 wore the light-blue jerseys adopted by New South Wales the previous year. During home internationals the light-blue New South Wales jerseys were worn when playing in Sydney and the maroon jerseys of Queensland were worn when playing an international in Brisbane. It was not until the 1961 tour of South Africa that Australia first wore the colours that we recognise today (gold shirts and green shorts) – chosen to avoid confusion with South Africa's more established green shirts with gold collars.

Australia's nickname, the Wallabies, derives from their first tour to the British Isles in 1908/1909, but the name's origins are unclear, other than it being a small, furry marsupial found only in Australia. Sources suggest that either the touring team came up with the name themselves during their long journey to the Britain, or that the British press endeavoured to coin a nickname for the tourists. The players came up with two suggestions, the Wallabies or the Wolves, and after a team vote, the former was chosen and has stuck. Furthermore, the team decided to perform an Aboriginal ritual challenge before each game, following the popularity of the 1905 New Zealand *haka* with the British. However, the players found this too embarrassing to perform. The name remained, but not the dance.

England

The first rugby club in the world to be formed was Guy's Hospital Club in London in 1843. Other clubs, which played various versions of football, formed soon after. By the 1860s, there were some 20 rugby clubs concentrated in the London area, with clubs steadily forming across the country, including Oxford and Cambridge universities. The two famous institutions met for the first Varsity Match in 1872. By 1870, several rugby clubs had been established across England and the first representative county match took place that same year between Yorkshire and Lancashire – a classic British rivalry.

The game's popularity grew at such a rapid pace throughout England that it became necessary to form a single ruling national union to manage club memberships, fixtures, rules and disputes. In December 1870, Edwin Ash, the secretary of the Richmond Club, and B.H. Burns, honorary secretary of Blackheath Club, jointly published a letter in the press, which read: 'Those who play the rugby-type game should meet to form a code of practice, as various clubs play to rules which differ from others, which makes the game difficult to play.' A positive response was received from this letter and on 26 January 1871, 32 representatives from 21 clubs met at the Pall Mall Restaurant, Cockspur Street in central London, to form the English Rugby Football Union (RFU). The meeting had initially been called primarily to address the challenge laid down by Scotland to play the first international, but the agenda had been expanded to include the issue of creating an English Rugby Union. These 21 founding member clubs were Blackheath, Richmond, Wellington College, Guy's Hospital, Harlequins, King's College, St Paul's School, Civil Service, Marlborough Nomads, Queen's House, West Kent, Wimbledon Hornets, Gipsies, Clapham Rovers, Flamingos, Lausanne, Addison, Mohicans, Belsize Park, Ravenscourt Park and Law Club. Of these original clubs eight still flourish today.

Lineout action from the 1905 England–New Zealand international at Crystal Palace in London. The game was won 15-0 by New Zealand.
Photo: New Zealand Rugby Museum

Did you know: The RFU founders believed that rugby was a worthwhile activity only if it contributed to the players' physical and moral wellbeing and hence should be kept amateur and non-commercial to uphold these values. However, the growth of the game made this difficult to control, as it generated large crowds and resulting cash. Players began joining the wealthier clubs, lured by better job offers set up by the clubs, and soon allegations of professionalism were brought to the RFU's attention.

In 1886, the issue of 'broken time' was first raised in Lancashire, northern England, where soccer and cricket players were being compensated by their clubs for loss of wages for time taken off from work to play sport, while rugby players were not. The issue came to a head when a meeting was held at the Westminster Palace Hotel in London on 20 September 1893. Two Yorkshire representatives of the English Rugby Union, J.A. Millar and M.N. Newsome, proposed that 'players be allowed compensation for bona fide loss of time'. The then secretary of the English RFU, George Rowland Hill (later Sir), proposed an amendment 'that this meeting, believing that the above principle is contrary to the true spirit of the game, declines to sanction the same'. This amendment was carried by 282 votes to 136 and with this, several of the northern clubs (many of whose players worked in the mines) promptly announced their withdrawal from the RFU. On 29 August 1895 at a meeting at the George Hotel in Huddersfield, 20 clubs from Yorkshire, Lancashire and Cheshire agreed to resign from the RFU and form the Northern Rugby Football Union, which in 1922 became known as the Rugby Football League. All rugby league players were banned from playing union rugby by the RFU, but the ban was temporarily lifted in 1939 during the war years, with many league players taking part in the so-called service internationals played between England and Scotland during World War II.

Fundamental differences between the games remain today. For instance, in rugby league the game has 13 players; there are no lineouts, no flankers, no rucks or mauls and scrums are uncontested. The two codes of rugby may never reunite, but there are fewer reasons today to prolong the tensions and prejudices of the past. In 1930, Lions rugby manager, James Baxter, was infamously quoted in reference to rugby league in Auckland, New Zealand by saying 'every city needs its sewer'. Take that!

This first meeting was chaired by Edwin Ash of the Richmond Club, with agenda items such as the desire to formulate acceptable rules and to sanction a challenge from Scotland to play the first international. During the meeting it was agreed that a ban on hacking would be introduced and the challenge by Scotland to play the first international was accepted. As a result, an English team of 20 players (ten of them former Rugby School pupils) travelled north to take on the might of the Scots in Edinburgh, only to lose to a bigger, fitter and better organised Scottish team. Following the international, a team of three lawyers (ex-Rugby School pupils) were tasked with writing the first set of rugby laws for the RFU, which they duly did.

After the formation of the RFU, several clubs from Scotland and Ireland subsequently joined. Membership fees were five shillings a year with an annual subscription of the same sum payable. One of the most important figures of the English RFU in its early days was Sir George Rowland Hill, secretary from 1881–1904 and president from 1904–1907. Hill was instrumental in consolidating the union and ensuring that rugby remained amateur, as conceived by its founders at that first meeting at the Pall Mall Restaurant. Like many other secretaries of the union, Hill had to deal with the issue of 'broken time' throughout his tenure, namely the controversial matter of whether amateur players should be compensated for their loss in wages as a direct result of their participation in the game. This was to become the longest-running saga in rugby's history, the catalyst for the formation of rugby league and the very same issue that ultimately resulted in the game of rugby union finally turning professional in 1995. To ensure the game remained amateur, the RFU instituted a series of draconian measures to maintain amateurism among the players. If a player was found to have participated in a fixture with or against anyone who had previously been paid any form of match fee, regardless of the sum, he was promptly banned from playing rugby union ever again. One can only imagine the loss of talented players to rugby league as a result of such silly rules. So strict was the RFU in ensuring that money stayed entirely out of the game that they banned outright the formation of club leagues in the game until 1987/1988. Only the County Championship was allowed to exist prior to this. Consequently, all club matches were officially categorised as 'friendlies' and even then it was extremely difficult to have such fixtures sanctioned by the RFU. In essence, the RFU had such a stranglehold on the game that it was slowly suffocating its development and success.

Despite such strict rulings on fixtures, England were granted permission to play their first international on 27 March 1871

Above: Action from the first test of the 2006 series between England and South Africa at Twickenham in London, England. The test was won 23-21 by England.
Photo: Scott Allen

Top right: One of the earliest images of rugby action during a test match, published in *The Graphic,* illustrating England pressing during the 1872 test between England and Scotland at The Kennington Oval in London, won 8 (1G 2T 1D)– 3 (1D) by England.
Image: Frédéric Humbert/www.flickr.com/photos/rugby_pioneers/creative commons license

Centre right: A rare photograph of the English and South African sides together after the 1913 test match, won 9-3 by the Grand Slam Springbok tourists who, with this victory, inflicted upon England their first-ever defeat at Twickenham.
Photo: Frédéric Humbert/www.flickr.com/photos/rugby_pioneers/creative commons license

Above: The England rugby team ready to play New Zealand at Crystal Palace in 1905, a match won 15-0 by New Zealand.
Photo: Frédéric Humbert/www.flickr.com/photos/rugby_pioneers/creative commons license

against Scotland in Edinburgh – a match lost by 1 $^{(1T)}$–4 $^{(1G\ 1T)}$. They avenged this defeat the following year in London. All future games between the two nations remained tightly fought contests, with England only achieving their first victory over Scotland in Scotland in 1883, in the process winning their first Triple Crown. England were to dominate the early years of the championship, but their form began to wane toward the end of the century, suffering their first championship whitewash in 1899. This poor form was quickly rectified when, in 1913 and 1914, they became the first team to win back-to-back Grand Slam championships. Following World War I, the 1920s were to become a golden era for English rugby as they notched up four Grand Slams in

Did you know: In 1863, the Blackheath Club of London attended the meetings that led to the formation of the Football Association (FA) and the genesis of soccer as an organised sport. However, Blackheath Club refused to join the FA, as they did not agree with the rules. Blackheath went on to become one of the leading rugby clubs in England and still exists, very much so, today.

1921, 1923, 1924 and 1928. On 4 January 1936, England recorded one of their most famous victories in their history when they defeated New Zealand, as winger Prince Alexander Obolensky scored a brace of tries to down the mighty All Blacks 13–0.

Lean times were to follow and it would not be until 1957 that England would record another Grand Slam. Much of this poor form can be attributed to the RFU: during these barren years, despite many great English players being produced, poor selection and management of these players ultimately led to their downfall and poor team form. Following their 1957 Grand Slam success, England again slid into a slump. The 1970s were the worst years in their history as they notched up five 'Wooden Spoons' in the Five Nations. However, in 1980, Bill Beaumont memorably led England to their first Grand Slam in 23 years and much hope was attached to this for the future. It proved to be a false dawn, as England failed to win another championship for the rest of the decade and were despatched from the 1987 RWC by Wales in the quarter-finals.

By the 1990s, under the leadership of a young Will Carling, England's form began to improve after they narrowly missed out on a Grand Slam when a determined Scotland side beat them to it in 1990. They made up for this in spectacular fashion during the following two seasons and claimed back-to-back Grand Slams, reaching the 1991 RWC final, convincingly beating South Africa in 1992 and recording a 15–9 victory over New Zealand in 1993. In preparation for the 1995 RWC England won another Grand Slam. However, in the 1995 RWC, after narrowly defeating Australia in the quarter-final, England were confronted with the wrath of New Zealand and Jonah Lomu in the Cape Town semi-final. The game was effectively over in 20 minutes after Lomu had blitzed England with four spectacular tries. England finished fourth in the tournament, suffering the ignominy of having to qualify for the 1999 RWC.

The rest of the 1990s were not overly spectacular for England despite three consecutive triple crowns from 1996 to 1998. They were embarrassingly dumped from the 1999 RWC by South Africa in a Paris quarter-final. They lost three consecutive chances of a Grand Slam in 1999, 2000 and 2001, losing the last game of each season (against Wales, Scotland and Ireland). In 2003, England recorded their first Grand Slam since 1995 in a season that would ultimately turn out to be the most successful in England's history, under the guidance of Clive Woodward and leadership of Martin Johnson, culminating in a triumphant England winning the 2003 RWC.

Since winning that RWC, a slump ensued, with many senior players retiring or incurring serious injuries. In the 40 internationals leading up to the following RWC, England won just 16 matches and suffered some record defeats, which included a sequence of seven consecutive losses. Not an ideal run as reigning world champions but, amazingly, England reached the 2007 RWC final, which they lost to South Africa but not without honour. One, however, gets the feeling that England's might is never far from the surface.

Swing Low, Sweet Chariot

During the mid-1980s, English rugby had reached an extremely low point, the team having lost 15 of their last 23 Five Nations internationals prior to their last Five Nations international of 1988 against Ireland. At half-time, the Irish led 3–0 and the mood of the home support was understandably sombre as they faced yet another defeat. But come the second half England cut loose, running in six tries and letting in none, to win 35–3 in spectacular fashion. During the second half rout, a new Twickenham hero by the name of Chris Oti emerged. A black player, Oti scored three of the tries, and to honour his incredible achievement a small section of the crowd (who were later identified as members of the Benedictine School of Douai) started singing the negro spiritual, *Swing Low, Sweet Chariot*. It was sung every time Chris Oti touched the ball, but was interpreted by some commentators as reflective of the Twickenham crowd's racist persuasion. Even though a small minority of racists had given the Twickenham crowd an underserved racist reputation in the

1980s, it was however claimed that the adoption of *Swing Low, Sweet Chariot* was not a taunt against Oti's ethnicity, but rather a salute to his prowess. As the tries continued to roll in, so the singing swelled. England played their next Twickenham international against Australia that autumn. Under the captaincy of Will Carling a convincing victory was registered, offering the Twickenham crowd plenty of opportunity to sing *Swing Low, Sweet Chariot* again. England was to embark on a period of great success following these two victories, and the song quickly became synonymous with the England team, and is today the 'national anthem' of Twickenham.

France

In historic times, a game known as *soulle* was played in Normandy and Brittany, northern France – an ancient form of football that continued to be played in these parts until the nineteenth century. It is believed that *soulle* was derived from games played by Roman soldiers, and some even suggest that all British forms of football are derived from *soulle* – the game having been brought across the English Channel with the Norman Conquest.

It is believed that rugby was first played in France in 1870 by a group of British students on a sports field in Le Havre. In 1877, British students again caught the locals' attentions in Paris by playing rugby matches in the Bois de Boulogne, and from that point the game of rugby began to take off in France, with locals beginning to participate. The development of rugby in Paris had a lot to do with its proximity to Britain and the number of university and professional people with British contacts living or working in France. In 1885, a Paris selection team became the first French team to tour abroad, making the trip across the English Channel to play the Civil Service team in Dulwich. In 1892, Paris hosted the first French club championship final, which was won by the Racing Club and refereed by Pierre de Coubertin, the organiser of the first modern Olympic Games four years later in Athens. Sports in general were becoming increasingly popular in France, and in 1887 an official multisport governing body was formed – the Union des Sociétés Françaises de Sports Athlétiques which governed all sports, including rugby. In 1920, the formation of the Fédération Française de Rugby (FFR) saw the management of rugby in France fall under this body, where it remains to this day. The FFR has had a tumultuous history – from introducing rugby to the Olympics to expulsion from the Five Nations in 1931 by the IRFB and barred from participating in any international fixtures against their member nations.

On New Year's Day 1906, France played their first international match against the all-conquering All Blacks, losing convincingly by 8–38. Following this first test, an annual fixture against England was arranged from that year on. Soon after, annual fixtures against Wales in 1908, Ireland in 1909 and Scotland in 1910 were organised. The French consistently lost all their early internationals, only managing their first victory on 2 January 1911 against Scotland in Paris by 16–15 – a shock to everyone! They were not to win another international until 1920 when they defeated Ireland in Dublin. But good times were not far off for the French, as they were to begin recording victories on a more regular basis.

From this point, the game developed at such a pace that it could not be properly managed by the Union des Sociétés Françaises de Sports Athlétiques or the FFR, with both club and international rugby becoming ill-disciplined, on and off the field. With this boom in the popularity of the game, top players were at such a premium that the richer clubs began to offer inducements to players. In 1912, the Scottish Rugby Union (SRU) kicked up such a fuss after Stade Bordelais had placed advertisements in the Scottish press, offering to find a well-paid job for a good flyhalf, that the French authorities had to ban the guilty club members for life to placate the IRFB. In 1930, 12 French clubs attempted to break away from the FFR to form their own union, to be called the French Amateur Rugby Union. When the IRFB in Britain got word of this they immediately suspended relations with the FFR until they could prove they had control over the game in France. Not since the breakaway of the league clubs in 1893 had the IRFB had to deal with such a crisis. A series of warnings were issued by the RFU to the French, but they fell on deaf ears and in 1931, the RFU issued their final warning, which read:

> 'Owing to the unsatisfactory condition of the game of Rugby Football as practised and played in France, neither our union, nor the clubs or unions under our jurisdiction, will fulfil or arrange fixtures with France, or French clubs, at home or away after the end of this season until we are satisfied that the control and conduct of the game have been placed on a satisfactory basis in all essentials.'

With France sent to Coventry and stripped of all international competition, the French immediately set about organising their own

Above left: Photograph of the English and French sides after the historical 1906 clash, the first ever, won 35-8 by England in Paris. *Photo*: Frédéric Humbert/www.flickr.com/photos/rugby_pioneers/creative commons license

Above: Rugby first being played in France by English and French students in the Bois de Boulogne, Paris. *Image*: Frédéric Humbert/www.flickr.com/photos/rugby_pioneers/creative commons license

Centre: Action from France (light grey) against Germany (white) in Paris, 1931. The match was convincingly won 34-0 by the French. *Photo*: Frédéric Humbert/www.flickr.com/photos/rugby_pioneers/creative commons license

Bottom: French scrumhalf Lucien Serin crosses for France's only try of the match against England at Twickenham in 1930, in a match ultimately won 11-5 by the English. *Photo*: Frédéric Humbert/www.flickr.com/photos/rugby_pioneers/creative commons license

competition and in 1934 created the Fédération Internationale de Rugby Amateur (FIRA) – an organisation designed to structure the game outside of the major rugby-playing nations. This proved to be a critical juncture in promoting the game to other European countries and dependencies. The founding members of FIRA were France, Italy, Germany, Portugal, Sweden, Romania, Spain, Holland, Czechoslovakia and Catalonia (an autonomous province of Spain). FIRA gradually expanded over the years (well after France had been readmitted into the Five Nations) to include other nations outside Europe, such as Tunisia, Morocco and Argentina, as well as all other European nations not in the home unions. This culminated in the formation of the official FIRA Championship in 1973/1974. During France's isolation, international fixtures were organised against these emerging nations, including games against Germany, Romania, Italy and Czechoslovakia – more often than not comfortably won by the French. However, it became clear that rugby standards were falling in France with the absence of top international competition, and in 1939 the French assured the IRFB that their clubs had cleaned up their act and that their championship had been suspended.

France was duly forgiven their sins by the IRFB, but with the outbreak of World War II a further period of six years was effectively added to their isolation before they could once again enjoy competitive internationals, taking on Scotland in the 1947 Five Nations tournament. The issue of the French paying their players continued, however, and in 1951 and 1952 France was accused of exactly the same offences that had led to their ban 20 years earlier. France once again promised the IRFB that they would drop the French championship and the matter was eventually resolved. With these antics finally over and the unspoken fear of the IRFB losing France to the game forever now dissipated, France was eventually offered full membership to the IRFB in 1978.

After World War II, success for France came in 1951 with their first win at Twickenham, their first victory over New Zealand in 1954, a series victory in South Africa in 1958 and their first outright championship victory in 1959. The series triumph in South Africa has since been identified as the great turning point in French rugby, which saw the French becoming a leading, at times dominant, force in world rugby. In the 1960s, they claimed three more outright championship wins and in 1968 registered their first Grand Slam. They achieved their second Grand Slam in 1977, with a pair following in 1981 and 1987. The French reached the final of the inaugural RWC after beating Australia in the match of the tournament, only to lose to New Zealand.

The greatest French achievement was their series victory over New Zealand, in New Zealand in 1994, with Jean-Luc Sadourny sealing the famous victory when he scored 'the try from the end of the world'. In true French fashion, however, they'd initially lost to Canada on the same tour, only to beat the All Blacks a few weeks later. After narrowly losing out on reaching the final of the 1995 RWC to a determined South Africa in the Durban rain, France became only the second nation in the history of the Five Nations Championship to wrap up back-to-back Grand Slam triumphs, which they achieved in 1997 and 1998.

In 1999, France again made the RWC final, this time defeating New Zealand in a spectacular semi-final and sending the All Blacks home without a tournament victory. In 2002, another Grand Slam was achieved, but in 2003, they were knocked out of the RWC tournament by the English after defeating Scotland and Ireland. 2004 was yet another Grand Slam year, followed by outright championship victories in 2006 and 2007, leading up to the 2007 RWC, hosted by themselves. Heavy defeats were suffered against the All Blacks in the winter prior to the World Cup and after a loss to the Argentinians in the opening game of the tournament, the French met New Zealand in a Cardiff quarter-final. Amazingly, France managed to turn a 0–13 deficit into a 20–18 victory and send the tournament favourites home once again without a win. This was to be France's high point of the tournament, as they lost to England in the semi-final and to Argentina again in the plate.

Ireland

The Irish will tell you that they in fact invented the game of rugby. According to Irish legend, William Webb Ellis was in fact born in Ireland, where he learned the 'handling game' before exporting it to Rugby School. Fact or fiction? Only the Irish can answer that – despite the fact that Webb Ellis himself recorded his birth place as Manchester, England. Records of various types of football played in Ireland date back to the mid-14th century, accounts which clearly indicate that the handling and carrying of the ball featured in these early forms of football. Ireland boasts two of the world's oldest rugby clubs. The first is Trinity College (sometimes referred to as Dublin University), with students who had learned the game while at English public schools forming the club in 1854. The other is the North of Ireland Football Club, established in 1859. Only Guy's Hospital Club of London outdates these two clubs. The first rugby game to be played in Ireland was in 1855 between the original and the new members of Trinity College. In 1868 Trinity College published a set of rules, which helped spread the game across Ireland. In 1873/1874, with the establishment of more clubs, the North of Ireland Football Club and Trinity College Club undertook the first overseas tour by an Irish side – to Scotland and England, where an attempt was made to arrange a test. This was unsuccessful, mainly because Ireland did not have a single, unified, national governing body for the sport.

With this in mind it was decided to establish a national union to govern the game. The exact date of the formation of the Irish rugby union is unknown due to the lack of archived minutes, but the Irish Rugby Football Union (IRFU) does celebrate *two* founding centenaries, as Ireland twice formed a union, firstly in 1874 and secondly in 1879. On 14 December 1874, Trinity College called a meeting in Dublin with seven clubs in attendance to form the Irish union. Representatives of the province of Ulster, however, were not invited to attend because of politics. Ulster was predictably angry at having been excluded, so formed its own union on 13 January 1875, known as the Northern Football Union of Ireland. The Irish Football Union had jurisdiction over clubs in the southern provinces of Leinster, Munster and some parts of Ulster, while the Northern Football Union of Ireland controlled the Belfast area. It was not until 1879 that the two unions merged to form the IRFU, agreeing to amalgamate on the following terms:

- A union to be known as the Irish Rugby Football Union is to be formed for the whole country
- A quota system is to be introduced to ensure that each union is well represented in the first Irish national team
- Branches are to be formed in Leinster, Munster and Ulster
- The union is to be run by a council of 18, made up of six from each province
- The council is to meet annually

Since this date, rugby in Ireland has done more to unite Irish people than divide them. Today, rugby is the only major Irish sport that has been consistently run on an all-Ireland basis, with little political and sectarian interference. Minor spats have occurred over the years regarding which flag should be raised during an international and which anthem should be sung. Only once have political troubles ruined fixtures: in 1972, Scotland and Wales refused to tour Ireland because of terrorist threats.

The first Irish international was played on 15 February 1875 under the jurisdiction of the Irish Football Union at The Kennington Oval Cricket Ground in London against England in a 20-a-side fixture. Twelve players were from Leinster and eight from Ulster. Ireland lost 0–7 [1G 1T 1D], with an Irish journalist stating that his team was 'immaculately innocent of training'. For their first international the Irish wore green and white hooped shirts but the following year in the return fixtures against England both sides wore white, despite the fact that the Irish were aware that this was England's chosen strip. It was not until the 1885/1886 season that Ireland would settle on the emerald-green jersey (which has slowly turned a darker shade of green in the modern professional era) with the shamrock badge.

Despite the influence of the IRFU and the first Irish rugby international, the game was still competing with association football, Gaelic football and hurling – all very popular sports in a country with a small population. With this in mind, a set of rules was drawn up by Charles Barrington and R.M. Wall of the IRFU, who sent a circular to other Irish disciplines in the hope of securing players who could become readily acquainted with the game of rugby. The four provincial branch unions – Ulster, Leinster, Munster and Connacht (with members elected to the IRFU) quickly organised their own competitions to ensure the success of the game and these competitions are today central to the game in Ireland.

Ireland struggled in its early years on the international scene, losing by large margins to the English; it took a full five years and eight internationals to even score in a match, let alone win. In 1877, Scotland were added to the international fixture list and in 1881 it was against the Scots on 19 February at Ormeau in Belfast that Ireland recorded their first test win by 3 [1G]–1[1T]. Ireland played their first set of complete internationals when Wales was added to the fixtures in 1882, eventually beating England for the first time in 1887. In 1894, Ireland completed their first Triple Crown success with victories over England (7–5), Scotland (5–0) and Wales (3–0). This was followed by a championship victory in 1896 and a second Triple Crown in 1899. Following this success, the first tour by an Irish rugby team was undertaken in the same year to Canada, where 17 tour members played 11 games and won ten.

In the early twentieth century, lean times followed and Ireland lost regularly. Hosting touring sides from South Africa and New Zealand, Ireland lost comprehensively 0–15 to the 1905 New Zealanders and 0–38 against Billy Millar's 1912 Grand Slam Springboks. It was not until 1935 that Ireland recorded another outright championship victory, but it was the immediate post-World War II years that have come to be known as Ireland's finest. In 1948, captain Karl Mullen's Irish side recorded their first Grand Slam success, with away victories over France on New Year's Day in Paris by 13–6 and narrowly over England at Twickenham by 11–10. Scotland were then seen off 6–0 in Dublin and with the championship secure, but the Triple Crown and Grand Slam titles still on the cards against Wales a fortnight later in Belfast, there was everything to play for. Ireland narrowly won 6–3 and went down in the history books as the first Irish side ever to win a Grand Slam. They followed this success the following season with a Triple Crown, with many Irish players of this era representing the Lions with distinction.

In 1910, Dr Tom Smyth became the first Irish Lions captain, followed Sam Walker (1938), Karl Mullen (1950), Robin Thompson (1955), Ronnie Dawson (1959), Tom Kiernan (1968), Willie-John McBride (1974), Cirian Fitzgerald (1983), Brian O'Driscoll (2005) and Paul O'Connell (2009) – an amazing statistic, considering Ireland's comparatively poor record in international rugby and small player pool. Ireland were denied a second Grand Slam in 1951, unbeaten through the championship but with a 3–3 draw against Wales. Consolation came in the form of a championship victory. Ireland's first win over a southern-hemisphere touring side was by 9–6 against Australia in Dublin in 1958, followed with a rare 9–6 win over the Springboks in 1965. Amazingly, the Irish have never managed to beat New Zealand in 22 attempts. The closest they came was in 1973 when they held the All Blacks to a 10–10 draw. However, in 1978, Munster memorably chalked up a historic 12–0 victory over the touring All Blacks, making them the only Irish side to beat New Zealand – a day that has gone down in Irish rugby folklore and which was very nearly repeated in 2008 in a 30-year-anniversary match with New Zealand who won at the death 18–16. It would be 23 long years before Ireland was to again win a championship outright, and in 1982, they notched up their fifth Triple Crown success thanks to the accuracy of Ollie Campbell's boot – a feat they repeated three years later when Michael Kiernan dropped 'that goal' against England in Dublin to win 13–10 and take the Triple Crown.

Following their mid-1980s successes, Ireland struggled until the end of 1990s, sustaining record defeats in the process, including humiliating defeats against New Zealand by 6–59 in 1992 and again in 1997 by 15–63; against South Africa by 0–33 in 1998 and against England by 3–35 in 1988 and 6–46 in 1997. In RWCs, Ireland have consistently disappointed and have yet to progress past the quarter-finals. In 1999 and 2007, they failed miserably when they were knocked out in the pool stages. In 2007, many touted the Irish as outsiders to win the conveted William Webb Ellis trophy because of their Triple Crown successes of 2004, 2006 and 2007, as well as victories over Australia and South Africa under the leadership of Brian O'Driscoll. But they reached new lows, notching up narrow victories over Namibia and Georgia before being comprehensively beaten and knocked out by France and Argentina. They made up for this disappointment in spectacular fashion in the 2009 Six Nations when they won their second Grand Slam.

 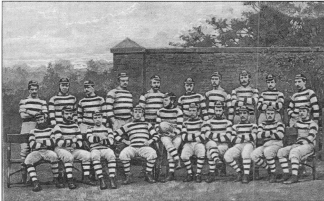

Above left: The 1898 Irish side that defeated England by 9-6 in Richmond after Louis Magee (seated second from left) and Harry Lindsay (seated fourth from right) had each scored crucial tries. *Photo*: Frédéric Humbert/www.flickr.com/photos/rugby_pioneers/creative commons license

Above right: Team portrait of the first-ever Irish rugby side to play in an international: against England at The Oval in 1875, a match won by England 7 [1G 1T 1D] – 0. *Image*: Frédéric Humbert/www.flickr.com/photos/rugby_pioneers/creative commons license

Italy

Rugby has an intrinsic, historical link with Italy, as primitive forms of football were played by the Romans, including the brutal *harpastum*. It is popularly believed that rugby was first brought to Milan University by students in 1910, who had learned the game while studying in France. It has since been established, however, that British communities first brought the game to Genoa somewhere between 1890 and 1895. The first recorded game of rugby union in Italy was a demonstration match played in 1910 in the northern city of Turin when Racing Club of Paris took on Servette of Geneva. This match introduced rugby to northern Italy, where it is still the most popular. The first match involving an Italian team was a year later, played between US Milanese and Voiron of France.

But the sport did not take off properly and remained a low-key game for many years. In his early political career, dictator Benito Mussolini attempted to use rugby as a vehicle for fascist unity in Italy. With his passion for indigenous Italian sports, he quickly latched onto the Roman origins of *harpastum* and rebranded rugby as *palla ovale* (oval ball). (Ironically, *harpastum* in fact predates the Romans to the ancient Greek kicking-and-throwing ball game known as *phaininda*, or *episkyros*, which he conveniently chose to ignore in his effort to promote the Italianness of rugby.) To manage the game of *palla ovale* Mussolini set up the Propaganda Committee in July 1911, but he quickly lost interest in the sport when he discovered that the national game was resistant to authority. So he had the national secretary of the Fascist Party, Augusto Turati, invent a game known as *volata* to replace soccer and rugby, both of which were identified as British sports, a fact Mussolini loathed. *Volata* was played by eight-man sides – essentially a hybrid between soccer and handball. With the advent of *volata*, rugby union suffered immeasurably during Mussolini's rule, until 1945 – a serious setback for the development of the game in Italy. Despite some 100 *volata* clubs existing during its height, the game never really took off and fascist efforts to popularise it were officially abandoned in 1933, with all references stricken from party records. It is no longer played today, dying a similar meat-hook demise to the bulky dictator. The Propaganda Committee disbanded in 1928 and with this, the ten or so remaining Italian rugby clubs met in 1928 to form the Federazione Italiana Rugby (FIR), essentially converting the management of the game to the FIR. This was a formative period for Italian rugby, with the first national championship completed the following year in 1929. Italy played their first international – against Spain on 20 May in Barcelona – going down 0–9.

Following this international, there were more fixtures for Italy through the 1930s – against Czechoslovakia, Catalonia, Romania, a French XV, Germany and Belgium. Their first recorded test victory was against Spain in 1930 when they won 3–0 in Milan, with other victories soon following. But the strength and quality of Italian rugby was exposed when they took on a French XV for the first time in 1935 in Rome, losing heavily by 6–44. This loss was followed by an equally heavy defeat to Germany a year later by 8–19 in Berlin. It was clearly evident that Italian rugby needed to radically improve in order for them to compete at top level. This occurred gradually, following their involvement as a founding member of FIRA with France the year before. They took part in the inaugural FIRA European Tournament in 1937 and through the management of FIRA, Italy organised and were ensured regular international fixtures against the likes of the USSR, Romania, Spain, Germany, Portugal, Czechoslovakia and France. With these fixtures, the game flourished in Italy in the national and international arenas following the setbacks during Mussolini's rule. In 1962 and 1963 Italy came to within a score of beating the French.

But France stopped playing international matches with Italy in 1967 after they inflicted a heavy 60–16 defeat over the Italians in Toulon; the two sides were not to meet again in a full international until 1995. Despite this, an improvement in the standard of Italian rugby and their emergence on the world rugby stage were recognised when their request to tour South Africa in 1973 was accepted – their first high-profile tour abroad. The Italian side was coached by ex-Springbok prop, Amos du Plooy, but struggled in South Africa. In total, they played nine tour matches against the weaker provincial sides and won just one – against the SA Africans. However, results aside, the tour was a great success. Interestingly, such was the importance of this tour for Italian rugby that international test caps were awarded for all their matches. Other unions immediately sat up and took notice of the Italian tour, with an Australia XV deciding to tour Italy later that year. However, the disparity between Italian rugby and top-flight international rugby was again evident when the Italians lost the only 'test' against the Australia XV by 21–59 in L'Aquila. The following year, Italy toured England for the first time and again, such was the magnitude and importance of the tour to the FIR that international caps were awarded for each match, despite none of the opposition being a national selection. All matches were lost, but the tour introduced Italian rugby to the British for the first time.

The steady improvement in Italian rugby is in no small part thanks to Italy's Mediterranean lifestyle and rich cultural history, which has attracted many famous players and coaches, including Andy Haden (New Zealand), David Campese (Australia), Rob Louw (South Africa), Michael Lynagh (Australia), Jannie Breedt (South Africa) and Naas Botha (South Africa), while coaches such as Carwyn

James (British and Irish Lions), Pierre Villepreux (France), John Kirwan (New Zealand), Pierre Berbizier (France), Nellie Smith (South Africa) and most recently, Nick Mallet (South Africa), ensure that the game continues to grow. In 1986, Australia became the second IRFB member side since France to award full international status to a match against Italy when the Italians toured Australia – a test won 39–18 by Australia. In 1987, Italy joined the IRFB and were invited to take part in the inaugural RWC and given the honour of playing the opening match against hosts New Zealand. In this RWC Italy went on to lose heavily, but ultimately finished the tournament strongly with an unexpected victory over Fiji, just failing to reach a quarter-final position because of their lower try count in their pool.

By the 1990s, Italy were playing regular internationals against the best in the world as they qualified for each of the 1991, 1995 and 1999 RWCs. In 1991, Italy put up a good account of themselves as they ran New Zealand close, eventually losing by just 21–31 in England; they beat the United States in the same tournament. In 1993, they won against a Scotland XV that was effectively a full-strength Scottish side in everything but name, and then again against a French XV in Treviso. This, coupled with consistent European Nations Cup victories, persuaded France once again to grant full international status to matches against Italy. Additionally, a series of high-profile victories brought Italy to the agenda of world rugby. They ran Australia extremely close in a two-test series in 1994 and beat Ireland in a 1995 RWC warm-up match – their first victory over a top-eight rugby nation. 1997 was a watershed year for Italian rugby, as they convincingly beat the Irish twice (home and away) and notched up their first, and so far only, victory over France, winning 40–32 in Grenoble. With these performances, the rugby world took notice and talk of including Italy in the Five Nations surfaced. Italy corroborated this idea of expanding the Five Nations with victories over Scotland in 1998 and narrow losses to Wales and England. In 1999, Italy was granted 2000 admission to the new Six Nations tournament. However, the new entrant could not have performed worse that year, twice conceding more than 100 points in a match, to New Zealand and South Africa, and losing by record margins to Wales, Scotland, Fiji and England. The 1999 RWC was a disaster for Italy: for the first time they lost all their pool matches. Things could not have looked any worse for them entering their first Six Nations tournament the next year. However, it started on a fairy-tale note as they beat Scotland 34–20 in their first Six Nations match, after a brilliant kicking performance by legendary flyhalf Diego Dominguez, who scored 29 points with the boot. Unfortunately, they were not to win again until 2003 when they beat Wales, with pickings being particularly slim until 2007 when they won back-to-back victories for the first time, to finish their highest on the log at fourth. To date, Italy have only managed to beat Scotland and Wales but none of the other three tournament members.

It was always going to be a tough ask for the Italians to enter the tournament and make an immediate impact, but after ten years heavy defeats are now rare, with touring to Rome no longer as easy a prospect as before. With most of their top players currently playing in European club competitions, standards are undoubtedly improving, but the hope of an Italian Six Nations Tournament win is still a long way off. Nevertheless, such has been the uplift in Italian rugby that its popularity has grown enormously; one should expect nothing but improvement in their game – especially when the Italian newspaper *La Gazzetta dello Sport* headlined the 27–53 loss to Ireland in 2007 with 'To lose like this is beautiful'.

In the 2007 RWC they had high expectations of reaching the quarter-finals, strategically playing a weakened side against New Zealand as they targeted their pool match with Scotland as their key to the next round. They were expected to win following their scintillating performance in Edinburgh earlier that year, which secured them their first Six Nations away victory by 37–17, but the boot of fullback David Bortolussi let them down and they lost 16–18. This remains one of Italy's greatest disappointments but they now have the 2011 RWC quarter-finals set firmly in their sights.

Italy have now come to be known as *li Azzurri* (the Blues) across the globe. Watch this space!

New Zealand

The first hint of rugby in today's most successful rugby nation in the world is from Christ's College in Christchurch, which recruited staff from English public schools. Christ's College is known to have had a set of football rules in 1862 with similarities to those used at Rugby School in England. A football club was founded in Christchurch the following year. Reports of rugby played at Christ's College, however, are sketchy and so it is now accepted that a small South Island town by the name of Nelson can formally lay claim to introducing rugby to New Zealand in 1870, because this is where rugby was played under the rules as written by Rugby School. Charles John Munro, educated at Sherborne in Dorset, England, and son of the president of the New Zealand chamber of commerce, is regarded as the Webb Ellis of New Zealand, since it was his enthusiasm for the game that led to Nelson founding the country's first rugby club in 1868. The players of the Nelson Football Club, having approved of the Rugby School rules, tested them out in a match against Nelson College on 14 May 1870, thereby writing themselves into history with the first official rugby match to be played in New Zealand. Within a year, Wellington had formed a club and by 1876 the leading clubs in New Zealand agreed to play to the rules decreed by the newly formed IRFB that had been approved in London five years earlier. However, early matches between clubs were rare events, as fields were rare in the mountainous countryside; communications were slow and uncertain and equipment scarce. Indeed, in 1872, the first match in Wanganui was delayed by two weeks in an attempt to find a ball. Some sides even travelled with their own goalposts to away matches!

The first meeting of the New Zealand Rugby Union (NZRU) was held in Wellington on 27 April 1893, with all major unions from the North Island and four from the South Island in attendance. The founding members were

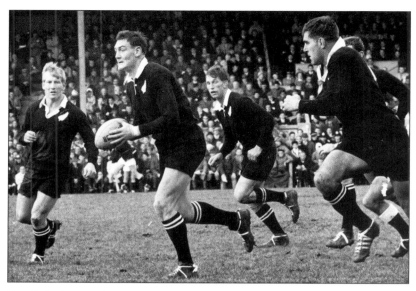

New Zealand captain Brian Lochore leads an All Black charge against France in the Wellington test of the 1968 series. In close support are scrumhalf Chris Laidlaw (left), flanker Kelvin Tremain (right) and lock Colin Meads (far right). New Zealand won the test 9-3 and the series 3-0.
Photo: New Zealand Rugby Museum

Auckland, Hawke's Bay, Manawatu, Marlborough, Nelson, South Canterbury, Taranaki, Wairarapa, Wanganui, Wellington and West Coast. Following the first tour from Australia (NSW) to New Zealand in 1882, tours between the two nations became commonplace. In 1888, the New Zealand Natives toured Great Britain, Australia and New Zealand on the longest tour in rugby history, playing an incredible 107 matches, and winning 78, losing 23 and drawing 6, in a tour lasting over a year. The tourists were very popular, often surprising their hosts by performing a Maori war dance, or *haka*, before a match, thereby establishing the tradition. Since this tour, Maori rugby has remained an vital part of the New Zealand game.

In recent times, however, many confuse Maori involvement in New Zealand rugby with the growing number of South Sea islanders plying their trade in New Zealand, where a professional career is very lucrative. Many islanders have gone on to represent New Zealand, which has helped New Zealand in no small part to become the dominating force that it is. However, it has also led to complaints levelled at New Zealand for 'buying' or 'poaching' players from poorer nations – a geographical privilege that other nations do not have (with the slight exception of Australia which granted citizenship to Fijians, Ilie Tabua and Lote Tuqiri). This led to an IRB ruling that once any player has played for a nation at senior level he may not represent another; and a player must have lived for a minimum of three years in a country before becoming eligible to play for that national side. Players such as Michael Jones, Stephen Bachop and Frank Bunce all represented Western Samoa at international level before playing for New Zealand. One of the first such players was the great Brian Williams of Western Samoa who played for New Zealand in the 1970s and 1980s. In more recent times, players such as Va'aiga Tuigamala (Samoa), Alama Leremia (Samoa), Joe Rokocoko (Fiji), Sitiveni Sivivatu (Fiji) and Tana Umaga (Samoa – his brother Mike played for Samoa) have represented New Zealand with distinction.

The first New Zealand tour abroad was to New South Wales in 1884 where eight games were played, and won. The team wore dark-blue jerseys with a gold fern badge. It was not until the New Zealand RFU was formed, with the first match being played under their jurisdiction (against New South Wales in 1894) that the team was kitted out in a black jersey with white fern and white shorts. The first evidence of black shorts being worn is from photographs of a 1901 match against New South Wales. As to how they earned the nickname All Blacks, there are two theories, both emanating from the 1905 'Originals' tour to the British Isles:

- Captain Billy Wallace remembers it originating from the *Daily Mail*, which initially used the term 'All Backs' for the first time following New Zealand's 63–0 win over Hartlepool Clubs, insinuating that the entire New Zealand team was made up of 'all backs' after the way the forwards had so slickly passed the ball. Reporting the subsequent game against Somerset, a printing error in the *Daily Mail* saw them being termed the 'All Blacks' for the first time, with the letter 'l' somehow appearing in the text. The *Daily Mail* then adopted this name for the team, which led to some confusion when the team toured Ireland, with the Irish supporters literally expecting to see a team made up entirely of black people.

- The second theory postulates that when the team arrived in the United Kingdom a reporter asked a New Zealand player the colour of the team's jersey, knickers and stockings. To each question the player answered with just one word: 'black'. The conversation ended with the player simply stating, 'We are all black'. The identity of the player remains unknown.

Despite the large number of tours completed between New Zealand and Australia, as well as a British Isles tour to New Zealand in 1888, New Zealand did not play an international until 15 August 1903, when they faced Australia at the Sydney Cricket Ground and won 22–3. Since then, New Zealand and Australia have played more internationals against each than anyone else in rugby history – a staggering 132. In 1904, the touring British side unexpectedly lost to New Zealand which sensitised the traditional northern home unions to the strength of New Zealand rugby. With this in mind, the first New Zealand side to tour beyond Australia was dubbed 'The Originals' when they toured the British Isles, France and the United States in 1905, playing 35 matches and losing just once, against Wales, an outcome still hotly contested today. Following the 1905 tour, Cliff Porter captained the New Zealand 'Invincibles', who, in 1925, toured the British Isles, France and Canada, this time winning all of the 32 matches played. They were denied a Grand Slam title, however, as there was no match against Scotland. Surprisingly, it was not until 1978 that New Zealand were to record a Grand Slam tour under the captaincy of Graham Mourie (after drawing against Scotland in 1964 and against Ireland in 1973), a feat that Tana Umaga's side emulated in 2005 and Richie McCaw's in 2008.

New Zealand have won almost every series they have played, with the real measure of New Zealand rugby prowess reflecting in their record of dominance in international rugby, winning an impressive 74.5 percent of all their matches. New Zealand share the world record of 17 consecutive international victories with South Africa and currently hold the world record for most consecutive home victories – 30 over a five-year period. They have completed a series whitewash over the Lions three times (1966, 1983 and 2005), recorded an RWC triumph in 1987 and an away-series victory over South Africa in 1996. Of the traditional top eight nations, New Zealand are unbeaten against Scotland and Ireland. They have won nine Tri-Nations titles, with only England and France of the northern hemisphere sides capable of posting occasional victories against them. Only five touring teams have managed a series win in New Zealand – South Africa in 1937 (dubbed by the New Zealand press as the greatest team to ever leave Africa), Australia in 1949 (when 30 of New Zealand's first-choice players were touring South Africa) and again in 1986, the Lions in 1971 and, most recently, France in 1994.

Surprisingly, in spite of this dominance, New Zealand have struggled to win the RWC. Ever since their lone 1987 triumph (a tournament some believe South Africa might have won had they been allowed to compete), New Zealand have consistently and fatally stumbled in each tournament, leading to premature exits. In 1991, David Campese and Australia outfoxed New Zealand in the Dublin semi-final (16–6). In 1995, Springbok Joel Stransky dropped them to defeat deep into extra time (12–15). In 1999, French flair overcame New Zealand dominance 31–43 in a remarkable French victory. In 2003, Stirling Mortlock broke New Zealand hearts in the semi-final with an 80-metre intercept (22–10) and in 2007, New Zealand failed for the first time to reach the semi-finals,when France stunned the world by beating them 20–18 in the Cardiff quarter-final, courtesy of a clear French forward pass.

Such a run of RWC defeats has led to the All Blacks being dubbed 'Chokers', but many believe they will shrug this moniker in 2011 when New Zealand host the Rugby World Cup in their own backyard – a venue where they have proved near-invincible. Regardless of previous setbacks, the All Blacks are truly the world's rugby powerhouse and have been for over a century.

The haka

Prior to the kick-off of an international, the New Zealand All Blacks perform a *haka*, popularly believed to be a type of war dance. In fact, the Maori word *haka* simply means a dance, or a song accompanied by a dance. Its origins are deeply rooted in Maori heritage. The first use of a *haka* is attributed to Chief Tinirau and his womenfolk. The story gpoes that Tinirau sought revenge for the killing of a tame whale by a priest called Kae. No one knew what this Kae looked like but they knew he had uneven teeth which overlapped. So Tinirau sent a hunting party of women to find Kae; when the woman arrived at Kae's village they performed a *haka* to force a smile from the village men, thereby unmasking Kae's identity. Kae was captured, taken to Tinirau's village and accordingly executed.

Left: The 1924 All Blacks to play Wales at Swansea. New Zealand went on to win comfortably by 19-0. *Photo*: New Zealand Rugby Museum

Middle left: The New Zealand team to play Australia on 3 September 1949 in Wellington. This was the first New Zealand side to play that day as later on the same day New Zealand played South Africa in Durban, which is to date the only time in rugby history that a nation has played two test matches on the same day on different continents! *Photo*: New Zealand Rugby Museum

Below: Team photograph of the first New Zealand test side: the 1903 team captained by James Duncan (middle row, third from right) which beat Australia on 15 August at the Sydney Cricket Ground by 22-3.
Photo: New Zealand Rugby Museum

New Zealand scrumhalf Sid Going leads the haka against the Irish in 1974 at Lansdowne Road, Dublin; a match won 15-6 by New Zealand.
Photo: New Zealand Rugby Museum

Team photograph of the third touring All Blacks side to the United Kingdom in 1935/36. *Photo*: New Zealand Rugby Museum

The 1967 All Blacks perform the haka to the Twickenham crowd prior to the New Zealand–England test, won 23-11 by New Zealand.
Photo: New Zealand Rugby Museum

All Black winger Bryan Williams in full flight against Australia in the third test of the 1972 series in Auckland. Ranging up in close support is his captain and flanker Ian Kirkpatrick. Both players scored a try to secure an emphatic 38-3 victory. *Photo*: New Zealand Rugby Museum

The 1905 All Blacks side to play England, lined up beneath the posts at Crystal Palace in London prior to kickoff. Inspirational captain Dave Gallaher is in the centre with the ball. *Photo*: New Zealand Rugby Museum

Above: The 'Originals' 1905 touring All Black side to the British Isles, captained by Dave Gallaher (centre with ball) after whom the Gallaher Cup is named.
Photo: Frédéric Humbert/www.flickr.com/photos/rugby_pioneers/creative commons license

Right: The 1903 New Zealand touring side to Australia: the first Kiwis to play an international, a match won 22-3 by New Zealand at the Sydney Cricket Ground in Sydney.
Photo: Frédéric Humbert/www.flickr.com/photos/rugby_pioneers/creative commons license

Bottom: The 1888 New Zealand 'Natives' who toured Great Britain, Australia and New Zealand, playing 107 matches in a year, winning 78.
Photo: Frédéric Humbert/www.flickr.com/photos/rugby_pioneers/creative commons license

The most commonly performed *haka* by the New Zealand team is known as *Ka Mate* or *Te Rauparaha*. Since 2005, they have occasionally performed a new *haka* for special fixtures, called *Kapa o Pango*. The *haka* has come to symbolise the power of the All Blacks and their status in world rugby, leaving an indelible impression of invincibility and ruthlessness on their opponents. It has over the years attracted some debate, with criticism from opposition and public alike, with some feeling it is an unfair attempt to intimidate the opposition prior to a match. However, most teams accept the *haka* as an integral part of New Zealand rugby heritage and face it. Some teams, however, choose to ignore the *haka* by turning their backs on the dance in order to insult the All Blacks – a tactic most often adopted by Australia and most recently by Italy during the 2007 RWC – but more often than not this simply further motivates the All Blacks and inevitably results in the opposition's defeat.

Often during the performance of the *haka* at away internationals, the home crowd will attempt to drown out the *haka* by singing their own national anthem, loudly, as Wales first did in their famous victory of 1905. In 2005, the All Blacks met the Welsh in a centenary match of the fixture, with the Welsh Rugby Union requesting that New Zealand repeat the sequence of events from the original match a century before. This involved the performance of the *haka* after the New Zealand anthem but before the Welsh anthem – which New Zealand agreed to. The following year, Wales requested the same pre-match format, but New Zealand refused and instead chose to perform the *haka* in their changing room. Captain Richie McCaw later defended this, stating that the *haka* was integral to New Zealand culture and All Blacks heritage and 'if the other team wants to mess around, we'll just do the *haka* in the shed'. The crowd, amidst some booing, were shown brief footage of the *haka* on the big screen.

The *Ka Mate haka* dates back to 1810 when a chief by the name of Te Rauparaha of Ngāti Toa iwi was being pursued by enemies. In a desperate attempt to save himself, the chief hid in a food-storage pit with a woman sitting over the entrance to conceal him. Here he thought he'd be safe as no man would ever sit beneath the genitals of a woman – especially a feared chief such as Te Rauparaha – with the enemy unlikely to search the pit, which proved to be true. Upon climbing out, Chief Te Rauparaha found someone standing over him; luckily it was a friend. In relief, Te Rauparaha performed a *haka* with the words: 'It is death, it is death; it is life, it is life; this is the man who enabled me to live as I climb up step by step toward sunlight.' These words are still used today and Chief Te Rauparaha's escape from death is commemorated in the *Ka Mate haka*, a celebration of life over death.

Ka Mate haka

Ringa Pakia	Slap the hands against the thighs
Uma tiraha	Puff out the chest
Turi whatia	Bend the knees
Hope whai ake	Let the hip follow
Waewae takahia kia kino	Stamp the feet as hard as you can
Ka mate, ka mate	'Tis death, 'tis death (or: I die, I die)
Ka ora, ka ora	'Tis life, 'tis life (or: I live, I live)
Ka mate, ka mate	'Tis death, 'tis death (or: I die, I die)
Ka ora, ka ora	'Tis life, 'tis life (or: I live, I live)
Tenei te tangata puhuruhuru	This is the hairy man that stands here
Nana nei I tiki mai whakawhiti te ra	Who brought the sun and caused it to shine
A upane, ka upane	A step toward, another step upward
A upane, ka upane	A step toward, another step upward
Whiti te ra, hi	The sun shines!

The first use of the *haka* by the All Blacks can be traced back to 1884 when the first New Zealand team to tour overseas (to Australia) performed a 'Maori war cry' before each match. Exactly which *haka* was chosen for these early games is unknown. When the New Zealand Natives toured the United Kingdom in 1888/1889, for example, they performed a *haka* using the words 'Ake ake kia kaha', which suggests that the *Ka Mate haka* was not the one performed. In 1903, when New Zealand played their first full international against Australia in Sydney it appears as though the *haka* had been composed specifically for the occasion, as it directly addressed 'the Wallabies' with its words. The first reference to the *Ka Mate* was during the 1905 New Zealand tour of the United Kingdom when New

Zealand performed the *Ka Mate* before the Scotland and Wales matches. Yet the *haka* has not been performed at every match. During the 1935/1936 tour of the United Kingdom, a *haka* was never performed on the field – and the *haka* was very rarely performed on home soil, the first time being at the crunch, series-deciding international against the 1921 touring Springboks. It was not until the 1987 RWC, hosted primarily by New Zealand, that the All Blacks consistently performed a *haka* prior to each home international.

On 28 August 2005, during the 2005 Tri-Nations at Carisbrook in Dunedin, the All Blacks, without announcement, performed a new, previously unseen *haka* against the 2004 Tri-Nations Champion Springboks – *the Kapa o Pango*. Written by Derek Lardelli of Ngati Porou, it is characterised by its more aggressive climax, with each player performing a throat-slitting action directed at the opposing team. The *Kapa o Pango* took over a year to compose, after lengthy consultations with many experts in Maori culture. Its words are more specifically related to the All Blacks, referring to the 'warriors in black' and the 'silver fern'. It serves only to complement the *Ka Mate*, rather than as a replacement and is essentially only used on special occasions. However, it has had to be slightly modified, with the throat-slitting action raising some critical comments from the public. The NZRU, in its defence, publicly stated that 'the throat-slitting gesture has a radically different meaning within Maori culture and *haka* traditions, specifically the drawing of vital energy into the heart and lungs', with composer Derek Lardelli stating that the gesture symbolises the cutting edge of sport and not the slaughter of opponents. Nevertheless, the action has since been removed to placate sensitive viewers.

Kapa o Pango haka

Kapa o Pango kia whakawhenua au I ahau!	All Blacks, let me become one with the land
Hi aue, hi!	do one
Ko Aotearoa e ngunguru nei!	This is our land that rumbles
Au, au, aue ha!	It's my time! It's my moment!
Ko Kapa o Pango e ngunguru nei!	This defines us as the All Blacks
Au, au, aue ha!	It's my time! It's my moment!
I ahaha!	I ahaha!
Ka tu te ihiihi	Our dominance
Ka tu te wanawana	Our supremacy will triumph
Ki runga ki te rangi e tu iho nei, tu iho nei, hi!	And be placed on high
Ponga ra!	Silver fern!
Kapa o Pango, aue hi!	All Blacks!
Ponga ra!	Silver fern!
Kapa o Pango, aue hi, ha!	All Blacks!

Scotland

The history of rugby in Scotland is interesting. Several hundred years before William Webb Ellis first ran with the ball, there are clear records of Romans based in Scotland playing a field ball game, *harpastum*, in their spare time, presumably to relax from their toils on the fringes of the Roman Empire, keeping the dastardly Picts and Scots at bay. There are also records from 1424 of a form of football that was often banned because of the public disorder it created and because it interfered with Sunday worship. Such games were traditionally played in the Border towns of Scotland where two villages would take part, trying and wrench the ball from each other in a running fracas that covered several square miles, often taking hours to finish. The most famous of these games was vividly described by Sir Walter Scott, illustrating the paucity of rules in a match involving several hundred players. During the game one individual somehow managed to work the ball out of a maul and throw it to a runner on the fringe (the Scots claim this incident as the seed of rugby union), who then sprinted toward the goal, only to be run down by a horse-mounted spectator! Today, the Border Ba' Games celebrate these ancient forms of football from which rugby more than likely evolved.

In the more recent orthodox history of the sport, soon after the formation of the RFU in 1871, the Scottish Football Union (SFU) was formed in 1873. Scottish pupils who attended institutions such as Rugby School and Oxford University brought the 'Rugby rules' back home to Scotland. The first club to be formed in Scotland was Edinburgh Academicals in 1858 which played according to these rules. They played in the first rugby game in the country, winning a 25-a-side match against Edinburgh University that same year. These two clubs were part of the six original clubs which formed the SFU, along with Glasgow Academicals, West of Scotland, Royal High

School Former Pupils and Merchistonians. Several Scottish clubs were initially affiliated to the English RFU, but quickly transferred their allegiance back across the border following the formation of the SFU, which brought a much-needed structure to Scottish rugby. Interestingly, the oldest fixture in rugby history is still played annually – between Edinburgh Academy and Merchiston Castle, which dates back to 11 December 1858.

Two years before the establishment of the SFU, the Scots had already played their first international. A year before this, in 1870, the Football Association staged an England–Scotland soccer international in London, but all the Scottish players were London residents – many with spurious claims to Scottish citizenship. 'True' Scottish rugby men found this situation highly unsatisfactory and due to the heightened interest in rugby in Scotland, pressure quickly began to mount to stage a rugby international against England. Following a meeting on 5 December 1870, representatives of four Scottish Clubs – Edinburgh Academicals, West of Scotland, Glasgow Academicals and the University of St Andrews – wrote to Mr B.H. Burns, the secretary of the Blackheath Club in London:

> 'For our own satisfaction, therefore, and with a view to really testing what Scotland can do against an English team, we, representing the whole footballing interest of Scotland, hereby challenge any team selected from the whole of England, to play us a match, twenty-a-side Rugby rules. If entered into we can promise England a hearty welcome and a first-rate match.'

Scotland indeed gave England 'a first-rate match', as they went on to win this first rugby international by a goal and a try to a try – an equivalent scoreline using the first valued scoring system of $4^{(1G\ 1T)}–1^{(1T)}$ – before 4,000 people at Raeburn Place in Edinburgh. Teams were 20 a side, with each half lasting 50 minutes. As well as having hosted and won the first international, Scotland can also lay claim to some other rugby firsts:

- Scotland staged the first-ever floodlit match in 1879 when Scottish club Langholm played in the first international club match against English club side Carlisle. The match was abandoned because it got too dark despite the lights being on!
- In 1883, Scotland invented the game of seven-a-side rugby when Melrose butcher, Ned Haig, devised the form of the game as a fundraiser for the ailing Border Club, which was short of players. The game became an overnight success and soon spread worldwide. In recognition of Scotland's contribution to the game of sevens, the IRFB granted Scotland the privilege of hosting the inaugural Sevens Rugby World Cup in 1993.
- The SRU owned Inverleith in Edinburgh – the first purpose-built rugby stadium, constructed in 1899. Murrayfield later became the permanent national rugby ground in 1924.
- In 1959, Murrayfield became the first rugby stadium in the world to install undersoil heating, thereby allowing rugby to be played in the harshest of winters.

Triggered by the purchase of Murrayfield in 1922, the SFU changed its name to the Scottish Rugby Union (SRU) in 1924. With the outbreak of World War II in 1939, rugby in Scotland was all but brought to a halt. The SRU cancelled all trial and international matches, encouraging member clubs to carry on as best they could. Some clubs closed down, while others amalgamated in an attempt to survive, playing matches against other local clubs and military bases within their vicinity. Murrayfield was offered to the nation and was taken over by the Royal Army Service Corps as a supply depot. Despite the war, the Armed Forces Sports Authorities managed to arrange two England–Scotland services internationals each year on a home-and-away basis, with Scotland's games initially played at Inverleith and then at Murrayfield in 1944.

Scotland are well known for being at the forefront of policing amateurism in the early days of rugby, which would often lead to international disputes – an attitude which began back in 1883 at the first sevens tournament in Melrose, when the SFU kicked up a fuss over the awarding of prizes to tournament winners. The union was also strict on travelling expenses and, following the New Zealand tour of 1905/1906, became extremely angry to learn that the tourists had been paid – or reimbursed for lost earnings – three shillings a day in expenses. The SFU was so fiercely pro-amateurism that they even refused to permit players to wear numbers on their jerseys until 1933, stating that 'the game should be for players and that numbering was only pandering to the unnecessary and promoted the intrusive involvement of spectators'. In the late 1920s, King George V was watching a Scottish international when he asked why Scotland were not wearing numbers. 'This is a rugby match, not a cattle auction,' one union official replied abrasively.

England remained Scotland's only international opponents until 1877, when Scotland played against and convincingly beat Ireland in Belfast. Wales joined the Scottish international calendar in 1883 and France in 1910, but not before the Scots had lost to New Zealand in 1905 and defeated South Africa in 1906. In 1879, Scotland and England first vied for the Calcutta Cup, which is the oldest international trophy in world rugby. England are the current holders.

Despite rugby union not being the national sport in Scotland (a distant second after soccer), Scotland have nevertheless managed to win three Grand Slams (1925, 1984 and 1990), ten Triple Crowns and 14 outright Five and Six Nations Championship victories – their most recent in 1999. Scotland is considered by the IRB to belong to the top-tier nations, although they are not as competitive as top sides like New Zealand or South Africa, mainly because of a small player pool. This can be partly attributed to the disparate popularity of the sport in the country, with rugby being popular only in the Border region. Farther north, soccer dominates, with rugby often only played at private schools.

The 1920s were halcyon days for the Scots. With four of their backline players coming from Oxford University, they clinched their celebrated Grand Slam in 1925 with a hard-fought 14–11 win against England. After World War II, however, Scottish rugby suffered a serious blow, with 17 consecutive defeats from 1951 to 1955, including a 44–0 drubbing by the 1951/1952 Springboks – a game that coined the now-classic quip, when a dejected Scottish fan remarked after the game, ' ... and they [the Scots] were lucky to get nil!'

In 1960, Scotland undertook their first international tour to South Africa. This was the first such short international tour to take place, with just three matches scheduled. Despite Scotland losing the international, the tour was seen as a great success and effectively laid the foundations that set the standard for all future short international tours. Following their success in 1929 it was 55 years before Scotland were to record another outright Five Nations championship victory, which they accomplished in style by securing their second Grand Slam in 1984. In the final match of the championship France, also undefeated, came to Edinburgh, looking like favourites to win the decider until, against all odds and deep into the game, Jim Calder secured the unexpected result with his match-winning try. They followed this up in 1990 with what is probably regarded as Scotland's most memorable Grand Slam. With narrow away victories over Ireland and Wales and a comfortable win over France, Scotland met England in Edinburgh for the Grand Slam decider – a fixture for which England were overwhelming favourites, having swept all before them with relative ease. Scotland meant business when they puposefully strode out onto the pitch, lifted by a passionate crowd in this all-important title match. David Sole's team triumphed after a young Tony Stanger beat English speedster Rory Underwood for what turned out to be the match-winning try.

Since then, pickings have been lean for Scotland. They have managed just one championship victory – in 1999 – after England surprisingly lost to Wales. Scotland embarrassingly lost all their matches in the 2004 Six Nations, but can boast having reached the quarter-finals of every RWC; they came close to making the final in 1991 were it not for the horrendous penalty miss by Gavin Hastings in front of the posts. In the new professional era Scotland have struggled more so than they did in the 1990s – and have only notched up one victory over a southern-hemisphere nation in the new millennium.

The famous image of All Black legend Colin Meads (facing the referee) being sent off in the 71st minute of the 1967 test against Scotland in Edinburgh by referee K. D. Kelleher of Ireland. Despite being reduced to 14 men New Zealand triumphed by 14-3.
Photo: New Zealand Rugby Museum

South Africa

Rugby was first introduced to South Africa in the 1860s by the British army, which had soldiers in its ranks who had attended Rugby School. In 1861 the principal of Diocesan College (aka Bishops) in Cape Town, George Ogilvie, introduced the 'Winchester Game' to the Cape – the version of rugby played at Winchester College in England at the time and which became the first version of rugby to be adopted in the Cape. With this, rugby fondly became known as 'Gog's Game' in the region, but by the 1870s the form of the game as played at Rugby School was formally adopted and became the accepted version in the Cape. Newspaper reports suggest that the first game of organised rugby to be played in South Africa was Civilians vs Military at Green Point Common in Cape Town on 23 August 1862. By 1875, the game had become a very popular pastime in the Cape, with games played on a regular basis between local teams and the British tommies. Rugby was part of the British colonial heritage in South Africa and was generally played by the English or 'English inclined' – but this was not long the case.

Dutch-speaking and Muslim communities soon took to playing rugby as well, and as a result of the consequent growth of the game in South Africa, clubs were formed to accommodate them. The first club was Hamiltons in Cape Town in 1875 which still thrives today. With the development of these early rugby clubs, a body was needed to regulate the laws and organise competitions. The Western Province Rugby Football Union (WPRFU) was founded in 1883 when Hamiltons Club called a meeting with the five other Cape Town clubs, followed by the Griqualand West Rugby Football Union (GWRFU) in 1886, the Eastern Province RFU in 1888 and the Transvaal RFU in 1889. As a result, a national union was needed to govern national rules and organise competitions between local unions and international unions. And so in 1889 the South African Rugby Board (SARB) was established in Kimberley; by 1891 it was sufficiently well organised to receive a touring side from the British Isles. The British team remained unbeaten throughout the tour and were ironically donated a cup by shipping tycoon Donald Currie, which the captain was to present to the first team which beat them. However, since no side did, the cup was awarded to Griqualand West who had provided the toughest opposition, a 3–0 win to the British. Griqualand West in turn donated the cup to SARB for South Africa's premier provincial tournament, which came to be known as the Currie Cup. This tour illustrated how far South Africa still had to improve; a basic statistical breakdown of the first three tours to South African by the British Isles in 1891, 1896 and 1903 highlights the growth of the game in South Africa from this point. In 1891, the British Isles remained unbeaten in all their 20 matches, winning the test series 3–0. In 1896, John Hammond's touring side won 19 of their 21 games, winning the test series 3–1, but in 1903, Mark Morrison's team could only manage 11 wins in their 22-match tour of South Africa, losing the test series 0–1. This was South Africa's

Did you know: Rugby the peacemaker. On 29 April 1902, as the Anglo-Boer War was drawing to a close a ceasefire was agreed upon so that the Brits and the Boers could play a rugby match.

Did you know: Herbert Castens captained South Africa in their first international on 30 July 1891 against the British Isles in Port Elizabeth. Castens was dropped for the second test match in Kimberley but for the third test in Cape Town, he was appointed referee – the only occasion in the history of rugby that a player has captained and refereed an international in the same series.

Did you know: In 1956, New Zealand won their first series against South Africa 3–1 in a dirty, hard-fought contest when New Zealand recruited their amateur, heavyweight boxing champion Kevin Skinner into their front row to deal with the Springbok props, Jaap Bekker and Chris Koch who had dominated in the second-test Springbok win.

Did you know: South Africa is the only test-playing nation that has never had a hat-trick of tries scored against it by an international player in a match.

Did you know: The only case of three brothers playing together in the same international is when South African's John, Dick and Freddie Luyt played together in the internationals vs Scotland, Wales and England on the 1912/1913 Springboks Grand Slam tour of the United Kingdom and France.

first test-series victory; they were not to lose another for 53 years – a record which still stands.

South Africa wore the green jersey for the first time when Barry Heatlie captained South Africa in their first test victory in 1896, the jerseys being supplied by Diocesan Old Boys' Club. It would not be till 12 September 1903 that South Africa were to wear green again, for the third international against the British Isles, when Heatlie was recalled as captain. Although the Diocesan Club had closed down, their attire was still available and South Africa won their second test match. In 1906, SARB finally settled on these colours. South Africa went on their first tour to the British Isles that year, captained by Paul Roos. The English press summoned captain Paul Roos, vice captain Paddy Caroline and team manager J.C. Carden before the first team practice, requesting that a nickname be provided for this first touring South African side. Roos replied that the unanimous decision was *der Springbokken*. The tour was a great success, with the Springboks winning 25 of their 28 matches and losing just one test to the Scots in Glasgow. A convincing series win over the 1910 British Isles made the rugby world take note of developments in South Africa and on the 1912/1913 tour of the United Kingdom all doubts were cast aside when Billy Millar's Sprinboks became the first touring side ever to complete the prized Grand Slam, including a 38–0 hammering of the Irish and a revenge 16–0 win over Scotland.

This level of success called for a clash with New Zealand, finally organised in 1921. The series was drawn, as was the 1928 series but in 1937, South Africa beat New Zealand away to become the unofficial world champions. A second Grand Slam success was recorded by Bennie Osler's team in 1931/1932, and in 1933 South Africa defeated Australia in the first and only five-test series ever played. After World War II, South Africa followed up their 1938 series victory over the British Lions with a resounding 4–0 whitewash of New Zealand and a third Grand Slam tour of the United Kingdom. In 1955, signs of a Springbok wilt were manifested when they shared the 1955 series with the Lions and lost a closely fought series to New Zealand away from home in 1956. In 1960/1961, South Africa recorded their fourth Grand Slam tour, a remarkable statistic considering Scotland have only managed such an achievement three times in a century and Ireland twice, while neither New Zealand nor Australia had yet achieved it. South Africa's lean times arrived in 1964/1965 when they lost seven internationals in a row. Results improved with series victories over France, the Lions and Australia, but on the 1969/1970 tour of the British Isles the effects of the South African government's apartheid practices became apparent ... enter apartheid.

Black and 'coloured' players (of mixed race) were racially discriminated against and not considered for national selection. As such, these players formed their own unions but the fact remained that only white players could belong to SARB which was affiliated to the IRFB, and therefore only players affiliated to SARB could play international rugby. So strict were the laws that the coloureds were forced to form their own union (South Africa Rugby Federation, SARF) and similarly the blacks the South African Rugby Association (SARA). However, only whites were eligible for national selection. As far back as 1921, race was brought to the fore in Springbok rugby during their tour of New Zealand when they the South African government objected to the 'ignominy' of having to play the New Zealand Maoris. Despite this prejudice, South Africa occasionally played abroad against 'non-whites', but ironically such players were not allowed to play in South Africa. This only really affected New Zealand and their Maori players. The NZRFU embarrassingly agreed to this ruling and did not select any Maoris to tour South Africa until the 1970 tour. By 1949, with apartheid written into law and institutionalised in South African society, white players had less chance to compete on the world stage as the international community gradually shunned South Africa. In 1967, New Zealand finally refused an invitation to tour South Africa when it was made clear that Maoris were unwelcome. South Africa quickly waived the rule. In 1970 New Zealand toured South Africa, with Maoris labelled 'honorary whites'. The disastrous tour of the British Isles in 1969/1970 heralded South Africa's isolation from world rugby, with angry anti-apartheid protests directed at the Springboks. Games were delayed or even cancelled, affecting the Springboks who did not win a test – a startling statistic considering they had previously only lost one test in the United Kingdom. The 1969/1970 tour to Britain was the last by a Springbok team for 22 years, until Naas Botha's Springboks played England in London in 1992. Similarly, the 1971 Springbok tour of Australia was also their last for 22 years until 1993. They were not to play in France for another 18 years and New Zealand for 13, while the British Lions did not tour South Africa for 17 years after their 1980 tour. South Africa did not play any test rugby during the years 1973, 1978, 1979, 1983, 1985, 1987, 1988, 1990 and 1991, relying heavily on 'rebel' tours such as the 1986 New Zealand Cavaliers, World XV outfits in 1977 and 1989, and a strange combination team from South America which toured in 1980 and 1982, and South America and Spain in 1984. In 1980, South Africa toured South America but were denied visas by Argentina. As a result, matches were played against unequal opposition in Chile, Uruguay and Paraguay.

In 1981, SARB amalgamated with SARA and SARF in a token move to appease international criticism, which made it technically possible to select black or coloured players for the national team. Errol Tobias (a 'coloured') was selected to play against the touring Irish at centre and thus became the first non-white player to represent South Africa. He was a fine centre and flyhalf who would surely have played more than his eventual six tests had he not had to compete with the great incumbent flyhalf of the time – Naas Botha. Avril Williams, uncle of Chester, became the second non-white Springbok, playing in both tests against the English in 1984. Despite international isolation, enthusiasm for the game still flourished in South Africa, with Currie Cup attendances regularly exceeding 50,000 a game. Opinion as to how to deal with South Africa in the international arena was divided. Some called for a complete boycott, while others felt maintaining contact was the best way to force change. For some, the gravest concern was the influence of South African money on the game (as illustrated by the 1986 New Zealand Cavaliers tour), which could potentially attract foreign players to South Africa, ruining the world game. Boycott was the strategy adopted, with South Africa not invited to participate in the RWCs of 1987 and 1991. In 1988, the president of SARB, Danie Craven, held talks with the African National Congress, resulting in the formation of the non-racist South African Rugby Football Union (SARFU) in 1992. With change in the air and readmission into international sport, times were uncertain for South African rugby. Arguments raged over whether or not the anthem, *Die Stem*, should be sung and whether the green and gold should be worn. South Africa was granted host-nation status for the 1995 RWC, when the first democratically elected president, Nelson Mandela, handed over the trophy to his captain, François Pienaar, allowing the nation to celebrate as one for the first time in their history. Rugby change in South Africa had begun. At international level, 39 non-white players have so far been selected. In 2008 Peter de Villiers was appointed the first non-white Springbok coach. Despite all these challenges unique to South African rugby, the Springboks remain one of the top rugby nations in the world and are the only team capable of regularly beating New Zealand. Since readmission in 1992, they have won two Tri-Nations titles (1998 and 2004) and boast the greatest success in RWC tournaments, having won twice in four attempts (1995 and 2007). Yet, the Springbok emblem is still seen by some to represent white supremacy and racial oppression. The badge is over a hundred years old and is worn with pride by white and black ambassadors for the Rainbow Nation. However, since the Springboks' triumph in 2007, calls to have the emblem scrapped have re-emerged, with controversial statements coming from the then sports minister, who stated the emblem was the property of the sports ministry and was in fact being used illegally without their authorisation – this despite the fact that Louis Luyt (SA Rugby President in 1996) had the trademark legally registered when the game went professional. Before that, the springbok emblem was the property of South African Rugby and was only 'given' to other sporting codes when applied for nicely. Prior to this, Sport Portfolio Committee chair, Butana Komphela, had stated: 'The springbok divides us. We have a responsibility to unite our country under one national emblem [the protea].' To compound matters, controversial Western Province/Stormers player, Luke Watson, allegedly stated that he 'wanted to vomit on the springbok jersey' and that 'the game was rotten

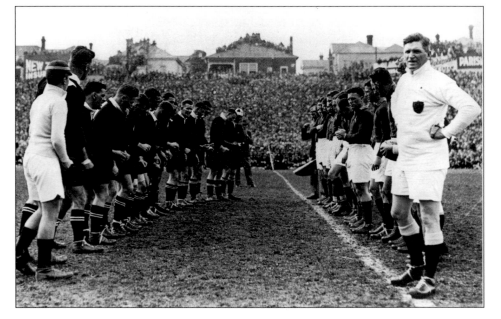

to the core [and] controlled by Dutchmen [Afrikaners]'. In 2009 a combination of the protea, worn on the left breast and the springbok on the right, was introduced for the British and Irish Lions tour. These things have a way of working themselves out; rugby is too much of a 'religion' in South Africa for it to be otherwise.

The All Blacks and Eden Park crowd cheer the 1937 Springboks prior to the final match of the tour, the decisive third test. The 1937 Springboks were popular tourists, described by a New Zealand newspaper as "the greatest team to ever leave New Zealand's shores" - a sentiment still believed by many today.
Photo: New Zealand Rugby Museum

Top left: 1906 Springbok squad.
Photo: Commons/wikimedia.org/creative commons license

Above: The 1937 Springbok squad. Seated centre is Danie Craven.
Photo: Commons/wikimedia.org/creative commons license

Left: 1924 Springbok squad. *Photo*: Commons/wikimedia.
org/creative commons license

The first South African side to wear green jerseys and win a test match; that against the British Isles in 1896, by 5-0 at Newlands in Cape Town. The side was captained by Barry Heatlie, seated middle.
Photo: Frédéric Humbert/www.flickr.com/photos/rugby_pioneers/creative commons license

All Blacks fullback Allan Hewson kicks for touch during the third and decisive 'Flour Bomb' test of the 1981 series against South Africa in Auckland, won 25-22 by New Zealand after a dubious late penalty was goaled by Hewson himself. Putting him under pressure is Bok winger Gerrie Germishuys while controversial referee Clive Norling looks on. *Photo*: New Zealand Rugby Museum

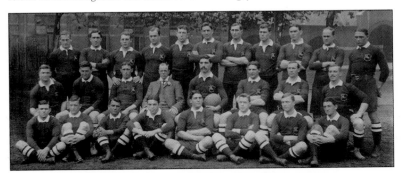

Centre: The first touring South African side to the British Isles in 1906-07, captained by Paul Roos (centre with ball) who is accredited for christening the South Africa rugby side '*der Springbokken*'. *Photo*: Frédéric Humbert/www.flickr.com/photos/rugby_pioneers/creative commons license

Bottom: The Springbok side that took on New Zealand in the first test of the 1928 series, a match won 17-0 by South Africa, which to this day remains a record defeat for the All Blacks against South Africa. Phil Mostert (seated fourth from left) was the Bok captain for the series. *Photo*: Frédéric Humbert/www.flickr.com/photos/rugby_pioneers/creative commons license

Wales

As was the case with the other home unions, various early forms of football were played in Wales before the game of rugby union was established. In the seventeenth century, a game known as *cnappan* was popular in Pembrokeshire and was played into the early twentieth century. *Cnappan* was an inter-village battle version of Tudor folk-football with inherent similarities to rugby and, as such, many Welsh rugby journalists and supporters believe that there is a direct link between rugby and *cnappan* and hence claim, as a nation, to be responsible for the development and evolution of the early forms of the game.

Rugby as we know it first began developing in Wales during the 1850s in colleges and schools, but with a slow start compared to the other home unions of the British Isles. Neath Football Club was the first club to be formed, in 1871. After the establishment of the Neath Club other clubs sprouted and rugby's popularity increased – especially among coalminers and factory workers. The growth in the sport's popularity soon led to rugby union being accepted as the Welsh national sport, enjoying an immense following. In March 1880, Wales became the last of the four home unions to form their own national union – the Welsh Rugby Football Union (WRFU), which was formalised at the Tenby Hotel in Swansea. Present at the meeting were the clubs Lampeter, Llandeilo, Llandovery, Cardiff, Newport, Swansea, Llanelli, Merthyr, Brecon, Pontypool and Bangor. Prior to this, the South Wales Union had been in operation since 1875 so the newly established WRFU was able to capitalise on the successful structures this union and its major clubs – Llanelli (1872), Newport (1874), Swansea (1875) and Cardiff (1876), commonly referred to as the 'Big Four' of Welsh rugby – had instituted.

The result of the formation of the WRFU was Wales's first international the following year, on 19 February 1881, when they took on England in Blackheath. Cynics suggest that the Welsh only established their union to compete in international rugby with the other home unions – a wish that was granted when they were thrashed by seven goals, six tries and one drop goal to nil (an equivalent scoreline today of 82–0). With this, the English refused to play against the Welsh until their standard of rugby improved. The result was slated by the nation and shortly thereafter, on 12 March 1881, at the Castle Hotel in Neath, the West Walians were included and the Welsh Rugby Union (WRU) was officially formed. With the poor performance of the Welsh in their first international, England refused to honour the following test, but Wales did play and manage to beat a very underprepared Irish side, some of whom walked off the pitch in disgust during the game. Scotland joined the Welsh international calendar in 1883 and Wales recorded their first international victory over England in 1890. This early success led to Wales's first Triple Crown in 1893, which was in part due to Wales adopting the four three-quarter system and eight forwards for the first time.

In 1896, the WRU was rocked with allegations of professionalism by the other home unions when the WRU bought a house for the great Welsh player, Arthur Gould, in appreciation for his huge contribution to Welsh rugby over his 12 years as an international player. Consequently, Ireland refused to play Wales the following year and Scotland went one further by refusing to play Wales for the following two years. England decided to ignore the issue, as many English clubs relied on the large gate-takings from their Welsh fixtures and stood to lose financially were they to shun the Welsh. Gould retired and the issue was slowly forgotten, as they generally are.

The twentieth century heralded a golden era in Welsh rugby. They enjoyed Triple Crown successes in 1900, 1902, 1905, 1908, 1909 and a first Grand Slam in 1908. Although this Grand Slam, as well as the 1909 one, was won during the Home Nations Championship, it is still regarded as a Grand Slam, considering the Welsh were to defeat France in both the 1908 and 1909 seasons despite France not yet being a part of the championship. They won their first official Grand Slam in the Five Nations in 1911. They lost just seven games from 1900 to 1911, a run that included beating the All Blacks in 1905 – one of the greatest achievements in Welsh rugby. Heading into the final test, the unbeaten All Blacks were heavy favourites, but a try by Welsh winger Teddy Morgan saw Wales win 3–0. However, the 'Did Deans score?' saga has raged to this day. New Zealand centre Bob Deans was denied a try which many claim was fairly scored. New Zealand felt they were robbed, with most neutrals stating it was a fair try. The referee was some distance behind play and unsighted. However, many felt that on the day Wales was the better team and deserved to win anyway.

Following these heady heydays, Welsh rugby entered a relative low – despite a first win at Twickenham in 1933 and defeating the 1935 All Blacks – and did not win another Grand Slam until 1950, followed by another in 1952. Following the successful inaugural tour by Scotland to South Africa in 1960, Wales undertook their first tour when they visited South Africa in 1964. Wales played four games, winning two and losing the international 3–24, Wales's heaviest defeat in more than 40 years.

Triple Crowns in 1965 and 1969 heralded the glorious Welsh rugby era of the 1970s, where they defeated all before them, with the exception of New Zealand and South Africa. Three Grand Slams and two Triple Crowns were recorded in the 1970s, with greats such as master scrumhalf Gareth Edwards, medical doctor/fullback J.P.R. Williams, generalissimo flyhalf Phil Bennett, flying winger J.J. Williams, ranging eighthman Mervyn Davies and Graham Price to the fore. But the retirement of many of these simply magical players at the end of the decade caused a Welsh slough where they regularly finished last in the Five Nations. A gloomy tournament whitewash in 1990 was a first for them, repeated in 1995 and 2003.

Wales have also fared disappointingly in RWCs, where aside from a third-place finish in 1987, they missed out on the quarter-finals in 1991, 1995 and 2007, have twice lost to Samoa in crunch fixtures, in 1991 and 1999, both in Cardiff, and most recently against a rampant Fijian side in 2007. The only glimmer of light in these dark years came in 2005, when a brilliant side captained by Michael Owen won the Grand Slam. But they defended their 2005 Grand Slam in appalling fashion, managing just a single victory in each of the 2006 and 2007 championships. In 2008, however, Ryan Jones led the Welsh to a second Grand Slam; this after failing to make the RWC play-off stages just months earlier and illustrating the true rollercoaster nature of Welsh form. But much like the French, the Welsh are mercurial to say the least, with a depth of latent talent far out of proportion to the size of the population, as witnessed by the massive influence Welsh players had on the 2009 British and Irish Lions tour to South Africa, with such superstars as Stephen Jones and Shane Williams dazzling for the tourists.

The 1910 Welsh side that outplayed France in 1910, a match won 49-14 by Wales in Swansea, in which Reggie Gibbs (seated far left) scored a hat-trick of tries and Jack Bancroft (standing, far left) scored a tournament record of eight conversions. *Photo*: Frédéric Humbert/www.flickr.com/photos/rugby_pioneers/creative commons license

An expectant home crowd watches Wales play England in 1905. Their expectations were certainly met as Wales trounced England by 25-0 in Cardiff. *Photo*: Frédéric Humbert/www.flickr.com/photos/rugby_pioneers/creative commons license

Top left: Action from the 1935 international between Wales and New Zealand in Cardiff. Wales notched up a famous 13-12 victory that day while wearing letters on their jerseys instead of the normal numbering. *Photo*: New Zealand Rugby Museum

Above: Cardiff euphoria in 1905 as Teddy Morgan's famous try is celebrated raucously by the Cardiff Arms Park crowd: a score which ultimately won the match for Wales against New Zealand by 3-0.
Photo: New Zealand Rugby Museum

Left: Lineout action from the 1980 centennial test match between Wales and New Zealand in Cardiff. Competing for the ball is All Black lock Andy Haden and Welsh lock Allan Martin. New Zealand went on to win by 23-3. *Photo*: New Zealand Rugby Museum

Far left: Injured Welsh captain Jack Wetter is assisted from the field during the 1924 match against New Zealand in Swansea. Such a loss for the Welsh was compounded by the fact that substitutes were not allowed in those days and with just 14 men they lost 0-19. *Photo:* New Zealand Rugby Museum

Left: Such was the demand to watch Wales play New Zealand in 1924 that fans clambered up anything to witness the match: in this case a telephone pole which is comfortably holding eight Welsh fans aloft at St Helen's in Swansea. Such vantage points, which allow free views of the action, have come to be termed 'The Scotsman Grandstand'. *Photo:* New Zealand Rugby Museum

Team photograph of the famous 1905 Welsh side that defeated New Zealand by 3-0 in Cardiff thanks to a try by winger Teddy Morgan (back row, third from right), who was also central in the controversial disallowed try for All Blacks centre Bob Deans. *Photo:* New Zealand Rugby Museum

Chapter Four
British and Irish Lions

Introduction

The British and Irish Lions are a combined touring side, comprising the best available players from all four the home unions, England, Scotland, Ireland and Wales. Affectionately known as the Lions, they were officially known as the British Isles Rugby Union Team until 2001. Tours by the British and Irish Lions to southern-hemisphere nations are undoubtedly a highlight in any nation's rugby calendar. Legendary Lions captain, Willie John McBride, stated that 'to tour with the Lions is the supreme prize'. Lions tours provide rare opportunity for the four home unions to put aside their historic rivalries as they come together and pool their talents to play side by side. The Lions have a great rugby tradition and an aura attached to them like no other rugby team in the world. Their tours of the top-tier southern-hemisphere nations are eagerly anticipated and intensely followed by fans across the globe, producing some of the most memorable rugby clashes of all time, and which are still talked about today. Tours played an important role in spreading rugby across the world during the game's early years; once the game was established, the Lions helped sustain its further development. Sometimes referred to as 'missionaries', they, however, never forced rugby onto unwilling populations, with tours only arranged on invitation from the southern nations. This missionary tag fell away once the original rugby 'pupils' became the 'teachers' – as was the case with South Africa and New Zealand, who began to dominate the Lions from 1903 on.

The name of the team and the history thereof is a complex topic, with a minefield of sensitivities involving the United Kingdom of Great Britain and Northern Ireland and the Republic of Ireland. Initially, the team was referred to as Great Britain; not a correct, all-encompassing term considering that Great Britain is the name of the largest island of the British Isles and incorporates only England, Wales and Scotland. The 1888 touring side to Australia was known as Great Britain but in 1891 the team was termed the British Isles by captain Bill MacLagen. According to the *Encyclopaedia Britannica*, the geographic term British Isles 'accommodates a group of islands off the northwest coast of continental Europe which comprise Great Britain, Ireland and a large number of smaller islands'. The term, however, remains controversial for the Irish whose government openly discourages its use. Being proudly independent, the Irish readily object to any association with Britain. Nevertheless, the touring name, the British Isles, stuck for 110 years, despite Irish players regularly being selected and often captaining the side. Several minor variations have occurred. In 1891, the team was initially called the English Rugby Football Team before tour captain Bill MacLagen changed the name to the British Isles Rugby Union Team. In 1908, a combined Welsh and English team toured under the name Anglo-Welsh and in 1910, the team sent to Argentina was called the English Rugby Union Team, but was later changed to the Combined British Rugby Union Team. In 1924, the team was nicknamed the Lions and the British Lions name stuck, being more commonly used than the official name. It was not until 2001 that the name was formally changed to the British and Irish Lions, with officials noting that the Republic of Ireland had not been a part of the UK for 79 years. Many saw this name change as unnecessary, arguing that the term British Isles has a stronger geographic resonance for rugby than any politcal ramifications. Here is a summary of the various names:

- 1888: Great Britain
- 1891–1908: British Isles
- 1908: Anglo-Welsh
- 1910: Combined British/British Isles
- 1924–2001: British Lions
- 2001–present: British and Irish Lions

For the most part in this book, the team is referred to by its correct title of the time. Match statistics and records are grouped together under the umbrella the British and Irish Lions.

The early Lions tours had no formal organisation, rarely involving representative selection, as a player's availability was almost as important as his ability. The 1899 Lions' tour to Australia was the first time selection was done from all four home unions. The 1924 tourists to South Africa were the first to be known as the British Lions and the first tour formally managed by the four home unions. (Previous tours had been essentially private affairs.) While, theoretically, the Lions toured with the primary aim of showcasing the best talent in British and Irish rugby; in practice they were – and would remain for much of the century – a selection of the best who could afford several months away from work. Early tours by the British Lions returned regular victories against the emerging southern-hemisphere nations but as these nations grew stronger, so the Lions found their tours increasingly tough. With this came the call to select the best players in a fair and unbiased manner. Ironically, this has led to excuses for poor performances, the argument being that players are selected, not on merit, but in the interests of national parity – an early form of quota selection. Tour logistics and organistaion were also iffy: the 1924 team, for example, only met for the first time when boarding the boat at Southampton.

There were concerns, however, that with the advent of professionalism, Lions tours would fall by the wayside, as with other international tours, but the team has survived and any such fears were finally quelled by the hugely successful 1997 Martin Johnson team. The subsequent tours to Australia in 2001 and New Zealand in 2005, however, highlighted the challenges confronting a modern Lions team: the large squad, the small numbers of tour matches, 'ethnic' divisions within the squad and the split in the squad between the 'test team' and the 'midweek team'. Nonetheless, a Lions tour remains a special experience for players and fans alike and is one of the few remaining bastions of traditional touring in today's world where visiting national teams tend to bypass invitation teams and provincial games. Today, Lions' fans travel abroad in huge numbers; just look at the seas of red in the stadia during the 2009 Lions tour to South Africa. The income generated for the host nation is a clear indication why the SANZAR unions are such strong supporters of Lions tours. Money aside, no other side in the history of rugby has evoked such memories, stirred such passion and won so many accolades in the game's history.

Because the Lions do not represent one nation they do not have a national flag or anthem. So in 2005, the Lions commissioned the song *The Power of Four* as the team's 'national anthem'. It was met with little support from the Lions' fans, with even the players not knowing the words. Oops!

Tours and test results

Tour no.	Year	Country toured	Tour captain	Played	Won	Lost	Drawn
1	1888	Australia	Bob Seddon (Scotland)	-	-	-	-
		New Zealand		-	-	-	-
2	1891	South Africa	Bill MacLagan (Scotland)	3	3	-	-
3	1896	South Africa	Johnny Hammond (England)	4	3	1	-
4	1899	Australia	Matthew Mullineux (England)	4	3	1	-
5	1903	South Africa	Mark Morrison (Scotland)	3	-	1	2
6	1904	Australia	'Darkie' Bedell-Sivright (Scotland)	3	3	-	-
		New Zealand		1	-	1	-
7	1908	New Zealand	Arthur Harding (Wales)	3	-	2	1
		Australia		-	-	-	-
8	1910	Argentina	John Raphael (England)	-	-	-	-
9	1910	South Africa	Tom Smyth (Ireland)	3	1	2	-
		Rhodesia		-	-	-	-
10	1924	South Africa	Ronald Cove-Smith (England)	4	-	3	1
		Rhodesia		-	-	-	-
11	1927	Argentina	David MacMyn (Scotland)	-	-	-	-
12	1930	New Zealand	Doug Prentice (England)	4	1	3	-
		Australia		1	-	1	-
13	1936	Argentina	Bernard Gadney (England)	-	-	-	-
14	1938	South Africa	Sam Walker (Ireland)	3	1	2	-
		Rhodesia		-	-	-	-

Tour no.	Year	Country toured	Tour captain	Played	Won	Lost	Drawn
15	1950	New Zealand	Karl Mullen (Ireland)	4	-	3	1
		Australia		2	2	-	-
16	1955	South Africa	Robin Thompson (Ireland)	4	2	2	-
		Rhodesia		-	-	-	-
		South West Africa		-	-	-	-
17	1959	New Zealand	Ronnie Dawson (Ireland)	4	1	3	-
		Australia		2	2	-	-
		Canada		-	-	-	-
18	1962	South Africa	Arthur Smith (Scotland)	4	-	3	1
		Rhodesia		-	-	-	-
		South West Africa		-	-	-	-
		Kenya		-	-	-	-
19	1966	New Zealand	Mike Campbell-Lamerton (Scotland)	4	-	4	-
		Australia		2	2	-	-
		Canada		-	-	-	-
20	1968	South Africa	Tom Kiernan (Ireland)	4	-	3	1
		Rhodesia		-	-	-	-
		South West Africa		-	-	-	-
21	1971	New Zealand	John Dawes (Wales)	4	2	1	1
		Australia		-	-	-	-
22	1974	South Africa	Willie-John McBride (Ireland)	4	3	-	1
		Rhodesia		-	-	-	-
		South West Africa		-	-	-	-
23	1977	New Zealand	Phil Bennett (Wales)	4	1	3	-
		Fiji		-	-	-	-
24	1980	South Africa	Bill Beaumont (England)	4	1	3	-
		South West Africa		-	-	-	-
25	1983	New Zealand	Ciaran Fitzgerald (Ireland)	4	-	4	-
26	1989	Australia	Finlay Calder (Scotland)	3	2	1	-
27	1993	New Zealand	Gavin Hastings (Scotland)	3	1	2	-
28	1997	South Africa	Martin Johnson (England)	3	2	1	-
29	2001	Australia	Martin Johnson (England)	3	1	2	-
30	2005	Argentina	Michael Owen (Wales)	1	-	-	1
		New Zealand	Brian O'Driscoll (Ireland)	3	-	3	-
31	2009	South Africa	Paul O'Connell (Ireland)	3	1	2	-
Totals:				105	38	57	10

Tours

Tour record	
Played	35
Won	27
Lost	2
Drawn	6
For	292
Against	98

Australia and New Zealand (1888)

It is an interesting piece of trivia that the origins of the Lions' rugby tours actually lies with cricket. Sporting entrepreneurs, Alfred Shaw and Arthur Shrewsbury, successfully undertook the first cricket tour to Australia in 1888; following the immense success of this, and realising the popularity of rugby in Australia, it quickly popped up that a rugby tour to Australia was next on their business agenda. Furthermore, early 'British' rugby tours followed this pattern of funding by private companies eager to exploit the burgeoning markets of the British Empire. The RFU denied the cricketing entrepreneurs their direct support on the grounds that they were not affiliated to any recognised sporting body. They saw no reason, however, to interfere with the tour as long as the promoters and the players did not infringe the principle that it was an amateur game. On this understanding, the RFU gave the two businessmen permission to organize the tour. Inevitably, the tour, prviate as it was, took place under a scandalous cloud of accusations of professionalism and, unfortunately for Shaw and Shrewsbury, it did not run as smoothly as their cricket tour. Yet despite these various challenges, this pioneer tour was successful enough to establish the concept of British rugby tours to the southern hemisphere.

And so it was that a squad of 21 players who had all been born in the four home nations, but representing only England, Scotland and Wales (although dominated by England) left for Australia. The squad was soon whittled down to 20 after J.P. Clowes was banned by the RFU for accepting £15 in expenses from the management's agent! Of these 21 players, only four had ever played for their country in an international. The team left home on 8 March 1888 and returned on 11 November 1888, captained by Bob Seddon of Scotland, with a total of 35 matches played under various different rules – including 21 matches under Australian Rules. No internationals were played – only matches against provincial, city and academic sides. The Lions won 27 matches in total.

This early tour (and others to follow) was fraught with travel difficulties across Australia's vast terrain, where transport was in the form of horse-drawn carriage or steam train, with journeys between venues taking four or five days. Such early Lions' tours would last in the region of four to six months, and with arduous sea journeys taking up to a month one way, one can appreciate that such a lengthy time away from home had a significant effect on a player's income which he'd forfeited in order to tour. Replacing injured players was not an option and with tour parties never exceeding 30 players, this was a frequent problem.

The first game of the first tour was played seven weeks after the tourists left Britain, on 28 April in New Zealand against Otago, and they remained unbeaten until their final game against Auckland. After nine matches in New Zealand, the Lions crossed the Tasman Sea for the Australian leg of the tour, where they were unbeaten. A switch of codes was made to make the contests more challenging. Tragedy struck when captain Bob Seddon drowned while sculling on the Hunter River after a game against Maitland in New South Wales on 13 August 1888. In honour of his memory, it was decided the tour should continue and Andrew Stoddart of England took over the captaincy. Stoddart was also the English cricket captain at the time: no other player has ever achieved this feat – captaining two different sports at national level at the same time. The tour was beset with injuries and twice the team had to call upon local Australian players to help them field 15 players. Matches played under Australian Rules were staged purely for the benefit of the organisers, as these games were guaranteed to draw far larger crowds than union rugby. Nonetheless, of the 19 matches played under Aussie Rules, the Lions were still unbeaten. It was then back across the Tasman for a further ten matches, where they remained unbeaten before returning home. The first British Isles tour proved an extremely successful venture and paved the way for future.

Tour record			Test-series record	
Played	20		Played	3
Won	20		Won	3
Lost	-		Lost	-
Drawn	-		Drawn	-
For	226		For	11
Against	1		Against	-

South Africa (1891)

With the success of the 1888 tour, the conservative British rugby administrators took to the idea and fully sanctioned and embraced a combined British team to tour overseas. The British were invited to South Africa following the formation of the SARB in 1889, with the costs of the tour underwritten by the Cape Colony Prime Minister, Cecil Rhodes. The invitation was accepted and the side became the first to travel under the auspices of the IRFB. This backing led to the 22-man party being billed as the 'English Rugby Football

Team', but in fact included four Scotsmen, including captain Bill MacLagan who saw to it that the team was given the British Isles tag it deserved. In total, 20 matches were played, including for the first time internationals, with the team destroying all their opposition, scoring a massive 226 points to just one, unbeaten in all 20 matches. The three-test series was comfortably won 3–0 and the team left Cape Town, having presented the famous Currie Cup to Griqualand West.

Tour record	
Played	21
Won	19
Lost	1
Drawn	1
For	310
Against	45

Test-series record	
Played	4
Won	3
Lost	1
Drawn	-
For	34
Against	16

South Africa (1896)

South African rugby quickly improved, with British touring teams finding it more difficult to win in South Africa. In 1896, the British Isles again toured South Africa, but this time were faced with much tougher opposition than in 1891 – proof enough that the game had taken root in the colonies and Boer republics. The tour was captained by Englishman Johnny Hammond (a veteran of the 1891 tour along with fellow forward Froude Hancock), bringing for the first time an element of experience to the squad. The squad was made up of players from England, Scotland and Ireland, and for the first time the party comprised significant Irish representation, following Ireland's domination of the Home Championship over the previous three seasons – six Irishman were included in the 21-man squad. (Two of them, Tom Crean and Robert Johnston, suggested to their teammates during the tour that they should limit themselves to four tumblers of champagne a day.) Despite the improved strength of the game in South Africa, the tourists still dominated, remaining unbeaten and winning the test series 3–1. South Africa, however, recorded their first international victory in the last test.

Tour record	
Played	21
Won	18
Lost	3
Drawn	-
For	333
Against	90

Test-series record	
Played	4
Won	3
Lost	1
Drawn	-
For	38
Against	23

Australia (1899)

In 1899, the Brish Isles were scheduled to tour South Africa, but with the outbreak of the Anglo–Boer War the tour was quickly cancelled and the destination changed. The 1899 British Isles squad to Australia was the first represented by players from all four home unions and featured at least one 'capped' international from each union. The 21-man squad featured seven international players (two English, two Irish, two Scottish and one Welsh) and was captained by London clergyman, Reverend Matthew Mullineux. He was a remarkable man who both arranged and managed the entire tour and to this day remains the only British Lions skipper never to have been capped by his country. Such was his leadership that he dropped himself following the first test defeat and handed the captaincy to Frank Stout – a decision that ultimately led to the test series victory. The tour started poorly for the tourists when they comprehensively lost the first test, followed by a loss to Queensland. There were mumblings from the Australian rugby public about the failing strength of this squad. However, this only served to motivate the British Isles, who upped their game, lost only once more and won the test series 3–1.

Tour record	
Played	22
Won	11
Lost	8
Drawn	3
For	231
Against	138

Test-series record	
Played	3
Won	-
Lost	1
Drawn	2
For	10
Against	18

South Africa (1903)

The 1903 British Isles tour to South Africa heralded a dominant era in South African rugby, which had improved immeasurably since the 1896 tour. Having lost just one of their previous 41 matches in South Africa, the tourists were this time to leave South African shores, having managed to win only half of their 22 matches, and this included losing the test series, for the first time. The tour was managed by Johnny Hammond who had featured in all three tours to South Africa (in 1891 as a player and in 1896 as captain), and was captained by Scotsman, Mark Morrison. The tourists were simply not good enough to compete and lost their first three matches in bruising encounters. Their backline in particular lacked the skills to counter the running of the South

Africans on the hard African fields. As such, much hope was pinned on the pack dominating. This, however, never materialised, as the South Africans began to make a name for themselves as tough scrummagers and completely dominated the Lions' pack. Despite losing the three-test series 0–1, it was a lot tighter than the score suggests, with the first two tests being drawn 10–10 and 0–0 respectively. The final and decisive game of the series was lost 0–8 by the British at a muddy Newlands – the first time the Lions had lost a series in South Africa. The tourists returned home unaware that it would take a Lions team another 78 years from their 1896 triumph to win a series again on South African soil.

Tour record	
Played	19
Won	16
Lost	2
Drawn	1
For	287
Against	84

Test-series record	
Played	4
Won	3
Lost	1
Drawn	-
For	53
Against	12

Australia and New Zealand (1904)

Not more than 12 months passed before the British Isles once again headed out for another tour – this time to Australia and New Zealand, with a series of test matches played for the first time in Australia and a single test against New Zealand. The voyage was arduous, and when the Lions team finally arrived at Auckland harbour two of the tour party had to be carried off the boat due to chronic seasickness. The tour was led by Scotsman, David Bedell-Sivright, who brought an element of experience to the side, having toured to South Africa the previous year. Unfortunately, the squad had not been selected to represent the very best of British rugby, with the forwards falling well short of the level required to compete against the robust emerging southern-hemisphere nations. However, their backline simply oozed class, with the likes of Percy Bush and William Llewellyn running rings around their Australian counterparts. The British Isles crushed the Australians in the test series 3–0, remaining unbeaten in Australia. It was a different matter in New Zealand, however, where opposition was a lot stiffer with the British Isles managing to win just three of their six matches, losing the only international. Future tours down under would follow a similar pattern – with matches in Australia won comfortably before playing New Zealand, with the test series inevitably lost.

Photograph of the crowd and scoreboard (note the advertising!) on the western bank of the old Athletic Park in Wellington prior to the 1904 international between New Zealand and the British Isles, won 9-3 by New Zealand. *Photo*: New Zealand Rugby Museum

Above left: The first-ever touring side from the United Kingdom, termed 'Great Britain', to the southern hemisphere, seen here on the boat to Australia and New Zealand in 1888. *Photo*: Frédéric Humbert/www.flickr.com/photos/rugby_pioneers/creative commons license

Above: The 1891 British Isles tourists to South Africa playing against South Africa at Newlands in the shadow of Table Mountain in Cape Town, a match won 4-0 by the tourists. *Photo*: Frédéric Humbert/www.flickr.com/photos/rugby_pioneers/creative commons license

Left: The 'founders' of British and Irish Lions Rugby: Alfred Shaw and Arthur Shrewsbury (standing fourth from left) with the first-ever touring side to the southern hemisphere in 1888. Tour captain Bob Seddon (standing far right) tragically drowned while on tour. *Photo*: Frédéric Humbert/www.flickr.com/photos/rugby_pioneers/creative commons license

Below left: Kick-off for the second test of the 1891 British Isles series versus South Africa in Kimberley. Played on a rock-hard field the British Isles won 3-0 to secure their first series win over South Africa. *Photo*: Frédéric Humbert/www.flickr.com/photos/rugby_pioneers/creative commons license

Above: The British Isles touring side to Australia and New Zealand, 1904. *Photo*: Frédéric Humbert/www.flickr.com/photos/rugby_pioneers/creative commons license

Left: The 1924 British Lions in South Africa, the first to be termed 'The Lions'. Dressed in their training gear the side struggled in South Africa and lost the test series 0-3 to the Springboks. *Photo*: Frédéric Humbert/www.flickr.com/photos/rugby_pioneers/creative commons license

Centre: All Black scrumhalf Frederick Roberts kicks a conversion during the first international against the British Lions in Dunedin, 1908. He is watched by teammate Charles Seeling and referee J. Duncan of New Zealand. *Photo*: New Zealand Rugby Museum

Bottom: Action from the first test of the 1904 series between Australia (light jerseys) and British Lions (hooped jerseys) in Sydney. The match was won 17-0 by the Lions and the series 3-0. *Photo*: Frédéric Humbert/www.flickr.com/photos/rugby_pioneers/creative commons license

Tour record	
Played	26
Won	16
Lost	9
Drawn	1
For	313
Against	201

Test-series record	
Played	3
Won	-
Lost	2
Drawn	1
For	8
Against	64

New Zealand and Australia (1908)

It was back to the Antipodes four years later under the leadership of the first Welsh captain, Arthur 'Boxer' Harding. The structure of the tour had changed, with more emphasis on competing against New Zealand. In the past, tours had centred on Australia, with matches in New Zealand tacked on, but following the All Blacks tour of the United Kingdom in 1905/1906, the British took note of the tourists' form and sailed directly to New Zealand in 1908, bypassing Australia, opting for a few matches there on the way home – none international. A full three-test series was played against New Zealand. The 28-man squad was made up entirely of Englishmen and Welshmen, this because the Irish and Scots had declined to participate in a tour which they saw mainly as a venture to prevent rugby league growth in Australia. As such, the team – since referred to as the 'Anglo-Welsh' – played in broad white and red hoops, representing the two nations' respective colours. The team was documented as a 'distinctively gentlemanly lot sent to convince the Kiwis of the virtues of the eight-man scrum and of pure amateurism'. They failed on both counts. The seven-man All Blacks scrum dominated and the Anglo-Welsh struggled to gel and compete at the backline, lacking the class of 1904. They managed just nine wins in New Zealand and lost the test series, despite drawing the second test, due mainly to the horrific Wellington weather conditions. They also failed to impress in Australia, despite lacklustre opposition. The team returned home knowing that in future they would need the full support of all four home unions to compete.

Action from the second test in Wellington of the 1908 series between New Zealand and the British Lions. Horrific weather conditions saw to it that the game ended in a low-scoring 3-3 draw. *Photo*: New Zealand Rugby Museum

Tour record	
Played	6
Won	6
Lost	-
Drawn	-
For	213
Against	31

'Test'-series record	
Played	1
Won	1
Lost	-
Drawn	-
For	28
Against	3

Argentina (1910)

This was a unique year for British Isles rugby in that they undertook two tours to the southern hemisphere in the same year. With Tom Smyth's side setting sail for South Africa, John Raphael of England led another squad on a maiden tour to Argentina for six matches, which included Argentina's first international – although not recognised by the British Isles as a capped test. However, the side was not as representative as the team that set sail for Cape Town and was billed on departure as the English Rugby Union team, but was correctly denoted as the Combined British team by their hosts upon arrival, as it contained three Scotsmen. The team remained unbeaten, encountering limited opposition and beating Argentina 28–3 in the 'test'.

Tour record	
Played	24
Won	13
Lost	8
Drawn	3
For	290
Against	236

Test-series record	
Played	3
Won	1
Lost	2
Drawn	-
For	23
Against	38

South Africa and Rhodesia (1910)

The 1910 tour to South Africa was a landmark for the British Isles, as this was the first under the official umbrella of all four home unions – basically, British Isles touring rugby as we know it today was born on this tour. This was an indication to their hosts that the British Isles were taking a more serious approach and not simply regarding it as an opportunity to spread their game to the colonies. The squad of 26 contained a record 12 internationals in the forwards, indicating the seriousness of intent in taking on the tough Springbok pack. It was an extremely physical tour, with four replacements having to be called upon as it progressed. These included Tom Richards – an Australian international player working on the South African gold mines at the time. He had toured the British Isles with Australia in 1908 and his inclusion in the British Isles squad was justified by the dubious fact that he had played a season in England with Bristol. The tour was captained by an Irishman, Dr Tom Smyth, for the first time. His team put up a much sterner challenge than their 1903 predecessors. The British Isles went down 1–2 in a tightly fought series, losing the final test 5–21 and having to play 70 minutes with just 14 players after they lost their fullback to injury. World War I interrupted further tours and it would be 14 years before they would sail again.

Tour record	
Played	21
Won	9
Lost	9
Drawn	3
For	175
Against	155

Test-series record	
Played	4
Won	-
Lost	3
Drawn	1
For	15
Against	43

South Africa and Rhodesia (1924)

On this tour the British Isles were nicknamed the Lions for the first time, coined by the South African media because of the heraldic beast portrayed on the team's official ties. From now on they would be known simply as the Lions. But the team struggled on the field and finished the tour with the dubious reputation as the worst British Isles side to ever have toured South Africa, having won just 9 of their 21 matches and none of the internationals. The team was captained by Englishman, Ronald Cove-Smith, who found it difficult to lift players against a Springbok team on the rise. British rugby was at a low ebb and the hard grounds of South Africa took their toll, often forcing the tourists to field players out of position (backs among forwards and vice versa) in an attempt to field 15 men. All three fullbacks and goal kickers were injured at the start of the tour and with no recognised kicker, they managed just eight successful kicks at goal in 24 matches – the worst record in their history. The side was eventually forced to call on an Irishman who happened to be living in Johannesburg to play four games for them to help alleviate the injury problem.

Tour record	
Played	9
Won	9
Lost	-
Drawn	-
For	295
Against	9

'Test'-series record	
Played	4
Won	4
Lost	-
Drawn	-
For	160
Against	3

Argentina (1927)

Following the success of the 1910 tour to Argentina, a second tour was undertaken in the hope of further developing the game to establish another rugby powerhouse in the southern hemisphere. The touring team comprised players from all four home unions, with the 23-man squad captained by Scotsman, David MacMyn. The tour was sponsored by the River Plate Union and paid for by donations and fundraising. It was a massive success for the tourists, who faced no real opposition in the nine matches, scoring 295 points to just nine. They easily won the four internationals (37–0, 46–0, 34–3 and 43–0), although caps were not awarded by the Lions. Despite the one-sided nature of the tour, they played to capacity crowds with the organisers turning a handsome profit. It was clear that the popularity of the game had spread across Argentina.

Tour record	
Played	27
Won	20
Lost	7
Drawn	-
For	620
Against	279

Test-series record	
Played	5
Won	1
Lost	4
Drawn	-
For	39
Against	59

New Zealand and Australia (1930)

Once again, the Lions bypassed Australia en route to New Zealand, but this time granted the Australians an international fixture on their way home. Little had changed from the last tour, with New Zealand an even more daunting prospect than before. The problem of player availability severely hindered the squad selection: more than one hundred players were approached before 29 eventually set sail – 16 Englishmen, seven Welshmen, five Irishmen and a lone Scot – under the captaincy of Englishman, Doug Prentice. Injury took its toll, with vice-captain, Wilfred Sobey, being so badly injured in the opening match that he retired from the tour. Red jerseys, white shorts, blue socks and green stocking tops were worn to represent each of the four home unions. New Zealand still played in white jerseys in the first test to avoid clashing with the Lions' older dark-blue strip until they changed their colours later in the tour. New Zealand's tactic of playing a rover proved crucial. (A rover is essentially a fourth loose forward who does not pack down in the 3-2-3 scrum formation and whose role it is to harass the scrumhalf, a tactic that starved the Lions of possession.) This so enraged the Lions' manager, James Baxter, that he condemned the All Blacks' rover as 'nothing more than a cheat' and upon returning to England, he had the IRFB rewrite the laws of scrummaging and eventually ban the practice outright. The Lions lost the test series 1–3 after winning the first game and left New Zealand for a series of seven matches in Australia where they failed to win the international, going down narrowly by 5–6 and then losing heavily 3–28 to New South Wales. It was a disappointing end to a tour that could have produced so much more.

Tour record	
Played	10
Won	10
Lost	-
Drawn	-
For	399
Against	12

'Test'-series record	
Played	1
Won	1
Lost	-
Drawn	-
For	23
Against	0

Argentina (1936)

Nine years after comprehensively sweeping aside all before them, the Lions returned to Argentina with the hope that they would receive stiffer opposition in the ten scheduled matches. It was not to be, as the team achieved greater success, scoring 399 points to just 12 against, and conceding but one try. They won the single international 23–0, again with caps not awarded by the Lions for the fixture. The 23-man squad was captained by Englishman, Bernard Gadney, and comprised ten internationals (including the famous Englishman of Russian heritage, Prince Alexander Obolensky), but it was not a truly representative squad, with no Welshmen included. It was a disappointment for the tourists to not face any strong opposition and it was clear that the game was not improving apace with the popularity in Argentina. This was the last Lions tour to Argentina until 2005.

Tour record	
Played	24
Won	17
Lost	7
Drawn	-
For	414
Against	284

Test-series record	
Played	3
Won	2
Lost	1
Drawn	-
For	36
Against	61

South Africa and Rhodesia (1938)

If ever there was a bleak prospect of touring success, then the 1938 Lions tour to South Africa was one of them, as the Springboks were unofficially world champions, following their series victory over New Zealand the year before. The Lions were seen as nothing more than fodder for the *Bokke*. However, the Lions proved otherwise, losing 1–2 in arguably the most entertaining test series contested between the two sides, with the possible exception of the 2009 tour, which was to produce surprisingly similar results. Captained by Irishman Sam Walker, the tour proved a great success for the Lions, who, despite losing the test series, won 17 of their 24 matches. In the test series they lost the first 12–26 in a game described by Danie Craven as 'the greatest test match ever played by South Africa', and in the following test they withered in the blistering 36°C Port Elizabeth heat, losing 3–19 in a match that came to be known as the 'Tropical Test'. In the final test the Lions turned a 3–13 half-time deficit into an famous 21–16 victory, so taking at least a share of the spoils and the honours. This would be the last Lions tour for 12 years, as World War II broke out in 1939.

Left: Lineout action from the second test between New Zealand and the British Lions in Christchurch, 1930. New Zealand went on to win by 13-10 and level the four-match series at one apiece. *Photo*: New Zealand Rugby Museum

Above: New Zealand centre Mark Nicholls drops a crucial goal during the third test of the 1930 series against the British Lions in Auckland. New Zealand won the test 15-10 and the series 3-1. *Photo*: New Zealand Rugby Museum

Below: Lineout action from the fourth test between New Zealand and the British Lions in 1930, won 22-8 by New Zealand in Wellington.
Photo: New Zealand Rugby Museum

Tour record	
Played	29
Won	22
Lost	6
Drawn	1
For	580
Against	205

Test-series record	
Played	6
Won	2
Lost	3
Drawn	1
For	63
Against	43

New Zealand and Australia (1950)

The first Lions team to tour after World War II was captained by Irishman Karl Mullen, and despite losing the four-test series 0–3, they could count themselves extremely unlucky not to have won the series, since all the tests were lost by very narrow margins. In the 1950s, this became a common pattern for the Lions, who never actually won a series but thrilled crowds with their style of rugby (especially the backline) that has left lasting memories to this day. To prevent a clash with their hosts' black jerseys, the Lions wore a new red jersey, replacing the navy blue. The tour introduced Irishman Jacky Kyle to New Zealand. He went on to be named among New Zealand Rugby Almanac's five players of the year along with Welsh winger Ken Jones. The backline was packed with talent and with the Welsh centre combination of Jack Matthews and Bleddyn Williams, the Lions played some exhilarating rugby. However, the All Blacks pack was much stronger and starved the dangerous Lions' backline of possession, pressing home their superiority to narrowly win the series. The All Blacks salvaged a draw in the dying moments of the first test after the Lions had led 9–3. In the second, the Lions struggled with 14 men after losing loose forward, Bill McKay to concussion, and lost the third and fourth tests by three points apiece. It was a disappointing end to a fine tour; the results were not a fair reflection of the closely fought contests. On the home leg, they played six matches in Australia, which included two comprehensive test wins, only to lose their last match of the tour to a New South Wales combination team.

Tour record	
Played	24
Won	18
Lost	5
Drawn	1
For	418
Against	271

Test-series record	
Played	4
Won	2
Lost	2
Drawn	-
For	49
Against	75

South Africa and Rhodesia (1955)

The 1955 tour was one of the most exhilarating in history and yielded an unprecedented 24 tries in the four-test series, which was eventually shared 2–2, making it the Lions' most successful tour to South Africa since 1896. It was the first time a Lions team toured by aeroplane, which significantly reduced travelling time. The team set new standards in dismantling the aura of the seemingly invincible Springboks, endearing themselves to their hosts at the same time. Superbly captained by Irishman Robin Thompson, the Lions' game was again dominated by their backline, as it has been in 1950, only this time they were even better. Welsh flyhalf Cliff Morgan was the kingpin of the backline, setting loose the English centre pairing of Jeff Butterfield and Phil Davies with Irish winger Tony O'Reilly (who turned 19 on the tour) on the outside to score a tour record of 16 tries. The tourists' game plan was simply to run the ball at all opportunities. This brought them victory in the first test in what is perhaps the greatest British Lions test match, which they narrowly won thanks to a last-second missed conversion by Springbok fullback Jack van der Schyff. The match produced nine tries in total, with the Lions running out 23–22 victors. Springbok backlash was severe as Tom van Vollenhoven scored a hat-trick in the second test to steer South Africa to a 25–9 win, only for the Lions to bounce back in a tighter third international to win by 9–6. Potentially facing their first series defeat since 1896, the Springboks refused to go down without a fight and comprehensively won the fourth test 22–8, thus ending one of the greatest Lions tours of all time.

Tour record	
Played	33
Won	27
Lost	6
Drawn	-
For	842
Against	353

Test-series record	
Played	6
Won	3
Lost	3
Drawn	-
For	83
Against	66

Australia, New Zealand and Canada (1959)

For the fourth successive tour, the 1959 Lions were again led by an Irishman, this time Ronnie Dawson, in a tour that included two games in Canada on the way home. The tour structure changed slightly, with the team reverting to playing in Australia prior to New Zealand. Again, the strategy of the Lions' game was to run the ball at all costs, with experienced players from the 1955 tour ensuring their continued success, thrilling the crowds once again. This was evident, with Tony O'Reilly easing past his 1955 record of 16 tries by scoring an amazing 22, closely followed by Peter Jackson with 19 – records which will surely never be broken. Following a 2–0 series win over Australia,

All Blacks captain and centre Ron Elvidge scores against the British Lions in the first test of the 1950 series in Dunedin. The match was drawn 9-9 but New Zealand went on to win the four-test series 3-0.
Photo: New Zealand Rugby Museum

Action from the first test between New Zealand and the Lions at Dunedin in 1950 showing the Lions winger breaking blindside from a scrum. The match was drawn 9-9.
Photo: New Zealand Rugby Museum

All Black legend Don Clarke dives over for a crucial try during the second test against the British Lions in Wellington in 1959. *Photo*: New Zealand Rugby Museum

Lions captain Ronnie Dawson of Ireland is under pressure from a seriously intent Kiwi captain Wilson Whineray (at right), during the 1959 series won 3-1 by New Zealand. *Photo*: New Zealand Rugby Museum.

Left: Lock Nev MacEwan secures lineout possesion during the first test of the 1959 series against the British Lions in Dunedin, controversially won 18-17 by New Zealand. *Photo*: New Zealand Rugby Museum.

Below: Fullback Don Clarke dives over to score the winning try in the second test of the 1959 series versus the British Lions in Wellington. This score took the game to 11-8 for New Zealand and remained the winning score. *Photo*: New Zealand Rugby Museum

Above: Captains Wilson Whineray of New Zealand and Ronnie Dawson of the British Lions lead their sides onto the pitch at Wellington for the second test of the 1959 series, won 3-1 by New Zealand.
Photo: New Zealand Rugby Museum

the Lions felt confident they could take on the might of New Zealand, only to be unlucky yet again and lose the series 1–3. It started with one of the most infamous Lions defeats when a world-record six penalty goals from All Black Don Clarke eclipsed four tries by the Lions for New Zealand to clinch the match 18–17. Another narrow 8–11 loss in the second test saw New Zealand seal the series in the third in Christchurch, winning 22–8, with the All Blacks pack dominating all facets of play. The tourists lifted themselves, however, for the fourth international to secure their second-ever win over the All Blacks and were able to leave New Zealand's shores with a modest share of the spoils and honour intact.

Tour record	
Played	25
Won	16
Lost	5
Drawn	4
For	401
Against	208

Test record	
Played	4
Won	-
Lost	3
Drawn	1
For	20
Against	48

South Africa, Rhodesia and Kenya (1962)

Following the drab, 'win-at-all-costs' victory by the Barbarians over South Africa in 1961, which centred around a massive pack, the Lions decided not to opt for a running game, but rather a massive set of forwards in order to counter the Boks' pack. However, the Springboks' scrum was more formidable than ever and up for the challenge. For the first time, the tour included a stopover match in Nairobi against a Kenyan/East African side, but the real business involved standing up to the Springboks' power. Despite failing to win a single test, the Lions came desperately close, drawing the first 3–3 but succumbing 0–3 in the next to Springbok flyhalf Keith Oxlee and 3–8 in the third. With this the series was lost, although the Lions could well have won had they taken their chances and not fallen victim to poor refereeing – specifically in the second test when a clear pushover try by the Lions was not awarded as the referee was unsighted. With the series wrapped up, the fourth test was a much looser affair, with the Springboks running riot, winning by 34–14 in Bloemfontein, with Springbok winger Mannetjies Roux in fine form, scoring two magnificent tries.

Tour record	
Played	35
Won	23
Lost	9
Drawn	3
For	524
Against	345

Test-series record	
Played	6
Won	2
Lost	4
Drawn	-
For	74
Against	87

Australia, New Zealand and Canada (1966)

Before the tour departed, the 1966 Lions squad was being talked about as one of the best ever. However, 1966 proved to be one of the British Lions' worst years, as they struggled in New Zealand under the leadership of Scotsman Mike Campbell-Lamerton. There was no doubt that the squad had the class and potential to beat the New Zealanders, with the likes of Mike Gibson and Willie-John McBride in the ranks but once again the Lions were dominated up front by their opponents. The tour started well with the Lions being unbeaten in Australia and winning the test series 2–0, but on arriving in New Zealand, they were brought down to earth with a bump, losing their first game to lowly Southland. They went on to lose three of their first five games, including a 6–20 walloping at the hands of Wellington. It became apparent that the Lions were out of their depth in a nation where rugby was stronger than ever, following the drubbing the All Blacks had inflicted on the Springboks the year before. The test series was a complete disaster: the Lions went down 0–4 and all by substantial margins. It was a dejected, weary team that left New Zealand to play twice in Canada en route home, with yet another defeat against British Columbia in Vancouver adding insult to injury for the Lions, despite an unconvincing win over Canada a few days later. It was a tour quickly forgotten by Lions supporters as they looked ahead for an improvement in 1968.

Tour record	
Played	20
Won	15
Lost	4
Drawn	1
For	377
Against	181

Test-series record	
Played	4
Won	3
Lost	-
Drawn	1
For	38
Against	61

South Africa and Rhodesia (1968)

Much was anticipated before the Lions tour to South Africa in 1968, which included such famous names as Gareth Edwards, Barry John, Mike Gibson, Gerald Davies and Willie-John McBride. Once again, however, the tourists left South Africa dejected, with nothing to show except for a draw in the second test. The hard fields of South Africa took their toll on the team and injuries ravaged the side, with Edwards, John, Gibson and Davies barely featuring in the tests because of injury. The forwards once again battled up front against one of the strongest Springbok packs in history, with the legendary Frik du Preez playing a blinder of a test series and scoring one of the greatest tries ever against a Lions team in the first test. The try tally following the test series endorsed the Springboks' superiority as they outscored the tourists by eight tries to one; it was only thanks to Kiernan's boot that the Lions made any impression at all, scoring 35 of his team's 38 points in the series. The 1968 tour ended a dismal era in the Lions' history. For an entire decade they had failed to win a single international against either New Zealand or South Africa. Few then could anticipate the rich harvest the 1970s were to yield.

Did you know: During the 1974 Lions tour of South Africa the Lions were playing the Orange Free State in Bloemfontein on a hot June day on a hard field in a tightly fought contest. A one-eyed Orange Free State player was giving the Lions a working over, dominating the lineouts – a situation captain McBride could not tolerate. The esteemed Lions leader decided the only way to eliminate the threat was to close his other eye. So McBride ordered his men to punch the lanky Afrikaner in his good eye during the next play and sure enough, the South African had to leave the field, blinded. This decision saw the Lions through to a narrow 11–9 victory ... on the blind side.

Tour record	
Played	26
Won	23
Lost	2
Drawn	1
For	580
Against	231

Test-series record	
Played	4
Won	2
Lost	1
Drawn	1
For	48
Against	42

New Zealand and Australia (1971)

Few would have thought that the Lions of 1971 would leave New Zealand victorious, after the team lost their first game against Queensland in Brisbane. As it was the team would lose just once more – against New Zealand in the second test. The team was led by the Welsh duo of captain John Dawes and coach Carwyn James who directed the Lions so memorably to impose a series defeat on New Zealand for the first time in history. British and Irish rugby was on a high, with several fine players from each of the home unions featuring in the squad – most notably from Wales who were to dominated European rugby in the 1970s, winning a Grand Slam that same year. For once, the Lions were able to field a pack that could match the class of their backline, which performed outstandingly with the wealth of possession. As a result Welsh flyhalf Barry John was able to commandingly marshall his backline – turning him into an instant star as a result of his genius – and take his team to a 2–1 test-series victory. John plundered 170 points, scoring in every game he played in. The Lions narrowly won the first test 9–3 but were convincingly outplayed in the second as the All Blacks bounced back to win 22–12, with forward Ian Kirkpatrick scoring one of the greatest individual tries of all time for the Kiwis, rivalling that of Frik du Preez's in 1968. In the third test John took complete control, dazzling the All Blacks and scoring ten of the team's 13 points in their 13–3 win. With this victory the Lions could not lose the series but it could be drawn, making the fourth test a needle affair. It was a tight contest in which the Lions found themselves 11–14 down deep into the second half. Then up stepped fullback J.P.R. Williams to kick the most audacious drop goal of his life from 45 metres out and tie the scores at 14 apiece, ensuring a series victory for the Lions. History had been made: the New Zealanders had at last been defeated at home in a series, something that hadn't happened since 1949.

Tour record	
Played	22
Won	21
Lost	-
Drawn	1
For	729
Against	207

Test-series record	
Played	4
Won	3
Lost	-
Drawn	1
For	79
Against	34

South Africa and Rhodesia (1974)

In 1974, the British Government wrote to the Lions requesting them not to tour apartheid South Africa. The Lions' hotel in London was stormed by protestors before their departure, but they stuck to their guns and toured. It turned out to be a welcome sporting decision, as the tour was one of the most successful in British Lions' history, with captain Willie-John McBride emulating the success of the 1891 side as they swept through South Africa unbeaten. Unbelievably, the mighty Springboks were well and truly crushed by an awesome Lions outfit that outscored them by ten tries to one in the test series. No team has ever achieved such a convincing series victory in South Africa since – and is unlikely to either. This was quite simply the greatest Lions team of all time. Their game plan was simple: attack and dominate the Springboks at the heart of their game – the forwards – even if it meant using illegal tactics. In this regard, the Lions' '99' call became notorious. When a player called out '99' he was soliciting mass retaliation from the entire team against perceived foul or dirty play. It did little to help the Lions' image, but it rattled their traditional bullying enemies and proved that a side that avoids physical or even dirty play will inevitably lose. Once achieved, the stellar backline had every chance to run at the opposition, with the team averaging 30 points per game. The Lions pack remained unchanged for the first three tests, while the Springboks panicked and chopped and changed their team from one defeat to the next: they used a total of 33 players in the series, a policy that surely contributed to the Boks' downfall. The first test was won 12–3 at a muddy Newlands, with the Lions being vociferously cheered by a large contingent of *nie blankes* ('non-whites') in the stands. The second test resulted in the Springboks recording their largest defeat in their history of 9–28 (five tries to zero). The third test was always going to be a very physical affair, as the Springboks were unlikely to lie down meekly and succumb to their first series defeat to the Lions since 1896. The point was illustrated when they picked bulky number 8 Gerrie Sonnekus as their scrumhalf. It was a tough, dirty test with the Lions using the '99' call several times, but in the end the Lions won 26–9, thereby securing their greatest test-series victory. Flying winger J.J. Williams became the first player to score two tries in successive tests against the Boks. The Lions were denied victory in the final test which ended in a controversial 13–13 draw, but nonetheless remained unbeaten in South Africa. Only one side had ever previously achieved this: their 1891 counterparts.

Tour record	
Played	26
Won	21
Lost	5
Drawn	-
For	607
Against	320

Test-series record	
Played	4
Won	1
Lost	3
Drawn	-
For	41
Against	54

New Zealand and Fiji (1977)

The 1977 Lions team arrived in New Zealand with as much hope of winning the series as their 1971 counterparts. Led by Welshman Phil Bennett, the team certainly had the talent to win but were soon to learn about All Black retribution: it became apparent that emulating the 1971 Lions was going to be a tough ask. The tour was beset with a series of on- and off-field issues and is one that most prefer to forget, after the Lions narrowly lost the test series 1–3. They were an experienced outfit and adopted a strategy of forward play in the wake of one of the wettest New Zealand winters in memory. The Lions lost just one provincial fixture and after narrowly losing the first test 12–16, they bounced back with a 13–9 victory in the second. New Zealand were too powerful in the third, scoring three tries to one to win 19–7 in preparation for the decisive final test that the tourists had to win in order to square the series. Indeed, it was a game they should have won but in a nail-biting finish, All Blacks eighthman, Laurie Knight, scored in injury time to win the match 10–9 and the All Blacks the series 3–1. It was a bitter ending for the Lions, as they deserved to share the series. A match in Fiji on the way home did little to ease their pain, losing this test 21–25, (no caps were awarded for this match by the tourists). Flyhalf Phil Bennett went on to describe this tour as one of the lowest moments of his career.

Tour record	
Played	18
Won	15
Lost	3
Drawn	-
For	401
Against	244

Test-series record	
Played	4
Won	1
Lost	3
Drawn	-
For	68
Against	77

South Africa (1980)

The 1980 Lions tour to South Africa received the same negative attention as the 1974 one, with the political situation even more fraught. However, due to the USSR's invasion of Afghanistan, political and media attention was briefly distracted and the team managed to sneak away. As the 1977 Lions had learned in New Zealand, so the 1980 Lions learned in South Africa. The hosts wanted revenge. This was the first of the Lions' short tours – a whistle-stop 18 matches in just ten weeks. Admirably captained by Englishman Bill Beaumont, the squad was decimated by injuries, with a record 15 replacements in the ten weeks. The tourists won all 14 of their provincial games and were a good match for the Springbok pack in the tests but could not compete with the pace of the Bok backline and loose forwards. The opening test was a thriller, which the Lions lost 22–26 in the dying minutes, ultimately outscored by five tries to one: only the boot of Irish flyhalf Tony Ward kept them in the match with a record haul of 18 points. The second test was a similar affair, producing some top-quality rugby and six tries in total as the

Left: All Blacks lock forward Colin Meads scores a spectacular try against the 1966 British Lions in Wellington, leaving five desperate Lions defenders in his wake. New Zealand went on to win the match by 16-12 and ultimately the series 4-0.
Photo: New Zealand Rugby Museum

Below: New Zealand captain Brian Lochore and British Lions captain Mike Campbell-Lamerton lead their respective sides out for the first test of the 1966 series in Dunedin. The match was won 20-3 by New Zealand and the series 4-0. *Photo*: New Zealand Rugby Museum

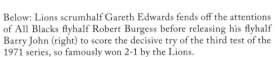

Below: Lions scrumhalf Gareth Edwards fends off the attentions of All Blacks flyhalf Robert Burgess before releasing his flyhalf Barry John (right) to score the decisive try of the third test of the 1971 series, so famously won 2-1 by the Lions.
Photo: New Zealand Rugby Museum

Legendary Irish and Lions lock forward Willie-John McBride secures and releases hard-earned lineout possession for his backline against New Zealand the 1971 series. *Photo*: New Zealand Rugby Museum

All Blacks scrumhalf Sid Going scores in the first test of the 1977 series against the British Lions in Wellington. New Zealand won the match 16-12 and the series 3-1. *Photo*: New Zealand Rugby Museum

Lions flyhalf and captain Phil Bennett kicks under pressure from All Blacks flanker Kevin Eveleigh during the second test of the 1977 series in Christchurch, won 13-9 by the Lions.
Photo: New Zealand Rugby Museum

Springboks triumphed 26–19 in Bloemfontein. The third international was crucial but unfortunately did not generate the same quality of rugby as the first two because of the horrific Port Elizabeth weather. The Lions led for most of the match and dominated throughout, but in the 70th minute lost concentration as a quick lineout by the Springboks led to a Gerrie Germishuys try in the corner, locking the scores at 10–10. This left mercurial Bok flyhalf Naas Botha with the unenviable task of kicking the series-winning conversion from the touchline in the driving rain. Unflappable, the little general slotted the kick, winning the match 12–10 and sealing the series. The Lions bounced back in the final test in Pretoria when Naas Botha had an off-day with the boot, the series finishing 3–1 to South Africa.

Tour record	
Played	18
Won	12
Lost	6
Drawn	-
For	478
Against	276

Test-series record	
Played	4
Won	-
Lost	4
Drawn	-
For	26
Against	78

New Zealand (1983)

One of the worst tours in the history of Lions rugby was attributed to the 1983 side led by Irishman Ciaran Fitzgerald, which failed to win a single international and lost two provincial matches. Numerous excuses were given, including a tough itinerary, injuries and poor selection, but in the end the 1983 Lions were simply unable to physically compete against a beefy New Zealand side. The All Blacks were riding a crest, following series victories against South Africa and France in 1981 and Australia in 1982. They dominated the Lions, despite being lucky to win the first test 16–12. The second test was played in a howling gale, with the All Blacks using the weather to their advantage to win 9–0. The third was won by New Zealand, despite being outscored two tries to one. In the final test, the Lions were completely outclassed, losing by the record scoreline of 6–38, which included a brilliant Stu Wilson hat-trick to bury the Lions and send them home without a victory. To this day, this is the heaviest defeat in the history of Lions rugby.

Tour record	
Played	12
Won	11
Lost	1
Drawn	-
For	360
Against	192

Test-series record	
Played	3
Won	2
Lost	1
Drawn	-
For	50
Against	60

Australia (1989)

The Lions were initially scheduled to tour South Africa in 1986, but the tour was hastily cancelled due to political pressure. The Lions quickly rescheduled and played instead on British soil for just the second time, to commemorate the centenary anniversary of the IRFB by taking on a World XV team which beat them 15–7. Three years later the Lions toured Australia. Following the success of the 1984 Grand Slam Wallabies, Australian rugby was granted the recognition it deserved and for the first time in 90 years received an exclusive Lions tour. From this tour on, all Lions test series would consist of three tests and not four. The team was captained by the Scot Finlay Calder, with much expected of his side. They went on to win the series after being comprehensively beaten in the first international. The Lions' game plan focused on the strength and physicality of their pack. However, the Wallaby backline outplayed them in the first test to win well by 30–12. After this defeat, few gave the Lions much chance of winning the second test, but they triumphed in a very physical game 19–12, following an all-out brawl during the first scrum of the match. All hinged, therefore, on the decisive third test, with tensions running high. However, one of the most exciting matches in history ensued as the Lions triumphed 19–18, in no small part to one of the most cringe-worthy errors in rugby history when David Campese, in his in-goal area, gave away the decisive try to his opposite winger, Ieuan Evans. It was a famous Lions series victory.

Tour record	
Played	13
Won	7
Lost	6
Drawn	-
For	314
Against	285

Test-series record	
Played	3
Won	1
Lost	2
Drawn	-
For	51
Against	57

New Zealand (1993)

Captained by Scotsman Gavin Hastings and coached for the second time by fellow countryman Ian McGeechan, this Lions side, many believed, could emulate the achievements of their 1971 counterparts. It was the last tour by the Lions during the era of amateur rugby with a record 30 players selected to compete in the 13 games scheduled games. The core of the team consisted of Englishmen, following their success in the Five Nations in 1991 and 1992, but despite this the team struggled, with a series of losses by the midweek side. The first test was controversially lost 18–20 after Frank Bunce scored a try in the opening minutes and sealed by a contentious Grant Fox penalty goal late in the match. The Lions bounced back in the second test with a record 20–7 victory with the series reaching a climax in the third and crucial international in Auckland. However, it was not to be: the Lions did not compete well, despite leading by ten points at one stage. New Zealand outplayed them to win comprehensively by 30–13 and take the series 2–1.

Tour record	
Played	13
Won	11
Lost	2
Drawn	-
For	480
Against	278

Test-series record	
Played	3
Won	2
Lost	1
Drawn	-
For	59
Against	66

South Africa (1997)

For the first time in 17 years, the Lions toured South Africa after the international sports ban had been lifted in 1992. Unofficial world champions at the time, the Springboks were considered heavy favourites, considering the poor form displayed by the northern-hemisphere nations during the 1990s. With Martin Johnson as captain and Ian McGeechan again as coach, the Lions produced one of the finest displays of touring rugby, triumphing against Gary Teichmann's Springboks. The 2–1 series win will go down as one of the greatest tactical victories of all time, planned to the minutest detail by master strategist Ian McGeechan who was without doubt the most influential man on the tour, of either side. This was the first Lions tour of the professional era and many believed that these traditional tours would fade away in the new commercial age of rugby. However, the Lions' success ensured that their tours would endure, able to compete with the RWC in terms of popularity and support. They were to lose just one game and won the first test in Cape Town against all odds, comprehensively defeating the Boks 25–16, courtesy of a brilliant Matt Dawson try. In the second test the Lions convincingly sealed the series with a Jeremy Guscott drop goal to win 18–15, despite being outscored by three tries to nil. The Boks had not selected a goal kicker (when will they ever learn?) and paid for it dearly, missing six attempts at goal by three different kickers. South Africa won the final test 35–16, but Lions wrote their names into the history books.

Tour record	
Played	10
Won	7
Lost	3
Drawn	-
For	449
Against	184

Test-series record	
Played	3
Won	1
Lost	2
Drawn	-
For	66
Against	77

Australia (2001)

For the first time in the history of the Lions, a foreigner, Kiwi Graham Henry was appointed as coach. Captained for the second successive time by Englishman Martin Johnson, and following the success of the 1997 South African tour, much was expected of the 2001 Lions. However, the challenge of beating the world champions on their home turf was to prove too much and the 2001 Lions became the first team to lose a series to Australia. A rift developed between the midweek and the test teams, fanned by the media and despite going up 1–0, they were eventually to lose the series 1–2. The first test was comprehensively won 29–13 by the Lions, with centre Brian O'Driscoll scoring one of the greatest Lions tries with his individual effort from behind the halfway line. Leading 1–0, many expected the Lions to win the second test, but the Wallabies recovered from a 6–11 half-time deficit to win 35–14. With a convincing victory apiece behind each team, the rugby world focused on the decisive third test. It was one of the most exciting matches in Lions' history with the teams locked at 23–23 with 12 minutes remaining. However, two penalties by Matt Burke saw the world champs through to a test-series victory and 20,000 rather glum Lions fans prepared to pack their bags.

Tour record	
Played	11
Won	7
Lost	4
Drawn	-
For	328
Against	220

Test-series record	
Played	3
Won	-
Lost	3
Drawn	-
For	40
Against	107

New Zealand (2005)

Following the success of the 1997 tour to Australia and the narrow loss in 2001, once again much was expected of the 2005 Lions in New Zealand, a side coached by English World Cup victor, Clive Woodward. If he could win a World Cup, the British Lions' board had confidence that he could win a series in New Zealand. To ensure he achieved this, Woodward was afforded all the resources he could wish for. He selected Irish centre Brian O'Driscoll to captain the 51-man squad – the largest Lions touring squad and one that will surely never be exceeded. In addition to the players, 44 people made up the management and back-room staff, including a tour lawyer. Despite this massive party, the Lions struggled in New Zealand, with Woodward making some bizarre selections and the Lions losing a physical match against the Maoris. Skipper O'Driscoll was lost to injury in the first minute of the first test, following a controversial off-the-ball spear tackle by All Black Tana Umaga and Keven Mealamu, and the test was comprehensively lost 3–21. Changes were made for the second test but the All Blacks ran riot, with Dan Carter in superb form as he amassed a record 33 points in a 48–18 win over the Lions. The third test yielded yet another vast scoreline in favour of the Kiwis (38–19), with the All Blacks securing a resounding test-series victories over the Lions.

Tour record	
Played	10
Won	7
Lost	2
Drawn	1
For	309
Against	169

Test-series record	
Played	3
Won	1
Lost	2
Drawn	-
For	74
Against	63

South Africa (2009)

For the third consecutive Lions tour to South Africa the side was captained by a lock forward: Irishman Paul O'Connell. The 2009 tour was one of the most anticipated in living memory as the World Champion Springboks prepared to exact revenge upon the Lions who had whipped them in 1997. It was the shortest tour in Lions history with ten matches scheduled over five weeks but with every aspect covered by wily coach Ian McGeechan, on his seventh Lions tour: two as a player, four as head coach and one as an assistant coach. Early games were disappointing as hefty ticket prices, coupled with the withdrawal of South African national players from provincial matches, resulted in small crowds witnessing one-sided affairs as the Lions went unbeaten into the test series. However, this was quickly forgotten as the test matches produced some of the most scintillating, physical encounters in a Lions series, perhaps to date. The first test was won 26-21 by South Africa thanks to some curious selections by McGeechan. After drawing the midweek match with the Emerging Springboks in Cape Town, all eyes were on the second test in Pretoria. In an epic nailbiter the Lions squandered a 19-8 lead late in the second half to lose 25-28 after a last-gasp, 54-metre penalty goal by replacement Bok flyhalf Morné Steyn effectively put paid to the tourists' hopes of a series win. It was a bitter pill for the Lions to swallow: they had thrown everything they had into the game; indeed six injured players were hospitalised overnight – four Lions and two Springboks. Only a record-equalling, deserved 28-9 victory in Johannesburg provided any gloss for the Lions who lost the series 1-2. Interestingly, the Lions outscored the Springboks 74–63 in aggregated points over the three-test series. Nonetheless, as clichéd as it sounds, rugby was the winner on this tour, with the future of Lions rugby assured: fans can now now look forward to the Lions tour to Australia in 2013.

Individual milestones	Player	Details
Longest test career	Willie-John McBride	Career from 04/08/1962–27/07/1974 (11 years, 11 months & 24 days)
Youngest test player	Tony O'Reilly	19 years & 91 days vs South Africa on 06/08/1955 in Johannesburg
Oldest test player	Neil Back	36 years & 160 days vs New Zealand on 25/06/2005 in Christchurch

Captain Paul O'Connell jumping for a lineout ball during the 2009 British and Irish Lions series against the Springboks. *Photo*: Andrew de Klerk

British and Irish Lions test summary

Home tests played	
Played	1
Won	0
Lost	0
Drawn	1
Points for	25
Points against	25
Average score	25.00 / 25.00
% Win	0.00
% Lose	0.00
% Draw	100.00

Away tests played	
Played	104
Won	38
Lost	57
Drawn	9
Points for	1,196
Points against	1,429
Average score	11.50 / 13.74
% Win	36.54
% Lose	54.81
% Draw	8.65

Total tests played	
Played	105
Won	38
Lost	57
Drawn	10
Points for	1,221
Points against	1,454
Average score	11.63 / 13.85
% Win	36.19
% Lose	54.29
% Draw	9.52

Opponent	Played	Won	Lost	Drawn
South Africa	47	17	23	6
New Zealand	38	6	29	3
Australia	20	15	5	0
Argentina	1	0	0	1
	105	38	57	10

Career records

Most capped players

Player	Caps	Country	Career	Points				
				T	C	P	DG	Total
Willie-John McBride	17	Ireland	04/08/1962–27/07/1974	-	-	-	-	-
Dickie Jeeps	13	England	06/08/1955–25/08/1962	-	-	-	-	-
Graham Price	12	Wales	18/06/1977–16/07/1983	1	-	-	-	4
Mike Gibson	12	Ireland	16/07/1966–14/08/1971	-	-	-	-	-
Gareth Edwards	10	Wales	08/06/1968–27/07/1974	-	-	-	1	3
Tony O'Reilly	10	Ireland	06/08/1955–19/09/1959	6	-	-	-	18
Rhys Williams	10	Wales	06/08/1955–19/09/1959	-	-	-	-	-
Andy Irvine	9	Scotland	13/07/1974–12/07/1980	2	1	6	-	28
Syd Millar	9	Ireland	06/06/1959–22/06/1968	-	-	-	-	-

Most tests as captain			
No.	Player	Country	Period
6	Martin Johnson	England	1997–01
6	Ronny Dawson	Ireland	1959

Most points in tests by a player

No.	Player	Country	Tests	Career	T	C	P	DG
67	Jonny Wilkinson	England	6	30/06/2001–02/07/2005	1	7	16	-
66	Gavin Hastings	Scotland	6	01/07/1989–03/07/1993	1	1	20	-
53	Stephen Jones	Wales	6	25/06/2005–04/07/2009	-	7	12	1
44	Phil Bennett	Wales	8	08/06/1974–13/08/1977	1	2	10	2
41	Neil Jenkins	Wales	4	21/06/1997–07/07/2001	-	1	13	-
35	Tom Kiernan	Ireland	5	04/08/1962–27/07/1968	-	1	11	-
30	Barry John	Wales	5	08/06/1968–14/08/1971	1	3	5	2
30	Stewart Wilson	Scotland	5	04/06/1966–10/09/1966	-	6	6	-
28	Andy Irvine	Scotland	9	13/07/1974–12/07/1980	2	1	6	-
26	Ollie Campbell	Ireland	7	14/06/1980–16/07/1983	-	1	7	1
26	Lewis Jones	Wales	3	29/07/1950–26/08/1950	1	4	4	1

Most tries in tests by a player

No.	Player	Country	Tests	Career
6	Tony O'Reilly	Ireland	10	06/08/1955–19/09/1959
5	John Williams	Wales	7	08/06/1974–30/07/1977
4	Malcolm Price	Wales	5	13/06/1959–29/08/1959
4	Willie Llewellyn	Wales	4	02/07/1904–13/08/1904
3	Gerald Davies	Wales	5	13/07/1968–14/08/1971
3	Ken Jones	Wales	6	23/06/1962–16/07/1966
3	Jeff Butterfield	England	4	06/08/1955–24/09/1955
3	Carl Aarvold	England	5	21/06/1930–30/08/1930
3	Jack Spoors	England	3	06/08/1910–03/09/1910
3	Alfred Bucher	Scotland	3	24/06/1899–12/08/1899

Most conversions in tests by a player

No.	Player	Country	Tests	Career
7	Stephen Jones	Wales	6	25/06/2005–04/07/2009
7	Jonny Wilkinson	England	6	30/06/2001–02/07/2005
6	Stewart Wilson	Scotland	5	04/06/1966–10/09/1966
4	Angus Cameron	Scotland	2	06/08/1955–20/08/1955
4	Lewis Jones	Wales	3	29/07/1950–19/08/1950
4	Chas. Adamson	England	4	24/06/1899–12/08/1899
4	Fred Byrne	England	4	30/07/1896–05/09/1896
3	Barry John	Wales	5	08/06/1968–14/08/1971
3	Doug Prentice	England	2	05/07/1930–30/08/1930

Most penalties in tests by a player

No.	Player	Country	Tests	Period
20	Gavin Hastings	Scotland	6	01/07/1989–03/07/1993
16	Jonny Wilkinson	England	6	30/06/2001–02/07/2005
13	Neil Jenkins	Wales	4	21/06/1997–07/07/2001
12	Stephen Jones	Wales	6	25/06/2005–04/07/2009
11	Tom Kiernan	Ireland	5	04/08/1962–27/07/1968
10	Phil Bennett	Wales	8	08/06/1974–13/08/1977
7	Ollie Campbell	Ireland	7	14/06/1980–16/07/1983
6	Andy Irvine	Scotland	9	13/07/1974–12/07/1980
6	Stewart Wilson	Scotland	5	04/06/1966–10/09/1966
5	Tony Ward	Ireland	1	31/05/1980
5	Barry John	Wales	5	08/06/1968–14/08/1971

Most drop goals in tests by a player

No.	Player	Country	Tests	Career
2	Rob Andrew	England	5	08/07/1989–30/07/1993
2	Phil Bennett	Wales	8	08/06/1974–13/08/1977
2	Barry John	Wales	5	08/06/1968–14/08/1971
2	David Watkins	Wales	6	04/06/1966–10/09/1966
2	Percy Bush	Wales	4	02/07/1904–13/08/1904

Match records

Most points in a match by a player

No.	Player	Country	Points				Versus	Venue	Date
			T	C	P	DG			
20	Stephen Jones	Wales	-	1	5	1	South Africa	Loftus Versfeld, Pretoria	27/06/2009
20	Jonny Wilkinson	England	-	1	6	-	Argentina	Millennium Stadium, Cardiff	23/05/2005
18	Jonny Wilkinson	England	1	2	3	-	Australia	Stadium Australia, Sydney	14/07/2001
18	Gavin Hastings	Scotland	-	-	6	-	New Zealand	Lancaster Park, Christchurch	12/06/1993
18	Tony Ward	Ireland	-	-	5	1	South Africa	Newlands, Cape Town	31/05/1980
17	Tom Kiernan	Ireland	-	1	5	-	South Africa	Loftus Versfeld, Pretoria	08/06/1968
16	Lewis Jones	Wales	1	2	2	1	Australia	GABBA, Brisbane	19/08/1950
15	Neil Jenkins	Wales	-	-	5	-	South Africa	Kings Park, Durban	28/06/1997
15	Neil Jenkins	Wales	-	-	5	-	South Africa	Newlands, Cape Town	21/06/1997
15	Gavin Hastings	Scotland	-	-	5	-	Australia	Sydney Football Stadium, Sydney	15/07/1989

Most tries in a match by a player

No.	Player	Country	Versus	Venue	Date
2	Shane Williams	Wales	South Africa	Coca-Cola Park, Johannesburg	04/07/2009
2	Tom Croft	England	South Africa	ABSA Stadium, Durban	20/06/2009
2	John Williams	Wales	South Africa	Boet Erasmus Stadium, Port Elizabeth	13/07/1974
2	John Williams	Wales	South Africa	Loftus Versfeld, Pretoria	22/06/1974
2	Gerald Davies	Wales	New Zealand	Lancaster Park, Christchurch	10/07/1971
2	Ken Jones	Wales	Australia	Lang Park, Brisbane	04/06/1966
2	Malcolm Price	Wales	New Zealand	Carisbrook, Dunedin	18/07/1959
2	Malcolm Price	Wales	Australia	Sydney Cricket Ground, Sydney	13/06/1959
2	Jimmy Nelson	Ireland	Australia	Sydney Cricket Ground, Sydney	26/08/1950
2	Carl Aarvold	England	New Zealand	Lancaster Park, Christchurch	05/07/1930
2	Willie Llewellyn	Wales	Australia	Sydney Cricket Ground, Sydney	02/07/1904
2	Alfred Bucher	Scotland	Australia	Sydney Cricket Ground, Sydney	05/08/1899

Most conversions in a match by a player

No.	Player	Country	Versus	Venue	Date
5	Stuart Wilson	Scotland	Australia	Lang Park, Brisbane	04/06/1966
4	Angus Cameron	Scotland	South Africa	Ellis Park, Johannesburg	06/08/1955
3	Stephen Jones	Wales	South Africa	ABSA Stadium, Durban	20/06/2009
3	Jonny Wilkinson	England	Australia	GABBA, Brisbane	30/06/2001

Most drop goals in a match by a player

No.	Player	Country	Versus	Venue	Date
2	Phil Bennett	Wales	South Africa	Boet Erasmus, Port Elizabeth	13/07/1974

Most penalties in a match by a player

No.	Player	Country	Versus	Venue	Date
6	Jonny Wilkinson	England	Argentina	Millennium Stadium, Cardiff	23/05/2005
6	Gavin Hastings	Scotland	New Zealand	Lancaster Park, Christchurch	12/06/1993
5	Stephen Jones	Wales	South Africa	Loftus Versfeld, Pretoria	27/06/2009
5	Neil Jenkins	Wales	South Africa	Kings Park, Durban	28/06/1997
5	Neil Jenkins	Wales	South Africa	Norwich Park Newlands, Cape Town	21/06/1997
5	Gavin Hastings	Scotland	Australia	Sydney Football Stadium, Sydney	15/07/1989
5	Tony Ward	Ireland	South Africa	Newlands, Cape Town	31/05/1980
5	Tom Kiernan	Ireland	South Africa	Loftus Versfeld, Pretoria	08/06/1968
4	Stephen Jones	Wales	New Zealand	Eden Park, Auckland	09/07/2005
4	Gavin Hastings	Scotland	New Zealand	Athletic Park, Wellington	26/06/1993

Most points in a match by the British & Irish Lions

No.	Result	Points				Versus	Venue	Date
		T	C	P	DG			
31	31–0	5	5	1	1	Australia	Lang Park, Brisbane	04/06/1966
29	29–13	4	3	1	-	Australia	GABBA, Brisbane	30/06/2001
28	28–9	3	2	3	-	South Africa	Coca-Cola Park, Johannesburg	04/07/2009
28	28–9	5	1	1	1	South Africa	Loftus Versfeld, Pretoria	22/06/1974
26	26–9	3	1	2	2	South Africa	Boet Erasmus Stadium, Port Elizabeth	13/07/1974
25	25–28	1	1	5	1	South Africa	Loftus Versfeld, Pretoria	27/06/2009
25	25–25	1	1	6	-	Argentina	Millennium Stadium, Cardiff	23/05/2005
25	25–16	2	-	5	-	South Africa	Norwich Park Newlands, Cape Town	21/06/1997
24	24–3	5	3	1	-	Australia	Sydney Cricket Ground, Sydney	13/06/1959
24	24–3	5	3	1	-	Australia	Sydney Cricket Ground, Sydney	26/08/1950
23	23–29	2	2	3	-	Australia	Stadium Australia, Sydney	14/07/2001
23	23–22	5	4	-	-	South Africa	Ellis Park, Johannesburg	06/08/1955

Most consecutive test wins

No.	Period	Opponents
6	30/07/1891–29/08/1896	South Africa, South Africa, South Africa, South Africa, South Africa & South Africa
3	08/06/1974–13/07/1974	South Africa, South Africa & South Africa
3	19/08/1950–06/08/1955	Australia, Australia & South Africa
3	02/07/1904–30/07/1904	Australia, Australia & Australia
3	22/07/1899–12/08/1899	Australia, Australia & Australia

Chapter Five
Pacific Islanders

Rugby is the principal sport played across the Pacific played by virtually all the island nations, including Fiji, Samoa and Tonga. International rugby was first played between these tiny island states when Fiji toured and beat Western Samoa 6–0 in Apia on 18 August 1924. The small population of these islands, however, means that the player pool from which to select is very restricted, with the result that they struggle to compete against the larger, established rugby nations of the world. With this in mind, the idea of forming a single, united Pacific Islanders side, selected from the best players that each island nation had to offer, made sense – a side which could take on the best – essentially a Pacific islands version of the British and Irish Lions.

The idea came to fruition in 2002 when the Pacific Islanders Rugby Alliance (PIRA) was formed, made up of the member unions of Fiji, Samoa, Tonga, Cook Islands and Niue. The structure of the side had to be organised quickly, as their first tour was already scheduled for 2004, with a tour to follow every other year from then on. A quota system to ensure fair representation from each nation was not adopted, while the coach is chosen by the PIRA board, who in turn is supported by the head coaches of Fiji, Samoa and Tonga.

Results aside, the first tour to Australia and New Zealand was an enormous success in introducing the combined side to the world. The islanders perform the *kailao* war dance before every match – a fierce dance of Tongan origin originally imported from Wallis Island, the purpose of which is to set the tone of the game. The Pacific Islanders competed impressively against full-strength sides from Australia (14–29), New Zealand (26–41) and South Africa (24–38). The next tour was in 2006 to Wales, Scotland and Ireland with a team made up of players who had previously only played for an island nation. This selection policy was adopted after the 2004 tour when some players had never played for an island nation and whose ambitions (it later transpired) were clearly to play for New Zealand. Two such players were Sione Lauaki and Sitiveni Sivivatu, who subsequently went on to play with distinction for the All Blacks. Once again, the Pacific Islanders failed to win any of the three internationals, but came close against Scotland (22–34), only to be hammered 17–61 by the Irish in the last international played at the old Lansdowne Road stadium.

The 2008 touring side was much more competitive. They lost to England 13–39, restricted France to a scoreline of 17–42 after they had been reduced to 14 men as early as the 20th minute and achieved their first victory of 25–17 over Italy in Reggio Emilia. The future of the side is far from clear but it is hoped that it will one day be included in an expanded Tri-Nations competition. This idea appears, however, to be a long way off and it seems more likely that they will continue touring every two years.

No.	Date	Venue	Versus	Score
		Pacific Islanders international matches		
1	03/07/2004	Adelaide Oval, Adelaide	Australia	14–29
2	07/10/2004	North Harbour Stadium, Albany	New Zealand	26–41
3	07/17/2004	Express Advocate Stadium, Gosford	South Africa	24–38
4	11/11/2006	Millennium Stadium, Cardiff	Wales	20–38
5	11/18/2006	Murrayfield, Edinburgh	Scotland	22–34
6	11/26/2006	Lansdowne Road, Dublin	Ireland	17–61
7	11/08/2008	Twickenham, London	England	13–39
8	11/15/2008	Stade Auguste Bonal, Sochaux	France	17–42
9	11/22/2008	Stadio Giglio, Reggio Emilia	Italy	25–17

Summary	
Played	9
Won	1
Lost	8
Drawn	0
Points for	178
Points against	339
Average score	19.78 / 37.67
% Win	11.11
% Lose	88.89
% Draw	0.00

Fiji

Rugby was introduced to Fiji by the British in the nineteenth century. The first recorded game was played in the town of Ba on Viti Levu Island in 1884 between British tommies and Fijian soldiers of the Native Constabulary. By 1900, game reporting was common in local newspapers. In 1904, a local club competition was organised in Suva after two clubs were formed: the Civil Service Club and Police Club, the oldest clubs in Fiji. In these early days of rugby, the game was referred to by locals as *Veicaqe vaka-Peritania* ('British-style football'). Their most regular opposition were visiting warship crews. In 1913, a group of New Zealand construction workers arrived in Suva to build a hotel, one of whom was a plumber, Paddy Sheehan, a one-time captain of Otago in Dunedin. He noted the disorganised, casual nature of the game and formed the Pacific Club. Three more clubs were also soon founded. A meeting was held in 1913 between the four clubs to form the Fiji Rugby Football Union. However, this union and its affiliated clubs catered mainly for expats so in 1915, the Fiji Native Rugby Football Union was formed to support local players. It was not until the two unions finally merged in 1945 that a united Fiji Rugby Union came into being.

In December 1913, Fiji got a feel for international rugby when an unofficial match against New Zealand, who were returning from their tour of North America, was arranged. This was the first representative game for Fiji with the side comprised mainly of Europeans. Fiji inevitably lost heavily (3–67), with Paddy Sheehan scoring their only try. It would be more than a decade before Fiji was to undertake their first tour when they visited Western Samoa and Tonga – and each of the players had to pay their own fares! They played their first test against Western Samoa on 18 August 1924 in Apia, winning 6–0, wearing an all-black strip. Uniquely, the game was played at 7 a.m. in order to allow their Samoan counterparts time to get to work on time after the game, with the players facing the additional challenge of having to dodge a large tree in the middle of the field. A three-test series followed against Tonga, which was drawn, with a return match against Western Samoa completing the tour.

In 1926, the first official overseas touring side, Auckland University College, arrived in Fiji. Tonga arrived later the same year for a three-test series in which Fiji wore their now-famous white jersey adorned with the palm-tree badge for the first time. The year 1938 turned out to be a momentous one for Fiji as they hosted the touring New Zealand Maori side, their first international opposition other than Tonga or Samoa. Such was the occasion that the Fijians wore rugby boots for the first time. The following year, Fiji undertook their first tour to a major rugby-playing nation when they toured New Zealand and became the first side to be unbeaten in New Zealand, including winning the only test of the tour against the Maoris by 14–4. It was at this match that they performed the *Cibi* for the first time – a Fijian war dance which they perform before every match to this day and which has its origins in Fiji's old military campaigns against their Pacific neighbours.

As expected, international rugby declined during World War II, but the war in fact resulted in the game improving, thanks to the vast increase in numbers of Allied servicemen stationed in the region, providing some stout competition for the local Fijian sides. After the war, Fiji embarked on their first tour of Australia in 1952. The Australians became the first major rugby nation to award full international status to the Fijian games. It was a tremendously successful tour for Fiji. They drew bumper crowds to all their matches and upset their hosts to win the second test 17–15, their first win over a top rugby nation. So successful was the Fijians' running, entertaining style of rugby that they again toured Australia in 1954 and once again shared the two-test series, winning the second test 18–16. These two tours and, more importantly, their two test victories, focused world attention on Fiji. In 1964, they were invited to tour the United Kngdom and France for the first time, with tests played against a Welsh XV (lost 22–28) and France (lost 3–22). In 1977, Fiji had their finest hour when they beat a British Lions XV by 25–21 (five tries to three), a full-strength Lions side in everything but name. International tours to Suva by top national sides became fairly common through the 1970s and 1980s. However, Australia remained the only nation to award international status to these matches until Wales did so on their tour in 1986, with the test won 22–15 by Wales.

In 1987, Fiji were invited to play in the inaugural RWC and reached the quarter-finals in a tough pool that included New Zealand, Argentina and Italy. By the 1991 RWC, the quality of rugby in Fiji had deteriorated to a point where they finished last in their pool and then failed to qualify for the 1995 tournament. During the 1999 tournament, they reached the quarter-final play-off before losing to England at Twickenham. In 2003 they failed to reach the play-off rounds after narrowly losing the crucial fixture to Scotland by 20–22. It was during the 2007 tournament that Fiji excelled beyond measure, playing some of the most sublime and entertaining rugby that the tournament has ever witnessed, beating Japan 35–31 and Canada 29–16, before playing the match of the tournament, beating Wales 38–34, scoring four fantastic running tries. This took them into the quarter-finals where they were to lose to eventual champions, South

Fiji test summary	
Played	267
Won	129
Lost	130
Drawn	8
Points for	5,436
Points against	5,173
% Win	48.31
% Lose	48.69
% Draw	3.0

Africa, by 20–37. However, this was a game they could very well have won after having played ten minutes of perhaps the finest rugby in Fijian history, to bring the scores to 20–23 with tries from deep within in their own half and against the run of play. One of the chief reasons why Fiji have failed to consistently impress on the world stage is the poaching of their top players, such as Ilie Tabua and Lote Tuqiri by neighbouring Australia, and Joe Rokocoko and Sitiveni Sivivatu by New Zealand, where players are attracted by lucrative contracts. In addition, simply getting their players to represent their country today is problematic, as the majority of top players are currently contracted to club sides in Europe, New Zealand and Australia where money calls the shots. To compound this, emphasis has been placed on sevens rugby by the Fiji Rugby Union – a form of the game where they have excelled at the highest level and can rightfully claim to be the best in the world after winning the sevens RWC in Hong Kong in 1997.

Match records: Fiji									
	No.	Versus	Result	Date	Venue	T	C	P	DG
Most points in a match by the team	120	Niue Island	120-0	10/091983	Apia	21	18	-	-
	No.	Player	Date	Versus	Venue	T	C	P	DG
Most points in a match by a player	36	Severo Koroduadua	10/09/1983	Niue Island	Apia	-	18	-	-
Most tries in a match by a player	6	Tevita Makutu	30/08/1979	Papua New Guinea	Suva				
	6	Senivalati Laulau	08/091983	Solomom Islands	Apia				
Most conversions in a match by a player	18	Severo Koroduadua	10/091983	Niue Island	Apia				
Most penalties in a match by a player	7	Nicky Little	08/07/2001	Samoa	Tokyo				
Most drop goals in a match by a player	3	Opeti Turuva	02/071994	Samoa	Nadi				

Career records: Fiji									
	No.	Player	Tests	Career	T	C	P	DG	Total
Most tests in a career	63	Nicky Little		02/07/1996–29/09/2007	2	113	133	2	641
Most points in a career	641	Nicky Little	63	02/07/1996–29/09/2007	2	113	133	2	
Most tries in a career	20	Senivalati Laulau	32	244/05/1980–09/11/1985					
Most conversions in a career	113	Nicky Little	63	02/07/1996–29/09/2007					
Most penalties in a career	133	Nicky Little	63	02/07/1996–29/09/2007					
Most drop goals in a career	6	Opeti Turuva	11	05/12/1990–22/05/1999					

Georgia

In Georgia an ancient indigenous sport known as *lelo* has many intrinsic similarities to rugby and led to the nickname of the national side, the *Lelos*, with the word since being adopted as the Georgian term for a try. *Lelo*, or more correctly, *lelo burti* (meaning 'field ball') is still played today by rural communities of this once Soviet republic on the Black Sea. A field is selected between two small rivers, with the men of one village taking on those of another. There is no limit on numbers and the aim is to simply carry a large, heavy ball over the opposing side's river by means of passing and brute force.

Various unsuccessful attempts to introduce rugby into Georgia began in 1928. In 1959, a Frenchman by the name of Jacques Haspekian managed to popularise the game among students in Tbilisi, with his first rugby session held on 15 October at the city racecourse with 20 people. However, once the similarities of *lelo* and rugby were noticed the game's popularity quickly grew. In short time the first rugby club was formed, the Georgian Polytechnical Institute Club, or GPI Club, known today as the Qochebi Club. By 1961, a few more rugby clubs were formed in Tbilisi and a three-team domestic competition was launched, known as the Tbilisi Championship and the Tbilisi Rugby Section was established to manage rugby in the city. 1962 was a milestone for Georgian rugby when a Georgian Club XV took on a foreign side for the first time, to be defeated by the touring Trud Moscow team from Russia. The same year, two Georgian clubs undertook their first tours abroad, to Russia and Latvia respectively, thereby introducing Georgian rugby to a wider audience for the first time. In 1964, the Georgia Rugby Federation was formed when the Tbilisi Rugby Section was restructured into an all-encompassing organisation to manage rugby across the state instead of just in Tbilisi. The Georgian Rugby Federation was affiliated to the Soviet Union Rugby Federation until 1992, with the best Georgian players being selected to play for the USSR national side. During this time, the Soviet Championship, introduced in the mid-1960s, was the premier club tournament in the region and was first won by a Georgian side, the Locomotivi Club of Tbilisi, in 1978. A clear improvement in Georgian rugby was evident when their sides went on to dominate the championship, winning from 1987 to 1990.

In 1989, the Georgian Rugby Federation, together with other FIRA nations, helped finance and host a tour by Zimbabwe and on 12 September 1989 Georgia played their first international, in Kutaisi, kicking off with a 16–3 win. The following year, Georgia undertook their first international tour, to Zimbabwe, where they played a two-test series which they drew 1–1 after losing the first test in Bulawayo. With independence in 1991, following the collapse of the Soviet Union, the Georgia Rugby Federation was renamed the Georgia Rugby Football Union and applied for IRFB membership, which was granted in 1992, with the union renamed the Georgia Rugby Union. In 1998, Georgia came within a whisker of qualifying for the 1999 RWC when they lost a two-test repechage play-off series against Tonga on points difference (repechage is a practice used in ladder competitions that allows participants who have failed to qualify by a small margin to continue to the next round).

However, in a young and unstable country the national side had limited resources with which to train, making do with what was available, most notably when they constructed scrum machines out of old Soviet tractors. Despite these challenges, rugby has grown rapidly to become one of the most popular sports in Georgia and since their affiliation to the IRFB in 1992, it has become a huge spectator sport. In 2001, 65,000 people filled the National Stadium in Tbilisi to watch Georgia take on Russia in the European Nations Cup and in 2002, the same two sides met for the most important match in both their history – a winner-takes-all fixture for a place in the 2003 RWC. Millions tuned in to their televisions as a full stadium in Tbilisi to witness an ecstatic 17–13 Georgian win. Against all expectations, Georgia had qualified for the 2003 RWC where the national side now played England (lost 6–84), Samoa (lost 9–46)

Georgia test summary	
Played	109
Won	66
Lost	38
Drawn	5
Points for	2,545
Points against	2,023
% Win	60.55
% Lose	34.86
% Draw	4.59

and South Africa (lost 19–46). They failed to win a game, losing their final fixture to Uruguay 12–24. The highlight of their campaign was their display against the Springboks against whom they scored their only try of the tournament. They again qualified for the 2007 RWC where it was clear that the game in Georgia had markedly improved and they came close to recording the greatest upset in the tournament's history against Ireland, just losing 10–14 after a disallowed try and three missed drop-goal attempts. They did, however, record their first RWC victory when they whipped Namibia 30–0, propelling the former Soviet Caucasian republic into wild celebration.

Georgia takes part in the annual European Nations Cup (a second-level competition for tier-two nations), which they won for the first time in 2001 (remaining unbeaten) and again in 2007/2008, following which they can officially lay claim to being the seventh-best side in Europe. However, the chances of Georgia being included in the premier European rugby tournament, the Six Nations, are far off unless a promotion and relegation system is one day introduced.

Match records: Georgia									
	No.	Versus	Result	Date	Venue	T	C	P	DG
Most points in a match by the team	98	Czech Republic	98-3	07/04/2007	Tbilisi	16	9	-	-
	No.	Player	Date	Versus	Venue	T	C	P	D
Most points in a match by a player	23	Pavle Jimsheladze	08/03/2003	Russia	Krasnodar	1	-	6	-
	23	Merab Kvirikashvili	07/04/2007	Czech Republic	Tbilisi	1	9	-	-
Most tries in a match by a player	3	Pavle Jimsheladze	23/03/1995	Bulgaria	Sofia				
	3	Archil Kavtarashvili	23/03/1995	Bulgaria	Sofia				
	3	Mamuka Gorgodze	12/06/2005	Czech Republic	Kutaissi				
	3	David Dadunashvili	07/04/2007	Czech Republic	Tbilisi				
	3	Malkhaz Urjukashvili	07/04/2007	Czech Republic	Tbilisi				
	3	Mamuka Gorgodze	26/04/2008	Spain	Tbilisi				
Most conversions in a match by a player	9	Pavle Jimsheladze	03/02/2002	Netherlands	Tbilisi				
	9	Merab Kvirikashvili	07/04/2007	Czech Republic	Tbilisi				
Most penalties in a match by a player	6	Pavle Jimsheladze	08/03/2003	Russia	Krasnodar				
Most drop goals in a match by a player	2	Davit Chavleishvili	199215/07/	Ukraine	Kiev				

Career records: Georgia									
	No.	Player	Tests	Career	T	C	P	DG	Total
Most tests in a career	57	Pavle Jimsheladze		23/03/1995–11/09/2007	9	61	48	3	320
Most points in a career	320	Pavle Jimsheladze	57	23/03/1995–11/09/2007	9	61	48	3	
Most tries in a career	15	Malkhaz Urjukashvili	55	12/10/1997–30/09/2007					
Most conversions in a career	61	Pavle Jimsheladze	57	23/03/1995–11/09/2007					
Most penalties in a career	48	Pavle Jimsheladze	57	23/03/1995–11/09/2007					
Most drop goals in a career	4	Kakha Machitidze	18	12/09/1989–28/03/1999					

Japan

Accounts of rugby first being played in Japan date back to 1874 when a crew of British sailors who had docked in Yokohama staged a game among themselves. At that time, rugby was played in Japan almost exclusively by the British for their own recreational purposes. In 1899, two teachers, Edward Clarke and Tanaka Ginnosuke, successfully introduced rugby to the locals – students of Keio University, Tokyo. Clarke, who was born in Japan, and Ginnosuke had both learned the game while studying abroad at Cambridge and on return decided to introduce it to the students. The Keio University Rugby Club was formed in the same year to become the first Japanese club for Japanese players. The club played its first game against the expatriate Yokohama Club in 1901, losing 5–35 and soon university games were attracting crowds of over 20,000. The game quickly spread to other prestigious Japanese learning institutions and by the 1920s, various regional unions had been formed.

On 30 November 1926, the Japan Rugby Football Union was formed to manage the game in Japan. In 1932, Japan hosted a tour by Canada in which they played their first international, beating the Canadians in Osaka 9–8 and winning the two-test series with a 38–5 victory in the second test. The tour was a success and two years later, Japan hosted an Australian university side with whom they drew the two-test series after winning the second test 14–9. A New Zealand university side toured in 1936 with evidence of rugby improving in Japan there for all to see as the New Zealanders struggled to win the series 1–0 after drawing the second match.

The development of the game took a heavy knock during the rise of Japanese militarism leading up to World War II. The government was staunchly supportive of all things indigenous, placing a strong emphasis on traditional Japanese martial arts while officially frowning on rugby and other foreign pastimes. Player numbers inevitably dropped during this period, as did the standard of rugby, but a small group of rugby enthusiasts remained to ensure its survival. Rugby began a slow revival after the war, with the occupying Allied powers encouraging support for the game. As the Japanese economy began to recover, major companies began to form rugby teams, partly as a marketing and publicity strategy and partly to provide recreational opportunities for their employees. Kobe Steel was the first such company team; these corporate teams still feature strongly in Japanese rugby today. Rugby in the universities once again became popular and in 1952, Oxford University became the first post-World War II side to tour Japan, followed by Cambridge University in 1953 and the Australian Universities in 1956 – Japan lost all the tests.

The Cherry Blossoms (the nickname derives from the emblem on the national jersey) have struggled to compete against the traditionally stronger rugby nations and have

An illustration of a rugby match in 1874 near Tokyo, Japan with Mount Fuji in the background. *Image*: Frédéric Humbert/www.flickr.com/photos/rugby_pioneers/ creative commons license

never won against any of the traditional top eight. They are, however, the dominating rugby force in Asia and instigated the 1969 formation of the Asian Cup Championship, which Japan have won more often than any other country, with only South Korea providing any form of resistance. Japan first played against a senior national selection side when an England XV toured in 1971 and lost the test series 0–2, although the second test was a closely fought affair: 6–3 in favour of the English XV. In 1973, Japan undertook their first tour of Great Britain and France, with France becoming the first top rugby nation to award full international status to a match against Japan, in Bordeaux on 27 October, won 30–18 by the French. To date, the most famous victories in Japanese rugby history include a 23–19 win over the Junior All Blacks in Wellington in 1968, 28–24 against a Scotland XV in Tokyo in 1989, and 44–29 against a full-strength Argentinian side in Tokyo in 1998.

Undoubtedly, one of the great achievements of Japanese rugby has been their qualification and appearance in every single RWC tournament where they have participated as Asia's top representative on each occasion. However, their performances in each of these tournaments have been disappointing, with their darkest hour occurring in the 1995 RWC when New Zealand trounced them with a record RWC score of 145–17, which set the development of rugby in Japan back by several years: public opinion was grossly critical of the national side's performance and with it the popularity of the game slumped. In all, Japan have managed just one win in RWCs: in 1991 when they beat a ramshackle Zimbabwe 52–8 in Belfast. In 2007, they staged a dramatic comeback to draw 12–12 with Canada. During the 2002 RWC qualifying programme, Japan defeated Chinese Taipei 155–3 in Tokyo to lay to rest the ghosts of the 1995 annihilation by New Zealand. This victory underlies Japan's domination of Asian rugby, again evident in the 2006 RWC qualifying event when they thrashed Hong Kong 52–3 and South Korea 54–0.

Despite Japan's poor performances in international fixtures against top-tier nations, the national side can still lay claim to several world records: most notably the try-scoring feats by their winger Daisuke Ohata who scored a world-record 69 tries in 58 tests, including eight in one match – a record unlikely to be bettered. Fullback Toru Kurihara holds the world record for scoring the most individual points in an international when on 21 July 2002 he scored 60 points through six tries and 15 conversions against Chinese Taipei in Tainan. On 8 May 1999, flyhalf Keiji Hirose became the first player ever to kick nine penalty goals in a test match, against Tonga. And the national side achieved the second-highest-ever tally in an international when they thumped Chinese Taipei 155–3 in Tokyo on 7 July 2002.

Today, Japan competes annually in the Pacific Nations Cup and the Asian Five Nations Tournament: they were champions in 2008 having been unbeaten.

Japan test summary	
Played	242
Won	78
Lost	157
Drawn	7
Points for	5,587
Points against	7,696
% Win	32.23
% Lose	64.88
% Draw	2.89

Match records: Japan									
	No.	Versus	Result	Date	Venue	T	C	P	DG
Most points in a match by the team	155	Chinese Taipei	155-3	07/07/2002	Tokyo	23	20	-	-
	No.	Player	Date	Versus	Venue	T	C	P	DG
Most points in a match by a player	60	Toru Kurihara	21/07/2002	Chinese Taipei	Taipei	6	15	-	-
Most tries in a match by a player	8	Daisuke Ohata	07/072002	Chinese Taipei	Tokyo				
Most conversions in a match by a player	15	Toru Kurihara	21/072002	Chinese Taipei	Taipei				
Most penalties in a match by a player	9	Keiji Hirose	08/05/1999	Tonga	Tokyo				
Most drop goals in a match by a player	2	Kensuke Iwabuchi	15/091998	Argentina	Tokyo				

Career records: Japan									
	No.	Player	Tests	Career	T	C	P	DG	Total
Most tests in a career	79	Yukio Motoki		15/05/1994–15/05/2005	9	-	-	-	45
Most points in a career	422	Keiji Hirose	38	19/02/1995–08/05/2005	5	77	79	2	
Most tries in a career	69	Daisuke Ohata	58	09/11/1996–25/11/2006					
Most conversions in a career	77	Keiji Hirose	38	19/02/1995–08/05/2005					
Most penalties in a career	79	Keiji Hirose	38	19/02/1995–08/05/2005					
Most drop goals in a career	5	Kyohei Morita	8	04/07/2004–15/05/2005					

Namibia

Rugby was first played in Namibia in 1916 after it had been introduced by South African soldiers who had invaded and seized the German colony in 1915. During its time under South African governance, the territory was known as South West Africa (SWA) and was considered a de facto fifth province by the South African government. Rugby became very popular and the 'national' side competed annually in South Africa's premier domestic rugby competition, the Currie Cup, but struggled against the stronger provincial teams in the tournament. This was mainly because SWA was restricted to only selecting white players due to South Africa's apartheid laws, and for a nation which boasts the lowest population density in the world – less than two people per square kilometre – this was a severely restrictive selection criterion given that the white rugby-playing population was a tiny percentage of the population. The team achieved their best-ever result in the 1989 tournament, a year before independence, when they finished third on the Currie Cup log.

There were, however, from a rugby perspective, some advantages to being ruled by South Africa, as top international touring sides to South Africa invariably visited SWA to play in Windhoek, which naturally improved the quality of rugby in the country. The first such side was the 1955 British Lions who won 9–0. This game is regarded by most to be Namibia's first international. However, because the country was effectively a South African dependency, the territory could not technically play international rugby as recognised by the IRFB, with touring sides treating SWA as a provincial fixture. The closest SWA came to beating a touring international team was a 14–14 draw with the Australians in 1961, a 13–13 draw with the French in 1975 and a tough, closely fought contest which they lost 16–23 to the all-conquering 1974 British Lions. During the Currie Cup competition, SWA's top players were eligible to play for South Africa. Some great 'South-Westers', such as Jan Ellis who played a then record 38 times for the Springboks, represented South Africa with distinction.

Officially, Namibia played their first rugby international on 12 January 1989, a year before their independence, when the side toured southern African neighbour Zimbabwe. For the tour, Zimbabwe granted full international status for the match against SWA, which was won 33–18 by the visitors at the Police Grounds in Harare. Following Namibia's independence on 21 March 1990, the national side performed admirably as they carried their Currie Cup form into the international arena for the first time. The Namibia Rugby Union was formed a few days later and joined the IRFB that month. Their first international match as an independent nation was played against a touring Portuguese side on 20 April 1990 in Windhoek, which the home side won emphatically by 86–9. It was a busy first year of international rugby as Namibia then lost a tight two-test series against both Wales and a touring French side, France A, before touring England and France for the first time later that year. The years in the tough Currie Cup tournament paid off in 1991 as the team achieved their greatest run of form, remaining unbeaten in ten tests, which included series victories over Italy, Ireland and Zimbabwe. It remains Namibia's greatest year with visiting sides struggling to overcome the harsh playing conditions of the desert, where, in many instances, grass is considered a luxury.

Independence came too late for Namibia to qualify for the 1991 RWC, but in 1993 they took part in the African qualifying rounds in an attempt to qualify as the second African country for inclusion in the 1995 tournament. They won round 1 in Nairobi in emphatic style with wins against Arabian Gulf (64–20), Kenya (60–9) and Zimbabwe (41–16) and were massive favourites to win the final round 2 in Casablanca. However, they put in a lame performance, losing to Côte d'Ivoire and drawing with Morocco, to see Côte d'Ivoire qualify ahead of them. This is one of Namibia's greatest disappointments in their international rugby history. From that point on, the quality of rugby in Namibia began to deteriorate, lacking the regular top-class competition they had once enjoyed in the Currie Cup years. They lost for the first time to Zimbabwe in 1996 (13–15), against a touring Tongan side in 1997 (14–20) and again to Zimbabwe (26–32). The prospects of qualifying for the 1999 tournament looked bleak, but the side raised their game beyond expectation, winning all but one of the five RWC qualifying fixtures in 1998, including a 22–10 revenge over Côte d'Ivoire in Casablanca.

With qualification for the 1999 RWC, Namibia has since gone on to qualify as Africa's second representative for every RWC. They have struggled, however, to compete in the world's premier rugby tournament and have yet to record a victory as they are more often than not on the receiving end of record scorelines. In 1999, they lost 11–72 to Canada and in 2003, suffered heavily in their pool, losing 14–67 to Argentina, 7–64 to Ireland before suffering the ignominy of losing by a record RWC margin of 0–142 against hosts Australia. Their only realistic chance of a victory was against Romania, but they lost this one 7–37. During the 2007 tournament, Namibia turned in their best RWC performance when they ran Ireland close to eventually lose 17–32 in a game they could very well have won. The rest of the tournament was a misery: they lost 10–87 to hosts France, 3–63 to Argentina and 0–30 to Georgia. Nicknamed the Welwitschias, after the country's unique indigenous desert plant, the team experienced a serious slump in form in 2005, losing heavily to Morocco (0–49). Several more recent defeats – against Tunisia (7–24), Kenya (26–30) and Uganda (19–20) – saw Namibia's IRB rankings slide considerably in recent years. Namibia competes annually in the Africa Cup and were champions in 2002 and 2004.

Namibia test summary	
Played	97
Won	52
Lost	44
Drawn	1
Points for	2,801
Points against	2,657
% Win	53.61
% Lose	45.36
% Draw	1.03

Match records: Namibia									
	No.	Versus	Result	Date	Venue	T	C	P	DG
Most points in a match by the team	112	Madagascar	112–0	15/062002	Windhoek	18	11	-	-
	No.	Player	Date	Versus	Venue	T	C	P	DG
Most points in a match by a player	35	Jaco Coetzee	07/07/1993	Kenya	Nairobi	3	7	2	-
Most tries in a match by a player	6	Gerhard Mans	20/04/1990	Portugal	Windhoek				
Most conversions in a match by a player	11	Moolman Olivier	20/04/1990	Portugal	Windhoek				
	11	Morné Schreuder	27/05/2006	Kenya	Windhoek				
Most penalties in a match by a player	5	Jaco Coetzee	22/06/1991	Italy	Windhoek				
	5	Rudi van Vuuren	23/01/1998	Portugal	Lisbon				
	5	Shaun McCulley	30/06/1990	France A	Windhoek				
Most drop goals in a match by a player	1	No player has ever kicked more than one drop goal in a match							

Career records: Namibia									
	No.	Player	Tests	Career	T	C	P	DG	Total
Most tests in a career	32	Herman Lindvelt		12/09/1998–22/09/2007	3	-	-	-	15
Most points in a career	344	Jaco Coetzee	28	09/06/1990–18/06/1994	6	84	46	3	
Most tries in a career	27	Gerhard Mans	22	02/06/1990–16/06/1994					
Most conversions in a career	84	Jaco Coetzee	28	09/06/1990–18/06/1994					
Most penalties in a career	46	Jaco Coetzee	28	09/06/1990–18/06/1994					
Most drop goals in a career	3	Jaco Coetzee	28	09/06/1990–18/06/1994					

Portugal

French students first introduced rugby to Portugal in the early twentieth century. The game remained low key and was generally only played in Lisbon during the early years. However, its popularity soon increased and in 1926, the Federação Portuguesa de Rugby, the Portuguese Rugby Federation, was formed to manage the game and organise the national championship, the Campeonato Nacional de Rugby. On 13 April 1935, Portugal played their first international when they took on neighbours Spain in Lisbon, losing 5–6. The following year the same two sides met for a return match in Madrid, with Portugal again losing, this time 9–16. Early international rugby competition for the Portuguese was scarce and it was not until 1966 that they won their first test in just their fifth international outing – against Spain in Madrid by 9–3. Regular competitive rugby was only realised in the mid-1960s when Portugal participated in the annual FIRA Championship against the likes of Romania, Germany, Spain, Belgium, the Netherlands, Poland, Denmark and Italy. They struggled to compete during these years and lost more than they won, more often than not by large margins and against nations where rugby was even younger and less popular than in Portugal.

Two of Portugal's most notable victories on the international stage occurred on 25 February 1972 in Coimbra, when they defeated Italy 9–6 for the first and only time in their history, and on 22 February 2003 when they beat Romania 16–15, in Lisbon, for the first time. Fixtures against the eight traditional powerhouse nations have been limited with Portugal yet to achieve a victory over any of these sides. The closest they came was in the 2007 RWC when they lost 10–56 to Scotland. In 1989, Portugal took part in the qualifying stages of the RWC for the first time, getting off to a winning start by beating Czechoslovakia 15–13 and advancing to the next qualification round, only to lose 3–32 to the Netherlands, thus failing to qualify. Since this first attempt to qualify for the RWC, Portugal has taken part in each and every qualification route in an attempt to play in the prestigious tournament. In the 1995 tournament, the Portuguese began well, beating Belgium 8–3 and Switzerland 32–0, before losing to Spain in a crucial match, leaving them with the daunting task of having to beat Wales in the following round. The match achieved little other than to indicate the great disparity that existed between the then Five Nations champions and Portugal, as they were outclassed by a whopping 11–102 in Lisbon. A second defeat to Spain saw the end of Portugal's qualification campaign.

In the 1999 tournament, Portugal again failed to qualify, playing the likes of Scotland and Spain. After losing the qualifying games in Edinburgh, Portugal had to win a home-and-away repechage showdown with Uruguay in order to qualify, but it was not to be as Portugal lost both matches by large margins. For the 2003 qualification process, Portugal didn't even progress past the first phase with the likelihood of them qualifying for 2007 but a wispy dream. However, this qualification disappointment saw Portugal turn their game around in dramatic fashion as they went on to produce some outstanding rugby, which saw them reach unprecedented rugby success. In 2003/2004, *Os Lobos*, 'the Wolves', as they are nicknamed, won the European Nations Cup for the very first time, including splendid away victories over comparative rugby heavyweights, Georgia and Russia. These feats saw Portuguese rugby being recognised on the world stage, as coach Tomaz Morais was nominated by the IRB as coach of the year – a remarkable achievement for a third-tier rugby nation. Portugal continued with this success going into the 2007 RWC in a gruelling but thrilling qualification process. Beginning with their defence of their European Nations Cup title in the 2004/2006 tournament, they finished a credible third – good enough to ensure an advance to the next round of qualification, together with Italy and Russia. Italy beat them comfortably; to advance further, Portugal had to beat Russia, which they did in magnificent style, winning 26–23 to advance through to the next round – a home-and-away series against Georgia, with the winner qualifying. Portugal lost this series and so entered the repechage round, which began with a home-and-away series against Morocco. Portugal won both encounters with an aggregate scoreline of 26–20 and reached the final round of qualification – a home-and-away test series against twice-RWC-qualifiers, Uruguay. In the most thrilling of repechage qualifying matches ever played, Portugal won 12–5 in Lisbon but lost 12–18 in Montevideo. However, based on their aggregate scores of 24–23 for the series, Portugal, against all odds, qualified for the 2007 RWC by a lone point, sending the nation into rugby heaven. As great an achievement as it was to qualify for the RWC, further progress was an extremely daunting prospect, as Portugal was pooled with New Zealand, Scotland, Italy and Romania. Many thought they were simply there to make up the numbers, but *Os Lobos* played with astounding commitment to become one of the most popular sides in the tournament, with passionate fans attending all their matches. The team scored a try in every single match, including a much-celebrated touchdown against New Zealand in which the hefty scoreline of 13–108 did Portugal little justice. They prevented Italy from scoring a bonus-point try in front of 50, 000 people at the Parc des Princes in Paris and came within a try of beating Romania, ultimately losing 10–14. Despite losing all four of their matches, the tournament was a special achievement for the only amateur side in the competition. Following the retirement of some of their star players after the RWC, a run of poor form has seen Portugal finish fifth in the European Nations Cup, their worst result since 2001/2002. However, their performance at the 2007 RWC warranted the IRB approving a grant to improve the quality of rugby in the country and much is expected of *Os Lobos* for the 2011 RWC.

Portugal test summary	
Played	200
Won	82
Lost	106
Drawn	12
Points for	3,199
Points against	4,493
% Win	41.0
% Lose	53.0
% Draw	6.0

Match records: Portugal									
	No.	Versus	Result	Date	Venue	T	C	P	DG
Most points in a match by the team	55	Netherlands	55–11	23/11/1996	Lisbon	6	5	5	0
	No.	Player	Date	Versus	Venue	T	C	P	DG
Most points in a match by a player	30	Thierry Teixeira	06/02/2000	Georgia	Lisbon	-	-	9	1
Most tries in a match by a player	3	Nuno Garváo	21/03/2004	Spain	Ibiza				
	3	Gonçalo Malheiro	10/06/2004	Barbarians	Lisbon				
Most conversions in a match by a player	4	Nuno Mourao	30/05/1998	Andorra	Lousa				
	4	João Queimado	08/04/1984	Denmark	Copenhagen				
	4	João Diogo Mota	13/05/2006	Ukraine	Lisbon				
	4	Pedro Cabral	16/02/2008	Czech Republic	Lisbon				
Most penalties in a match by a player	9	Thierry Teixeira	06/02/2000	Georgia	Lisbon				
Most drop goals in a match by a player	2	João Queimado	17/03/1985	Morocco	Rabat				

Career records: Portugal									
	No.	Player	Tests	Career	T	C	P	DG	Total
Most tests in a career	84	Joaquim Ferreira		03/04/1992–25/09/2007	3	-	-	-	15
Most points in a career	231	Gonçalo Malheiro	37	30/05/1998–01/12/2007	7	23	36	14	
Most tries in a career	13	Diogo Mateus	63	06/02/2000–14/03/2009					
	13	Nuno Durão	46	26/03/1983–02/03/1996					
	13	António Aguilar	49	06/03/1999–14/03/2009					
Most conversions in a career	23	Gonçalo Malheiro	37	30/05/1998–01/12/2007					
Most penalties in a career	36	Gonçalo Malheiro	37	30/05/1998–01/12/2007					
Most drop goals in a career	14	Gonçalo Malheiro	37	30/05/1998–01/12/2007					

Romania

Romanian students returning from their studies in France brought rugby to Romania. Stadiul Roman, formed in 1913, was Romania's first exclusively rugby-playing club. Rugby was also played by the Bucharest Romanian Tennis Club at the time. So rapid was the spread of the game's popularity in Bucharest that by 1914 there were 17 rugby clubs and a healthy national club championship. This growth and the number of clubs warranted the formation of the Federația Romănă de Rugby, the Romanian Rugby Federation, or FRR, to manage the club championship. Rugby developed at such a pace that on 1 July 1919, Romania was able to field a national side in Paris to take on the United States – their first international, which they lost 0–21. In 1924, Romania sent a national side to compete in the 1924 Paris Olympic Games, but the contest was a harsh lesson for the Romanians, losing heavily to France and the United States, to claim the tournament bronze medal. The Oaks, as they have come to be known, won their first international against Czechoslovakia in 1927 and by the 1930s Romania was playing regular international matches against other European nations in the FIRA Championship, they being co-founders with France. By this time the sport had begun to spread to other parts of the country; in 1939, Brașov became the first town outside of Bucharest to form a rugby club, at an aircraft factory, no less.

With regular international competition, the national side improved dramatically; in 1960 Romania managed to beat a full-strength French side 11–5 in Bucharest. They remained unbeaten against the French for the next three years, including draws in 1961 and 1963 and a 3–0 win in 1962. The improvement in the game is largely attributed to the ruling communist regime which used sport as a propaganda tool during the Cold War. Any international success, especially against top nations, generally Western, was presented as a direct result of the efficacy of communist ideology; to ensure continued rugby success large wadges of cash were pumped into the game by the state. Top players were employed by the army or police whose sides, Steaua and Dynamo, practised six days a week in state-of-the-art training facilities.

Such a nurturing environment inevitably bred a class national side that became extremely competitive against the best in the world. With victories over France under their belt, Romania was ensured an annual fixture with the French, against whom they recorded more stunning wins in 1968, 1974, 1976, 1980, 1982 and 1990. These caught the rugby world's attention, as did Romania's narrow 12–13 loss to a Wales XV in Cardiff and their 13–13 draw with an Ireland XV in Dublin in 1980, which were essentially full-strength sides in everything but name. Such form proved that they were competitive enough to warrant full international status by the top nations. In September 1981, Romania played against their second top nation, after France, when they took on Scotland in Edinburgh, losing 6–12 but denying the Scots any tries. That same year they lost 6–14 to New Zealand in Bucharest after having had two tries disallowed but it wasn't long before they recorded their first victory over a top nation other than France: in 1983 they played Wales for the first time, in Bucharest, recording a convincing 24–6 win. The following year they proved they weren't a flash in the pan by beating Five Nations Grand Slam champions, Scotland, 28–22 in Bucharest, clear evidence they were a team whose star was on the rise and who could beat the best when given the opportunity. They reinforced this by running England close at 15–22 at Twickenham in 1985. A 15–9 win against Wales in Cardiff in 1988 sparked the first debate about expanding the Five Nations into a Six Nations, to include Romania.

However, coinciding with the revolution and the clumsy execution of the brutal communist dictator, Nicolae Ceausescu (and his wife), this was as good as it got for Romania and the game fell into a rapid decline from 1989, with heavy defeats to England (3–58) and Scotland (0–32) – a direct result of the political turmoil. Considering the game was state-run and state-funded, it inevitably suffered massively as funds dried up. To make matters worse, the 1989/1990 revolution claimed the lives of several leading Romanian rugby players and administrators, including captain Florică Murariu, an army officer who was shot dead at a roadblock. Today, roughly one-third of the number of clubs exist compared to the 1970s and early 1980s. Yet despite this demise of the game in Romania, the Oaks have still managed occasional international success, including a 18–12 victory over Scotland in Bucharest in 1991 and their first away win over France in 1990 by 12–6 in Auch. The advent of professionalism was perhaps the final undoing of Romanian rugby, as virtually all their top players left the essentially amateur domestic game to play professionally in France, a significant loss of talent and resources for a game that was already struggling to stay afloat. A measure of the decline in Romanian rugby came in 2001 when they lost by a record 0–134 to England, while top club side Dinamo Bucharest lost 0–151 to England's Saracens Club.

Romania test summary	
Played	342
Won	192
Lost	141
Drawn	9
Points for	7,373
Points against	6,301
% Win	56.14
% Lose	41.23
% Draw	2.63

The Oaks have competed in every single RWC since they were invited by the IRFB to take part in the 1987 tournament when the FRR became affiliated with the IRFB. They have, however, never proceeded past the pool stages. Their best performances were lone wins in each of the 1987, 1991, 1999, 2003 and 2007 tournaments. Romania competes annually in the European Nations Cup, being champions in 2000, 2001/2002 and 2004/2006. Even with results slowly improving, Romania can sadly no longer claim to be the best European side outside of those competing in the Six Nations, with Georgia now rightfully claiming this title, and Portugal hot on their heels.

Match records: Romania									
	No.	Versus	Result	Date	Venue	T	C	P	DG
Most points in a match by the team	100	Bulgaria	100–0	21/09/1976	Burgas	18	14	-	-
	No.	Player	Date	Versus	Venue	T	C	P	DG
Most points in a match by a player	32	Ionut Tofan	05/10/2002	Spain	Iasi	2	8	2	-
	5	Gheorghe Rascanu	02/05/1972	Morocco	Bucharest				
Most tries in a match by a player	5	Cornel Popescu	18/10/1986	Portugal	Birlad				
	5	Ionel Rotaru	13/04/1996	Portugal	Bucharest				
Most conversions in a match by a player	12	Virgil Popisteanu	13/04/1996	Portugal	Bucharest				
Most penalties in a match by a player	6	Petre Mitu	04/02/2001	Portugal	Lisbon				
Most drop goals in a match by a player	3	Valeriu Irimescu	29/10/1967	West Germany	Bucharest				
	3	Dumitru Alexandru	17/10/1976	Poland	Nowy Dwor				

Career records: Romania									
	No.	Player	Tests	Career	T	C	P	DG	Total
Most tests in a career	77	Adrian Lungu		13/04/1980–03/06/1995	3	-	-	-	12
Most points in a career	316	Ionut Tofan	60	04/10/1997–18/09/2007	12	53	46	4	
Most tries in a career	33	Petre Motrescu	34	20/04/1973–30/04/1980					
Most conversions in a career	53	Ionut Tofan	60	04/10/1997–18/09/2007					
Most penalties in a career	54	Neculai Nichitean	28	14/04/1990–01/06/1997					
Most drop goals in a career	13	Dumitru Alexandru	47	14/03/1974–20/09/1988					

Team photograph of the Romanian rugby side at the 1924 Paris Olympic Games who finished as bronze medallists. *Photo*: Frédéric Humbert/www.flickr.com/photos/rugby_pioneers/creative commons license

Samoa

Following the Treaty of Berlin in 1878, the island group of Samoa was split up between Germany and the United States in 1899 and named Western Samoa and American Samoa respectively. During World War I Western Samoa was seized by the Allies and mandated to New Zealand under the 1919 Treaty of Versailles. Rugby was first introduced in 1920 by the Marist Brothers, a Catholic order, and with such a Kiwi connection it was inevitable that rugby would become the most popular sport in Samoa. Today, it is indeed the national sport. Nicknamed *Manu Samoa* (*manu* means warrior; the word stems from a famous Samoan chief who ruled some ten generations ago), the national side was officially known as Western Samoa until 1997 when the country's name was changed to Samoa. Like New Zealand and the other island nations, Samoa always performs a war dance before each game – the *siva tau* – first performed at the 1991 RWC, replacing the 'gentler' *ma'ulu'ulu moa*, as the *siva tau* was considered more aggressive and effective in psyching the players up.

In 1924, the Apia Rugby Union, effectively the national union, was formed to manage the game in Western Samoa and affiliated to the New Zealand Rugby Union. It was later named the Western Samoa Rugby Football Union after independence and was re-named the Samoa Rugby Football Union in 1997. With the formation of the Apia Rugby Union, Western Samoa's first international was played on 18 August 1924 against Fiji at the Racecourse Ground in Apia. Western Samoa lost 0–6. They exacted revenge a month later when they won their first test in Apia 9–3. International games were sparse in these early years and, aside from a single test against Fiji in 1928, it was not until 1955 that Western Samoa would again play international rugby, against a touring Fijian side in a three-test series in Apia, which they lost 0–3. In 1956, they played Tonga for the first time in Nuku'alofa, losing 8–24, and in 1960 the New Zealand Maoris provided Western Samoa their first taste of a wider rugby world when they visited, winning the two-test series comfortably. Western Samoa struggled in these early years, coming last in the first South Pacific Championship in 1963, and it was not until 1971 that they notched up their second test victory, against New Caledonia in the fourth South Pacific Championship. In the absence of Tonga and Fiji, Western Samoa won the championship that year, defeating Tahiti, New Caledonia and Cook Islands. In 1975, Western Samoa recorded their first victory over Tonga, and in 1976, undertook their first tour to a major rugby-playing nation, to New Zealand where they lost a two-test series against the Maoris. Their rugby was beginning to take on the stamp it is famous for today: aggressive defence characterised by blockbusting tackling often bordering on the illegal. Western Samoa won the first 'traditional tri-series' between the three island nations and following this form, Wales became the first top-tier nation to award full international status to Western Samoa when they toured in 1986, winning the test 32–14. In 1987, Western Samoa were not invited to play in the inaugural RWC, but a year later, with IRFB affiliation secured, undertook their first tour to the United Kingdom and Ireland, losing both tests. They toured mainland Europe in 1989, beating West Germany 54–6 and Belgium 37–8, but lost the big one 24–32 to Romania.

These tours abroad saw an improvement in Western Samoan rugby as they began to win more regularly. In 1990, they qualified for their first RWC, the 1991 tournament, where they achieved their greatest triumph. They defeated co-hosts Wales 16–13 at the National Stadium in Cardiff; to this day the greatest upset in the tournament's history, as the islanders' thunderous tackling, rabid commitment and some favourable refereeing decisions saw them reach the quarter-finals against all odds, at which point their campaign was abruptly squashed by Scotland. They repeated this form in the 1995 RWC, with victories over Italy (42–18) and Argentina (32–26) in East London, once again qualifying for the quarter-finals. Tasked with beating the Springboks in Johannesburg they lost 14–42 in a match marred by the islanders' ferocious tackling, much of which was downright brutal. In the 1999 tournament they again made the play-offs, this time the quarter-final play-offs, following a magnificent 38–31 win over hosts Wales at the new Millennium Stadium, but this was to be the last of Samoa's great performances in RWCs, failing to reach the play-offs in both the 2003 and 2007 tournaments, the latter their worst showing, barely scraping a 25–21 victory over United States, before losing to Tonga, England and South Africa.

Samoa's close ties with New Zealand are certainly behind their success, as the majority of their players play their first-class rugby in New Zealand. However, this relationship has gleaned mixed success, as many top Samoans have been lost to the All Blacks, which has become a bigger snag in the professional era as earnings are higher in New Zealand, especially at international level. Players lost to the All Blacks include Brian Williams, whose son Gavin plays for Samoa; Va'aiga Tuigamala; Michael Jones; Tana Umaga, whose brother Mike played for Western Samoa; Mils Muliaina; Jerry Collins and Isaia Toeava. Economic challenges, and others, have led to some severe highs and lows for *Manu Samoa*, whose performance is normally dictated by player availability. When they can select their best players from abroad they inevitably give the best a run for their money, as in

Samoa test summary	
Played	172
Won	75
Lost	92
Drawn	5
Points for	3,438
Points against	3,859
% Win	43.60
% Lose	43.49
% Draw	2.91

1994 when they thumped Wales 34–9 in Apia, Ireland 40–25 in Dublin in 1996, Italy 17–9 in 2001 in L'Aquila and Argentina 28–12 in Buenos Aires in 2005. The ability to consistently replicate these performances has eluded them, however, with Samoa regularly conceding record defeats against the top nations, as was the case in 2008 when they lost 14–101 to New Zealand in New Plymouth.

Match records: Samoa									
	No.	Versus	Result	Date	Venue	T	C	P	DG
Most points in a match by the team	74	Korea	74–4	08/04/1990	Tokyo	13	8	2	-
	No.	Player	Date	Versus	Venue	T	C	P	DG
Most points in a match by a player	24	Roger Warren	29/05/2004	Tonga	Apia	-	-	8	-
Most tries in a match by a player	4	Tupo Fa'amasino	28/05/1991	Tonga	Nuku'alofa				
	4	Elvis Seveali'I	10/06/2001	Japan	Apia				
	4	Alesana Tuilagi	02/07/2005	Tonga	Apia				
Most conversions in a match by a player	8	Andy Aiolupo	08/04/1990	Korea	Tokyo				
Most penalties in a match by a player	8	Roger Warren	29/05/2004	Tonga	Apia				
Most drop goals in a match by a player	1	No player has ever kicked more than one drop goal in a match							

Career records: Samoa									
	No.	Player	Tests	Career	T	C	P	DG	Total
Most tests in a career	65	Brian Lima		23/06/1990–22/09/2007	31	-	-	-	150
Most points in a career	184	Earl Va'a	29	12/11/1996–01/11/2003	5	33	31	-	
Most tries in a career	31	Brian Lima	65	23/06/1990–22/09/2007					
Most conversions in a career	35	Andy Aiolupo	18	29/10/1988–06/08/1994					
Most penalties in a career	35	Darren Kellett	13	05/06/1993–16/12/1995					
Most drop goals in a career	2	Darren Kellett	13	05/06/1993–16/12/1995					
	2	Roger Warren	12	29/05/2004–03/09/2008					
	2	Steven Bachop	17	01/06/1991–20/10/1999					

Spain

Despite rugby having to compete for popularity in soccer-mad Spain, the sport has remained well liked, being most followed in Madrid and Valladolid. Funding for the game has increased following the recent improvement of the national side. Rugby was first introduced to Spain in the early 1920s by the French and in 1923 the Federación Española de Rugby, the Spanish Rugby Federation, was formed to manage the burgeoning game. Spain played their first rugby international against a French XV on 1 March 1927 in Madrid, losing heavily by 6–66. The following year, Spain toured France and lost the only international of the tour against a French XV by 6–53 in Bordeaux. In 1929, Spain won their first international when they defeated Italy 9–0 in Barcelona and played Germany for the first time, losing 15–24. In 1931, Spain undertook a successful tour to Morocco, enjoying international success in a series for the first time, winning 1–0 after drawing the all-important second test in Rabat. Following wins over neighbours Portugal in 1935 and 1936, it was not until 1951 that Spain would again compete on the international stage.

With meagre victories in the 1950s over the likes of Belgium, they lost heavily against the stronger teams, such as a French XV, Italy and West Germany. However, results improved in the 1960s as they competed in the FIRA B Championship against Portugal, Czechoslovakia, Belgium, Poland, the Netherlands and Yugoslavia. In 1973, Spain was promoted to the FIRA A Championship where they competed against Romania, a French XV and Italy. Spain found the going tough and regularly lost – badly – with only a 10–3 victory over Italy in 1977 detracting from their dismal form. In 1979, Spain was relegated to FIRA B. They remained unbeaten in the

1979/1980 FIRA B Championship and were once more promoted to the A league for the 1980/1981 tournament, but failed to win a single match and were yet again demoted. Here they stayed for the next two years, during which time their form began to improve, thus attracting the New Zealand Maoris to Spain in 1982. However, the only test of the tour indicated the disparity that existed between Spanish rugby and other leading nations, as the Maoris won 66–3. Argentina toured the same year, with Spain providing sterner opposition in the only test to lose 19–28 in Madrid. After winning the 1984 FIRA B Championship and drawing a two-test series with Zimbabwe in Zimbabwe, Spain were duly promoted again. By the late 1980s, Spain was starting to prod better sides, such as Scotland A and England B but usually lost by large margins.

They were not invited to take part in the 1987 RWC and failed to qualify for both the 1991 and 1995 tournaments, playing among others, Wales – the first time Spain was awarded full international status against a tier-one team. It was an RWC qualifying game held on 21 May 1994 in Madrid and, after beating Portugal by more than 100 points just a few days before, Wales was expected to win well. However, Spain played with passion and commitment to lose by 0–54, with the scoreline doing scant justice to their performance. This, coupled with their magnificent 11–3 win against Romania a month earlier – just their second victory over the Slavs – saw Spanish rugby improve in leaps and bounds in their quest to qualify for the 1999 RWC. The side went on to win nine consecutive internationals in 1996/1997, including RWC qualifying games, and in 1998 Spain enjoyed their greatest rugby achievement when they qualified for the 1999 RWC. It was a big ask, pooled with defending champions South Africa, co-hosts Scotland and Uruguay. However, the Spaniards competed in soldierly fashion, losing 15–27 to Uruguay, 3–47 to South Africa and 0–48 to Scotland – not too shabby when one compares the essentially amateur background of Spanish rugby to the high-tech professionalism of South Africa and Scotland. Following this, Spain failed to qualify in the final stages of both the 2003 and 2007 RWCs, losing their way against teams such as Romania and Georgia.

After the 1999 RWC, Spain competed in the European Nations Cup for the first time in 2000, where they now compete annually, and finished third, their best finish to date. Most of Spain's finest victories have played out at their national rugby stadium at the Madrid University ground. These include keeping Italy score-free in a 10–0 win in 1972; a 10–3 win against Italy in 1977, the last time they beat Italy; beating Romania 6–0, for the first time, in 1992 and a free-scoring 36–32 victory over Georgia in 2000. In addition, their 30–18 defeat of Zimbabwe in 1984 to share the series honours in Harare still ranks highly for the Spaniards.

Spain test summary	
Played	303
Won	126
Lost	168
Drawn	10
Points for	5,333
Points against	6,723
% Win	41.57
% Lose	55.44
% Draw	3.3

Match records: Spain									
	No.	Versus	Result	Date	Venue	T	C	P	DG
Most points in a match by the team	90	Czech Republic	90–8	02/04/1995	Madrid	14	10	-	-
	No.	Player	Date	Versus	Venue	T	C	P	DG
Most points in a match by a player	23	Andrei Kovalenco	09/05/2008	Portugal	Elche	-	1	7	-
	23	Esteban Roque Segovia	20/11/2004	Hungary	Madrid	-	4	5	-
Most tries in a match by a player	3	Ferran Velazco Querol	06/04/2002	Netherlands	Murcia				
	3	Cesar Sempere Padilla	20/11/2004	Hungary	Madrid				
	3	Cesar Sempere Padilla	13/11/2005	Poland	Madrid				
	3	Cesar Sempere Padilla	05/05/2007	Czech Republic	Prague				
Most conversions in a match by a player	9	Esteban Roque Segovia	27/03/2005	Slovenia	Ljubliana				
Most penalties in a match by a player	7	Andrei Kovalenco	09/05/2008	Portugal	Elche				
Most drop goals in a match by a player	2	Cesar Sempere Padilla	05/11/2005	Japan	Tokyo				

Career records: Spain									
	No.	Player	Tests	Career	T	C	P	DG	Total
Most tests in a career	93	Francisco Puertas Soto		18/05/1985–16/10/1999	6	5	12	1	78
Most points in a career	264	Esteban Roque Segovia	19	20/11/2004–23/05/2007	1	53	50	1	
Most tries in a career	22	Cesar Sempere Padilla	31	20/11/2004–15/03/2009					
Most conversions in a career	53	Esteban Roque Segovia	54	20/11/2004–23/05/2007					
Most penalties in a career	50	Esteban Roque Segovia	54	20/11/2004–23/05/2007					
Most drop goals in a career	2	Cesar Sempere Padilla	31	20/11/2004–15/03/2009					
	2	Ferran Velazco Querol	50	08/11/1997–27/05/2006					

Tonga

Tonga boasts the unique distinction of being the only Pacific island nation that was never colonised, with the result that rugby was only introduced in 1900 by Australian missionaries teaching in Tongan schools. The game slowly took off with visiting sailors playing local Tongan sides, but coupled with the return of Tongans who had learned the game studying or working abroad, rugby soon became the most popular island game. It is now the national sport, with Tonga's *sipi tau* war dance performed before every international. The Tongan Rugby Football Union (TRFU) was formed in 1923 to manage the game in Tonga, which was shambolic, with games randomly being arranged around the island. With the advent of organised rugby it was just a year later that the *Ikale Tahi*, the Sea Eagles, as the Tongan side is called, played their first international against the visiting Fijians on 25 August 1924 at the Teufaiva Sports Ground in the capital Nuku'alofa. This series has since been dubbed the Pacific Derby, as it is the original and oldest Pacific rugby fixture still played today. The Tongans won the test 9–6, the first in a three-match series, and went on to tie the series after losing the second and drawing the third. The tour was a great success so it was decided that a three-test series should be played between the two sides every other year on a home-and-away basis. Tonga undertook their first tour in 1926 to Fiji to play a three-test series, which they won 2–1, along with the title of the unofficial champions of the Pacific Ocean. However, due to the historical enmity between the two nations, games are brutally physical, with warlike hostility clearly re-enacted on the field. The level of physicality reached a point of such violence during the notorious all-important third and deciding test of the 1928 series that it had to be abandoned, with Tonga in a bloody 11–8 lead. Tonga won the series but has since lost all further series to Fiji who now dominate the Pacific Derby.

In 1954, an Australian XV side became the first from a major rugby nation to tour Tonga, however, no internationals were played. It wasn't until 1956 that Tonga played fresh international opposition and beat Western Samoa 24–8 in Nuku'alofa, which they followed up by beating the Samoans in a three-test series in Apia the following year. In 1960, the New Zealand Maoris visited Tonga for a once-off test in Nuku'alofa, won 27–16 by Tonga. Following a poor run of form in the mid-1960s, Tonga upped their game in 1969 in spectacular fashion when they toured their first major rugby-playing nation, New Zealand. On the trip they played the New Zealand Maoris in a two-test series and won both tests convincingly: 26–19 in Christchurch and 19–6 in Auckland. Following successful tours by Fiji to Australia a few years earlier, Australia invited Tonga to tour in 1973. The Wallabies were expected to win, and win well, as Tonga had had mixed success during the early games. Tonga lost the first test in Sydney 12–30, but a week later in Brisbane turned the form books around in dramatic style to record their greatest-ever victory by beating Australia 16–11 (four tries to two). Tonga were then invited to tour the United Kingdom for the first time, losing the two tests, against a Scotland XV 8–44 and a Wales XV 7–26. In 1979, Tonga won the South Pacific Games in Suva for the first time, defeating arch rivals Fiji in a tense final by 6–3.

Wales became the second top-tier side to award international status to Tongan games when they toured in 1986, winning the only test 7–15 in a match infamous for being one of the dirtiest games of rugby ever played. In 1987, the TRFU, now affiliated to the IRFB, was invited to take part in the first RWC where they were pooled with Canada, Ireland and Wales and lost all their matches. They failed to qualify for the 1991 tournament, but after winning the 1994 South Pacific Championship, on try count, they edged out Fiji on an aggregate scoreline of 34–25 to qualify for the 1995 RWC. After losing to France and Scotland, Tonga won their first RWC match when they beat Côte d'Ivoire in Rustenburg by 29–11.

They qualified for the 1999 RWC; their form going into the tournament could not have been better – they'd shocked France in June 1999 to win 20–16 in Nuku'alofa, a result which rivals their 1973 victory over Australia. In the tournament Tonga had mixed fortunes,

Tonga test summary	
Played	210
Won	79
Lost	126
Drawn	5
Points for	3,892
Points against	4,824
% Win	37.62
% Lose	60.0
% Draw	2.38

losing a 9–45 physical encounter with New Zealand, achieving a thrilling 28–25 victory over Italy after fullback Sateki Tuipuloto kicked a last-gasp, winning drop goal, only to be trounced 10–101 by England.

To qualify for the 2003 RWC Tonga successfully completed a gruelling eight-match qualification process, which ended with record 84–12 and 119–0 victories over Papua New Guinea and Korea respectively. Pooled with Italy, Wales, Canada and New Zealand, they failed to win a match, but they qualified for the 2007 RWC, producing some stupendous rugby: after beating the United States 25–15 and Samoa 19–15, they very nearly achieved a massive upset, taking South Africa to the wire, but losing 25–30, with just the bounce of the ball in the final minute denying them victory. They went on to lose 20–36 to England, but were one of the most popular sides in the tournament.

Match records: Tonga									
	No.	Versus	Result	Date	Venue	T	C	P	DG
Most points in a match by the team	119	Korea	119–0	21/03/2003	Nuku'alofa	17	17	-	-
	No.	Player	Date	Versus	Venue	T	C	P	DG
Most points in a match by a player	44	Pierre Hola	21/03/2003	Korea	Nuku'alofa	2	17	-	-
Most tries in a match by a player	5	Benhur Kivalu	24/06/2006	Cook Islands	Avarua				
Most conversions in a match by a player	17	Pierre Hola	21/03/2003	Korea	Nuku'alofa				
Most penalties in a match by a player	4	Sateki Tu'ipulotu	19/02/1995	Japan	Tokyo				
	4	Kusitafu Tonga	25/05/2001	Fiji	Nuku'alofa				
	4	Sateki Tu'ipulotu	10/11/2001	Scotland	Edinburgh				
	4	Fangatapu Apikotoa	23/07/2005	Samoa	Nuku'alofa				
	4	Pierre Hola	16/09/2007	Samoa	Montpellier				
Most drop goals in a match by a player	1	No player has ever kicked more than one drop goal in a match							

Career records: Tonga									
	No.	Player	Tests	Career	T	C	P	DG	Total
Most tests in a career	41	Siua Taumalolo		1996–2007	12	4	10	-	98
Most points in a career	278	Pierre Hola	35	18/09/1998–05/07/2008	11	56	35	2	
Most tries in a career	12	Siua Taumalolo	41	1996–2007					
Most conversions in a career	56	Pierre Hola	35	18/09/1998–05/07/2008					
Most penalties in a career	35	Sateki Tu'ipulotu	35	18/09/1998–05/07/2008					
Most drop goals in a career	2	Pierre Hola	35	18/09/1998–05/07/2008					

United States of America

Rugby in America has struggled to compete in popularity over the years with American football, baseball, basketball, ice hockey, athletics and lately, soccer. There has always been massive potential for America to become a rugby powerhouse if their talent and player base were exploited more aggressively, especially considering the huge numbers who play American football through high school and into college. Because rugby is not played in schools, most registered players only start playing the game after graduation. Additionally, the sheer size of the country creates enormous logistical and selection issues. Just bringing a side together to train and play a match is a challenge in itself, let alone selecting a national team from fifty states. Rugby was first introduced to the USA by British immigrants in the mid-nineteenth century and by 1872 there were several rugby clubs in the San Francisco Bay area. On 14 May 1874, the first recorded game of rugby in America was played between Harvard University and McGill University from Canada, essentially the first rugby tour to take place between the two countries. However, it was in California where the game prospered and in 1882, a Californian side, the first all-American rugby side constituted, played and lost 4–7 to the British expatriate Phoenix Rugby Club.

As American football evolved from rugby union, many clubs opted for the new game and rugby suffered. The first recorded game of American football took place in 1869 and by the beginning of the twentieth century it was by far and away the most popular contact sport in the USA. Despite this, a small core of rugby players remained in California and on 16 November 1912, the USA played their first international match, against a touring Australian side on the California Field in Berkeley, which was won 12–8 by the Australians. A year later, a full-strength New Zealand side arrived, with an international game played at the same venue, which the All Blacks won by a then world-record 51–3 scoreline. Following World War I, the US Olympic Committee agreed to sanction a side to compete in the 1920 Olympic Games. However, it received no financial backing due to the fact that California was the only state playing rugby in the United States. This was America's first trip abroad with the French XV strong favourites to win. America, however, put in a stout performance to record their first international victory, upsetting the French by 8–0 to claim the gold medal. Following this magnificent feat, the French invited the USA to tour after the Olympic Games, with some success for the Americans who won three of their four matches, only losing the test match 5–14 against a full-strength French side in Paris.

Amazingly, despite the Californians' terrific success on behalf of the United States at the games, there was little interest in the team's achievements – or in the sport for that matter – due to the massive increase in popularity of American football. As the 1924 Paris Olympic Games approached, rugby as a sport resurfaced in America when France officially challenged America to defend their title. Once again, the US Olympic Committee granted permission to send a side, but no funds. A mixed bunch of old Californian players and American football players formed a hodge-podge team and sailed for France. Full international status was granted to all games, with America easily beating Romania 39–0, to meet France in the final that what was to become American finest rugby hour. Before a packed Olympic Stadium, the USA stunned their French hosts to win 17–3 and reclaim the gold medal in what is still to this day America's only win over a top international rugby-playing nation. Shortly after the 1924 Olympics, the International Olympic Committee removed rugby as an Olympic sport, which had a profound impact on rugby in America: without Olympic incentive the sport collapsed completely.

It was not until the early 1960s that rugby was once again played in America, with steady growth through the 1960s and into the 1970s. The United States of America Rugby Football Union, known today as USA Rugby, was formed in 1975. On 31 January 1976, America played Australia, a momentous occasion for USA Rugby, as it had been a full 52 years since their previous international; it was also the first test match where the team played as the Eagles, the Bald eagle being the national bird logoed on their jerseys. Played in Anaheim, California, the Eagles performed stoically, going down a creditable 12–24. From this point, international rugby in America prospered: the side played France in the same same year, Canada for the first time in 1977, toured England in 1977 and beat Canada for the first time in 1978. However, regular success was slow in coming: after beating Canada in 1978, it was not until 1984 that they won again, again against Canada. Record scorelines were regularly conceded against top sides but, nonetheless, the United States were invited to take part in the inaugural RWC in 1987. The Americans played some good rugby, beating Japan 21–18 in their first RWC match, before losing 12–47 to Australia and 6–34 to England. They qualified for the 1991 RWC, only to lose all their matches, and then failed to qualify for the 1995 tournament. Despite this failure, 1995 witnessed one of their greatest victories when they beat Canada in Canada for the first time by 15–14 in Markham. They backed up this form by qualifying for the 1999 RWC, but it was in the 2003 tournament that the USA produced their best performances when they were extremely unlucky to lose 18–19 to Fiji, but beat Japan convincingly by 39–26 in Gosford and lost competitively against Scotland (15–39) and France (14–41). The USA again lost all their matches in the 2007 RWC, but found some success when a blinder of a try – scored by green-card Zimbabwean immigrant, winger Takudzwa Ngwenya against South Africa – was voted the IRB Try of the Year.

USA test summary	
Played	169
Won	52
Lost	115
Drawn	2
Points for	3,257
Points against	4,774
% Win	30.77
% Lose	68.05
% Draw	1.18

Match records: USA									
	No.	Versus	Result	Date	Venue	T	C	P	DG
Most points in a match by the team	91	Barbados	91–0	01/07/2006	San Francisco	13	13	-	-
	No.	Player	Date	Versus	Venue	T	C	P	DG
Most points in a match by a player	26	Chris O'Brien	07/11/1989	Uruguay	Montevideo	3	7	-	-
	26	Mike Hercus	30/05/2004	Russia	Tokyo				
	26	Mike Hercus	01/07/2006	Barbados	San Francisco	-	13	-	-
Most tries in a match by a player	4	Vaea Anitoni	06/07/1996	Japan	San Francisco				
	4	Brian Hightower	07/06/1997	Japan	San Francisco				
	4	Vaea Anitoni	08/04/1998	Portugal	Lisbon				
Most conversions in a match by a player	13	Mike Hercus	01/07/2006	Barbados	San Francisco				
Most penalties in a match by a player	6	Matt Alexander	18/09/1996	Canada	Hamilton				
Most drop goals in a match by a player	1	No player has ever kicked more than one drop goal in a match							

Career records: USA									
	No.	Player	Tests	Career	T	C	P	DG	Total
Most tests in a career	62	Luke Gross		06/01/1996–31/10/2003	-	-	-	-	-
Most points in a career	423	Mike Hercus	42	22/06/2002–22/11/2008	9	84	67	3	
Most tries in a career	26	Vaea Anitoni	46	13/06/1992–15/07/2000					
Most conversions in a career	84	Mike Hercus	42	22/06/2002–22/11/2008					
Most penalties in a career	67	Mike Hercus	42	22/06/2002–22/11/2008					
Most drop goals in a career	3	Mike Hercus	42	22/06/2002–22/11/2008					

Action from the 1920 international between France and United States in Paris, a match won 14-5 by the French.
Photo: Frédéric Humbert/www.flickr.com/photos/rugby_pioneers/creative commons license

Uruguay

For many, rugby in Uruguay is famous more because of the survival technique adopted by members of the Stella Maris Old Christians rugby side from Montevideo, whose plane crashed high up in the Andes and were forced to eat the flesh of their dead colleagues to survive, than the exploits of the national side on the rugby field. It is believed that rugby was first introduced into Uruguay by fellow South Americans from Chile and Argentina in the early twentieth century and became most popular in the capital, Montevideo. On 5 August 1948, there were sufficient players to select a national side for Uruguay's first international against Chile in Buenos Aires, which they lost 3–21. This saw the game's popularity rise and in 1951 the Unión de Rugby del Uruguay (URU) was formed. Following this, *Los Teros*, as the Uruguayan side has come to be known after the national bird on their emblem, the southern lapwing, or *tero*, played their next international during the 1951 Buenos Aires Pan American Games. During these games the first South American Rugby Championship was held between Argentina, Chile, Brazil and Uruguay, with mixed success for Uruguay. They lost heavily in their first international against Argentina (0–62), but sneaked in narrow victories over Chile and Brazil to claim the runners-up spot.

Virtually all of Uruguay's international competition was generated through the South American Championship, playing Argentina, Chile, Brazil, Paraguay, Peru and Venezuela. A few friendly internationals were played against various touring sides, as in 1960 when Uruguay was trounced 0–59 by a French XV. Montevideo hosted the championship for the first time in 1961, but the hosts let the home crowd down as they suffered heavy defeats against Chile and Argentina to finish a disappointing third. In the 1960s, Uruguay didn't do well in the championship, but by the 1970s, with rugby quality improving, they finished runners-up twice, in 1973 and 1977. In 1976, a New Zealand XV side captained by Graham Mourie scheduled a lone match in Uruguay at the beginning of their tour to Argentina, against the Uruguayan national side. Uruguay's performed admirably, despite losing 3–64. In the 1979 championship, Uruguay put in a fine showing against South American rugby giants, Argentina, who were unbeaten against Uruguay, with the latter losing narrowly by just 16–19. They were pipped to the runners-up spot by Chile on points difference that year, but in the following championship in 1981, Uruguay became the first nation other than Argentina to win the championship – thanks to Argentina not competing that year. With the return of Argentina, Uruguay were again relegated to the runners-up position, a spot they held for the next two decades

The 1980s saw other sides touring, such as Spain in 1987 and the United States in 1989. Uruguay was not invited to take part in the 1987 RWC, nor did they attempt to qualify for the 1991 tournament, but in 1993 they tried gamely for RWC inclusion when the South American Championship that year doubled as RWC qualifyiers with the winner into the 1995 RWC in South Africa. Uruguay came close: they beat Paraguay 67–3 and Chile 14–6 but lost crucially against Argentina 10–19. They played Canada for the first time in 1995 at the Montevideo Pan American Games, losing 9–28, but stepped up the pace when they beat Spain 47–10 later that year. In 1998, Uruguay began their qualification odyssey for their first RWC shwoing after they beat Morocco in the deciding home-and-away repechage series by a 36–24 aggregate scoreline. This was an important achievement for *Los Teros* who were pooled with Spain, co-hosts Scotland and defending champions South Africa. Uruguay performed with passion and intent, recording their first RWC victory in their opening game against Spain by 27–15 in Galashiels. They then lost 12–43 to Scotland in Edinburgh and went on to niggle South Africa in their final match, losing 3–39 in Glasgow after the Springboks had been reduced to 14 men. This tournament showing boosted the popularity of rugby in Uruguay no end. After losing all their matches in the 2001 Pan American Games by slim margins, Uruguay attempted to qualify for the 2003 RWC in a series of games against Chile, Canada and the United States. Their bid started poorly, losing all three of their away fixtures, but in the return home matches they were unbeaten, recording a memorable 25–23 win over Canada for the first time in a thrilling encounter; they beat the United States for the first time a week later 10–9 and reinforced this with a solid 34–23 victory over Chile. This was enough to guarantee a place in the 2003 RWC in Australia, where Uruguay found the standard of rugby somewhat higher than it had been four years earlier. They were thumped 6–72 by South Africa in their opening game and then pulverised 13–60 by Samoa, before raising their game to beat Georgia 24–12 in Sydney, thereby ensuring they'd won at least one RWC match in each of the tournaments they'd had played in. Their last match was woebegone, losing 13–111 to eventual champions England, which did little to enhance the popularity of rugby back home. Despite a record 92–8 win over Venezuela in the 2004 South American Championship, the quality of their game was deteriorating. After a record 3–134 hiding

Uruguay test summary	
Played	152
Won	61
Lost	90
Drawn	1
Points for	2,990
Points against	3,995
% Win	40.13
% Lose	59.21
% Draw	0.66

at the hands of South Africa in 2005 it appeared inevitable that Uruguay would not qualify for the 2007 RWC. This proved to be the case: they lost a repechage series to the USA and then lost the final all-important repechage series to Portugal.

Match records: Uruguay									
	No.	Versus	Result	Date	Venue	T	C	P	DG
Most points in a match by the team	93	Paraguay	93–3	10/10/1998	Asuncion				
	No.	Player	Date	Versus	Venue	T	C	P	DG
Most points in a match by a player	29	Juan Menchaca	07/09/2002	Chile	Montevideo	-	1	5	4
Most tries in a match by a player	4	Benjamin Bono	04/05/2002	Paraguay	Mendoza				
Most conversions in a match by a player	7	Ricardo Sierra	06/10/2001	Paraguay	Montevideo				
Most penalties in a match by a player	6	Federico Sciarra	01/05/1999	Morocco	Casablanca				
	6	Juan Menchaca	01/05/2002	Chile	Mendoza				
	6	Matias Arocena	15/06/2008	Georgia	Bucharest				
Most drop goals in a match by a player	4	Juan Menchaca	07/09/2002	Chile	Montevideo				

Career records: Uruguay									
	No.	Player	Tests	Career	T	C	P	DG	Total
Most tests in a career	66	Diego Ormaechea		06/10/1979–15/10/1999	14	-	-	-	70
Most points in a career	222	Juan Menchaca	36	13/03/1999–24/03/2007	4	20	49	5	
Most tries in a career	14	Diego Ormaechea	66	06/10/1979–15/10/1999					
Most conversions in a career	20	Juan Menchaca	36	13/03/1999–24/03/2007					
Most penalties in a career	49	Juan Menchaca	36	13/03/1999–24/03/2007					
Most drop goals in a career	5	Juan Menchaca	36	13/03/1999–24/03/2007					

Zimbabwe

Rugby was introduced to Rhodesia, now Zimbabwe, in 1980 by Cecil Rhodes's Pioneer Column which occupied the territory of Mashonaland in 1890. During the trek north to Fort Salisbury (later Harare), rugby games were played between the wagoneers and troopers of the occupying force. The first two clubs were formed in Bulawayo in 1894: Queen's Rugby Club and Bulawayo Athletics Club. The following year, the Rhodesia Rugby Football Union was constituted to organise and oversee the first tour abroad by a Rhodesian side: to South Africa to participate in the 1898 Currie Cup. In 1901, the first interprovincial match was played in Rhodesia between Matabeleland and Mashonaland in Salisbury, but such were the 'roads' that it took the visiting Matabeles ten days by mule coach to reach Salisbury.

As a British colony, Rhodesia was, from a rugby perspective, considered a province of South Africa, much like South West Africa, so overseas touring sides to South Africa regularly played against the Rhodesians. The first such side was the 1910 British Isles team that played and beat Rhodesia by 24–11 in Bulawayo. Rhodesia next played the British Lions in 1924, followed by New Zealand for the first time in 1928. In 1933, an Australian side became the first tourists to play a two-'test' series against Rhodesia and won comfortably. In 1949, Rhodesia achieved its greatest rugby success of all time when the won the two-test series against the mighty All Blacks 1–0 after winning the first test 10–8 in Salisbury and drawing the second 3–3 in Bulawayo. During a three-match series against Australia in 1953, Rhodesia managed to draw the second match in Kitwe, Northern Rhodesia 8–8, but this was their last such success, as the all-conquering 1974 British Lions was the last touring side to play Rhodesia, thrashing them 42–6 in Salisbury in the only test.

By the 1960s, a number of Rhodesian players were considered good enough to play for the Springboks, including Des van Jaarsveldt, the first Rhodesian to captain South Africa in an international. He played just one test, against Scotland in 1960, before being summarily dropped as the staunchly Afrikaner-nationalist South African authorities could not condone an *uitlander* as Springbok skipper. Other

Rhodesians of note to have played for the Springboks include flyhalf Ian Robertson, centre David Smith and winger Ray Mordt, the latter duo continuing their rugby careers with distinction in South Africa after Zimbabwean independence.

With civil war raging in the 1970s and Rhodesia a political pariah, international tours stopped after the 1974 British Lions' visit. Until 1980, Rhodesia was restricted to the Currie Cup, which it competed for ferociously. As an internationally recognised independent state, following independence on 18 April 1980, Zimbabwe climbed back into the international rugby arena, but cut ties with South Africa and pulled out of the Currie Cup, which ultimately sealed Zimbabwe's fate as a competitve international rugby nation. Zimbabwe played their first international against Kenya in Nairobi, winning 34–24. They competed well in their early internationals, regularly beating the likes of Kenya and Spain through the 1980s and were unlucky to lose narrowly to Romania in a two-test series in 1982. In 1986, during the shared two-test series with the Soviet Union, Richard Tsimba became the first black player to represent the country. Because of South African isolation, the IRFB invited Zimbabwe as Africa's sole representative to partcipate in the inaugural RWC in 1987. The team struggled, losing narrowly to Romania 20–21, before being walloped 21–60 by Scotland and 12–70 by France. However, they ended the year on a high when they won the first African Championship, beating Kenya 44–12 in the Nairobi final.

With the dawning of the professional era of the 1990s, Zimbabwe fell by the wayside. In 1989, they managed to win just once, against Kenya, while losing a home series to Spain 0–2 and failing to win a test on their tour to Europe. The following year, Zimbabwe qualified for the 1991 RWC, beating Côte d'Ivoire, Morocco and Tunisia in Harare, but their 24–13 win over Tunisia was to be their last for three years as they went on to lose 15 tests in a row, including their first against Namibia. Clearly out of their depth in the 1991 RWC, they lost all their games by large margins: Ireland 11–55, Scotland 12–51 and Japan 8–52. Their next win would be against Kenya in an RWC qualifying match on 3 July 1993. In 1994 they failed to qualify for the RWC for the first time, losing to Namibia and Côte d'Ivoire in Casablanca.

Zimbabwe's 1991 qualification was to be their last achievement of any note. Political turmoil and economic collapse have effectively killed the game. In 1998, Wales became the last top side to grant full international status to a Zimbabwean match. A trickle of victories included a first-ever 15–13 win against neighbours Namibia in 1996 and another over the same side in 2001 by 27–26. In subsequent years, Zimbabwean rugby plumbed the depths, losing to the likes of Uganda, Zambia and Madagascar. In the African Championship, they lost by record scores to Namibia (8–68) and South Africa u23 (20–71 and 29–78). This is a rugby tragedy for a nation that consistently produces top players at school level, even today. As with other disciplines such as cricket, football and tennis, Zimbabwean sportsman of international ability pack their bags and leave. Fine players who have gone on to represent their adopted country with distinction include David Smith, Ray Mordt, Gary Teichmann, Adrian Garvey, Bobby Skinstad, Tonderai Chavanga, Tendai 'The Beast' Mtawarira and Brian Mujati – all to South Africa; Andy Marinos to Wales; David Pocock to Australia; Takudzwa Ngwenya to the United States and Scott Gray and Paul Johnstone to Scotland. However, with a reasonably robust sporting culture and infrastructure still evident at school and club level, coupled with a whiff of political change and economic turnaround in the air, who knows; perhaps Zimbabwe might one day claw its way back. The international rugby community certainly hopes so.

Zimbabwe test summary	
Played	115
Won	39
Lost	75
Drawn	1
Points for	2,622
Points against	3,144
% Win	33.91
% Lose	65.22
% Draw	0.87

Match records: Zimbabwe									
	No.	Versus	Result	Date	Venue	T	C	P	DG
Most points in a match by the team	130	Botswana	130–10	07/09/1996	Bulawayo	20	15	-	-
	No.	Player	Date	Versus	Venue	T	C	P	DG
Most points in a match by a player	27	Doug Trivella	21/06/1997	Italy A	Harare	2	4	3	-
Most tries in a match by a player	4	Shaun Landman	03/07/1993	Kenya	Nairobi				
Most conversions in a match by a player	4	Ian Noble	03/07/1993	Kenya	Nairobi				
	4	Doug Trivella	21/06/1997	Italy A	Harare				
Most penalties in a match by a player	6	Kennedy Tsimba	16/09/1998	Côte d'Ivoire	Casablanca				
Most drop goals in a match by a player	2	Anthony Papenfus	09/05/1998	Namibia	Windhoek				

Career records: Zimbabwe									
	No.	Player	Tests	Career	T	C	P	DG	Total
Most tests in a career	20	Brendan Dawson		05/05/1990–19/09/1998	3	-	-	-	14
Most points in a career	72	Kennedy Tsimba	6	21/06/1997–19/09/1998	4	5	14	-	
Most tries in a career	8	Victor Olonga	14	22/05/1993–19/09/1998					
Most conversions in a career	8	Ian Noble	6	22/05/1993–14/06/1994					
Most penalties in a career	14	Kennedy Tsimba	6	21/06/1997–19/09/1998					
	14	Andy Ferreira	7	23/05/1987–06/10/1991					
Most drop goals in a career	3	Anthony Papenfus	4	21/06/1997–09/05/1998					

Above: Ian Robertson, verstaile Rhodesian flyhalf/fullback and Springbok fullback. *Photo: The Chronicle*

Above left: The Rhodesian rugby squad prior to a Currie Cup match against the Orange Free State, 26 May 1979. Seated extreme right is talented fullback Leroy Duberley who was killed in action a few months later when the helicopter he was in was shot down over Mozambique. A minute's silence was observed the following Saturday at the Currie Cup match in Durban, won incidentally by Rhodesia.

Ray Mordt, powerful Rhodesian and Springbok winger, sails into his opposite number Gerrie Germishuys during a 1978 Currie Cup clash in Salisbury (Harare). *Photo: The Herald*

Chapter Seven
International test matches

This chapter details only those matches that are recognised as capped internationals by the ten tier-one rugby nations. To avoid duplication, match statistics for a particular series are given only once, under the heading of the team that appears first alphabetically. For example, to find all match details for England vs Australia, refer to the listings for Australia vs England. Also, for clarification, the chapter does not only list tier-one vs tier-one countries, but all tier-one vs tier-two and -three, and international invitations teams.

The story of the rugby 'cap' can be traced back to Rugby School when in 1839 the school first decided to adopt a team uniform. A unique part of the rugby uniform was a small velvet cap, which came to represent the ultimate honour of representing Rugby School at rugby. The cap idea was soon adopted by English clubs, eventually becoming a symbol of national and international achievement. Today, a player who represents his country receives a cap for each international game. So a capped international is defined as any player who has represented his country in an international match. Each union can award caps at their own discretion, with some unions being stricter than others in the criteria. South Africa, for example, has never awarded caps for matches against the New Zealand Maori team, while all other unions have, barring New Zealand of course. Wales even awarded caps for matches against the British Barbarians in the early 1990s, which no other union has done. International caps were previously not awarded by top-tier sides playing tier-two and tier-three teams prior to the 1980s, with the exception of France which awarded caps for matches against FIRA nations during and after their years of isolation from the Five Nations.

With the advent of professionalism, there are now a plethora of international cups, plates, shields and trophies on offer, often frowned upon by the crustier rugby-union traditionalists. The most recent is the Hillary Shield, competed for between England and New Zealand. The oldest international rugby trophy is the Calcutta Cup, contested between England and Scotland since 1879. There is some fascinating rugby history associated with some of the older trophies. This chapter includes records of all international matches ever played by the top ten tier-one rugby nations, with details of any trophies associated with each country.

To help the reader analyse scorelines for early internationals played before the implementation of the first official scoring system by the IRFB in 1891, these have have been converted to a numerical format using the original 1886 scoring system. Prior to this, match results were simply registered by what goals or tries were scored. Take, for example, the 1872 encounter between England and Scotland, won by 1G 2T 1D to 1D – strange reading to many: using the 1886 system, England would have won by a scoreline of 8–3. Such matches are shown with the converted numerical score shadowed by the superscripted older score of the time, for example:

5 February 1872, Kennington Oval, London
England   8 [1G 2T 1DG]   T: Hamersley, D'Aguilar, Finney; C: Isherwood; DG: Freeman
Scotland   3 [1DG]   DG: Cathcart

Displayed at the start of each match-result section is an at-a-glance summary (in a grey box) of the matches played between two countries. These summary boxes only appear if two countries have played each other four times or more.

Key to abbreviations used in this chapter:

T: Try	C: Conversion	PG: Penalty goal	DG: Drop goal
GM: Goal from a mark	For: points for	Against: points against	* point scorer/s unknown

Argentina

Argentina vs Australia (Puma Trophy)

The Puma Trophy was instituted as a perpetual trophy between Australia and Argentina. The trophy, a bronze statue of a puma, was first competed for in 2000 but is not awarded for any internationals played in RWCs. Australia has dominated the contests, but Argentina has won on four occasions, most famously in the 1987 two-test series when Hugo Porta hoofed Australia into defeat.

27 October 1979, Ferro Carril Oeste Stadium, Buenos Aires
Argentina 24 T: Madero (2); C: Porta (2); PG: Porta; DG: Porta (3)
Australia 13 T: Crowe; PG: P McLean (2); DG: Melrose

3 November 1979, Ferro Carril Oeste Stadium, Buenos Aires
Australia 17 T: Moon (2), Batch; C: P McLean; PG: P McLean
Argentina 12 T: Petersen; C: Porta; PG: Porta; DG: Porta

31 July 1983, Ballymore, Brisbane
Argentina 18 T: Miguens, Petersen; C: Porta (2); PG: Porta; DG: Porta
Australia 3 PG: Campese

7 August 1983, Sydney Cricket Ground, Sydney
Australia 29 T: Moon (2), penalty try, Roche, Campese; C: Campese (3); PG: Campese
Argentina 13 T: Milano; PG: Porta (2); DG: Porta

6 July 1986, Ballymore, Brisbane
Australia 39 T: Papworth (2), Grigg, Campese; C: Lynagh (4); PG: Lynagh (5)
Argentina 19 T: Cuesta-Silva, Turnes, J Lanza; C: Porta, Madero; PG: Porta

12 July 1986, Sydney Cricket Ground, Sydney
Australia 26 T: Campese (2), Tuynman; C: Lynagh; PG: Lynagh (4)
Argentina 0

31 October 1987, Velez Sarsfield Stadium, Buenos Aires
Argentina 19 T: Cuesta-Silva; PG: Porta (4); DG: Porta
Australia 19 T: Williams, Cutler, Lynagh; C: Lynagh (2); PG: Lynagh

7 November 1987, Velez Sarsfield Stadium, Buenos Aires
Argentina 27 T: Mendi; C: Porta; PG: Porta (5); DG: Porta (2)
Australia 19 T: Williams (2); C: Lynagh; PG: Lynagh (3)

4 October 1991, Stradey Park, Llanelli (RWC, Pool 3)
Australia 32 T: Campese (2), Horan (2), Kearns; C: Lynagh (3); PG: Lynagh (2)
Argentina 19 T: Teran (2); C: del Castillo; PG: del Castillo; DG: Arbizu (2)

30 April 1995, Ballymore, Brisbane
Australia 53 T: Lynagh (2), Campese, Eales, Pini, Smith, Ofahengaue; C: Lynagh (3); PG: Lynagh (4)
Argentina 7 T: Pichot; C: Arbizu

6 May 1995, Sydney Football Stadium, Sydney
Australia 30 T: Campese (2), Wilson; PG: Lynagh (5)
Argentina 13 T: Arbizu; C: Crexell; PG: Crexell, Meson

1 November 1997, Ferro Carril Oeste Stadium, Buenos Aires
Australia 23 T: Finegan; PG: Knox (6)
Argentina 15 PG: Giannantonio (5)

8 November 1997, Ferro Carril Oeste Stadium, Buenos Aires
Argentina 18 T: Pichot, Martin; C: Giannantonio; PG: Giannantonio (2)
Australia 16 T: Finegan, Tune; PG: Knox (2)

17 June 2000, Ballymore, Brisbane
Australia 53 T: Latham (4), Roff (2), Williams (2), Connors; C: Roff (4)
Argentina 6 PG: Cilley (2)

24 June 2000, Bruce Stadium, Canberra
Australia 32 T: Roff, Latham, Mortlock; C: Mortlock; PG: Mortlock (5)
Argentina 25 T: Corletto, Mendez; PG: Contepomi (5)

3 November 2002, River Plate Stadium, Buenos Aires
Australia 17 T: Mortlock; PG: Burke (3), Flatley
Argentina 6 PG: Contepomi (2)

10 October 2003, Stadium Australia, Sydney (RWC, Pool A)
Australia 24 T: Sailor, Roff; C: Flatley; PG: Flatley (4)
Argentina 8 T: Corletto; PG: F Contepomi

Puma Trophy			Current Holder: Australia				Number of titles: Australia 2, Argentina 0	
No.	Date	Venue		Result			Series	Holder
1	17/06/2000	Ballymore, Brisbane	Australia	53–6	Argentina		2–0	Australia
2	24/06/2000	Bruce Stadium, Canberra	Australia	32–35	Argentina			
3	03/11/2002	River Plate Stadium, Buenos Aires	Argentina	6–17	Australia		0–1	Australia

Argentina vs Brazil

Argentina vs Brazil	
Played:	11
Won:	11
Lost:	0
Drawn:	0
For:	860
Against:	38

Average score:
78.18–3.45

Argentina percentages:
Won:	100%
Lost:	0%
Drawn:	0%

13 September 1951, GEBA, Buenos Aires
Argentina 72*
Brazil 0

12 October 1961, Carrasco Polo Club, Montevideo
Argentina 60 T: Goti (5), Neri (4), Montes de Oca, González del Solar, Hogg, Lavayén, penalty try; C: Olivieri (8), Goti
Brazil 0

19 August 1964, San Pablo
Argentina 30 T: Neri (2), Contepomi, Dartiguelongue, Etchegaray, Goti, McCormick, Molina Berro; C: Molina Berro (2), Queirolo
Brazil 8* T: (1); C: (1); PG: (1)

12 October 1971, Carrasco Polo Club, Montevideo
Argentina 50 T: Rodríguez-Jurado (5), Carracedo (3), Constante, Otaola, Braceras, Loyola C: Rodríguez-Jurado (2), Cutler (2); PG: Porta, Rodríguez-Jurado
Brazil 6 PG: Smith (2)

20 October 1973, Clube Atlético, São Paulo
Argentina 96 T: Pérez-Leiros (3), Sanz (3), Walther (3),Travaglini (2), Porta (2), Carracedo, Bottarini, Etchegaray, Insúa, Miguens; C: Porta (7), Morgan (2); PG: Porta DG: Rodríquez-Jurado
Brazil 0

27 September 1975, Asuncion
Argentina 64 T: Bach (2), de Forteza (2), Ventura (2), Bozzo, Brouchou, d'Agnilo, Devoto, Minquez, penalty try; C: de Forteza (6), Capalbo (2)
Brazil 6* PG: (2)

24 October 1977, Cancha del Atletico, Tucuman
Argentina 78 T: Sansot (3), Morgan (3), Alvarez (2), Ventura (2), Badano, Iachetti, Passaglia; C: Sansot (4), Capalbo (3); PG: Sansot (4)
Brazil 6 PG: Bishop (2)

9 October 1979, Stade Francais Field, Santiago
Argentina 109 T: Sartori (3), Morgan (3), Terán (3), Cerioni (2), Paz (2), Puccio, Dip, Courreges, Negri, Memoli, penalty try; C: Dip (9), Sanguinetti (6); DG: Escalante
Brazil 3 PG: Bishop

8 October 1989, Carrasco Polo Club, Montevideo
Argentina 103 T: Jorge (6), Schacht (3), Soler (3), Loffreda (2), Branca, Camerlinckx, Garretón, Halle, Sanés, Silvestre; C: Mesón (10); PG: Mesón
Brazil 0

ARGENTINA

1 October 1991, Belgrano Stadium, Buenos Aires
Argentina 84 T: Mendy (5), Tolomei (4), Etchegoyen (2), Rossi, Garzón, Marguery, Rocca, penalty try; C: Mendy (10)
Brazil 6 PG: Segatto (2)

2 October 1993 Clube Atlético, São Paulo
Argentina 114 T: Jorge (8), Tolomei (3), Cuesta-Silva (2), Paz-Posse, Mesón, Merlot, Pérez, Salvat; C: Mesón (10), Criscuolo (2)
Brazil 3 PG: Volga

Argentina vs British and Irish Lions

23 May 2005, Millennium Stadium, Cardiff
British Lions 25 T: Smith; C: Wilkinson; PG: Wilkinson (6)
Argentina 25 T: Nunez Piossek; C: Todeschini; PG: Todeschini(6)

Argentina vs British and Irish Lions XV

Argentina vs British and Irish Lions XV	
Played:	6
Won:	0
Lost:	6
Drawn:	0
For:	6
Against:	211

Average score:
1–35.17

Argentina percentages:
Won:	0%
Lost:	100%
Drawn:	0%

12 June 1910, GEBA, Buenos Aires
British Lions XV 28 T: Monks (2), Raphael, Ward, Fraser; C: Harrison (2), Raphael; PG: Harrison; DG: Monks
Argentina 3 T: MacCarthy

31 July 1927, GEBA, Buenos Aires
British Lions XV 37 T: Wilson (2), Hammett, Kelly, Aarvold, Spong, Payne, MacMyn; C: Hammett (3); PG: Hammett; DG: Spong
Argentina 0

7 August 1927, GEBA, Buenos Aires
British Lions XV 46 T: Aarvold (4), Kelly (2), Spong, Payne, MacMyn, McIlwaine; C: Hammett (6); DG: Hammett
Argentina 0

14 August 1927, GEBA, Buenos Aires
Brit Lions XV 34 T: Taylor (3), Hamilton-Smythe (2), Douty, McIlwaine; C: Hammett (5); PG: Hammett
Argentina 3 GM: Torino

21 August 1927, Belgrano Stadium, Buenos Aires
British Lions XV 43 T: Aarvold (3), Kelly (2), Wilson, Spong, Sobey, Coghlan, McIlwaine, MacMyn; C: Wilson (5)
Argentina 0

16 August 1936, GEBA, Buenos Aires
British Lions XV 23 T: Boyle (2), Unwin, Tallent; C: Brett (2); PG: Brett; DG: Shaw
Argentina 0

Argentina vs Canada

Argentina vs Canada	
Played:	9
Won:	6
Lost:	3
Drawn:	0
For:	277
Against:	159

Average score:
30.78–17.67

Argentina percentages:
Won:	66.67%
Lost:	33.33%
Drawn:	0%

3 October 1981, GEBA, Buenos Aires
Argentina 35 T: Campo (2), Loffreda, Allen, Baetti; C: Porta (3); PG: Porta (2); DG: Porta
Canada 0

30 March 1990, Swanguard Stadium, Burnaby
Canada 15 T: Palmer; C: Wyatt; PG Wyatt (3)
Argentina 6 PG: Vidou (2)

16 June 1990, Velez Sarsfield Stadium, Buenos Aires
Canada 19 T: Stuart; PG: Rees (4); DG: Rees
Argentina 15 T: Bunader (2), Garzon; PG: Meson

10 March 1995, Ferro Carril Oeste Stadium, Buenos Aires
Argentina 29 T: Meson; PG Meson (8)
Canada 26 T: Stanley (2), Lytton, MacKinnon; C: Graf (2), Ross

21 September 1996, Fletchers Field, Markham
Argentina 41 T: Solari (2), Bartolucci (2), Martin; C: Quesada (2); PG: Quesada (4)
Canada 21 T: Wirachowski, Hendry; C: Ross; PG: Ross (3)

26 May 2001, Fletchers Field, Markham
Argentina   20   T: Roldan; PG: Contepomi (2); DG: Fernandez-Miranda (3)
Canada   6   PG: Stewart (2)

30 August 2003, Cricket & Rugby Club, Buenos Aires
Argentina   62   T: Nunez-Piossek (2), Fernandez-Lobbe (2), Pichot, Contepomi, Longo, Martin, Alvarez-Kairelis; C: Contepomi (7); PG: Contepomi
Canada   22   T: Pritchard, Stanley, Tkachuk; C: Ross (2); PG: Ross

2 July 2005, Kingsland, Calgary
Canada   22   T: Smith; C: Daypuck; PG: Daypuck (5)
Argentina   15   T: Tiesi (2); C: Fernandez-Miranda; PG: Fernandez-Miranda

Argentina vs Chile

Argentina vs Chile	
Played:	28
Won:	28
Lost:	0
Drawn:	0
For:	1 150
Against:	173

Average score:
41.07–6.18

Argentina percentages:
Won:	100%
Lost:	0%
Drawn:	0%

20 September 1936, Estadio Playa Ancha, Valparaiso
Argentina   29*
Chile   0

27 September 1936, Estadio Playa Ancha, Valparaiso
Argentina   31*
Chile   3*

21 August 1938, GEBA, Buenos Aires
Argentina   33*
Chile   3*

16 September 1951, GEBA, Buenos Aires
Argentina   13*
Chile   3*

18 September 1958, Prince of Wales Country Club, Santiago
Argentina   14*
Chile   0

7 October 1961, Carrasco Polo Club, Montevideo
Argentina   11   T: Montes de Oca, Oliveri; C: Goti; PG: de Oliveri
Chile   3   T: de Braun

22 August 1964, San Pablo
Argentina   30   T: Etchegaray, Goti, Loyola, Otano, Schmitt; C: Molina Berro (3); PG: Molina, Berro (2); DG: Queirolo
Chile   8*   T: (2) C: (1)

30 September 1967, San Isidro, Buenos Aires
Argentina   18   T: España, Silva, Verardo, Chesta; C: Méndez (3)
Chile   0

11 October 1969, Prince of Wales Country Club, Santiago
Argentina   54   T: Pascual (3), Rodríguez-Jurado (2), Walther (2), Otaño, Silva, Anthony, Martínez, Benzi; C: Seaton (9)
Chile   0

10 October 1971, Carrasco Polo Club, Montevideo
Argentina   20   T: Martínez-Mosquera (2), Otaola, Martínez C: Rodríguez-Jurado PG: Cutler (2)
Chile   3   PG: Cabrera

21 October 1973, Clube Atlético, São Paulo
Argentina   60   T: Rodríguez-Jurado (2), Travaglini (2), Morgan, Carracedo, Casas, Sanz, Virasoro; C: Morgan (6); PG:Morgan (4)
Chile   3   PG: Marsano

28 September 1975, Asuncion
Argentina   45   T: Alvarez (2), Lucke, Minguez, Muniz, Sanguinetti; C: de Forteza (3); PG: Sanguinetti (2), de Forteza; DG: de Forteza (2)
Chile   3*   PG: (1)

ARGENTINA

30 October 1977, Cancha del Atletico, Tucuman
Argentina 25 T: Alvarez (2), Morgan, Sansot; C: Capalbo (3); PG: Sansot
Chile 10 T: MacGregor; PG: Planellas (2)

6 October 1979, Stade Francais Field, Santiago
Argentina 34 T: Terán (2), Negri, Sanguinetti, Ramallo, Paz; C: Sanguinetti, Becar-Varela; PG: Saguinetti, Becar-Verela
Chile 15 T: Ramírez; C: Pionella; PG: Pienella (3)

16 July 1983, Estadio San Isidro, Buenos Aires
Argentina 46 T: Scolni (3), Lanza (2), Annichini (2), Dassen, Cuesta-Silva, de Chazal; C: Piccardo (3)
Chile 6 PG: Montebruno; DG: Montebruno

19 September 1985, Asuncion
Argentina 59 T: Silva (4), Annichini (2), Branca, Cash, Cuesta-Silva, Porta; C: Porta (8); PG: Porta
Chile 6* PG: (2)

3 October 1987, Stade Francais, Santiago
Argentina 47 T: Gerosa (2), Milano (2), Madero (2), Loffreda, Franchi; C: Baetti (6); PG: Baetti
Chile 9 PG: Planella (2); DG: Planella

10 October 1989, Carrasco Polo Club, Montevideo
Argentina 36 T: Schacht (2), Angelillo, Cóppola, Loffreda; C: Dominguez (2); PG: Dominguez (4)
Chile 9 T: Muñoz; C: Planella; PG: Planella

15 August 1991, Prince of Wales Country Club, Santiago
Argentina 41 T: Terán (2), Cuesta-Silva (2), Camardón, Santamarina; C: Mesón (4); PG: Mesón; DG: Arbizu (2)
Chile 6 PG: Gili (2)

11 October 1993, Jorge Newbery Gimnasia, Buenos Aires
Argentina 70 T: Jorge (4), Tolomei (2), Salvat, Merlo, Posse, Irazoqui; C: Arbizu (7); PG: Arbizu (2)
Chile 7 T: Encinas; C: Venegas

30 September 1995, Prince of Wales Country Club, Santiago
Argentina 78 T: Salvat (3), Crexell (2), Jurado (2), Cremaschi, Fernandez-Miranda, Mendez-Azpillaga, penalty try;
C: Luna (5), Cilley (2); PG: Luna (3)
Chile 3* PG: (1)

4 October 1997, Medoza Rugby Club Ground, Mendoza
Argentina 50 T: Ruiz (2), Muliero (2), Durand, Legora, Gravano; C: Mesón (6); PG: Mesón
Chile 10 T: Pizarro; C: González; PG: González

10 October 1998, Prince of Wales Country Club, Santiago
Argentina 25 T: Bartolucci, Brolese, Molina; C: Altube (2); PG: Altube, Contepomi
Chile 17 T: Manzur, Sahid; C: González (2); PG: González

4 May 2002, Mendoza Rugby Club Ground, Mendoza
Argentina 57 T: Senillosa (3), Stortoni, Nunez-Piossek, Simone, Nannini, Gaitan, Roncero; C: J Fernandez-Miranda (6)
Chile 13 T: Broussain; C: Gonzalez; PG: González (2)

30 April 2003, Luis Franzini Stadium, Montevideo
Argentina 49 T: Ostiglia (2), Borges, Freixas, Nannini, Senillosa, Durand; C: J Fernandez-Miranda (4); PG: J Fernandez-Miranda;
DG: Senillosa
Chile 3 PG: González

25 April 2004, Prince of Wales Country Club, Santiago
Argentina 45 T: Nunez-Piossek (2), Bosch, Aramburu, Dande, Borges; C: Bustos (6); PG: Bustos
Chile 3 PG: Cristián Onetto

1 July 2006, Prince of Wales Country Club, Santiago
Argentina 60 T: Ledesma (2), Serra-Miras, Borges, Avramovic, Carballo, Scelzo, Carizza, Leguizamon, Gambarini;
C: Todeschini (4), Serra-Miras
Chile 13 T: Gajardo; C: Berti; PG: Berti; DG: Berti

14 August 2007, Estadio San Isidro, Buenos Aires
Argentina 70 T: Fernandez-Lobbe (2), Serra (2), Longo, Bosch, M Contepomi, F Contepomi, Gaitan, Scelzo;
C: F Contepomi (10)
Chile 14 T: Berti (2) C: Berti (2)

19 November 2005, Stadio Luigi Ferraris, Genoa
Argentina 39 T: Stortoni, Aramburu, Tiesi, Morey; C: Contepomi (2); PG: Contepomi (5)
Italy 22 T: Canale; C: Pez; PG: Pez (5)

18 November 2006, Stadio Flaminio, Rome
Argentina 23 T: Avramovic, Todeschini; C: Todeschini (2); PG: Todeschini (3)
Italy 16 T: Stanojevic; C: Bortolussi; PG: Bortolussi (3)

9 June 2007, Estadio Malvinas Argentinas, Mendoza
Argentina 24 T: Leonelli, Serra Miras; C: Serra Miras; PG: Serra Mira (4)
Italy 6 PG: Bortolussi (2)

28 June 2008, Estadio Olimpico, Cordoba
Italy 13 T: Canavosio; C: Marcato; PG: Marcato (2)
Argentina 12 PG: Hernandez (2), Bosch (2)

15 November 2008, Stadio Olimpico, Turin
Argentina 22 T: Carballo; C: Contepomi; PG: Contepomi (5)
Italy 14 T: Masi; PG: Marcato (2); DG: Marcato

Argentina vs Japan

Argentina vs Japan	
Played:	5
Won:	4
Lost:	1
Drawn:	0
For:	205
Against:	139
Average score:	
41–27.80	
Argentina percentages:	
Won:	80%
Lost:	20%
Drawn:	0%

15 May 1993, Cancha del Atletico, Tucuman
Argentina 30 T: Cuesta-Silva, Arbizu, Silvetti, Sporleder; C: Cremaschi, Crexell; PG: Cremaschi (2)
Japan 27 T: Horikoshi, Kajihara; C: Hosokawa; PG: Hosokawa (5)

22 May 1993, Ferro Carril Oeste Stadium, Buenos Aires
Argentina 45 T: Roby, Cremaschi, Cuesta-Silva, Arbizu, Camardon; C: Meson (4); PG: Meson (4)
Japan 20 T: Masuho; PG: Hosokawa (5)

15 September 1998, Chichibunomiya Stadium, Tokyo
Japan 44 T: Ohata (2), McCormick, Watanabe; C: Watanabe (2), Murata; PG: Watanabe (3), Murata; DG: Iwabuchi (2)
Argentina 29 T: Corleto, Ledesma, Martin, Pfister; C: Lobrauco (2), Fuselli; DG: Fuselli

16 October 1999, Millennium Stadium, Cardiff (RWC, Pool D)
Argentina 33 T: Albanese, Pichot; C: Contepomi; PG: Quesada (7)
Japan 12 PG: Hirose (4)

23 April 2005, Cricket & Rugby Club, Buenos Aires
Argentina 68 T: Higgs (2), Genoud (2), Bosch, Ayerza, Albina, Leguizamon, penalty try; C: Todeschini (5), Fernandez-Miranda (2); PG: Todeschini (3)
Japan 36 T: Tachikawa, Ohata, Motoki, Onozawa; C: Morita (2); PG: Morita (3); DG: Morita

Argentina vs Junior Springboks

Argentina vs Junior Springboks	
Played:	5
Won:	1
Lost:	4
Drawn:	0
For:	26
Against:	116
Average score:	
5.2–23.2	
Argentina percentages:	
Won:	20%
Lost:	80%
Drawn:	0%

16 July 1932, Ferro Carril Oeste Stadium, Buenos Aires
Junior Boks 42 T: Gage (3), D'Alton (2), Cunningham, Apsey, Moodie, Smit, Cornell; C: Jordaan (6)
Argentina 0

23 July 1932, Ferro Carril Oeste Stadium, Buenos Aires
Junior Boks 34 T: Gage (2), Cornell, Elliot, Seymour, Robertson, Apsey; C: Jordaan (2); PG: Jordaan (3)
Argentina 3 T: Escary

12 September 1959, GEBA, Buenos Aires
Junior Boks 14 T: Wentzel, Taylor, Holton, Gericke; C: Gericke
Argentina 6 T: Hogg; PG: Raimundez

3 October 1959, GEBA, Buenos Aires
Junior Boks 20 T: Twigge (4), Bezuidenhout; C: Wentzel PG: Gericke
Argentina 6 PG: Guastella; DG: Guastella

19 June 1965, Ellis Park, Johannesburg
Argentina 11 T: Pascual, España, Loyola; C: Poggi
Junior Boks 6 T: du Preez (2)

ARGENTINA

Argentina vs Namibia

14 October 2003, Central Coast Stadium, Gosford (RWC, Pool A)

Argentina	67	T:Gaitan (3), Bouza (2), N Fernandez-Miranda, J Fernandez-Miranda, Mendez, penalty try (2); C: Quesada (7); PG: Quesada
Namibia	14	T: Grobler, Husselman; C: Wessels (2)

22 September 2007, Stade Velodrome, Marseille (RWC, Pool D)

Argentina	63	T:Leguizamon (2), MContepomi, F Contepomi, Tiesi, Corleto, penalty try, Todeschini, Roncero; C: F Contepomi (4), Todeschini (2); PG: F Contepomi (2)
Namibia	3	PG: Schreude

Argentina vs New Zealand

Argentina vs New Zealand	
Played:	13
Won:	0
Lost:	12
Drawn:	1
For:	180
Against:	585
Average score:	
13.84–45	
Argentina percentages:	
Won:	0%
Lost:	92.31%
Drawn:	7.69%

26 October 1985, Ferro Carril Oeste Stadium, Buenos Aires

New Zealand	33	T: Kirwan (2), Crowley, Hobbs; C: Crowley; PG: Crowley (4); DG: Fox
Argentina	20	T: J Lanza, Cuesta-Silva; PG: Porta (3); DG: Porta

3 November 1985, Ferro Carril Oeste Stadium, Buenos Aires

Argentina	21	PG: Porta (4); DG: Porta (3)
New Zealand	21	T: Kirwan (2), Mexted, Green; C: Crowley; PG: Crowley

1 June 1987, Athletic Park, Wellington (RWC, Pool 3)

New Zealand	46	T: Kirk, Brooke, Stanley, Earl, Crowley, Whetton; C: Fox (2); PG: Fox (6)
Argentina	15	T: J Lanza; C: Porta; PG: Porta (3)

15 July 1989, Carisbrook, Dunedin

New Zealand	60	T: Gallagher (3), Kirwan (2), Wright (2), Jones (2), penalty try; C: Fox (7); PG: Fox (2)
Argentina	9	T: Turnes; C: Baetti; PG: Baetti

29 July 1989, Athletic Park, Wellington

New Zealand	49	T: Wright (2), Deans (2), Gallagher, Kirwan, Whetton; C: Fox (6); PG: Fox (3)
Argentina	12	T: Dengra; C: Gomez; PG: Gomez (2)

6 July 1991, Velez Sarsfield Stadium, Buenos Aires

New Zealand	28	T: Wright, Earl; C: Fox; PG: Fox (5); DG: Crowley
Argentina	14	T: Garreton, Carreras; PG: del Castillo (2)

13 July 1991, Velez Sarsfield Stadium, Buenos Aires

New Zealand	36	T: Z Brooke, M Jones, Kirwan, Wright; C: Fox (4); PG: Fox (4)
Argentina	6	PG: del Castillo (2)

21 June 1997, Athletic Park, Wellington

New Zealand	93	T: Spencer (2), Cullen (2), Umaga (2), Jones, Marshall, Kronfeld, Fitzpatrick, Browne, Brooke, Stensness, penalty try; C: Spencer (10); PG: Spencer
Argentina	8	T: Solari; PG: Quesada

28 June 1997, Waikato Stadium, Hamilton

New Zealand	62	T: Randell, Brown, Cullen, Stensness, Kronfeld, Allen, R Brooke, Spencer, Umaga; C: Spencer (6), Cullen; PG: Spencer
Argentina	10	T: Grau; C: Quesada; PG: Quesada

23 June 2001, Lancaster Park, Christchurch

New Zealand	67	T: Alatini (2), Wilson (2), Umaga, Randell, Jack, MacDonald, Howlett, Holler; C: Mehrtens (3), Brown (4); PG: Mehrtens
Argentina	19	T: Arbizu, Camardon; PG: Contepomi (3)

1 December 2001, River Plate Stadium, Argentina

New Zealand	24	T: Lomu, Robertson C: Mehrtens; PG: Mehrtens (4)
Argentina	20	T: Arbizu (2) C: Contepomi (2); PG: Contepomi (2)

26 June 2004, Waikato Stadium, Hamilton

New Zealand	41	T: Tuiali'i, Umaga, Rokocoko, Tuitupou, Muliaina; C: Mehrtens (5); PG: Mehrtens (2)
Argentina	7	T: Aramburu C: Senillosa

25 June 2006, Velez Sarsfield Stadium, Buenos Aires

New Zealand	25	T: MacDonald, Carter, Hamilton; C: Carter (2); PG: Carter (2)
Argentina	19	T: Durand; C: Todeschini; PG: Todeschini (4)

Argentina vs New Zealand XV

Argentina vs New Zealand XV	
Played:	4
Won:	0
Lost:	4
Drawn:	0
For:	30
Against:	80

Average score:
7.5–20

Argentina percentages:
Won:	0%
Lost:	100%
Drawn:	0%

30 October 1976, Ferro Carril Oeste Stadium, Buenos Aires
New Zealand XV 21 T: Wilson, Sloane C: Rowlands (2); PG: Rowlands (3)
Argentina 9 PG: Varela (2); DG: Porta

6 November 1976, Ferro Carril Oeste Stadium, Buenos Aires
New Zealand XV 26 T: Rollerson, Ma Taylor, Mu Taylor, Cron; C: Rowlands (2); PG: Rolands (2)
Argentina 6 PG: Sansot, Porta

8 September 1979, Carisbrook, Dunedin
New Zealand XV 18 PG: Wilson (5); DG: Dunn
Argentina 9 PG: Porta DG: Porta (2)

15 September 1979, Athletic Park, Wellington
New Zealand XV 15 T: Cunningham, Loveridge; C: Wilson (2); PG: Wilson
Argentina 6 PG: Porta (2)

Argentina vs Oxford and Cambridge XV (Oxbridge)

Argentina vs Oxbridge	
Played:	8
Won:	2
Lost:	5
Drawn:	1
For:	48
Against:	126

Average score:
6–15.75

Argentina percentages:
Won:	25,00%
Lost:	62,50%
Drawn:	12,50%

29 August 1948, GEBA, Buenos Aires
Oxbridge 17*
Argentina 0

5 September 1948, GEBA, Buenos Aires
Oxbridge 39*
Argentina 0

26 August 1956, GEBA, Buenos Aires
Oxbridge 25 T: Davies (2), Braco; C: Currie (2); PG: Currie (4)
Argentina 6 PG: Fernández del Casal (2)

16 September 1956, GEBA, Buenos Aires
Oxbridge 11 T: Watson, Lawrence; C: Richards; PG: Richards
Argentina 3 PG: Fernández del Casal

11 September 1965, GEBA, Buenos Aires
Argentina 19 T: Scharenburg, Rodríguez-Jurado; C: Poggi (2); PG: Poggi (3)
Oxbridge 19 T: Frankcom, Gibson, Houston, James; C: Wilson (2); PG: Wilson

18 September 1965, GEBA, Buenos Aires
Oxbridge 9 T: Frankcom; DG: Gibson (2)
Argentina 3 PG: Poggi

28 August 1971, Ferro Carril Oeste Stadium, Buenos Aires
Argentina 11 T: Morgan, Walther, Anthony; C: Harris-Smith
Oxbridge 3 PG: Sevilla

4 September 1971, Ferro Carril Oeste Stadium, Buenos Aires
Argentina 6 T: Incola; DG: Harris-Smith
Oxbridge 3 T: P Carrol

ARGENTINA

Argentina vs Paraguay
Played: 16
Won: 16
Lost: 0
Drawn: 0
For: 1,311
Against: 58

Average score:
81.94–3.63

Argentina percentages:
Won: 100%
Lost: 0%
Drawn: 0%

Argentina vs Paraguay

16 October 1971, Carrasco Polo Club, Montevideo
Argentina 61 T: Loyola (3), Rodríguez-Jurado (2), Porta (2), penalty try (2), Carracedo, Velásquez, Braceras, Foster; C: Porta (2), Rodríguez-Jurado (4), Cutler (2); PG: Cutler; DG: Porta
Paraguay 0

14 October 1973, Clube Atlético, São Paulo
Argentina 98 T: Morgan (6), Matarazzo (3), Gradín (3), Rodríguez-Jurado (2), Faríello (2), Altberg, Carracedo; C: Morgan (13)
Paraguay 3 PG: Burt

25 September 1975, San José Rugby Club Ground, Asunción
Argentina 93 T: Alvarez (3), Brouchou (3), Miguens (2), Cato, Giargia, Iachetti, Lucke, Minguez, Muniz, Sanguinetti; C: de Forteza (11), Sanguinetti; PG: de Forteza (3)
Paraguay 0

29 October 1977, Cancha del Atletico, Tucuman
Argentina 77 T: Alvarez (4), Balfour (2), Morgan (2), Truco, Allen, Terán, penalty try; C: Guarrochena (10); PG: Guarrochena (3)
Paraguay 3 PG: Moscarda

7 October 1979, Sausalito, Viña del Mar
Argentina 76 T: Morgan (3), Courreges (2), Sanguinetti (2), Ramallo (2), Terán, Escalante, Puccio, Morgan, Ventura; C: Dip (6), Escalante; PG: Dip (2)
Paraguay 13 T: Gimenez, Taboada; C: Mongelos; PG: Mongelos

20 July 1983, Estadio San Isidro, Buenos Aires
Argentina 43 T: Scolni (4), Lanza, Dassen, Cordeiro, Ventura, Cubelli; C: Sauze (2); DG: Sauze
Paraguay 3 PG: Mongelos

21 September 1985, San José Rugby Club Ground, Asunción
Argentina 102 T: Merlo (3), de la Arena (3), Annichini (2), Lanza (2), Milano (2), Visca (2), Baeck, Branca, Cubelli, Petersen, Sanes; C: Porta (13)
Paraguay 3* PG: (1)

30 September 1987, Stade Francais Field, Santiago
Argentina 62 T: Baetti (2), Caminotti, Mendy, Madero, Mesón, Carreras, Coria, Franchi, Vidou, penalty try; C: Baetti (9)
Paraguay 4 T: Duarte

12 October 1989, Montevideo
Argentina 75 T: Bertranou (2), Camerlinckx (2), Cóppola (2), Schacht (2), Soler (2), Branca, Jorge, Mesón, Silvestre; C: Dominguez (4), Mesón (4); PG: Dominguez
Paraguay 7 T: Cáceres; PG: García

28 September 1991, Club San José Field, Asuncion
Argentina 37 T: Herrera, Garzón, Pitinari, Rossi, Damioli, Etchegoyen; C: Méndez (2); PG: Méndez (3)
Paraguay 10 T: Nuñez PG: Mateaude (2)

16 October 1993, Jorge Newbery Gimnasia, Buenos Aires
Argentina 51 T: Meson (2), Tolomei (2), Cuesta-Silva, Marguery, Arbizu, Camardon; C: Meson (4); PG: Meson
Paraguay 3 PG: Matiauda

24 September 1995, San José Rugby Club Ground, Asunción
Argentina 103 T: Cuesta-Silva (3), Mendez (3), Salvat (3), Luna (2), Angelillo, Cremaschi, Portillo, Sugasti, Viel-Temperley; C: Cremaschi (7), Luna (3); PG: Cremaschi
Paraguay 9* PG: (2) DG: (1)

13 September 1997, Aranduroga Rugby Club Ground, Corrientes
Argentina 78 T: Gómez Coli (3), Rotondo (3), Giannantonio, Ravé, Carmona, Aguirre, Brandi, Díaz; C: Luna (9)
Paraguay 0

3 October 1998, San José Rugby Club Ground, Asunción
| Argentina | 59 | T: Grande (5), Ohanián, Díaz, Durand, Stortoni, Olina C: Molina, Fuselli, Altubel; PG: Fuselli |
| Paraguay | 0 | |

1 May 2002, Mendoza Rugby Club Ground, Mendoza
| Argentina | 152 | T: Soler (5), Nunez-Piossek (4), Stortoni (3), Sporleder (3), Senillosa (3), Bouza (2), Phelan, Gaitan, Nannini, Cruz-Legora; C: Cilley (16) |
| Paraguay | 0 | |

27 April 2003, Luis Franzini Stadium, Montevideo
| Argentina | 144 | T: Nunez-Piossek (9), Sambucetti (3), Senillosa (2), Borges (2), Albina (2), Sporleder (2), Bartolucci, Schusterman, Nannini, Hernandez; C: Bustos (9), Hernandez (2), F Fernandez-Miranda |
| Paraguay | 0 | |

Argentina vs Peru

11 September 1958, Clube Stade Francais, Santiago
| Argentina | 44* |
| Peru | 0 |

<table>
<tr><td colspan="2">Argentina vs Romania</td></tr>
<tr><td>Played:</td><td>7</td></tr>
<tr><td>Won:</td><td>7</td></tr>
<tr><td>Lost:</td><td>0</td></tr>
<tr><td>Drawn:</td><td>0</td></tr>
<tr><td>For:</td><td>274</td></tr>
<tr><td>Against:</td><td>89</td></tr>
<tr><td colspan="2">Average score:</td></tr>
<tr><td colspan="2">39.14–12.71</td></tr>
<tr><td colspan="2">Argentina percentages:</td></tr>
<tr><td>Won:</td><td>100%</td></tr>
<tr><td>Lost:</td><td>0%</td></tr>
<tr><td>Drawn:</td><td>0%</td></tr>
</table>

Argentina vs Romania

8 September 1973, Ferro Carril Oeste Stadium, Buenos Aires
| Argentina | 15 | T: Dumas; C: Porta; PG: Porta (3) |
| Romania | 9 | PG: Florescu, Durbac; DG: Nicolescu |

15 September 1973, Ferro Carril Oeste Stadium, Buenos Aires
| Argentina | 24 | T: Rodríquez-Jurado (2), Matarazzo, Alonso; C: Porta; PG: Porta; DG: Porta |
| Romania | 3 | DG: Duta |

31 October 1992, Dinamo Stadion, Bucharest
| Argentina | 21 | T: Camardón, le Fort, penalty try; C: Mesón (3) |
| Romania | 18 | T: Dumitras (2); C: Nichitean; PG: Nichitean (2) |

14 October 1995, Ferro Carril Oeste Stadium, Buenos Aires
| Argentina | 51 | T: Cuesta-Silva (2), Jurado, Luna, Mendez; C: Luna (4); PG: Luna (6) |
| Romania | 16 | T: Girbu; C: Besarau; PG: Besarau (2); DG: Besarau |

18 October 1997, Stade Jacques Fouroux, Auch
| Argentina | 45 | T: Scelzo (2), Simone (2), Albanese, Soler; C: J Fernandez-Miranda (3); PG: J Fernandez-Miranda (3) |
| Romania | 18 | T: Gontineac, Tofan; C: Tofan; PG: Tofan (2) |

8 August 1998, Centro Cordoba, Buenos Aires
| Argentina | 68 | T: Pichot (2), Martin, Albanese, Soler, Arbizu, Fernandez-Lobbe, Sporleder, Camerlinckx, penalty try; C: Quesada (9) |
| Romania | 22 | T: Gontineac, Draguceanu, penalty try; C: Mitu (2); PG: Mitu |

22 October 2003, Aussie Stadium, Sydney (RWC, Pool A)
| Argentina | 50 | T: Hernandez (2), Bouza (2), Gaitan, Contepomi, N Fernandez-Miranda; C: J Fernandez-Miranda (4), Quesada (2); PG: J Fernandez-Miranda |
| Romania | 3 | PG: Tofan |

Argentina vs Samoa

13 October 1991, Sardis Road, Pontypridd (RWC, Pool 3)
| Western Samoa | 35 | T: Tagaloa (2), Lima (2), Bunce, Bacho; C: Vaea (4); PG: Vaea |
| Argentina | 12 | T: Teran; C: Arbizu; PG: Arbizu, Laborde |

30 May 1995, Basil Kenyon Stadium, East London (RWC – Pool B)
| Western Samoa | 32 | T: Lam, Leaupepe, Harder; C: Kellett; PG: Kellett (5) |
| Argentina | 26 | T: Crexwell, penalty try; C: Cilley (2); PG: Cilley (4) |

10 October 1999, Stradey Park, Llanelli (RWC, Pool D)
| Argentina | 32 | T: Allub; PG: Quesada (8); DG: Quesada |
| Samoa | 16 | T: Paramore; C: Leaega; PG: Leaega (3) |

3 December 2005, Cricket & Rugby Club, Buenos Aires
| Samoa | 28 | T: Tupai, Sititi, Tagicakibau; C: Warren (2); PG: Warren (2); DG: Warren |
| Argentina | 12 | T: Fernandez-Lobbe, Agulla; C: Fernandez-Miranda |

<table>
<tr><td colspan="2">Argentina vs Samoa</td></tr>
<tr><td>Played:</td><td>4</td></tr>
<tr><td>Won:</td><td>1</td></tr>
<tr><td>Lost:</td><td>3</td></tr>
<tr><td>Drawn:</td><td>0</td></tr>
<tr><td>For:</td><td>82</td></tr>
<tr><td>Against:</td><td>111</td></tr>
<tr><td colspan="2">Average score:</td></tr>
<tr><td colspan="2">20.5–27.75</td></tr>
<tr><td colspan="2">Argentina percentages:</td></tr>
<tr><td>Won:</td><td>25%</td></tr>
<tr><td>Lost:</td><td>75%</td></tr>
<tr><td>Drawn:</td><td>0%</td></tr>
</table>

ARGENTINA

Argentina vs Scotland

10 November 1990, Murrayfield, Edinburgh
Scotland   49   T: Stanger (2), K Milne (2), Moore, Armstrong, Gray, G Hastings, Chalmers
                           C: G Hastings (5); PG: G Hastings
Argentina   3   PG: Meson

4 June 1994, Ferro Carril Oeste Stadium, Buenos Aires
Argentina   16   T: Teran; C: Meson; PG: Meson (3)
Scotland   15   PG: M Dods (5)

11 June 1994, Ferro Carril Oeste Stadium, Buenos Aires
Argentina   19   T: Martin; C: Meson; PG: Meson (3); DG: del Castilla
Scotland   17   T: Logan; PG: Shiel (2), M Dods; DG: Townsend

21 August 1999, Murrayfield, Edinburgh
Argentina   31   T: Bartolucci (2), Albanese; C: Quesada (2); PG: Quesada (3); DG: Quesad
Scotland   22   T: Metcalfe, Tait, Walton; C: Logan (2); PG: Logan

18 November 2001, Murrayfield, Edinburgh
Argentina   25   T: Corletto; C: Contepomi; PG: Contepomi (6)
Scotland   16   T: Townsend, Lee; PG: Townsend (2)

12 November 2005, Murrayfield, Edinburgh
Argentina   23   T: Leonelli, penalty try; C: Todeschini (2); PG: Todeschini (3)
Scotland   19   T: Parks; C: Paterson; PG: Paterson (3); DG: Parks

7 October 2007, Stade de France, Paris (RWC, Q/F)
Argentina   19   T: Longo; C: F Contepomi; PG: F Contepomi (3); DG: Hernandez
Scotland   13   T: Cusiter; C: Paterson; PG: Paterson, Parks

7 June 2008, Estadio Gigante de Arroyito, Rosario
Argentina   21   T: Tejeda, Tiesi; C: Todeschini; PG: Todeschini (3)
Scotland   15   PG: Paterson (5)

14 June 2008, Velez Sarsfield Stadium, Buenos Aires
Scotland   26   T: Ford, Morrison; C: Paterson (2); PG: Paterson (4)
Argentina   14   T: Fernandez-Lobbe, Agulla; C: Todeschini (2)

Argentina vs Scotland XV

13 September 1969, GEBA, Buenos Aires
Argentina   20   T: Travaglini (2), Walther; C: Harris-Smith; PG: Harris-Smith;
                           DG: Harris-Smith (2)
Scotland XV   3   T: Smith;

27 September 1969, GEBA, Buenos Aires
Scotland XV   6   T: Carmichael; PG: Blaikie
Argentina   3   T: Otano

24 November 1973, Murrayfield, Edinburgh
Scotland XV   12   PG: Morgan (3); DG: Telfer
Argentina   11   T: Travaglini, Porta; DG: Porta

Argentina vs South Africa (Danie Craven Cup)

Argentina vs South Africa	
Played:	13
Won:	0
Lost:	13
Drawn:	0
For:	272
Against:	544

Average score:
20.92–41.85

Argentina percentages:

Won:	0%
Lost:	100%
Drawn:	0%

Officially, South Africa and Argentina met for the first time on 6 November 1993, but in reality it was on 26 April 1980 when Argentina toured South Africa under the guise of 'South America', in an effort to sneak under the boycott radar. Argentina has lost all 13 encounters, the most recent a match to celebrate Nelson Mandela's 90th birthday. Some of the scores have been tight, notably in 2003 when a last-minute, wide-out penalty goal by Louis Koen stole a 26–25 victory for the Springoks in Port Elizabeth. The Danie Craven Cup, named after the legendary Springbok and administrator, and an avid Argentinophile himself, is competed for when the teams meet.

6 November 1993, Ferro Carrill Oeste, Buenos Aires
South Africa 29 T: Small (2), van der Westhuizen, Joubert; C: Stransky (3); PG: Stransky
Argentina 26 T: Meson, Salvat; C: Meson (2); PG: Meson (4)

13 November 1993, Ferro Carrill Oeste, Buenos Aires
South Africa 52 T: Small (2), Strauss (2), Johnson, Williams, van der Westhuizen; C: Johnson (4); PG: Johnson (3)
Argentina 23 T: Camardon, Jorge; C: Meson (2); PG: Meson (2); DG: Arbizu

8 October 1994, Boet Erasmus Stadium, Port Elizabeth
South Africa 42 T: Roux (2), Strauss, Stransky, Williams; C: Stransky (4); PG: Stransky (3)
Argentina 22 T: Teran, Pfister, Loffreda; C: del Castillo (2); PG: del Castillo

15 October 1994, Ellis Park, Johannesburg
South Africa 46 T: Badenhorst (2), Williams, Stransky, Andrews, van der Westhuizen, Straueli; C: Stransky (4); PG: Stransky
Argentina 26 T: Llanes, Cilley; C: Cilley (2); PG: Cilley (4)

9 November 1996, Ferro Carril Oeste, Buenos Aires
South Africa 46 T: Andrews, Venter, Small, le Roux, Joubert, van der Westhuizen, penalty try; C: Honiball (3), Joubert; PG: Honiball
Argentina 15 T: Martin, Camardon; C: Cilley; PG: Cilley

16 November 1996, Ferro Carril Oeste, Buenos Aires
South Africa 44 T: Kruger (2), Venter, le Roux, Mulder, Olivier; C: Honiball (4); PG: Honiball (2)
Argentina 21 T: Martin, Miranda; C: Cilley; PG: Cilley (2) Quesada

12 November 2000, Estadio Monumental Antonio Vespucio Liberti, Buenos Aires
South Africa 37 T: Paulse (2), Andrews, Fleck, van Straaten; C: Montgomery (3); PG: van Straaten (2)
Argentina 33 T: Orengo, Contepomi, Simone; C: Quesada (3); PG: Quesada (4)

29 June 2002, PAM Brink Stadium, Springs
South Africa 49 T: Terblanche (2), Davidson, Pretorius, Jacobs, Conradie; C: Pretorius (5); PG: Pretorius (3)
Argentina 29 T: Lobbe, Penalty try; C: Quesada (2); PG: Quesada (5)

28 June 2003, Eastern Province Rugby Football Union Stadium, Port Elizabeth
South Africa 26 T: Coetzee, Russell; C: Koen (2); PG: Koen (4)
Argentina 25 T: Piossek, Contepomi, Hernandez; C: Quesada (2); PG: Quesada (2)

4 December 2004, Estadio Jose Amalfitani, Buenos Aires
South Africa 39 T: du Toit (2), Cronje, du Preez, Joubert; C: du Toit (4); PG: du Toit (2)
Argentina 7 T: Bouza; C: Fernandez Miranda

5 November 2005, Estadio Jose Amalfitani, Buenos Aires
South Africa 34 T: Smith, Fourie, Montgomery; C: Montgomery (2); PG: Montgomery (3), Pretorius; DG: Conradie
Argentina 23 T: Durand, M Contepomi, Leonelli; C: F Contepomi; PG: F Contepomi (2)

14 October 2007, Stade de France, Paris (RWC, S/F)
South Africa 37 T: Habana (2), Rossouw, du Preez; C: Montgomery (4); PG: Montgomery (3)
Argentina 13 T: M Contepomi; C: F Contepomi; PG: F Contepomi (2)

9 August 2008, Coca-Cola Park, Johannesburg
South Africa 63 T: van Niekerk (2), Pietersen (2), Spies, du Plessis, Jacobs, Nokwe, du Preez; C: James (9)
Argentina 9 PG: Contepomi (3)

ARGENTINA

Argentina vs SA Gazelles

Played: 6
Won: 2
Lost: 4
Drawn: 0
For: 60
Against: 71

Average score:
10–11.83

Argentina percentages:
Won: 33.33%
Lost: 66.67%
Drawn: 0%

Argentina vs Spain

Played: 4
Won: 4
Lost: 0
Drawn: 0
For: 149
Against: 75

Average score:
37.25–18.75

Argentina percentages:
Won: 77.78%
Lost: 22.22%
Drawn: 0%

Argentina vs USA

Played: 8
Won: 8
Lost: 0
Drew: 0
For: 247
Against: 119

Average score:
30.88–14.88

Argentina percentages:
Won: 100%
Lost: 0%
Draw: 0%

Argentina vs South African Gazelles

24 September 1966, GEBA, Buenos Aires
SA Gazelles   9   T: Bennet; PG: Pretorius; DG: Uys
Argentina   3   PG: Gradín

1 October 1966, GEBA, Buenos Aires
SA Gazelles   20   T: Wilkens, Bond, Meiring; C: Pretorius; PG: Pretorius (3)
Argentina   15   T: Rodríguez-Jurado; PG: Poggi, Gradin; DG: Poggi (2)

17 July 1971, Boet Erasmus Stadium, Port Elizabeth
SA Gazelles   12   T: Swartz, Holm; PG: van Deventer; DG: van Deventer
Argentina   6   PG: Espagnol (2)

7 August 1971, Loftus Versfeld, Pretoria
Argentina   12   PG: Harris-Smith (2); DG: Harris-Smith (2)
SA Gazelles   0

21 October 1972, Ferro Carril Oeste Stadium, Buenos Aires
SA Gazelles   14   T: Fourie, Swartz, Cronjé; C: Snyman
Argentina   6   PG: E Morgan (2)

4 November 1972, Ferro Carril Oeste Stadium, Buenos Aires
Argentina   18   T: E Morgan (2), Porta, Travaglini; C: Porta
SA Gazelles   16   T: J Snyman, Borgen; C: D Snyman; PG: D Snyman (2)

Argentina vs Spain

23 November 1982, Campo Universitaria, Madrid
Argentina   28   T: Ure (2), Travaglini, Porta; C: Porta (3); PG: Porta; DG: Porta
Spain   19   T: Longhey, Sanch; C: Moriche; PG: Moriche (3)

17 August 1987, Estadio Mundialista, Mar del Plata
Argentina   40   T: Cuesta (2), Scolni, Madero, Miguens, Ricci; C: Porta (5); PG: Porta (2)
Spain   12   T: Azkargorta; C: Puertas; PG: Puertas (2)

26 September 1992, Velez Sarsfield Stadium, Buenos Aires
Argentina   38   T: Mendez (2), Arbizu, de la Arena, Salvat; C: Mendez (5); PG: Mendez
Spain   10   T: Altuna, Etxebarría

24 October 1992, Campo Universitario, Madrid
Argentina   43   T: Cuesta (2), Camardón, Jorge, Méndez, Mesón; C: Mesón (5); PG: Mesón
Spain   34   T: Altuna, de la Calle, Puerta, Torres; C: Sánchez (4); PG: Sánchez (2)

Argentina vs United States of America

11 November 1989, Velez Sarsfield Stadium, Buenos Aires
Argentina   23   T: Mesón, Loffreda, penalty try; C: Mesón; PG: Mesón (3)
USA   6   PG: O'Brien (2)

7 April 1990, Santa Barbara
Argentina   13   T: Camerlinckx, Loffreda; C: Vidou; PG: Vidou
USA   6   T: Leversee; C: O'Brien

28 May 1994, George Allen Field, Long Beach
Argentina   28   T: Terán, Noriega, Santamarina; C: Mesón (2); PG: Mesón (3)
USA   22   T: Takau, Anitoni, Bachelet; C: Williams (2); PG: Williams

20 June 1994, Ferro Carril Oeste Stadium, Buenos Aires
Argentina   16   T: Jorge, Sporleder; PG: Mesón; DG: Mesón
USA   11   T: Takau; PG: Williams (2)

14 September 1996, Nepean
Argentina   29   T: Simone, Bartolucci, Travaglini; C: Meson; PG: Meson (2), Quesada (2)
USA   26   T: Bachelet, Lumkong; C: Alexander (2); PG: Alexander (4)

15 August 1998, Cricket & Rugby Club, Buenos Aires

| Argentina | 52 | T: Soler (2), Contepomi, Mendez, Camerlinckx, Penalty try; C: Quesada (5); PG: Quesada (4) |
| USA | 24 | T: Blom, Anitoni; C: Blom; PG: Williams (4) |

23 May 2001, Mohawk Sports Park, Hamilton

| Argentina | 44 | T: Martin (2), Stortoni, Orengo, Contepomi, Longo, Soler; C: Contepomi (3); PG: Contepomi |
| USA | 16 | T: Timoteo; C: Wells; PG: Wells (3) |

23 August 2003, Cricket & Rugby Club, Buenos Aires

| Argentina | 42 | T: Gaitan, Durand, Bouza, Reggiardo, Corleto, penalty try; C: Contepomi (3); PG: Contepomi (2) |
| USA | 8 | T: Liddington; PG: Sherman |

Argentina vs Uruguay

Argentina vs Uruguay	
Played:	32
Won:	32
Lost:	0
Drawn:	0
For:	1,397
Against:	309
Average score:	
42.33–9.66	
Argentina percentages:	
Won:	100%
Lost:	0%
Drawn:	0%

9 September 1951, GEBA, Buenos Aires

| Argentina | 62 | T: U O'Farrell (7), Ehrman (2), Farrell (2), Morea (2), Swain, J O'Farrell, penalty try; C: Fernandez del Casal (6), Bazan |
| Uruguay | 0 | |

15 September 1958, Everton Club Field, Santiago

| Argentina | 50* | |
| Uruguay | 3* | |

14 October 1961, Carrasco Polo Club, Montevideo

| Argentina | 36 | T: Neri (4), Goti (2), Scharemberg, Guidi; C: Oliveri (6) |
| Uruguay | 3 | PG: Moor-Davies |

15 August 1964, São Paulo

| Argentina | 25 | T: Goti (2), Lasalle, Loyola, Neri, Schmitt; C: Molina Berro (2); DG: Molina, Berro |
| Uruguay | 6* | PG: (1); DG: (1) |

27 September 1967, Estadio CA, San Isidro

| Argentina | 38 | T: Pascual (2), España (2), Méndez, Poggi, Scharenberg, Travaglini, Walther C: Méndez (3), Poggi; PG: Poggi |
| Uruguay | 6 | T: Magri; PG: Cassarino |

4 October 1969, Prince of Wales Country Club, Santiago

| Argentina | 41 | T: Walther (2), Benzi (2), Martínez, Pascual, Silva, Carbone, penalty try; C: Poggi (2), Seaton (2); PG: Seaton (2) |
| Uruguay | 6 | T: Sartori PG: Bacot |

17 October 1971, Carrasco Polo Club, Montevideo

| Argentina | 55 | T: Rodríguez-Jurado (3), Loyola, Porta, Otaola, Costante, Silva, Fernández, Nicola; C: Rodríguez-Jurado (4), Cutler (4); PG: Rodríguez-Jurado; DG: Porta (2) |
| Uruguay | 6 | PG: Smith (2) |

16 October 1973, Clube Atlético, São Paulo

| Argentina | 55 | T: Morgan (3), Sanz (2), Carracedo, Porta, Harris-Smith, Matarazzo; C: Morgan (5); PG: Morgan (3) |
| Uruguay | 0 | |

21 September 1975, Asuncion

| Argentina | 30 | T: Escalante, Sanguinetti; C: Sanguinetti (2); PG: Sanguinetti (3) DG: Escalante, Landajo, Sanguinetti |
| Uruguay | 15* | T: (1); C: (1); PG: (3) |

21 August 1976, Montevideo

| Argentina | 47* | |
| Uruguay | 0 | |

28 October 1977, Cancha del Atletico, Tucuman

| Argentina | 70 | T: Morgan (3), Terán (2), Truco, Capalbo, D'Agnilo, Balfour, Passaglia, penalty try; C: Capalbo (7); PG: Capalbo (4) |
| Uruguay | 0 | |

4 October 1979, Stade Francais Field, Santiago

| Argentina | 19 | T: Ventura, Argerich; C: Sanguinetti; PG: Beccar-Varela (3) |
| Uruguay | 16 | T: Smith; PG: Cerbino (4) |

ARGENTINA

23 July 1983, Estadio CA, San Isidro
| Argentina | 29 | T: Annichini (2), Lanza, Piaccardo, Serrano; C: Piccardo (3); PG: Piccardo |
| Uruguay | 6 | PG: Ubilla (2) |

17 September, 1985 Asuncion
| Argentina | 63 | T: Baeck (2), Cuesta-Silva (2), J Lanza (2), P Lanza, Minguez, Petersen, Turnes; C: Porta (7); PG: Porta (3) |
| Uruguay | 16* | T: (2); C: (1); PG: (2) |

27 September 1987, Stade Francais Field, Santiago
| Argentina | 41 | T: Gerosa (2), Loffreda (2), Madero, Angelillo, Mendy; C: Baetti (5); PG: Baetti |
| Uruguay | 21 | PG: Silva (6); DG: Brancatto |

14 October 1989, Montevideo
| Argentina | 34 | T: Jorge (2), Schacht (2); C: Mesón (3); PG: Mesón (4) |
| Uruguay | 14 | T: Ormaechea, Ubilla; PG: Nicolaa (2) |

21 September 1991, Estadio CA, San Isidro
| Argentina | 32 | T: Salvat (2), Damioli, Buabse; C: Méndez (2); PG: Méndez (4) |
| Uruguay | 9 | T: Sciarra; C: Nicola; PG: Ubilla |

23 October 1993, Wanderers Club, Montevideo
| Argentina | 19 | T: Corral; C: Meson; PG: Meson (4) |
| Uruguay | 10 | T: Ormaechea; C: Terra; PG: Terra |

4 March 1995, Ferro Carril Oeste Stadium, Buenos Aires
| Argentina | 44 | T: Arbizu (3), Viel-Temperley (2), Crexell; C: Meson (4); PG: Meson (2) |
| Uruguay | 3* | PG: (1) |

8 October 1995, Estadio Posadas, Misiones
| Argentina | 52 | T: Jurado (2), Nougues, Crexell, Luna, Martin, Teran; C: Luna (4); PG: Luna (3) |
| Uruguay | 37* | |

8 June 1996, Carrasco Polo Club, Montevideo
| Argentina | 37 | T: Soler (2), Criscuolo, Pichot, Sporleder; C: Cilley (3); PG: Cilley (2) |
| Uruguay | 18* | T: (2); C: (1); PG: (2) |

18 September 1996, Mohawk Sports Park, Nepean
| Argentina | 54 | T: Giannantonio (2), Camardon, Orengo, Quesada, Barrea, Hasan, Martin; C: Quesada (7) |
| Uruguay | 20* | T: (2); C: (2); PG: (2) |

27 September 1997, Carrasco Polo Club, Montevideo
| Argentina | 56 | T: Orengo (2), Albanese, Soler, Diaz-Alberdi, Ugartemendia, N Fernandez-Miranda, Promanzio; C: J Fernandez-Miranda (5); PG: J Fernandez-Miranda; DG: J Fernandez-Miranda |
| Uruguay | 17 | T: Ormaechea, penalty try; C: Reyes (2); PG: Reyes |

4 June 1998, Cricket & Rugby Club, Buenos Aires
| Argentina | 72 | T: Soler (3), Reggiardo, Allub, Fernandez-Lobbe, Llanes, Phelan, Ohanian, Solari, Giannantonio, Fernandez-Miranda; C: Arbizu (4), Quesada, Giannantonio |
| Uruguay | 5 | T: Viana |

18 August 1998, Estadio CA, San Isidro
| Argentina | 55 | T: Bouza, Jurado, Simone, Reggiardo, Sporleder, Fernandez-Lobbe, penalty try (2); C: J Fernandez-Miranda (4), Todeschini (2); DG: J Fernandez-Miranda |
| Uruguay | 0 | |

17 October 1998, Cancha del Atletico, Tucuman
| Argentina | 30 | T: Grande, Lobrauco, Brolese, Martin; C: Contepomi (2); PG: Contepomi (2) |
| Uruguay | 14 | T: Vecino, Sánchez; C: Sciarra (2) |

19 May 2001, Richardson Stadium, Kingston
| Argentina | 32 | T: Nunez-Piossek, Orengo, Soler, Dande; C: Contepomi (3); PG: Contepomi (2) |
| Uruguay | 27 | T: Ibarra, Mendaro C: Menchaca PG: Menchaca (5) |

28 April 2002, Mendoza Rugby Club Ground, Mendoza
| Argentina | 35 | T: Nunez-Piossek (2), Soler (2), Senillosa, J Fernandez-Miranda; C: J Fernandez-Miranda; PG: J Fernandez-Miranda |
| Uruguay | 21 | T: Grille (2); C: Menchaca; PG: Menchaca (2); DG: Aguirre |

3 May 2003, Luis Franzini Stadium, Montevideo
| Argentina | 32 | T: Nunez-Piossek (2), Senillosa (2), Contepomi, Ostiglia; C: J Fernandez-Miranda |
| Uruguay | 0 | |

27 August 2003, Estadio CA, San Isidro
Argentina 57 T: Corleto (2), Alvarez-Kairelis (2), Nunez-Piossek, Pichot, Reggiardo, Mendez, Scelzo; C: Quesada (6)
Uruguay 0

28 April 2004, Prince of Wales Country Club, Santiago
Argentina 69 T: Nunez-Piossek (2), Lopez-Flemming (2), Henn, Galindo, Leonelli, Mendez, Senillosa, penalty try;
C: Senillosa (8); PG: Senillosa
Uruguay 10 T: Mosquera; C: Perez del Castillo; PG: Pereira

8 July 2006, Cricket & Rugby Club, Buenos Aires
Argentina 26 T: Avramovic (2); C: Todeschini (2); PG: Todeschini (4)
Uruguay 0

Argentina vs Venezuela

1 May 2004, Prince of Wales Country Club, Santiago
Argentina 147 T: Higgs (5), Senillosa (3), Boffelli (2), Borges (2), Lopez-Fleming (2), Leonelli-Morey (2), Aramburu, Albina,
Guinazu, Bouza, Sanz, Galindo, Contepomi; C: Bustos (9), Senillosa (7)
Venezuela 7 T: Pino; C: Aguilar

Argentina vs Wales

Argentina vs Wales	
Played:	11
Won:	4
Lost:	7
Drawn:	0
For:	289
Against:	315

Average score:	
26.27–28.63	

Argentina percentages:	
Won:	36.37%
Lost:	63.63%
Drawn:	0%

9 October 1991, National Stadium, Cardiff (RWC, Pool 3)
Wales 16 T: Arnold; PG: Ring (3), Rayer
Argentina 7 T: Simon; PG: del Castillo

21 November 1998, Stradey Park, Llanelli
Wales 43 T: Charvis (2), James, Taylor; C: Jenkins (4); PG: Jenkins (5)
Argentina 30 T: Contepomi, Pichot, Sporleder, penalty try; C: Contepomi (2);
PG: Contepomi (2)

5 June 1999, Ferro Carril Oeste Stadium, Buenos Aires
Wales 36 T: James, Sinkinson, C Wyatt; C: Jenkins (3); PG: Jenkins (4); DG: Jenkins
Argentina 26 T: Bartolucci, Quesada; C: Quesada (2); PG: Quesada (4)

12 June 1999, Ferro Carril Oeste Stadium, Buenos Aires
Wales 23 T: G Jenkins; PG: N Jenkins (5); DG: N Jenkins
Argentina 16 T: Orengo; C: Cilley; PG: Contepomi(3)

1 October 1999, Millennium Stadium, Cardiff (RWC, Pool D)
Wales 23 T: Taylor, Charvis; C: Jenkins (2); PG: Jenkins (3)
Argentina 18 PG: Quesada (6)

10 November 2001, Millennium Stadium, Cardiff
Argentina 30 T: Contepomi, Camardon; C: Contepomi; PG: Contepomi (5); DG: Contepomi
Wales 16 T: Morris; C: Harris; PG: Harris (3)

12 June 2004, El Stadio Atletico, Tucuman
Argentina 50 T: Borges (2), Longo, M Contepomi, Gaitan, F Contepomi;
C: F Contepomi (4); PG: F Contepomi (4)
Wales 44 T: Peel, Forster, Charvis, Parker, Luscombe; C: Henson (5); PG: Henson (3)

19 June 2004, Velez Sarsfield Stadium, Buenos Aires
Wales 35 T: Williams (3), Robinson; C: Henson (3); PG: Henson (3)
Argentina 20 T: Aramburu, Durand, Borge; C: Senillosa; PG: Senillosa

11 June 2006, Estadio Raúl Conti, Puerto Madryn
Argentina 27 T: Leguizamon, Piossek, Leonelli; C: Todeschini (3); PG: Todeschini (2)
Wales 25 T: M Jones, Evans, Hook; C: N Robinson (2); PG: N Robinson (2)

17 June 2006, Velez Sarsfield Stadium, Buenos Aires
Argentina 45 T: Tiesi (2), J-M Fernandez Lobbe; C: Todeschini (3); PG: Todeschini (8)
Wales 27 T: Delve, S Williams, Byrne; C: Hook (2), N Robinson; PG: Hook (2)

18 August 2007, Millennium Stadium, Cardiff
Wales 27 T: G Thomas, A Jones, M Jones; C: Hook (3); PG: Hook (2)
Argentina 20 T: Corleto (2); C: Todeschini (2); PG: Todeschini (2)

Argentina vs Wales XV

14 August 1968, GEBA, Buenos Aires
Argentina   9   T: Anthony; PG: Seaton (2)
Wales XV   5   T: Turner; C: Dawes

28 August 1968, GEBA, Buenos Aires
Argentina   9   T: penalty try; PG: Seaton (2)
Wales XV   9   T: Ferguson; PG: Fergsuon (2)

16 October 1976, National Stadium, Cardiff
Wales XV   20   T: T Davies, Edwards; PG: Bennett (4)
Argentina   19   T: Gauweloose, Beccar-Varela; C: Porta; PG: Beccar-Varela (2), Porta

Argentina vs World XV

9 August 1980, Ferro Carril Oeste Stadium, Buenos Aires
Argentina   36   T: Mastai (2), Sansot (2), Campo, Silva, Ure; C: Porta (4)
World XV   22   T: Fouroux, Fenwick, Slemen, Scott; C: Slemen (2), O'Brien

25 June 1983, Athletic Club, Atlanta
Argentina   28   T: Palma, Madero, Campo, Courreges; C: Loffreda (2), Sansot; PG: Loffred; DG: Madero
World XV   20   T: Cunningham, Berbizier, Pardo-Vidal; C: Ella; PG: Ella, Campese

17 April 1999, Buenos Aires Cricket & Rugby Club, Buenos Aires
Argentina   49   T: Martin (2), Simone (2), Ledesma, Albanese, Corleto; C: Cilley (3), Quesada (3), Porta
World XV   31   T: Tenana (2), Sanders, Mather, Arancibia; C: Chalmers (3)

Argentina: summaries and records

Home matches	
Played	161
Won	85
Lost	69
Drawn	7
Points for	4,116
Points against	3,042
Average score	25.57/18.89
Win %	52.80
Lose %	42.86
Draw %	4.35

Away matches	
Played	107
Won	50
Lost	55
Drawn	2
Points for	2,777
Points against	2,355
Average score	25.95/22.01
Win %	46.73
Lose %	51.4
Draw %	1.87

Neutral venues	
Played	56
Won	46
Lost	9
Drawn	1
Points for	2,589
Points against	726
Average score	46.23/12.96
Win %	82.14
Lose %	16.07
Draw %	1.79

Total matches	
Played	324
Won	181
Lost	133
Drawn	10
Points for	9,482
Points against	6,123
Average score	29.27/18.9
Win %	55.06
Lose %	41.05
Draw %	3.09

Most capped players: Argentina							
Player	Caps	Career	T	C	PG	DG	Total
Lisandro Arbizu	87	13/07/1991–17/06/2005	17	14	14	11	188
Rolando Martin	87	04/06/1994–26/10/2003	20	-	-	-	100
Pedro Sporleder	78	27/10/1990–22/10/2003	14	-	-	-	70
Federico Méndez Azpillaga	75	27/10/1990–23/05/2005	14	-	-	-	70
Agustin Pichot	73	30/04/1995–19/10/2007	12	-	-	-	60

ARGENTINA

Most tests as captain: Argentina

No.	Player	Period
48	Lisandro Arbizu	1992–2003
38	Hugo Porta	1977–1990
31	Agustin Pichot	2000–2007
21	Pedro Sporleder	1996–1999
15	Hector Silva	1967–1971

Most points by a player in a career: Argentina

No.	Player	Tests	Career	Points			
				T	C	PG	DG
595	Hugo Porta	58	10/10/1971–17/04/1999	11	85	100	28
494	Gonzalo Quesada	38	14/09/1996–26/10/2003	4	72	103	7
476	Felipe Contepomi	65	10/10/1998–15/11/2008	11	56	101	2
373	Santiago Meson	34	30/09/1987–04/10/1997	9	68	63	1
276	Federico Todeschini	22	08/08/1998–14/06/2008	4	38	60	-

Most tries by a player in a career: Argentina

No.	Player	Tests	Career
30	José-Mariá Núñez-Piossek	28	19/05/2001–09/08/2008
28	Diego Cuesta Silva	63	16/07/1983–21/10/1995
24	Gustavo Jorge	23	08/10/1989–20/06/1994
20	Rolando Martin	87	13/07/1991–17/06/2005
18	Facundo Soler	26	22/06/1996–04/05/2002
18	Uriel o'Farrel	3	13/09/1951–16/09/1951

Most conversions by a player in a career: Argentina

No.	Player	Tests	Career
85	Hugo Porta	58	10/10/1971–17/04/1999
72	Gonzalo Quesada	38	14/09/1996–26/10/2003
68	Santiago Meson	34	30/09/1987–04/10/1997
56	Felipe Contepomi	65	10/10/1998–15/11/2008
42	Juan Fernandez-Miranda	34	17/09/1997–09/06/2007

Most penalties by a player in a career: Argentina

No.	Player	Tests	Career
103	Gonzalo Quesada	38	14/09/1996–26/10/2003
101	Felipe Contepomi	65	10/10/1998–15/11/2008
100	Hugo Porta	58	10/10/1971–17/04/1999
63	Santiago Meson	34	30/09/1987–04/10/1997
60	Federico Todeschini	22	08/08/1998–14/06/2008

ARGENTINA

Most drop goals by a player in a career: Argentina

No.	Player	Tests	Career
28	Hugo Porta	58	10/10/1971–17/04/1999
11	Lisandro Arbizu	86	13/07/1991–17/06/2005
7	Gonzalo Quesada	38	14/09/1996–26/10/2003
6	Juan Martin Hernandez	32	13/09/1969–16/10/1973
6	Tomas Harris-Smith	7	13/091969–16/10/1973

Most points by a player in a match: Argentina

No.	Player	Points				Versus	Venue	Date
		T	C	PG	DG			
50	Eduardo Morgan	6	13	-	-	Paraguay	Clube Atlético, São Paulo	14/10/1973
45	José-Mariá Nuñez-Piossek	9	-	-	-	Paraguay	Luis Franzini Stadium, Montevideo	2704//2003
40	Gustavo Jorge	8	-	-	-	Brazil	Clube Atlético, São Paulo	02/10/1993
40	Cristian Mendy	5	10	-	-	Brazil	Belgrano Stadium, Buenos Aires	01/10/1991
36	Martin Sansot	3	6	4	-	Brazil	Cancha del Atlético, Tucuman	24/10/1977

Most tries by a player in a match: Argentina

No.	Player	Versus	Venue	Date
11	Uriel O'Farrell	Brazil	GEBA, Buenos Aires	13/09/1951
9	José-Mariá Nuñez-Piossek	Paraguay	Luis Franzini Stadium, Montevideo	27/04/2003
8	Gustavo Jorge	Brazil	Clube Atlético, São Paulo	02/10/1993
7	Uriel O'Farrell	Uruguay	GEBA, Buenos Aires	09/09/1951
6	Gustavo Jorge	Brazil	Carrasco Polo Club, Montevideo	08/10/1989
6	Eduardo Morgan	Paraguay	Clube Atlético, São Paulo	10/14/1973

Most conversions by a player in a match: Argentina

No.	Player	Versus	Venue	Date
16	Jose Cilley	Paraguay	Mendoza Rugby Club Stadium, Mendoza	01/05/2002
13	Hugo Porta	Paraguay	Asuncion	21/09/1985
13	Eduardo Morgan	Paraguay	Clube Atlético, São Paulo	14/10/1973
11	Eduardo de Forteza	Paraguay	Asuncion	25/09/1975
10	Felipe Contepomi	Chile	Estadio San Isidro, Buenos Aires	14/08/2007
10	Santiago Meson	Brazil	Clube Atlético, São Paulo	02/10/1993
10	Cristian Mendy	Brazil	Belgrano Stadium, Buenos Aires	01/10/1991
10	Santiago Meson	Brazil	Carrasco Polo Club, Montevideo	08/10/1989
10	Pablo Guarrochena	Paraguay	Cancha del Atletico, Tucuman	29/10/1977

Most penalties by a player in a match: Argentina

No.	Player	Versus	Venue	Date
8	Federico Todeschini	Wales	Velez Sarsfield Stadium, Buenos Aires	17/06/2006
8	Gonzalo Quesada	Samoa	Stradey Park, Llanelli	10/10/1999
8	Santiago Meson	Canada	Ferro Carril Oeste Stadium, Buenos Aires	10/03/1995
7	Federico Todeschini	Italy	Stadio Flaminio, Rome	16/11/2002
7	Gonzalo Quesada	Ireland	Stade Felix Bollaert, Lens	20/10/1999
7	Gonzalo Quesada	Japan	Millennium Stadium, Cardiff	16/10/1999
7	Gonzalo Quesada	Canada	Cricket & Rugby Club, Buenos Aires	22/08/1998
7	Santiago Meson	France	Stade Marcel Saupin, Nantes	14/11/1992
7	Hugo Porta	France	Ferro Carril Oeste Stadium, Buenos Aires	29/06/1974

Most drop goals by a player in a match: Argentina

No	Player	Versus	Venue	Date
3	Juan Martin Hernández	Ireland	Parc des Princes, Paris	30/09/2007
3	Juan Fernandez-Miranda	Canada	Fletchers Field, Markham	26/05/2001
3	Hugo Porta	New Zealand	Ferro Carril Oeste Stadium, Buenos Aires	03/11/1985
3	Hugo Porta	Australia	Ferro Carril Oeste Stadium, Buenos Aires	27/10/1979

Most points in a match by Argentina

No.	Result	T	C	PG	DG	Versus	Venue	Date
152	152–0	24	16	-	-	Paraguay	Mendoza Rugby Club Ground, Mendoza	01/05/2002
147	147–7	23	16	-	-	Venezuela	Prince of Wales Country Club, Santiago	01/05/2004
144	144–0	24	12	-	-	Paraguay	Luis Franzini Stadium, Montevideo	27/04/2003
114	114–3	18	12	-	-	Brazil	Clube Atlético, São Paulo	02/10/1993
109	109–3	19	15	1	-	Brazil	Prince of Wales Country Club, Santiago	09/10/1979

Most consecutive test wins by Argentina

No.	Period	Details
10	26/09/1992–23/10/1993	Spain (H), Spain (H), Romania (A), France (A), Japan (H), Japan (H), Brazil (A), Chile (H), Paraguay (H), Uruguay (A)
7	07/10/1961–25/07/1965	Chile (N), Brazil (N), Uruguay (A), Uruguay (N), Brazil (A), Chile (N), Section Paloise (H)
7	07/08/1971–17/10/1971	SA Gazelles (A), Oxford and Cambridge (H), Oxford and Cambridge (H), Chile (N), Brazil (N), Paraguay (N), Uruguay (A)
7	04/11/1972–21/10/1973	SA Gazelles (H), Romania (H), Romania (H), Paraguay (N), Uruguay (N), Brazil (A), Chile (N)

Milestones

Longest test career	Hugo Porta	10/10/1971–17/04/1999 (27 years & 188 days)
Oldest test player	Hugo Porta	47 years & 217 days on 17/04/1999 vs World XV in Buenos Aires

Above: Wallaby fullback Jim Lenehan attempts to drop a goal during the first test of the second Bledisloe Cup series of 1962 in Wellington. His attempt was in vain under the pressure of All Black flanker Waka Nathan and the match was drawn 9-9. *Photo*: New Zealand Rugby Museum

Above left: Argentina's Hugo Porta in action. *Photo*: UAR

Left: Great All Black scrumhalf Sid Going scores one of his ten career test tries, this one against the Wallabies in the third test of the 1972 Bledisloe Cup series won 3-0 by New Zealand. Unable to stop Going is Wallaby flyhalf Geoff Richardson. *Photo*: New Zealand Rugby Museum

Below: 1927 Waratahs in training. *Photo* ARU

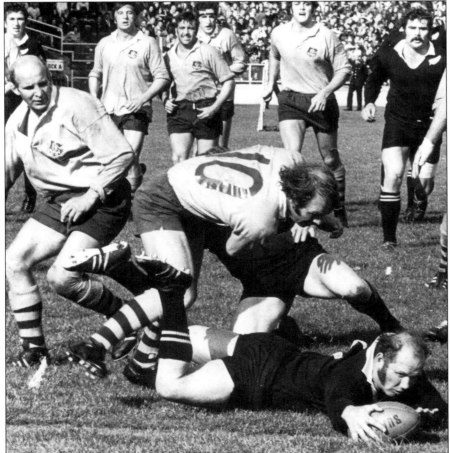

208

Australia

Wallabies

Australia vs British Lions	
Played:	20
Won:	5
Lost:	15
Drawn:	0
For:	195
Against:	335

Average score:
9.75–16.75

Australia percentages:
Won:	25%
Lost:	75%
Drawn:	0%

Australia vs Argentina (Puma Trophy) *see page 182*

Australia vs British and Irish Lions (Tom Richards Trophy)

Introduced for the 2001 British and Irish Lions tour of Australia, a series won 2–1 by Australia for the first time in their history, the Tom Richards Trophy is played for whenever Australia and the British and Irish Lions meet. Made of crystal, it has a portrait of Tom Richards etched into the glass as well as the emblems of both teams. Tom Richards is the only Australian to have represented both Australia and the British Lions in rugby union. In 1905, Richards's father immigrated to South Africa to try his luck on the Witwatersrand goldfields. A keen rugby player, Tom followed his father but wasn't eligible for Springbok selection because of residence issues. He returned to Australia and was selected to tour the British Isles in 1908 with the Wallabies, returning to South Africa after the tour. In 1910, the British Isles toured South Africa, but were decimated through injury woes. Richards, who'd once played with Gloucester Rugby Club in England, was called up as a replacement, a dubious qualification to say the least. Nevertheless, he went down in history for his dual national representation.

24 June 1899, Sydney Cricket Ground, Sydney
Australia	13	T: Colton, Evans, Spragg; C: Spragg (2)
British Lions	3	T: Nicholls

22 July 1899, GABBA, Brisbane
British Lions	11	T: Nicholls, Adamson, Smith; C: Adamson
Australia	0	

5 August 1899, Sydney Cricket Ground, Sydney
British Lions	11	T: Bucher (2), Tims; C: Adamson
Australia	10	T: Spragg (2); C: Spragg (2)

12 August 1899, Sydney Cricket Ground, Sydney
British Lions	13	T: Bucher, Adamson; C: Adamson (2); PG: Adamson
Australia	0	

2 July 1904, Sydney Cricket Ground, Sydney
British Lions	17	T: Llewellyn (2), Bush; C: O'Brien, Harding; DG: Bush
Australia	0	

23 July 1904, GABBA, Brisbane
British Lions	17	T: O'Brien, Llewellyn, Bush; C: Bush (2); DG: Bush
Australia	3	T: Burdon

30 July 1904, Sydney Cricket Ground, Sydney
British Lions	16	T: Llewellyn, Gape, Morgan, Swannell; C: O'Brien, Bush
Australia	0	

30 August 1930, Sydney Cricket Ground, Sydney
Australia	6	T: Malcom, McGhie
British Lions	5	T: Novis; C: Prentice

19 August 1950, GABBA, Brisbane
British Lions	19	T: Jones, Williams; C: Jones (2); PG: Jones (2); DG: Jones
Australia	6	T: Cross; PG: Gardner

26 August 1950, Sydney Cricket Ground, Sydney
British Lions	24	T: Nelson (2), Kyle, John, MacDonald; C: Robins (2), Jones; PG: Jones
Australia	3	T: Burke

6 June 1959, Exhibition Ground, Brisbane
British Lions	17	T: O'Reilly, Smith; C: Risman; PG: Hewitt (2); DG: Scotland
Australia	6	PG: Donald (2)

AUSTRALIA

13 June 1959, Sydney Cricket Ground, Sydney

British Lions	24	T: Price (2), Risman, O'Reilly, Dawson; C: Hewitt (2), Scotland; PG: Scotland
Australia	3	PG: Donald

28 May 1966, Sydney Cricket Ground, Sydney

British Lions	11	T: Kennedy, McLoughlin; C: Rutherford; PG: Rutherford
Australia	8	T: Miller; C: Ruebner; PG: Ruebner

4 June 1966, Lang Park, Brisbane

British Lions	31	T: Jones (2), Bebb, Watkins, Murphy; C: Wilson (5); PG: Wilson; DG: Watkins
Australia	0	

1 July 1989, Sydney Football Stadium, Sydney

Australia	30	T: Walker, Gourley, Maguire, Martin; C: Lynagh (4); PG: Lynagh; DG: Lynagh
British Lions	12	PG: Hastings (2), Chalmers; DG: Chalmers

8 July 1989, Ballymore, Brisbane

British Lions	19	T: Hastings, Guscott; C: Andrew; PG: Hastings, Andrew; DG: Andrew
Australia	12	T: Martin; C: Lynagh; PG: Lynagh (2)

15 July 1989, Sydney Football Stadium, Sydney

British Lions	19	T: Evans; PG: Hastings (5)
Australia	18	T: Williams; C: Lynagh; PG: Lynagh (4)

30 June 2001, GABBA, Brisbane

British Lions	29	T: Robinson, Quinnell, O'Driscoll, James; C: Wilkinson (3); PG: Wilkinson
Australia	13	T: Walker, Grey; PG: Walker

7 July 2001, Colonial Stadium, Melbourne

Australia	35	T: Roff (2), Burke; C: Burke; PG: Burke (6)
British Lions	14	T: Back; PG: Wilkinson (3)

14 July 2001, Stadium Australia, Sydney

Australia	29	T: Herbert (2); C: Burke (2); PG: Burke (5)
British Lions	23	T: Robinson, Wilkinson; C: Wilkinson (2); PG: Wilkinson (3)

Tom Richards Trophy		Current holder: Australia				Number of titles: Australia 1, British Lions 0		
No.	Date	Venue	Result			Series	Holder
1	30/06/2001	GABBA, Brisbane	Australia	13–29	British Lions		
2	07/07/2001	Colonial Stadium, Brisbane	Australia	35–14	British Lions	2 - 1	Australia
3	14/07/2001	Stadium Australia, Sydney	Australia	29–23	British Lions		

Australia vs Canada	
Played:	6
Won:	6
Lost:	0
Drawn:	0
For:	283
Against:	60

Average score:
47.17–10

Australia percentages:

Won:	100%
Lost:	0%
Drawn:	0%

Australia vs Canada

15 June 1985, Sydney Cricket Ground, Sydney

Australia	59	T: Burke (2), Lane (2), Grigg (2), Calcraft, Kassulke, Farr-Jones; C: Lynagh (7); PG: Lynagh (3)
Canada	3	DG: Wyatt

23 June 1985, Ballymore, Brisbane

Australia	43	T: Burke (3), Grigg, Cutler, Tuynman, Farr-Jones; C: Lynagh (3); PG: Lynagh (2); DG: Lynagh
Canada	15	T: Tucker; C: Wyatt; PG: Wyatt (3)

9 October 1993, Kingsland Stadium, Calgary

Australia	43	T: Campese (3), Horan, Daly, D Smith; C: Lynagh (2); PG: Lynagh (3)
Canada	16	T: Jackart, Kennedy; PG: Graf (2)

31 May 1995, Boet Erasmus Stadium, Port Elizabeth (RWC, Pool A)

Australia	27	T: Tabua, Roff, Lynagh; C: Lynagh (3); PG: Lynagh (2)
Canada	11	T: Charron; PG: Rees (2)

29 June 1996, Ballymore, Brisbane
Australia   74   T: Burke (3), Wilson (2), Campese, Tune, Horan, Herbert, Payne; C: Burke (9); PG: Burke (2)
Canada   9   PG: Ross (3)

29 September 2007, Stade Chaban Delmas, Bordeaux (RWC Pool B)
Australia   37   T: Mitchell (2), Baxter, Freier, Latham, Smith; C: Shepherd (2); PG: Huxley
Canada   6   PG: Pritchard (2)

Australia vs England	
Played:	36
Won:	21
Lost:	14
Drawn:	1
For:	774
Against:	519
Average score:	
21.5–14.42	
Australia percentages:	
Won:	58,33%
Lost:	38,89%
Drawn:	2,78%

Australia vs England (Cook Cup)

Australia and England first met on 9 January 1909 in London, but first played for the Cook Cup on 12 July 1997, after the two had contracted to play each other biannually for ten years on a home-and-away basis. The Cook Cup, which is not played for during RWC internationals, was named after the renowned English explorer, navigator and cartographer, Captain James Cook, who died in 1779. Captain Cook represents a notable English-Australian connection in that he was the first Briton to make landfall on the eastern coastline of Australia 1770. The crystal cup was designed by Royal Doulton in London. Australia triumphed 25–6 in the first Cook Cup international at the Sydney Football Stadium. However, the series was to be decided through two tests that year, with the second played at Twickenham in November, which ended in a 15–15 draw, securing the first title for Australia. In 1998 Australia inflicted a record score against England in Brisbane, winning 76–0 in a match featuring young debutant Jonny Wilkinson. Australia ran in 11 tries, but in the subsequent meeting at Twickenham later that year could muster only a one-point 12–11 victory, without scoring a try, but retaining the cup. The following few years saw the Cook Cup being decided over single internationals, with the 1999 match featuring a celebration of a century of Australian rugby. To mark the occasion the two teams faced off in the same colour strips they had worn 100 years earlier; Australia wearing the New South Wales light blue and England dark navy blue. Australia won 22–15. It was not until the following year that England were to claim their first Cook Cup victory after winger Dan Luger scored a hotly debated last-second TMO try to seal the deal by 22–19. England held on to their title of Cook Cup Champions for four years, including a 25–14 victory in Melbourne in 2003, England's first on Australian soil. The two teams met again that year in the memorable RWC final when after nearly 100 minutes of rugby, Jonny Wilkinson dropped a goal deep into extra-time to clinch the cup. In 2004, the Cook Cup was again played for over two games, with Australia exacting revenge in style, thrashing England 51–15 in Brisbane and then narrowly holding out 21–19 in London later that year, courtesy of some wayward kicking by England flyhalf Charlie Hodgson. England claimed the cup the following year in a one-off match at Twickenham by 26–16. In 2006, the trophy was once again contested over two matches, with Australia comprehensively winning both to reclaim the cup.

9 January 1909, Rectory Field, Blackheath
Australia   9   T: Russell (2), N Rowe
England   3   T: Mobbs

7 January 1928, Twickenham, London
England   18   T: Tucker, Taylor, Laird, Periton; C: Richardson (3)
Australia   11   T: Towers (2), E Ford; C: Lawton

3 January 1948, Twickenham, London
Australia   11   T: Windon (2), Walker; C: Tonkin
England   0

1 February 1958, Twickenham, London
England   9   T: Phillips, Jackson; PG: Hetherington
Australia   6   PG: Lenehan; DG: Curley

AUSTRALIA

4 June 1963, Sydney Cricket Ground, Sydney
Australia	18	T: Jones, Walsham, Heinrich, Davies; C: Ryan (3)
England	9	T: Phillips, Clarke, Godwin

7 January 1967, Twickenham, London
Australia	23	T: Brass, Catchpole; C: Lenehan; PG: Lenehan, Hawthorne; DG: Hawthorne (3)
England	11	T: Ashby; C: Hosen; PG: Hosen (2)

17 November 1973, Twickenham, London
England	20	T: Old, Neary, Ripley; C: Rossborough; PG: Rossborough (2)
Australia	3	PG: Fairfax

24 May 1975, Sydney Cricket Ground, Sydney
Australia	16	T: Loane; PG: Brown (2); DG: Brown, Wright
England	9	T: Squires; C: Butler; DG: Butler

31 May 1975, Ballymore, Brisbane
Australia	30	T: Price, Smith, Fay, Weatherstone, Monaghan; C: Brown, Wright; PG: Brown, Wright
England	21	T: Squires, Uttley; C: Old (2); PG: Old (3)

3 January 1976, Twickenham, London
England	23	T: Corless, Duckham, Lampowski; C: Hignell; PG: Hignell (3)
Australia	6	PG: P Mclean (2)

2 January 1982, Twickenham, London
England	15	T: Jeavons; C: Dodge; PG: Rose (3)
Australia	11	T: Moon (2); PG: McLean

3 November 1984, Twickenham, London
Australia	19	T: M Ella, Lynagh, Poidevin; C: Lynagh (2); PG: Lynagh
England	3	PG: Barnes

23 May 1987, Concord Oval, Sydney (RWC, Pool 1)
Australia	19	T: Campese, Poidevin; C: Lynagh; PG: Lynagh (3)
England	6	T: Harrison; C: Webb

29 May 1988, Ballymore, Brisbane
Australia	22	T: Williams; PG: Lynagh (6)
England	16	T: R Underwood, Bailey; C: Webb; PG: Webb (2)

12 June 1988, Concord Oval, Sydney
Australia	28	T: Campese, G Ella, Lynagh, Carter; C: Lynagh (3); PG: Lynagh (2)
England	8	T: Richards, R Underwood

5 November 1988, Twickenham, London
England	28	T: Morris, Halliday, R Underwood (2); C: Webb (3); PG: Webb (2)
Australia	19	T: Leeds, Campese, Grant; C: Lynagh (2); PG: Lynagh

27 July 1991, Sydney Football Stadium, Sydney
Australia	40	T: Campese (2), Roebuck, Ofahengaue (2); C: Lynagh (4); PG: Lynagh (4)
England	15	T: Guscott; C: Webb; PG: Webb (3)

2 November 1991 Twickenham, London (RWC, Final)
Australia	12	T: Daly; C: Lynagh; PG: Lynagh (2)
England	6	PG: Webb (2)

11 June 1995, Newlands, Cape Town (RWC, Q/F)
England	25	T: A Underwood; C: Andrew; PG: Andrew (5); DG: Andrew
Australia	22	T: Smith; C: Lynagh; PG: Lynagh (5)

12 July 1997, Sydney Football Stadium, Sydney
Australia	25	T: Burke, Tune, Gregan, Horan; C: Burke; PG: Eales
England	6	PG: Stimpson; DG: Catt

15 November 1997, Twickenham, London
England	15	PG: Catt (5)
Australia	15	T: Gregan, Tune; C: Roff; PG: Roff

6 June 1998, Suncorp Stadium, Brisbane
Australia   76   T: Larkham (3), Tune (3), Kefu, Horan (2), Gregan, Burke; C: Burke (4), Larkham (2); PG: Burke (3)
England   0

28 November 1998, Twickenham, London
Australia   12   PG: Eales (4)
England   11   T: Guscott; PG: Catt (2)

26 June 1999, Stadium Australia, Sydney
Australia   22   T: Tune (2), Roff, Wilson; C: Roff
England   15   T: Perry (2); C: Wilkinson; PG: Wilkinson

18 November 2000, Twickenham, London
England   22   T: Luger; C: Wilkinson; PG: Wilkinson (4); DG: Wilkinson
Australia   19   T: Burke; C: Burke; PG: Burke (4)

10 November 2001, Twickenham, London
England   21   PG: Wilkinson (5); DG: Wilkinson (2)
Australia   15   T: Burke, Latham; C: Burke; PG: Burke

16 November 2002, Twickenham, London
England   32   T: Cohen (2); C: Wilkinson (2); PG: Wilkinson (6)
Australia   31   T: Flatley (2), Sailor; C: Burke (2); PG: Burke (4)

21 June 2003, Colonial Stadium, Melbourne
England   25   T: Greenwood, Tindall, Cohen; C: Wilkinson (2); PG: Wilkinson (2)
Australia   14   T: Sailor; PG: Roff (3)

22 November 2003, Stadium Australia, Sydney (RWC, Final)
England   20   T: Robinson; PG: Wilkinson (4); DG: Wilkinson
Australia   17   T: Tuqiri; PG: Flatley (4)

26 June 2004, Suncorp Stadium, Brisbane
Australia   51   T: Rathbone (3), Paul (2), Tuqiri; C: Roff (3); PG: Roff (5)
England   15   T: Hill, Dallaglio; C: Hodgson; PG: Hodgson

27 November 2004, Twickenham, London
Australia   21   T: Paul, Latham; C: Flatley; PG: Giteau (3)
England   19   T: Moody, Lewsey, Cueto; C: Tindall (2)

12 November 2005, Twickenham, London
England   26   T: Cohen, Cueto; C: Hodgson, Barkley; PG: Hodgson (2), Barkley; DG: Hodgson
Australia   16   T: Mitchell; C: Rogers; PG: Rogers (3)

11 June 2006, Telstra Stadium, Sydney
Australia   34   T: Latham, Gerrard, Blake; C: Mortlock (2); PG: Mortlock (5)
England   3   PG: Barkley

17 June 2006, Telstra Dome, Melbourne
Australia   43   T: Gerrard (2), Smith, Tuqiri, Chisholm, Larkham; C: Mortlock (5); PG: Mortlock
England   18   T: Chuter, Varndell; C: Goode; PG: Goode; DG: Goode

6 October 2007, Stade Velodrome, Marseille (RWC, Q/F)
England   12   PG: Wilkinson (4)
Australia   10   T: Tuqiri C: Mortlock PG: Mortlock

15 November 2008, Twickenham, London
Australia   28   T: Ashley-Cooper; C: Giteau; PG: Giteau (6), Mortlock
England   14   T: Easter; PG: Cipriani (2); DG: Armitage

AUSTRALIA

Cook Cup			Current holder: Australia			Number of titles: Australia 6, England 5	
No.	Date	Venue	Result			Series	Holder
1	12/07/1997	Sydney Football Stadium, Sydney	Australia	25–6	England	1–0	Australia
2	15/11/1997	Twickenham, London	England	15–15	Australia		
3	06/06/1998	Suncorp Stadium, Brisbane	Australia	76–0	England	2–0	Australia
4	28/11/1998	Twickenham, London	England	11–12	Australia		
5	26/06/1999	Stadium Australia, Sydney	Australia	22–15	England	1–0	Australia
6	18/11/2000	Twickenham, London	England	22–19	Australia	1–0	England
7	10/11/2001	Twickenham, London	England	21–15	Australia	1–0	England
8	16/11/2002	Twickenham, London	England	32–31	Australia	1–0	England
9	21/06/2003	Colonial Stadium, Melbourne	Australia	14–25	England	0–1	England
10	26/06/2004	Suncorp Stadium, Brisbane	Australia	51–15	England	2–0	Australia
11	27/11/2004	Twickenham, London	England	19–21	Australia		
12	12/11/2005	Twickenham, London	England	26–16	Australia	1–0	England
13	11/06/2006	Telstra Stadium, Sydney	Australia	34–3	England	2–0	Australia
14	17/06/2006	Telstra Dome, Melbourne	Australia	43–18	England		
15	15/11/2008	Twickenham, London	England	14–28	Australia	0–1	Australia

Australia vs Fiji

Australia vs Fiji	
Played:	18
Won:	25
Lost:	2
Drawn:	1
For:	497
Against:	218

Average score:
27.61–12.11

Australia percentages:

Won:	83.33%
Lost:	11.12%
Drawn:	5.55%

26 July 1952, Sydney Cricket Ground, Sydney
Australia 15 T: Jones, Stapleton, Johnson, Solomon; PG: Baker
Fiji 9 T: Valewai, Ranavue; PG: Ranavue

9 August 1952, Sydney Cricket Ground, Sydney
Fiji 17 T: Salabogi, Ralagi; C: Vatabua; PG: Vatabua, Ranavue; DG: Ranavue
Australia 15 T: Stapleton, Cox, Shehadie, Windon; DG: Solomon

5 June 1954, Exhibition Ground, Brisbane
Australia 22 T: Cameron, Phipps, Cross, Jones, Tate; C: Barker, Tooth; PG: Barker
Fiji 19 T: Naborisi, Cavalevu, Domoni, Buroglevu; C: Vatabua (2); PG: Vatabua

26 June 1954, Sydney Cricket Ground, Sydney
Fiji 18 T: Seruvatu, Sankuru; PG: Ranavue (3), Nawalu
Australia 16 T: Cross, Shehadie; C: Barker (2); PG: Barker (2)

10 June 1961, Exhibition Ground, Brisbane
Australia 24 T: Lisle, R Thornett, MacGrath, Cleary, Phelps, Catchpole; C: Dowse (3)
Fiji 6 PG: Bose (2)

17 June 1961, Sydney Cricket Ground, Sydney
Australia 20 T: Cleary (2), Reid, Ellwood; C: Dowse; PG: Dowse (2)
Fiji 14 T: Nabou, Rasou, Lovodua; C: Bose; PG: Tawase

1 July 1961, Olympic Park, Melbourne
Australia 3 T: Lisle
Fiji 3 T: Levula

19 September 1972, Backhurst Park, Suva
Australia 21 T: Thompson, Sullivan, Burnett, Stumbles; C: Thompson; DG: Fairfax
Fiji 19 T: Varo (2); C: Batisbasaga; PG: Batisbasaga (3)

12 June 1976, Sydney Cricket Ground, Sydney
Australia 22 T: Batch (2), Ryan, Pearse; PG: P McLean (2)
Fiji 6 T: Tuiese; C: Naituyaga

19 June 1976, Ballymore, Brisbane
Australia 21   T: Ryan (2); C: P McLean (2); PG: P McLean (2); DG: P McLean
Fiji 9   PG: Raitilava (3)

26 June 1976, Sydney Cricket Ground, Sydney
Australia 27   T: Batch, Pearse, Ryan; PG: P McLean (5)
Fiji 17   T: Nasave, Matalau, Viriviri; C: Nasave; PG: Nasave

24 May 1980, National Stadium, Suva
Australia 22   T: Martin, Moon; C: P McLean; PG: P McLean (3); DG: P Mclean
Fiji 9   PG: Vinetaki, Waiseke; DG: Radrodo

9 June 1984, National Stadium, Suva
Australia 16   T: Campese; PG: Lynagh (4)
Fiji 3   PG: Turuva

10 August 1985, Ballymore, Brisbane
Australia 52   T: Farr-Jones (2), Grigg, Reynolds, Cutler, Lawton, Papworth; C: Knox (3); PG: Knox (3); DG: Knox (2), Campese
Fiji 28   T: Nawalu, Niuqila, Cama, Talawadua; C: Koroduadua (3); PG: Koroduadua (2)

17 August 1985, Sydney Cricket Ground, Sydney
Australia 31   T: Campese (2), Grigg, McIntyre, Cutler; C: Knox; PG: Knox (3)
Fiji 9   PG: Koroduadua (2); DG: Koroduadua

18 September 1998, Paramatta Stadium, Sydney
Australia 66   T: Smith (2), Larkham (2), Roff, Little, Finegan, Grey, Paul; C: Eales (9); PG: Eales
Fiji 20   T: Koroi, Serevi; C: Serevi (2); PG: Serevi (2)

9 June 2007, Subiaco Oval, Perth
Australia 49   T: Tuqiri (2), Staniforth (2), Huxley, Norton-Knight, Larkham, Ashley-Cooper; C: Huxley (3); PG: Huxley
Fiji 0

23 September 2007, Stade de la Mosson, Montpellier (RWC, Pool B)
Australia 55   T: Mitchell (3), Giteau (2), Ashley-Cooper, Hoiles; C: Giteau (4); PG: Giteau (3); DG: Barnes
Fiji 12   T: Ratuva, Neivua; C: Bai

Australia vs France (Trophée des Bicentenaires)

Australia vs France	
Played:	40
Won:	22
Lost:	16
Drawn:	2
For:	805
Against:	688
Average scores:	
20.13 – 17.2	
Australia percentages:	
Won:	55%
Lost:	40%
Drawn:	5%

The Trophée des Bicentenaires was donated by the Fédération Française de Rugby in 1988 to celebrate both countries' rugby centenaries: when Australia hosted its first tour in 1888 and France formed the Union des Sociétés Françaises de Sports Athlétiques in 1887. The trophy is today played for in perpetuity between the two and is a bronze sculpture featuring two players in a tackle. Although the trophy dates from 1988, it was first contested in 1989 when Australia started off as holders of the trophy based on the results of the most recent matches between the two sides. The trophy is played for each time the sides meet in a test, excluding RWC games. In the event of a drawn one-off test or drawn two-test series the current holder retains the trophy. It only passes to the other if they win a series or one-off international. Australia has won the Trophée des Bicentenaires ten times, in 1989, 1990, 1993, 1997, 1998, 2000, 2002, 2008 and 2009, while France had to wait 12 years until 2001 when they narrowly won the one-off test in Marseille. France have since won the trophy twice, in 2004 and 2005 and Australia are the current holders, winning the one-off test in June 2009.

22 January 1928, Stade Colombes, Paris
Australia 11   T: Ford, Towers, Wallace; C: Lawton
France 8   T: Bonamy, Camel; C: Behotequy

11 January 1948, Stade Colombes, Paris
France 13   T: Basquet (2), Pomathios; C: Alvarez (2)
Australia 6   PG: Tonkin (2)

9 March 1958, Stade Colombes, Paris
France 19   T: Crauste, Quaglio, Rancoule; C: A Labazuy (2); DG: M Prat, A Labazuy
Australia 0

AUSTRALIA

26 August 196, Sydney Cricket Ground, Sydney
| France | 15 | T: Lacroix, Pique, Bouguyon; DG: P Albaladejo (2) |
| Australia | 8 | T: Heinrich; C: Elwood; PG: Elwood |

11 February 1967, Stade Colombes, Paris
| France | 20 | T: L Camberabero; C: G Camberabero; PG: G Camberabero (4); DG: G Camberabero |
| Australia | 14 | T: G Davis, Johnson; C: Hawthorne; PG: Hawthorne; DG: Hawthorne |

17 August 1968, Sydney Cricket Ground, Sydney
| Australia | 11 | T: Smith; C: McGill; PG: McGill; DG: Ballesty |
| France | 10 | T: W Spanghero, Boujet; C: Villepreux, Boujet |

20 November 1971, Stade Toulouse, Toulouse
| France | 11 | T: Skréla, Bertranne; PG: Villepreux |
| Australia | 13 | T: L'Estrange (2); C: McGill; PG: J McLean |

27 November 1971, Stade Colombes, Paris
| France | 18 | T: Boffeli; C: Villepreux; PG: Villepreux (4) |
| Australia | 9 | PG: McGill, J McLean (2) |

17 June 1972, Sydney Cricket Ground, Sydney
| Australia | 14 | T: Taafe, Taylor; PG: Fairfax (2) |
| France | 14 | T: Lux (2), Saisset; C: Villepreux |

25 June 1972, Ballymore, Ballymore
| France | 16 | T: Maso (2), W Spanghero; C: Villepreux, Cabrol |
| Australia | 15 | PG: Fairfax (5) |

24 October 1976, Stade Municipal, Bordeaux
| France | 18 | T: Bertranne, Cholley, Paparemborde; C: Droitecourt (3) |
| Australia | 15 | PG: P McLean (4); DG: P McLean |

30 October 1976, Parc des Princes, Paris
| France | 34 | T: Harize, Averous, Rives, Bertranne, Aguirre, Cholley; C: Aguirre (2); PG: Aguirre; DG: Astre |
| Australia | 6 | PG: P McLean (2) |

5 July 1981, Ballymore, Brisbane
| Australia | 17 | T: Poidevin, O'Connor, Moon; C: McLean; PG: Richards |
| France | 15 | T: Mesny; C: Gabernet; PG: Blanco, Gabernet; DG: Vivies |

11 July 1981, Sydney Cricket Ground, Sydney
| Australia | 24 | T: Hall, O'Connor; C: P McLean (2); PG: P McLean (4) |
| France | 14 | T: Lacans, Elissalde; DG: Ellissalde, Sallefranque |

13 November 1983, Stade Municipal, Clermont Ferrand
| France | 15 | PG: Lescarboura (3); DG: Lescarboura, Lafond |
| Australia | 15 | T: Roche; C: Campese; PG: Campese; DG: M Ella, Hawker |

19 November 1983, Parc des Princes, Paris
| France | 15 | T: Estéve; C: Lescarboura; PG: Gabernet, Lescarboura (2) |
| Australia | 6 | PG: Campese; DG: M Ella |

21 June 1986, Sydney Cricket Ground, Sydney
| Australia | 27 | T: Campese; C: Lynagh; PG: Lynagh (6); DG: Lynagh |
| France | 14 | T: Blanco (2), Sella; C: Lescarboura |

13 June 1987, Concord Oval, Sydney (RWC, S/F)
| France | 30 | T: Blanco, Sella, Lorieux, lagisquet; C: Camberabero (4); PG: Camberabero (2) |
| Australia | 24 | T: Campese, Codey; C: Lynagh (2); PG: Lynagh (3); DG: Lynagh |

4 November 1989, Stade Municipal, Strasbourg
| Australia | 32 | T: Horan (2), Campese, Williams; C: Lynagh (2); PG: Lynagh (4) |
| France | 15 | PG: Camberabero (4); DG: Camberabero |

11 November 1989, Stade Municipal, Lille
| France | 25 | T: Lagisquet, Andrieu; C: Lacroix; PG: Lacroix (5) |
| Australia | 19 | T: Kearns, Farr-Jones; C: Lynagh; PG: Lynagh (3) |

9 June 1990, Sydney Football Stadium, Sydney
Australia   21   T: Martin; C: Lynagh; PG: Lynagh (5)
France   9   PG: Camberabero (3)

24 June 1990, Ballymore, Brisbane
Australia   48   T: Carozza, Cornish, Gavin, Little, Campese, penalty try; C: Lynagh (6); PG: Lynagh (4)
France   31   T: Blanco (2), Armary, Lacombe; C: Camberabero (3); PG: Camberabero (3)

30 June 1990, Sydney Football Stadium, Sydney
France   28   T: Camberabero, Mesnel; C: Camberabero; PG: Camberabero (2), Blanco; DG: Camberabero (3)
Australia   19   T: Campese, Daly; C: Lynagh; PG: Lynagh (2); DG: Lynagh

30 October 1993, Stade Municipal, Bordeaux
France   16   T: Hueber; C: Lacroix; PG: Lacroix; DG: Penaud, Sadourny
Australia   13   T: Gavin; C: Lynagh; PG: Lynagh (2)

6 November 1993, Parc des Princes, Paris
Australia   24   T: Roebuck, Gavin; C: Roebuck; PG: Roebuck (4)
France   3   PG: Lacroix

21 June 1997, Sydney Football Stadium, Sydney
Australia   29   T: Hardy (2); C: Eales (2); PG: Eales (5)
France   15   T: Bernat-Salle, Castaignede; C: Dourthe; PG: Dourthe

28 June 1997, Ballymore, Brisbane
Australia   26   T: Harry, Tune, Little; C: Eales; PG: Eales (3)
France   19   T: Castaignede; C: Lamaison; PG: Lamaison (4)

21 November 1998, Stade de France, Paris
Australia   32   T: Bowman, Wilson, Kefu; C: Eales; PG: Eales (5)
France   21   T: Carbonneau, Lombard; C: Lamaison; PG: Lamaison (3)

6 November 1999, Millennium Stadium, Cardiff (RWC, Final)
Australia   35   T: Tune, Finegan; C: Burke (2); PG: Burke (7)
France   12   PG: Lamaison (4)

4 November 2000, Stade de France, Paris
Australia   18   PG: Burke (6)
France   13   T: Galthie; C: Lamaison; PG: Lamaison (2)

17 November 2001, Stade Velodrome, Marseille
France   14   T: Marsh; PG: Traille (2), Michalak
Australia   13   T: Tune; C: Flatley; PG: Burke (2)

22 June 2002, Colonial Stadium, Melbourne
Australia   29   T: Latham, Larkham; C: Burke (2); PG: Burke (5)
France   17   T: Poux; PG: Gelez (3), Traille

29 June 2002, Stadium Australia, Sydney
Australia   31   T: Mortlock (2), Burke, Herbert; C: Mortlock; PG: Burke (2); DG: Gregan
France   25   T: Rougerie (2), Marconais; C: Merceron (2); PG: Merceron (2)

13 November 2004, Stade de France, Paris
France   27   T: Brusque, Michalak; C: Elissalde; PG: Elissalde (5)
Australia   14   T: Gregan; PG: Giteau (2), Flatley

2 July 2005, Suncorp Stadium, Brisbane
Australia   37   T: Turinui (2), Larkham, Latham, Sailor, Paul; C: Giteau, Rogers; PG: Giteau
France   31   T: Heymans, Laharrague, Traille, Candelon; C: Elissalde (4); PG: Elissalde

5 November 2005, Stade Velodrome, Marseille
France   26   T: Heymans, Martin; C: Elissalde (2); PG: Elissalde(3), Michalak
Australia   16   T: Mitchell; C: Rogers; PG: Rogers (3)

28 June 2008, ANZ Stadium, Sydney
Australia   34   T: Giteau, Sharpe, Elsom, Mortlock; C: Giteau (4); PG: Giteau (2)
France   13   T: Palisson; C: Trinh-Duc; PG: Yachvili (2)

AUSTRALIA

5 July 2008, Suncorp Stadium, Brisbane
Australia	40	T: Cross (2), Hynes, Horwill; C: Giteau (4); PG: Giteau (4)
France	10	T: Trinh-Duc; C: Yachvili; PG: Trinh-Duc

22 November 2008, Stade de France, Paris
Australia	18	T: Moore, Hynes; C: Giteau; PG: Giteau (2)
France	13	T: penalty try; C: Skrela; PG: Skrela; DG: Medard

27 June 2009 ANZ Stadium, Sydney
Australia	22	T: Giteau; C: Giteau; PG: Giteau (5)
France	6	PG: Yachvili, Beauxis

Trophée des Bicentenaires			Current holder: Australia			Number of titles: Australia 10, France 3	
No.	Date	Venue	Result			Series	Holder
1	04/11/1989	Stade Municipal, Strasbourg	France	15–32	Australia	1–1	Australia
2	11/11/1989	Stade Municipal, Lille	France	25–19	Australia		
3	09/06/1990	Sydney Football Stadium, Sydney	Australia	21–9	France	2–1	Australia
4	24/06/1990	Ballymore, Brisbane	Australia	48–31	France		
5	30/06/1990	Sydney Football Stadium, Sydney	Australia	19–28	France		
6	30/10/1993	Stade Municipal, Bordeaux	France	16–13	Australia	1–1	Australia
7	06/11/1993	Parc des Princes, Paris	France	3–24	Australia		
8	21/06/1997	Sydney Football Stadium, Sydney	Australia	29–15	France	2–0	Australia
9	28/06/1997	Ballymore, Brisbane	Australia	26–19	France		
10	21/11/1998	Stade de France, Paris	France	21–32	Australia	0–1	Australia
11	04/11/2000	Stade de France, Paris	France	13–18	Australia	0–1	Australia
12	17/11/2001	Stade Vélodrome, Marseille	France	14–13	Australia	1–0	France
13	22/06/2002	Colonial Stadium, Melbourne	Australia	29–17	France	2–0	Australia
14	29/06/2002	Stadium Australia, Sydney	Australia	31–25	France		
15	13/11/2004	Stade de France, Paris	France	27–14	Australia	1–0	France
16	02/07/2005	Suncorp Stadium, Brisbane	Australia	37–31	France	1–1	France
17	05/11/2005	Stade Velodrome, Marseille	France	26–16	Australia		
18	28/06/2008	ANZ Stadium, Sydney	Australia	34–13	France	2–0	Australia
19	05/07/2008	Suncorp Stadium, Brisbane	Australia	40–10	France		
20	22/11/2008	Stade de France, Paris	France	13–18	Australia	0–1	Australia
21	27/06/2009	ANZ Stadium, Sydney	Australia	22–6	France	1–0	Australia

Zealand government office in Melbourne, earning Melbourne the nickname of the 'capital of New Zealand'. Between 1931 and 1981 the trophy was contested irregularly. New Zealand won the trophy 18 times and Australia four in this period. From 1982 to 1995 the cup was played for on an annual basis, either as a series of two or three matches, or at times as a one-off match. During this period, New Zealand won the trophy 11 times and Australia three. Since 1996, the cup has been incoporated into the annual Tri-Nations tournament, until 1998 as a three-match series: the two Tri-Nations matches and a third game independent of the Tri-Nations. From 1999, the cup was played for exclusively within the Tri-Nations, when Australia and New Zealand played each other twice as per the tournament fixtures. However, in order for the non-holder to regain the trophy within the Tri-Nations they had to win the series outright, with critics pointing out that, due to the parity of the two teams, each would invariably win their home games, leaving a tied series and legions of frustrated fans. The 2006 Tri-Nations' extension saw the return of three-game contests for the Bledisloe Cup, with each team playing each other three times except during RWC years.

15 August 1903, Sydney Cricket Ground, Sydney
New Zealand   22   T: Asher, R McGregor, Tyler; C: Wallace; PG: Wallace; GM: Wallace (2)
Australia   3   PG: Wickham

2 September 1905, Tahuna Park, Dunedin
New Zealand   14   T: McMinn (2), Cross, Wrigley; C: Francis
Australia   3   T: McLean

20 July 1907, Sydney Cricket Ground, Sydney
New Zealand   26   T: Mitchinson (3), Seeling, Hughes, Francis; C: Wallace (4)
Australia   6   PG: Carmichael; GM: Carmichael

3 August 1907, GABBA, Brisbane
New Zealand   14   T: Wallace (2), Seeling, Francis; C: Wallace
Australia   5   T: Messenger; C: Messenger

10 August 1907, Sydney Cricket Ground, Sydney
New Zealand   5   T: Mitchinson; C: Wallace
Australia   5   T: Wood; C: Messenger

25 June 1910, Sydney Cricket Ground, Sydney
New Zealand   6   T: Wilson, Fuller
Australia   0

27 June 1910, Sydney Cricket Ground, Sydney
Australia   11   T: Gilbert (2), Hodgens; C: Row
New Zealand   0

2 July 1910, Sydney Cricket Ground, Sydney
New Zealand   28   T: Burns (2), Stohr (2), Paterson, Mitchinson, Mitchell, Paton; C: O'Leary (2)
Australia   13   T: Gilbert, Row; C: Row (2); PG: Row

6 September 1913, Athletic Park, Wellington
New Zealand   30   T: Lynch (3), McKenzie (2), Murray, Gray, Roberts; C: Roberts (3)
Australia   5   T: Carr; C: McMahon

13 September 1913, Carisbrook, Dunedin
New Zealand   25   T: Brown, Cummings, Hasell, Taylor, Wilson; C: O'Leary (3); DG: O'Leary
Australia   13   T: Jones (2), Suttor; C: Simpson (2)

20 September 1913, Lancaster Park, Christchurch
Australia   16   T: Suttor (2), Jones, Thompson; C: Hughes (2)
New Zealand   5   T: Fanning; C: O'Leary

18 July 1914, Sydney Cricket Ground, Sydney
New Zealand   5   T: McNeece; C: Graham
Australia   0

1 August 1914, GABBA, Brisbane
New Zealand   17   T: Taylor (3), R Roberts, Lynch; C: E Roberts
Australia   0

AUSTRALIA

15 August 1914, Sydney Cricket Ground, Sydney
New Zealand   22   T: R Roberts (2), Francis (2), McKenzie, Taylor; C: R Roberts, E Roberts
Australia   7   T: Wogan; DG: Dwyer

6 July 1929, Sydney Cricket Ground, Sydney
Australia   9   T: Gordon; PG: Lawton (2)
New Zealand   8   T: Oliver; C: Nepia; PG: Nepia

20 July 1929, Exhibition Ground, Brisbane
Australia   17   T: McGhie, Crossman, Ford; C: Lawton; PG: Lawton (2)
New Zealand   9   T: Grenside, Porter; PG: Cundy

27 July 1929, Sydney Cricket Ground, Sydney
Australia   15   T: J Ford, King; PG: Lawton (2), Towers
New Zealand   13   T: McWilliams, Stringfellow, Grenside; C: Lilburne (2)

12 September 1931, Eden Park, Auckland
New Zealand   20   T: Hart, Ball; C: Bush; PG: Bush (4)
Australia   13   T: Towers (2), Cowper; C: Ross (2)

2 July 1932, Sydney Cricket Ground, Sydney
Australia   22   T: Cerutti (2), Bridle, Cowper; C: Lawton (2); PG: Lawton (2)
New Zealand   17   T: Hore, Purdue, Bullock-Douglas; C: Pollock (2); DG: Pollock

16 July 1932, Exhibition Ground, Brisbane
New Zealand   21   T: Bullock-Douglas (2), Ball, Page; C: Pollock; PG: Collins; DG: Pollock
Australia   3   T: Steggall

23 July 1932, Sydney Cricket Ground, Sydney
New Zealand   21   T: Kilby, McLean, Solomon, Manchester, Palmer; C: Collins (2), Pollock
Australia   13   T: Hemingway, Bridle, Cowper; C: Ross, Cowper

11 August 1934, Sydney Cricket Ground, Sydney
Australia   25   T: Towers (2), Bridle, McLean; C: Ross (2); PG: Ross (3)
New Zealand   11   T: Hore, Knight, Max; C: Collins

25 August 1934, Sydney Cricket Ground, Sydney
New Zealand   3   T: Hore
Australia   3   T: Loudon

5 September 1936, Athletic Park, Wellington
New Zealand   11   T: Hart, Hadley, Watt; C: Pollock
Australia   6   T: McLaughlin; PG: Rankin

12 September 1936, Carisbrook, Dunedin
New Zealand   38   T: Mitchell (2), Hart (2), Reid (2), Rankin (2), Watt; C: Pollock (4); PG: Pollock
Australia   13   T: McLaughlin, Bridle; C: Rankin (2); PG: Rankin

23 July 1938, Sydney Cricket Ground, Sydney
New Zealand   24   T: Saxton (2), Sullivan, Parkhill; C: Taylor (3); PG: Taylor (2)
Australia   9   PG: Carpenter (3)

6 August 1938, Exhibition Ground, Brisbane
New Zealand   20   T: Phillips, Milliken, Bowman, Mitchell; C: Taylor (2); DG: Morrison
Australia   14   T: Carpenter (2), Collins; C: Carpenter; PG: Carpenter

13 August 1938, Sydney Cricket Ground, Sydney
New Zealand   14   T: Saxton, Bowman; C: Taylor; PG: Taylor (2)
Australia   6   T: Ramsay PG: Hayes

14 September 1946, Carisbrook, Dunedin
New Zealand   31   T: Argus (2), Haig, Elliott, Finlay, Smith, White; C: Scott (5)
Australia   8   T: Eastes, Allan; C: Livermore

28 September 1946, Eden Park, Auckland
New Zealand   14   T: Elvidge; C: Scott; PG: Scott (3)
Australia   10   T: Eastes, MacBride; C: Piper (2)

14 June 1947, Exhibition Ground, Brisbane
New Zealand   13   T: Penalty try, Argus, Arnold; C: Scott (2)
Australia   5   T: Cornforth; C: Piper

28 June 1947, Sydney Cricket Ground, Sydney
New Zealand   27   T: Argus, Kearney, Mason; C: Scott (3); PG: Scott (3), Thornton
Australia   14   T: McLean; C: Allan; PG: Allan (3)

3 September 1949, Athletic Park, Wellington
Australia   11   T: Garner (2), Windon; C: Cawsey
New Zealand   6   T: Moore; PG: Kelly

24 September 1949, Eden Park, Auckland
Australia   16   T: Solomon, Windon, Emery; C: Allan, Cawsey; PG: Allan
New Zealand   9   T: Roper; DG: Smith; PG: O'Callaghan

23 June 1951, Sydney Cricket Ground, Sydney
New Zealand   8   T: Skinner; C: Cockerill; PG: Cockerill
Australia   0

7 July 1951, Sydney Cricket Ground, Sydney
New Zealand   17   T: Jarden (2), N Wilson, Lynch; C: Cockerill; DG: Lynch
Australia   11   T: Tooth, Shehadie; C: Rothwell; PG: Rothwell

21 July 1951, GABBA, Brisbane
New Zealand   16   T: Tanner, Lynch, Bell, Haig; C: Cockerill (2)
Australia   6   PG: Rothwell, Cottrell

6 September 1952, Lancaster Park, Christchurch
Australia   14   T: Stapleton, Barker, Windon; C: Cottrell; DG: Solomon
New Zealand   9   T: Fitzgerald, White; PG: Bell

13 September 1952, Athletic Park, Wellington
New Zealand   15   T: Hotop, Robinson; PG: Jarden, Bowden; DG: Hotop
Australia   8   T: Windon; C: Cottrell; PG: Cottrell

29 August 1955, Athletic Park, Wellington
New Zealand   16   T: Clark, Vodanovich, Jarden; C: Jarden (2); PG: Jarden
Australia   8   T: Jones; C: Tooth; PG: Stapleton

3 September 1955, Carisbrook, Dunedin
New Zealand   8   T: Jarden; C: Jarden; DG: Elsom
Australia   0

17 September 1955, Eden Park, Auckland
Australia   8   T: Stapleton, Hughes; C: Stapleton
New Zealand   3   T: Jarden

25 May 1957, Sydney Cricket Ground, Sydney
New Zealand   25   T: MacEwan, Hemi, McMullen, Walsh; C: D Clarke (2); PG: D Clarke (3)
Australia   11   T: Cross; C: Tooth; PG: Tooth (2)

1 June 1957, Exhibition Ground, Brisbane
New Zealand   22   T: Dixon, McMullen, Brown, Meads; C: D Clarke (2); DG: Brown; GM: D Clarke
Australia   9   T: Morton; PG: Tooth (2)

23 August 1958, Athletic Park, Wellington
New Zealand   25   T: Whineray (2), Walsh (2), Graham, McMullen, Jones; C: D Clarke (2)
Australia   3   T: Ellwood

6 September 1958, Lancaster Park, Christchurch
Australia   6   T: Morton; PG: Curley
New Zealand   3   T: Brown

20 September 1958, Epsom Showgrounds, Auckland
New Zealand   17   T: Meads; C: D Clarke; PG: D Clarke (4)
Australia   8   T: Carroll; C: Curley; PG: Curley

26 May 1962, Exhibition Ground, Brisbane
New Zealand   20   T: B Watt (2), MacEwan, Tremain; C: D Clarke; PG: D Clarke; DG: D Clarke
Australia   6   PG: Scott (2)

4 June 1962, Sydney Cricket Ground, Sydney
New Zealand   14   T: Nathan, Watt; C: D Clarke; PG: D Clarke (2)
Australia   5   T: R Thornett; C: Scott

AUSTRALIA

25 August 1962, Athletic Park, Wellington
New Zealand   9   T: Morrisey; PG: D Clarke (2)
Australia   9   PG: Chapman (3)

8 September 1962, Carisbrook, Christchurch
New Zealand   3   PG: Clarke
Australia   0

22 September 1962, Eden Park, Auckland
New Zealand   16   T: Morrissey, Heeps, Herewini; C: Clarke (2); DG: Herewini
Australia   8   T: Lenehan; C: Chapman; PG: Chapman

15 August 1964, Carisbrook, Dunedin
New Zealand   14   T: McLeod; C: Williment; PG: Williment (2); DG: Moreton
Australia   9   T: Marks; PG: Casey (2)

22 August 1964, Lancaster Park, Christchurch
New Zealand   18   T: Murdoch, Moreton, Rangi, Gray; C: Clarke (3)
Australia   3   T: Marks

29 August 1964, Athletic Park, Wellington
Australia   20   T: E Boyce (2); C: Casey; PG: Casey (3); DG: Hawthorne
New Zealand   5   T: Murdoch; C: Clarke

19 August 1967, Athletic Park, Wellington
New Zealand   29   T: Steel (2), Davis, Tremain; C: Williment (4); PG: Williment (2); DG: Herewini
Australia   9   T: Batterham (2); PG: Batterham

15 June 1968, Sydney Cricket Ground, Sydney
New Zealand   27   T: Kirkpatrick (3), Kirton, Steel, Laidlaw; C: McCormick (3); PG: McCormick
Australia   11   T: Cardy; C: McGill; PG: McGill (2)

22 June 1968, Ballymore, Brisbane
New Zealand   19   T: Lister, Thorne, penalty try; C: McCormick (2); PG: McCormick (2)
Australia   18   T: Hipwell; PG: McGill (5)

19 August 1972, Athletic Park, Wellington
New Zealand   29   T: Dougan, Going, Sutherland, Williams, P Whiting; C: Morris (3); DG: Morris
Australia   6   PG: J McLean (2)

2 September 1972, Lancaster Park, Christchurch
New Zealand   30   T: Kirkpatrick (2), Williams, Sutherland, P Whiting; C: Morris (2); PG: Morris (2)
Australia   17   T: J McLean (2), Cole; C: J McLean; DG: Richardson

16 September 1972, Eden Park, Auckland
New Zealand   38   T: Kirkpatrick, Sutherland, Scown, Going, Whiting, Williams; C: Morris (4); PG: Morris (2)
Australia   3   PG: J McLean

25 May 1974, Sydney Cricket Ground, Sydney
New Zealand   11   T: D Robertson, Kirkpatrick; PG: Karam
Australia   6   T: Price; C: P McLean

1 June 1974, Ballymore, Brisbane
Australia   16   T: Hipwell, Monaghan; C: P McLean; PG: P McLean (2)
New Zealand   16   T: Hurst, Leslie; C: Karam; PG: Karam (2)

8 June 1974, Sydney Cricket Ground, Sydney
New Zealand   16   T: Batty, Stevens, Kirkpatrick; C: Karam (2)
Australia   6   PG: P McLean (2)

19 August 1978, Athletic Park, Wellington
New Zealand   13   T: Williams; PG: B Wilson (3)
Australia   12   T: Batch; C: Wright; PG: Wright (2)

26 August 1978, Lancaster Park, Christchurch
New Zealand   22   T: Taylor, Seear, S Wilson; C: B Wilson (2); PG: B Wilson; DG: Bruce
Australia   6   PG: Wright; DG: Wright

9 September 1978, Eden Park, Auckland
Australia   30   T: Cornelsen (4), Pearse; C: Wright, Melrose; PG: Wright; DG: Melrose
New Zealand   16   T: Ashworth, S Wilson; C: McKechnie; PG: McKechnie (2)

28 July 1979, Sydney Cricket Ground, Sydney
Australia 12 PG: P McLean (3); DG: Melrose
New Zealand 6 PG: Wilson; DG: Taylor

21 June 1980, Sydney Cricket Ground, Sydney
Australia 13 T: Hawker, Martin; C: Gould; DG: Ella
New Zealand 9 PG: Codlin (3)

28 June 1980, Ballymore, Brisbane
New Zealand 12 T: Reid; C: Codlin; PG: Codlin (2)
Australia 9 T: Moon; C: Gould; PG: Gould

12 July 1980, Sydney Cricket Ground, Sydney
Australia 26 T: Grigg (2), O'Connor, Carson; C: Gould (2); PG: Gould; DG: Ella
New Zealand 10 T: Fraser; PG: Codlin (2)

14 August 1982, Lancaster Park, Christchurch
New Zealand 23 T: Mexted, Mourie, Pokere, Fraser; C: Hewson (2); PG: Hewson
Australia 16 T: Hawker, Campese; C: Gould; PG: Gould (2)

28 August 1982, Athletic Park, Wellington
Australia 19 T: G Ella, Campese; C: Gould; PG: Gould (3)
New Zealand 16 T: Shaw, Fraser; C: Hewson; PG: Hewson (2)

11 September 1982, Eden Park, Auckland
New Zealand 33 T: Hewson, Shaw; C: Hewson (2); PG: Hewson (5); DG: Hewson, Smith
Australia 18 T: Gould; C: Gould; PG: Gould (3); DG: Hawker

20 August 1983, Sydney Cricket Ground, Sydney
New Zealand 18 T: Taylor; C: Hewson; PG: Hewson (4)
Australia 8 T: Slack, Poidevin

21 June 1984, Sydney Cricket Ground, Sydney
Australia 16 T: Reynolds, Moon; C: M Ella; PG: M Ella; DG: Gould
New Zealand 9 PG: Hewson (2); DG: Hewson

4 August 1984, Ballymore, Brisbane
New Zealand 19 T: Pokere; PG: Deans (5)
Australia 15 T: M Ella; C: M Ella; PG: M Ella (2), Campese

18 August 1984, Sydney Cricket Ground, Sydney
New Zealand 25 T: Stone, Clamp; C: Deans; PG: Deans (5)
Australia 24 T: Campese; C: M Ella; PG: M Ella (5), Campese

29 June 1985, Eden Park, Auckland
New Zealand 10 T: Green; PG: Crowley (2)
Australia 9 T: Black; C: Lynagh; PG: Lynagh

9 August 1986, Athletic Park, Wellington
Australia 13 T: Campese, Burke; C: Lynagh; PG: Lynagh
New Zealand 12 T: Brooke-Cowden; C: Cooper; PG: Cooper (2)

23 August 1986, Carisbrook, Dunedin
New Zealand 13 T: Kirk; PG: Cooper (2); DG: Cooper
Australia 12 PG: Lynagh (3); DG: Lynagh

6 September 1986, Eden Park, Auckland
Australia 22 T: Leeds, Campese; C: Lynagh; PG: Lynagh (4)
New Zealand 9 PG: Crowley (3)

25 July 1987, Concord Oval, Sydney
New Zealand 30 T: Fitzpatrick (2), Kirwan, Green; C: Fox; PG: Fox (3); DG: Fox
Australia 16 T: Papworth; PG: Leeds (3); DG: Hawker

3 July 1988, Concord Oval, Sydney
New Zealand 32 T: Kirwan (2), McDowell, A Whetton, Schuster; C: Fox (3); PG: Fox (2)
Australia 7 T: Williams; PG: Lynagh

16 July 1988, Ballymore, Brisbane
Australia 19 T: Grant, Williams; C: Leeds; PG: Leeds (3)
New Zealand 19 T: M Jones, Wright, Kirwan; C: Fox (2); PG: Fox

AUSTRALIA

30 July 1988, Concord Oval, Sydney
New Zealand 30 T: Deans, Gallagher, Kirwan; C: Fox (3); PG: Fox (4)
Australia 9 T: Walker; C: Lynagh; PG: Leeds

5 August 1989, Eden Park, Auckland
New Zealand 24 T: Gallagher, Loe; C: Fox (2); PG: Fox (4)
Australia 12 T: Campese; C: Lynagh; PG: Lynagh (2)

21 July 1990, Lancaster Park, Christchurch
New Zealand 21 T: Fitzpatrick, Innes, Crowley, Kirwan; C: Fox; PG: Fox
Australia 6 PG: Lynagh (2)

4 August 1990, Eden Park, Auckland
New Zealand 27 T: Fitzpatrick, Z Brooke, G Bachop; C: Fox (3); PG: Fox (2); DG: Fox
Australia 17 T: Horan, Ofahengaue; PG: Lynagh (2); DG: Lynagh

18 August 1990, Athletic Park, Wellington
Australia 21 T: Kearns; C: Lynagh; PG: Lynagh (5)
New Zealand 9 PG: Fox (2); DG: Fox

10 August 1991, Sydney Football Stadium, Sydney
Australia 21 T: Gavin, Egerton; C: Lynagh (2); PG: Lynagh (3)
New Zealand 12 T: I Jones; C: Fox; PG: Fox (2)

24 August 1991, Eden Park, Auckland
New Zealand 6 PG: Fox (2)
Australia 3 PG: Lynagh

27 October 1991, Lansdowne Road, Dublin (RWC, S/F)
Australia 16 T: Campese, Horan; C: Lynagh; PG: Lynagh (2)
New Zealand 6 PG: Fox (2)

14 July 1992, Sydney Football Stadium, Sydney
Australia 16 T: Campese, Horan; PG: Lynagh (2)
New Zealand 15 T: Tuigamala, Bunce; C: Fox; PG: Fox

19 July 1992, Ballymore, Brisbane
Australia 19 T: Carozza (2); PG: Lynagh (3)
New Zealand 17 T: Timu, Kirwan; C: Fox (2) PG: Fox

25 July 1992, Sydney Football Stadium, Sydney
New Zealand 26 T: Bunce, Joseph; C: Fox (2); PG: Fox (3) DG: Fox
Australia 23 T: Farr-Jones, Herbert; C: Lynagh (2); PG: Lynagh (3)

17 July 1993, Carisbrook, Dunedin
New Zealand 25 T: Fitzpatrick, Bunce; PG: Fox (5)
Australia 10 T: Horan; C: Kelaher; PG: Kelaher

17 August 1994, Sydney Football Stadium, Sydney
Australia 20 T: Little, Kearns; C: Knox (2); PG: Knox (2)
New Zealand 16 T: Howarth; C: Howarth; PG: Howarth (3)

22 July 1995, Eden Park, Auckland
New Zealand 28 T: Lomu C: Mehrtens; PG: Mehrtens (5); DG: Mehrtens (2)
Australia 16 T: Ofahengaue; C: Roff; PG: Roff (2), Burke

29 July 1995, Sydney Football Stadium, Sydney
New Zealand 34 T: Bunce (2), Mehrtens, Lomu, Wilson; C: Mehrtens (3); PG: Mehrtens
Australia 23 T: Ofahengaue, Smith; C: Burke (2); PG: Burke (3)

6 July 1996, Athletic Park, Wellington
New Zealand 43 T: M Jones, Cullen, Lomu, Marshall, Wilson, Z Brooke; C: Mehrtens (2); PG: Mehrtens (3)
Australia 6 PG: Burke (2)

27 July 1996, Lang Park, Brisbane
New Zealand 32 T: Marshall, Bunce; C: Mehrtens (2); PG: Mehrtens (6)
Australia 25 T: Gregan, Burke; PG: Burke (5)

5 July 1997, Lancaster Park, Christchurch
New Zealand 30 T: Z Brooke (2), Kronfeld (2); C: Spencer (2); PG: Spencer (2)
Australia 13 T: Horan; C: Eales; PG: Eales (2)

26 July 1997, Melbourne Cricket Ground, Melbourne
New Zealand   33   T: Bunce, Wilson, Cullen; C: Spencer (3); PG: Spencer (4)
Australia   18   T: Little, Gregan; C: Burke; PG: Burke (2)

16 August 1997, Carisbrook, Dunedin
New Zealand   36   T: Randall, Cullen, Marshall; C: Spencer (3); PG: Spencer (5)
Australia   24   T: Roff, Larkham (2), Tune; C: Knox (2)

11 July 1998, Melbourne Cricket Ground, Melbourne
Australia   24   T: Burke (2); C: Burke; PG: Burke (4)
New Zealand   16   T: Kronfeld, I Jones; PG: Mehrtens, Spencer

1 August 1998, Lancaster Park, Christchurch
Australia   27   T: Bowman, Larkham, Little, Burke; C: Eales (2); PG: Burke
New Zealand   23   T: Cullen, Lomu; C: Mehrtens (2); PG: Mehrtens (3)

29 August 1998, Sydney Football Stadium, Sydney
Australia   19   T: Burke; C: Eales; PG: Eales (4)
New Zealand   14   T: Cullen; PG: Mehrtens (2); DG: Mehrtens

24 July 1999, Eden Park, Auckland
New Zealand   34   T: Marshall; C: Mehrtens; PG: Mehrtens (9)
Australia   15   T: Gregan, Herbert; C: Burke; PG: Burke

28 August 1999, Stadium Australia, Sydney
Australia   28   T: Connors; C: Burke; PG: Burke (7)
New Zealand   7   T: Mehrtens; C: Mehrtens

15 July 2000, Stadium Australia, Sydney
New Zealand   39   T: Umaga, Alatini, Cullen, Lomu, Marshall; C: Mehrtens (4); PG: Mehrtens (2)
Australia   35   T: Mortlock (2), Latham, Roff, Paul; C: Mortlock (2); PG: Mortlock (2)

5 August 2000, Westpac Trust Stadium, Wellington
Australia   24   T: Mortlock, Roff; C: Mortlock; PG: Mortlock (3), Eales
New Zealand   23   T: Cullen (2); C: Mehrtens (2); PG: Mehrtens (3)

11 August 2001, Carisbrook, Dunedin
Australia   23   T: Burke, penalty try; C: Burke (2); PG: Burke (3)
New Zealand   15   T: Lomu, Wilson; C: Mehrtens; PG: Brown

1 September 2001, Stadium Australia, Sydney
Australia   29   T: Latham, Kefu; C: Burke, Flatley; PG: Burke (4), Walker
New Zealand   26   T: Howlett, Alatini; C: Mehrtens (2); PG: Mehrtens (4)

13 July 2002, Lancaster Park, Christchurch
New Zealand   12   PG: Mehrtens (4)
Australia   6   PG: Burke (2)

3 August 2002, Stadium Australia, Sydney
Australia   16   T: Sharpe, Rogers; PG: Burke (2)
New Zealand   14   T: McCaw; PG: Mehrtens (3)

26 July 2003, Stadium Australia, Sydney
New Zealand   50   T: Rokocoko (3), Howlett, Umaga, Carter, Mauger; C: Spencer (2), Carter; PG: Spencer (3)
Australia   21   T: Burke, Sailor, Rogers; PG: Burke (2)

16 August 2003, Eden Park, Auckland
New Zealand   21   T: Howlett (2); C: Spencer; PG: Spencer (3)
Australia   17   T: Smith PG: Flatley (4)

14 November 2003, Stadium Australia, Sydney (RWC, S/F)
Australia   22   T: Mortlock; C: Flatley; PG: Flatley (5)
New Zealand   10   T: Thorne; C: MacDonald; PG: MacDonald

17 July 2004, Westpac Trust Stadium, Wellington
New Zealand   16   T: Howlett; C: Carter; PG: Carter (3)
Australia   7   T: Mortlock; C: Giteau

7 August 2004, Telstra Stadium, Sydney
New Zealand   18   PG: Carter (4), Spencer, Mehrtens
Australia   23   T: Tuqiri; PG: Giteau (4), Burke (2)

AUSTRALIA

13 August 2005, Telstra Stadium, Sydney
New Zealand 30
Australia 13

T: Weepu, McCaw, Rokocoko; C: Carter (2), McAlister; PG: Carter (3)
T: Mitchell; C: Giteau; PG: Giteau (2)

3 September 2005, Eden Park, Auckland
New Zealand 34
Australia 24

T: Howlett (3), McCaw; C: MacDonald; PG: McAlister (3), MacDonald
T: Chisholm, Gerrard, Tuqiri, Johanssan; C: Rogers (2)

8 July 2006, Jade Stadium, Christchurch
New Zealand 32
Australia 12

T: Mealamu (2), McCaw, Toeava; C: Carter (3); PG: Carter (2)
T: Tuqiri, Fava; C: Mortlock

29 July 2006, Suncorp Stadium, Brisbane
New Zealand 13
Australia 9

T: Rokocoko; C: Carter; PG: Carter; DG: Carter
PG: Mortlock (3)

19 August 2006, Eden Park, Auckland
New Zealand 34
Australia 27

T: Eaton, Jack, McAlister; C: Carter (2); PG: Carter (5)
T: Tuqiri (2), Elsom; C: Mortlock (3); PG: Mortlock (2)

30 June 2007, Melbourne Cricket Ground, Melbourne
Australia 20
New Zealand 15

T: Ashley-Cooper, Staniforth; C: Giteau (2); PG: Mortlock (2)
T: Gear, Woodcock; C: Carter; PG: Carter

21 July 2007, Eden Park, Auckland
New Zealand 26
Australia 12

T: Woodcock; PG: Carter (7)
PG: Mortlock (3); DG: Giteau

26 July 2008, ANZ Stadium, Sydney
Australia 34
New Zealand 19

T: Cross, Hynes, Elsom, Horwill; C: Giteau (4); PG: Giteau; DG: Giteau
T: Muliaina, Hore, Ellis; C: Carter (2)

2 August 2008, Eden Park, Auckland
New Zealand 39
Australia 10

T: Woodcock (2), Nonu (2); C: Carter (2); PG: Carter (5)
T: Ashley-Cooper; C: Giteau; PG: Giteau

13 September 2008, Suncorp Stadium, Brisbane
New Zealand 28
Australia 24

T: Muliaina, Woodcock, Weepu, Carter; C: Carter (4)
T: Ashley-Cooper, Horwill, Cross; C: Giteau (3); PG: Giteau

1 November 2008, Hong Kong Stadium, Hong Kong
New Zealand 19
Australia 14

T: Sivivatu, McCaw; PG: Carter (3)
T: Mitchell (2); C: Giteau (2)

No.	Date	Venue	Result			Series	Holder
			Bledisloe Cup — Current holder: New Zealand — Number of titles: New Zealand 37, Australia 12				
1	12/09/1931	Eden Park Auckland	New Zealand	20–13	Australia	1–0	New Zealand
2	02/07/1932	Sydney Cricket Ground, Sydney	Australia	17–22	New Zealand		
3	16/07/1932	Exhibition Ground, Brisbane	Australia	3–21	New Zealand	1–2	New Zealand
4	23/07/1932	Sydney Cricket Ground, Sydney	Australia	21–13	New Zealand		
5	11/08/1934	Sydney Cricket Ground, Sydney	Australia	25–11	New Zealand		
6	25/08/1934	Sydney Cricket Ground, Sydney	Australia	3–3	New Zealand	1–0	Australia
7	05/09/1936	Athletic Park, Wellington	New Zealand	11–6	Australia		
8	12/09/1936	Carisbrook, Dunedin	New Zealand	38–13	Australia	2–0	New Zealand
9	23/07/1938	Sydney Cricket Ground, Sydney	Australia	9–24	New Zealand		
10	06/08/1938	Exhibition Ground, Brisbane	Australia	14–20	New Zealand	0–3	New Zealand
11	13/08/1938	Sydney Cricket Ground, Sydney	Australia	6–14	New Zealand		
12	14/09/1946	Carisbrook, Dunedin	New Zealand	31–8	Australia		
13	29/09/1946	Eden Park Auckland	New Zealand	14–10	Australia	2–0	New Zealand
14	14/06/1947	Exhibition Ground, Brisbane	Australia	5–13	New Zealand		
15	28/06/1947	Sydney Cricket Ground, Sydney	Australia	14–27	New Zealand	0–2	New Zealand
16	03/09/1949	Athletic Park, Wellington	New Zealand	6–11	Australia		
17	24/09/1949	Eden Park Auckland	New Zealand	9–16	Australia	0–2	Australia
18	23/06/1951	Sydney Cricket Ground, Sydney	Australia	0–8	New Zealand		
19	07/07/1951	Sydney Cricket Ground, Sydney	Australia	11–17	New Zealand	0–3	New Zealand
20	21/07/1951	GABBA, Brisbane	Australia	6–16	New Zealand		
21	06/09/1952	Lancaster Park, Christchurch	New Zealand	9–14	Australia		
22	13/09/1952	Athletic Park, Wellington	New Zealand	15–8	Australia	1–1	New Zealand
23	29/08/1955	Athletic Park, Wellington	New Zealand	16–8	Australia		
24	03/09/1955	Carisbrook, Dunedin	New Zealand	8–0	Australia	2–1	New Zealand
25	17/09/1955	Eden Park Auckland	New Zealand	3–8	Australia		
26	25/05/1957	Sydney Cricket Ground, Sydney	Australia	11–25	New Zealand		
27	01/06/1957	Exhibition Ground, Brisbane	Australia	9–22	New Zealand	0–2	New Zealand
28	23/08/1958	Athletic Park, Wellington	New Zealand	25–3	Australia		
29	06/09/1958	Lancaster Park, Christchurch	New Zealand	3–6	Australia	2–1	New Zealand
30	20/09/1958	Epsom Showgrounds, Auckland	New Zealand	17–8	Australia		
31	26/05/1962	Exhibition Ground, Brisbane	Australia	6–20	New Zealand		
32	04/06/1962	Sydney Cricket Ground, Sydney	Australia	5–14	New Zealand		
33	25/08/1962	Athletic Park, Wellington	New Zealand	9–9	Australia	4–0	New Zealand
34	08/09/1962	Carisbrook, Dunedin	New Zealand	3–0	Australia		
35	22/09/1962	Eden Park Auckland	New Zealand	16–8	Australia		
36	15/08/1964	Carisbrook, Dunedin	New Zealand	14–9	Australia		
37	22/08/1964	Lancaster Park, Christchurch	New Zealand	18–3	Australia	2–1	New Zealand
38	29/08/1964	Athletic Park, Wellington	New Zealand	5–20	Australia		
39	19/08/1967	Athletic Park, Wellington	New Zealand	29–9	Australia	1–0	New Zealand

AUSTRALIA

No.	Date	Venue	Result			Series	Holder
40	15/06/1968	Sydney Cricket Ground, Sydney	Australia	11–27	New Zealand	0–2	New Zealand
41	22/06/1968	Ballymore, Brisbane	Australia	18–19	New Zealand		
42	19/08/1972	Athletic Park, Wellington	New Zealand	29–6	Australia	3–0	New Zealand
43	02/09/1972	Lancaster Park, Christchurch	New Zealand	30–17	Australia		
44	16/09/1972	Eden Park Auckland	New Zealand	38–3	Australia		
45	25/05/1974	Sydney Cricket Ground, Sydney	Australia	6–11	New Zealand	0–2	New Zealand
46	01/06/1974	Ballymore, Brisbane	Australia	16–16	New Zealand		
47	08/06/1974	Sydney Cricket Ground, Sydney	Australia	6–16	New Zealand		
48	19/08/1978	Athletic Park, Wellington	New Zealand	13–12	Australia	2–1	New Zealand
49	26/08/1978	Lancaster Park, Christchurch	New Zealand	22–6	Australia		
50	09/09/1978	Eden Park Auckland	New Zealand	16–30	Australia		
51	28/07/1979	Sydney Cricket Ground, Sydney	Australia	12–6	New Zealand	1–0	Australia
52	21/06/1980	Sydney Cricket Ground, Sydney	Australia	13–9	New Zealand	2–1	Australia
53	28/06/1980	Ballymore, Brisbane	Australia	9–12	New Zealand		
54	12/07/1980	Sydney Cricket Ground, Sydney	Australia	26–10	New Zealand		
55	14/08/1982	Lancaster Park, Christchurch	New Zealand	23–16	Australia	2–1	New Zealand
56	28/08/1982	Athletic Park, Wellington	New Zealand	16–19	Australia		
57	11/09/1982	Eden Park Auckland	New Zealand	33–18	Australia		
58	20/08/1983	Sydney Cricket Ground, Sydney	Australia	8–18	New Zealand	0–1	New Zealand
59	21/07/1984	Sydney Cricket Ground, Sydney	Australia	16–9	New Zealand	1–2	New Zealand
60	04/08/1984	Ballymore, Brisbane	Australia	15–19	New Zealand		
61	18/08/1984	Sydney Cricket Ground, Sydney	Australia	24–25	New Zealand		
62	29/06/1985	Eden Park Auckland	New Zealand	10–9	Australia	1–0	New Zealand
63	09/08/1986	Athletic Park, Wellington	New Zealand	12–13	Australia	1–2	Australia
64	23/08/1986	Carisbrook, Dunedin	New Zealand	13–12	Australia		
65	06/09/1986	Eden Park Auckland	New Zealand	9–22	Australia		
66	25/07/1987	Concord Oval, Sydney	Australia	16–30	New Zealand	0–1	New Zealand
67	03/07/1988	Concord Oval, Sydney	Australia	7–32	New Zealand	0–2	New Zealand
68	16/07/1988	Ballymore, Brisbane	Australia	19–19	New Zealand		
69	30/07/1988	Concord Oval, Sydney	Australia	9–30	New Zealand		
70	05/08/1989	Eden Park Auckland	New Zealand	24–12	Australia	1–0	New Zealand
71	21/07/1990	Lancaster Park, Christchurch	New Zealand	21–6	Australia	2–1	New Zealand
72	04/08/1990	Eden Park Auckland	New Zealand	27–17	Australia		
73	18/08/1990	Athletic Park, Wellington	New Zealand	9–21	Australia		
74	10/08/1991	Sydney Football Stadium, Sydney	Australia	21–12	New Zealand	1–1	New Zealand
75	24/08/1991	Eden Park Auckland	New Zealand	6–3	Australia		
76	04/07/1992	Sydney Football Stadium, Sydney	Australia	16–15	New Zealand	2–1	Australia
77	19/07/1992	Ballymore, Brisbane	Australia	19–17	New Zealand		
78	25/07/1992	Sydney Football Stadium, Sydney	Australia	23–26	New Zealand		
79	17/07/1993	Carisbrook, Dunedin	New Zealand	25–10	Australia	1–0	New Zealand

No.	Date	Venue	Result			Series	Holder
80	17/08/1994	Sydney Football Stadium, Sydney	Australia	20–16	New Zealand	1–0	Australia
81	22/07/1995	Eden Park Auckland	New Zealand	28–16	Australia	2–0	New Zealand
82	29/07/1995	Sydney Football Stadium, Sydney	Australia	23–34	New Zealand		
83	06/07/1996	Athletic Park, Wellington	New Zealand	43–6	Australia	2–0	New Zealand
84	27/07/1996	Suncorp Stadium, Brisbane	Australia	25–32	New Zealand		
85	05/07/1997	Lancaster Park, Christchurch	New Zealand	30–13	Australia	3–0	New Zealand
86	26/07/1997	Melbourne Cricket Ground, Melbourne	Australia	18–33	New Zealand		
87	16/08/1997	Carisbrook, Dunedin	New Zealand	36–24	Australia		
88	11/07/1998	Melbourne Cricket Ground, Melbourne	Australia	24–16	New Zealand	3–0	Australia
89	01/08/1998	Lancaster Park, Christchurch	New Zealand	23–27	Australia		
90	29/08/1998	Sydney Football Stadium, Sydney	Australia	19–14	New Zealand		
91	24/07/1999	Eden Park Auckland	New Zealand	34–15	Australia	1–1	Australia
92	28/08/1999	Stadium Australia, Sydney	Australia	28–7	New Zealand		
93	15/07/2000	Stadium Australia, Sydney	Australia	35–39	New Zealand	1–1	Australia
94	05/08/2000	Westpac Trust Stadium, Wellington	New Zealand	23–24	Australia		
95	11/08/2001	Carisbrook, Dunedin	New Zealand	15–23	Australia	2–0	Australia
96	01/09/2001	Stadium Australia, Sydney	Australia	29–26	New Zealand		
97	13/07/2002	Jade Stadium, Christchurch	New Zealand	12–6	Australia	1–1	Australia
98	03/08/2002	Stadium Australia, Sydney	Australia	16–14	New Zealand		
99	26/07/2003	Telstra Stadium, Sydney	Australia	21–50	New Zealand	2–0	New Zealand
100	16/08/2003	Eden Park Auckland	New Zealand	21–17	Australia		
101	17/07/2004	Westpac Stadium, Wellington	New Zealand	16–7	Australia	1–1	New Zealand
102	07/08/2004	Telstra Stadium, Sydney	Australia	23–18	New Zealand		
103	13/08/2005	Telstra Stadium, Sydney	Australia	13–30	New Zealand	2–0	New Zealand
104	03/09/2005	Eden Park Auckland	New Zealand	34–24	Australia		
105	08/07/2006	Jade Stadium, Christchurch	New Zealand	32–12	Australia	3–0	New Zealand
106	29/07/2006	Suncorp Stadium, Brisbane	Australia	9–13	New Zealand		
107	19/08/2006	Eden Park Auckland	New Zealand	34–27	Australia		
108	30/06/2007	Melbourne Cricket Ground, Melbourne	Australia	20–15	New Zealand	1–1	New Zealand
109	21/07/2007	Eden Park Auckland	New Zealand	26–12	Australia		
110	26/07/2008	ANZ Stadium, Sydney	Australia	34–19	New Zealand	3–1	New Zealand
111	02/08/2008	Eden Park Auckland	New Zealand	39–10	Australia		
112	13/09/2008	Suncorp Stadium, Brisbane	Australia	24–28	New Zealand		
113	01/11/2008	Hong Kong Stadium, Hong Kong	New Zealand	19–14	Australia		

AUSTRALIA

AUSTRALIA

Australia vs New Zealand Maoris

From 1922 to 1958, the ARU granted full caps with 16 tests played. However, since then, the ARU has not awarded full international status to Maori games.

24 June 1922, Royal Agricultural Showground, Sydney
NZ Maoris	25	T: Potaka, Tresize, Gemmell, Broughton; C: Akuira (2); PG: Akuira, Taiapa, Jacob
Australia	22	T: Raymond (3), Taylor, Walker, Fox; C: Taylor (2)

26 June 1922, Royal Agricultural Showground, Sydney
Australia	28	T: Raymond, Cooney, Shute, Taylor, Davis, McKay; C: Taylor, Nothling; PG: Taylor, Humphreys
NZ Maoris	13	T: Phillips, Taituha; C: Akuira, Jacob; PG: Akuira

8 July 1922, University Oval, Sydney
NZ Maoris	23	T: Barclay (4), Taituha, Bannister; C: Taiapa; PG: Taiapa
Australia	22	T: Raymond, Wogan, Shute, McKay; C: Stanley (3); DG: Nothling

16 June 1923, Royal Agricultural Showground, Sydney
Australia	27	T: Crossman (2), Sheehan, Raymond; C: Mingay (3); PG: Nothling (3)
NZ Maoris	23	T: Potaka (2), Walker, Gemmell, Keepa; C: Tureia (4)

23 June 1923, Royal Agricultural Showground, Sydney
Australia	21	T: Bowers (2), Sheehan, Crossman, Raymond; C: Stanley (2), Nothling
NZ Maoris	16	T: Gemmell (2), Taituha, Walker; C: Taiapa, Tureia

25 June 1923, Royal Agricultural Showground, Sydney
Australia	14	T: Greatorex (2), Walker, Crossman; C: Crossman
NZ Maoris	12	T: Mill, Bevan, Gemmell; PG: Taiapa

22 September 1928, Athletic Park, Wellington
NZ Maoris	9	PG: Nepia (3)
Australia	8	T: Towers, Rosenblum; C: Croft

9 September 1931, Showgrounds Oval, Palmerston North
Australia	14	T: Steggall, Bonis, Judd; C: Ross; PG: Ross
NZ Maoris	3	T: MacDonald

23 September 1936, Showgrounds Oval, Palmerston North
Australia	31	T: McLean (3), Kelaher, Richards, Ramsay; C: Rankin (3), Gibbons, Kelly; PG: Rankin
NZ Maoris	6	T: McKinley; PG: Pepere

25 September 1946, Rugby Park, Hamilton
NZ Maoris	20	T: Smith (2), Gardiner, Paewai, Marriner; C: Isaacs; PG: Isaacs
Australia	0	

4 June 1949, Sydney Cricket Ground, Sydney
NZ Maoris	12	T: Smith, Lanigan, Hohaia, Stirling
Australia	3	T: Windon

11 June 1949, Exhibition Ground, Brisbane
Australia	8	T: Fogarty, Windon; C: Piper
NZ Maoris	8	T: Couch; C: Kenny; PG: Kenny

25 June 1949, Sydney Cricket Ground, Sydney
Australia	18	T: Brockhoff (2), Blomley, Windon; C: Piper (3)
NZ Maoris	3	PG: Kenny

14 June 1958, Exhibition Ground, Brisbane
Australia	15	T: Morton; PG: Lenehan (4)
NZ Maoris	14	T: Emery, Grbich; C: Whatarau; PG: Whatarau (2)

28 June 1958, Sydney Cricket Ground, Sydney
Australia	3	PG: Donald
NZ Maoris	3	PG: Walters

5 July 1958, Olympic Park, Melbourne
NZ Maoris	13	T: Raureti, Whatarau, Koopu; C: Whatarau (2)
Australia	6	PG: Donald (2)

AUSTRALIA

Australia vs New Zealand XV

Australia vs New Zealand XV	
Played:	24
Won:	6
Lost:	18
Drawn:	0
For:	257
Against:	459

Average score:
10.71–19.13

Australia percentages:
Won:	25%
Lost:	75%
Draw:	0%

The matches listed here from 1920 to 1928 are not recognised as full internationals by New Zealand on the grounds that these matches were not fully representative of Australia's international rugby. During World War I, competitive rugby in Australia all but shut down, with only six clubs managing to re-establish in 1919, all based in New South Wales, with a New South Wales team managing to play New Zealand regularly both home and away. This team undertook the famous Waratahs tour to the United Kingdom in 1927/1928. Any Queenslander or Victorian who wished to play competitive rugby union had no option but to join the New South Wales Rugby Union. As only one state union existed no domestic fixtures took place, so a national side could only be chosen from the New South Wales Union. The ARU, however, has subsequently recognised these matches against New Zealand as full Australian internationals on the basis that the New South Wales team essentially comprised of players from New South Wales, Queensland and Victoria. With the re-formation of the Queensland Rugby Union in 1929, New Zealand once again recognised fixtures against Australia as full internationals.

24 July 1920, Sydney Cricket Ground, Sydney
| New Zealand XV | 26 | T: Belliss (2), Baird, Donald, Steel, Storey; C: Roberts (2); DG: Tilyard |
| Australia | 15 | T: Wogan, Lawton, Fox; C: Lawton (3) |

31 July 1920, Sydney Cricket Ground, Sydney
| New Zealand XV | 14 | T: Storey (2), Steel, West; C: Roberts |
| Australia | 6 | T: Bond; PG: Lawton |

7 August 1920, Sydney Cricket Ground, Sydney
| New Zealand XV | 24 | T: Roberts (2), Belliss, Moffitt, Steel, Storey; C: Roberts (3) |
| Australia | 13 | T: Mingay (2), Marrott; C: Wogan, Mingay |

3 September 1921, Lancaster Park, Christchurch
| Australia | 17 | T: Raymond, Walker, Smith, Carr; C: Loudon; PG: Loudon |
| New Zealand XV | 0 | |

29 July 1922, Royal Agricultural Showground, Sydney
| New Zealand XV | 26 | T: Richardson (2), Belliss, Dickinson, Nicholls, Steel, White; C: Nicholls; PG: Nicholls |
| Australia | 19 | T: Raymond, Wogan, Newman; PG: Stanley (2); DG: Stanley |

5 August 1922, Royal Agricultural Showground, Sydney
| Australia | 14 | T: Stanley; C: Stanley; PG: Stanley (3) |
| New Zealand XV | 8 | T: Dickinson, Steel; C: Badeley |

7 August 1922, Royal Agricultural Showground, Sydney
| Australia | 8 | T: Raymond, Marrott; C: Stanley |
| New Zealand XV | 6 | T: Brownlie (2) |

25 August 1923, Carisbrook, Dunedin
| New Zealand XV | 19 | T: Belliss, McMeeking, Tilyard; C: Sinclair (2); PG: Sinclair (2) |
| Australia | 9 | T: Stanley, Sheehan, Smith |

1 September 1923, Lancaster Park, Christchurch
| New Zealand XV | 34 | T: Brownlie, Donald, Lucas, Potaka, Richardson, Pringle, Williams; C: Sinclair (5); PG: Sinclair |
| Australia | 6 | T: Erasmus, Marrott |

15 September 1923, Athletic Park, Wellington
| New Zealand XV | 38 | T: Stewart (2), Lucas (2), Morgan, Nicholls, Paewai, Tunnicliff; C: McLean (4); PG: McLean (2) |
| Australia | 11 | T: Nothling, Stanley; C: Stanley; PG: Nothling |

5 July 1924, Royal Agricultural Showground, Sydney
| Australia | 20 | T: Crossman, Stanley, Smith, Thorn, Greatorex; C: Nothling; PG: Stanley |
| New Zealand XV | 16 | T: Cooke, Hart, Masters; C: Nepia, Richardson; PG: Nepia |

12 July 1924, Royal Agricultural Showground, Sydney
| New Zealand XV | 21 | T: Lucas (3), Svenson (2), Munro, Cooke |
| Australia | 5 | T: Greatorex; C: Thorn |

16 July 1924, Royal Agricultural Showground, Sydney
New Zealand XV   38   T: Porter (3), Brown, Cooke, Couples, Lucas, Munro, Svenson, White; C: Nicholls (4)
Australia   8   T: Stanley; C: Nothling; PG: Nothling

13 June 1925, Royal Agricultural Showground, Sydney
New Zealand XV   26   T: Elvy (2), Wise (2), Kirkpatrick, Lomas, Righton; C: Dickson; PG: Dickson
Australia   3   T: Greatorex

20 June 1925, Royal Agricultural Showground, Sydney
New Zealand XV   4   DG: Harris
Australia   0

23 June 1925, Royal Agricultural Showground, Sydney
New Zealand XV   11   T: Law, Walter, Wise; C: Johnson
Australia   3   PG: Ross

19 September 1925, Eden Park, Auckland
New Zealand XV   36   T: Brownlie (2), Cooke (2), Finlayson, McGregor, Mill, Robilliard; C: Nicholls (6)
Australia   10   T: Morrissey, Bowers; C: Lawton (2)

10 July 1926, Royal Agricultural Showground, Sydney
Australia   26   T: Bowers, Crossman, Sheehan, Ford; C: Ross PG: Ross (4)
New Zealand XV   20   T: Brownlie, Lomas, Porter, Stewart; C: Nicholls; PG: Nicholls (2)

17 July 1926, Royal Agricultural Showground, Sydney
New Zealand XV   11   T: Elvy, Svenson; C: Nicholls; PG: Nicholls
Australia   6   T: Woods; PG: Ross

20 July 1926, Royal Agricultural Showground, Sydney
New Zealand XV   14   T: Cooke, Svenson; C: Nicholls; PG: Nicholls (2)
Australia   0

29 July 1926, Royal Agricultural Showground, Sydney
New Zealand XV   28   T: Robilliard (3), Mill (2), Cooke; C: Nicholls (5)
Australia   21   T: Wallace, Towers; PG: Towers (3), Crossman (2)

5 September 1928, Athletic Park, Wellington
New Zealand XV   15   T: Cooke; PG: Bradanovich (4)
Australia   12   T: Rosenblum (2), White; PG: White

8 September 1928, Carisbrook, Dunedin
New Zealand XV   16   T: Knight, Porter, Robinson; C: Bradanovich (2); PG: Bradanovich
Australia   14   T: Loudon, O'Connor, Malcolm, Hemmingway; C: George

15 September 1928, Lancaster Park, Christchurch
Australia   11   T: Smairl, Hemmingway, Loudon; C: Towers
New Zealand XV   8   T: McClymont; C: Oliver; PG: Oliver

Australia vs Pacific Islanders

3 July 2004, Adelaide Oval, Adelaide
Australia   29   T: Mortlock (2), Giteau (2), Cannon; C: Roff, Burke
Pacific Islanders   14   T: Lauaki, Bobo; C: Baikeinuku (2)

Australia vs Romania

3 June 1995, Danie Craven Stadium, Stellenbosch (RWC Pool A)
Australia   42   T: Roff (2), Foley, Burke, Smith, Wilson; C: Burke (2), Eales (4)
Romania   3   DG: Ivanciuc

3 October 1999, Ravenhill, Belfast (RWC, Pool E)
Australia   57   T: Kefu (3), Roff (2), Little, Horan, Paul, Burke; C: Burke (5), Eales
Romania   9   PG: Mitu (3)

18 October 2003, Suncorp Stadium, Brisbane (RWC, Pool A)
Australia   90   T: Rogers (3), Burke (2), Larkham (2), Flatley, Roff, Mortlock, Giteau, Tuqiri, Smith; C: Flatley (11);
                            PG: Flatley
Romania   8   T: Toderasc; PG: Tofan

Australia vs Samoa

Australia vs Samoa

Played:	4
Won:	4
Lost:	0
Drawn:	0
For:	181
Against:	26

Average score:
45.25–6.5

Australia percentages:

Won:	100%
Lost:	0%
Drawn:	0%

9 October 1991, Pontypool Park, Pontypool (RWC, Pool 3)
Australia   9   PG: Lynagh (3)
Western Samoa   3   PG: Vaea

6 August 1994, Sydney Football Stadium, Sydney
Australia   73   T: Little (2), Smith (2), Campese, Gavin, Pini, Junee, Gregan, Howard,
                          Ofahengaue; C: Knox (6); PG: Knox (2)
Western Samoa   3   PG: Kellett

26 September 1998, Ballymore, Brisbane
Australia   25   T: Crowley, Ofahengaue, Herbert; C: Eales (2); PG: Eales (2)
Samoa   13   T: Clarke, Paramore; PG: Va'a

11 June 2005, Telstra Stadium, Sydney
Australia   74   T: Sharpe (2), Mortlock (2), Sailor (2), Chisholm, Elsom, Rathbone, Latham,
                          Turinui, Rogers; C: Giteau (5), Mortlock (2)
Samoa   7   T: Fanolua; C: Talapusi

Australia vs Scotland (Hopetoun Cup)

Australia vs Scotland

Played:	25
Won:	18
Lost:	7
Drawn:	0
For:	636
Against:	297

Average score:
25.44–11.88

Australia percentages:

Won:	72%
Lost:	28%
Drawn:	0%

Australia were to play Scotland on their first tour to the Britain in 1908, but the SRFU found out that the Australians were each receiving three shillings a day expenses. So outraged were the Scots, claiming the tourists were acting as professionals, that they refused to play them. Relations had improved by the time the Waratahs toured in 1927 and the first test took place on 17 December 1927 in Edinburgh, won by the Scots. Today, the two nations play for the Hopetoun Cup, a crystal cup designed by Royal Doulton, a perpetual trophy first contested in 1998. In the spirit of the two unions, it was named after the Seventh Earl of Hopetoun, a Scot by the name of John Adrian Louis Hope who was Governor General of Australia in 1901. Australia have dominated each series, with Scotland yet to win one.

17 December 1927, Murrayfield, Edinburgh
Scotland   10   T: Graham, Welsh; C: Drysdale (2)
Australia   8   T: E Ford, J Ford; C: Lawton

22 November 1947, Murrayfield, Edinburgh
Australia   16   T: Kearney, Tonkin, Howell, Cooke; C: Piper (2)
Scotland   7   PG: McDonald; DG: Hepburn

15 February 1958, Murrayfield, Edinburgh
Scotland   12   T: Weatherstone, Stevenson; PG: A Smith (2)
Australia   8   T: Thornett, Donald; C: Lenehan

17 December 1966, Murrayfield, Edinburgh
Scotland   11   T: Chisholm, Boyle; C: Wilson; PG: Wilson
Australia   5   T: Brass; C: Lenehan

2 November 1968, Murrayfield, Edinburgh
Scotland   9   T: Hinshelwood; PG: Blaikie (2)
Australia   3   PG: Smith

6 June 1970, Sydney Cricket Ground, Sydney
Australia   23   T: Batterham (2), Cole (2), Hipwell, Rosenblum; C: McGill; PG: McGill
Scotland   3   PG: Lauder

6 December 1975, Murrayfield, Edinburgh
Scotland   10   T: Renwick, Dick; C: Morgan
Australia   3   PG: McLean

19 December 1981, Murrayfield, Edinburgh
Scotland   24   T: Renwick; C: Irvine; PG: Irvine (5;) DG: Rutherford
Australia   15   T: Poidevin, Moon, Slack; PG: P McLean

AUSTRALIA

4 July 1982, Ballymore, Brisbane
Scotland 12 T: Robertson; C: Irvine; PG: Irvine; DG: Rutherford
Australia 7 T: Hawker; PG: Hawker

10 July 1982, Sydney Cricket Ground, Sydney
Australia 33 T: Gould (2), O'Connor; C: P McLean (3); PG: P McLean (5)
Scotland 9 PG: Irvine (3)

8 December 1984, Murrayfield, Edinburgh
Australia 37 T: Campese (2), M Ella, Farr-Jones; C: Lynagh (3); PG: Lynagh (5)
Scotland 12 PG: Dods (4)

19 November 1988, Murrayfield, Edinburgh
Australia 32 T: Lawton (2), Campese (2), Gourley; C: Lynagh (3); PG: Lynagh (2)
Scotland 13 T: G Hastings, Robertson; C: G Hastings; PG: G Hastings

13 June 1992, Sydney Football Stadium, Sydney
Australia 27 T: Campese (2), Carozza, Lynagh; C: Lynagh; PG: Lynagh (3)
Scotland 12 T: Wainwright; C: G Hastings; PG: G Hastings (2)

21 June 1992, Ballymore, Brisbane
Australia 37 T: Carozza (2), Horan (2), Eales; C: Lynagh; PG: Lynagh (5)
Scotland 13 T: Lineen, Sole; C: Chalmers; PG: Chalmers

9 November 1996, Murrayfield, Edinburgh
Australia 29 T: Waugh, Herbert; C: Burke (2); PG: Burke (5)
Scotland 19 T: Logan, Stanger; PG: Shepherd (3)

22 November 1997, Murrayfield, Edinburgh
Australia 37 T: Larkham (2), Gregan, Roff, Ofahengaue; C: Eales (3); PG: Eales (2)
Scotland 8 T: Murray; PG: Hodge

13 June 1998, Sydney Football Stadium, Sydney
Australia 45 T: Tune (2), Wilson, Burke, Horan; C: Burke (4); PG: Burke (4)
Scotland 3 PG: Lee

20 June 1998, Ballymore, Brisbane
Australia 33 T: Tune, Larkham, Grey, Ofahengaue; C: Burke (2); PG: Burke (3)
Scotland 11 T: Hodge; PG: Lee (2)

11 November 2000, Murrayfield, Edinburgh
Australia 30 T: Burke, Latham, Roff; C: Burke (3); PG: Burke (3)
Scotland 9 PG: Townsend (3)

8 November 2003, Suncorp Stadium, Brisbane (RWC, Q/F)
Australia 33 T: Mortlock, Gregan, Lyons; C: Flatley (3); PG: Flatley (4)
Scotland 16 T: Russell; C: Paterson; PG: Paterson (2); DG: Paterson

13 June 2004, Telstra Dome, Melbourne
Australia 35 T: Tuqiri (2), Giteau, Sailor; C: Roff (2), Burke; PG: Roff (3)
Scotland 15 PG: Parks (5)

19 June 2004, Telstra Stadium, Sydney
Australia 34 T: Tuqiri (2), Sailor, Turunui, Roff; C: Roff (3); PG: Roff
Scotland 13 T: Cusiter; C: Parks; PG: Parks (2)

6 November 2004, Murrayfield, Edinburgh
Australia 31 T: Rathbone (2), Tuqiri, Mortlock; C: Giteau (4); PG: Giteau
Scotland 14 T: Lamont, Southwell; C: Paterson (2)

20 November 2004, Hampden Park, Glasgow
Australia 31 T: Tuqiri, Waugh, Giteau, Gregan; C: Giteau (3), Flatley; PG: Giteau
Scotland 17 T: Hogg; PG: Paterson (4)

25 November 2006, Murrayfield, Edinburgh
Australia 44 T: Gerrard (2), Larkham, Moore, Latham; C: Mortlock (5); PG: Mortlock (3)
Scotland 15 T: Webster, Lamont C: Paterson PG: Paterson

No.	Date	Venue	Result			Series	Holder
			Hopetoun Cup Current holder: Australia		Number of titles: Australia 5, Scotland 0		
1	13/06/1998	Sydney Football Stadium, Sydney	Australia	45–3	Scotland	2–0	Australia
2	20/06/1998	Ballymore, Brisbane	Australia	33–11	Scotland		
3	11/11/2000	Murrayfield, Edinburgh	Scotland	9–30	Australia	0–1	Australia
4	13/06/2004	Telstra Dome, Melbourne	Australia	35–15	Scotland	2–0	Australia
5	19/06/2004	Telstra Stadium, Sydney	Australia	34–13	Scotland		
6	06/11/2004	Murrayfield, Edinburgh	Scotland	14–31	Australia	0–2	Australia
7	20/11/2004	Hampden Park, Glasgow	Scotland	17–31	Australia		
8	25/11/2006	Murrayfield, Edinburgh	Scotland	15–44	Australia	0–1	Australia

Australia vs South Africa

Played: 65
Won: 26
Lost: 38
Drawn: 1
For: 1,074
Against: 1,184

Average score:
16.52–18.22

Australia percentages:
Won: 40%
Lost: 58.47%
Drawn: 1.53%

Australia vs South Africa (Nelson Mandela Challenge Plate)

South Africa and Australia first met officially in 1933 in a five-test series, although the Springboks had toured Australia in 1921, winning three matches against the Waratahs but not recognised by South Africa as internationals. The five-test series of 1933 is to date the only such series of its kind in rugby history; South Africa won 3–2. The first encounter on Australian soil was in 1937 when, en route to New Zealand, South Africa won a two-test series 2–0. Fixtures between the two nations were frequent after World War II, with a series being played about every four years. In 1953, Australia toured South Africa and became the first side in 15 years to beat the South Africans when they won 18–14 at Newlands. Such was the occasion that the South African crowd cheered Australian captain John Solomon off the field with a standing ovation. In 1969, South Africa won 4–0 and in 1971 toured Australia to become South Africa's first 'Invincibles', as they left Australia with 13 wins and a clean sheet. The 1971 tour was overshadowed by off-the-field troubles and anti-apartheid demonstrations, which ensured that the two sides were not to meet again for the next 21 years during South Africa's years of isolation. South Africa won the 1971 tests 3–0. However, the series was not remembered for its rugby but for the angry politcal demonstrations which saw Queensland declare a state of emergency and arrange for the test to be switched from Ballymore to the securer Exhibition Ground. Demonstrators attempted to saw down the goalposts in Sydney, with no fewer than 700 arrests during the tour. Hotels and airlines cancelled Springbok reservations as the tourists became increasingly secretive in their movements. Twenty-one years later, the two sides met again under happier circumstances in Cape Town in a one-off test. A year later world champions Australia won the 1993 series. Since 1996, the two teams have met on an annual basis following the advent of the Tri-Nations tournament. Since 2000,they have competed for the Nelson Mandela Challenge Plate: named after South Africa's first post-apartheid president, it is a leather-clad silver plate with a 24-carat gold rim and a central gold disc showing a Wallaby and a Springbok. The idea was that the plate would be contested bi-annually in a one-off international outside the Tri-Nations, but this evolved to an annual challenge within the Tri-Nations. The first Nelson Mandela Challenge Plate match was on 8 July 2000 in Melbourne. Nelson Mandela addressed the crowd, and a massive television audience via satellite, prior to kick-off. Australia won. The plate was next contested during the 2002 Tri-Nations and was won 33–31 by South Africa at the death in an Ellis Park thriller. The 2004 challenge was held off until 2005 because of British and Irish Lions scheduling issues. For the first time, the 2005 challenge was played over a two-test series in matches which did not double up as Tri-Nations tests. The series was drawn 1–1 and the plate retained by South Africa. With the plate challenge officially incorporated into the Tri-Nations series the following year, Australia reclaimed it, winning the 2006 three-test series 2–1. In 2007 Australia retained the plate after sharing the series 1–1, but the Wallabies refused to acknowledge the plate as anything meaningful as South Africa had fobbed them off with essentially a Springbok 'B' side (which only just lost 17–25). A sour taste lingered, with both sides guilty of unbecoming behaviour: Australia for bad manners and South Africa for insulting the Wallabies with a second-string side, keeping back its star players for the forthcoming RWC. Despite failing to regain the plate in 2008, South Africa inflicted some revenge by humiliating Australia with a record 53-8 defeat in Johannesburg.

AUSTRALIA

8 July 1933, Newlands, Cape Town
South Africa	17	T: Bergh (2), Craven, Osler; C: Brand; PG: Brand
Australia	3	PG: Billman

22 July 1933, Kingsmead, Durban
Australia	21	T: Loudon, Cerutti, Bennett, Sturtridge; C: Billman (3); PG: Billman
South Africa	6	T: Waring; PG: Brand

12 August 1933, Ellis Park, Johannesburg
South Africa	12	T: M Louw, Turner; C: Brand; DG: Osler
Australia	3	T: Cowper

26 August 1933, Crusader Ground, Port Elizabeth
South Africa	11	T: White, S Louw; C: Osler; PG: Brand
Australia	0	

2 September 1933, Springbok Park, Bloemfontein
Australia	15	T: Kelleher, Steggle, Bridle; C: Ross; DG: Cowper
South Africa	4	DG: Brand

26 June 1937, Sydney Cricket Ground, Sydney
South Africa	9	T: Bastard, Bergh; PG: Brand
Australia	5	T: Towers; C: Towers

17 July 1937, Sydney Cricket Ground, Sydney
South Africa	26	T: van Reenen (2), Bergh, Babrow, Williams, Turner; C: Brand (4)
Australia	17	T: Hodgson, Kelaher, O'Brein; C: Rankin; PG: Rankin (2)

22 August 1953, Ellis Park, Johannesburg
South Africa	25	T: Lategan, Marais, Oelofse, du Rand, Muller; C: Marais, Buchler; PG: Marais, Buchler
Australia	3	PG: Sweeney

5 September 1953, Newlands, Cape Town
Australia	18	T: Jones, Stapleton, Cross, Johnson; C: Colbert (2), Stapleton
South Africa	14	T: Ochse, van Wyk, du Rand, Koch; C: Marais

19 September 1953, Kingsmead, Durban
South Africa	18	T: R Bekker, Rossouw, van Wyk, H Bekker; C: Rens (3)
Australia	8	T: Cross; C: Colbert; PG: Solomon

26 September 1953, Crusader Ground, Port Elizabeth
South Africa	22	T: Koch, Oelofse; C: Rens (2); PG: Rens (2); DG: Rens, Buchler
Australia	9	T: Stapleton PG: Barker (2)

26 May 1956, Sydney Cricket Ground, Sydney
South Africa	9	T: Nel, Retief; PG: Viviers
Australia	0	

2 June 1956, Exhibition Ground, Brisbane
South Africa	9	T: Dryburgh, Retief; DG: van Vollenhoven
Australia	0	

5 August 1961, Ellis Park, Johannesburg
South Africa	28	T: van Zyl (3), Gainsford, Oxlee, Engelbrecht, Pelser, Hopwood; C: Claassen (2)
Australia	3	PG: Dowse

12 August 1961, Boet Erasmus Stadium, Port Elizabeth
South Africa	23	T: van Zyl, Roux, Oxlee; C: Oxlee; PG: Oxlee (3); DG: Wilson
Australia	11	T: Cleary; C: Dowse; PG: Dowse (2)

13 July 1963, Loftus Versfeld, Pretoria
South Africa	14	T: Bedford, Cilliers C: Oxlee; PG: Oxlee (2)
Australia	3	T: McMullen

10 August 1963, Newlands, Cape Town
Australia	9	T: Boyce; PG: Casey, Hawthorne
South Africa	5	T: penalty try; C: Oxlee

24 August 1963, Ellis Park, Johannesburg
Australia   11   T: Williams; C: Casey; PG: Casey (2)
South Africa   9   PG: Smith (3)

7 September 1963, Boet Erasmus Stadium, Port Elizabeth
South Africa   22   T: Gainsford, Naudé, Malan; C: Oxlee (2); PG: Oxlee (2), Naudé
Australia   6   PG: Casey; DG: Casey

19 June 1965, Sydney Cricket Ground, Sydney
Australia   18   T: Lenehan, S Boyce; PG: Ellwood (4)
South Africa   11   T: Engelbrecht (2); C: Naudé; PG: Naudé

26 June 1965, Lang Park, Brisbane
Australia   12   PG: Ellwood (2), Lenehan (2)
South Africa   8   T: Gainsford, Truter; C: Naudé

2 August 1969, Ellis Park, Johanneburg
South Africa   30   T: Nomis (2), Roux, Ellis, Greyling; C: Visagie (3); PG: Visagie (3)
Australia   11   T: Forman; C: Rosenblum; PG: Rosenblum (2)

16 August 1969, Kings Park, Durban
South Africa   16   T: Engelbrecht (2), Visagie; C: Visagie (2); PG: Visagie
Australia   9   PG: Ballesty (3)

6 September 1969, Newlands, Cape Town
South Africa   11   T: Ellis, Visagie; C: Visagie; PG: Visagie
Australia   3   PG: Ballesty

20 September 1969, Free State Stadium, Bloemfontein
South Africa   19   T: Olivier (2), Roux; C: Visagie (2); PG: Visagie (2)
Australia   8   T: Knight; C: Ballesty; PG: Ballesty

17 July 1971, Sydney Cricket Ground, Sydney
South Africa   19   T: JF Viljoen, JT Viljoen, Ellis; C: McCallum (2); PG: McCallum; DG: Visagie
Australia   11   T: R McLean; C: McGill; PG: McGill (2)

31 July 1971, Exhibition Ground, Brisbane
South Africa   14   T: Visagie (2), JT Viljoen; C: McCallum; PG: McCallum
Australia   6   PG: McGill (2)

7 August 1971, Sydney Cricket Ground, Sydney
South Africa   18   T: Cronje, Visagie, Ellis; C: Visagie (3); PG: Visagie
Australia   6   T: Cole; PG: J McLean

22 August 1992, Newlands, Cape Town
Australia   26   T: Carroza (2), Campese; C: Lynagh; PG: Lynagh (3)
South Africa   3   PG: Botha

31 July 1993, Sydney Football Stadium, Sydney
South Africa   19   T: Small (2), Muller; C: van Rensburg (2)
Australia   12   PG: Roebuck (4)

14 August 1993, Ballymore, Brisbane
Australia   28   T: Little (2), Horan; C: Roebuck (2); PG: Roebuck (3)
South Africa   20   T: Stransky, Olivier; C: Stransky (2); PG: Stransky (2)

21 August 1993, Sydney Football Stadium, Sydney
Australia   19   T: Horan; C: Roebuck; PG: Roebuck (4)
South Africa   12   T: Small, Pienaar; C: Stransky

25 May 1995, Newlands, Cape Town (RWC, Pool A)
South Africa   27   T: Hendriks, Stransky; C: Stransky; PG: Stransky (4); DG: Stransky
Australia   18   T: Lynagh, Kearns; C: Lynagh; PG: Lynagh (2)

13 July 1996, Sydney Football Stadium, Sydney
Australia   21   T: Roff, Horan; C: Burke; PG: Burke (3)
South Africa   16   T: Hendriks; C: Honiball; PG: Joubert, Honiball (2)

AUSTRALIA

3 August 1996, Free State Stadium, Bloemfontein
South Africa	25	T: Stransky; C: Stransky; PG: Stransky (6)
Australia	19	T: Tune; C: Eales; PG: Burke, Eales (3)

2 August 1997, Suncorp Stadium, Brisbane
Australia	32	T: Manu, Tune (2), Larkham; C: Knox (3); PG: Knox (2)
South Africa	20	T: du Randt, Andrews, de Beer; C: de Beer; PG: de Beer

23 August 1997, Loftus Versfeld, Pretoria
South Africa	61	T: Dalton, Erasmus, Andrews, Rossouw, de Beer, Montgomery (2), Brosnihan; C: de Beer (6); PG: de Beer (3)
Australia	22	T: Knox, Roff, Little; C: Knox (2); PG: Knox

18 July 1998, Subiaco Oval, Perth
South Africa	14	T: van der Westhuizen; PG: Montgomery (3)
Australia	13	T: Tune, Gregan; PG: Burke

22 August 1998, Ellis Park, Johannesburg
South Africa	29	T: Garvey, Skinstad; C: Montgomery (2); PG: Montgomery (5)
Australia	15	PG: Burke (5)

17 July 1999, Suncorp Stadium, Brisbane
Australia	32	T: Roff (2), Horan, Burke; C: Burke (3); PG: Burke (2)
South Africa	6	PG: van Straaten (2)

14 August 1999, Norwich Park Newlands, Cape Town
South Africa	10	T: Fleck; C: de Beer; PG: de Beer
Australia	9	PG: Burke (3)

30 October 1999, Twickenham, London (RWC, S/F)
Australia	27	PG: Burke (8); DG: Larkham
South Africa	21	PG: de Beer (6); DG: de Beer

8 July 2000, Colonial Stadium, Melbourne
Australia	44	T: Mortlock (2), Little, Kefu, Larkham; C: Mortlock (2); PG: Mortlock (5)
South Africa	23	T: Paulse (2), Swanepoel; C: Koen; PG: Koen (2)

29 July 2000, Stadium Australia, Sydney
Australia	26	T: Mortlock, Paul; C: Mortlock (2); PG: Mortlock (4)
South Africa	6	PG: van Straaten (2)

26 August 2000, ABSA Stadium, Durban
Australia	19	T: Latham; C: Mortlock; PG: Mortlock (4)
South Africa	18	PG: van Straaten (6)

28 July 2001, Minolta Loftus, Pretoria
South Africa	20	T: Skinstad; PG: van Straaten (5)
Australia	15	PG: Burke (4), Edmonds

18 August 2001, Subiaco Oval, Perth
Australia	14	T: Grey; PG: Burke (3)
South Africa	14	T: Andrews; PG: van Straaten (3)

27 July 2002, GABBA, Brisbane
Australia	38	T: Latham (2), Mortlock, Tune; C: Burke (3); PG: Burke (3), Mortlock
South Africa	27	T: Joubert (2), Skinstad, Russell; C: Pretorius (2); PG: Pretorius

17 August 2002, Ellis Park, Johannesburg
South Africa	33	T: Paulse (2), van Niekerk, Russell, Greeff; C: Greeff (4)
Australia	31	T: Kefu, Cannon, Rogers; C: Burke (2); PG: Burke (3); DG: Gregan

12 July 2003, Newlands, Cape Town
South Africa	26	T: Matfield, Russell; C: Koen (2); PG: Koen (4)
Australia	22	T: Waugh, Sailor, Roff; C: Burke (2); DG: Burke

2 August 2003, Suncorp Stadium, Brisbane
Australia	29	T: Waugh, Rogers; C: Flatley (2); PG: Flatley (5)
South Africa	9	PG: Koen (3)

31 July 2004, Subiaco Oval, Perth
Australia   30   T: Larkham, Rathbone, Tuqiri, Latham; C: Giteau, Burke; PG: Giteau (2)
South Africa   26   T: van der Westhuyzen, de Villiers, du Toit; C: Montgomery; PG: Montgomery (3)

21 August 2004, ABSA Stadium, Durban
South Africa   23   T: Matfield, van Nierkerk; C: Montgomery (2); PG: Montgomery (3)
Australia   19   T: Smith, Mortlock, Tuqiri; C: Giteau (2)

9 July 2005, Telstra Stadium, Sydney
Australia   30   T: Giteau (2), Larkham, Rogers, Mitchell C: Giteau; PG: Giteau
South Africa   12   PG: Montgomery (4)

23 July 2005, Ellis Park, Johannesburg
South Africa   33   T: de Villiers, Fourie, Habana; C: Montgomery (3); PG: Montgomery (4)
Australia   20   T: Paul, Lyons, Larkham; C: Mortlock; PG: Giteau

30 July 2005, Securicor Loftus, Pretoria
South Africa   22   T: Paulse; C: Montgomery; PG: Montgomery (3); DG: Montgomery, Pretorius
Australia   16   T: Smith; C: Giteau; PG: Giteau (3)

20 August 2005, Subiaco Oval, Perth
South Africa   22   T: Habana (2); PG: Montgomery (3); DG: Montgomery
Australia   19   T: Rathbone; C: Rogers; PG: Rogers (3), Giteau

15 July 2006, Suncorp Stadium, Brisbane
Australia   49   T: Giteau (2), Holmes, Paul, Latham, Chisholm; C: Mortlock (5); PG: Mortlock (2); DG: Larkham
South Africa   0

5 August 2006, Telstra Stadium, Sydney
Australia   20   T: Gerrard, Rogers; C: Mortlock (2); PG: Mortlock (2)
South Africa   18   T: Fourie, Montgomery; C: James; PG: James (2)

9 September 2006, Ellis Park, Johannesburg
South Africa   24   T: du Preez, Paulse; C: Pretorius; PG: Pretorius (3); DG: Pretorius
Australia   16   T: Larkham; C: Mortlock; PG: Mortlock (3)

16 June 2007, Newlands, Cape Town
South Africa   22   T: Fourie; C: Montgomery; PG: Montgomery (3); DG: Steyn (2)
Australia   19   T: Giteau; C: Mortlock; PG: Mortlock (4)

7 July 2007, Telstra Stadium, Sydney
Australia   25   T: Hoiles, Gerrard, Giteau; C: Mortlock (2); PG: Mortlock (2)
South Africa   17   T: van Heerden, Paulse; C: Hougaard (2); PG: Hougaard

19 July 2008, Subiaco Oval, Perth
Australia   16   T: Mortlock, Tuqiri; PG: Giteau; DG: Barnes
South Africa   9   PG: Steyn (2), James

23 August 2008, The ABSA Stadium, Durban
Australia   27   T: Robinson, Mortlock, Tuqiri; C: Giteau (3); PG: Giteau (2)
South Africa   15   T: Jacobs (2); C: Montgomery; PG: James

30 August 2008, Coca-Cola Park, Johannesburg
South Africa   53   T: Nokwe (4), Bekker, Ndungane, Pienaar, Jacobs; C: James (3), Montgomery (2); PG: James
Australia   8   T: Mitchell; PG: Giteau

AUSTRALIA

AUSTRALIA

Nelson Mandela Challenge Plate		Current holder: Australia			Number of titles: Australia 4, South Africa 2		
No.	Date	Venue	Result			Series	Holder
1	08/07/2000	Colonial Stadium, Melbourne	Australia	44–23	South Africa	1–0	Australia
2	17/08/2002	Ellis Park, Johannesburg	South Africa	33–31	Australia	1–0	South Africa
3	09/07/2005	Telstra Stadium, Sydney	Australia	30–12	South Africa	1–1	South Africa
4	23/07/2005	Ellis Park, Johannesburg	South Africa	33–20	Australia		
5	15/07/2006	Suncorp Stadium, Brisbane	Australia	49–0	South Africa	2–1	Australia
6	05/08/2006	Telstra Stadium, Sydney	Australia	20–18	South Africa		
7	09/09/2006	Ellis Park, Johannesburg	South Africa	24–16	Australia		
8	16/06/2007	Newlands, Cape Town	South Africa	22–19	Australia	1–1	Australia
9	07/07/2007	Telstra Stadium, Sydney	South Africa	17–25	Australia		
10	19/07/2008	Subiaco Oval, Perth	Australia	16–9	South Africa	1–2	Australia
11	23/08/2008	The ABSA Stadium, Durban	South Africa	15–27	Australia		
12	30/08/2008	Coca-Cola Park, Johannesburg	South Africa	53–8	Australia		

Australia vs South Africa XV

The three matches listed below are not recognised as capped internationals by South Africa on the grounds that they were not fully representative of an Australian international rugby side. The ARU has since recognised these matches against the touring 1921 South Africans as full Australian internationals on the basis that the New South Wales union and team at the time were composed of players from New South Wales, Queensland and Victoria.

25 June 1921, Royal Agricultural Showground, Sydney
South African XV   25   T: van Heerden (5), Meyer (2); C: P Morkel (2)
Australia   10   T: Nothling, Carr; C: Mingay (2)

27 June 1921, Royal Agricultural Showground, Sydney
South African XV   16   T: Meyer (2), H Morkel (2); C: de Villiers (2)
Australia   11   T: Carr, Holdsworth, Davis; C: Nothling

2 July 1921, University Ground, Sydney
South African XV   28   T: Ellis, Clarkson, Meyer, Kruger, J Morkel, Mostert; C: P Morkel (3); DG: Strauss
Australia   9   T: Sheehan, McKay PG: Mingay

Australia vs South Korea

17 May 1987, Ballymore, Brisbane
Australia   65   T: Burke (3), Grigg (2), Slack (2), Cook, Gould, B Smith, Miller, James, Farr-Jones; C: Smith (5); PG: Smith
South Korea   18   T: Jung, Beak; C: Sin (2); PG: Sin (2)

Australia vs Spain

1 November 2001, Campo Universitaria, Madrid
Australia   92   T: Latham (3), Roff (2), Grey, Foley, Smith, Kefu, Stiles, Bond, Cockbain, Herbert; C: Burke (10), Flatley (2); PG: Burke
Spain   10   T: Villau-Cabeza C: Martinez PG: Alonso-Lasheras

Australia vs Tonga

Australia vs Tonga	
Played:	4
Won:	3
Lost:	1
Drawn:	0
For:	167
Against:	42

Average score:
41.75–10.5

Australia percentages:

Won:	75%
Lost:	25%
Drawn:	0%

23 June 1973, Sydney Cricket Ground, Sydney

Australia	30	T: Stephens (2), Cole, Richardson, Hipwell, penalty try; C: McGill (2), Richardson
Tonga	12	T: Tupi, Latu; C: Ma'ake (2)

30 June 1973, Ballymore, Brisbane

Tonga	16	T: Vave, Latu, Mafi, Kavapulu
Australia	11	T: Cole, Tindall; PG: McGill

4 July 1993, Ballymore, Brisbane

Australia	52	T: Campese (2), Corozza, Little, Gavin, Morgan, Johnstone; C: Roebuck (3), Lynagh; PG: Roebuck (3)
Tonga	14	T: Fenukitau, penalty try; C: Vave (2)

21 September, 1998 Bruce Stadium, Canberra

Australia	74	T: Little (4), Edmonds (2), Roff, Horan, Whitaker, Finnegan, Paul, Robinson; C: Edmonds (5), Eales (2)
Tonga	0	

Australia vs United States of America

Australia vs USA	
Played:	6
Won:	6
Lost:	0
Drawn:	0
For:	254
Against:	63

Average score:
42.33–10.5

Australia percentages:

Won:	100%
Lost:	0%
Drawn:	0%

16 November 1912, St Ignatius Ground, Berkeley

Australia	12	T: Meibusch (2), Carroll; PG: Prentice
USA	8	T: Harrigan; C: Erb; PG: Erb

31 January 1976, Glover Field, Anaheim

Australia	24	T: Ryan, Price, Pearse; C: Hindmarsh (3); PG: Hindmarsh (2)
USA	12	PG: Oxman (4)

9 July 1983, Sydney Cricket Ground, Sydney

Australia	49	T: Campese (4), Slack (2), Ross, Roche, Hanley ;C: Gould (4), Campese; DG: M Ella
USA	3	PG: Meyerseick

31 May 1987, Ballymore, Brisbane (RWC, Pool 1)

Australia	47	T: Leeds (2), penalty try, Smith, Slack, Papworth, Campese, Codey; C: Lynagh (6); PG: Lynagh
USA	12	T: Nelson; C: Nelson; PG: Nelson; DG: Horton

8 July 1990, Ballymore, Brisbane

Australia	67	T: Lynagh (2), Williams (2), Daly, McKenzie, Little, Kearns, Gavin, Farr-Jones, Slattery, Campese; C: Lynagh (8); DG: Campese
USA	9	T: Leversee; C: O'Brien; PG: O'Brien

14 October 1999, Thomond Park, Limerick (RWC, Pool E)

Australia	55	T: Stanifort (2), Larkham, Foley, Burke, Strauss, Latham, Whitaker; C: Burke (5), Roff; PG: Burke
USA	19	T: Grobler; C: Dalzell; PG: Dalzell (3); DG: Niu

Australia vs Wales (James Bevan Trophy)

The trophy was commissioned and donated by International Business Wales, the economic arm of the Welsh Assembly Government, to celebrate 100 years of rugby between the two nations. It is named after the Melbourne-born and Welsh-raised rugby player who, in 1881, by a twist of fate became the first captain of the Welsh rugby team. Bevan's father was born in Scotland and immigrated to Australia in 1848. On the voyage out he met his future wife, with whom he had three children. In 1866, tragedy struck when Mr and Mrs Bevan were among 251 who drowned when the Melbourne-bound SS *London* sank in heavy seas. With no relatives in Australia, the young James was sent with his one surviving sister to live with their closest relatives in Wales, thus making him eligible to play for his adopted country. Wales began as holders of the trophy based on the results of recent matches. It was first contested during the two-test series of 2007, won 2–0 by Australia. It is played for each time the two sides meet, except in RWCs. In the event of a drawn test or series, the current holder retains the trophy. Wales are the current holders after winning the thrilling 2008 autumn international by 21-18 in Cardiff.

AUSTRALIA

Australia vs Wales

Played:	28
Won:	17
Lost:	10
Drawn:	1
For:	645
Against:	399

Average score:
23.04–14.25

Australia percentages:

Won:	60.71%
Lost:	35.72%
Drawn:	3.57%

12 December 1908, Cardiff Arms Park, Cardiff
Wales 9 T: Travers, Hopkins; PG: Winfield
Australia 6 T: Richards, Russell

26 November 1927, Cardiff Arms Park, Cardiff
Australia 18 T: Wallace (2), King, Sheehan; C: Lawton (3)
Wales 8 T: Finch, Lewis; C: Rees

20 December 1947, Cardiff Arms Park, Cardiff
Wales 6 PG: Tamplin (2)
Australia 0

4 January 1958, Cardiff Arms Park, Cardiff
Wales 9 T: Collins; PG: T Davies; DG: C James
Australia 3 T: Miller

3 December 1966, Cardiff Arms Park, Cardiff
Australia 14 T: Lenehan, Cardy; C: Lenehan; PG: Lenehan; DG: Hawthorne
Wales 11 T: Dawes, Morgan; C: Price; PG: Price

21 June 1969, Sydney Cricket Ground, Sydney
Wales 19 T: Davies, Taylor, Morris; C: Jarrett (2); PG: Jarrett (2)
Australia 16 T: McGill, Smith; C: McGill (2); PG: McGill (2)

10 November 1973, National Stadium, Cardiff
Wales 24 T: T Davies, Morris, Windsor; PG: Bennett (4)
Australia 0

20 December 1975, National Stadium, Cardiff
Wales 28 T: JJ Williams (3), Edwards; C: Fenwick (2), Martin; PG: Fenwick (2)
Australia 3 PG: P McLean

11 June 1978, Ballymore, Brisbane
Australia 18 T: Loane; C: P McLean; PG: P McLean (2); DG: P McLean, Monaghan
Wales 8 T: T Davies, Holmes

17 June 1978, Sydney Cricket Ground, Sydney
Australia 19 T: Crowe; DG: P McLean; PG: P McLean (4)
Wales 17 T: T Davies, B Williams; PG: W Davies (2); DG: W Davies

5 December 1981, National Stadium, Cardiff
Wales 18 T: R Moriarty; C: G Evans; PG: G Evans (3); DG: W Davies
Australia 13 T: Slack, M Cox; C: P McLean; PG: P McLean

24 November 1984, National Stadium, Cardiff
Australia 28 T: Lawton, Tuynman, M Ella, Lynagh; C: Gould (3); PG: Gould (2)
Wales 9 T: Bishop; C: Wyatt; PG: Wyatt

18 June 1987, International Stadium, Rotorua (RWC, 3/4 play-off)
Wales 22 T: Roberts, P Moriarty, Hadley; C: Thorburn (2); PG: Thorburn (2)
Australia 21 T: Burke, Grigg; C: Lynagh (2); PG: Lynagh (2); DG: Lynagh

22 July 1991, Ballymore, Brisbane
Australia 63 T: Lynagh (2), Kearns (2), Gavin (2), Ofahengaue, Horan, Roebuck, Campese, Egerton, Little; C: Lynagh (6); PG: Lynagh
Wales 6 PG: Thorburn; DG: A Davies

12 October 1991, National Stadium, Cardiff (RWC, Pool 3)
Australia 38 T: Roebuck (2), Slattery, Campese, Horan, Lynagh; C: Lynagh (4); PG: Lynagh (2)
Wales 3 PG: Ring

21 November 1992, National Stadium, Cardiff
Australia 23 T: Wilson, McCall, Campese; C: Roebuck; PG: Roebuck (2)
Wales 6 PG: C Stephens (2)

9 June 1996, Ballymore, Brisbane
Australia   56   T: Roff, Murdoch, Howard, Caputo, Morgan, Manu, Wilson; C: Burke (6); PG: Burke (3)
Wales   25   T: Proctor, Taylor, Llewellyn; C: Jenkins (2); PG: Jenkins (2)

22 June 1996, Sydney Football Stadium, Sydney
Australia   42   T: Finegan, Burke, Roff, Foley, Morgan, Horan; C: Burke (2), Eales; PG: Burke (2)
Wales   3   PG: Jenkins

1 December 1996, National Stadium, Cardiff
Australia   28   T: Burke, Brial, penalty try; C: Burke (2); PG: Burke (3)
Wales   19   T: J Thomas; C: Davies; PG: Davies (4)

23 October 1999, Millennium Stadium, Cardiff (RWC, Q/F)
Australia   24   T: Gregan (2), Tune; C: Burke (3); PG: Burke
Wales   9   PG: Jenkins (3)

25 November 2001, Millennium Stadium, Cardiff
Australia   21   PG: Burke (7)
Wales   13   T: Gavin Thomas; C: Harris; PG: Harris (2)

14 June 2003, Stadium Australia, Sydney
Australia   30   T: Sailor (2), Latham, Paul, Grey ;C: Roff; PG: Flatley
Wales   10   T: Robinson; C: S Jones; PG: S Jones

26 November 2005, Millennium Stadium, Cardiff
Wales   24   T: S Williams, penalty try; C: S Jones; PG: S Jones (4)
Australia   22   T: Tuqiri, Sharpe, Latham; C: Rogers (2); PG: Rogers

4 November 2006, Millennium Stadium, Cardiff
Wales   29   T: S Williams, M Williams; C: Hook (2); PG: Hook (3), S Jones, Henson
Australia   29   T: Shepherd (2), Giteau, Latham; C: Giteau (3); PG: Giteau

26 May 2007, Telstra Stadium, Sydney
Australia   29   T: Palu, Sharpe, Giteau, Hoiles; C: Mortlock (3); PG: Mortlock
Wales   23   T: Robinson, G Thomas; C: Hook (2); PG: Hook (2); DG: Hook

2 June 2007, Suncorp Stadium, Brisbane
Australia   31   T: Ioane, Mitchell, Huxley; C: Mortlock (2); PG: Mortlock (4)
Wales   0

15 September 2007, Millennium Stadium, Cardiff (RWC, Pool B)
Australia   32   T: Latham (2), Giteau, Mortlock; C: Mortlock (2), Giteau; PG: Mortlock; DG: Barnes
Wales   20   T: J Thomas, S Williams; C: Hook (2); PG: Hook, S Jones

29 November 2008, Millennium Stadium, Cardiff
Wales   21   T: S Williams, Byrne; C: S Jones; PG: S Jones (2); DG: S Jones
Australia   18   T: Chisholm, Ioane; C: Giteau; PG: Giteau; DG: Giteau

James Bevan Trophy		Current holder: Wales				Number of titles: Australia 1, Wales 1	
No.	Date	Venue	Result			Series	Holder
1	26/05/2007	Telstra Stadium, Sydney	Australia	29–23	Wales	2–0	Australia
2	02/06/2007	Suncorp Stadium, Brisbane	Australia	31–0	Wales		
3	29/11/2008	Millennium Stadium, Cardiff	Wales	21–18	Australia	1–0	Wales

Australia: summaries and record

Home matches	
Played	262
Won	152
Lost	101
Drawn	9
Points for	5,993
Points against	4,040
Average score	22.87/15.42
Win %	58.02
Lose %	38.55
Draw %	3.44

Away matches	
Played	216
Won	86
Lost	125
Drawn	5
Points for	3,398
Points against	3,709
Average score	15.73/17.17
Win %	39.81
Lose %	57.87
Draw %	2.31

Neutral venues	
Played	16
Won	12
Lost	4
Drawn	0
Points for	550
Points against	202
Average score	34.38/12.63
Win %	75
Lose %	25
Draw %	0

Total matches	
Played	494
Won	250
Lost	230
Drawn	14
Points for	9,941
Points against	7,951
Average score	20.12/16.1
Win %	50.61
Lose %	46.56
Draw %	2.83

Most capped players: Australia							
Player	Caps	Career	T	C	PG	DG	Total
George Gregan	139	18/06/1994–06/10/2007	18	-	-	3	99
Stephen Larkham	102	22/06/1996–08/09/2007	25	2	-	2	135
David Campese	101	14/08/1982–01/12/1996	64	8	7	2	315
George Smith	99	04/11/2000–27/06/2009	9	-	-	-	45
Joe Roff	86	31/05/1995–03/07/2004	30	20	18	-	244
John Eales	86	22/07/1991–01/09/2001	2	31	34	-	173

Most tests as captain; Australia		
No.	Player	Period
59	George Gregan	2001–2007
55	John Eales	1996–2001
36	Nick Farr-Jones	1988–1992
28	Stirling Mortlock	2006–2009
19	Andrew Slack	1984–1987

Most points by a player in a career: Australia							
No.	Player	Tests	Career	T	C	PG	DG
911	Michael Lynagh	72	09/06/1984–11/06/1995	17	140	177	9
878	Matthew Burke	81	21/08/1993–21/08/2004	29	104	174	1
489	Stirling Mortlock	78	17/06/2000–27/06/2009	29	61	74	-
442	Matt Giteau	67	16/11/2002–27/06/2009	23	69	60	3
315	David Campese	101	14/08/1982–01/12/1996	64	8	7	2

Most tries by a player in a career: Australia

No.	Player	Tests	Career
64	David Campese	101	14/08/1982–01/12/1996
40	Chris Latham	78	21/11/1998–06/10/2007
30	Lote Tuqiri	66	07/06/2003–13/09/2008
30	Joe Roff	86	31/05/1995–03/07/2004
30	Tim Horan	80	05/08/1989–17/06/2000

Most conversions by a player in a career: Australia

No.	Player	Tests	Career
140	Michael Lynagh	72	09/06/1984–11/06/1995
104	Matt Burke	81	21/08/1993–21/08/2004
69	Matt Giteau	67	16/11/2002–27/06/2009
61	Stirling Mortlock	78	17/06/2000–27/06/2009
31	John Eales	86	22/07/1991–01/09/2001

Most penalties by a player in a career: Australia

No.	Player	Tests	Career
177	Michael Lynagh	72	09/06/1984–11/06/1995
174	Matt Burke	81	21/08/1993–21/08/2004
74	Stirling Mortlock	78	17/06/2000–27/06/2009
62	Paul McLean	30	25/05/1974–10/07/1982
60	Matt Giteau	67	16/11/2002–27/06/2009

Most drop goals by a player in a career: Australia

No.	Player	Tests	Career
9	Michael Lynagh	72	09/06/1984–11/06/1995
9	Phil Hawthorne	21	25/08/1962–19/08/1967
8	Mark Ella	25	21/06/1980–08/12/1984
4	Paul McLean	30	25/05/1974–10/07/1982

Most points by a player in a match: Australia

No.	Player	T	C	PG	DG	Versus	Venue	Date
42	Mat Rogers	2	16	-	-	Namibia	Adelaide Oval, Adelaide	25/10/2003
39	Matt Burke	3	9	2	-	Canada	Ballymore, Brisbane	29/06/1996
30	Elton Flatley	1	11	1	-	Romania	Suncorp Stadium, Brisbane	18/10/2003
29	Stirling Mortlock	2	2	5	-	South Africa	Colonial Stadium, Melbourne	08/07/2000
28	Michael Lynagh	2	3	4	-	Argentina	Ballymore, Brisbane	30/04/1995

AUSTRALIA

Most tries by a player in a match: Australia

No.	Player	Versus	Venue	Date
5	Chris Latham	Namibia	Adelaide Oval, Adelaide	25/10/2003
4	Lote Tuqiri	Italy	Telstra Dome, Melbourne	25/06/2005
4	Chris Latham	Argentina	Ballymore, Brisbane	17/06/2000
4	Jason Little	Tonga	Bruce Stadium, Canberra	21/09/1998
4	David Campese	United States	Sydney Cricket Ground, Sydney	09/07/1983
4	Greg Cornelsen	New Zealand	Eden Park, Auckland	09/09/1978

Most conversions by a player in a match: Australia

No.	Player	Versus	Venue	Date
16	Mat Rogers	Namibia	Adelaide Oval, Adelaide	25/10/2003
11	Elton Flatley	Romania	Suncorp Stadium, Brisbane	18/10/2003
10	Matt Burke	Spain	Campo Universitaria, Madrid	01/11/2001
9	John Eales	Fiji	Paramatta Stadium, Sydney	18/09/1998
9	Matt Burke	Canada	Ballymore, Brisbane	29/06/1996

Most penalties by a player in a match: Australia

No.	Player	Versus	Venue	Date
8	Matt Burke	South Africa	Twickenham, London	30/10/1999
7	Matt Burke	Wales	Millennium Stadium, Cardiff	25/11/2001
7	Matt Burke	France	Millennium Stadium, Cardiff	06/11/1999
7	Matt Burke	New Zealand	Stadium Australia, Sydney	28/08/1999

Most drop goals by a player in a match: Australia

No.	Player	Versus	Venue	Date
3	Phil Hawthorne	England	Twickenham, London	07/01/1967
2	David Knox	Fiji	Ballymore, Brisbane	10/08/1985
2	Mark Ella	Ireland	Lansdowne Road, Dublin	10/11/1984

Most points in a match by Australia

No.	Result	Points				Versus	Venue	Date
		T	C	PG	DG			
142	142–0	22	16	-	-	Namibia	Adelaide Oval, Adelaide	25/10/2003
92	92–10	13	12	1	-	Spain	Campo Universitaria, Madrid	01/11/2001
91	91–3	13	10	2	-	Japan	Stade Gerland, Lyon	08/09/2007
90	90–8	13	11	1	-	Romania	Suncorp Stadium, Brisbane	18/10/2003
76	76–0	11	6	3	-	England	Suncorp Stadium, Brisbane	06/06/1998

Most consecutive test wins by Australia		
No.	Period	Details
10	28/08/1999–08/07/2000	New Zealand (H), Romania (N), Ireland (A), United States (N), Wales (A), South Africa (N), France (N), Argentina (H), Argentina (H), South Africa (H)
10	29/08/1998–17/07/1999	New Zealand (H), Fiji (H), Tonga (H), Samoa (H), France (A), England (A), Ireland (H), Ireland (H), England (H), South Africa (H)
10	04/10/1991–19/07/1992	Argentina (N), Western Samoa (N), Wales (A), Ireland (A), New Zealand (N), England (A), Scotland (H), Scotland (H), New Zealand (H), New Zealand (H)

Milestones		
Longest test career	Kiwi Cooke	02/07/1932–11/01/1948 (15 years, 6 months & 10 days)
Youngest test player	Brian Ford	18 years & 90 days on 01/06/1957 vs New Zealand in Brisbane
Oldest test player	Tony Miller	38 years & 113 days on 19/08/1967 vs New Zealand in Wellington

Australian flyhalf Phil Hawthorne in space against New Zealand during the third test of the second Bledisloe Cup series of 1962 in Auckland. Ready to tackle Hawthorne is All Black winger Rod Heeps (right) while flanker Waka Nathan (left) moves up in defence. *Photo*: New Zealand Rugby Museum

AUSTRALIA

England

ENGLAND RUGBY ®

England vs Argentina *see* page 187

England vs Australia (Cook Cup) *see* page 211

England vs Canada

England vs Canada	
Played:	6
Won:	6
Lost:	0
Drawn:	0
For:	273
Against:	73

Average score:
45.5–12.17

England percentages:
Won:	100%
Lost:	0%
Drawn:	0%

17 October 1992, Wembley, London
England   26   T: Hunter (2), Guscott, Winterbottom; PG: Webb (2)
Canada   13   T: Graf; C: Rees; PG: Rees (2)

10 December 1994, Twickenham, London
England   60   T: R Underwood (2), Catt (2), A Underwood, Bracken; C: Andrew (6); PG: Andrew (6)
Canada   19   T: Lougheed (2), Evans; C: Rees (2)

28 August 1999, Twickenham, London
England   36   T: Luger, Dawson, Perry, Greenwood (2); C: Wilkinson (4); PG: Wilkinson
Canada   11   T: Stanley; PG: Rees (2)

2 June 2001, Fletcher's Field, Markham
England   22   T: Lewsey (2), Bracken, West; C: Walder
Canada   10   T: Fauth; C: Ross; PG: Ross

9 June 2001, Burnaby
England   59   T: Shaw (2), Walder (2), penalty try, Worsley, Noon, Wood; C: Walder (5); PG: Walder (3)
Canada   20   T: Baugh, Fauth; C: Ross (2); PG: Ross (2)

13 November 2004, Twickenham, London
England   70   T: Robinson (3), Lewsey (2), Cueto (2), Greenwood, Tindall, Hodgson, Moody, Vyvyan; C: Paul (3), Hodgson (2)
Canada   0

England vs Fiji

England vs Fiji	
Played:	4
Won:	4
Lost:	0
Drawn:	0
For:	156
Against:	71

Average score: 39–17.75

England percentages:
Won:	100%
Lost:	0%
Drawn:	0%

16 June 1988, National Stadium, Suva
England   25   T: Underwood (2), Barley; C: Barnes (2); PG: Barnes (3)
Fiji   12   PG: Koroduadua (3); DG: Koroduadua

4 November 1989, Twickenham, London
England   58   T: Underwood (5), Skinner, Bailey, Linnett, Guscott, Ackford; C: Hodgkinson (5), Andrew; PG: Hodgkinson (2)
Fiji   23   T: Eranavula, Rasari, Savai, Teleru; C: Koroduadua (2); PG: Koroduadua

20 July 1991, National Stadium, Suva
England   28   T: Probyn, Andrew, R Underwood; C: Webb (2); PG: Webb (2); DG: Andrew (2)
Fiji   12   T: Seru; C: Serevi; PG: Serevi; DG: Serevi

20 October 1999, Twickenham, London (RWC, Q/F play-off)
England   45   T: Luger, Back, Beal, Greening; C: Wilkinson, Dawson; PG: Wilkinson (7)
Fiji   24   T: Satala, Tikomaimakogia, Nakauta; C: Little (3); PG: Little

England vs France

England vs France

Played:	92
Won:	50
Lost:	35
Drawn:	7
For:	1,388
Against:	1,094

Average score:
15.09–11.89

England percentages:

Won:	54.35%
Lost:	38.04%
Drawn:	7.61%

One of the most anticipated games in the rugby calendar is the annual England–France fixture which has come to be known as *Le Crunch* since the Five Nations match of 1991. Strangely, *Le Crunch* was initially all about an apple – the famous Golden Delicious variety – which is grown in France. An advert on UK television promoted the apple with the catchphrase 'Try le crunch', which is now symbolic of the annual cross-Channel clash. England were the first home union to play France, on 22 March 1906 in Paris and since then it has been a permanent annual fixture, being interrupted only by the World Wars. France struggled to compete against the English in the early the twentieth century, only winning their first game in 1927. They were not to win at Twickenham until 1951. In more recent times, the two sides have occasionally met in warm-up games during RWC years, but their traditional Six Nations clash produces rugby of the finest quality.

22 March 1906, Parc des Princes, Paris
England 35 T: Hudson (4), Hogarth, Kewney, Mills, Peters, Stoop; C: Cartwright (4)
France 8 T: Lesieur, Muhr; C: Branlat

5 January 1907, Athletic Ground, Richmond
England 41 T: Lambert (5), Birkett, Nanson, Shewring, Slocock; C: Hill (5); DG: Birkett
France 13 T: Communeau, Muhr; C: Maclos (2); PG: Maclos

1 January 1908, Stade Olympique Yves-du-Manoir, Paris
England 19 T: Birkett, Lambert, Lapage, Mills, Portus; C: Roberts (2)
France 0

30 January 1909, Welford Road, Leicester
England 22 T: Hutchinson (2), Johns, Mobbs, Simpson, Tarr; C: Jackett (2)
France 0

3 March 1910, Parc des Princes, Paris
England 11 T: Hudson (2), Berry; C: Chapman
France 3 T: Communeau

28 January 1911, Twickenham, London
England 37 T: Lambert (2), Pillman (2), Mann, A Stoop, Wodehouse; C: Lambert (5); PG: Lambert (2)
France 0

8 April 1912, Parc des Princes, Paris
England 18 T: Birkett, Brougham, Eddison, Roberts; C: Pillman; DG: Coverdale
France 8 T: Dufau, Falliot; C: Boyau

25 January 1913, Twickenham, London
England 20 T: Coates (3), Pillman (2), Poulton; C: Greenwood
France 0

13 April 1914, Stade Olympique Yves-du-Manoir, Paris
England 39 T: Poulton (4), Lowe (3), Davies, Watson; C: Greenwood (6)
France 13 T: André, Capmau, Lubin-Lebrere; C: Besset (2)

31 January 1920, Twickenham, London
England 8 T: Davies; C: Greenwood; PG: Greenwood
France 3 T: Crabos

28 March 1921, Stade Olympique Yves-du-Manoir, Paris
England 10 T: Blakiston, Lowe; C: Hammett (2)
France 6 PG: Crabos (2)

25 February 1922, Twickenham, London
England 11 T: Voyce; C: Day; PG: Day (2)
France 11 T: Cassayet, Got, Lasserre; C: Crabos

ENGLAND

2 April 1923, Stade Olympique Yves-du-Manoir, Paris
England 12 T: Conway, Wakefield; C: Luddington; DG: Davies
France 3 PG: Beguet

23 February 1924, Twickenham, London
England 19 T: Jacob (3), Catcheside, Young; C: Conway (2)
France 7 T: Ballarin; DG: Behoteguy

13 April 1925, Stade Olympique Yves-du-Manoir, Paris
England 13 T: Hamilton-Wickes, Wakefield; C: Luddington (2); GM: Luddington
France 11 T: Barthe, Besson, Cluchague; C: Ducousso

27 February 1926, Twickenham, London
England 11 T: Aslett (2), Kittermaster; C: Francis
France 0

2 April 1927, Stade Olympique Yves-du-Manoir, Paris
France 3 T: Vellat
England 0

25 February 1928, Twickenham, London
England 18 T: Periton (2), Palmer (2); C: Richardson (3)
France 8 T: Galia, Jaureguy; C: Verger

1 April 1929, Stade Olympique Yves-du-Manoir, Paris
England 16 T: Aarvold (2), Gummer, Periton; C: Stanbury (2)
France 6 T: Houdet, Ribere

22 February 1930, Twickenham, London
England 11 T: Periton, Reeve, Robson; C: Black
France 5 T: Serin; C: Ambert

6 April 1931, Stade Olympique Yves-du-Manoir, Paris
France 14 T: Clady, Galia; DG: Baillette, Gerald
England 13 T: Burland, Smeddle, Tallent; C: Black (2)

19 April 1947, Twickenham, London
England 6 T: Guest, Roberts
France 3 PG: Prat

29 March 1948, Stade Olympique Yves-du-Manoir, Paris
France 15 T: Pomathios, Prat, Soro; C: Alvarez; DG: Bergougnan
England 0

26 February 1949, Twickenham, London
England 8 T: Cannell; C: Holmes; DG: Preece
France 3 DG: Alvarez

25 February 1950, Stade Olympique Yves-du-Manoir, Paris
France 6 T: Cazenave, Pilon
England 3 T: Smith

24 February 1951, Twickenham, London
France 11 T: Basquet, Prat; C: Prat; DG: Prat
England 3 T: Boobyer

5 April 1952, Stade Olympique Yves-du-Manoir, Paris
England 6 PG: Hall (2)
France 3 T: Pomathios

28 February 1953, Twickenham, London
England 11 T: Butterfield, Evans, Woodward; C: Hall
France 0

10 April 1954, Stade Olympique Yves-du-Manoir, Paris
France 11 T: Boniface, M Prat; C: J Prat; DG: J Prat
England 3 T: Wilson

26 February 1955, Twickenham, London
France   16   T: Baulon, Celeya; C: Vannier (2); DG: J Prat (2)
England   9   T: Higgins; PG: Hazell (2)

14 April 1956, Stade Olympique Yves-du-Manoir, Paris
France   14   T: Dupuy, Pauthe; C: Labazuy; PG: Labazuy (2)
England   9   T: Thompson; PG: Allison (2)

23 February 1957, Twickenham, London
England   9   T: Jackson (2), Evans
France   5   T: Darrouy; C: Vannier

1 March 1958, Stade Olympique Yves-du-Manoir, Paris
England   14   T: Thompson (2), Jackson; C: Hastings; PG: Hastings
France   0

28 February 1959, Twickenham, London
England   3   PG: Hetherington
France   3   PG: Labazuy

27 February 1960, Stade Olympique Yves-du-Manoir, Paris
France   3   PG: Vannier
England   3   T: Weston

25 February 1961, Twickenham, London
England   5   T: Harding; C: Willcox
France   5   T: Crauste; C: Vannier

24 February 1962, Stade Olympique Yves-du-Manoir, Paris
France   13   T: Crauste (3); C: Albaladejo (2)
England   0

23 February 1963, Twickenham, London
England   6   PG: Willcox (2)
France   5   T: G Boniface; C: Albaladejo

22 February 1964, Stade Olympique Yves-du-Manoir, Paris
England   6   T: Phillips; PG: Hosen
France   3   T: Darrouy

27 February 1965, Twickenham, London
England   9   T: Payne; PG: Rutherford (2)
France   6   T: Darrouy; PG: Dedieu

26 February 1966, Stade Olympique Yves-du-Manoir, Paris
France   13   T: A Boniface, Gachassin, Graurin; C: Lacaze (2)
England   0

25 February 1967, Twickenham, London
France   16   T: Dourthe, Duprat; C: G Camberabero (2); DG: G Camberabero; PG: G Camberabero
England   12   DG: Finlan; PG: Hosen (3)

24 February 1968, Stade Olympique Yves-du-Manoir, Paris
France   14   T: Gachassin; C: G Camberabero; DG: G Camberabero, Lacaze; PG: G Camberabero
England   9   DG: Weston; PG: Hiller (2)

22 February 1969, Twickenham, London
England   22   T: Fielding, Rollitt, Webb; C: Hiller (2); PG: Hiller (3)
France   8   T: Bonal C: Lacaze DG: Lacaze

18 April 1970, Stade Olympique Yves-du-Manoir, Paris
France   35   T: Berot, Bonal, Bourgarel, Dauga, Lux, Trillo; C: Villepreux (4); DG: Berot, Villepreux; PG: Villepreux
England   13   T: Spencer, Taylor; C: Jorden (2); PG: Jorden

27 February 1971, Twickenham, London
England   14   T: Hiller; C: Hiller; PG: Hiller (3)
France   14   T: Bertranne, Cantoni; C: Villepreux; DG: Berot; PG: Villepreux

ENGLAND

26 February 1972, Stade Olympique Yves-du-Manoir, Paris
France 37 T: Duprat (2), Biemouret, Lux, Sillieres, W Spanghero; C: Villepreux (5); PG: Villepreux
England 12 T: Beese; C: Old; PG: Old (2)

24 February 1973, Twickenham, London
England 14 T: Duckham (2); PG: Jorden (2)
France 6 T: Bertranne; C: Romeu

2 March 1974, Parc des Princes, Paris
France 12 T: Romeu; C: Romeu; DG: Romeu; PG: Romeu
England 12 T: Duckham; C: Old; DG: Evans; PG: Old

1 February 1975, Twickenham, London
France 27 T: Etchenique, Gourdon, Guilbert, Spanghero; C: Paries (4); PG: Paries
England 20 T: Duckham, Rossborough; DG: Rossborough; PG: Rossborough (3)

20 March 1976, Parc des Princes, Paris
France 30 T: Paparemborde (2), Romeu, Bastiat, Foroux, Gourdon; C: Romeu (3)
England 9 T: Dixon; C: Butler; PG: Butler

19 February 1977, Twickenham, London
France 4 T: Sangali
England 3 PG: Hignell

21 January 1978, Parc des Princes, Paris
France 15 T: Averous, Gallion; C: Aguirre (2); PG: Aguirre
England 6 DG: Old (2)

3 March 1979, Twickenham, London
England 7 T: Bennett; PG: Bennett
France 6 T: Costes; C: Aguirre

2 February 1980, Parc des Princes, Paris
England 17 T: Carleton, Preston; DG: Horton (2); PG: Hare
France 13 T: Averous, Rives; C: Caussade; PG: Caussade

21 March 1981, Twickenham, London
France 16 T: Lacans, Pardo; C: Laporte; DG: Laporte (2)
England 12 PG: Rose (4)

20 February 1982, Parc des Princes, Paris
England 27 T: Woodward, Carleton; C: Hare (2); PG: Hare (5)
France 15 T: Pardo; C: Sallefranque; DG: Lescarboura; PG: Sallefranque (2)

15 January 1983, Twickenham, London
France 19 T: Estéve, Sella, Paparemborde; C: Blanco (2); PG: Camberabero
England 15 DG: Cusworth; PG: Hare (4)

3 March 1984, Parc des Princes, Paris
France 32 T: Codorniou (2), Sella, Estéve, Begu, Gallion; C: Lescarboura; PG: Lescarboura; DG: Lescarboura
England 18 T: Underwood, Hare; C: Hare (2); PG: Hare (2)

2 February 1985, Twickenham, London
England 9 PG: Andrew (2); DG: Andrew
France 9 DG: Lescarboura (3)

15 March 1986, Parc des Princes, Paris
France 29 T: Sella, Laporte, Blanco, penalty try; C: Laporte (2); PG: Laporte (3)
England 10 T: Dooley; PG: Barnes (2)

21 February 1987, Twickenham, London
France 19 T: Bonneval, Sella; C: Berot; PG: Berot (2); DG: Mesnel
England 15 PG: Rose (4); DG: Andrew

16 January 1988, Parc des Princes, Paris
France 10 T: Rodriguez; PG: Berot (2)
England 9 PG: Webb (2); DG: Cusworth

4 March 1989, Twickenham, London
England   11   T: Carling, Robinson; PG: Andrew
France   0

3 February 1990, Parc des Princes, Paris
England   26   T: Guscott, Carling, R Underwood; C: Hodgkinson; PG: Hodgkinson (4)
France   7   T: Lagisquet; PG: Charvet

16 March 1991, Twickenham, London
England   21   T: R Underwood; C: Hodgkinson; PG: Hodgkinson (4); DG: Andrew
France   19   T: Saint-André, Mesnel, Camberabero; C: Camberabero (2); PG: Camberabero

19 October 1991, Parc des Princes, Paris (RWC, Q/F)
England   19   T: R Underwood, Carling; C: Webb; PG: Webb (3)
France   10   T: Lafond; PG: Lacroix (2)

15 February 1992, Parc des Princes, Paris
England   31   T: R Underwood, Morris, Webb, penalty try; C: Webb (3); PG: Webb (3)
France   13   T: Viars, Penaud; C: Viars; PG: Viars

16 January 1993, Twickenham, London
England   16   T: Hunter; C: Webb; PG: Webb (3)
France   15   T: Saint-André (2); C: Camberabero; PG: Camberabero

5 March 1994, Parc des Princes, Paris
England   18   PG: Andrew (5); DG: Andrew
France   14   T: Benazzi; PG: Lacroix (3)

4 February 1995, Twickenham, London
England   31   T: A Underwood (2), Guscott; C: Andrew (2); PG: Andrew (4)
France   10   T: Viars; C: Lacroix; PG: Lacroix

22 June 1995, Loftus Versfeld, Pretoria (RWC, 3/4 play-off)
France   19   T: Roumat, N'Tamack; PG: Lacroix (3)
England   9   PG: Andrew (3)

20 January 1996, Parc des Princes, Paris
France   15   PG: Lacroix (3); DG: Lacroix, Castaignede
England   12   PG: Grayson (2); DG: Grayson (2)

1 March 1997, Twickenham, London
France   23   T: Lamaison, Leflamand; C: Lamaison (2); PG: Lamaison (2); DG: Lamaison
England   20   T: Dallaglio; PG: Grayson (4); DG: Grayson

7 February 1998, Stade de France, Paris
France   24   T: Bernat-Salles, Dominici; C: Lamaison; PG: Lamaison (2); DG: Castaignede, Sadourny
England   17   T: Back; PG: Grayson (4)

20 March 1999, Twickenham, London
England   21   PG: Wilkinson (7)
France   10   T: Comba; C: Castaignede; PG: Castaignede

19 February 2000, Stade de France, Paris
England   15   PG: Wilkinson (5)
France   9   PG: Dourthe (3)

7 April 2001, Twickenham, London
England   48   T: Catt, Greening, Balshaw, Perry, Hill, Greenwood; C: Wilkinson (6); PG: Wilkinson (2)
France   19   T: Bernat-Salles; C: Merceron; PG: Merceron (3); DG: Merceron

2 March 2002, Stade de France, Paris
France   20   T: Merceron, Harinordoquy; C: Merceron (2); PG: Merceron (2)
England   15   T: Robinson, Cohen; C: Wilkinson; PG: Wilkinson

15 February 2003, Twickenham, London
England   25   T: Robinson; C: Wilkinson; PG: Wilkinson (5); DG: Wilkinson
France   17   T: Magne, Poitrenoud, Traille; C: Merceron

ENGLAND

30 August 2003, Stade Velodrome, Marseille
France   17   T: Brusque; PG: Michalak (3); DG: Michalak
England   16   T: Tindall; C: Grayson; PG: Grayson (3)

6 September 2003, Twickenham, London
England   45   T: Cohen (2), Robinson, Balshaw, Lewsey; C: Wilkinson (3), Grayson; PG: Wilkinson (4)
France   14   T: Rougerie; PG: Merceron (2) DG: Jauzion

15 November 2003, Telstra Stadium, Sydney (RWC, S/F)
England   24   PG: Wilkinson (5) DG: Wilkinson (3)
France   7   T: Betsen; C: Michalak

27 March 2004, Stade de France, Paris
France   24   T: Harinordoquy, Yachvili; C: Yachvili; PG: Yachvili (4)
England   21   T: Cohen, Lewsey; C: Barkley; PG: Barkley (3)

13 February 2005, Twickenham, London
France   18   PG: Yachvili (6)
England   17   T: Barkley, Lewsey; C: Hodgson (2); PG: Hodgson

12 March 2006, Stade de France, Paris
France   31   T: Fritz, Traille, Dominici; C: Yachvili (2); PG: Yachvili (4)
England   6   PG: Hodgson, Goode

11 March 2007, Twickenham, London
England   26   T: Flood, Tindall; C: Flood, Geraghty; PG: Flood (3), Geraghty
France   18   PG: Skrela (3), Yachvili (3)

11 August 2007, Twickenham, London
France   21   T: Pelous, Chabel; C: Ellisalde; PG: Skrela (2), Ellisalde
England   15   PG: Barkley (4); DG: Gomarsall

18 August 2007, Stade Velodrome, Marseille
France   22   T: Jauzion; C: Elissalde; PG: Elissalde (4), Michalak
England   9   PG: Wilkinson (3)

13 October 2007, Stade de France, Paris (RWC, S/F)
England   14   T: Lewsey; PG: Wilkinson (2); DG: Wilkinson
France   9   PG: Beauxis (3)

23 February 2008, Stade de France, Paris
England   24   T: Sackey, Wigglesworth; C: Wilkinson; PG: Wilkinson (3); DG: Wilkinson
France   13   T: Nallet; C: Traille; PG: Parra, Yachvili

15 March 2009, Twickenham, London
England   34   T: Flutey (2), Cueto, Armitage, Worsley; C: Flood (3); PG: Flood
France   10   T: Szarzewski, Malzieu

England vs Georgia

12 October 2003, Subiaco Oval, Perth (RWC, Pool C)
England   84   T: Greenwood (2), Cohen (2), Robinson, Tindall, Dawson, Thompson, Dallaglio, Back, Regan, Luger; C: Wilkinson (5), Grayson (4); PG: Wilkinson (2)
Georgia   6   PG: Urjukashvili, Jimsheladze

ENGLAND

England vs Ireland (Millennium Trophy)

England vs Ireland	
Played:	122
Won:	70
Lost:	44
Drew:	8
For:	1,439
Against:	970

Average score:
11.8–7.95

England percentages:

Won:	57.38%
Lost:	36.06%
Draw:	6.56%

England vs Ireland is the second-oldest international fixture in the world, with the two countries first meeting on 15 February 1875 at The Oval in London. England have had the upper hand in the series since its inception, with Ireland managing only brief periods of domination in the late 1940s, mid-1970s and most recently, the mid-2000s. The Millennium Trophy is contested annually between Ireland and England as part of the Six Nations championship. The trophy, in the shape of a horned Viking helmet, was initiated in 1988 for Dublin's millennial celebrations and was donated by Digital. To celebrate Dublin's millennium and to introduce the trophy, an additional fixture between England and Ireland was arranged following the Five Nations. The city adopted the slogan 'Dublin's great in '88', with the Irish adamant that England would not win the game and ruin their celebrations. This was sadly not to be, as the English won 21–10 to claim the first Millennium Trophy.

15 February 1875, Kennington Oval, London
England 7 (1G 1T 1D)
Ireland 0
T: Michell, Cheston, Nash; C: Pearson, Nash

13 December 1875, Rathmines, Dublin
England 4 (1G 1T)
Ireland 0
T: Clark, Kewley; C: Pearson

5 February 1877, Kennington Oval, London
England 8 (2G 2T)
Ireland 0
T: Adams, Hornby, Hutchinson (2); C: Stokes (2)

11 March 1878, Lansdowne Road, Dublin
England 7 (2G 1T)
Ireland 0
T: Gardner, Penny, Turner; C: Pearson (2)

5 February 1879, Kennington Oval, London
England 11 (2G 2T 1D)
Ireland 0
T: Adams, Evanson, Rowley, Twynam; C: Stokes (2); DG: Stokes

4 February 1880, Lansdowne Road, Dublin
England 4 (1G 1T)
Ireland 1 (1T)
T: Ellis, Markendale; C: Stokes
T: Cuppaidge

2 February 1881, Whalley Range, Manchester
England 8 (2G 2T)
Ireland 0
T: Sawyer, Taylor (3); C: Stokes (2)

6 February 1882, Lansdowne Road, Dublin
Ireland 2 (2T)
England 2 (2T)
T: Johnstone, Stokes
T: Bolton, Hunt

5 February 1883, Whalley Range, Manchester
England 6 (1G 3T)
Ireland 1 (1T)
T: Bolton, Tatham, Twynam, Wade; C: Evanson
T: Forrest

4 February 1884, Lansdowne Road, Dublin
England 3 (1G)
Ireland 0
T: Bolton; C: Sample

7 February 1885, Whalley Range, Manchester
England 2 (2T)
Ireland 1 (1T)
T: Bolton, Hawcridge
T: Greene

6 February 1886, Lansdowne Road, Dublin
England 1 (1T)
Ireland 0
T: Wilkinson

5 February 1887, Lansdowne Road, Dublin
Ireland 6 (2G)
England 0
T: Montgomery, Tillie; C: Rambaut (2)

ENGLAND

15 March 1890, Rectory Field, Blackheath
England   3 (3T)   T: Rogers, Morrison, Stoddart
Ireland   0

7 February 1891, Lansdowne Road, Dublin
England   9   T: Lockwood (2), Wilson (2), Toothill; C: Lockwood (2)
Ireland   0

6 February 1892, Whalley Range, Manchester
England   7   T: Evershed, Percival; C: Woods
Ireland   0

4 February 1893, Lansdowne Road, Dublin
England   4   T: Bradshaw, Taylor
Ireland   0

3 February 1894, Rectory Field, Blackheath
Ireland   7   T: J Lytle; DG: Forrest
England   5   T: Lockwood; C: Taylor

2 February 1895, Lansdowne Road, Dublin
England   6   T: Fegan, Thomas
Ireland   3   T: L Magee

1 February 1896, Meanwood Road, Leeds
Ireland   10   T: Sealy, Stevenson; C: Bulger (2)
England   4   DG: Byrne

6 February 1897, Lansdowne Road, Dublin
Ireland   13   T: Gardiner (2), Bulger; GM: Bulger
England   9   T: Robinson; PG: Byrne (2)

5 February 1898, Athletic Ground, Richmond
Ireland   9   T: Lindsay, Magee; PG: Bulger
England   6   T: Robinson; PG: Byrne

4 February 1899, Lansdowne Road, Dublin
Ireland   6   T: Allen; PG: Magee
England   0

3 February 1900, Athletic Ground, Richmond
England   15   T: Robinson (2), Gordon-Smith; C: Alexander; DG: Gordon-Smith
Ireland   4   DG: Allison

9 February 1901, Lansdowne Road, Dublin
Ireland   10   T: Davidson, Gardiner; C: Irwin (2)
England   6   T: Robinson; PG: Alexander

8 February 1902, Welford Road, Leicester
England   6   T: Cooper, Williams
Ireland   3   T: F Gardiner

14 February 1903, Lansdowne Road, Dublin
Ireland   6   T: Ryan; PG: Corley
England   0

13 February 1904, Rectory Field, Blackheath
England   19   T: Moore (2), Vivyan (2), Simpson; C: Vivyan (2)
Ireland   0

11 February 1905, Mardyke, Cork
Ireland   17   T: Moffatt (2), Allen, Maclear, Wallace; C: Maclear
England   3   T: Coopper

10 February 1906, Welford Road, Leicester
Ireland   16   T: Tedford (2), Maclear, Purdon; C: Gardiner, Maclear
England   6   T: Jago, Mills

> **Did you know**: Irishman D.B. Walkington was selected to play against England in 1887. He had to play with a monocle due to his poor eyesight, an item he carefully removed every time he had to make a tackle!

9 February 1907, Lansdowne Road, Dublin
Ireland 17 T: Caddell (2), Tedford, Thrift; C: Parke; GM: Parke
England 9 T: Imrie, Slocock; PG: Pickering

8 February 1908, Athletic Ground, Richmond
England 13 T: Hudson (2), Williamson; C: Wood (2)
Ireland 3 PG: Parke

13 February 1909, Lansdowne Road, Dublin
England 11 T: Palmer (2), Mobbs; C: Palmer
Ireland 5 T: Parke; C: Pinion

12 February 1910, Twickenham, London
England 0
Ireland 0

11 February 1911, Lansdowne Road, Dublin
Ireland 3 T: T Smyth
England 0

10 February 1912, Twickenham, London
England 15 T: Roberts (2), Birkett, Brougham, Poulton
Ireland 0

8 February 1913, Lansdowne Road, Dublin
England 15 T: Coates (2), Pillman, Ritson; PG: Greenwood
Ireland 4 DG: Lloyd

14 February 1914, Twickenham, London
England 17 T: Lowe (2), Davies, Pillman, Roberts; C: Chapman
Ireland 12 T: Jackson, Quinn; C: Lloyd; DG: Lloyd

14 February 1920, Lansdowne Road, Dublin
England 14 T: Lowe, Mellish, Myers, Wakefield; C: Greenwood
Ireland 11 T: Dickson, Lloyd; C: Lloyd; PG: Lloyd

12 February 1921, Twickenham, London
England 15 T: Blakiston, Brown, Lowe; C: Cumberlege; DG: Lowe
Ireland 0

11 February 1922, Lansdowne Road, Dublin
England 12 T: Lowe, Maxwell-Hyslop, Smallwood, Gardner
Ireland 3 T: Wallis

10 February 1923, Welford Road, Leicester
England 23 T: Lowe, Corbett, Price, Smallwood, Voyce; C: Conway (2); DG: Davies
Ireland 5 T: McClelland; C: Crawford

9 February 1924, Ravenhill, Belfast
England 14 T: Catcheside (2), Corbett, Hamilton-Wickes; C: Conway
Ireland 3 T: Douglas

14 February 1925, Twickenham, London
England 6 T: Smallwood (2)
Ireland 6 T: T Hewitt, H Stephenson

13 February 1926, Lansdowne Road, Dublin
Ireland 19 T: Cussen (2), F Hewitt, G Stephenson; C: G Stephenson (2); PG: G Stephenson
England 15 T: Haslett, Periton, Young; C: Francis (3)

12 February 1927, Twickenham, London
England 8 T: Gibbs, Laird; C: Stanbury
Ireland 6 T: H McVicker; PG: G Stephenson

11 February 1928, Lansdowne Road, Dublin
England 7 T: Richardson; DG: Richardson
Ireland 6 T: Arigho, Sugden

ENGLAND

261

ENGLAND

9 February 1929, Twickenham, London
Ireland	6	T: Davy, Sugden
England	5	T: Smeddle; C: Wilson

8 February 1930, Lansdowne Road, Dublin
Ireland	4	DG: Murray
England	3	T: Novis

14 February 1931, Twickenham, London
Ireland	6	T: McMahon; PG: Murray
England	5	T: Black; C: Black

13 February 1932, Lansdowne Road, Dublin
England	11	T: Burland; C: Burland; PG: Burland (2)
Ireland	8	T: Waide; C: Murray; PG: Murray

11 February 1933, Twickenham, London
England	17	T: Novis (2), Booth, Gadney, Sadler; C: Kendrew
Ireland	6	T: Hunt; PG: Murray

10 February 1934, Lansdowne Road, Dublin
England	13	T: Fry (2), Meikle; C: Gregory (2)
Ireland	3	T: Morgan

9 February 1935, Twickenham, London
England	14	T: Giles; C: Boughton; PG: Boughton (3)
Ireland	3	T: O'Connor

8 February 1936, Lansdowne Road, Dublin
Ireland	6	T: Bailey, Boyle
England	3	T: Sever

13 February 1937, Twickenham, London
England	9	T: Butler, Sever; PG: Cranmer
Ireland	8	T: Moran (2); C: Bailey

12 February 1938, Lansdowne Road, Dublin
England	36	T: Giles, Bolton, Marshall, Nicholson, Prescott, Unwin, Reynolds; C: Parker (6); PG: Parker
Ireland	14	T: Bailey, Cromey, Daly, Mayne; C: Crowe

11 February 1939, Twickenham, London
Ireland	5	T: Irwin; C: McKibbin
England	0	

8 February 1947, Lansdowne Road, Dublin
Ireland	22	T: O'Hanlon (2), Mullan (2), McKay; C: Mullan (2); PG: Mullan
England	0	

14 February 1948, Twickenham, London
Ireland	11	T: Kyle, McKay, McKee; C: Mullan
England	10	T: Guest (2); C: Uren (2)

12 February 1949, Lansdowne Road, Dublin
Ireland	14	T: O'Hanlon, McKee; C: Norton; PG: Norton (2)
England	5	T: van Ryneveld; C: Holmes

11 February 1950, Twickenham, London
England	3	T: Roberts
Ireland	0	

10 February 1951, Lansdowne Road, Dublin
Ireland	3	PG: McKibbon
England	0	

29 March 1952, Twickenham, London
England	3	T: Boobyer
Ireland	0	

14 February 1953, Lansdowne Road, Dublin
Ireland   9   T: Mortell; PG: Henderson (2)
England   9   T: Evans; PG: Hall (2)

13 February 1954, Twickenham, London
England   14   T: Butterfield, Regan, Wilson; C: King; PG: King
Ireland   3   PG: Murphy-O'Connor

12 February 1955, Lansdowne Road, Dublin
Ireland   6   T: O'Reilly; PG: Henderson
England   6   T: Butterfield, Hastings

11 February 1956, Twickenham, London
England   20   T: Butterfield, Evans, Jackson; C: Currie; PG: Currie (2), Allison
Ireland   0

9 February 1957, Lansdowne Road, Dublin
England   6   T: Jackson; PG: Challis
Ireland   0

8 February 1958, Twickenham, London
England   6   T: Ashcroft; PG: Hetherington
Ireland   0

14 February 1959, Lansdowne Road, Dublin
England   3   PG: Risman
Ireland   0

13 February 1960, Twickenham, London
England   8   T: Marques; C: Rutherford; DG: Sharp
Ireland   5   T: Culliton; C: Kiernan

11 February 1961, Lansdowne Road, Dublin
Ireland   11   T: Kavanagh; C: Moffett; PG: Moffett (2)
England   8   T: Roberts, Rogers; C: Risman

10 February 1962, Twickenham, London
England   16   T: Roberts, Sharp, Wade; C: Sharp (2); PG: Sharp
Ireland   0

9 February 1963, Lansdowne Road, Dublin
Ireland   0
England   0

8 February 1964, Twickenham, London
Ireland   18   T: Flynn (2), Casey, Murphy; C: Kiernan (3)
England   5   T: Rogers; C: Willcox

13 February 1965, Lansdowne Road, Dublin
Ireland   5   T: Lamont; C: Kiernan
England   0

12 February 1966, Twickenham, London
England   6   T: Greenwood; PG: Ruherford
Ireland   6   T: McGrath; PG: Kiernan

11 February 1967, Lansdowne Road, Dublin
England   8   T: McFadyean; C: Hosen; PG: Hosen
Ireland   3   PG: Kiernan

10 February 1968, Twickenham, London
England   9   DG: Finlan; PG: Hiller (2)
Ireland   9   PG: Kiernan (3)

8 February 1969, Lansdowne Road, Dublin
Ireland   16   T: Bresnihan, Murphy; C: Kiernan; DG: McGann; PG: Kiernan (2)
England   15   T: Duckham; PG: Hiller (4)

ENGLAND

14 February 1970, Twickenham, London
England 9   T: Shackleton; DG: Hiller (2)
Ireland 3   PG: Kiernan

13 February 1971, Lansdowne Road, Dublin
England 9   PG: Hiller (3)
Ireland 6   T: Duggan, Grant

12 February 1972, Twickenham, London
Ireland 16   T: Flynn, Grace; C: Kiernan; DG: McGann; PG: Kiernan
England 12   T: Ralston; C: Hiller; PG: Hiller (2)

10 February 1973, Lansdowne Road, Dublin
Ireland 18   T: Grace, Milliken; C: McGann (2); DG: McGann; PG: McGann
England 9   T: Neary; C: Jorden; PG: Jorden

16 February 1974, Twickenham, London
Ireland 26   T: Gibson (2), Moloney, Moore; C: Gibson (2); DG: Quinn; PG: Ensor
England 21   T: Squires; C: Old; PG: Old (5)

18 January 1975, Lansdowne Road, Dublin
Ireland 12   T: Gibson, McCombe; C: McCombe (2)
England 9   T: Stevens; C: Old; DG: Old

6 March 1976, Twickenham, London
Ireland 13   T: Grace; DG: McGann; PG: McGann (2)
England 12   PG: Old (4)

5 February 1977, Lansdowne Road, Dublin
England 4   T: Cooper
Ireland 0

18 March 1978, Twickenham, London
England 15   T: Dixon, Slemen; C: Young (2); PG: Young
Ireland 9   DG: Ward; PG: Ward (2)

17 February 1979, Lansdowne Road, Dublin
Ireland 12   T: MacLennan; C: Ward; DG: Ward; PG: Ward
England 7   T: Bennett; PG: Bennett

19 January 1980, Twickenham, London
England 24   T: Scott, Slemen, Smith; C: Hare (3) PG: Hare (2)
Ireland 9   PG: Campbell (3)

7 March 1981, Lansdowne Road, Dublin
England 10   T: Dodge, Rose; C: Rose
Ireland 6   DG: Campbell, MacNeill

6 February 1982, Twickenham, London
Ireland 16   T: MacNeill, McLoughlin; C: Campbell; PG: Campbell (2)
England 15   T: Slemen; C: Rose; PG: Rose (3)

19 March 1983, Lansdowne Road, Dublin
Ireland 25   T: Slattery, Campbell; C: Campbell; PG: Campbell (5)
England 15   PG: Hare (5)

18 February 1984, Twickenham, London
England 12   PG: Hare (3); DG: Cusworth
Ireland 9   PG: Ward (3)

30 March 1985, Lansdowne Road, Dublin
Ireland 13   T: Mullin; PG: Kiernan (2); DG: Kiernan
England 10   T: Underwood; PG: Andrew (2)

1 March 1986, Twickenham, London
England 25   T: Richards (2), Davies, penalty try; C: Andrew (3); PG: Andrew
Ireland 20   T: Ringland, Mullin, McCall; C: Kiernan; PG: Kiernan (2)

7 February 1987, Lansdowne Road, Dublin
Ireland 17
England 0

T: Kiernan, Matthews, Crossan; C: Kiernan; PG: Kiernan

19 March 1988, Twickenham, London
England 35
Ireland 3

T: Oti (3), Rees, Underwood (2); C: Webb, Andrew (3); PG: Webb
DG: Kiernan

23 April 1988, Lansdowne Road, Dublin
England 21
Ireland 10

T: R Underwood, Harding; C: Webb (2); PG: Webb (3)
T: S Smith, MacNeill; C: Kiernan

18 February 1989, Lansdowne Road, Dublin
England 16
Ireland 3

T: Moore, Richards; C: Andrew; PG: Andrew (2)
PG: Kiernan

20 January 1990, Twickenham, London
England 23
Ireland 0

T: Probyn, Egerton, Guscott, R Underwood; C: Hodgkinson (2); PG: Hodgkinson

2 March 1991, Lansdowne Road, Dublin
England 16
Ireland 7

T: R Underwood, Teague; C: Hodgkinson; PG: Hodgkinson (2)
T: Geoghegan; PG: B Smith

1 February 1992, Twickenham, London
England 38
Ireland 9

T: Webb (2), Morris, Guscott, R Underwood, Halliday; C: Webb (4); PG: Webb (2)
T: Keyes; C: Keyes; PG: Keyes

20 March 1993, Lansdowne Road, Dublin
Ireland 17
England 3

T: Galwey; PG: Elwood (2); DG: Elwood (2)
PG: Webb

19 February 1994, Twickenham, London
Ireland 13
England 12

T: Geoghegan; C: Elwood; PG: Elwood (2)
PG: Callard (4)

21 January 1995, Lansdowne Road, Dublin
England 20
Ireland 8

T: Carling, Clarke, A Underwood; C: Andrew; PG: Andrew
T: Foley; PG: Burke

17 March 1996, Twickenham, London
England 28
Ireland 15

T: Sleightholme; C: Grayson; PG: Grayson (6); DG: Grayson
PG: Mason (4); DG: Humphreys

15 February 1997, Lansdowne Road, Dublin
England 46
Ireland 6

T: Sleightholme (2), Hill, Underwood (2), Gomarsall; C: Grayson (2); PG: Grayson (4)
PG: Elwood (2)

4 April 1998, Twickenham, London
England 35
Ireland 17

T: de Glanville, Perry, Cockerill, Catt; C: Grayson (3); PG: Grayson (3)
T: Hickie (2); C: Elwood (2); PG: Elwood

6 March 1999, Lansdowne Road, Dublin
England 27
Ireland 15

T: Perry, Rodber; C: Wilkinson; PG: Wilkinson (4); DG: Grayson
PG: Humphreys (5)

5 February 2000, Twickenham, London
England 50
Ireland 18

T: Cohen (2), Healey (2), Back, Tindall; C: Wilkinson (4); PG: Wilkinson (4)
T: Maggs, Galwey; C: Humphreys; PG: Humphreys (2)

20 October 2001, Lansdowne Road, Dublin
Ireland 20
England 14

T: Wood; PG: Humphreys (3), O'Gara (2)
T: Healey; PG: Wilkinson (3)

16 February 2002, Twickenham, London
England 45
Ireland 11

T: Greenwood (2), Wilkinson, Cohen, Kay, Worsley; C: Wilkinson (6); PG: Wilkinson
T: O'Gara; PG: Humphreys (2)

30 March 2003, Lansdowne Road, Dublin

| England | 42 | T: Greenwood (2), Dallaglio, Tindall, Luger; C: Wilkinson (3), Grayson; PG: Wilkinson; DG: Wilkinson (2) |
| Ireland | 6 | PG: Humphreys; DG: Humphreys |

6 March 2004, Twickenham, London

| Ireland | 19 | T: Dempsey; C: O'Gara; PG: O'Gara (4) |
| England | 13 | T: Dawson; C: Grayson; PG: Grayson (2) |

27 February 2005, Lansdowne Road, Dublin

| Ireland | 19 | T: O'Driscoll; C: O'Gara; PG: O'Gara (2); DG: O'Gara (2) |
| England | 13 | T: Corry; C: Hodgson; PG: Hodgson; DG: Hodgson |

18 March 2006, Twickenham, London

| Ireland | 28 | T: Horgan (2), Leamy; C: O'Gara (2); PG: O'Gara (3) |
| England | 24 | T: Noon, Borthwick; C: Goode; PG: Goode (4) |

24 February 2007, Croke Park, Dublin

| Ireland | 43 | T: Dempsey, D Wallace, Horgan, Boss; C: O'Gara (3), P Wallace; PG: O'Gara (5) |
| England | 13 | T: Strettle; C: Wilkinson; PG: Wilkinson (2) |

15 March 2008, Twickenham, London

| England | 33 | T: Sackey, Tait, Noon; C: Cipriani (3); PG: Cipriani (4) |
| Ireland | 10 | T: Kearney; C: O'Gara; PG: O'Gara |

28 February 2009, Croke Park, Dublin

| Ireland | 14 | T: O'Driscoll; PG: O'Gara (2); DG: O'Driscoll |
| England | 13 | T: Armitage; C: Goode; PG: Flood, Armitage |

Millenium Trophy			Current holder: Ireland			Number of titles: England 14, Ireland 8	
No.	Date	Venue	Result				Holder
1	23/04/1988	Lansdowne Road, Dublin	Ireland	10–21	England	England
2	18/02/1989	Lansdowne Road, Dublin	Ireland	3–16	England	England
3	20/01/1990	Twickenham, England	England	23–0	Ireland	England
4	02/03/1991	Lansdowne Road, Dublin	Ireland	7–16	England	England
5	01/02/1992	Twickenham, England	England	38–9	Ireland	England
6	20/03/1993	Lansdowne Road, Dublin	Ireland	17–3	England	Ireland
7	19/02/1994	Twickenham, England	England	12–13	Ireland	Ireland
8	21/01/1995	Lansdowne Road, Dublin	Ireland	8–20	England	England
9	17/03/1996	Twickenham, England	England	28–15	Ireland	England
10	15/02/1997	Lansdowne Road, Dublin	Ireland	6–46	England	England
11	04/04/1998	Twickenham, England	England	35–17	Ireland	England
12	06/03/1999	Lansdowne Road, Dublin	Ireland	15–27	England	England
13	05/02/2000	Twickenham, England	England	50–18	Ireland	England
14	20/10/2001	Lansdowne Road, Dublin	Ireland	20–14	England	Ireland
15	16/02/2002	Twickenham, England	England	45–11	Ireland	England
16	30/03/2003	Lansdowne Road, Dublin	Ireland	6–42	England	England
17	06/03/2004	Twickenham, England	England	13–19	Ireland	Ireland
18	27/02/2005	Lansdowne Road, Dublin	Ireland	19–13	England	Ireland
19	18/03/2006	Twickenham, England	England	24–28	Ireland	Ireland
20	24/02/2007	Croke Park, Dublin	Ireland	43–13	England	Ireland
21	15/03/2008	Twickenham, England	England	33–10	Ireland	England
22	28/02/2009	Croke Park, Dublin	Ireland	14–13	England	Ireland

England vs Italy

8 October 1991, Twickenham, London
England 36 T: Guscott (2), Webb, Underwood; C: Webb (4); PG: Webb (4)
Italy 6 T: Cuttitta; C: Dominguez

31 May 1995, Kings Park, Durban (RWC, Pool B)
England 27 T: A Underwood, R Underwood; C: Andrew; PG: Andrew (5)
Italy 20 T: Cuttitta, Vaccari; C: Dominguez (2); PG: Dominguez (2)

23 November 1996, Twickenham, London
England 54 T: Gomarsall (2), Sleighthome, Dallaglio, Johnson, Rodber, Sheasby; C: Catt (5); PG: Catt (3)
Italy 21 T: Vaccari, Troncon, Alancio; C: Dominguez (3)

22 November 1998, McAlpine Stadium, Huddersfield
England 23 T: Luger, Greenwood; C: Grayson (2); PG: Grayson (3)
Italy 15 PG: Dominguez (4); DG: Dominguez

2 October 1999, Twickenham, London (RWC, Pool B)
England 67 T: Dawson, Hill, de Glanville, Perry, Wilkinson, Back, Luger, Corry; C: Wilkinson (6); PG: Wilkinson (5)
Italy 7 T: Dominguez; C: Dominguez

18 March 2000, Stadio Olympio, Rome
England 59 T: Healey (3), Dawson (2), Cohen (2), penalty try; C: Wilkinson (4), King; PG: Wilkinson (2); DG: Back
Italy 12 T: Martin, Stoica; C: Dominguez

17 February 2001, Twickenham, London
England 80 T: Healey (2), Balshaw (2), Cohen, Regan, Worsley, Greenwood, Wilkinson, Dallaglio; C: Wilkinson (9); PG: Wilkinson (4)
Italy 23 T: Dallan, Checchinato; C: Scanavacca (2); PG: Scanavacca (3)

7 April 2002, Stadio Flaminio, Rome
England 45 T: Greenwood (2), Dallaglio, Healey, Cohen, Robinson; C: Wilkinson (5), Dawson; PG: Wilkinson
Italy 9 PG: Dominguez (3)

9 March 2003, Twickenham, London
England 40 T: Lewsey (2), Thompson, Simpson-Daniel, Tindall, Luger; C: Wilkinson (4), Dawson
Italy 5 T: Bergamasco

15 February 2004, Stadio Flaminio, Rome
England 50 T: Robinson (3), Balshaw, Lewsey, Grayson, Jones; C: Grayson (3); PG: Grayson (3)
Italy 9 PG: Wakarua (2); DG: Wakarua

12 March 2005, Twickenham, London
England 39 T: Cueto (3), Thompson, Balshaw, Hazell; C: Hodgson (2), Goode; PG: Hodgson
Italy 7 T: Troncon; C: Peens

11 February 2006, Stadio Flaminio, Rome
England 31 T: Tindall, Hodgson, Cueto, Simpson-Daniel; C: Hodgson (4); PG: Hodgson
Italy 16 T: Mi Bergamasco; C: Pez; PG: Pez; DG: Pez (2)

10 February 2007, Twickenham, London
England 20 T: Robinson; PG: Wilkinson (5)
Italy 7 T: Scanavacca; C: Scanavacca

10 February 2008, Stadio Flaminio, Rome
England 23 T: Sackey, Flood; C: Wilkinson (2); PG: Wilkinson (3)
Italy 19 T: Picone; C: Bortolussi; PG: Bortolussi (4)

7 February 2009, Twickenham, London
England 36 T: Ellis (2), Goode, Flutey, Cueto; C: Goode (4); PG: Goode
Italy 11 T: Mi Bergamasco; PG: McLean (2)

ENGLAND

England vs Japan

30 May 1987, Concord Oval, Sydney (RWC, Pool 1)
England 60 T: Underwood (2), Rees, Salmon, Richards, Simms, Harrison (3), Redman; C: Webb (7); PG: Webb (2)
Japan 7 T: Miyamoto; PG: Matsuo

England vs Netherlands

14 November 1998, McAlpine Stadium, Huddersfield
England 110 T: Back(4), Guscott (4), Beal, penalty try, Corry, Greenwood, Cockerill, Dawson, Healey, Luger; C: Grayson (15)
Netherlands 0

England vs New Zealand (Hillary Shield)

England vs New Zealand
Played: 32
Won: 6
Lost: 25
Drawn: 1
For: 402
Against: 765

Average score:
12.56–23.91

England percentages:
Won: 18.75%
Lost: 78.13%
Drawn: 3.12%

The New Zealand–England clash has consistently produced matches of the highest order since the teams first met at Crystal Palace, London in 1905. Despite New Zealand dominating the series, matches are usually tightly fought, physical affairs, with England twice having famously won in New Zealand. Undoubtedly, England's most glorious triumph came in 1936 when they beat the All Blacks 13-0 at Twickenham but have yet to manage a larger victory margin. New Zealand have achieved many memorable victories over England: none more so than the annihilation of England in the 1995 RWC semi-final, when a young Jonah Lomu scored four scintillating tries. In recent times, New Zealand have achieved comfortable victories, including their record win at Twickenham in 2006. Today, the two sides play for the Hillary Shield, first contested at Twickenham in 2008. The shield is named after New Zealander Sir Edmund Hillary who on 29 May 1953 became the first man to scale Mount Everest. Hillary, who died in 2008, was an avid rugby fan who maintained close links with both countries and is unrivalled as the most famous New Zealander of all time. His wife June presented the shield to the first winning captain, Richie McCaw of New Zealand. The All Blacks are the current holders.

2 December 1905, Crystal Palace, London
New Zealand 15 T: McGregor (4), Newton
England 0

3 January 1925, Twickenham, London
New Zealand 17 T: Svenson, Steel, Parker, M Brownlie; C: Nichols; PG: Nichols
England 11 T: Cove Smith, Kittermaster; C: Conway; PG: Corbett

4 January 1936, Twickenham, London
England 13 T: Obolensky (2), Sever; DG: Cranmer
New Zealand 0

30 January 1954, Twickenham, London
New Zealand 5 T: Dalzell; C: Scott
England 0

25 May 1963, Eden Park, Auckland
New Zealand 21 T: Caulton (2), D Clarke; C: D Clarke (3); PG: D Clarke; DG: D Clarke
England 11 T: Ranson; C: Hosen; PG: Hosen (2)

1 June 1963, Lancaster Park, Christchurch
New Zealand 9 T: McKay, Walsh; GM: D Clarke
England 6 T: Phillips; PG: Hosen

4 January 1964, Twickenham, London
New Zealand 14 T: Caulton, Meads; C: D Clarke; PG: D Clarke (2)
England 0

4 November 1967, Twickenham, London
New Zealand 23 T: Kirton (2), Birtwistle, Laidlaw, Dick; C: McCormick (4)
England 11 T: Lloyd (2); C: Rutherford; PG: Larter

6 January 1973, Twickenham, London
New Zealand   9   T: Kirkpatrick; C: Karam; DG: Williams
England   0

15 September 1973, Eden Park, Auckland
England   16   T: Squires, Stevens, Neary; C: Rossborough (2)
New Zealand   10   T: Batty, Hurst; C: Lendrum

25 November 1978, Twickenham, London
New Zealand   16   T: Oliver, Johnstone; C: McKechnie; PG: McKechnie (2)
England   6   PG: Hare; DG: Hare

24 November 1979, Twickenham, London
New Zealand   10   T: Fleming; PG: R Wilson (2)
England   9   PG: Hare (3)

19 November 1983, Twickenham, London
England   15   T: Colclough; C: Hare; PG: Hare (3)
New Zealand   9   T: Davie; C: Deans; PG: Deans

1 June 1985, Lancaster Park, Christchurch
New Zealand   18   PG: Crowley (6)
England   13   T: Harrison, Teague; C: Barnes; PG: Barnes

8 June 1985, Athletic Park, Wellington
New Zealand   42   T: Green (2), Kirwan, Mexted, Shaw, Hobbs; C: Crowley (3); PG: Crowley (3); DG: Smith
England   15   T: Hall, Harrison; C: Barnes (2); DG: Barnes

3 October 1991, Twickenham, London (RWC, Pool 1)
New Zealand   18   T: M Jones; C: Fox; PG: Fox (4)
England   12   PG: Webb (3); DG: Andrew

27 November 1993, Twickenham, London
England   15   PG: Callard (4); DG: Andrew
New Zealand   9   PG: Wilson (3)

18 June 1995, Newlands, Cape Town (RWC, S/F)
New Zealand   45   T: Lomu (4), Kronfeld, Bachop; C: Mehrtens (3); PG: Mehrtens; DG: Mehrtens, Z Brooke
England   29   T: R Underwood (2), Carling (2); C: Andrew (3); PG: Andrew

22 November 1997, Old Trafford, Manchester
New Zealand   25   T: Wilson, Jones, Randell; C: Mehrtens (2); PG: Mehrtens (2)
England   8   T: de Glanville; PG: Catt

6 December 1997, Twickenham, London
England   26   T: Rees, Hill, Dallaglio; C: Grayson; PG: Grayson (3)
New Zealand   26   T: Mehrtens, Little; C: Mehrtens (2); PG: Mehrtens (4)

20 June 1998, Carisbrook, Dunedin
New Zealand   64   T: Cullen (2), Randell (2), Wilson (2), Kronfeld, Lomu, Mayerhofler; C: Mehrtens (5); PG: Mehrtens (3)
England   22   T: Cockerill, Dawson, Beim; C: Stimpson (2); PG: Stimpson

27 June 1998, Eden Park, Auckland
New Zealand   40   T: Wilson (2), Maka, Vidiri, Randell, Mayerhofler; C: Mehrtens (2), Spencer (3)
England   10   T: Dawson; C: Dawson; PG: Dawson

9 October 1999, Twickenham, London (RWC, Pool B)
New Zealand   30   T: Wilson, Lomu, Kelleher; C: Mehrtens (3); PG: Mehrtens (3)
England   16   T: de Glanville; C: Wilkinson; PG: Wilkinson (3)

9 November 2002, Twickenham, London
England   31   T: Moody, Wilkinson, Cohen; C: Wilkinson (2); PG: Wilkinson (3); DG: Wilkinson
New Zealand   28   T: Lomu (2), Howlett, Lee; C: Blair (2), Mehrtens (2)

14 June 2003, Athletic Park, Wellington
England   15   PG: Wilkinson (4); DG: Wilkinson
New Zealand   13   T: Howlett; C: Spencer; PG: Spencer (2)

> **Did you know**: The first player to be sent off in a test was All Black Cyril Brownlie, who was sent off against England on 3 January 1925 at Twickenham in a notoriously dirty match? New Zealand still went on to win by 17–11.

12 June 2004, Carisbrook, Dunedin
New Zealand 36   T: Spencer, Rokocoko, Howlett; C: Carter(3); PG: Carter (5)
England 3   PG: Hodgson

19 June 2004, Eden Park, Auckland
New Zealand 36   T: Rokocoko (3), Carter, Spencer; C: Carter (4); PG: Carter
England 12   PG: Hodgson (4)

19 November 2005, Twickenham, London
New Zealand 23   T: Umaga, Mealamu; C: Carter (2); PG: Carter (3)
England 19   T: Corry; C: Hodgson; PG: Hodgson (4)

5 November 2006, Twickenham, London
New Zealand 41   T: Mauger, Rokocoko, Hayman, Carter; C: Carter (3); PG: Carter (5)
England 20   T: Noon, Cohen, Perry; C: Hodgson; PG: Hodgson

14 June 2008, Eden Park, Auckland
New Zealand 37   T: Smith, Carter, Muliaina, Sivivatu; C: Carter (4); PG: Carter (3)
England 20   T: Ojo (2); C: Barkley (2); PG: Barkley (2)

21 June 2008, AMI Stadium, Christchurch
New Zealand 44   T: Kahui, Carter, Nonu, Lauaki, Cowan; C: Carter (4), Donald; PG: Carter (3)
England 12   T: Care, Varndell; C: Barkley

29 November 2008, Twickenham, London
New Zealand 32   T: Muliaina (2), Nonu; C: Carter; PG: Carter (5)
England 6   PG: Flood, Armitage

Hillary Shield		Current holder: New Zealand				Number of titles: New Zealand 1, England 0	
No	Date	Venue	Result			Series	Holder
1	29/11/2008	Twickenham, London	England	6–32	New Zealand	0–1	New Zealand

England vs New Zealand Maoris

16 February 1889, Rectory Field, Blackheath
England 7 [1G 4T]   T: Bedford (2), Evershed, Stoddart, Sutcliffe; C: Sutcliffe
NZ Maoris 0

England vs Pacific Islanders

8 November 2008, Twickenham, London
England 39   T: Sackey (2), Cipriani, Kennedy, Mears; C: Cipriani (4); PG: Cipriani (2)
Pacific Islanders 13   T: Rabeni; C: Hola; PG: Hola, Bai

England vs Romania

England vs Romania	
Played:	4
Won:	4
Lost:	0
Drawn:	0
For:	268
Against:	21

Average score: 67–5.25

England percentages:
Won:	100%
Lost:	0%
Drawn:	0%

England vs Romania

5 January 1985, Twickenham, London
England 22   T: Smith; PG: Andrew (4); DG: Andrew (2)
Romania 15   PG: Alexandru (5)

13 May 1989, Dinamo Stadion, Bucharest
England 58   T: Oti (4), Guscott (3), Probyn, Richards; C: Hodgkinson (8);
                    PG: Hodgkinson; DG: Andrew
Romania 3   PG: Constantin

12 November 1994, Twickenham, London
England 54   T: A Underwood (2), R Underwood, Carling, Rodber, penalty try;
                    C: Andrew (6); PG: Andrew (4)
Romania 3   PG: Ivancuic

17 November 2001, Twickenham, London
England 134   T: Robinson (4), Luger (3), Cohen (3), Hodgson (2), Moody (2), Tindall (2),
                    Healey, Sanderson, Regan, Worsley; C: Hodgson (14); PG: Hodgson (2)
Romania 0

England vs Samoa

England vs Samoa	
Played:	5
Won:	5
Lost:	0
Drawn:	0
For:	190
Against:	78

Average score:
38–15.60

England percentages:

Won:	100%
Lost:	0%
Drawn:	0%

4 June 1995, Kings Park, Durban (RWC, Pool B)

England	44	T: Underwood (2), Back, penalty try; C: Callard (3); PG: Callard (5); DG: Catt
Western Samoa	22	T: Sini (2), Umaga; C: Fa'amasino (2); PG: Fa'amasino

16 December 1995, Twickenham, London

England	27	T: Dallaglio, Underwood; C: Grayson; PG: Grayson (5)
Western Samoa	9	PG: Kellett (3)

26 October 2003, Colonial Stadium, Melbourne (RWC, Pool C)

England	35	T: Back, penalty try, Balshaw, Vickery; C: Wilkinson (3); PG: Wilkinson (2); DG: Wilkinson
Samoa	22	T: Sititi; C: Va'a; PG: Va'a (5)

26 November 2005, Twickenham, London

England	40	T: Voyce (2), Hodgson, Ellis, Varndell; C: Hodgson (3); PG: Hodgson (3)
Samoa	3	PG: Vili

22 September 2007, Stade de la Beaujoire, Nantes (RWC, Pool A)

England	44	T: Sackey (2), Corry (2); C: Wilkinson (3); PG: Wilkinson (4); DG: Wilkinson (2)
Samoa	22	T: Poluleuligaga; C: Crichton; PG: Crichton (5)

England vs Scotland (Calcutta Cup)

England vs Scotland	
Played:	126
Won:	67
Lost:	42
Drawn:	17
For:	1,436
Against:	1,078

Average score:
11.4–8.56

England percentages:

Won:	53.17%
Lost:	33.33%
Drawn:	13.5%

England first played Scotland on 27 March 1871 at Raeburn Place in Edinburgh. The symbol of this historic match is the Calcutta Cup, a trophy awarded to the winner of the annual Six Nations game between England and Scotland, the oldest rugby trophy in the world, dating back to 1879. It is currently held by Scotland who claimed the trophy by defeating England 15–9 at Murrayfield in the 2008 Six Nations Championship. On Christmas Day 1872, a game of rugby football was played in Calcutta, India between 20 players representing England and 20 from Scotland, Ireland and Wales. The match was such a success that it was repeated a week later and ultimately led to the formation of the Calcutta Football Club in January 1873. The club joined the RFU in 1874 and despite the Indian climate not being suitable for rugby, the club prospered. However, when the club's free bar was discontinued membership dipped alarmingly. Other sports, such as tennis and polo, considered more suited to the local climate, eroded the number of 'gentlemen' available for rugby. With the drop in membership, the remaining members decided to disband but were keen to perpetuate the name of the club. They withdrew the club's funds from the bank in silver rupees and had them melted down and made into a cup which they presented to the RFU in 1878 with the proviso that it should be competed for annually. The cup is of Indian workmanship, approximately 45cm in height, the body finely engraved with three King cobras forming the handles; the domed lid is surmounted by an elephant which was copied from the Viceroy's own stock and is complete with a howdah: the ornate carriage for riding on the back of an elephant. The inscription on the wooden base reads:

The Calcutta Cup – presented to the Rugby Football Union by the Calcutta Football Club as an international challenge cup to be played for annually by England and Scotand, 1878

The base has plates attached which record the date of each match, with the name of the winning country and the names of the two captains. Interestingly, there is an anomaly in the records of the winning country on the base of the cup as it was first played for in 1879, but the plinth shows records going back to the first international in 1871: before the cup's existence. The original trophy is in a fragile state following years of poor treatment and cannot travel. In 1988, a prime example of such mistreatment took place when it was damaged by some drunken players, including English number 8 Dean Richards and Scottish flanker John Jeffrey who took the cup on a late-night Edinburgh binge, purportedly playing football with it along Princes Street. Jeffrey received a six-month ban from the SRU and Richards given a one-match ban by the English RFU. The Calcutta Club's initial wish was that the trophy be used as rugby's equivalent to the FA Cup. However, the RFU refused to turn the Calcutta Cup into a knock-out competition for club sides, believing that such 'competitiveness' ran against the amateur ethos of rugby. It was decided instead by the RFU that the cup should be presented to the winner of the annual England–Scotland game. The first Calcutta Cup match was played at Raeburn Place in Edinburgh on 10 March 1879, which ended in a draw and it was not until the following year, on 28 February 1880, that England became the first winners of the cup when they beat Scotland in Manchester. As of 2009, 116 Calcutta Cup matches have taken place.

27 March 1871, Raeburn Place, Edinburgh
Scotland   4 (1G 1T)   T: R Birkett, Green; C: Tobin
England   1 (1T)   T: Cross

5 February 1872, Kennington Oval, London
England   8 (1G 2T 1D)   T: Hamersley, D'Aguilar, Finney; C: Isherwood; DG: Freeman
Scotland   3 (1D)   DG: Cathcart

3 March 1873, Hamilton Crescent, Glasgow
Scotland   0
England   0

23 February 1874, Kennington Oval, London
England   3 (1D)   DG: Freeman
Scotland   1 (1T)   T: Finlay

8 March 1875, Raeburn Place, Edinburgh
Scotland   0
England   0

6 March 1876, Kennington Oval, London
England   4 (1G 1T)   T: Lee, Collins; C: Stokes
Scotland   0

5 March 1877, Raeburn Place, Edinburgh
Scotland   3 (1D)   DG: Cross
England   0

4 March 1878, Kennington Oval, London
England   0
Scotland   0

10 March 1879, Raeburn Place, Edinburgh
Scotland   3 (1D)   DG: Finlay
England   3 (1G)   T: Burton; C: Stokes

28 February 1880, Whalley Range, Manchester
England   9 (2G 3T)   T: Taylor (2), Burton, Fry, Gurdon; C: Stokes (2)
Scotland   3 (1G)   T: Brown; C: Cross

19 March 1881, Raeburn Place, Edinburgh
Scotland   4 (1G 1T)   T: Ainslie, Brown; C: Begbie
England   4 (1T 1D)   T: Rowley; DG: Stokes

4 March 1882, Whalley Range, Manchester
Scotland   2 (2T)   T: R Ainslee (2)
England   0

3 March 1883, Raeburn Place, Edinburgh
England   2 (2T)   T: Rotherham, Bolton
Scotland   1 (1T)   T: Reid

1 March 1884, Rectory Field, Blackheath
England   3 (1G)   T: Kindersley; C: Bolton
Scotland   1 (1T)   T: Jamieson

13 March 1886, Raeburn Place, Edinburgh
Scotland 0
England 0

5 March 1887, Whalley Range, Manchester
England 1 (1T) T: Jeffery
Scotland 1 (1T) T: Morton

1 March 1890, Raeburn Place, Edinburgh
England 6 (1G 1T) T: Evershed, Dyson; C: Jowett
Scotland 0

7 March 1891, Athletic Ground, Richmond
Scotland 9 T: W Neilson, J Orr; C: MacGregor (2); DG: Clauss
England 3 T: Lockwood; C: Alderson

5 March 1892, Raeburn Place, Edinburgh
England 5 T: Bromet; C: Lockwood
Scotland 0

4 March 1893, Headingley, Leeds
Scotland 8 DG: Boswell, Campbell
England 0

17 March 1894, Raeburn Place, Edinburgh
Scotland 6 T: Boswell (2)
England 0

9 March 1895, Athletic Ground, Richmond
Scotland 6 T: G Neilson; PG: G Neilson
England 3 PG: Byrne

14 March 1896, Old Hampden Park, Glasgow
Scotland 11 T: Fleming, Gedge, Gowans; C: Scott
England 0

13 March 1897, Fallowfield, Manchester
England 12 T: Fookes, Robinson; C: Byrne; DG: Byrne
Scotland 3 T: Bucher

12 March 1898, Powderhall, Edinburgh
Scotland 3 T: McEwan
England 3 T: Royds

11 March 1899, Rectory Field, Blackheath
Scotland 5 T: Gillespie; C: Thomson
England 0

10 March 1900, Inverleith, Edinburgh
Scotland 0
England 0

9 March 1901, Rectory Field, Blackheath
Scotland 18 T: Gillespie, Welsh, Timms, Fell; C: Gillespie (3)
England 3 T: Robinson

15 March 1902, Inverleith, Edinburgh
England 6 T: Williams, Taylor
Scotland 3 T: Fell

21 March 1903, Athletic Ground, Richmond
Scotland 10 T: Dallas, Simson; DG: Timms
England 6 T: Dobson, Forrest

19 March 1904, Inverleith, Edinburgh
Scotland 6 T: Crabbie, MacDonald
England 3 T: Vivyan

ENGLAND

18 March 1905, Athletic Ground, Richmond
Scotland 8   T: Simson, Stronach; C: Scott
England 0

17 March 1906, Inverleith, Edinburgh
England 9   T: Mills, Raphael, Simpson
Scotland 3   T: Purves

16 March 1907, Rectory Field, Blackheath
Scotland 8   T: Purves, Simson; C: Geddes
England 3   T: Peters

21 March 1908, Inverleith, Edinburgh
Scotland 16   T: MacLeod (2); C: Geddes; DG: Purves, Schulze
England 10   T: Birkett, Slocock; C: Lambert (2)

20 March 1909, Athletic Ground, Richmond
Scotland 18   T: Tennent (2), Gilray, Simson; C: Cunningham (3)
England 8   T: Mobbs, Watson; C: Palmer

19 March 1910, Inverleith, Edinburgh
England 14   T: Birkett (2), Berry, Ritson; C: Chapman
Scotland 5   T: MacPherson; C: MacCullum

18 March 1911, Twickenham, London
England 13   T: Birkett, Lawrie, Wodehouse; C: Lagden (2)
Scotland 8   T: Simson, Sutherland; C: Cunningham

16 March 1912, Inverleith, Edinburgh
Scotland 8   T: Sutherland, Usher; C: MacCullum
England 3   T: Holland

15 March 1913, Twickenham, London
England 3   T: Brown
Scotland 0

21 March 1914, Inverleith, Edinburgh
England 16   T: Lowe (3), Poulton; C: Harrison (2)
Scotland 15   T: Will (2), Huggan; C: Turner; DG: Bowie

20 March 1920, Twickenham, London
England 13   T: Harris, Kershaw, Lowe; C: Greenwood (2)
Scotland 4   DG: Bruce-Lockhart

19 March 1921, Inverleith, Edinburgh
England 18   T: Brown, Edwards, King, Woods; C: Hammett (3)
Scotland 0

18 March 1922, Twickenham, London
England 11   T: Lowe (2), Davies; C: Conway
Scotland 5   T: Dykes; C: Bertram

17 March 1923, Inverleith, Edinburgh
England 8   T: Smallwood, Voyce; C: Luddington
Scotland 6   T: Gracie, McLaren

15 March 1924, Twickenham, London
England 19   T: Catcheside, Myers, Wakefield; C: Conway (3); DG: Myers
Scotland 0

21 March 1925, Murrayfield, Edinburgh
Scotland 14   T: Nelson, Wallace; C: Drysdale, Gillies; DG: Waddell
England 11   T: Hamilton-Wickes, Wakefield; C: Luddington; PG: Luddington

20 March 1926, Twickenham, London
Scotland 17   T: Smith (2), Waddell; C: Waddell (2); DG: Dykes
England 9   T: Tucker, Voyce, Webb

19 March 1927, Murrayfield, Edinburgh
Scotland 21 T: Smith (2), Dykes, MacPherson, Scott; C: Gillies; DG: Waddell
England 13 T: Gibbs, Laird; C: Stanbury, Stark; PG: Stark

17 March 1928, Twickenham, London
England 6
Scotland 0 T: Hanley, Laird

16 March 1929, Murrayfield, Edinburgh
Scotland 12 T: I Smith (2), Brown, Nelson
England 6 T: Meikle, Novis

15 March 1930, Twickenham, London
England 0
Scotland 0

21 March 1931, Murrayfield, Edinburgh
Scotland 28 T: MacKintosh (2), Smith (2), Ford, Logan; C: Allan (5)
England 19 T: Tallent (2), Reeve (2); C: Black (2); PG: Black

19 March 1932, Twickenham, London
England 16 T: Aavold (2), Black, Tanner; C: Burland (2)
Scotland 3 T: Smith

18 March 1933, Murrayfield, Edinburgh
Scotland 3 T: Fyfe
England 0

17 March 1934, Twickenham, London
England 6 T: Booth, Meikle
Scotland 3 T: Shaw

16 March 1935, Murrayfield, Edinburgh
Scotland 10 T: Fyfe, Lambie; C: Fyfe (2)
England 7 T: Booth; DG: Cranmer

21 March 1936, Twickenham, London
England 9 T: Bolton, Candler, Cranmer
Scotland 8 T: Shaw; C: Fyfe; PG: Fyfe

20 March 1937, Murrayfield, Edinburgh
England 6 T: Sever, Unwin
Scotland 3 PG: D Shaw

19 March 1938, Twickenham, London
Scotland 21 T: Renwick (2), Shaw (2), Dick; PG: Crawford (2)
England 16 T: Unwin; DG: Reynolds ;PG: Parker (3)

18 March 1939, Murrayfield, Edinburgh
England 9 PG: Heaton (3)
Scotland 6 T: Murdoch, Shaw

15 March 1947, Twickenham, London
England 24 T: Bennett, Guest, Henderson, Holmes; C: Heaton (4); DG: Hall
Scotland 5 T: Jackson; C: Geddes

20 March 1948, Murrayfield, Edinburgh
Scotland 6 T: Drummond, Young
England 3 PG: Uren

19 March 1949, Twickenham, London
England 19 T: van Ryneveld (2), Guest, Hosking, Kennedy; C: Travers (2)
Scotland 3 PG: Wilson

18 March 1950, Murrayfield, Edinburgh
Scotland 13 T: Sloan (2), Abercrombie; C: Gray (2)
England 11 T: Smith (2); C: Hofmeyr; PG: Hofmeyr

ENGLAND

17 March 1951, Twickenham, London
England   5   T: White; C: Hook
Scotland   3   T: Cameron

15 March 1952, Murrayfield, Edinburgh
England   19   T: Evans, Winn, Woodward, Kendall-Carpenter; C: Hall (2); DG: Agar
Scotland   3   T: Johnston

21 March 1953, Twickenham, London
England   26   T: Bazley (2), Adkins, Butterfield, Stirling, Woodward; C: Hall (4)
Scotland   8   T: Henderson, Weatherstone C: Thomson

20 March 1954, Murrayfield, Edinburgh
England   13   T: Wilson (2), Young; C: Gibbs (2)
Scotland   3   T: Elgie

19 March 1955, Twickenham, London
England   9   T: Beer, Sykes; PG: Hazell
Scotland   6   T: Cameron; PG: Cameron

17 March 1956, Murrayfield, Edinburgh
England   11   T: Williams; C: Currie; PG: Currie (2)
Scotland   6   T: Stevenson; PG: Smith

16 March 1957, Twickenham, London
England   16   T: Davies, Higgins, Thompson; C: Challis (2); PG: Challis
Scotland   3   PG: Scotland

15 March 1958, Murrayfield, Edinburgh
Scotland   3   PG: Elliot
England   3   PG: Hastings

21 March 1959, Twickenham, London
England   3   PG: Risman
Scotland   3   PG: Scotland

19 March 1960, Murrayfield, Edinburgh
England   21   T: Roberts, Syrett, Young; C: Rutherford (3); DG: Sharp; PG: Rutherford
Scotland   12   T: A Smith; PG: Scotland (3)

18 March 1961, Twickenham, London
England   6   T: Roberts; PG: Horrocks-Taylor
Scotland   0

17 March 1962, Murrayfield, Edinburgh
Scotland   3   PG: Scotland
England   3   PG: Willcox

16 March 1963, Twickenham, London
England   10   T: Drake-Lee, Sharp; C: Willcox (2)
Scotland   8   T: Glasgow; C: Coughtrie; DG: Scotland

21 March 1964, Murrayfield, Edinburgh
Scotland   15   T: Glasgow, Bruce, Telfer; C: Wilson (3)
England   6   T: Rogers; PG: Hosen

20 March 1965, Twickenham, London
England   3   T: Hancock
Scotland   3   DG: Chisholm

19 March 1966, Murrayfield, Edinburgh
Scotland   6   T: Whyte; PG: Blaikie
England   3   DG: McFadyean

18 March 1967, Twickenham, London
England   27   T: McFadyean (2), Taylor, Webb; C: Hosen (3); DG: Finlan; PG: Hosen (2)
Scotland   14   T: Hinshelwood, Turner; C: Wilson; PG: Wilson (2)

16 March 1968, Murrayfield, Edinburgh
England   8   T: Coulman; C: Hiller; PG: Hiller
Scotland   6   DG: Connell; PG: Wilson

15 March 1969, Twickenham, London
England   8   T: Duckham (2); C: Hiller
Scotland   3   PG: Brown

21 March 1970, Murrayfield, Edinburgh
Scotland   14   T: Biggar, Turner; C: P Brown; PG: P Brown (2)
England   5   T: Spencer; C: Hiller

20 March 1971, Twickenham, London
Scotland   16   T: P Brown, Paterson, Rae; C: P Brown (2); DG: Paterson
England   15   T: Hiller, Neary; PG: Hiller (3)

27 March 1971, Murrayfield, Edinburgh
Scotland   26   T: Frame (2), Steele, Rea, P Brown; C: A Brown (4); PG: P Brown
England   6   PG: Hiller; DG: Cowman

18 March 1972, Murrayfield, Edinburgh
Scotland   23   T: P Brown, MacEwan; DG: Telfer; PG: P Brown (3), A Brown
England   9   PG: Old (3)

17 March 1973, Twickenham, London
England   20   T: Dixon (2), Evans, Squires; C: Jorden (2)
Scotland   13   T: Steele (2); C: Irvine; PG: Morgan

2 February 1974, Murrayfield, Edinburgh
Scotland   16   T: Irvine, Lauder; C: Irvine; PG: Irvine (2)
England   14   T: Cotton, Neary; DG: Rossborough; PG: Old

15 March 1975, Twickenham, London
England   7   T: Morley; PG: Bennett
Scotland   6   PG: Morgan (2)

21 February 1976, Murrayfield, Edinburgh
Scotland   22   T: Lawson (2), Leslie; C: Irvine (2); PG: Irvine (2)
England   12   T: Maxwell; C: Old; PG: Old (2)

15 January 1977, Twickenham, London
England   26   T: Kent, Slemen, Uttley, Young; C: Hignell (2); PG: Hignell (2)
Scotland   6   PG: Irvine (2)

4 March 1978, Murrayfield, Edinburgh
England   15   T: Nelmes, Squires; C: Young (2); PG: Dodge
Scotland   0

3 February 1979, Twickenham, London
England   7   T: Slemen; PG: Bennett
Scotland   7   T: Rutherford; PG: Irvine

15 March 1980, Murrayfield, Edinburgh
England   30   T: Carleton (3), Slemen, Smith; C: Hare (2); PG: Hare (2)
Scotland   18   T: Tomes, Rutherford; C: Irvine (2); PG: Irvine (2)

21 February 1981, Twickenham, London
England   23   T: Davies, Slemen, Woodward; C: Hare; PG: Hare (3)
Scotland   17   T: Munro (2), Calder; C: Irvine; PG: Irvine

16 January 1982, Murrayfield, Edinburgh
Scotland   9   DG: Rutherford; PG: Irvine (2)
England   9   PG: Dodge (2), Rose

5 March 1983, Twickenham, London
Scotland   22   T: Laidlaw, Smith; C: Dods; DG: Robertson; PG: Dods (3)
England   12   DG: Horton; PG: Hare (3)

ENGLAND

4 February 1984, Murrayfield, Edinburgh
Scotland   18   T: Johnstone, Kennedy; C: Dods (2); PG: Dods (2)
England   6   PG: Hare (2)

16 March 1985, Twickenham, London
England   10   T: Smith; PG: Andrew (2)
Scotland   7   T: Robertson; PG: Dods

15 February 1986, Murrayfield, Edinburgh
Scotland   33   T: Duncan, Rutherford, S Hastings; C: G Hastings (3); PG: G Hastings (5)
England   6   PG: Andrew (2)

4 April 1987, Twickenham, London
England   21   T: Rose, penalty try; C: Rose (2); PG: Rose (3)
Scotland   12   T: Robertson; C: G Hastings; PG: G Hastings (2)

5 March 1988, Murrayfield, Edinburgh
England   9   PG: Webb (2); DG: Andrew
Scotland   6   PG: G Hastings (2)

4 February 1989, Twickenham, London
England   12   PG: Andrew (2), Webb (2)
Scotland   12   T: Jeffrey; C: Dods; PG: Dods (2)

17 March 1990, Murrayfield, Edinburgh
Scotland   13   T: Stanger; PG: Chalmers (3)
England   7   T: Guscott; PG: Hodgkinson

16 February 1991, Twickenham, London
England   21   T: Heslop; C: Hodgkinson; PG: Hodgkinson (5)
Scotland   12   PG: Chalmers (4)

26 October 1991, Murrayfield, Edinburgh (RWC, S/F)
England   9   PG: Webb (2); DG: Andrew
Scotland   6   PG: G Hastings (2)

18 January 1992, Murrayfield, Edinburgh
England   25   T: R Underwood, Morris; C: Webb; PG: Webb (4); DG: Guscott
Scotland   7   T: White; PG: G Hastings

6 March 1993, Twickenham, London
England   26   T: A Underwood, Guscott, R Underwood; C: Webb; PG: Webb (3)
Scotland   12   PG: G Hastings (3); DG: Chalmers

5 February 1994, Murrayfield, Edinburgh
England   15   PG: Callard (5)
Scotland   14   T: Wainwright; PG: G Hastings (2); DG: Townsend

18 March 1995, Twickenham, London
England   24   PG: Andrew (7); DG: Andrew
Scotland   12   PG: G Hastings (2); DG: Chalmers (2)

2 March 1996, Murrayfield, Edinburgh
England   18   PG: Grayson (6)
Scotland   9   PG: Dods (3)

1 February 1997, Twickenham, London
England   41   T: Gomarsall, de Glanville, Carling, penalty try; C: Grayson (3); PG: Grayson (5)
Scotland   13   T: Ericksson; C: Shepherd; PG: Shepherd (2)

22 March 1998, Murrayfield, Edinburgh
England   34   T: Penalty try, Dawson, Healey, Grayson; C: Grayson (4); PG: Grayson; DG: Grayson
Scotland   20   T: Stanger, Longstaff; C: Lee (2); PG: Chalmers (2)

20 February 1999, Twickenham, London
England   24   T: Rodber, Luger, Beal; C: Wilkinson (3); PG: Wilkinson
Scotland   21   T: Tait (2), Townsend; C: Logan (3)

2 April 2000, Murrayfield, Edinburgh
Scotland   19   T: Hodge; C: Hodge; PG: Hodge (4)
England   13   T: Dallaglio; C: Wilkinson; PG: Wilkinson (2)

3 March 2001, Twickenham, London
England   43   T: Balshaw (2), Dallaglio (2), Hill, Greenwood; C: Wilkinson (5); PG: Wilkinson
Scotland   3   PG: Logan

2 February 2002, Murrayfield, Edinburgh
England   29   T: Robinson (2), Tindall, Cohen; C: Wilkinson (2), Hodgson; PG: Wilkinson
Scotland   3   PG: Hodge

22 March 2003, Twickenham, London
England   40   T: Robinson (2), Cohen, Lewsey; C: Wilkinson (3), Grayson; PG: Wilkinson (4)
Scotland   9   PG: Paterson (3)

21 February 2004, Murrayfield, Edinburgh
England   35   T: Cohen, Balshaw, Lewsey, Grewcock; C: Grayson (3); PG: Grayson (3)
Scotland   13   T: Danielli; C: Paterson; PG: Paterson (2)

19 March 2005, Twickenham, London
England   43   T: Noon (3), Worsley, Lewsey, Ellis, Cueto; C: Hodgson (4)
Scotland   22   T: S Lamont, Craig, Taylor; C: Paterson (2); PG: Paterson

25 February 2006, Murrayfield, Edinburgh
Scotland   18   PG: Paterson (5); DG: Parks
England   12   PG: Hodgson (4)

3 February 2007, Twickenham, London
England   42   T: Robinson (2), Wilkinson, Lund; C: Wilkinson (2); PG: Wilkinson (5); DG: Wilkinson
Scotland   20   T: Taylor, Dewey; C: Paterson (2); PG: Paterson (2)

8 February 2008, Murrayfield, Edinburgh
Scotland   15   PG: Paterson (4), Parks
England   9   PG: Wilkinson (3)

21 March 2009, Twickenham, London
England   26   T: Monye, Flutey, Tait; C: Flood; PG: Flood (2); DG: Care
Scotland   12   PG: Paterson (3), Godman

ENGLAND

Calcutta Cup			Current holder: England		Number of tiles: England 63, Scotland 39	
No.	Date	Venue	Result			Holder
1	02/03/1879	Raeburn Place, Edinburgh	Scotland	3-3	England	Drawn
2	07/03/1880	Whalley Range, Manchester	England	4-0	Scotland	England
3	06/03/1881	Raeburn Place, Edinburgh	Scotland	4-4	England	Drawn
4	04/03/1882	Whalley Range, Manchester	England	0-2	Scotland	Scotland
5	03/03/1883	Raeburn Place, Edinburgh	Scotland	1-2	England	England
6	01/03/1884	Rectory Field, Blackheath	England	3-1	Scotland	England
7	13/03/1886	Raeburn Place, Edinburgh	Scotland	0-0	England	Drawn
8	05/03/1887	Whalley Range, Manchester	England	1-1	Scotland	Drawn
9	01/03/1890	Raeburn Place, Edinburgh	Scotland	0-6	England	England
10	07/03/1891	Athletic Ground, Richmond	England	3-9	Scotland	Scotland
11	05/03/1892	Raeburn Place, Edinburgh	Scotland	0-5	England	England
12	04/03/1893	Headingley, Leeds	England	0-8	Scotland	Scotland
13	17/03/1894	Raeburn Place, Edinburgh	Scotland	6-0	England	Scotland
14	09/03/1895	Athletic Ground, Richmond	England	3-6	Scotland	Scotland
15	14/03/1896	Old Hampden Park, Glasgow	Scotland	11-0	England	Scotland
16	13/03/1897	Fallowfield, Manchester	England	8-3	Scotland	England
17	12/03/1898	Powderhall, Edinburgh	Scotland	3-3	England	Drawn
18	11/03/1899	Rectory Field, Blackheath	England	0-5	Scotland	Scotland
19	10/03/1900	Inverleith, Edinburgh	Scotland	0-0	England	Drawn
20	09/03/1901	Rectory Field, Blackheath	England	3-18	Scotland	Scotland
21	15/03/1902	Inverleith, Edinburgh	Scotland	3-6	England	England
22	21/03/1903	Athletic Ground, Richmond	England	6-10	Scotland	Scotland
23	19/03/1904	Inverleith, Edinburgh	Scotland	6-3	England	Scotland
24	18/03/1905	Athletic Ground, Richmond	England	0-8	Scotland	Scotland
25	17/03/1906	Inverleith, Edinburgh	Scotland	3-9	England	England
26	16/03/1907	Rectory Field, Blackheath	England	3-8	Scotland	Scotland
27	21/03/1908	Inverleith, Edinburgh	Scotland	16-10	England	Scotland
28	20/03/1909	Athletic Ground, Richmond	England	8-18	Scotland	Scotland
29	19/03/1910	Inverleith, Edinburgh	Scotland	5-14	England	England
30	18/03/1911	Twickenham, London	England	13-8	Scotland	England
31	16/03/1912	Inverleith, Edinburgh	Scotland	8-3	England	Scotland
32	15/03/1913	Twickenham, London	England	3-0	Scotland	England
33	21/03/1914	Inverleith, Edinburgh	Scotland	15-16	England	England
34	20/03/1920	Twickenham, London	England	13-4	Scotland	England
35	19/03/1921	Inverleith, Edinburgh	Scotland	0-18	England	England
36	18/03/1922	Twickenham, London	England	11-5	Scotland	England
37	17/03/1923	Inverleith, Edinburgh	Scotland	6-8	England	England
38	15/03/1924	Twickenham, London	England	19-0	Scotland	England
39	21/03/1925	Murrayfield, Edinburgh	Scotland	14-11	England	Scotland

No.	Date	Venue		Result		Holder
40	20/03/1926	Twickenham, London	England	9–17	Scotland	Scotland
41	19/03/1927	Murrayfield, Edinburgh	Scotland	21–13	England	Scotland
42	17/03/1928	Twickenham, London	England	6–0	Scotland	England
43	16/03/1929	Murrayfield, Edinburgh	Scotland	12–6	England	Scotland
44	15/03/1930	Twickenham, London	England	0–0	Scotland	Drawn
45	21/03/1931	Murrayfield, Edinburgh	Scotland	28–19	England	Scotland
46	19/03/1932	Twickenham, London	England	16–3	Scotland	England
47	18/03/1933	Murrayfield, Edinburgh	Scotland	3–0	England	Scotland
48	17/03/1934	Twickenham, London	England	6–3	Scotland	England
49	16/03/1935	Murrayfield, Edinburgh	Scotland	10–7	England	Scotland
50	21/03/1936	Twickenham, London	England	9–8	Scotland	England
51	20/03/1937	Murrayfield, Edinburgh	Scotland	3–6	England	England
52	19/03/1938	Twickenham, London	England	16–21	Scotland	Scotland
53	18/03/1939	Murrayfield, Edinburgh	Scotland	6–9	England	England
54	15/03/1947	Twickenham, London	England	24–5	Scotland	England
55	20/03/1948	Murrayfield, Edinburgh	Scotland	6–3	England	Scotland
56	19/03/1949	Twickenham, London	England	19–3	Scotland	England
57	18/03/1950	Murrayfield, Edinburgh	Scotland	13–11	England	Scotland
58	17/03/1951	Twickenham, London	England	5–3	Scotland	England
59	15/03/1952	Murrayfield, Edinburgh	Scotland	3–19	England	England
60	21/03/1953	Twickenham, London	England	26–8	Scotland	England
61	20/03/1954	Murrayfield, Edinburgh	Scotland	3–13	England	England
62	19/03/1955	Twickenham, London	England	9–6	Scotland	England
63	17/03/1956	Murrayfield, Edinburgh	Scotland	6–11	England	England
64	16/03/1957	Twickenham, London	England	16–3	Scotland	England
65	15/03/1958	Murrayfield, Edinburgh	Scotland	3–3	England	Drawn
66	21/03/1959	Twickenham, London	England	3–3	Scotland	Drawn
67	19/03/1960	Murrayfield, Edinburgh	Scotland	12–21	England	England
68	18/03/1961	Twickenham, London	England	6–0	Scotland	England
69	17/03/1962	Murrayfield, Edinburgh	Scotland	3–3	England	Drawn
70	16/03/1963	Twickenham, London	England	10–8	Scotland	England
71	21/03/1964	Murrayfield, Edinburgh	Scotland	15–6	England	Scotland
72	20/03/1965	Twickenham, London	England	3–3	Scotland	Drawn
73	19/03/1966	Murrayfield, Edinburgh	Scotland	6–3	England	Scotland
74	18/03/1967	Twickenham, London	England	27–14	Scotland	England
75	16/03/1968	Murrayfield, Edinburgh	Scotland	6–8	England	England
76	15/03/1969	Twickenham, London	England	8–3	Scotland	England
77	21/03/1970	Murrayfield, Edinburgh	Scotland	14–5	England	Scotland
78	20/03/1971	Twickenham, London	England	15–16	Scotland	Scotland
79	18/03/1972	Murrayfield, Edinburgh	Scotland	23–9	England	Scotland

ENGLAND

ENGLAND

No.	Date	Venue	Result			Holder
80	17/03/1973	Twickenham, London	England	20–13	Scotland	England
81	02/02/1974	Murrayfield, Edinburgh	Scotland	16–14	England	Scotland
82	15/03/1975	Twickenham, London	England	7–6	Scotland	England
83	21/02/1976	Murrayfield, Edinburgh	Scotland	22–12	England	Scotland
84	15/01/1977	Twickenham, London	England	26–6	Scotland	England
85	04/03/1978	Murrayfield, Edinburgh	Scotland	0–15	England	England
86	03/02/1979	Twickenham, London	England	7–7	Scotland	Drawn
87	15/03/1980	Murrayfield, Edinburgh	Scotland	18–30	England	England
88	21/02/1981	Twickenham, London	England	23–17	Scotland	England
89	16/01/1982	Murrayfield, Edinburgh	Scotland	9–9	England	Drawn
90	05/03/1983	Twickenham, London	England	12–22	Scotland	Scotland
91	04/02/1984	Murrayfield, Edinburgh	Scotland	18–6	England	Scotland
92	16/03/1985	Twickenham, London	England	10–7	Scotland	England
93	15/02/1986	Murrayfield, Edinburgh	Scotland	33–6	England	Scotland
94	04/04/1987	Twickenham, London	England	21–12	Scotland	England
95	05/03/1988	Murrayfield, Edinburgh	Scotland	6–9	England	England
96	04/02/1989	Twickenham, London	England	12–12	Scotland	Drawn
97	17/03/1990	Murrayfield, Edinburgh	Scotland	13–7	England	Scotland
98	16/02/1991	Twickenham, London	England	21–12	Scotland	England
99	18/01/1992	Murrayfield, Edinburgh	Scotland	7–25	England	England
100	06/03/1993	Twickenham, London	England	26–12	Scotland	England
101	05/02/1994	Murrayfield, Edinburgh	Scotland	14–15	England	England
102	18/03/1995	Twickenham, London	England	24–12	Scotland	England
103	02/03/1996	Murrayfield, Edinburgh	Scotland	9–18	England	England
104	01/02/1997	Twickenham, London	England	41–13	Scotland	England
105	22/03/1998	Murrayfield, Edinburgh	Scotland	20–34	England	England
106	20/02/1999	Twickenham, London	England	24–21	Scotland	England
107	02/04/2000	Murrayfield, Edinburgh	Scotland	19–13	England	Scotland
108	03/03/2001	Twickenham, London	England	43–3	Scotland	England
109	02/02/2002	Murrayfield, Edinburgh	Scotland	3–29	England	England
110	22/03/2003	Twickenham, London	England	40–9	Scotland	England
111	21/02/2004	Murrayfield, Edinburgh	Scotland	13–35	England	England
112	19/03/2005	Twickenham, London	England	43–22	Scotland	England
113	25/02/2006	Murrayfield, Edinburgh	Scotland	18–12	England	Scotland
114	03/02/2007	Twickenham, London	England	42–20	Scotland	England
115	08/02/2008	Murrayfield, Edinburgh	Scotland	15–9	England	Scotland
116	21/03/2009	Twickenham, London	England	26–12	Scotland	England

England vs South Africa

England–South Africa games have produced some memorable rugby since the first match more than a century ago at Crystal Palace in 1906. One has tended to dominate the other over different periods; South Africa for more than the first half of the twentieth century from 1906 right through to 1961 with their immensely powerful touring sides. England's first victory was in 1969, followed by a shock victory three years later when they beat the much-favoured Springboks in South Africa. South Africa comprehensively beat England 2–0 in 1984, but apartheid isolation meant that it was not until 1992 that the two sides met again. After the drawn series of 1994, South Africa dominated the English for the next six years, losing just once, in 1998. The 1999 Springbok victory in Paris in the quarter-final of the RWC will forever be remembered as one of South Africa's greatest victories. Flyhalf Jannie de Beer forced Martin Johnson's team out of the RWC through perhaps the greatest goal-kicking display ever witnessed in rugby as he kicked a South African record of 34 points in the match, including a world-record haul of five drop goals, all in the second half (described by the English press as England's water torture: 'drop, drop, drop ...') . Following South Africa's win in 2000, however, they were not to beat the English for the next six seasons as they suffered the wrath of Jonny Wilkinson's deadly left boot as he kicked 99 points in five encounters over this period. In 2006, South Africa reversed the trend, winning at Twickenham, and in 2007 notched up four consecutive wins, inflicting record scorelines and defeats on the English, most memorably in the 2007 pool A encounter by 36–0 and again during the RWC final. In 2008, South Africa thumped England at Twickenham 42–6, a record defeat for England at that ground.

England vs South Africa	
Played:	31
Won:	12
Lost:	18
Drawn:	1
For:	480
Against:	640

Average score:
15.48–20.65

England percentages:

Won:	38.7%
Lost:	58.07%
Drawn:	3.23%

8 December 1906, Crystal Palace, London
| England | 3 | T: Brooks |
| South Africa | 3 | T: Millar |

4 January 1913, Twickenham, London
| South Africa | 9 | T: J Morkel; PG: D Morkel (2) |
| England | 3 | T: Poulton |

2 January 1932, Twickenham, London
| South Africa | 7 | T: Bergh; DG: Brand |
| England | 0 | |

5 January 1952, Twickenham, London
| South Africa | 8 | T: du Toit; C: Muller; PG: Muller |
| England | 3 | T: Winn |

7 January 1961, Twickenham, London
| South Africa | 5 | T: Hopwood; C: du Preez |
| England | 0 | |

20 December 1969, Twickenham, London
| England | 11 | T: Larter, Pullin; C: Hiller; PG: Hiller |
| South Africa | 8 | T: Greyling; C: Visagie; PG: Visagie |

3 June 1972, Ellis Park, Johannesburg
| England | 18 | T: Morley; C: Doble; PG: Doble (4) |
| South Africa | 9 | PG: Snyman (3) |

2 June 1984, Boet Erasmus Stadium, Port Elizabeth
| South Africa | 33 | T: Gerber, C du Plessis, Louw; C: Heunis (3); PG: Heunis (5) |
| England | 15 | PG: Hare (4); DG: Horton |

9 June 1984, Ellis Park, Johannesburg
| South Africa | 35 | T: Gerber (3), Stofberg, Sonnekus, Tobias; C: Heunis (3), Tobias; PG: Heunis |
| England | 9 | PG: Hare (3) |

14 November 1992, Twickenham, London
| England | 33 | T: Underwood, Guscott, Morris, Carling; C: Webb (2); PG: Webb (3) |
| South Africa | 16 | T: Strauss C: Botha; PG: Botha (2); DG: Botha |

ENGLAND

4 June 1994, Loftus Versfeld, Pretoria
England	32	T: Clarke, Andrew; C: Andrew (2); PG: Andrew (5); DG: Andrew
South Africa	15	PG: Joubert (5)

11 June 1994, Newlands, Cape Town
South Africa	27	T: le Roux, Joubert; C: Joubert; PG: Joubert (2), le Roux (3)
England	9	PG: Andrew (3)

18 November 1995, Twickenham, London
South Africa	24	T: Williams (2), van der Westhuizen; PG: Stransky (3)
England	14	T: de Glanville; PG: Callard (3)

29 November 1997, Twickenham, London
South Africa	29	T: Garvey, Andrews, Swanepoel, Snyman; C: Honiball (2), Montgomery; PG: Honiball
England	11	T: Greenstock; PG: Catt (2)

4 July 1998, Norwich Park Newlands, Cape Town
South Africa	18	T: van der Westhuizen, Terblanche; C: Montgomery; PG: Montgomery (2)
England	0	

5 December 1998, Twickenham, London
England	13	T: Guscott; C: Dawson; PG: Dawson (2)
South Africa	7	T: Rossouw; C: Montgomery

24 October 1999, Stade de France, Paris (RWC, Q/F)
South Africa	44	T: van der Westhuizen, Rossouw; C: de Beer (2); PG: de Beer (5); DG: de Beer (5)
England	21	PG: Grayson (6), Wilkinson

17 June 2000, Loftus Versfeld, Pretoria
South Africa	18	PG: van Straaten (6)
England	13	T: Luger; C: Stimpson; PG: Stimpson (2)

24 June 2000, Free State Stadium, Bloemfontein
England	27	PG: Wilkinson (8); DG: Wilkinson
South Africa	22	T: van der Westhuizen; C: Montgomery; PG: van Straaten (4), Montgomery

2 December 2000, Twickenham, London
England	25	T: Greenwood; C: Wilkinson; PG: Wilinson (6)
South Africa	17	T: van Straaten; PG: van Straaten (4)

24 November 2001, Twickenham, London
England	29	T: Luger; PG: Wilkinson (7); DG: Catt
South Africa	9	PG: van Straaten (3)

23 November 2002, Twickenham, London
England	53	T: penalty try, Back, Hill, Cohen, Dallaglio, Greenwood (2); C: Stimpson (2), Gomarsall (2), Wilkinson, Dawson; PG: Wilkinson (2)
South Africa	3	PG: Pretorius

18 October 2003, Subiaco Oval, Perth (RWC, Pool C)
England	25	T: Greenwood; C: Wilkinson; PG: Wilkinson (4); DG: Wilkinson (2)
South Africa	6	PG: Koen (2)

20 November 2004, Twickenham, London
England	32	T: Hodgson, Cueto; C: Hodgson (2); PG: Hodgson (5); DG: Hodgson
South Africa	16	T: Habana; C: Montgomery; PG: Montgomery (3)

18 November 2006, Twickenham, London
England	23	T: Cueto, Vickery; C: Goode (2); PG: Hodgson (2), Goode
South Africa	21	T: James, Ndungane; C: James; PG: James (2); DG: Steyn

25 November 2006, Twickenham, London
South Africa	25	T: van der Linde; C: Pretorius; PG: Pretorius (2); DG: Pretorius (4)
England	14	T: Cueto; PG: Goode (3)

26 May 2007, Vodacom Park, Bloemfontein
South Africa	58	T: Habana (2), van der Linde, Steyn, Burger, Willemse, de Villiers; C: Montgomery (7); PG: Montgomery (3)
England	10	T: Simpson-Daniel; C: Wilkinson; PG: Wilkinson

2 June 2007, Loftus Versfeld, Pretoria
South Africa   55   T: Habana (2), Spies (2), Burger, Montgomery, Botha, Januarie; C: Montgomery (5), James; PG: Montgomery
England   22   T: Scarbrough; C: Wilkinson; PG: Wilkinson (5)

14 September 2007, Stade de France, Paris (RWC, Pool A)
South Africa   36   T: Pietersen (2), Smith; C: Montgomery (3); PG: Montgomery (4), Steyn
England   0

20 October 2007, Stade de France, Paris (RWC, Final)
South Africa   15   PG: Montgomery (4), Steyn
England   6   PG: Wilkinson (2)

22 November 2008, Twickenham, London
South Africa   42   T: Rossouw, Pienaar, Jacobs, Fourie, Habana; C: Pienaar (3), Steyn; PG: Pienaar (3)
England   6   PG: Cipriani (2)

England vs Tonga

15 October 1999, Twickenham, London (RWC, Pool B)
England   101   T: Greenwood (2), Healey (2), Luger (2), Perry, Greening (2), Guscott (2), Dawson, Hill; C: Grayson (12); PG: Grayson (4)
Tonga   10   T: Tiueti; C: S Tu'ipulotu; PG: S Tu'ipulotu

28 September 2007, Parc des Princes, Paris (RWC, Pool A)
England   36   T: Sackey (2), Tait, Farrell C: Wilkinson (2) PG: Wilkinson (2) PG: Wilkinson (2)
Tonga   20   T: Hufanga, T'Pole C: Hola (2) PG: Hola (2)

England vs United States of America

England vs USA	
Played:	5
Won:	5
Lost:	0
Drawn:	0
For:	253
Against:	52

Average score:
50.6–10.4

England percentages:
Won:	100%
Lost:	0%
Drawn:	0%

3 June 1987, Concord Oval, Sydney (RWC, Pool 1)
England   34   T: Winterbottom (2), Dooley, Harrison; C: Webb (3); PG: Webb (4)
USA   6   T: Purcell, C: Nelson

11 October 1991, Twickenham, London
England   37   T: Underwood (2), Carling, Skinner, Heslop; C: Hodgkinson (4); PG: Hodgkinson (3)
USA   9   T: Nelson; C: Williams; PG: Williams

21 August 1999, Twickenham, London
England   106   T: Guscott (4), Back (2), Luger (2), Perry (2), Hill, Dawson, de Glanville, Greening, Johnson, penalty try; C: Wilkinson (13)
USA   8   T: Sucher; PG: Dalzell

16 June 2001, Boxer Stadium, San Francisco
England   48   T: Lewsey (2), Lloyd (2), West, P Sanderson, Moody, Worsley; C: Walder (4)
USA   19   T: Niciqa (2), Grobler; C: Wells (2)

8 September 2007, Stade Felix Bollaert, Lens (RWC, Pool A)
England   28   T: Robinson, Barkley, Rees; C: Barkley (2); PG: Barkley (3)
USA   10   T: Moeakiola; C: Hercus; PG: Hercus

England vs Uruguay

2 November 2003 Suncorp Stadium, Brisbane (RWC, Pool C)
England   111   T: Lewsey (5), Balshaw (2), Catt (2), Gomarsall (2), Robinson (2), Moody, Luger, Abbott, Greenwood; C: Grayson (11), Catt (2)
Uruguay   13   T: Lemoine; C: Menchaca; PG: Menchaca (2)

England vs Wales	
Played:	118
Won:	53
Lost:	53
Drawn:	12
For:	1,500
Against:	1,309

Average score:
12.71–11.09

England percentages:

Won:	44.92%
Lost:	44.92%
Drawn:	10.16%

England vs Wales

On 19 February 1881, England played Wales for the first time, at Richardson's Field. The result was extremely one-sided, with England winning by 30 $^{(7G\ 6T\ 1D)}$–0 (an equivalent scoreline today of 82–0). Welsh rugby duly improved and in 1890 they beat the English. The series is the most closely fought in the game's history: in 118 clashes during 128 years of rugby each has won 53 times, with 12 games drawn. In five generations of rugby each has enjoyed periods of domination. The Welsh are remembered for their glory years of the 1970s, the English dominating in the 1990s and early years of the millennium, posting some record scores in the process. It is one of the most hotly anticipated fixtures on the international calendar, with the two nations never forgetting their competitive history. In 1977, Welsh captain Phil Bennett was quoted as saying of the English in a pre-game pep talk:

'Look what these bastards have done to Wales. They've taken our coal, our water and our steel. They buy our homes and live in them for a fortnight every year. What have they given us? Absolutely nothing. We've been exploited, raped, controlled and punished by the English – and that's who you are playing this afternoon.'

19 February 1881, Richardson's Field, Blackheath		
England	30 $^{(7G\ 6T\ 1D)}$	T: Burton (4), Budd, Fernandes, Hunt, Rowley, Taylor, Twynam, Vassal (3); C: Stokes (6), Hunt; DG: Hunt
Wales	0	

16 December 1882, St Helen's, Swansea		
England	10 $^{(2G\ 4T)}$	T: Wade (3), Bolton, Henderson, Thomson; C: Evanson (2)
Wales	0	

5 January 1884, Cardigan Fields, Leeds		
England	5 $^{(1G\ 2T)}$	T: Rotherham, Wade, Twynam; C: Bolton
Wales	3 $^{(1G)}$	T: Allen; C: Lewis

3 January 1885, St Helen's, Swansea		
England	7 $^{(1G\ 4T)}$	T: Hawcridge, Kindersley, Ryalls, Teggin, Wade; C: Payne
Wales	4 $^{(1G\ 1T)}$	T: Jordan (2); C: Taylor

2 January 1886, Rectory Field, Blackheath		
England	5 $^{(2T\ 1GM)}$	T: Wade, Wilkinson; GM: Stoddart
Wales	3 $^{(1G)}$	T: Stadden; C: Taylor

8 January 1887, Stradey Park, Llanelli		
Wales	0	
England	0	

15 February 1890, Crown Flatt, Dewsbury		
Wales	1 $^{(1T)}$	T: Stadden
England	0	

3 January 1891, Rodney Parade, Newport		
England	7	T: Christopherson (2), Budworth; C: Alderson (2)
Wales	3	T: Pearson; C: Bancroft

2 January 1892, Rectory Field, Blackheath		
England	17	T: Alderson, Evershed, Hubbard, Nichol; C: Lockwood (2), Alderson
Wales	0	

7 January 1893, Cardiff Arms Park, Cardiff		
Wales	12	T: Gould (2), Biggs; C: Bancroft; PG: Bancroft
England	11	T: Marshall (3), Lohden; C: Stoddart

6 January 1894, Birkenhead Park, Birkenhead
England   24   T: Bradshaw, Morfitt, Lockwood, Taylor; C: Lockwood (3), Taylor; GM: Taylor
Wales   3   T: Parfitt

5 January 1895, St Helen's, Swansea
England   14   T: Carey, Leslie-Jones, Thomson, Woods; C: Mitchell
Wales   6   T: Elsey, Graham

4 January 1896, Rectory Field, Blackheath
England   25   T: Cattell (2), Fookes (2), Morfitt (2), Mitchell; C: Taylor, Valentine
Wales   0

9 January 1897, Rodney Parade, Newport
Wales   11   T: Pearson, Boucher, Jones; C: Bancroft
England   0

2 April 1898, Rectory Field, Blackheath
England   14   T: Fookes (2), F Stout, P Stout; C: Byrne
Wales   7   T: Huzzey; DG: Huzzey

7 January 1899, St Helen's, Swansea
Wales   26   T: Llewellyn (4), Huzzey (2); C: Bancroft (4)
England   3   T: Robinson

6 January 1900, Kingsholm, Gloucester
Wales   13   T: Hellings, Trew; C: Bancroft (2); PG: Bancroft
England   3   T: Nicholson

5 January 1901, Cardiff Arms Park, Cardiff
Wales   13   T: Hodges, Nicholls, Williams; C: Bancroft (2)
England   0

11 January 1902, Rectory Field, Blackheath
England   8   T: Dobson, Robinson; C: Alexander
Wales   9   T: Gabe, Osborne; PG: Strand-Jones

10 January 1903, St Helen's, Swansea
Wales   21   T: Hodges (3), Owen, Pearson; C: Strand-Jones (3)
England   5   T: Dobson; C: Taylor

9 January 1904 Welford Road, Leicester
England   14   T: Elliot (2), Brettargh; C: F Stout; PG: Gamlin
Wales   14   T: Llewellyn, Morgan; C: Winfield (2); GM: Winfield

14 January 1905, Cardiff Arms Park, Cardiff
Wales   25   T: Morgan (2), Gabe, Harding, D Jones, Llewellyn, Watkins; C: Davies (2)
England   0

13 January 1906, Athletic Ground, Richmond
Wales   16   T: Hodges, Maddocks, Morgan, C Pritchard; C: Winfield (2)
England   3   T: Hudson

12 January 1907, St Helen's, Swansea
Wales   22   T: Maddocks (2), Williams (2), Brown, Gibbs; C: Gibbs (2)
England   0

18 January 1908, Ashton Gate, Bristol
Wales   28   T: Gabe (2), Bush, Gibbs, Trew; C: Winfield (2), Bush; PG: Winfield; DG: Bush
England   18   T: Birkett (2), Lapage, Williamson; C: Wood (2), Roberts

16 January 1909, Cardiff Arms Park, Cardiff
Wales   8   T: Hopkins, Williams; C: Bancroft
England   0

15 January 1910, Twickenham, London
England   11   T: Chapman, Solomon; C: Chapman; PG: Chapman
Wales   6   T: Gibbs, Webb

ENGLAND

21 January 1911, St Helen's, Swansea
| Wales | 15 | T: Gibbs, Morgan, Spiller, Pugsley; PG: Birt |
| England | 11 | T: Roberts, Kewney, Scholfield; C: Lambert |

20 January 1912, Twickenham, London
| England | 8 | T: Brougham, Pym; C: Chapman |
| Wales | 0 | |

18 January 1913, Cardiff Arms Park, Cardiff
| England | 12 | T: Coates, Pillman; C: Greenwood; DG: Poulton |
| Wales | 0 | |

17 January 1914, Twickenham, London
| England | 10 | T: Brown, Pillman; C: Chapman (2) |
| Wales | 9 | T: W Watts; C: Bancroft; DG: Hirst |

17 January 1920, St Helen's, Swansea
| Wales | 19 | T: Powell, Shea; C: Shea; DG: Shea (2); PG: Shea |
| England | 5 | T: Day; C: Day |

15 January 1921, Twickenham, London
| England | 18 | T: Smallwood (2), Kershaw, Lowe; C: Hammett; DG: Davies |
| Wales | 3 | T: Ring |

21 January 1922, Cardiff Arms Park, Cardiff
| Wales | 28 | T: Bowen, Delahay, I Evans, Parker, Hiddlestone, Palmer, Richards, Whitfield; C: Rees (2) |
| England | 6 | T: Day, Lowe |

20 January 1923, Twickenham, London
| England | 7 | T: Price; DG: Smallwood |
| Wales | 3 | T: Michael |

19 January 1924, St Helen's, Swansea
| England | 17 | T: Catcheside (2), Jacob, Locke, Myers; C: Conway |
| Wales | 9 | T: Johnson, T Jones, Owen |

17 January 1925, Twickenham, London
| England | 12 | T: Hamilton-Wickes, Kittermaster, Voyce; PG: Armstrong |
| Wales | 6 | T: Thomas, James |

16 January 1926, Cardiff Arms Park, Cardiff
| Wales | 3 | T: Andrews |
| England | 3 | T: Wakefield |

15 January 1927, Twickenham, London
| England | 11 | T: Corbett; C: Stanbury; GM: Corbett; PG: Stanbury |
| Wales | 9 | T: Andrews, Harding; PG: Male |

21 January 1928, St Helen's, Swansea
| England | 10 | T: Taylor, Laird; C: Richardson (2) |
| Wales | 8 | T: Bartlett, D John; C: Jones |

19 January 1929, Twickenham, London
| England | 8 | T: Wilkinson(2); C: Wilson |
| Wales | 3 | T: Morley |

18 January 1930, Cardiff Arms Park, Cardiff
| England | 11 | T: Reeve (2); C: Black; PG: Black |
| Wales | 3 | T: Jones-Davies |

17 January 1931, Twickenham, London
| England | 11 | T: Burland; C: Burland; PG: Black (2) |
| Wales | 11 | T: Jones-Davies, Morley; C: Bassett; GM: Powell |

16 January 1932, St Helen's, Swansea
| Wales | 12 | T: Boon; C: Bassett; DG: Boon; PG: Bassett |
| England | 5 | T: Coley; C: Barr |

21 January 1933, Twickenham, London
Wales   7   T: Boon; DG: Boon
England   3   T: Elliot

20 January 1934, Cardiff Arms Park, Cardiff
England   9   T: Meikle (2), Warr
Wales   0

19 January 1935, Twickenham, London
England   3   PG: Boughton
Wales   3   T: Wooller

18 January 1936, St Helen's, Swansea
Wales   0
England   0

16 January 1937, Twickenham, London
England   4   DG: Sever
Wales   3   T: Wooller

15 January 1938, Cardiff Arms Park, Cardiff
Wales   14   T: McCarley, I Rees; C: Jenkins; PG: Jenkins (2)
England   8   T: Candler, Sever; C: Freakes

21 January 1939, Twickenham, London
England   3   T: Teden
Wales   0

18 January 1947, Cardiff Arms Park, Cardiff
England   9   T: White; C: Gray; DG: Hall
Wales   6   T: Stephens, Evans

17 January 1948, Twickenham, London
England   3   PG: Newman
Wales   3   T: K Jones

15 January 1949, Cardiff Arms Park, Cardiff
Wales   9   T: L Williams (2), Meredith
England   3   DG: Hall

21 January 1950, Twickenham, London
Wales   11   T: Cale, C Davies; C: L Jones; PG: L Jones
England   5   T: Smith; C: Hofmeyr

20 January 1951, St Helen's, Swansea
Wales   23   T: Matthews (2), Thomas (2), K Jones; C: L Jones (4)
England   5   T: Rittson-Thomas; C: Hewitt

19 January 1952, Twickenham, London
England   6   T: Agar, Woodward
Wales   8   T: K Jones (2); C: M Thomas

17 January 1953, Cardiff Arms Park, Cardiff
England   8   T: Cannell; C: Hall; PG: Woodward
Wales   3   PG: Davies

16 January 1954, Twickenham, London
England   9   T: Woodward (2), Winn
Wales   6   T: Rowlands; PG: Rowlands

22 January 1955, Cardiff Arms Park, Cardiff
Wales   3   PG: Edwards
England   0

21 January 1956, Twickenham, London
Wales   8   T: Davies, Robbins; C: Owen
England   3   PG: Allison

19 January 1957, Cardiff Arms Park, Cardiff
England   3   PG: Allison
Wales   0

18 January 1958, Twickenham, London
England   3   T: Thompson
Wales   3   PG: T Davies

17 January 1959, Cardiff Arms Park, Cardiff
Wales   5   T: Bebb; C: T Davies
England   0

16 January 1960, Twickenham, London
England   14   T: Roberts (2); C: Rutherford; PG: Rutherford (2)
Wales   6   PG: T Davies (2)

21 January 1961, Cardiff Arms Park, Cardiff
Wales   6   T: Bebb (2)
England   3   T: Young

20 January 1962, Twickenham, London
England   0
Wales   0

19 January 1963, Cardiff Arms Park, Cardiff
England   13   T: Owen, Phillips; C: Sharp (2); DG: Sharp
Wales   6   T: Hayward; PG: Hodgson

18 January 1964, Twickenham, London
England   6   T: Perry, Ranson
Wales   6   T: Bebb (2)

16 January 1965, Cardiff Arms Park, Cardiff
Wales   14   T: S Watkins (2), H Morgan; C: T Price; DG: Watkins
England   3   PG: Rutherford

15 January 1966, Twickenham, London
Wales   11   T: Pask; C: T Price; PG: T Price (2)
England   6   T: Perry; PG: Rutherford

15 April 1967, Cardiff Arms Park, Cardiff
Wales   34   T: G Davies (2), Jarrett, Morris, Bebb; C: Jarrett (5); DG: Raybould; PG: Jarrett (2)
England   21   T: Barton (2), Savage; PG: Hosen (4)

20 January 1968, Twickenham, London
England   11   T: McFadyean, Redwood; C: Hiller; PG: Hiller
Wales   11   T: Edwards, Wanbon; C: Jarrett; DG: John

12 April 1969, National Stadium, Cardiff
Wales   30   T: M Richards (4), John; C: Jarrett (3); DG: John; PG: Jarrett (2)
England   9   PG: Hiller (3)

28 February 1970, Twickenham, London
Wales   17   T: T Davies, John, J Williams, Hopkins; C: J Williams; DG: John
England   13   T: Duckham, Novak; C: Hiller (2); PG: Hiller

16 January 1971, National Stadium, Cardiff
Wales   22   T: G Davies (2), Bevan; C: Taylor (2); DG: John (2); PG: J Williams
England   6   T: Hannaford; PG: Rossborough

15 January 1972, Twickenham, London
Wales   12   T: J Williams; C: John; PG: John (2)
England   3   PG: Hiller

20 January 1973, National Stadium, Cardiff
Wales   25   T: J Bevan (2), G Davies, Edwards, A Lewis; C: Bennett; PG: Taylor
England   9   DG: Cowman; PG: Doble (2)

16 March 1974, Twickenham, London
England   16   T: Duckham, Ripley; C: Old; PG: Old (2)
Wales   12   T: T Davies; C: Bennett; PG: Bennett (2)

15 February 1975, National Stadium, Cardiff
Wales   20   T: G Davies, Fenwick, JJ Williams; C: Martin; PG: Martin (2)
England   4   T: Horton

17 January 1976, Twickenham, London
Wales   21   T: J Williams (2), Edwards; C: Fenwick (3); PG: Martin
England   9   PG: Hignell (3)

5 March 1977, National Stadium, Cardiff
Wales   14   T: Edwards, J Williams; PG: Fenwick (2)
England   9   PG: Hignell (3)

4 February 1978, Twickenham, London
Wales   9   PG: Bennett (3)
England   6   PG: Hignell (2)

17 March 1979, National Stadium, Cardiff
Wales   27   T: E Rees, D Richards, Ringer, M Roberts, JJ Williams; C: Martin, Fenwick; DG: W Davies
England   3   PG: Bennett

16 February 1980, Twickenham, London
England   9   PG: Hare (3)
Wales   8   T: E Rees, Squire

17 January 1981, National Stadium, Cardiff
Wales   21   T: W Davies; C: Fenwick; DG: W Davies; PG: Fenwick (4)
England   19   T: Hare; PG: Hare (5)

6 March 1982, Twickenham, London
England   17   T: Carleton, Slemen; PG: Hare (3)
Wales   7   T: J Lewis; DG: W Davies

5 February 1983, National Stadium, Cardiff
Wales   13   T: Squire; DG: Dacey; PG: Wyatt (2)
England   13   T: Carleton; DG: Cusworth; PG: Hare (2)

17 March 1984, Twickenham, London
Wales   24   T: Hadley; C: H Davies PG: H Davies (4); DG: Dacey (2)
England   15   PG: Hare (5)

20 April 1985, National Stadium, Cardiff
Wales   24   T: J Davies, Roberts; C: Thorburn (2); PG: Thorburn (3); DG: J Davies
England   15   T: Smith; C: Andrew; PG: Andrew (2); DG: Andrew

17 January 1986, Twickenham, London
England   21   PG: Andrew (6); DG: Andrew
Wales   18   T: Bowen; C: Thorburn; PG: Thorburn (3); DG: J Davies

7 March 1987, National Stadium, Cardiff
Wales   19   T: S Evans; PG: Wyatt (5)
England   12   PG: Rose (4)

8 June 1987, Ballymore, Brisbane (RWC, Q/F)
Wales   16   T: Roberts, Jones, Devereux; C: Thorburn (2)
England   3   PG: Webb

6 February 1988, Twickenham, London
Wales   11   T: Hadley (2); DG: J Davies
England   3   PG: Webb

18 March 1989, National Stadium, Cardiff
Wales   12   T: Hall; C: Thorburn; PG: Thorburn (2)
England   9   PG: Andrew (2); DG: Andrew

17 February 1990, Twickenham, London
England   34   T: Carling, Hill, R Underwood (2); C: Hodgkinson (3); PG: Hodgkinson (4)
Wales   6   T: P Davies; C: Thorburn

19 January 1991, National Stadium, Cardiff
England   25   T: Teague; PG: Hodgkinson (7)
Wales   6   PG: Thorburn, Jenkins

7 March 1992, Twickenham, London
England   24   T: Carling, Skinner, Dooley; C: Webb (3); PG: Webb (2)
Wales   0

6 February 1993, National Stadium, Cardiff
Wales   10   T: I Evans; C: N Jenkins; PG: N Jenkins
England   9   PG: Webb (2); DG: Guscott

19 March 1994, Twickenham, London
England   15   T: R Underwood, Rodber; C: Andrew; PG: Andrew
Wales   8   T: Walker; PG: N Jenkins

18 February 1995, National Stadium, Cardiff
England   23   T: Ubogu, R Underwood (2); C: Andrew; PG: Andrew (2)
Wales   9   PG: Jenkins (3)

3 February 1996, Twickenham, London
England   21   T: A Underwood, Guscott; C: Grayson; PG: Grayson (3)
Wales   15   T: Taylor, Howley; C: A Thomas; PG: A Thomas

15 March 1997, National Stadium, Cardiff
England   34   T: Stimpson, Underwood, Hill, de Glanville; C: Catt (4); PG: Catt (2)
Wales   13   T: Howley; C: Davies; PG: Davies (2)

21 February 1998, Twickenham, London
England   60   T: Rees (2), Greenwood, Dallaglio, Healey, Back, Bracken, Dawson; C: Grayson (7); PG: Grayson (2)
Wales   26   T: Bateman (2), G Thomas, Gibbs; C: Jenkins (3)

11 April 1999, Wembley Stadium, London
Wales   32   T: Howarth, Gibbs; C: Jenkins (2); PG: Jenkins (6)
England   31   T: Luger, Hanley, Hill; C: Wilkinson (2); PG: Wilkinson (4)

4 March 2000, Twickenham, London
England   46   T: Greening, Back, Hill, Dallaglio, Cohen; C: Wilkinson (3); PG: Wilkinson (5)
Wales   12   PG: Jenkins (3); DG: Jenkins

3 February 2001, Millennium Stadium, Cardiff
England   44   T: Greenwood (3), Dawson (2), Cohen; C: Wilkinson (4); PG: Wilkinson (2)
Wales   15   T: Howley, Quinnell; C: Jenkins; PG: Jenkins

23 March 2002, Twickenham, London
England   50   T: Luger (2), Greenwood, Wilkinson, Stimpson; C: Wilkinson (5); PG: Wilkinson (4); DG: Wilkinson
Wales   10   T: Harris; C: Harris; PG: Harris

22 February 2003, Millennium Stadium, Cardiff
England   26   T: Greenwood, Worsley; C: Wilkinson (2); PG: Wilkinson (2); DG: Wilkinson (2)
Wales   9   PG: Sweeney (3)

23 August 2003, Millennium Stadium, Cardiff
England   43   T: Moody, Luger, Worsley, Abbott, West; C: King (2), Walder; PG: King (3); DG: King
Wales   9   PG: S Jones (3)

9 November 2003, Suncorp Stadium, Brisbane (RWC, Q/F)
England   28   T: Greenwood; C: Wilkinson; PG: Wilkinson (6); DG: Wilkinson
Wales   17   T: S Jones, Charvis, M Williams; C: Harris

20 March 2004, Twickenham, London
England   31   T: Cohen (2), Worsley; C: Barkley (2); PG: Barkley (4)
Wales   21   T: Thomas, Taylor; C: S Jones; PG: S Jones (3)

5 February 2005, Millennium Stadium, Cardiff
Wales 11 T: S Williams; PG: S Jones, Henson
England 9 PG: Hodgson (3)

3 February 2006, Twickenham, London
England 47 T: Cueto, Moody, Tindall, Dallaglio, Dawson, Voyce; C: Hodgson (2), Goode (2); PG: Hodgson (3)
Wales 13 T: Martyn Williams; C: S Jones; PG: S Jones (2)

17 March 2007, Millennium Stadium, Cardiff
Wales 27 T: Hook, Horsman; C: Hook; PG: Hook (4); DG: Hook
England 18 T: Ellis, Robinson; C: Flood; PG: Flood; DG: Flood

4 August 2007, Twickenham, London
England 62 T: Easter (4), Perry, Borthwick, Robinson, Tait, Dallaglio; C: Wilkinson (7); PG: Wilkinson
Wales 5 T: D James

2 February 2008, Twickenham, London
Wales 26 T: Byrne, Phillips; C: Hook (2); PG: Hook (4)
England 19 T: Flood; C: Wilkinson; PG: Wilkinson (3); DG: Wilkinson

14 February 2009, Millennium Stadium, Cardiff
Wales 23 T: Halfpenney; PG: S Jones (5), Halfpenney
England 15 T: Sackey, Armitage; C: Flood; DG: Goode

England vs World XV

17 April 1971, Twickenham, London
World XV 28 T: Williams (3), Kirkpatrick (2), Marais; C: Villepreux (5)
England 11 T: Hiller; C: Hiller; PG: Hiller (2)

England: summaries and records

Home matches	
Played	312
Won	194
Lost	91
Drawn	27
Points for	5,610
Points against	3,141
Average score	17.98/10.07
Win %	62.18
Lose %	29.17
Draw %	8.65

Away matches	
Played	285
Won	118
Lost	146
Drawn	21
Points for	3,519
Points against	3,888
Average score	12.35/13.64
Win %	41.4
Lose %	51.23
Draw %	7.37

Neutral venues	
Played	22
Won	16
Lost	6
Drew	0
For	709
Against	403
Average	32.23/18.32
Win %	72.73
Lose %	27.27
Draw %	0

Total matches	
Played	619
Won	328
Lost	243
Drawn	48
Points for	9,838
Points against	7,432
Average score	15.89/12.01
Win %	52.99
Lose %	39.26
Draw %	7.75

Most capped players: England							
Player	Caps	Career	Points				
			T	C	PG	DG	Total
Jason Leonard	114	28/07/1990–15/02/2004	1	-	-	-	5
Lawrence Dallaglio	85	18/11/1995–20/10/2007	17	-	-	-	85
Rory Underwood	85	18/02/1984–17/03/1996	49	-	-	-	210
Martin Johnson	84	16/01/1993–22/11/2003	2	-	-	-	10
Matt Dawson	77	16/12/1995–18/03/2006	16	6	3	-	101

ENGLAND

Most tests as captain: England		
No.	Player	Period
59	Will Carling	1988–1996
39	Martin Johnson	1998–2003
22	Lawrence Dallaglio	1997–2004
21	Bill Beaumont	1978–1982
17	Martin Corry	2005–2007

Most points by a player in a career: England				Points			
No.	Player	Tests	Career	T	C	PG	DG
1032	Jonny Wilkinson	70	04/04/1998–15/03/2008	6	144	209	29
400	Paul Grayson	32	16/12/1995–06/03/2004	2	78	72	6
396	Rob Andrew	71	05/01/1985–15/03/1997	2	33	86	21
296	Jonathan Webb	33	23/05/1987–20/03/1993	4	41	66	-
259	Charlie Hodgson	31	17/11/2001–14/06/2008	6	44	44	3

Most tries by a player in a career: England			
No.	Player	Tests	Career
49	Rory Underwood	85	18/02/1984–17/03/1996
31	Ben Cohen	57	05/02/2000–25/11/2006
31	Will Greenwood	55	15/11/1997–27/11/2004
30	Jeremy Guscott	65	13/05/1989–15/10/1999
28	Jason Robinson	51	17/02/2001–20/10/2007

Most conversions by a player in a career: England			
No.	Player	Tests	Career
144	Jonny Wilkinson	70	04/04/1998–15/03/2008
78	Paul Grayson	32	16/12/1995–06/03/2004
44	Charlie Hodgson	31	17/11/2001–14/06/2008
41	Jonathan Webb	33	23/05/1987–20/03/1993
35	Simon Hodgkinson	14	13/05/1989–11/10/1991

Most penalties by a player in a career: Emgland			
No.	Player	Tests	Career
209	Jonny Wilkinson	70	04/04/1998–15/03/2008
86	Rob Andrew	71	05/01/1985–15/03/1997
72	Paul Grayson	32	16/12/1995–06/03/2004
67	Dusty Hare	25	16/03/1974–09/06/1984
66	Jonathan Webb	33	23/05/1987–20/03/1993

Most drop goals by a player in a career: England

No.	Player	Tests	Career
29	Jonny Wilkinson	70	04/04/1998–15/03/2008
21	Rob Andrew	71	05/01/1985–15/03/1997
6	Paul Grayson	32	16/12/1995–06/03/2004
4	Les Cusworth	12	24/11/1979–06/02/1988
4	John Horton	13	04/02/1978–09/06/1984
4	Andy Goode	16	12/03/2005–13/06/2009

Most points by a player in a match: England

No.	Player	Points				Versus	Venue	Date
		T	C	PG	DG			
44	Charlie Hodgson	2	14	2	-	Romania	Twickenham, London	17/11/2001
36	Paul Grayson	-	12	4	-	Tonga	Twickenham, London	15/10/1999
35	Jonny Wilkinson	1	9	4	-	Italy	Twickenham, London	17/02/2001
32	Jonny Wilkinson	1	6	5	-	Italy	Twickenham, London	02/10/1999
30	Jonny Wilkinson	1	5	4	1	Wales	Twickenham, London	23/03/2002
30	Paul Grayson	-	15	-	-	Holland	McAlpine Stadium, Huddersfield	14/11/1998
30	Rob Andrew	-	6	6	-	Canada	Twickenham, London	10/12/1994

Most tries by a player in a match: England

No	Player	Versus	Venue	Date
5	Josh Lewsey	Uruguay	Suncorp Stadium, Brisbane	02/11/2003
5	Rory Underwood	Fiji	Twickenham, London	04/11/1989
5	Daniel Lambert	France	Athletic Ground, Richmond	05/01/1907

Most conversions by a player in a match: England

No.	Player	Versus	Venue	Date
15	Paul Grayson	Holland	McAlpine Stadium, Huddersfield	14/11/1998
14	Charlie Hodgson	Romania	Twickenham, London	17/11/2001
13	Jonny Wilkinson	United States	Twickenham, London	21/08/1999
12	Paul Grayson	Tonga	Twickenham, London	15/10/1999
11	Paul Grayson	Uruguay	Suncorp Stadium, Brisbane	02/11/2003

Most penalties by a player in a match: England

No.	Player	Versus	Venue	Date
8	Jonny Wilkinson	South Africa	Free State Stadium, Bloemfontein	24/06/2000
7	Jonny Wilkinson	South Africa	Twickenham, London	24/11/2001
7	Jonny Wilkinson	Fiji	Twickenham, London	20/10/1999
7	Jonny Wilkinson	France	Twickenham, London	20/03/1999
7	Rob Andrew	Scotland	Twickenham, London	18/03/1995
7	Simon Hodgkinson	Wales	National Stadium, Cardiff	19/01/1991

ENGLAND

No.	Player	Versus	Venue	Date
3	Jonny Wilkinson	France	Stadium Australia, Sydney	15/11/2003

Most drop goals by a player in a match

Most points in a match by England

No.	Result	Points				Versus	Venue	Date
		T	C	PG	DG			
134	134–0	20	14	2	-	Romania	Twickenham, London	17/11/2001
111	111–13	17	13	-	-	Uruguay	Suncorp Stadium, Brisbane	02/11/2003
110	110–0	16	15	-	-	Holland	McAlpine Stadium, Huddersfield	14/11/1998
106	106–8	16	13	-	-	United States	Twickenham, London	21/08/1999
101	101–10	13	12	4	-	Tonga	Twickenham, London	15/10/1999

Most consecutive test wins by England

No.	Period	Details
14	23/03/2002–23/08/2003	Wales (H), Italy (A), Argentina (A), New Zealand (H), Australia (H), South Africa (H), France (H), Wales (A), Italy (H), Scotland (H), Ireland (A), New Zealand (A), Australia (A), Wales (A)
11	24/06/2000–16/06/2001	South Africa (A), Australia (H), Argentina (H), South Africa (H), Wales (A), Italy (H), Scotland (H), France (H), Canada (A), Canada (A), United States (A)
10	06/09/2003–21/02/2004	France (H), Georgia (N), South Africa (N), Samoa (N), Uruguay (N), Wales (N), France (N), Australia (A), Italy (A), Scotland (A)
10	12/11/1994–1/06/1995	Romania (H), Canada (H), Ireland (A), France (H), Wales (A), Scotland (H), Argentina (N), Italy (N), Western Samoa (N), Australia (N)
10	16/12/1882–06/02/1886	Wales (A), Ireland (H), Scotland (A), Wales (H), Ireland (A), Scotland (H), Wales (A), Ireland (H), Wales (H), Ireland(A)

Milestones

Longest test career	Jason Leonard	28/07/1990–15/02/2004 (13 years, 6 months & 19 days)
Youngest test player	Colin Laird	18 years & 134 days on 15/01/1927 vs Wales
Oldest test player	Frederick Gilbert	38 years & 362 days on 10/02/1923 vs Ireland

England dribbling forward against New Zealand during the first-ever international between the two sides at Crystal Palace in London, 1905. New Zealand won comfortably by 15-0. *Photo*: New Zealand Rugby Museum

Above left: All Black lock forwards Colin Meads (left) and Sam Strahan (right) soar in a lineout versus England at Twickenham in 1967. New Zealand went on to win the match by 23-11. *Photo*: New Zealand Rugby Museum

Above right: New Zealand captain and flanker Ian Kirkpatrick scores the only try of the 1973 England vs New Zealand international at Twickenham, London in 1973. English centre Peter Preece is too late to stop Kirkpatrick. New Zealand won by 9-0. *Photo*: New Zealand Rugby Museum

England flanker Tony Neary scores a brilliant try against New Zealand to help secure one of England's most famous test victories when they won by 16-10 in Auckland, 1973. All Black winger Bryan Williams is too late to stop him, much to the delight of a beaming English prop Fran Cotton (left).
Photo: New Zealand Rugby Museum

Top left: The 1892 England side to take on Scotland at Raeburn Place in Edinburgh and who triumphed by 5-0 after forward William Bromet (back row middle) scored the only try of the match. *Photo*: Frédéric Humbert/www.flickr.com/photos/rugby_pioneers/creative commons license

Above: An unidentified English player is high-tackled during the 1930 clash versus France in a match won 11-5 by England at Twickenham, London. *Photo*: Frédéric Humbert/www.flickr.com/photos/rugby_pioneers/creative commons license

Above: Lions flyhalf Bev Risman (of England) dives over in spectacular fashion to score the winning try against New Zealand in the fourth test of the 1959 series in Auckland. *Photo*: New Zealand Rugby Museum

Left: English scrumhalf Jon Webster clears from the base of a scrum under the scrutiny of All Black flanker Ken Stewart during the 1973 test won 16-10 by England in Auckland. *Photo*: New Zealand Rugby Museum

29 January 1972, Stade Olympique Yves-du-Manoir, Paris
Ireland   14   T: Moloney, McLoughlin; PG: Kiernan (2)
France   9   T: Lux; C: Villepreux; PG: Villepreux

29 April 1972, Lansdowne Road, Dublin
Ireland   24   T: Duggan, Flynn, Moloney; C: Kiernan (3); PG: Kiernan (2)
France   14   T: Duprat (2), Lux; C: Villepreux

14 April 1973, Lansdowne Road, Dublin
Ireland   6   PG: Gibson (2)
France   4   T: Phliponneau

19 January 1974, Parc des Princes, Paris
France   9   T: Boffelli; C: Aguirre; PG: Berot
Ireland   6   PG: Ensor (2)

1 March 1975, Lansdowne Road, Dublin
Ireland   25   T: Ensor, Grace, McBride; C: McCombe (2); DG: McCombe (2); PG: McCombe
France   6   DG: Paries; PG: Paries

7 February 1976, Parc des Princes, Paris
France   26   T: Pecune, Cholley, Fouroux, Rives; C: Rives, Bastiat; PG: Romeu (2)
Ireland   3   PG: Robbie

19 March 1977, Lansdowne Road, Dublin
France   15   T: Bastiat; C: Aguirre; PG: Aguirre (2), Romeu
Ireland   6   PG: Gibson, Quinn

18 February 1978, Parc des Princes, Paris
France   10   T: Gallion; PG: Aguirre (2)
Ireland   9   PG: Ward (3)

20 January 1979, Lansdowne Road, Dublin
Ireland   9   PG: Ward (3)
France   9   T: Caussade; C: Aguirre; PG: Aguirre

1 March 1980, Parc des Princes, Paris
France   19   T: Gourdon (2); C: Aguirre; DG: Pedeutour; PG: Aguirre (2)
Ireland   18   T: McLennan; C: Campbell; DG: Campbell; PG: Campbell (3)

7 February 1981, Lansdowne Road, Dublin
France   19   T: Pardo; DG: Laporte (2); PG: Laporte (2), Gabernet
Ireland   13   T: MacNeill; PG: Campbell (3)

20 March 1982, Parc des Princes, Paris
France   22   T: Blanco, Mesny; C: Gabernet; PG: Blanco (2), Gabernet (2)
Ireland   9   PG: Campbell (3)

19 February 1983, Lansdowne Road, Dublin
Ireland   22   T: Finn (2); C: Campbell; PG: Campbell (4)
France   16   T: Blanco, Estéve; C: Blanco; PG: Blanco (2)

21 January 1984, Parc des Princes, Paris
France   25   T: Gallion, Sella; C: Lescarboura; PG: Lescarboura (4); DG: Lescarboura
Ireland   12   PG: Campbell (4)

2 March 1985, Lansdowne Road, Dublin
Ireland   15   PG: Kiernan (5)
France   15   T: Estéve, Codorniou; C: Lescarboura (2); PG: Lescarboura

1 February 1986, Parc des Princes, Paris
France   29   T: Berbizier, Marocco, Sella; C: Laporte; PG: Laporte (3), Blanco; DG: Lafond
Ireland   9   PG: Kiernan (3)

21 March 1987, Lansdowne Road, Dublin
France   19   T: Champ (2); C: Berot; PG: Berot (3)
Ireland   13   T: Ringland, Bradley; C: Kiernan; PG: Kiernan

FRANCE

20 February 1988, Parc des Princes, Paris
France 25 T: Blanco, Lagisquet, Sella, Camberabero, Carminati; C: Camberabero; DG: Berot
Ireland 6 PG: Kiernan (2)

21 January 1989, Lansdowne Road, Dublin
France 26 T: Lagisquet (2), Blanco, Lafond; C: Lafond (2); PG: Lafond (2)
Ireland 21 T: Mullin; C: Kiernan; PG: Kiernan (5)

3 March 1990, Parc des Princes, Paris
France 31 T: Mesnel (2), Lagisquet; C: Camberabero (2); PG: Camberabero (5)
Ireland 12 PG: Kiernan (4)

2 February 1991, Lansdowne Road, Dublin
France 21 T: Lagisquet, Cabannes; C: Camberabero (2); PG: Camberabero (3)
Ireland 13 T: S Smith; PG: Kiernan (3)

21 March 1992, Parc des Princes, Paris
France 44 T: Penaud (2), Viars (2), Cecillon, Cabannes, Sadourny; C: Viars (5); PG: Viars (2)
Ireland 12 PG: McAleese (4)

20 February 1993, Lansdowne Road, Dublin
France 21 T: Saint-André, Sella; C: Camberabero; PG: Camberabero (2); DG: Camberabero
Ireland 6 PG: Malone (2)

15 January 1994, Parc des Princes, Paris
France 35 T: Benetton, Lacroix, Merle, Saint-André; C: Lacroix (3); PG: Lacroix (3)
Ireland 15 PG: Elwood (5)

4 March 1995, Lansdowne Road, Dublin
France 25 T: Delaigue, Cecillon, N'Tamack, Saint-André; C: N'Tamack; PG: N'Tamack
Ireland 7 T: Geoghegan; C: Elwood

10 June 1995, Kings Park, Durban (RWC, Q/F)
France 36 T: Saint-André, N'Tamack; C: Lacroix; PG: Lacroix (8)
Ireland 12 PG: Elwood (4)

17 February 1996, Parc des Princes, Paris
France 45 T: N'Tamack (2), Castel (2), Accoceberry, Campan, Saint-André; C: Castaignede (5)
Ireland 10 T: penalty try; C: Humphreys; PG: Humphreys

18 January 1997, Lansdowne Road, Dublin
France 32 T: Venditti (3), Galthie; C: Castaignede (3); PG: Castaignede (2)
Ireland 15 PG: Elwood (5)

7 March 1998, Stade de France, Paris
France 18 T: Bernat-Salles, Ibanez; C: Lamaison; PG: Lamaison (2)
Ireland 16 T: Hickie; C: Elwood; PG: Elwood (3)

6 February 1999, Lansdowne Road, Dublin
France 10 T: N'Tamack; C: Castaignede; PG: Castaignede
Ireland 9 PG: Humphreys (3)

19 March 2000, Stade de France, Paris
Ireland 27 T: O'Driscoll (3); C: O'Gara (2), Humphreys; PG: Humphreys (2)
France 25 T: Lasucq; C: Merceron; PG: Merceron (6)

17 February 2001, Lansdowne Road, Dublin
Ireland 22 T: O'Driscoll; C: O'Gara; PG: O'Gara (5)
France 15 T: Pelouse, Bernat-Salles; C: Lamaison; PG: Lamaison

6 April 2002, Stade de France, Paris
France 44 T: Betsen (2), Brusque (2), Rougerie; C: Merceron (2); PG: Merceron (5)
Ireland 5 T: Wood

8 March 2003, Lansdowne Road, Dublin
Ireland 15 PG: Humphreys (4); DG: Murphy
France 12 PG: Gelez (4)

9 November 2003, Colonial Stadium, Melbourne (RWC, Q/F)
France	43	T: Magne, Dominici, Harinordoquy, Crenca; C: Michalak (4); PG: Michalak (5)
Ireland	21	T: O'Driscoll (2), Maggs; C: Humphreys (3)

14 February 2004, Stade de France, Paris
France	35	T: Clerc, Pape, Jauzion, Elissalde; C: Michalak (3); PG: Michalak (3)
Ireland	17	T: Foley, Howe; C: O'Gara (2); PG: O'Gara

12 March 2005, Lansdowne Road, Dublin
France	26	T: Dominici (2), Baby; C: Yachvili; PG: Yachvili (2); DG: Delaigue
Ireland	19	T: O'Driscoll; C: O'Gara; PG: O'Gara (4)

11 February 2006, Stade de France, Paris
France	43	T: Heymans (2), Marty (2), Rougerie, Magne; C: Elissalde (5); PG: Elissalde
Ireland	31	T: Trimble, O'Gara, D'Arcy, O'Callaghan; C: O'Gara (4); PG: O'Gara

11 February 2007, Croke Park, Dublin
France	20	T: Ibanez, Clerc; C: Skrela, Beauxis; PG: Skrela (2)
Ireland	17	T: O'Gara; PG: O'Gara (4)

21 September 2007, Stade de France, Paris (RWC, Pool D)
France	25	T: Clerc (2); PG: Elissalde (5)
Ireland	3	DG: O'Gara

9 February 2008, Stade de France, Paris
France	26	T: Clerc (3), Heymans; C: Elissalde (3)
Ireland	21	T: penalty try, Wallace; C: O'Gara; PG: O'Gara (3)

7 February 2009, Croke Park, Dublin
Ireland	30	T: Heaslip, O'Driscoll, D'Arcy; C: O'Gara (3); PG: O'Gara (3)
France	21	T: Harinordoquy, Medard; C: Beauxis; PG: Beauxis; DG: Beauxis (2)

France vs Ireland XV

26 January 1946, Lansdowne Road, Dublin
France	4	DG: Bergougnan
Ireland XV	3	PG: Thorpe

France vs Italy	
Played:	30
Won:	29
Lost:	1
Drawn:	0
For:	895
Against:	295

Average score:
29.83–9.83

France percentages:
Won:	96.67%
Lost:	3.33%
Drawn:	0%

France vs Italy (Giuseppe Garibaldi Trophy)

These two teams met for the first time in 1937 during France's isolation from the Five Nations, in a game that was comfortably won by France. They next met in 1952 and played annually until 1967 when a 60–16 French victory (equivalent to 82–22 today) proved that Italy's place on the French international calendar was a mismatch and no longer required. In 1995, the contest was rekindled and just two years later Italy recorded their first, and so far only, victory over the French. Today, the Giuseppe Garibaldi Trophy is awarded annually to the winner of the Six Nations international between the two. It was designed by former French captain Jean-Pierre Rives and was first awarded in 2007 when France beat Italy 39–3. Giuseppe Garibaldi, an Italian revolutionary born in France in 1807, is regarded as the father of a unified Italy. He was also a French army general and the trophy was mooted as a fitting way to commemorate the bicentenary of his birth, given Garibaldi's common links. Curiously, this is the only rugby trophy that has 'godfathers' responsible for its safekeeping: former Italian international Diego Dominguez and former French international Jean-François Tordo.

17 October 1937, Parc des Princes, Paris
France	43	T: Celhay (4), Delgue (2), Bergese, Goyard, Milliand; C: Desclaux (3), Thiers (3); DG: Bonnus
Italy	5	T: Visentin; C: Vigliano

17 May 1952, Arena Civica, Milan
France	17	T: Basquet, Bienes, Roge; C: Prat; PG: Prat (2)
Italy	8	T: Percudani; C: Turcato; PG: Cecchetto-Milani

FRANCE

26 April 1953, Stade Gerland, Lyon
France 22   T: Porthault (2), Domec; C: Desclaux (2); PG: Bertrand; DG: Desclaux (2)
Italy 8   T: Gerosa; C: Battaglini; PG: Battaglini

24 April 1954, Stadio Olympio, Rome
France 39   T: Boniface, Larrequy, Lepatey (2), Murillo (2), Prat; C: Prat (6); PG: Prat (2)
Italy 12   T: Gabrielli, Lanfranchi; PG: Dari (2)

10 April 1955, Stade Lesdiguieres, Grenoble
France 24   T: Baulon, Dufau, Rancoule (2); C: Vannier (3); PG: Vannier (2)
Italy 0

2 April 1956, Stadio Plebiscito, Padua
France 16   T: Baulon, Roge (2); C: Vannier (2); PG: Vannier
Italy 3   T: Cantoni

21 April 1957, Stade Armandie, Agen
France 38   T: Darrouy (2), Dupuy (2), Mauduy (2), Domenech, Haget; C: Cassagne (5), Vannier (2)
Italy 6   T: Malosti; PG: Lanfranchi

7 April 1958, Naples
France 11   T: Danos, Mommejat; C: Vannier; PG: Vannier
Italy 3   PG: Lanfranchi

29 March 1959, Stade le Beajoire, Nantes
France 22   T: Bouquet, Dupuy (2), Moncla, Rancoule; C: Labazuy (2); PG: Labazuy
Italy 0

17 April 1960, Stadio di Monigo, Treviso
France 26   T: Casaux (2), Meyer, Rancoule; C: Vannier (4); DG: Albaladejo (2)
Italy 0

2 April 1961, Stade Municipal, Chambery
France 17   T: Bouquet, Boniface, Domenech, Rancoule; C: Vannier; PG: Vannier
Italy 0

22 April 1962, Stadio Mompiano, Brescia
France 6   T: Saux; PG: Boniface
Italy 3   PG: Lanfranchi

14 April 1963, Stade Lesdiguieres, Grenoble
France 14   T: Darrouy, Dupuy (2), Lira; C: Dedieu
Italy 12   T: Augeri, Levorato; PG: Perrini (2)

29 March 1964, Stadio Comunale, Parma
France 12   T: Boniface; PG: Albaladejo (3)
Italy 3   DG: Martini

18 April 1965, de la Croix du Prince, Pau
France 21   T: Boniface, Darrouy (2), Gruarin, Rupert; C: Lacaze (3)
Italy 0

9 April 1966, Naples
France 21   T: Dauga, Darrouy, Lagrange, Maso; C: Lacaze (3); DG: Lacaze
Italy 0

26 March 1967, Stade Mayol, Toulon
France 60   T: Arnaudet (3), Gachassin (2), Cabanier, Dauga, Darrouy, Lux, Rupert, Sitjar; C: G Camberabero (9);
            PG: G Camberabero (2); DG: G Camberabero
Italy 13   T: Degli Antoni, Prosperini, Salmaso; C: Zitti (2)

14 October 1995, Ferro Carril Oeste Stadium, Buenos Aires
France 34   T: Carminati, N'Tamack, Sadourney (2); C: Deylaud (4); PG: Deylaud (2)
Italy 22   T: Troncon; C: Bonomi; PG: Bonomi (4); DG: Bonomi

22 March 1997, Stade Lesdiguieres, Grenoble
Italy 40   T: Francescato, Croci, Gardner, Vaccari; C: Dominguez (4); PG: Dominguez (4)
France 32   T: Bondouy (2), Sadourny, penalty try; C: Aucagne (3); PG: Aucagne (2)

18 October 1997, Stade Jacques Fouroux, Auch
France 30   T: Califano, Saint-Andre; C: Lamaison; PG: Lamaison (6)
Italy 19   T: Vaccari; C: Dominguez; PG: Dominguez (3); DG: Dominguez

1 April 2000, Stade de France, Paris
France 42   T: Penaud (2), Castaignede, Benazzi, Pelous; C: Dourthe (4); PG: Dourthe (3)
Italy 31   T: Troncon (2), Martin, Stoica; C: Dominguez (4); DG: Dominguez

3 March 2001, Stadio Flaminio, Rome
France 30   T: Bonetti, Sadourney, Bernat-Salles; C: Lamaison (3); PG: Lamaison (3)
Italy 19   T: Perziano; C: Dominguez; PG: Dominguez (4)

2 February 2002, Stade de France, Paris
France 33   T: Traille, Betsen; C: Traille; PG: Merceron (7)
Italy 12   PG: Dominguez (4)

23 March 2003, Stadio Flaminio, Rome
France 53   T: Traille (2), Rougerie (2), Betsen, Michalak, Castaignede; C: Yachvili (6); PG: Yachvili (2)
Italy 27   T: Pez, Bergamasco, Persico, Phillips; C: Pez (2); PG: Pez

21 February 2004, Stade de France, Paris
France 25   T: Harinordoquy (2), Elhorga; C: Elissalde (2); PG: Elissalde, Traille
Italy 0

19 March 2005, Stadio Flaminio, Rome
France 56   T: Marty (2), Nyanga, Jauzion, Laharrague, Lamboley, Mignoni; C: Yachvili (4), Michalak (2); PG: Yachvili (3)
Italy 13   T: Robertson; C: Peens; PG: Peens (2)

25 February 2006, Stade de France, Paris
France 37   T: Lievremont, Nyanga, de Villiers, Rougerie, Michalak; C: Yachvili (3); PG: Elissalde, Yachvili
Italy 12   PG: Pez (3); DG: Pez

3 February 2007, Stadio Flaminio, Rome
France 39   T: Chabal (2), Dominici, Heymans, Jauzion; C: Skrela (4); PG: Skrela, Beauxis
Italy 3   PG: Pez

9 March 2008, Stade de France, Paris
France 25   T: David, Floch, Rougerie; C: Yachvili (2); PG: Yachvili (2)
Italy 13   T: Castrogiovani; C: Marcato; PG: Marcato (2)

21 March 2009, Stadio Flaminio, Rome
France 50   T: Medard (2), Chabal, Trinh-Duc, Heymans, Nallet, Malzieu; C: Parra (3); PG: Parra (3)
Italy 8   T: Parisse; PG: Marcato

Guiseppe Garibaldi Trophy		Current holder: France				Number of titles: France 3, Italy 0		
No.	Date	Venue		Result			Series	Holder
1	03/02/2007	Stadio Flaminio, Rome	Italy	3–39	France		0–1	France
2	09/03/2008	Stade de France, Paris	France	25–13	Italy		1–0	France
3	21/03/2009	Stadio Flaminio, Rome	Italy	8–50	France		0–1	France

France vs Japan

27 October 1973, Stade Municipal, Bordeaux
France 30   T: Delaigue, Barrau, Bertranne, Saisset, Skrela; C: Cabrol (5)
Japan 18   T: Ohigashi, Sakata, Shimazaki; PG: Ueyama, Shimazaki

18 October 2003, Dairy Farmers Stadium, Townsville (RWC, Pool B)
France 51   T: Rougerie (2), Pelous, Dominici, Crenca, Michalak; C: Michalak (5), Merceron; PG: Michalak (3)
Japan 29   T: Konia, Ohata; C: Kurihara (2); PG: Kurihara (5)

FRANCE

FRANCE

France vs Kiwis

At the end of World War II, the New Zealand Army toured Britain and France in 1945/1946 and were known as the 'Kiwis'. The French awarded test caps for the game against the Kiwis but were beaten by a strong Kiwi side that played entertaining rugby of the highest quality.

10 March 1946, Stade Olympique Yves-du-Manoir, Paris
Kiwi's	14	T: Sheratt (2), Blake; C: Scott; PG: Scott
France	9	T: Pebeyre, Baladie, Terreau

France vs Namibia

8 October 1999, Stade Lescure, Bordeaux (RWC, Pool C)
France	47	T: Mola (3), Mignoni, Bernat-Salles, N'Tamack; C: Dourthe (3), Lamaison; PG: Dourthe (3)
Namibia	13	T: A Samuelson; C: van Dyk; PG: van Dyk (2)

16 September 2007, Stade Municipal, Toulouse (RWC, Pool D)
France	87	T: Clerc (3), Nallet (2), Chabal (2), Heymans, Marty, Dusautoir, Bonnaire, Elissalde, Ibanez; C: Elissalde (11)
Namibia	10	T: Langenhoven; C: Losper; DG: Wessels

France vs New Zealand (Dave Gallaher Cup)

France vs New Zealand	
Played:	48
Won:	12
Lost:	35
Drawn:	1
For:	636
Against:	1,158
Average score:	
13.25–24.13	
France percentages:	
Won:	25%
Lost:	72.92%
Drawn:	2.08%

This popular series is named in memory of the charismatic All Blacks captain Dave Gallaher who was killed during World War I. On 4 October 1917, Sergeant David Gallaher incurred wounds during the Battle of Passchendaele (officially known as the Third Ypres) that led to his death eight days later. He was captain of the first All Blacks touring team to the British Isles, France and North America, known as 'The Originals' and which in January 1906 provided France with their first-ever international opposition. His death caused great distress in New Zealand where he was already a national hero, with his sacrifice officially commemorated by the Auckland Rugby Union in 1922 with the inaugural Gallaher Shield for their club championship. The 1924 touring New Zealand 'Invincibles' visited his grave in France; a photograph of the side lined up at his headstone has since become an iconic image of the nation's sporting and cultural history. The All Blacks of 2000 also visited the grave when the Dave Gallaher Cup was officially introduced. It is awarded to the winner of a particular test match between France and New Zealand, but not during RWC encounters. Until 2007 the Dave Gallaher Cup was based on a unique challenge-match system whereby the holding union defended the cup from the challenging union. The dates for these matches were mutually agreed upon and if they were to meet twice or more in a series then it was usually the first match of that series that would count as the challenge match. The first such match was won by New Zealand in 2000 and despite France winning the second test of the series, New Zealand held the trophy based on the first result. In the 2004 game in Paris, New Zealand added a red poppy to their jerseys in memory of Gallaher, the first and only time that another insignia has joined the silver fern on the All Blacks shirt. The last challenge match was played on 9 June 2007 in Wellington which saw New Zealand win 61–10. As of 2009 the format was changed. The challenge match system was scrapped and an aggregate-score system was instead adopted with the team scoring the most points in the series winning the trophy. It was under this new ruling that France won the Gallaher Trophy for the first time when they beat New Zealand 37-36 on aggregate score, despite sharing the series at a game each. In 2006, the *Train du Rugby* travelled to 110 towns throughout France to mark the centenary of French rugby; aboard was the Dave Gallaher Cup (won by New Zealand that year). To date, the trophy has been contested eight times with France the current holders and the All Blacks victorious on six previous occasions as well as retaining the cup in 2002 when the Paris test was drawn. Over the years the French have proved New Zealand's bogey side, regularly inflicting on them shock defeats in matches notorious for their physicality. France won a series in New Zealand in 1994, winning their first Dave Gallaher Trophy away and twice bundled New Zealand out of RWCs, in 1999 and 2007 in remarkable come-from-behind victories that will be forever remembered. Between RWCs, New Zealand have dominated the French and recently have won regularly by record margins both home and away.

1 January 1906, Parc des Princes, Paris
New Zealand   38   T: Wallace (3), Abbott (2), Hunter (2), Harper (2), Glasgow; C: Wallace (2), Tyler, Abbott
France   8   T: Cessieux, Jerome; C: Pujol

18 January 1925, Stade des Ponts Jumeaux, Toulouse
New Zealand   30   T: Cooke (2), White, Porter, Steel, Svenson, Irvine, Richardson; C: Nicholls (3)
France   6   T: Cassayet, Ribere

27 February 1954, Stade Olympique Yves-du-Manoir, Paris
France   3   T: J Prat
New Zealand   0

22 July 1961, Eden Park, Auckland
New Zealand   13   T: McKay, O'Sullivan; C: D Clarke (2); DG: D Clarke
France   6   DG: Albaladejo (2)

5 August 1961, Athletic Park, Wellington
New Zealand   5   T: Tremain; C: D Clarke
France   3   T: Dupuy

19 August 1961, Lancaster Park, Christchurch
New Zealand   32   T: Graham, Little, Meads, Tremain, Yates; C: D Clarke (4); PG: D Clarke (3)
France   3   T: Crauste

8 February 1964, Stade Olympique Yves-du-Manoir, Paris
New Zealand   12   T: Caulton, Gray; PG: Herewini; DG: Laidlaw
France   3   PG: Albaladejo

25 November 1967, Stade Olympique Yves-du-Manoir, Paris
New Zealand   21   T: Going, Dick, Steel, Kirkpatrick; C: McCormick (3); PG: McCormick
France   15   T: Campaes; PG: Villepreux (3); DG: Gachassin

13 July 1968, Lancaster Park, Christchurch
New Zealand   12   T: Kirton; PG: McCormick (3)
France   9   PG: Villepreux (2); DG: Lacaze

27 July 1968, Athletic Park, Wellington
New Zealand   9   PG: McCormick (3)
France   3   PG: Villepreux

10 August 1968, Eden Park, Auckland
New Zealand   19   T: Going (2); C: McCormick (2); PG: McCormick (2); DG: Cottrell
France   12   T: Trillo, Carrere, Lux; DG: Dourthe

10 February 1973, Parc des Princes, Paris
France   13   T: Dourthe, Bertranne; C: Romeu; PG: Romeu
New Zealand   6   PG: Karam (2)

11 November 1977, Stade Municipal, Toulouse
France   18   T: Paparemborde; C: Romeu; PG: Romeu (3); DG: Romeu
New Zealand   13   T: Williams; PG: Williams, McKechnie; DG: Robertson

19 November 1977, Parc des Princes, Paris
New Zealand   15   T: Wilson; C: McKechnie; PG: McKechnie, Seear; DG: McKechnie
France   3   PG: Romeu

7 July 1979, Lancaster Park, Christchurch
New Zealand   23   T: S Wilson, Watts, Donaldson; C: B Wilson; PG: B Wilson (3)
France   9   T: Mesny; C: Aguirre; DG: Caussade

14 July 1979, Eden Park, Auckland
France   24   T: Averous, Codorniou, Caussade, Gallion; C: Caussade; PG: Aguirre; DG: Caussade
New Zealand   19   T: S Wilson, Mourie; C: B Wilson; PG: B Wilson (3)

14 November 1981, Stade Municipal, Toulouse
New Zealand   13   T: Wilson; PG: Hewson (2); DG: Hewson
France   9   PG: Laporte (2); DG: Gabernet

21 November 1981, Parc des Princes, Paris
New Zealand   18   T: Wilson, penalty try; C: Hewson (2); PG: Hewson (2)
France   6   PG: Laporte, Blanco

FRANCE

16 June 1984, Lancaster Park, Christchurch
New Zealand 10 T: Taylor; PG: Hewson (2)
France 9 T: Blanco; C: Lescarboura; PG: Lescarboura

23 June 1984, Eden Park, Auckland
New Zealand 31 T: B Smith, Taylor, Dalton; C: Hewson (2); PG: Hewson (5)
France 18 T: Lescarboura (2), Bonneval; PG: Lescarboura (2)

28 June 1986, Lancaster Park, Christchurch
New Zealand 18 T: Brewer; C: Cooper; PG: Cooper (2); DG: Botica (2)
France 9 DG: Lescarboura (3)

8 November 1986, Stade Municipal, Toulouse
New Zealand 19 T: W Shelford; PG: Crowley (3); DG: Stone, Crowley
France 7 T: Sella; PG: Berot

15 November 1986, Le Beajoire Stadium, Nantes
France 16 T: Charvet, Lorieux; C: Berot; PG: Berot (2)
New Zealand 3 PG: Crowley

20 June 1987, Eden Park, Auckland (RWC, Final)
New Zealand 29 T: Jones, Kirk, Kirwan; C: Fox; PG: Fox (4); DG: Fox
France 9 T: Berbizier; C: Camberabero; PG: Camberabero

17 June 1989, Lancaster Park, Christchurch
New Zealand 25 T: Wright (2), A Whetton; C: Fox (2); PG: Fox (3)
France 17 T: Blanco (2), Cecillon; C: Berot; PG: Beroty

1 July 1989, Eden Park, Auckland
New Zealand 34 T: Stanley, Fitzpatrick, Deans, A Whetton; C: Fox (3); PG: Fox (4)
France 20 T: Rouge-Thomas, Cecillon; PG: Blanco (4)

3 November 1990, Le Beajoire Stadium Nantes
New Zealand 24 T: Innes, A Whetton; C: Fox (2); PG: Fox (3); DG: Fox
France 3 PG: Camberabero

10 November 1990, Parc des Princes, Paris
New Zealand 30 T: Crowley, M Jones; C: Fox (2); PG: Fox (6)
France 12 PG: Camberabero (3); DG: Camberabero

26 June 1994, Lancaster Park, Christchurch
France 22 T: Benetton; C: Lacroix; PG: Lacroix (2); DG: Deylaud (2), Sadourny
New Zealand 8 T: Bunce; PG: Cooper

3 July 1994, Eden Park, Auckland
France 23 T: N'Tamack, Sadourny; C: Lacroix, Deylaud; PG: Lacroix (2), Deylaud
New Zealand 20 T: Fitzpatrick; PG: Cooper (5)

11 November 1995, Stade Municipal, Toulouse
France 22 T: Sadourny, Dourthe, Saint-André; C: Castaignede (2); PG: Castaignede
New Zealand 15 PG: Culhane (5)

18 November 1995, Parc des Princes, Paris
New Zealand 37 T: Lomu, Jones, Rush, Bunce; C: Culhane; PG: Culhane (5)
France 12 T: Saint-André (2); C: Castaignede

26 June 1999, Athletic Park, Wellington
New Zealand 54 T: Umaga (3), Cullen (2), Marshall (2); C: Mehrtens (5); PG: Mehrtens (3)
France 7 T: Mola; C: Castaignede

31 October 1999, Twickenham, London (RWC, S/F)
France 43 T: Lamaison, Dominci, Dourthe, Bernat-Salles; C: Lamaison (4); PG: Lamaison (3); DG: Lamaison (2)
New Zealand 31 T: Lomu (2), Wilson; C: Mehrtens (2); PG: Mehrtens (4)

11 November 2000, Stade de France, Paris
New Zealand 39 T: Howlett, Cullen; C: Mehrtens; PG: Mehrtens (9)
France 26 T: Bernat-Salles, Pelous; C: Lamaison (2); PG: Lamaison (4)

18 November 2000, Stade Velodrome, Marseille
France 42 T: Garbajosa, Magne, Galthie; C: Lamaison (3); PG: Lamaison (5); DG: Lamaison (2)
New Zealand 33 T: Marshall, Howlett, Slater; C: Mehrtens (3); PG: Mehrtens (4)

30 June 2001, Westpac Trust Stadium, Wellington
New Zealand   37   T: Wilson, Lomu, Thorne, Howlett; C: Brown (4); PG: Brown (3)
France   12   PG: Skrela (4)

16 November 2002, Stade de France, Paris
France   20   T: Magne, Brusque; C: Gelez (2); PG: Gelez (2)
New Zealand   20   T: Meeuws, Umaga; C: Mehrtens (2); PG: Mehrtens (2)

28 June 2003, Jade Stadium, Christchurch
New Zealand   31   T: Rokocoko (3); C: Carter (2); PG: Carter (4)
France   23   T: Marconnet, Jauzion; C: Michalak, Merceron; PG: Michalak, Traille; DG: Michalak

20 November 2003, Stadium Australia, Sydney (RWC, 3/4 play-off)
New Zealand   40   T: Jack, Howlett, Rokocoko, Thorn, Muliaina, Holah; C: Carter (4), MacDonald
France   13   T: Elhorga; C: Yachvili; PG: Yachvili; DG: Yachvili

27 November 2004, Stade de France, Paris
New Zealand   45   T: So'oialo, Collins, Carter, Kelleher, Nonu; C: Carter (4); PG: Carter (4)
France   6   PG: Michalak (2)

11 November 2006, Stade Gerland, Lyon
New Zealand   47   T: Sivivatu (2), McCaw, Carter, Smith, Rokocoko, McAlister; C: Carter (3); PG: Carter (2)
France   3   DG: Fritz

18 November 2006, Stade de France, Paris
New Zealand   23   T: Rokocoko, Nonu; C: Carter (2); PG: Carter (3)
France   11   T: Heymans; PG: Yachvili (2)

2 June 2007, Eden Park, Auckland
New Zealand   42   T: Mauger (2), Sivivatu (2), So'oialo; C: Carter, Weepu, Evans (2); PG: Carter, Weepu, Evans
France   11   T: Coux; PG: Boyet (2)

9 June 2007, Westpac Stadium, Wellington
New Zealand   61   T: Rokocoko (2), Oliver, Kelleher, MacDonald, Collins, Toeava, Mealamu, Evans; C: McAlister (5);
                                 PG: McAlister (2)
France   10   T: J Laharrague; C: Boyet; PG: Boyet

6 October 2007, Millennium Stadium, Cardiff (RWC, Q/F)
France   20   T: Dusautoir, Jauzion; C: Beauxis, Elissalde; PG: Beauxis (2)
New Zealand   18   T: McAlister, So'oialo; C: Carter; PG: Carter (2)

13 June 2009, Carisbrook, Dunedin
France   27   T: Trinh-Duc, Servat, Medard; C: Dupuy (3); PG: Dupuy (2)
New Zealand   22   T: Messam, Nonu; PG: Donald (4)

20 June 2009, Westpac Stadium, Wellington
New Zealand   14   T: Nonu; PG: Donald (2), McAlister
France   10   T: Heymans; C: Dupuy; PG: Yachvili

| Dave Gallaher Cup | | Current holder: France | | | Number of titles: New Zealand 7, France 1 | |
No.	Date	Venue	Result			Winner
1	11/11/2000	Stade de France, Paris	France	26–39	New Zealand	New Zealand
2	30/06/2001	Westpac Trust Stadium, Wellington	New Zealand	37–12	France	New Zealand
3	16/11/2002	Stade de France, Paris	France	20–20	New Zealand	New Zealand
4	28/06/2003	Jade Stadium, Christchurch	New Zealand	31–23	France	New Zealand
5	27/11/2004	Stade de France, Paris	France	6–45	New Zealand	New Zealand
6	11/11/2006	Stade Gerland, Lyon	France	3–47	New Zealand	New Zealand
7	02/06/2007	Eden Park, Auckland	New Zealand	42–11	France	New Zealand
8	13/06/2009	Carisbrook, Dunedin	New Zealand	22–27	France	France
9	20/06/2009	Westpac Stadium Wellington	New Zealand	14–10	France	

FRANCE

France vs New Zealand Maoris

26 December 1926, Stade Olympique Yves-du-Manoir, Paris
NZ Maoris 12 T: Barclay (2), Rika, Falwasser
France 3 T: Ribere

France vs Pacific Islanders

15 November 2008, Stade Auguste Bonal, Sochaux
France 42 T: Szarzewski, Tillous-Bordes, Heymans, Picamoles, Médard; C: Skréla (4); PG: Skréla (3)
Pacific Islanders 17 T: Taione; PG: Bai (4)

France vs Romania	
Played:	49
Won:	39
Lost:	8
Drawn:	2
For:	1,277
Against:	451

Average score:
26.02–9.2

France percentages:
Won:	79.59%
Lost:	16.33%
Drawn:	4.08%

France vs Romania

4 May 1924, Stade Olympique Yves-du-Manoir, Paris
France 61 T: Jaurequy (4), Got (2), Gerintes (2), Dupouy (2), Behotequy (2), Etcheberry; C: Bequet (8); PG: Bequet, Behotequy
Romania 3 PG: Florian

15 May 1938, Dinamo Stadion, Bucharest
France 11 T: Blond, Caunegre, le Goff; C: Desclaux
Romania 8 T: Andries; C: Irimia; PG: Irimia

19 May 1957, Dinamo Stadoin, Bucharest
France 18 T: Vignes; PG: Vannier (4); DG: Vannier
Romania 15 PG: Penciu (2), Ionescu; DG: Penciu, Ionescu

15 December 1957, Stade Municipal, Bordeaux
France 39 T: Dupuy (3), Boniface (2), Crauste, Vannier, Viqier; C: Vannier (6); PG: Vannier
Romania 0

5 June 1960, Dinamo Stadion, Bucharest
Romania 11 T: Barbu; C: Penciu; DG: Penciu (2)
France 5 T: Moncla; C: Vannier

12 November 1961, Parc Municipal, Bayonne
France 5 T: Lacaze; C: Marracq
Romania 5 T: Moraru; C: Penciu

11 November 1962, Dinamo Stadion, Bucharest
Romania 3 PG: Penciu
France 0

15 December 1963, Stade Toulouse, Toulouse
France 6 T: Dupuy, Gachassin
Romania 6 T: Rahtopol; DG: Penciu

29 November 1964, Dinamo Stadion, Bucharest
France 9 T: Camberabero, Gachassin; DG: Camberabero
Romania 6 T: Wusek; PG: Peciu

28 November 1965, Stade Gerland, Lyon
France 8 T: G Boniface (2); C: A Boniface
Romania 3 DG: Dragomirescu

27 November 1966, Dinamo Stadion, Bucharest
France 9 T: Duprat, Salut; PG: Lacaze
Romania 3 PG: Penciu

10 December 1967, Stade le Beajoire, Nantes
France 11 T: Capendequy; C: Lacaze; PG: Lacaze; DG: Lacaze
Romania 3 PG: Penciu

1 December 1968, Dinamo Stadion, Bucharest
Romania 15 PG: Irimescu (4); DG: Irimescu
France 14 T: Bonal; C: Paries; PG: Paries (3)

14 December 1969, Stade Maurice Trelut, Tarbes
France   14   T: Dauga; C: Dehez; PG: Dehez (2); DG: Dehez
Romania   9   PG: Irimescu (2); DG: Irimescu

29 November 1970, Dinamo Stadion, Bucharest
France   14   T: Pebeyre; C: Villepreux; PG: Villipreux (3)
Romania   3   PG: Irimescu

11 December 1971, Parc Sauclieres, Beziers
France   31   T: Cantoni, Dourthe, Dubertrand, Maso; C: Villepreux (3); PG: Villepreux (3)
Romania   12   PG: Irimescu (2); DG: Durbac, Nicolescu

26 November 1972, Stade 1 Mai, Constanta
France   15   T: Trillo; C: Romeu; PG: Romeu (3)
Romania   6   PG: Nica (2)

11 November 1973, Valence
France   7   T: Bertranne; DG: Romeu
Romania   6   PG: Durbac (2)

13 October 1974, Dinamo Stadion, Bucharest
Romania   15   T: Marica; C: Durbac; PG: Durbac (2), Nica
France   10   T: Gourdon; PG: Romeu (2)

23 November 1975, Stade Municipal, Bordeaux
France   36   T: Dubertrand (3), Bastiat, Fouroux, Pecune; C: Romeu (3); PG: Romeu, Bastiat
Romania   12   PG: Bucos (3); DG: Bucos

14 November 1976, Dinamo Stadion, Bucharest
Romania   15   T: Alexandru, Murariu, Paraschiv; DG: Bucos
France   12   T: Bastiat; C: Aquirre; PG: Aquirre (2)

10 December 1977, Stade Marcel Michelin, Clermont-Ferrand
France   9   PG: Romeu (3)
Romania   6   PG: Bucos; DG: Alexandru

3 December 1978, Dinamo Stadion, Bucharest
France   9   PG: Aquirre (2); DG: Caussade
Romania   6   PG: Constantin (2)

2 December 1979, Stade de Sapiac, Montauban
France   30   T: Joinel, Codorniou, Bertranne C: Aquirre (2), Caussade; PG: Caussade (2), Aquirre; DG: Aquirre
Romania   12   PG: Constantin (3); DG: Constantin

23 November 1980, Dinamo Stadion, Bucharest
Romania   15   T: Bors; C: Constantin; PG: Constantin (3)
France   0

1 November 1981, de l'Egassiairal, Narbonne
France   17   T: Elissalde, Blanco; PG: Gabernet (2); DG: Laporte
Romania   9   PG: Constantin (3)

31 October 1982, Dinamo Stadion, Bucharest
Romania   13   T: Paraschiv; PG: Ion, Podarascu; DG: Podarascu
France   9   T: Fabre; C: Camberabero; DG: Camberabero

4 December 1983, Stade Ernest Wallan, Toulouse
France   26   T: Esteve, Gallion, Lagisquet, Lescarboura; C: Lescarboura (2); PG: Lescarboura; DG: Lescarboura
Romania   15   T: Radulescu; C: Podarascu; PG: Podarascu (3)

10 November 1984, Dinamo Stadion, Bucharest
France   18   T: Sella, Lescarboura; C: Lescarboura (2); PG: Lescarboura (2)
Romania   3   PG: Alexandru

12 April 1986, Stade Nord, Lille
France   25   T: Charvet, Bonneval, Sella, Erbani, Lagisquet; C: Laporte; PG: Laporte
Romania   13   T: David, Hodorca; C: Ignat; PG: Ignat

FRANCE

25 October 1986, Dinamo Stadion, Bucharest
| France | 20 | T: Andrieu, Blanco, Berot; C: Berot; PG: Berot (2) |
| Romania | 3 | PG: Nastese |

28 May 1987, Athletic Park, Wellington (RWC, Pool 4)
| France | 55 | T: Charvet (2), Andrieu, Sella, Laporte, Erbani, Camberabero, Lagisquet (2); C: Laporte (8); PG: Laporte |
| Romania | 12 | PG: Bezuscu (4) |

11 November 1987, Stade Armandie, Agen
| France | 49 | T: Lagisquet (2), Andrieu (2), Berot, Ondarts, penalty try; C: Berot (6); PG: Berot (3) |
| Romania | 3 | DG: Alexandru |

26 November 1988, Dinamo Stadion, Bucharest
| France | 16 | T: Blanco, Lagisquet; C: Berot; PG: Berot (2) |
| Romania | 12 | T: Neaga; C: Ignat; PG: Ignat (2) |

24 May 1990, Stade Jacques Fouroux, Auch
| Romania | 12 | PG: Ignat (3); DG: Ignat |
| France | 6 | PG: Lescarboura (2) |

22 June 1991, Dinamo Stadion, Bucharest
| France | 33 | T: Blanco, Camberabero, Cecillon, Simon; C: Camberabero; PG: Camberabero (5) |
| Romania | 21 | T: Dumitras; C: Nichitean; PG: Nichitean (5) |

4 October 1991, Parc Sauclieres, Beziers (RWC, Pool 4)
| France | 30 | T: Saint-André, Roumat, Lafond, penalty try; C: Camberabero; PG: Camberabero (4) |
| Romania | 3 | PG: Nichitean |

28 May 1992, Stade Municipal Jules Deschaseaux, Le Havre
| France | 25 | T: Saint-André, Cadieu, Galthie, penalty try; C: Lacroix (2), Viars; PG: Viars |
| Romania | 6 | PG: Racean (2) |

20 May 1993, Dinamo Stadion, Bucharest
| France | 37 | T: Bernat-Salles (3), Cecillon; C: Viars (4); PG: Viars (3) |
| Romania | 20 | T: Leonte, Neaga; C: Nichitean (2); PG: Nichitran (2) |

17 October 1993, Parc Municipal, Brive
| France | 51 | T: Bernat-Salles (3), Sella, Loppy, Merle; C: Lacroix (6); PG: Lacroix (3) |
| Romania | 0 | |

8 April 1995, Dinamo Stadion, Bucharest
| France | 24 | T: Sadourny, penalty try; C: Lacroix; PG: Lacroix (4) |
| Romania | 15 | PG: Nichitean (2); DG: Nichitean (3) |

17 October 1995, Stadio Cancha del Atletico, Tucuman
| France | 52 | T: Arlettaz (2), Carminati, Castiagnede, Delaigue, Lievremont, Pelous; C: Castaignede (4); PG: Castaignede (2); DG: Castaignede |
| Romania | 8 | T: Negreci; DG: Maftei |

20 April 1996, Stade Jean Alric, Aurillac
| France | 64 | T: Califano (3), Glas (2), Labrousse (2), Moni, N'tamack, Penaud; C: Dourthe (7) |
| Romania | 12 | PG: Popisteanu (3); DG: Popisteanu |

1 June 1997, Dinamo Stadium, Bucharest
| France | 51 | T: Venditti (2), Viars (2), Merle, Bernat-Salles (2), Lievremont, Penaud; C: Lamaison (2), Viars |
| Romania | 20 | T: Gontineac, Radoi; C: Nichitean (2); PG: Nichitean (2) |

22 October 1997, Stade Antoine Beguere, Lourdes
| France | 39 | T: Benazzi, Merle, Saint-Andre, Tournaire, penalty try; C: Lamaison (4); PG: Lamaison (2) |
| Romania | 3 | PG: Tofan |

3 June 1999, Stade J-P Antoine, Castres
| France | 62 | T: Bernat-Salles, Crenca, dal Maso, Galthie, Sarramea, Mola (2), Delmotte (2); C: Lamaison (7); PG: Lamaison |
| Romania | 8 | T: Constantin; PG: Mitu |

28 May 2000, Dinamo Stadium, Bucharest
| France | 67 | T: Dominici (3), Ibanez (2), Benazzi, Merceron, Souverbie, Elissalde, Nallet; C: Dourthe (7); PG: Dourthe |
| Romania | 20 | T: Brezoianu, Mavrodin, Solomie; C: Vusec PG: Vusec |

22 August 2003, Stade Felix-Bollaert, Lens
France   56   T: Betsen, Crenca, Magne, Rougerie, Jauzion, Harinordoquy, Liebenberg, Traille; C: Michalak (7), Merceron
Romania   8   T: Brezoianu; PG: Dumbrava

17 June 2006, Cotroceni Stadium, Bucharest
France   62   T: Jauzion, Martin, Dusautoir, Traille, Marconnet, Castaignede, Szarzewski, Laharrague, Marty; C: Traille (6), Castaignede; PG: Traille
Romania   14   T: Fercu; PG: Vlaicu (3)

France vs Samoa

12 June 1999, Apia Stadium, Apia
France   39   T: Magne, Mignoni, Artiguste, dal Maso, Castaignede; C: Castaignede (4); PG: Castaignede (2)
Samoa   22   T: Leaupepe; C: Schuster; PG: Schuster (3), Bachop (2)

France vs Scotland	
Played:	82
Won:	45
Lost:	34
Drawn:	3
For:	1,111
Against:	969
Average score:	
13.55–11.82	
France percentages:	
Won:	54.88%
Lost:	41.46%
Drawn:	3.66%

France vs Scotland

Scotland was the last of the four home nations to play France in a test, in 1910, the same year that France was first included in the Five Nations. Scotland won comfortably that day but, incredibly, lost the following year in Paris, letting France record their first Five Nations victory. The 1913 game was not a happy occasion regardless of the fact that the Scots won 21–3: the English referee so incensed the Parisian crowd that he and some of the Scottish players were jeered and jostled off the pitch at the end of the game. Scotland were so furious with their French hosts that they refused to play them the following year. However, during Word War I time was the healer and since then two have met happily every year expect during World War II. Each has taken turns in dominating the series, but with the French holding the upper hand as of now. The two have met three times in RWCs, producing the first draw in an RWC, in 1987 at 20 all. Scotland have yet to beat France in an RWC.

22 January 1910, Inverleith, Edinburgh
Scotland   27   T: Tennent (3), Robertson (2), Angus, Gowlland; C: MacCallum (3)
France   0

2 January 1911, Stade Olympique Yves-du-Manoir, Paris
France   16   T: Laterrade, Failliot (2), Peyroutou; C: Descamps (2)
Scotland   15   T: MacCallum, Munro, Abercrombie; C: Turner; DG: Pearson

20 January 1912, Inverleith, Edinburgh
Scotland   31   T: Gunn, Sutherland (2), Pearson, Will, Turner; C: Turner (5); PG: Pearson
France   3   T: Communeau

1 January 1913, Parc des Princes, Paris
Scotland   21   T: Stewart (3), Gordon (2); C: Turner (3)
France   3   T: Sebedio

1 January 1920, Parc des Princes, Paris
Scotland   5   T: Crole; C: Kennedy
France   0

22 January 1921, Inverleith, Edinburgh
France   3   T: Billac
Scotland   0

2 January 1922, Stade Olympique Yves-du-Manoir, Paris
France   3   T: Jaureguy
Scotland   3   T: Browning

20 January 1923, Inverleith, Edinburgh
Scotland   16   T: McClaren (2), Bryce, Liddell; C: Drysdale (2)
France   3   GM: Beguet

FRANCE

1 January 1924, Stade Charlety, Paris
France   12   T: Jaureguy, Piquiral, Galau, Moureu
Scotland   10   T: Wallace; DG: Waddell; PG: Davies

24 January 1925, Inverleith, Edinburgh
Scotland   25   T: Smith (4), Wallace (2), Gillies; C: Gillies, Drysdale
France   4   DG: du Manoir

2 January 1926, Stade Olympique Yves-du-Manoir, Paris
Scotland   20   T: Wallace (3), MacMyn, Bannerman; C: Drysdale; PG: Gillies
France   6   T: Piquiral; PG: Gonnet

22 January 1927, Murrayfield, Edinburgh
Scotland   23   T: Waddell (2), Smith (2); C: Gillies (3), Drysdale; PG: Gilles
France   6   T: Piquiral, Hutin

2 January 1928, Stade Olympique Yves-du-Manoir, Paris
Scotland   15   T: Simmers, Paterson, Dykes, Douty, Scott
France   6   T: Haget, Camel

19 January 1929, Murrayfield, Edinburgh
Scotland   6   T: Paterson; PG: Brown
France   3   T: Behoteguy

1 January 1930, Stade Olympique Yves-du-Manoir, Paris
France   7   T: Bioussa; DG: Magnanou
Scotland   3   T: Simmers

24 January 1931, Murrayfield, Edinburgh
Scotland   6   PG: Allan (2)
France   4   DG: Servole

1 January 1947, Stade Olympique Yves-du-Manoir, Paris
France   8   T: Lassegue, Terreau; C: Prat
Scotland   3   PG: Geddes

24 January 1948, Murrayfield, Edinburgh
Scotland   9   T: Jackson; PG: Murdoch (2)
France   8   T: Lacaussade; C: Alvarez; PG: Prat

15 January 1949, Stade Olympique Yves-du-Manoir, Paris
Scotland   8   T: Elliot, Kininmonth; C: Alardice
France   0

14 January 1950, Murrayfield, Edinburgh
Scotland   8   T: MacDonald, Budge; C: Bruce-Lockhart
France   5   T: Merquey; C: Prat

13 January 1951, Stade Olympique Yves-du-Manoir, Paris
France   14   T: Mias, Porthault; C: Prat; PG: Prat (2)
Scotland   12   T: Rose (2); PG: Gray (2)

12 January 1952, Murrayfield, Edinburgh
France   13   T: J Prat, Basquet; C: J Prat (2); PG: J Prat
Scotland   11   T: Cordial; C: Thomson; PG: Thomson (2)

10 January 1953, Stade Olympique Yves-du-Manoir, Paris
France   11   T: Bordeau; C: Bertrand; DG: Carabignac; PG: Bertrand
Scotland   5   T: Rose; C: Cameron

9 January 1954, Murrayfield, Edinburgh
France   3   T: Brejassou
Scotland   0

8 January 1955, Stade Olympique Yves-du-Manoir, Paris
France   15   T: Boniface, J Prat, Domenech, Dufau; PG: Vannier
Scotland   0

FRANCE

14 January 1956, Murrayfield, Edinburgh
Scotland   12   T: Kemp (2); PG: Smith, Cameron
France   0

12 January 1957, Stade Olympique Yves-du-Manoir, Paris
Scotland   6   DG: Scotland; PG: Scotland
France   0

11 January 1958, Murrayfield, Edinburgh
Scotland   11   T: Stevenson, Hastie; C: Chisholm; PG: Chisholm
France   9   T: Dupuy; PG: Vannier (2)

10 January 1959, Stade Olympique Yves-du-Manoir, Paris
France   9   T: Moncla; DG: Lacaze (2)
Scotland   0

9 January 1960, Murrayfield, Edinburgh
France   13   T: Meyer, Mericq, Moncla; C: Vannier (2)
Scotland   11   T: A Smith (2); C: Elliot; PG: Elliot

7 January 1961, Stade Olympique Yves-du-Manoir, Paris
France   11   T: Boniface; C: Albaladejo; DG: Albaladejo; PG: Albaladejo
Scotland   0

13 January 1962, Murrayfield, Edinburgh
France   11   T: Rancoule; C: Albaladejo; PG: Albaladejo (2)
Scotland   3   PG: Smith

12 January 1963, Stade Olympique Yves-du-Manoir, Paris
Scotland   11   T: Thomson; C: Scotland; DG: Scotland; PG: Scotland
France   6   DG: A Boniface; PG: Albaladejo

4 January 1964, Murrayfield, Edinburgh
Scotland   10   T: Laughland, Thomson; C: Wilson (2)
France   0

9 January 1965, Stade Olympique Yves-du-Manoir, Paris
France   16   T: Gachassin, Pique, Darrouy (2); C: Didieu (2)
Scotland   8   T: Henderson (2); C: Scotland

15 January 1966, Murrayfield, Edinburgh
Scotland   3   T: Whyte
France   3   PG: Lacaze

14 January 1967, Stade Olympique Yves-du-Manoir, Paris
Scotland   9   DG: Simmers; PG: Wilson (2)
France   8   T: Duprat, Carrere; C: Gachassin

13 January 1968, Murrayfield, Edinburgh
France   8   T: Duprat, Campaes; C: G Camberabero
Scotland   6   T: Keith; PG: Wilson

11 January 1969, Stade Olympique Yves-du-Manoir, Paris
Scotland   6   T: J Telfer; PG: Blaikie
France   3   PG: Villepreux

10 January 1970, Murrayfield, Edinburgh
France   11   T: Dauga, Lux; C: Paries; DG: Paries
Scotland   9   T: Smith; PG: Lauder (2)

16 January 1971, Stade Olympique Yves-du-Manoir, Paris
France   13   T: Sillieres, Villepreux; C: Villepreux (2); PG: Villepreux
Scotland   8   T: Steele; C: P Brown; PG: Smith

15 January 1972, Murrayfield, Edinburgh
Scotland   20   T: Telfer, Renwick, Frame; C: A Brown; DG: Telfer; PG: P Brown
France   9   T: Dauga; C: Villepreux; PG: Villepreux

FRANCE

13 January 1973, Parc des Princes, Paris
France 16   T: Dourthe; DG: Romeu; PG: Romeu (3)
Scotland 13   T: Lawson; DG: McGeechan; PG: Brown (2)

16 March 1974, Murrayfield, Edinburgh
Scotland 19   T: McHarg, Dick; C: Irvine; PG: Morgan, Irvine (2)
France 6   DG: Romeu; PG: Romeu

15 February 1975, Parc des Princes, Paris
France 10   T: Dourthe; DG: Astre; PG: Paries
Scotland 9   PG: Irvine (3)

10 January 1976, Murrayfield, Edinburgh
France 13   T: Dubertrand; PG: Romeu (3)
Scotland 6   DG: Morgan; PG: Renwick

5 March 1977, Parc des Princes, Paris
France 23   T: Harize, Bertranne, Paco, Paparemborde; C: Romeu (2); PG: Romeu
Scotland 3   PG: Irvine

4 February 1978, Murrayfield, Edinburgh
France 19   T: Gallion, Haget; C: Aguirre; PG: Aguirre (3)
Scotland 16   T: Shedden, Irvine; C: Morgan; DG: Morgan; PG: Morgan

17 March 1979, Parc des Princes, Paris
France 21   T: Belascain, Malquier (2); DG: Aguerre; PG: Aguerre, Aguirre
Scotland 17   T: Irvine, Dickson, Robertson; C: Irvine; PG: Irvine

16 February 1980, Murrayfield, Edinburgh
Scotland 22   T: Rutherford, Irvine (2); C: Irvine, Renwick; PG: Irvine (2)
France 14   T: Gallion, Gabernet; DG: Caussade; PG: Gabernet

17 January 1981, Parc des Princes, Paris
France 16   T: Blanco, Bertranne; C: Caussade; PG: Vivies, Gabernet
Scotland 9   T: Rutherford; C: Renwick; PG: Irvine

6 March 1982, Murrayfield, Edinburgh
Scotland 16   T: Rutherford; DG: Renwick; PG: Irvine (3)
France 7   T: Rives; PG: Sallefranque

5 February 1983, Parc des Princes, Paris
France 19   T: Estève (2); C: Blanco; PG: Blanco (3)
Scotland 15   T: Robertson; C: Dods; DG: Gossman (2); PG: Dods

17 March 1984, Murrayfield, Edinburgh
Scotland 21   T: Calder; C: Dods; PG: Dods (5)
France 12   T: Gallion; C: Lescarboura; PG: Lescarboura; DG: Lescarboura

16 February 1985, Parc des Princes, Paris
France 11   T: Blanco (2); PG: Lescarboura
Scotland 3   PG: Dods

17 January 1986, Murrayfield, Edinburgh
Scotland 18   PG: G Hastings (6)
France 17   T: Berbizier, Sella; PG: Laporte (2); DG: Laporte

7 March 1987, Parc des Princes, Paris
France 28   T: Bonneval (3), Berot; PG: Berot (3); DG: Mesnel
Scotland 22   T: Beattie, S Hastings; C: G Hastings; PG: G Hastings (4)

23 May 1987, Lancaster Park, Christchurch (RWC, Pool 4)
Scotland 20   T: White, Duncan; PG: G Hastings (4)
France 20   T: Sella, Berbizier, Blanco; C: Blanco; PG: Blanco (2)

6 February 1988, Murrayfield, Edinburgh
Scotland 23   T: G Hastings, Tukalo; PG: G Hastings (4); DG: Cramb
France 12   T: Lagisquet; C: Berot; PG: Berot; DG: Lescarboura

18 March 1989, Parc des Princes, Paris
France   19   T: Berbizier, Blanco, Lagisquet; C: Berot (2); PG: Berot
Scotland   3   PG: Dods

17 February 1990, Murrayfield, Edinburgh
Scotland   21   T: F Calder, Tukalo; C: Chalmers (2); PG: Chalmers (2), G Hastings
France   0

19 January 1991, Parc des Princes, Paris
France   15   PG: Camberabero (2); DG: Camberabero (2), Blanco
Scotland   9   PG: Chalmers (2); DG: Chalmers

7 March 1992, Murrayfield, Edinburgh
Scotland   10   T: Edwards; PG: G Hastings (2)
France   6   PG: Lafond (2)

6 February 1993, Parc des Princes, Paris
France   11   T: Lacroix; PG: Camberabero (2)
Scotland   3   PG: G Hastings

19 March 1994, Murrayfield, Edinburgh
France   20   T: Sadourny, Saint-André; C: Lacroix, Montlaur; PG: Lacroix (2)
Scotland   12   PG: G Hastings (4)

18 February 1995, Parc des Princes, Paris
Scotland   23   T: G Hastings, Townsend; C: G Hastings (2); PG: G Hastings (3)
France   21   T: Saint-André (2), Sadourny; PG: Lacroix; DG: Deylaud

3 June 1995, Loftus Versfeld, Pretoria (RWC, Pool D)
France   22   T: N'Tamack; C: Lacroix; PG: Lacroix (5)
Scotland   19   T: Wainwright; C: G Hastings; PG: G Hastings (4)

3 February 1996, Murrayfield, Edinburgh
Scotland   19   T: Dods (2); PG: Dods (3)
France   14   T: Benazzi; PG: Lacroix (2), Castaignede

15 March 1997, Parc des Princes, Paris
France   47   T: Benazzi, del Maso, Leflamand, Magne; C: Lamaison (3); PG: Lamaison (6); DG: Sadourny
Scotland   20   T: Tait (2); C: Shepherd (2); PG: Shepherd (2)

21 February 1998, Murrayfield, Edinburgh
France   51   T: Lievremont (2), Califano, Carbonneau, Bernat-Salles (2), Castaignede; C: Lamaison (2), Castaignede (3);
                      PG: Lamaison, Castaignede
Scotland   16   T: Stanger; C: Chalmers; PG: Chalmers (3)

10 April 1999, Stade de France, Paris
Scotland   36   T: M Leslie (2), Tait (2), Townsend; C: Logan (4); PG: Logan
France   22   T: N'Tamack, Juillet, Dominici; C: Aucagne (2); PG: Aucagne

4 March 2000, Murrayfield, Edinburgh
France   28   T: Magne (2), Castaignede; C: Merceron (2); PG: Merceron (3)
Scotland   16   T: Nicol; C: Paterson; PG: Paterson (2), Logan

4 February 2001, Stade de France, Paris
France   16   T: Bernat-Salles; C: Lamaison; PG: Lamaison (3)
Scotland   6   PG: Logan (2)

23 March 2002, Murrayfield, Edinburgh
France   22   T: Marsh (2), Galthie; C: Merceron (2); PG: Merceron
Scotland   10   T: Redpath; C: Laney; PG: Laney

23 February 2003, Stade de France, Paris
France   38   T: Pelous, Poitrenaud, Traille, Rougerie; C: Gelez (3); PG: Gelez (4)
Scotland   3   PG: Paterson

25 October 2003, Stadium Australia, Sydney (RWC, Pool B)
France   51   T: Betsen, Harinordoquy, Michalak, Galthie, Brusque; C: Michalak (4); PG: Michalak (4);
                      DG: Michalak, Brusque
Scotland   9   PG: Paterson (3)

FRANCE

21 March 2004, Murrayfield, Edinburgh
France   31   T: Jauzion (2), Magne; C: Yachvili (2); PG: Yachvili (4)
Scotland   0

5 February 2005, Stade de France, Paris
France   16   T: Traille; C: Michalak; PG: Delaigue (2); DG: Delaigue
Scotland   9   PG: Paterson (3)

4 February 2006, Murrayfield, Edinburgh
Scotland   20   T: Lamont (2); C: Paterson (2); PG: Paterson (2)
France   16   T: Bonnaire, Bruno; PG: Elissalde (2)

17 March 2007, Stade de France, Paris
France   46   T: Harinordoquy, Jauzion, Marty, Heymans, Milloud, Vermeulen; C: Beauxis (5); PG: Beauxis (2)
Scotland   19   T: Walker, S Lamont, E Murray; C: Paterson (2)

3 February 2008, Murrayfield, Edinburgh
France   27   T: Clerc (2), Malzieu; C: Elissalde (2), Skrela; PG: Traille (2)
Scotland   6   PG: Parks; DG: Parks

14 February 2009, Stade de France, Paris
France   22   T: Ouedraogo; C: Beauxis; PG: Beauxis (5)
Scotland   13   T: T Evans; C: Paterson; PG: Godman (2)

France vs South Africa	
Played:	36
Won:	10
Lost:	20
Drawn:	6
For:	531
Against:	709

Average score:
14.75–19.69

France percentages:
Won:	27.77%
Lost:	55.56%
Drawn:	16.67%

France vs South Africa

On 3 January 1907, South Africa played against a French XV in Paris and won by 55–6, but it was not until 11 January 1913 that the two sides officially met in Bordeaux where South Africa won 38–5. Their next game was not until 1952. French rugby improved immeasurably from this point and in 1958 France stunned the world when they won a series in South Africa: one of the first great upsets in world rugby. However, South Africa were not to lose another series to the French until 1993, achieving record scorelines in the late 1970s and early 1980s. The two sides met in the epic 1995 rain-soaked RWC semi-final, and in 1996 and 1997 South Africa won back-to-back series in France, including a record 52–10 whipping of the French at the Parc des Princes. Following the loss, the French have somewhat dominated the series losing just twice. Of the 36 matches played, six have been drawn – a remarkable statistic comparatively, proving just how tight the series has been, and is.

11 January 1913, Route du Medoc, Bordeaux
South Africa   38   T: W Morkel, D Morkel (2), Francis, R Luyt, McHardy (2), Ledger, J Morkel; C: D Morkel (2), G Morkel (2); PG: D Morkel
France   5   T: Bruneau; C: André

16 February 1952, Stade Olympique Yves-du-Manoir, Paris
South Africa   25   T: Johnstone (2), Dinkelmann, Muller, Delport, van Wyk; C: Muller, Johnstone; PG: Johnstone
France   3   DG: Carbignac

26 July 1958, Newlands, Cape Town
South Africa   3   T: Lochner
France   3   DG: Danos

16 August 1958, Ellis Park, Johannesburg
France   9   PG: Lacaze; DG: Lacaze, Martine
South Africa   5   T: Fourie; C: Gerber

18 February 1961, Stade Olympique Yves-du-Manoir, Paris
France   0
South Africa   0

25 July 1964, PAM Brink Stadium, Springs
France   8   T: Darrouy; C: Albaladejo; PG: Albaladejo
South Africa   6   T: Stewart; PG: Stewart

15 July 1967, Kings Park, Durban
South Africa   26   T: Dirksen (2), Greyling (2), Ellis; C: H de Villiers (4); PG: H de Villiers
France   3   T: Dourthe

22 July 1967, Free State Stadium, Bloemfontein
South Africa   16   T: Olivier, Dirkson, Engelbrecht; C: H de Villiers (2); PG: Naudé
France   3   PG: Villepreux

29 July 1967, Ellis Park, Johannesburg
France   19   T: Cabanier, Trillo; C: G Camberabero (2); DG: G Camberabero (2); PG: Lacaze
South Africa   14   T: Olivier, Ellis; C: Visagie; PG: Naudé (2)

12 August 1967, Newlands, Cape Town
South Africa   6   DG: Visagie; PG: H de Villiers
France   6   T: Spanghero; PG: G Camberabero

9 November 1968, Stade Municipal, Bordeaux
South Africa   12   PG: Visagie (4)
France   9   T: Dauga (2), Bonal

16 November 1968, Stade Olympique Yves-du-Manoir, Paris
South Africa   16   T: Engelbrecht, D de Villiers, Nomis; C: Visagie (2); PG: Visagie
France   11   T: Cester; C: Paries; DG: Puget, Paries

12 June 1971, Free State Stadium, Bloemfontein
South Africa   22   T: Muller, Viljoen; C: McCallum (2); PG: McCallum (3); DG: Visagie
France   9   T: Trillo; PG: Berot (2)

19 June 1971, Kings Park, Durban
South Africa   8   T: Cronje; C: McCallum; DG: Visagie
France   8   T: Bertranne; C: Berot; DG: Cantoni

23 November 1974, Stade Municipal, Toulouse
South Africa   13   T: Stapelberg; PG: Bosch (2), C Fourie
France   4   T: Bertranne

30 November 1974, Parc des Prince, Paris
South Africa   10   T: Stapelberg; PG: Bosch (2)
France   8   T: Gourdon, Dourthe

21 June 1975, Free State Stadium, Bloemfontein
South Africa   38   T: Whipp, Grobler, Cockrell, Oosthuizen, Pope; C: Bosch (2), D Snyman; PG: Bosch (3), D Snyman
France   25   T: Skrela, Paparemborde, Averous, Harize; C: Pesteil (3); PG: Pesteil

28 June 1975, Loftus Versfeld, Pretoria
South Africa   33   T: C Fourie, du Plessis; C: Bosch (2); PG: Bosch (6), C Fourie
France   18   T: E Paparemborde; C: Romeu; DG: Romeu; PG: Romeu (3)

8 November 1980, Loftus Versfeld, Pretoria
South Africa   37   T: Pienaar, Germishuys, Serfontein, Stofberg, Kahts; C: Botha (4); PG: Botha (3)
France   15   T: Dintrans; C: Vivies; PG: Vivies (3)

17 October 1992, Stade Gerland, Lyons
South Africa   20   T: Small, Gerber; C: Botha (2); PG: Botha; DG: Botha
France   15   T: Penaud (2); C: Viars; PG: Viars

24 October 1992, Parc des Princes, Paris
France   29   T: Roumat, Penaud; C: Lacroix (2); PG: Lacroix (5)
South Africa   16   T: Gerber; C: Botha; PG: Botha (2); DG: Botha

26 June 1993, Kings Park, Durban
South Africa   20   T: Schmidt; PG: van Rensburg (5)
France   20   T: Saint-André; PG: Lacroix (3); DG: Hueber, Penaud

3 July 1993, Ellis Park, Johannesburg
France   18   PG: Lacroix (4); DG: Lacroix (2)
South Africa   17   T: Small; PG: van Rensburg (4)

FRANCE

17 June 1995, Kings Park, Durban (RWC, S/F)
South Africa	19	T: Kruger; C: Stransky; PG: Stransky (4)
France	15	PG: Lacroix (5)

30 November 1996, Stade Lescure, Bordeaux
South Africa	22	T: Small, Joubert; PG: Honiball (4)
France	12	PG: Dourthe (4)

7 December 1996, Parc des Princes, Paris
South Africa	13	T: Dalton; C: Honiball; PG: Honiball (2)
France	12	PG: Dourthe (4)

15 November 1997, Stade Gerland, Lyon
South Africa	36	T: Montgomery, Rossouw, Muir, Small, Dalton; C: Honiball (4); PG: Honiball
France	32	T: Merle, Glas, Califano; C: Lamaison; PG: Lamaison (5)

22 November 1997, Parc des Princes, Paris
South Africa	52	T: Rossouw (4), Snyman, Honiball, Teichmann; C: Honiball (7); PG: Honiball
France	10	T: Ibanez; C: Lamaison; PG: Lamaison

16 June 2001, Ellis Park, Johannesburg
France	32	T: Dominici. Merceron; C: Merceron (2); PG: Merceron (6)
South Africa	23	T: Paulse; PG: Montgomery (6)

23 June 2001, ABSA Stadium, Durban
South Africa	20	T: Krige; PG: James (5)
France	15	PG: Merceron (4); DG: Merceron

10 November 2001, Stade de France, Paris
France	20	T: Ibanez; PG: Gelez (4), Traille
South Africa	10	T: Rossouw; C: van Straaten; PG: van Straaten

9 November 2002, Stade Velodrome, Marseille
France	30	T: Clerc, Heymans; C: Gelez; PG: Gelez (5); DG: Castaignede
South Africa	10	T: van Nierkerk; C: Pretorius; PG: Pretorius

18 June 2005, The ABSA Stadium, Durban
South Africa	30	T: Habana (2), de Villiers; C: Montgomery (3); PG: Montgomery (2); DG: Montgomery
France	30	T: Nyanga, Pape, Bonnaire, Candelon; C: Elissalde (2); PG: Elissalde; DG: Michalak

25 June 2005, Eastern Province Rugby Football Union Stadium, Port Elizabeth
South Africa	27	T: Habana (2), de Villiers; C: Montgomery (3); PG: Montgomery (2)
France	13	T: Michalak; C: Michalak; PG: Michalak, Yachvili

26 November 2005, Stade de France, Paris
France	26	T: Svarzewski, Michalak, Rougerie; C: Elissalde; PG: Elissalde (2), Michalak
South Africa	20	T: J Botha, Fourie; C: Montgomery (2); PG: Montgomery, Bosman

24 June 2006, Newlands, Cape Town
France	36	T: Clerc (2), Traille, Heymans; C: Yachvili (2); PG: Yachvili (2); DG: Traille, Fritz
South Africa	26	T: Russell; PG: Montgomery (7)

France vs Tonga

26 May 1995, Loftus Versfeld, Pretoria (RWC, Pool D)
France	38	T: Lacroix (2), Hueber, Saint-André; C: Lacroix (3); PG: Lacroix (3); DG: Delaigue
Tonga	10	T: T Va'enuku; C: Tu'ipulotu; PG: Tu'ipulotu

16 June 1999, Teufaiva Stadium, Nuku'alofa
Tonga	20	T: Taumalolo (2), Taunaholo; C: Tu'ipulotu; PG: Tu'ipulotu
France	16	T: Sarramea; C: Lamaison; PG: Lamaison (3)

19 November 2005, Stade Municipal, Toulouse
France	43	T: Clerc (2), Lievremont, Rougerie, Jauzion; C: Yachvili (3); PG: Yachvili (4)
Tonga	8	T: Vaki; DG: Vunipola

FRANCE

FRANCE

France vs United States of America

France vs USA	
Played:	7
Won:	6
Lost:	1
Drawn:	0
For:	181
Against:	93

Average score:
25.86–13.29

France percentages:
Won:	85.71%
Lost:	14.29%
Drawn:	0%

10 October 1920, Stade Olympique Yves-du-Manoir, Paris
France 14 T: Billac, Borde, Got, Jaurequy; C: Struxianco
USA 5 T: MacDonald; C: Doe

18 May 1924, Stade Olympique Yves-du-Manoir, Paris
USA 17 T: Farrish (2), Patrick, Rodgers, Manelli; C: Doe
France 3 T: Gallau

12 June 1976, North Field, Chicago
France 33 T: Averous, Rousset, Romeu; C: Romeu (3); PG: Romeu (5)
USA 14 T: Fraumann (2); PG: Scott (2)

13 July 1991, Observatory Park, Denver
France 41 T: Blanco (2), Lafond, Courtoils, Champ, Mesnel, Saint-André, Cecillon; C: Camberabero (3); PG: Camberabero
USA 9 PG: O'Brein (3)

20 July 1991, Colorado Springs
France 10 T: Mesnel, Blanco; C: Camberabero
USA 3 PG: Williams

31 October 2003, WIN Stadium, Wollongong (RWC, Pool B)
France 41 T: Liebenberg (3), Poux, Bru; C: Merceron (2); PG: Merceron (3); DG: Yachvili
USA 14 T: Schubert, Hercus; C: Hercus (2)

3 July 2004, Rentschler Stadium, Hartford
France 39 T: Tabacco, Valbon, Barrau, Lievremont, de Villiers C: Peclier (4); PG: Peclier (2)
USA 31 T: Paga, Hercus, Naivalu, van Zyl, Mo'unga; C: Hercus (3)

France vs Wales

France vs Wales	
Played:	86
Won:	40
Lost:	43
Drawn:	3
For:	1,241
Against:	1,268

Average score:
14.43–14.74

France percentages:
Won:	46.51%
Lost:	50%
Drawn:	3.49%

After England added France to their calendar in 1906, Wales followed suit in 1908 to become the next home union to include the European newcomers in their diary. Wales completely dominated the French in the early encounters, winning by record scores as they racked up their Grand Slams of 1909, 1910 and 1911, including the emphatic, demoralising 14–49 loss for the French in their first Five Nations game. It would take France until 1928 to beat Wales and until 1948 to defeat them in Wales, in Swansea by 11–3. Following this, French form improved and by the late 1950s they were regularly winning home and away against Wales. Their clashes with the great Welsh sides of the 1970s produced some of the most entertaining and physical matches the Five Nations had seen in decades. Welsh form dipped in the 1980s as the French posted 12 victories in a row from 1983 to 1993. Matches in the late 1990s and the new century have been very entertaining affairs, regularly producing large scorelines, such as the 67-point thriller in 1999 when Wales unbelievably turned a 1998 0–51 drubbing into a 34–33 win in Paris. Two years later Wales won another high-scoring match by 43–35, only to lose the following year by 33–37, both classic encounters of the highest order. Of late, France have dominated the Welsh, having only lost twice: during Wales's Grand Slam campaign of 2005 and 2008.

2 March 1908, Cardiff Arms Park, Cardiff
Wales 36 T: Gibbs (4), Jones, Morgan (2), Trew (2); C: Winfield (2), Gibbs; PG: Winfield
France 4 DG: Vareilles

23 February 1909, Stade Olympique Yves-du-Manoir, Paris
Wales 47 T: Baker (3), Trew (3), Jones (2), Williams (2), Watts; C: Bancroft (6), Trew
France 5 T: Sagot; C: Sagot

1 January 1910, St Helen's, Swansea
Wales 49 T: Gibbs (3), Morgan (2), Maddocks (2), Trew, J Jones, Gronow; C: Bancroft (8); PG: Bancroft
France 14 T: Lafitte, Mauriat; C: Menrath; PG: Menrath (2)

FRANCE

28 February 1911, Parc des Princes, Paris
Wales   15   T: Morgan, Williams, Owen; C: Bancroft (3)
France   0

25 March 1912, Rodney Parade, Newport
Wales   14   T: Davies (2), Plummer, Jones; C: Thomas
France   8   T: Lesieur, Larribeau; C: Boyau

27 February 1913, Parc des Princes, Paris
Wales   11   T: C Lewis, Davies, Williams; C: C Lewis
France   8   T: Failliot, André; C: Struxiano

2 March 1914, St Helen's, Swansea
Wales   31   T: Wetter (2), Uzzell (2), Hirst, Rev. Davies, Evans; C: Bancroft (5)
France   0

17 February 1920, Stade Olympique Yves-du-Manoir, Paris
Wales   6   T: B Williams, Powell
France   5   T: Jaureguy; C: Struxiano

26 February 1921, Cardiff Arms Park, Cardiff
Wales   12   T: J Williams, Hodder; PG: Jenkins (2)
France   4   DG: Lasserre

23 March 1922, Stade Olympique Yves-du-Manoir, Paris
Wales   11   T: Whitfield, Cummins, I Evans; C: Jenkins
France   3   T: Jaureguy

24 February 1923, St Helen's, Swansea
Wales   16   T: Harding, M Thomas, Baker; C: A Jenkins (2); PG: Rees
France   8   T: Lalande, Lasserre; C: Larrieu

27 March 1924, Stade Olympique Yves-du-Manoir, Paris
Wales   10   T: Finch, Rickards; DG: Griffiths
France   6   T: Behoteguy, Lubin-Lebrere

28 February 1925, Cardiff Arms Park, Cardiff
Wales   11   T: Finch (2), Delahay; C: Parker
France   5   T: de Laborderie; C: Ducousso

5 April 1926, Stade Olympique Yves-du-Manoir, Paris
Wales   7   T: Watkins; DG: Cornish
France   5   T: Gerintes; C: Gonnet

26 February 1927, St Helen's, Swansea
Wales   25   T: Roberts (2), Harding (2), Thomas, Andrews, Morgan; C: Male (2)
France   7   T: Prevost; DG: Verger

9 April 1928, Stade Olympique Yves-du-Manoir, Paris
France   8   T: Houdet (2); C: Behoteguy
Wales   3   T: Powell

23 February 1929, Cardiff Arms Park, Cardiff
Wales   8   T: Arthur, Barrell; C: Parker
France   3   T: A Camel

21 April 1930, Stade Olympique Yves-du-Manoir, Paris
Wales   11   T: Skym; DG: Morgan, Powell
France   0

28 February 1931, St Helen's, Swansea
Wales   35   T: Ralph (2), Davey, Fender, Lang, Williams, Arthur; C: Bassett (5); DG: Powell
France   3   T: Petit

22 February 1947, Stade Olympique Yves-du-Manoir, Paris
Wales   3   PG: Tamplin
France   0

21 February 1948, St Helen's, Swansea
France   11   T: Basquet, Terreau, Pomathios; C: Alvarez
Wales   3   PG: O Williams

26 March 1949, Stade Olympique Yves-du-Manoir, Paris
France   5   T: Lassegue; C: Alvarez
Wales   3   T: K Jones

25 March 1950, Cardiff Arms Park, Cardiff
Wales   21   T: K Jones (2), John, Matthews; C: L Jones (3); PG: L Jones
France   0

7 April 1951, Stade Olympique Yves-du-Manoir, Paris
France   8   T: Alvarez; C: Prat; PG: Alvarez
Wales   3   PG: K Jones

22 March 1952, St Helen's, Swansea
Wales   9   DG: A Thomas; PG: L Jones (2)
France   5   T: Pomathios; C: J Prat

28 March 1953, Stade Olympique Yves-du-Manoir, Paris
Wales   6   T: Griffiths (2)
France   3   PG: Bertrand

27 March 1954, Cardiff Arms Park, Cardiff
Wales   19   T: Griffiths, B Williams; C: Evans (2); PG: Evans (3)
France   13   T: Martine, Baulon; C: J Prat (2); PG: J Prat

26 March 1955, Stade Olympique Yves-du-Manoir, Paris
Wales   16   T: Thomas, Morris; C: Owen (2); PG: Owen (2)
France   11   T: Baulon; C: Vannier; DG: M Prat; PG: Vannier

24 March 1956, Cardiff Arms Park, Cardiff
Wales   5   T: Williams; C: Owen
France   3   T: Bouquet

23 March 1957, Stade Olympique Yves-du-Manoir, Paris
Wales   19   T: Prosser, Howells, Faull, B Meredith; C: T Davies (2); PG: T Davies
France   13   T: Dupuy, Prat, Sanac; C: Bouquet (2)

29 March 1958, Cardiff Arms Park, Cardiff
France   16   T: Danos, Tarricq; C: Labazuy (2); DG: Vannier (2)
Wales   6   T: Collins; PG: T Davies

4 April 1959, Stade Olympique Yves-du-Manoir, Paris
France   11   T: Moncla (2); C: Labazuy; PG: Labazuy
Wales   3   PG: T Davies

26 March 1960, Cardiff Arms Park, Cardiff
France   16   T: Celaya, Lacroix, Meficq, Dupuy; C: Vannier, Albaladejo
Wales   8   T: Cresswell; C: N Morgan; PG: N Morgan

25 March 1961, Stade Olympique Yves-du-Manoir, Paris
France   8   T: Boniface, Saux; C: Vannier
Wales   6   T: Pask, Bebb

24 March 1962, Cardiff Arms Park, Cardiff
Wales   3   PG: Coslett
France   0

23 March 1963, Stade Olympique Yves-du-Manoir, Paris
France   5   T: G Boniface; C: Albaladejo
Wales   3   PG: Hodgson

21 March 1964, Cardiff Arms Park, Cardiff
Wales   11   T: S Watkins; C: Bradshaw; PG: Bradshaw (2)
France   11   T: Crauste; C: Albaladejo; PG: Albaladejo (2)

27 March 1965, Stade Olympique Yves-du-Manoir, Paris
France   22   T: G Boniface (2), Herrero (2); C: Didieu (2); DG: Lasserre; PG: Didieu
Wales   13   T: Dawes, S Watkins, Bebb; C: T Price (2)

FRANCE

26 March 1966, Cardiff Arms Park, Cardiff
Wales	9	T: S Watkins; PG: Bradshaw (2)
France	8	T: Duprat, Rupert; C: Lacaze

1 April 1967, Stade Olympique Yves-du-Manoir, Paris
France	20	T: G Camberabero, Dauga, Dourthe; C: G Camberabero; PG: G Camberabero; DG: G Camberabero (2)
Wales	14	T: Bebb; C: T Price; DG: D Watkins; PG: T Price (2)

23 March 1968, Cardiff Arms Park, Cardiff
France	14	T: L Camberabero, Carrere; C: G Camberabero; DG: G Camberabero; PG: G Camberabero
Wales	9	T: W Jones; PG: D Rees (2)

22 March 1969, Stade Olympique Yves-du-Manoir, Paris
France	8	T: Campaes; C: Villepreux; PG: Villepreux
Wales	8	T: Edwards, M Richards; C: Jarrett

4 April 1970, National Stadium, Cardiff
Wales	11	T: Morris; C: J Williams; PG: J Williams (2)
France	6	T: Cantoni, Bonal

27 March 1971, Stade Olympique Yves-du-Manoir, Paris
Wales	9	T: Edwards, John; PG: John
France	5	T: Dauga; C: Villepreux

25 March 1972, National Stadium, Cardiff
Wales	20	T: T Davies, J Bevan; PG: John (4)
France	6	PG: Villepreux (2)

24 March 1973, Parc des Princes, Paris
France	12	DG: Romeu; PG: Romeu (3)
Wales	3	DG: Bennett

16 February 1974, National Stadium, Cardiff
Wales	16	T: JJ Williams; DG: Edwards; PG: Bennett (3)
France	16	T: Lux DG: Romeu; PG: Romeu (3)

18 January 1975, Parc des Princes, Paris
Wales	25	T: Fenwick, Cobner, T Davies, Edwards, G Price; C: Fenwick; PG: Fenwick
France	10	T: Gourdon; PG: Taffary (2)

6 March 1976, National Stadium, Cardiff
Wales	19	T: JJ Williams; PG: Bennett (2), Fenwick (2), Martin
France	13	T: Gourdon, Averous; C: Romeu; PG: Romeu

5 February 1977, Parc des Princes, Paris
France	16	T: Skréla, Harize; C: Romeu; PG: Romeu (2)
Wales	9	PG: Fenwick (3)

18 March 1978, National Stadium, Cardiff
Wales	16	T: Bennett (2); C: Bennett; DG: Edwards, Fenwick
France	7	T: Skréla; DG: Vivies

17 February 1979, Parc des Princes, Paris
France	14	T: Gourdon (2); PG: Aguirre (2)
Wales	13	T: Holmes; PG: Fenwick (3)

19 January 1980, National Stadium, Cardiff
Wales	18	T: E Rees, Holmes, D Richards, G Price; C: W Davies
France	9	T: Marchal; C: Caussade; DG: Caussade

7 March 1981, Parc des Princes, Paris
France	19	T: Gabernet; PG: Laporte (3), Gabernet (2)
Wales	15	T: D Richards; C: G Evans; PG: G Evans (3)

6 February 1982, National Stadium, Cardiff
Wales	22	T: Holmes; PG: G Evans (6)
France	12	T: Blanco; C: Sallefranque; PG: Sallefranque, Martinez

Most points by a player in a match: France

No.	Player	Points				Versus	Venue	Date
		T	C	PG	DG			
30	Didier Camberabero	3	9	-	-	Zimbabwe	Eden Park, Auckland	02/06/1987
28	Frédérick Michalak	1	4	4	1	Scotland	Stadium Australia, Sydney	25/10/2003
28	Christophe Lamaison	1	4	3	2	New Zealand	Twickenham, London	31/10/1999
27	Jean-Baptiste Elissalde	1	11	-	-	Namibia	Stade Municipal, Toulouse	16/09/2007
27	Gérald Merceron	1	2	6	-	South Africa	Ellis Park, Johannesburg	16/06/2001
27	Christophe Lamaison	-	3	5	2	New Zealand	Stade Velodrome, Marseille	18/11/2000
27	Guy Camberabero	-	9	2	1	Italy	Stade Mayol, Toulon	26/03/1967

Most tries by a player in a match: France

No.	Player	Versus	Venue	Date
4	Maurice Celhay	Italy	Parc des Princs, Paris	17/10/1937
4	Adolphe Jaureguy	Romania	Stade Olympique Yves-du-Manoir, Paris	04/05/1924

Most conversions by a player in a match: France

No.	Player	Versus	Venue	Date
11	Jean-Baptiste Elissalde	Namibia	Stade Municipal, Toulouse	16/09/2007
9	Didier Camberabero	Zimbabwe	Eden Park, Auckland	02/06/1987
9	Guy Camberabero	Italy	Stade Mayol, Toulon	26/03/1967
8	Guy Laporte	Romania	Athletic Park, Wellington	28/05/1987
8	Louis Beguet	Romania	Stade Olympique Yves-du-Manoir, Paris	04/05/1924

Most penalties by a player in a match: France

No.	Player	Versus	Venue	Date
8	Thierry Lacroix	Ireland	Kings Park, Durban	10/06/1995
7	Gérald Merceron	Italy	Stade de France, Paris	02/02/2002
6	Dimitri Yachvili	England	Twickenham, London	13/02/2005
6	Frédérick Michalak	Fiji	Suncorp Stadium, Brisbane	11/10/2003
6	Gérald Merceron	South Africa	Ellis Park, Johannesburg	16/06/2001
6	Gérald Merceron	Ireland	Stade de France, Paris	19/03/2000
6	Christophe Lamaison	Italy	Stade Jacques Fouroux, Auch	18/10/1997
6	Christophe Lamaison	Scotland	Parc des Princes, Paris	15/03/1997
6	Jean-Michel Aguirre	Argentina	Ferro Carril Oeste Stadium, Buenos Aires	02/07/1977

Most drop goals by a player in a match: France

No.	Player	Versus	Venue	Date
3	Didier Camberabero	Australia	Sydney Football Stadium, Sydney	30/06/1990
3	Jean-Patrick Lescarboura	New Zealand	Lancaster Park, Christchurch	28/06/1986
3	Jean-Patrick Lescarboura	England	Twickenham, London	02/02/1985
3	Pierre Albaladejo	Ireland	Stade Olympique Yves-du-Manoir, Paris	09/04/1960

FRANCE

No.	Result	Points				Versus	Venue	Date
		T	C	PG	DG			
87	87–10	13	11	-	-	Namibia	Stade Municipal, Toulouse	16/09/2007
77	77–10	12	7	1	-	Fiji	Stade Geoffroy-Guichard, St Ettiene	24/11/2001
70	70–12	13	9	-	-	Zimbabwe	Eden Park, Auckland	02/06/1987
67	67–20	10	7	1	-	Romania	Dinamo Stadium, Bucharest	28/05/2000
64	64–7	9	5	3	-	Georgia	Stade Velodrome, Marseille	30/09/2007
64	64–12	10	7	-	-	Romania	Stade Jean Alric, Aurillac	20/04/1996

Most points in a match by France

No.	Peroid	Details
10	06/04/1931–17/10/1937	England (H), Germany (H), Germany (A), Germany (H), Germany (A), Germany (H), Germany (A), Germany (A), Germany (H), Italy (H)

Most consecutive test wins by France

Longest test career	Francis Haget	20/06/19–07/06/1987 (12 years, 11 months & 19 days)
Youngest test player	Claude Dourthe	18 years & 7 days on 27/11/1966 vs Romania in Bucharest
Oldest test player	Alfred Roques	37 years & 329 days on 12/01/1963 vs Scotland in Paris

Milestones

Action from the 1954 international between France and New Zealand in Paris showing the French backline ranging forward to plunder a famous 3-0 victory for the French, their first-ever over New Zealand. *Photo*: New Zealand Rugby Museum

Left: An unidentified and very brave Frenchman tackles legendary New Zealand fullback Don Clarke during the second test of the 1961 series in Wellington. New Zealand won the match by 5-3 after Clarke's boot sealed victory with the crucial conversion of Kelvin Tremain's try.
Photo: New Zealand Rugby Museum

Above: Capatin Brian Lochore prepares to clear the ball during the 1967 internationalagainst France in Paris, won 21-15 by New Zealand.
Photo: New Zealand Rugby Museum

Below left: Action from the 1967 France vs New Zealand international in Paris at the Stade Olympique Yves-du-Manoir. New Zealand won the match by 21-15. *Photo*: New Zealand Rugby Museum

Above left: French winger Adolphe Jaureguy races away to score one of his two tries to secure France their first-ever win over Ireland, by 15-7 in 1920 at Lansdowne Road in Dublin. *Photo*: Frédéric Humbert/www.flickr.com/photos/rugby_pioneers/creative commons license

Above right: A French player gathers a loose ball during the first-ever international between France and Wales played at Cardiff Arms Park in Cardiff and won 36-4 by Wales. *Photo*: Frédéric Humbert/www.flickr.com/photos/rugby_pioneers/creative commons license

Lineout action from France's inaugural test match, that against New Zealand, on 1 January 1906 at the Parc des Princes in Paris. The match was won 38-8 by New Zealand. *Photo*: Frédéric Humbert/www.flickr.com/photos/rugby_pioneers/creative commons license

Above left: A view of Rugby School from The Close, the field where the game of rugby first happened. *Photo*: Andrew de Klerk

Top right: Rugby being played in Toronto during the 1890s. *Image*: Frédéric Humbert/www.flickr.com/photos/rugby_pioneers/creative commons license

Above right: Famous rugby caps of a bygone era. *Image*: Frédéric Humbert/www.flickr.com/photos/rugby_pioneers/creative commons license

Left: Unsubtle Springbok supporters' banner prior to a French match. The literal translation of the Afrikaans text bottom right reads: 'Looks like a Zuma/Shaik story'. *Photo*: Andrew de Klerk

All Black eighthman Murray Mexted releases the ball to his forwards under French pressure during the first test in Christchurch in 1984, won 10-9 by New Zealand. *Photo*: New Zealand Rugby Museum

Action from the one-off Bledisloe Cup fixture of 1985 played in Auckland. The match was won 10-9 by New Zealand.
Photo: New Zealand Rugby Museum

Above: Lions supporters come out en masse for the second test against the Springboks at Loftus Versveld in 2009. *Photo*: Andrew de Klerk

Right: Italian eighthman Carlo Checchinato. *Photo*: Federazione Italiana Rugby

Below: The 2008 Bledisloe Cup champions New Zealand celebrate after defeating Australia 19-14 at the first neutral-venue Bledisloe test match, played in Hong Kong. New Zealand won the series by 3-1. *Photo*: www.allblacks.com

Above: The Springboks playing the All Blacks, 26 August 2006.
Photo: Andrew de Klerk

Right: 2008 IRB player of the year Shane Williams in full flight during the 2009 British and Irish Lions tour to South Africa. Williams holds the Welsh record of 46 tries in 65 tests. *Photo*: Andrew de Klerk

Argentinean scrumhalf Agustín Pichot chips over England winger Paul Sackey as prop forward Perry Freshwater and fullback Iain Balshaw move up in defence at Twickenham in 2006. Pichot was instrumental in leading Argentina to a famous 25-18 victory. *Photo*: Unión Argentina de Rugby

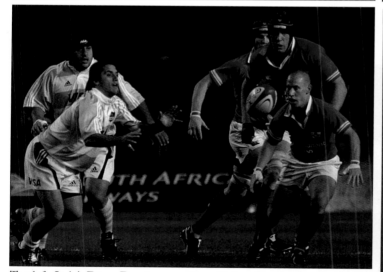

Top left: Italy's Diego Dominguez. *Photo*: Federazione Italiana Rugby

Top right: Former Italian captain Alessandro Troncon.
Photo: Federazione Italiana Rugby.

Above: Argentinean captain and scrumhalf Agustín Pichot in action during the 2004 autumn clash against Ireland at Lansdowne Road, won 21-19 by Ireland. In close support is prop Rodrigo Roncero as Irish flanker Simon Easterby, lock Paul O'Connell and scrumhalf Peter Stringer move up to cover. *Photo*: Unión Argentina de Rugby

A French lineout in their game against the Springboks on 18 June 2005. *Photo*: Andrew de Klerk

Top left: All Springbok action. *Photo*: Andrew de Klerk

Above: Kiwi captain Graham Mourie, with a sweaty Aussie jersey draped over his shoulders, holds the Bledisloe Cup aloft. *Photo*: New Zealand Rugby Museum

Left: The state-of-the-art Millennium Stadium in Cardiff. *Photo*: Welsh Rugby Union

Below: England vs Argentina on 11 November 2006 at Twickenham. *Photo*: PatrickK/commons.wikimedia.org/ creative commons license

Above: Scotland scrumhalf Mike Blair takes a quick tap penalty against South Africa during the RWC warm-up international in August 2007 at Murrayfield. The match was comfortably won 27-3 by South Africa after they led 24-3 at half time. *Photo*: Adrian van de Vyver

Above right: The victorious 2003 RWC English side. In front from left: Lewis Moody, Neil Back, Mike Tindall, Josh Lewsey, Phil Vickery, Trevor Woodman and Jason Leonard. Ben Cohen holds the camera and Lawrence Dallaglio the cup. The statue could be Wellington, approving no doubt. *Photo*: bombdog/commons.wikimedia.org/creative commons license

Below: A determined Schalk Burger in customary pose.
Photo: Jomike/commons.wikimedia.org/creative commons license

Above: The 2007 RWC. England against the All Blacks. England doggedly clawed their way into the final, but lost to South Africa. *Photo*: unofficialenglandrugby/commons.wikimedia.org/creative commons license

Top: South Africa on a lap of honour at the Stade de France in Paris during the 2007 RWC, after their 37-13 demolition of Argentina in the semifinal. *Photo*: Scott Allen

Above: Bryan Habana holds the William Webb Ellis trophy aloft for the South African fans during their victory parade following the 2007 RWC. Captain John Smit is on the left and winger Akona Ndungane on the right. *Photo*: EMiLiA/ commons.wikimedia.org/creative commons license

Right: Wallabies vs Springboks lineout, July 2007. *Photo*: Stephanie/commons.wikimedia.org/creative commons license

Above: Percy Montgomery scoring a try against Samoa in the 2007 RWC. *Photo*: Jomike/commons.wikimedia.org/creative commons license

Below: 2005 Tri-Nations. The Wallabies, unfazed, watch the intimidating haka performed by the All Blacks at Eden Park. *Photo*: Daniel Weisser/commons.wikimedia.org/creative commons license

Top: The 2007 RWC Australia against Japan. *Photo*: TwoWings/commons.wikimedia.org/creative commons license

Above: Argentina playing France in the 2007 RWC. *Photo*: Chmouel/commons.wikimedia.org/creative commons license

Below: Two of the best loose forwards in the modern game: South Africa's Schalk Burger and New Zealand's captain Richie McCaw. *Photo*: Thys Lombard

The recognition due women's rugby has travelled a long, hard road. In the early days, the IRFB and national unions refused to consider the women's game due to social sensibilities: indeed, the rugby pitch was deemed an uncouth and inappropriate place for a woman, let alone the stands! The first account of women playing rugby was when a proposed women's rugby tour to New Zealand in 1891 was hastily cancelled due to public dismay at the very thought of such an event taking place, with shock and horror abounding. In many countries women were banned outright from playing rugby but following the first women's rugby international between France and the Netherlands in 1982 (won 4–0 by France) the game has grown, with women's matches now common on the international calendar. In 1991, the first Women's Rugby World Cup was held but it was not until 1998 that the tournament was officially recognised by the IRB. The table below summarises the tournament, with New Zealand's Black Ferns dominating (*see* photo). The next Women's Rugby World Cup will be held in England in 2010. *Photo:* allblacks.com

Year	Host	Winner
1991	Wales	USA
1994	Scotland	England
1998	Netherlands	New Zealand
2002	Spain	New Zealand
2006	Canada	New Zealand

Top: A pair of Scotland's finest: Chris Paterson (left) and Gavin Hastings (right): *Photo* Scottish Rugby/PAI

Left: Scott Hastings. *Photo*: Scottish Rugby/PAI

Above: South African captain John Smit fending off the attentions of Richie McCaw. Springbok scrumhalf Ricky Januarie looks on. *Photo*: Thys Lombard

Top: John Smit (left) and South Africa's most capped player, Percy Montgomery, who is now the Springbok kicking coach.
Photo: Thys Lombard

Above: Unstoppable Springbok winger Bryan Habana has largely redefined the winger's role in the modern game, with powerhouse tackles following up on kick-offs, 22 dropouts and up-and-unders, which has in no small part contributed to the Springbok successes of recent years. *Photo*: Thys Lombard

Ireland

IRFU

Ireland vs Argentina *see page 191*

Ireland vs Australia (Lansdowne Cup) *see page 219*

Ireland vs Canada

Ireland vs Canada	
Played:	5
Won:	4
Lost:	0
Drawn:	1
For:	186
Against:	63

Average score:
40.25–14.25

Ireland percentages:
Won:	80%
Lost:	0%
Drawn:	20%

30 May 1987, Carisbrook, Dunedin (RWC, Pool 2)
Ireland	46	T: Crossan (2), Bradley, Spillane, Ringland, McNeill; C: Kiernan (5); PG: Kiernan (2); DG: Kiernan, Ward
Canada	19	T: Cardinal; PG: Rees (3), Wyatt; DG: Rees

30 November 1997, Lansdowne Road, Dublin
Ireland	33	T: Nolan (2), McGuinass, Maggs, Costello; C: Elwood; PG: Elwood (2)
Canada	11	T: Cardinal; PG: Rees (2)

17 June 2000, Fletchers Field, Markham
Canada	27	T: Stanley, Murphy, Stewart; C: Stewart (3); PG: Stewart (2)
Ireland	27	T: Horgan, Bishop, Easterby; PG: O'Gara (3), Humphreys

8 November 2008, Thomond Park, Limerick
Ireland	55	T: Kearney (2), Bowe (2), Earls, Heaslip, D Wallace, Quinlan; C: O'Gara (5), P Wallace; PG: O'Gara
Canada	0	

23 May 2009, Thunderbird Stadium, Vancouver
Ireland	25	T: Buckley, Murphy, Whitten; C: Keatley (2); PG: Keatley (2)
Canada	6	PG: Pritchard (2)

Ireland vs England (Millennium Trophy) *see page 259*

Ireland vs Fiji

18 November 1995, Lansdowne Road, Dublin
Ireland	44	T: Johns, Francis, R Wallace, Staples, P Wallace; C: Burke (5); PG: Burke (3)
Fiji	8	T: Waqa; PG: Waqa

17 November 2002, Lansdowne Road, Dublin
Ireland	64	T: Murphy (2), Maggs (3), O'Driscoll, Bishop, Dawson, Foley; C: Humphreys (5); PG: Humphreys (3)
Fiji	17	T: Doviverata, Narruhn; C: Little, Serevi; PG: Little

Ireland vs France *see page 302*

Ireland vs Georgia

14 November 1998, Lansdowne Road, Dublin
Ireland	70	T: Dempsey (2), Scally, Costello, Johns, Wallace, Maggs, Bell, Duignan, O'Shea; C: Elwood (10)
Georgia	0	

28 September 2002, Lansdowne Road, Dublin
Ireland	63	T: O'Driscoll (2), Dempsey, Maggs, Hickie, Quinlan, G Easterby, S Easterby; C: O'Gara (5), Humphreys (2); PG: O'Gara (3)
Georgia	14	T: Katsadze, Khamashuridze; C: Uriukashvili (2)

15 September 2007, Stade Toulouse, Toulouse (RWC, Pool D)
Ireland	14	T: Best, Dempsey; C: O'Gara (2)
Georgia	10	T: Shkinin; C: Kvirikashvili; PG: Kvirikashvili

Ireland vs Italy

Ireland vs Italy	
Played:	17
Won:	14
Lost:	3
Drawn:	0
For:	565
Against:	312

Average score:
33.24–18.35

Ireland percentages:

Won:	83.35%
Lost:	16.65%
Drawn:	0%

31 December 1988, Lansdowne Road, Dublin

Ireland	31	T: Crossan (2), Aherne, Matthews (2); C: Cunningham; PG: Danaher (2); DG: Dean
Italy	15	T: Brunello; C: Troiani; PG: Troiani (3)

6 May 1995, Stadio di Monigo, Treviso

Italy	22	T: Vaccari; C: Dominguez; PG: Dominguez (4); DG: Dominguez
Ireland	12	PG: Burke (4)

4 January 1997, Lansdowne Road, Dublin

Italy	37	T: Dominguez, Vaccari (2), Cuttitta; C: Dominguez (4); PG: Dominguez (3)
Ireland	29	T: Bell PG: Burke (8)

20 December 1997, Campo Arcoveggio, Bologna

Italy	37	T: Dominguez, Pilat, Stoica; C: Dominguez (2); PG: Dominguez (6)
Ireland	22	T: O'Mahony; C: Elwood; PG: Humphreys (4), Elwood

10 April 1999, Lansdowne Road, Dublin

Ireland	39	T: O'Shea (2), Dempsey, Johns, Bishop; C: Elwood; PG: Elwood (4)
Italy	30	T: Baroni, Cristofoletto, Roselli; C: Dominguez (3); PG: Dominguez; DG: Dominguez (2)

4 March 2000, Lansdowne Road, Dublin

Ireland	60	T: Horgan (2), Dempsey, Wood, Dawson, O'Driscoll; C: O'Gara (6); PG: O'Gara (6)
Italy	13	T: Moscardi C: Dominguez; PG: Dominguez (2)

3 February 2001, Stadio Flaminio, Rome

Ireland	41	T: Henderson (3), Horgan, O'Gara; C: O'Gara (2); PG: O'Gara (4)
Italy	22	T: Pilat, Checchinato, Bergamasco; C: Pez (2); PG: Pilat

23 March 2002, Lansdowne Road, Dublin

Ireland	32	T: Kelly (2), Hickie; C: O'Gara; PG: Humphreys (4), O'Gara
Italy	17	T: de Carli, Bergamasco; C: Dominguez (2); DG: Peens

22 February 2003, Stadio Flaminio, Rome

Ireland	37	T: Stringer, Kelly, Humphreys, Murphy, O'Driscoll; C: Humphreys (3); PG: Humphreys (2)
Italy	13	T: Dallan; C: Pez; PG: Dominguez, Pez

30 August 2003, Thomond Park, Limerick

Ireland	61	T: Hickie (4), Kelly, Byrne, Dempsey, Humphreys; C: Humphreys (6); PG: Humphreys (3)
Italy	6	PG: Peens (2)

20 March 2004, Lansdowne Road, Dublin

Ireland	19	T: O'Kelly, O'Driscoll, Horgan; C: O'Gara (2)
Italy	3	PG: de Marigny

6 February 2005, Stadio Flaminio, Rome

Ireland	28	T: Murphy, Stringer, Hickie; C: O'Gara (2); PG: O'Gara (3)
Italy	17	T: Castrogiovanni; PG: de Marigny (3), Orquera

3 February 2006, Lansdowne Road, Dublin

Ireland	26	T: Flannery, Bowe; C: O'Gara (2); PG: O'Gara (4)
Italy	16	T: Mirco Bergamasco; C: Pez; PG: Pez (2), Griffen

17 March 2007, Stadio Flaminio, Rome

Ireland	51	T: Dempsey (2), Hickie (2), Easterby, D'Arcy, Horgan, O'Gara; C: O'Gara (4); PG: O'Gara
Italy	24	T: Bortolami, de Marigny; C: Scanavacca; PG: Pez (2); DG: Pez (2)

24 August 2007, Ravenhill, Belfast

Ireland	23	T: Trimble, O'Gara; C: O'Gara (2); PG: O'Gara (2); DG: O'Gara
Italy	20	T: Troncon, Pratichettie C: Bortolussi, de Marigny; PG: Bortolussi; DG: Bortolussi

2 February 2008, Croke Park, Lansdowne Road
Ireland 16 T: Dempsey; C: O'Gara; PG: O'Gara (3)
Italy 11 T: Parisse; PG: Bortolussi (2)

15 February 2009, Stadio Flaminio, Rome
Ireland 38 T: Fitzgerald (2), Bowe, D Wallace, O'Driscoll; C: O'Gara (4), Kearney; PG: O'Gara
Italy 9 PG: McLean (3)

Ireland vs Japan

Ireland vs Japan	
Played:	5
Won:	5
Lost:	0
Drawn:	0
For:	251
Against:	83

Average score:
50.2–16.6

Ireland percentages:
Won:	100%
Lost:	0%
Drawn:	0%

9 October 1991, Lansdowne Road, Dublin (RWC, Pool 2)
Ireland 32 T: Mannion (2), O'Hara, Staples; C: Keyes (2); PG: Keyes (4)
Japan 16 T: Hayashi, Kajihara, Yoshida; C: Yoshida (2)

31 May 1995, Free State Stadium, Bloemfontein (RWC, Pool C)
Ireland 50 T: Corkery, Francis, Geoghegan, Halvey, Hogan, penalty try (2); C: Burke (6); PG: Burke
Japan 28 T: Latu, Izawa, Hirao, Takura; C: Yoshida(4)

11 November 2000, Lansdowne Road, Dublin
Ireland 78 T: Hickie (3), O'Driscoll (2), Howe (2), Murphy, Stringer, Henderson, Clohessy; C: O'Gara (10); PG: O'Gara
Japan 9 PG: Hirose (3)

12 June 2005, Nagai Stadium, Osaka
Ireland 44 T: Bowe, Maggs, Best, Sheahan; C: Staunton (2), Humphreys; PG: Staunton (4), Humphreys (2)
Japan 12 PG: Morita (4)

19 June 2005, Prince Chichibu Memorial Ground, Tokyo
Ireland 47 T: Duffy (2), Sheahan (2), Wallace, Humphreys, Dempsey; C: Humphreys (6)
Japan 18 T: Ohata (2); C: Hirose; PG: Hirose (2)

Ireland vs Namibia

Ireland vs Namibia	
Played:	4
Won:	2
Lost:	2
Drew:	0
For:	117
Against:	65

Average score:
29.25–16.25

Ireland percentages:
Won:	50%
Lost:	50%
Draw:	0%

20 July 1991, South West Stadium, Windhoek
Namibia 15 T: Stoop; C: Coetzee; PG Coetzee (2); DG: Coetzee
Ireland 6 T: penalty try; C: Mullin

27 July 1991, South West Stadium, Windhoek
Namibia 26 T: Stoop, Coetzee, Mans, Maritz, Barnard; C: Coetzee (3)
Ireland 15 T: Staples, Cunningham; C: Staples (2); DG: Curtis

19 October 2003, Aussie Stadium, Sydney (RWC, Pool A)
Ireland 64 T: Quinlan (2), Horgan (2), Miller (2), Dempsey, Kelly, Hickie, Easterby; C: O'Gara (7)
Namibia 7 T: Powell; C: Wessels

9 September 2007, Stade Chaban-Delmas, Bordeaux (RWC, Pool D)
Ireland 32 T: Easterby, Trimble (2), O'Driscoll, penalty try; C: O'Gara (2); PG: O'Gara
Namibia 17 T: Niewenhuis, van Zyl; C: Wessels (2); PG: Wessels

IRELAND

Ireland vs New Zealand

Played: 22
Won: 0
Lost: 21
Drawn: 1
For: 213
Against: 560

Average score:
9.68–25.45

Ireland percentages:
Won: 0%
Lost: 95.45%
Drawn: 4.55%

Ireland vs New Zealand

If one considers that this is one of the oldest fixtures on any rugby calendar, dating back to 25 November 1905, then it is remarkable that in more than a century of international matches, Ireland have never once beaten the All Blacks. Early games between the two were tight affairs and in 1973 the Irish came close when they held New Zealand to a 10–10 draw. In recent times, however, the margins of victory have been much greater, with New Zealand regularly inflicting heavy defeats on the Irish and piling up record scores in the process. In 2001, the two sides produced the match of this series, with the lead changing hands several times before New Zealand ran out winners by six tries to three in Dublin. The trend looks set to continue for the Irish as the strength of New Zealand rugby continues to increase.

25 November 1905, Lansdowne Road, Dublin
New Zealand   15   T: Deans (2), McDonald; C: Wallace (3)
Ireland   0

1 November 1924, Lansdowne Road, Dublin
New Zealand   6   T: Svenson; PG: Nicholls
Ireland   0

7 December 1935, Lansdowne Road, Dublin
New Zealand   17   T: Mitchell, Oliver, Hart; C: Gilbert; PG: Gilbert (2)
Ireland   9   T: Beamish; PG: Bailey, Siggins

9 January 1954, Lansdowne Road, Dublin
New Zealand   14   T: Clark, Stuart; C: Scott; PG: Scott; DG: Scott
Ireland   3   PG: Henderson

7 December 1963, Lansdowne Road, Dublin
New Zealand   6   T: Tremain; PG: Clarke
Ireland   5   T: Fortune; C: Kiernan

20 January 1973, Lansdowne Road, Dublin
Ireland   10   T: Grace; PG: McGann (2)
New Zealand   10   T: Going, Wyllie; C: Karam

23 November 1974, Lansdowne Road, Dublin
New Zealand   15   T: Karam; C: Karam; PG: Karam (3)
Ireland   6   PG: Ensor (2)

5 June 1976, Athletic Park, Wellington
New Zealand   11   T: B Robertson, Kirkpatrick; PG: Mains
Ireland   3   PG: McGann

4 November 1978, Lansdowne Road, Dublin
New Zealand   10   T: Dalton; DG: Bruce (2)
Ireland   6   PG: Ward (2)

18 November 1989, Lansdowne Road, Dublin
New Zealand   23   T: Gallagher, Wright, Shelford; C: Fox; PG: Fox (3)
Ireland   6   PG: B Smith (2)

30 May 1992, Carisbrook, Dunedin
New Zealand   24   T: Henderson, Clarke, Bunce (2); C: G Cooper (4)
Ireland   21   T: Cunningham (2), Staples; C: Russell (3); PG: Russell

6 June 1992, Athletic Park, Wellington
New Zealand   59   T: Bunce (2), Pene (2), I Jones, Clarke, Timu, M Cooper (2), Kirwan,
                                Strachan; C: M Cooper (6); PG: M Cooper
Ireland   6   T: Furlong; C: Russell

27 May 1995, Ellis Park, Johannesburg (RWC, Pool C)
New Zealand   43   T: Lomu (2), Kronfeld, Bunce, Osborne; C: Mehrtens (3) PG: Mehrtens (4)
Ireland   19   T: Halpin, McBride, Corkery; C: Elwood (2)

15 November 1997, Lansdowne Road, Dublin

New Zealand	63	T: Wilson (2), Osborne (2), Marshall, Mehrtens, Ieremia; C: Mehrtens (5); PG: Mehrtens (6)
Ireland	15	T: Wood (2); C: Elwood; PG: Elwood

17 November 2001, Lansdowne Road, Dublin

New Zealand	40	T: Jack, Thorne, Howlett, Mauger, Lomu, Hewitt; C: Mehrtens (5)
Ireland	29	T: Maggs, Hickie, Miller; C: Humphreys; PG: Humphreys (2); DG: Humphreys (2)

15 June 2002, Carisbrook, Dunedin

New Zealand	15	T: Howlett, MacDonald; C: Mehrtens; PG: Mehrtens
Ireland	6	PG: O'Gara; DG: O'Driscoll

22 June 2002, Eden Park, Auckland

New Zealand	40	T: MacDonald (2), Ralph, Kelleher, Holah; C: Mehrtens (3); PG: Mehrtens (3)
Ireland	8	T: Longwell; DG: O'Driscoll

12 November 2005, Lansdowne Road, Dublin

New Zealand	45	T: Howlett (2), Sivivatu (2), Weepu; C: Evans (4); PG: Evans (4)
Ireland	7	T: Horan; C: Humphreys

10 June 2006, Waikato Stadium, Hamilton

New Zealand	34	T: Howlett, Muliaina, Flavell; C: McAlister (2); PG: McAlister (5)
Ireland	23	T: Trimble, B O'Driscoll; C: O'Gara (2); PG: O'Gara (3)

17 June 2006, Eden Park, Auckland

New Zealand	27	T: Kelleher, Dermody, McAlister; C: McAlister (3); PG: McAlister (2)
Ireland	17	T: O'Connell, Flannery; C: O'Gara (2); PG: O'Gara

7 June 2008, Westpac Stadium, Wellington

New Zealand	21	T: Sivivatu, Nonu; C: Carter; PG: Carter (3)
Ireland	11	T: P Wallace; PG: O'Gara (2)

15 November 2008, Croke Park, Dublin

New Zealand	22	T: Nonu, Thorn, penalty try; C: Carter (2); PG: Carter
Ireland	3	PG: O'Gara

Ireland vs New Zealand Maoris

1 December 1888, Lansdowne Road, Dublin

NZ Maoris	13 [4G 1T]	T: Keogh (2), Ellison, Elliot, Wynyard; C: McCausland (4)
Ireland	4 [1G 1T]	T: Woods, Waites; C: Stevenson

Ireland vs Pacific Islanders

26 November 2006, Lansdowne Road, Dublin

Ireland	61	T: Easterby (2), O'Kelly, Wallace, Hickie, R Best, Horgan, O'Connell; C: Wallace (6); PG: Wallace (3)
Pacific Islanders	17	T: Rabeni, Pisi, Fa'atau C: Pisi

Ireland vs Romania

Ireland vs Romania	
Played:	8
Won:	8
Lost:	0
Drew:	0
For:	346
Against:	92
Average score:	
43.25–11.5	
Ireland percentages:	
Won:	100%
Lost:	0%
Draw:	0%

1 November 1986, Lansdowne Road, Dublin

Ireland	60	T: Crossan (3), Mullin (2), Dean (2), Anderson, Bradley, McNeill; C: Kiernan (7); PG: Kiernan (2)
Romania	0	

13 November 1993, Lansdowne Road, Dublin

Ireland	25	T: Geoghegan; C: Elwood; PG: Elwood (6)
Romania	3	PG: Constantin

21 November 1998, Lansdowne Road, Dublin

Ireland	53	T: penalty try (2), Bell (2), O'Shea, Scally, Ward; C: Elwood (3), Humphreys (3); PG: Elwood (2)
Romania	35	T: Viereanu (2), Solomie, Fugici, Brezoianu; C: Mitu (2) PG: Mitu (2)

15 October 1999, Lansdowne Road, Dublin (RWC, Pool E)

Ireland	44	T: O'Shea (2), O'Cuinneagain, Ward, Tierney; C: Elwood (5); PG: Elwood (2); DG: O'Driscoll
Romania	14	T: Sauan PG: Mitu (3)

IRELAND

2 June 2001, Dinamo Stadium, Bucharest

| Ireland | 37 | T: Bell, Foley, Galwey, Maggs; C: Humphreys (3), Burke; PG: Humphreys (3) |
| Romania | 3 | PG: Tofan |

7 September 2002, Thomond Park, Limerick

| Ireland | 39 | T: Hayes, Henderson, O'Driscoll, Gleeson, penalty try; C: O'Gara (3), Humphreys; PG: O'Gara (2) |
| Romania | 8 | T: Maftei PG: Tofan |

11 October 2003, Central Coast Stadium, Gosford (RWC, Pool A)

| Ireland | 45 | T: Hickie (2), Horgan, Wood, Costello; C: Humphreys (3), O'Gara; PG: Humphreys (4) |
| Romania | 17 | T: penalty try, Maftei; C: Tofan, Andrei; PG: Tofan |

26 November 2005, Lansdowne Road, Dublin

| Ireland | 43 | T: Trimble (2), Best, O'Connor, Murphy, Dempsey; C: Humphreys (5); PG: Humphreys |
| Romania | 12 | PG: Mitu (4) |

Ireland vs Russia

21 September 2002, Central Stadium, Krasnoyarsk

| Ireland | 35 | T: Dempsey (2), Wood, O'Kelly; C: O'Gara (3); PG: O'Gara (3) |
| Russia | 3 | PG: Pieterse |

Ireland vs Samoa

Ireland vs Samoa	
Played:	4
Won:	3
Lost:	1
Drew:	0
For:	149
Against:	84
Average:	
37.25–21	
Ireland percentages:	
Won:	75%
Lost:	25%
Draw:	0%

29 October 1988, Lansdowne Road, Dublin

| Ireland | 49 | T: Crossan (2), Kiernan, Matthews, Mullin, Sexton, Francis, McBride; C: Kiernan (4); PG: Kiernan (2); DG: Sexton |
| Western Samoa | 22 | T: Young (2), Ah'Kuoi, Koko; C: Aiolupo (2), Crichton |

12 November 1996, Lansdowne Road, Dublin

| Western Samoa | 40 | T: Vaega (2), Leaupepe, Patu, So'oalo; C: Va'a (3); PG: Va'a (3) |
| Ireland | 25 | T: Wallace; C: Mason; PG: Mason (6) |

11 November 2001, Lansdowne Road, Dublin

| Ireland | 35 | T: Sheahan, Staunton, Murphy, Howe; C: O'Gara (3); PG: O'Gara (3) |
| Samoa | 8 | T: So'oala; PG: Va'a |

20 June 2003, Apia Park, Apia

| Ireland | 40 | T: O'Gara (2), Miller; C: O'Gara (2); PG: O'Gara (5), Burke; DG: O'Gara |
| Samoa | 14 | T: Fanuatanu, Va'a; C: Va'a (2) |

Ireland vs Scotland (Centenary Quaich)

Ireland vs Scotland	
Played:	123
Won:	55
Lost:	63
Drawn:	5
For:	1,261
Against:	1,327
Average score:	
10.25–10.79	
Ireland percentages:	
Won:	44.72%
Lost:	51.22%
Drawn:	4.06%

On 19 February 1877, Scotland and Ireland met in Belfast for the first time, kicking off the third-oldest rugby fixture in history. Scotland won this first encounter with ease and continued to dominate until the 1914. Irish rugby grew in strength following World War I with Ireland winning 22 of the 27 encounters from 1926 to 1959. The two teams generally shared the spoils in the 1970s and 1980s, with Scotland enjoying a 12-match unbeaten run from 1989 to 1999. In 2000, Ireland broke the spell in spectacular fashion, racking up a record 44–22 win in Dublin. The Irish have since gone on to dominate the Scots, having lost just twice in the first decade of the millennium. In 1989, the two Celtic neighbours first competed for the Centenary Quaich, which is today contested on an annual basis during the Six Nations Championship. A *quaich* is a shallow two-handled cup, Scotland's traditional whisky-drinking vessel, derived from the Gaelic word *cuach*. The cup, painstakingly carved from wood, originated in the Highlands of Scotland, its history stretching back to the mists of time. Its two handles make it a perfect cup for sharing; ideal considering their history and the love they both share for whisk(e)y. The Centenary Quaich is only competed for in matches played during the Six Nations tournament.

19 February 1877, Ormeau, Belfast
Scotland   20 (4G 2T 2DG)
Ireland   0

T: MacKenzie (3), Pocock, Irvine, Reid; C: Cross (4); DG: MacKenzie (2)

17 February 1879, Ormeau, Belfast
Scotland   7 (1G 1T 1DG)
Ireland   0

T: Brown, Somerville; C: Cross; DG: Cross

14 February 1880, Hamilton Crescent, Glasgow
Scotland   11 (1G 2T 2D)
Ireland   0

T: Ewart (2), Masters; C: Cross; DG: Finlay (2)

19 February 1881, Ormeau, Belfast
Ireland   3 (1DG)
Scotland   1 (1T)

DG: Bagot
T: Graham

18 February 1882, Hamilton Crescent, Glasgow
Scotland   2 (2T)
Ireland   0

T: McCowan, Brown

17 February 1883, Ormeau, Belfast
Scotland   4 (1G 1T)
Ireland   0

T: Reid, Somerville; C: Maclagan

16 February 1884, Raeburn Place, Edinburgh
Scotland   8 (2G 2T)
Ireland   1 (1T)

T: Peterkin, Tod, D Wauchope, Asher; C: Berry (2)
T: McIntosh

21 February 1885 Ormeau, Belfast
Scotland   1 (1T)
Ireland   0

T: Jamieson

7 March 1885 Raeburn Place, Edinburgh
Scotland   5 (1G 2T)
Ireland   0

T: Reid, Peterkin, D Wauchope; C: Veitch

20 February 1886 Raeburn Place, Edinburgh
Scotland   14 (3G 2T 1DG)
Ireland   0

T: D Wauchope (2), Morrison (2), Macfarlan; C: Macfarlan (3); DG: Asher

19 February 1887 Ormeau, Belfast
Scotland   8 (1G 2T 1GM)
Ireland   0

T: Maclagan, McEwan, Morton; C: Berry; GM: Berry

10 March 1888 Raeburn Place, Edinburgh
Scotland   3 (1G)
Ireland   0

T: Macfarlan; C: Berry

16 February 1889 Ormeau, Belfast
Scotland   3 (1DG)
Ireland   0

DG: Stevenson

22 February 1890 Raeburn Place, Edinburgh
Scotland   5 (1T 1DG)
Ireland   0

T: J Orr; DG: Boswell

21 February 1891 Ballynafeigh, Belfast
Scotland   14
Ireland   0

T: Wotherspoon (3), Clauss, MacGregor; C: Boswell (3); DG: McEwan

20 February 1892 Raeburn Place, Edinburgh
Scotland   2
Ireland   0

T: Millar

18 February 1893 Ballynafeigh, Belfast
Ireland   0
Scotland   0

IRELAND

24 February 1894 Lansdowne Road, Dublin
Ireland   5   T: Wells; C: J Lytle
Scotland   0

2 March 1895 Raeburn Place, Edinburgh
Scotland   6   T: Welsh, Campbell
Ireland   0

15 February 1896 Lansdowne Road, Dublin
Ireland   0
Scotland   0

20 February 1897 Powderhall, Edinburgh
Scotland   8   T: Turnbull; C: T Scott; PG: T Scott
Ireland   3   T: Bulger

19 February 1898 Balmoral Showgrounds, Belfast
Scotland   8   T: T Scott (2); C: T Scott
Ireland   0

18 February 1899, Inverleith, Edinburgh
Ireland   9   T: Campbell, Reid, Sealy
Scotland   3   PG: Donaldson

24 February 1900, Lansdowne Road, Dublin
Ireland   0
Scotland   0

23 February 1901, Inverleith, Edinburgh
Scotland   9   T: Gillespie, Welsh (2)
Ireland   5   T: Doran; C: Irvine

22 February 1902, Balmoral Showgrounds, Belfast
Ireland   5   T: G Doran; C: Corley
Scotland   0

28 February 1903, Inverleith, Edinburgh
Scotland   3   T: Crabbie
Ireland   0

27 February 1904, Lansdowne Road, Dublin
Scotland   19   T: Bedell-Sivright (2), Timms, MacDonald, Simson; C: MacDonald (2)
Ireland   3   T: Moffatt

25 February 1905, Inverleith, Edinburgh
Ireland   11   T: Tedford, Wallace, Moffatt; C: MacLear
Scotland   5   T: Timms; C: Forrest

24 February 1906, Lansdowne Road, Dublin
Scotland   13   T: Bedell-Sivright, Munro; C: MacCallum (2); GM: MacLeod
Ireland   6   T: Parke, Robb

23 February 1907, Inverleith, Edinburgh
Scotland   15   T: Sanderson, Purves, Frew; C: MacLeod, Geddes (2)
Ireland   3   PG: Parke

29 February 1908, Lansdowne Road, Dublin
Ireland   16   T: Thrift (2), Thompson, Beckett; C: Parke, Hinton
Scotland   11   T: MacLeod, Martin; C: MacLeod; PG: MacLeod

27 February 1909, Inverleith, Edinburgh
Scotland   9   T: Lindsay-Watson, McGregor, Kyle
Ireland   3   PG: Parke

26 February 1910, Balmoral Showgrounds, Belfast
Scotland   14   T: Dobson, Walter (2), Stuart; C: MacCallum
Ireland   0

25 February 1911, Inverleith, Edinburgh
Ireland   16   T: O'Callaghan, Foster, Adams, Quinn; C: Hinton, Lloyd
Scotland   10   T: Simson, Angus; DG: Munro

24 February 1912, Lansdowne Road, Dublin
Ireland   10   T: Foster; DG: Lloyd; PG: Lloyd
Scotland   8   T: Turner, Will; C: MacCallum

22 February 1913, Inverleith, Edinburgh
Scotland   29   T: Stewart (4), Usher, Bowie, Purves; C: Turner (4)
Ireland   14   T: Schute, Stokes; C: Lloyd (2); DG: Lloyd

28 February 1914, Lansdowne Road, Dublin
Ireland   6   T: Quinn, McNamara
Scotland   0

28 February 1920, Inverleith, Edinburgh
Scotland   19   T: Crole (2), Angus, Browning; C: Kennedy (2); PG: Kennedy
Ireland   0

26 February 1921, Lansdowne Road, Dublin
Ireland   9   T: Cussen, Stephenson, Cunningham
Scotland   8   T: Hume, Sloan; C: Maxwell

25 February 1922, Inverleith, Edinburgh
Scotland   6   T: Bryce, Liddell
Ireland   3   T: Clarke

24 February 1923, Lansdowne Road, Dublin
Scotland   13   T: Liddell, McQueen, Browning; C: Browning (2)
Ireland   3   T: Cussen

23 February 1924, Inverleith, Edinburgh
Scotland   13   T: Waddell (2), Bertram; C: Drysdale (2)
Ireland   8   T: G Stephenson (2); C: G Stephenson

28 February 1925, Lansdowne Road, Dublin
Ireland   8   T: H Stephenson; C: Crawford; PG: Crawford
Scotland   14   T: Wallace, McMyn; C: Drysdale, Dykes; DG: Waddell

27 February 1926, Murrayfield, Edinburgh
Ireland   3   T: Gage
Scotland   0

26 February 1927, Lansdowne Road, Dublin
Ireland   6   T: Pike, Ganly
Scotland   0

25 February 1928, Murrayfield, Edinburgh
Ireland   13   T: Ganly, Davy, Stephenson; C: Stephenson (2)
Scotland   5   T: Kerr; C: Drysdale

23 February 1929, Lansdowne Road, Dublin
Scotland   16   T: MacPherson, Simmers, Bannerman, I Smith; C: Dykes, Allan
Ireland   7   T: Arigho; DG: Davy

22 February 1930, Murrayfield, Edinburgh
Ireland   14   T: Davy (3), Crowe; C: Murray
Scotland   11   T: Ford, MacPherson, Waters; C: Waters

28 February 1931, Lansdowne Road, Dublin
Ireland   8   T: Sugden, Pike; C: Murray
Scotland   5   T: MacIntosh; C: Allan

27 February 1932, Murrayfield, Edinburgh
Ireland   20   T: Lightfoot (2), Hunt, Waide; C: Murray (4)
Scotland   8   T: Wood, Simmers; C: Allan

IRELAND

1 April 1933, Lansdowne Road, Dublin
Scotland   8   DG: Jackson, Lind
Ireland   6   T: Crowe, Murray

24 February 1934, Murrayfield, Edinburgh
Scotland   16   T: Dick (2), Crawford; C: Shaw (2); PG: Allan
Ireland   9   T: Russell (2), O'Connor

23 February 1935, Lansdowne Road, Dublin
Ireland   12   T: O'Connor, Lawlor, Bailey, Ridgeway
Scotland   5   T: Shaw; C: Fyfe

22 February 1936, Murrayfield, Edinburgh
Ireland   10   T: Walker, McMahon; DG: Hewitt
Scotland   4   DG: Murdoch

27 February 1937, Lansdowne Road, Dublin
Ireland   11   T: Alexander, McMahon, Moran; C: Bailey
Scotland   4   DG: W Shaw

26 February 1938, Murrayfield, Edinburgh
Scotland   23   T: Forrest (2), MacRae, Drummond; C: Crawford (2); DG: Dorward; PG: Drummond
Ireland   14   T: Cromey, O'Loughlin, Moran, Morgan; C: Walker

25 February 1939, Lansdowne Road, Dublin
Ireland   12   T: Moran, Torrens; PG: McKibbin; GM: Sayers
Scotland   3   T: Innes

22 February 1947, Murrayfield, Edinburgh
Ireland   3   T: Mullan
Scotland   0

28 February 1948, Lansdowne Road, Dublin
Ireland   6   T: Mullan, Kyle
Scotland   0

26 February 1949, Murrayfield, Edinburgh
Ireland   13   T: McCarthy (2); C: Norton (2); PG: Norton
Scotland   3   PG: Allardice

25 February 1950, Lansdowne Road, Dublin
Ireland   21   T: Blayney, Curtis, Crowe; C: Norton (3); PG: Norton (2)
Scotland   0

24 February 1951, Murrayfield, Edinburgh
Ireland   6   T: O'Brien; DG: Henderson
Scotland   5   T: Sloan; C: Thomson

23 February 1952, Lansdowne Road, Dublin
Ireland   12   T: Lane, Kyle, Henderson; PG: Henderson
Scotland   8   T: Davisdon; C: Thomson; PG: Thomson

28 February 1953, Murrayfield, Edinburgh
Ireland   26   T: McCarthy, Byrne (3), Mortell, Kavanagh; C: Gregg (4)
Scotland   8   T: Henderson; C: I Thomson; PG: I Thomson

27 February 1954, Ravenhill, Belfast
Ireland   6   T: Mortell (2)
Scotland   0

26 February 1955, Murrayfield, Edinburgh
Scotland   12   T: Swann; DG: Cameron; PG: Elgie (2)
Ireland   3   PG: Kelly

25 February 1956, Lansdowne Road, Dublin
Ireland   14   T: Henderson, O'Reilly, Kyle, O'Meara; C: Pedlow
Scotland   10   T: Michie, Smith; C: McClung (2)

23 February 1957, Murrayfield, Edinburgh
Ireland 5 T: O'Sullivan; C: Berkery
Scotland 3 PG: Scotland

1 March 1958, Lansdowne Road, Dublin
Ireland 12 T: Pedlow (2); PG: Henderson, Berkery
Scotland 6 T: Smith, Weatherstone

28 February 1959, Murrayfield, Edinburgh
Ireland 8 T: Dooley; C: Hewitt; PG: Hewitt
Scotland 3 PG: Scotland

27 February 1960, Lansdowne Road, Dublin
Scotland 6 T: Thomson; DG: Scotland
Ireland 5 T: Wood; C: Hewitt

25 February 1961, Murrayfield, Edinburgh
Scotland 16 T: Douglas, Ross (2); C: Scotland (2); PG: Scotland
Ireland 8 T: Kavanagh, Hewitt; C: Moffett

24 February 1962, Lansdowne Road, Dublin
Scotland 20 T: Smith (2), Cowan; C: Scotland; DG: Coughtrie; PG: Scotland (2)
Ireland 6 T: Hunter; PG: Hunter

23 February 1963, Murrayfield, Edinburgh
Scotland 3 PG: Coughtrie
Ireland 0

22 February 1964, Lansdowne Road, Dublin
Scotland 6 PG: Wilson (2)
Ireland 3 PG: Kiernan

27 February 1965, Murrayfield, Edinburgh
Ireland 16 T: McGrath, Young, Murphy; C: Kiernan (2); DG: Gibson
Scotland 6 DG: Laughland; PG: Wilson

26 February 1966, Lansdowne Road, Dublin
Scotland 11 T: Hinshelwood (2), Grant; C: Wilson
Ireland 3 PG: Kiernan

25 February 1967, Murrayfield, Edinburgh
Ireland 5 T: Murphy; C: Kiernan
Scotland 3 PG: Wilson

24 February 1968, Lansdowne Road, Dublin
Ireland 14 T: Duggan (2), Bresnihan; C: Kiernan; PG: Kiernan
Scotland 6 PG: Wilson (2)

22 February 1969, Murrayfield, Edinburgh
Ireland 16 T: Duggan, McGann, Gibson, Bresnihan; C: Moroney (2)
Scotland 0

28 February 1970, Lansdowne Road, Dublin
Ireland 16 T: Molloy, Goodall, Gibson, Brown; C: Kiernan (2)
Scotland 11 T: Lauder, M Smith; C: C Smith; DG: Robertson

27 February 1971, Murrayfield, Edinburgh
Ireland 17 T: Duggan (2), Grant; C: Gibson; PG: Gibson (2)
Scotland 5 T: Frame; C: P Brown

24 February 1973, Murrayfield, Edinburgh
Scotland 19 T: Forsyth; DG: Morgan (2), McGeechan; PG: Morgan (2)
Ireland 14 T: McMaster, Kiernan; PG: McGann (2)

2 March 1974, Lansdowne Road, Dublin
Ireland 9 T: Milliken; C: Gibson; PG: McKinney
Scotland 6 PG: Irvine (2)

IRELAND

1 February 1975, Murrayfield, Edinburgh
Scotland 20   T: Renwick, Steele; DG: Morgan, McGeechan; PG: Irvine (2)
Ireland 13   T: Dennison, Grace; C: McCombe; PG: McCombe

20 March 1976, Lansdowne Road, Dublin
Scotland 15   DG: Wilson; PG: Irvine (4)
Ireland 6   PG: McGann (2)

19 February 1977, Murrayfield, Edinburgh
Scotland 21   T: Gammell (2), Madsen; DG: Morgan; PG: Irvine (2)
Ireland 18   T: Gibson; C: Gibson; DG: Quinn; PG: Gibson (2), Quinn

21 January 1978, Lansdowne Road, Dublin
Ireland 12   T: McKinney; C: Ward; PG: Ward (2)
Scotland 9   PG: Morgan (3)

3 March 1979, Murrayfield, Edinburgh
Scotland 11   T: Rutherford, Irvine; PG: Irvine
Ireland 11   T: Patterson (2); PG: Ward

2 February 1980, Lansdowne Road, Dublin
Ireland 22   T: Keane, Kennedy; C: Campbell; DG: Campbell; PG: Campbell (3)
Scotland 15   T: Johnston (2); C: Irvine (2); PG: Irvine

21 March 1981, Murrayfield, Edinburgh
Scotland 10   T: Hay; DG: Rutherford; PG: Irvine
Ireland 9   T: Irwin C: Campbell; PG: Campbell

20 February 1982, Lansdowne Road, Dublin
Ireland 21   DG: Campbell; PG: Campbell (6)
Scotland 12   T: Rutherford; C: Irvine; PG: Renwick (2)

15 January 1983, Murrayfield, Edinburgh
Ireland 15   T: Kiernan; C: Campbell; PG: Campbell (3)
Scotland 13   T: Laidlaw; DG: Renwick; PG: Dods (2)

3 March 1984, Lansdowne Road, Dublin
Scotland 32   T: Laidlaw (2), Robertson, Dods, penalty try; C: Dods (3); PG: Dods (2)
Ireland 9   T: Kiernan; C: Murphy; PG: Murphy

2 February 1985, Murrayfield, Edinburgh
Ireland 18   T: Ringland (2); C: Kiernan (2); PG: Kiernan; DG: Kiernan
Scotland 15   PG: Dods (4); DG: Robertson

15 March 1986, Lansdowne Road, Dublin
Scotland 10   T: Laidlaw; PG: G Hastings (2)
Ireland 9   T: Ringland; C: Kiernan; PG: Kiernan

21 February 1987, Murrayfield, Edinburgh
Scotland 16   T: Laidlaw, Tukalo; C: G Hastings; DG: Rutherford (2)
Ireland 12   T: Lenehan; C: Kiernan; PG: Kiernan; DG: Kiernan

16 January 1988, Lansdowne Road, Dublin
Ireland 22   T: Mullin, MacNeill, Bradley; C: Kiernan (2); PG: Kiernan; DG: Kiernan
Scotland 18   T: Laidlaw, S Hastings; C: G Hastings (2); PG: G Hastings (2)

4 March 1989, Murrayfield, Edinburgh
Scotland 37   T: Tukalo (3), Jeffrey, Cronin; C: Dods (4); PG: Dods (3)
Ireland 21   T: Mullin (2), Dunlea; C: Kiernan (3); PG: Kiernan

3 February 1990, Lansdowne Road, Dublin
Scotland 13   T: White (2); C: Chalmers; PG: Chalmers
Ireland 10   T: J Fitzgerald; PG: Kiernan (2)

16 March 1991, Murrayfield, Edinburgh
Scotland 28   T: G Hastings, Stanger, S Hastings; C: Chalmers (2); PG: Chalmera (3), G Hastings
Ireland 25   T: Crossan, Geohegan, Robinson, Mullin; C: B Smith (3); DG: B Smith

12 October 1991, Murrayfield, Edinburgh (RW, Pool 2)
Scotland 24 T: Shiel, Armstrong; C: G Hastings (2); PG: G Hastings (3); DG: Chalmers
Ireland 15 PG: Keyes (4); DG: Keyes

15 February 1992, Lansdowne Road, Dublin
Scotland 18 T: Stanger, Nicol; C: G Hastings (2); PG: G Hastings (2)
Ireland 10 T: Wallace; PG: Keyes (2)

16 January 1993, Murrayfield, Edinburgh
Scotland 15 T: Stark, Stanger; C: G Hastings; PG: G Hastings
Ireland 3 PG: Malone

5 March 1994, Lansdowne Road, Dublin
Ireland 6 PG: Elwood (2)
Scotland 6 PG: G Hastings (2)

4 February 1995, Murrayfield, Edinburgh
Scotland 26 T: Joiner, Cronin; C: G Hastings (2); PG: G Hastings (4)
Ireland 13 T: Mullin, Bell; PG: Burke

20 January 1996, Lansdowne Road, Dublin
Scotland 16 T: McKenzie, Dods; PG: Dods; DG: Townsend
Ireland 10 T: Clohessy; C: Elwood; PG: Elwood

1 March 1997, Murrayfield, Edinburgh
Scotland 38 T: Tait, Walton, Weir, Stanger, Townsend; C: Shepherd (5); PG: Shepherd
Ireland 10 T: Hickie; C: Humphreys PG: Humphreys

7 February 1998, Lansdowne Road, Dublin
Scotland 17 T: Tait; PG: Shepherd (2), Chalmers (2)
Ireland 16 T: penalty try; C: Humphreys; PG: Humphreys (2); DG: Humphreys

20 March 1999, Murrayfield, Edinburgh
Scotland 30 T: C Murray (2), Townsend, Grimes; C: Logan (2); PG: Logan (2)
Ireland 13 T: Humphreys; C: Humphreys; PG: Humphreys (2)

19 February 2000, Lansdowne Road, Dublin
Ireland 44 T: O'Kelly, Horgan, O'Driscoll, Humphreys, Wood; C: Humphreys (3), O'Gara (2); PG: O'Gara (2), Humphreys
Scotland 22 T: Logan, Metcalfe, Graham; C: Logan (2); PG: Logan

29 September 2001, Murrayfield, Edinburgh
Scotland 32 T: Pountney, Smith, J Leslie, Henderson; C: Townsend, Paterson (2); PG: Paterson (2)
Ireland 10 T: Dempsey; C: Humphreys; PG: O'Gara

2 March 2002, Lansdowne Road, Dublin
Ireland 43 T: O'Driscoll (3), Horgan, Easterby; C: Humphreys (2), O'Gara; PG: Humphreys (4)
Scotland 22 T: Leslie; C: Laney; PG: Laney (5)

16 February 2003, Murrayfield, Edinburgh
Ireland 36 T: Hickie, Murphy, Humphreys; C: Humphreys (3); PG: Humphreys (5)
Scotland 6 PG: Ross (2)

6 September 2003, Murrayfield, Edinburgh
Ireland 29 T: Maggs, Hickie, Horgan, Wallace; C: O'Gara (3); PG: O'Gara
Scotland 10 T: Webster; C: Paterson; PG: Paterson

27 March 2004, Lansdowne Road, Dublin
Ireland 37 T: D'Arcy (2), Murphy, Wallace, Stringer; C: O'Gara(3); PG: O'Gara (2)
Scotland 16 T: Hogg; C: Paterson; PG: Paterson (2); DG: Parks

12 February 2005, Murrayfield, Edinburgh
Ireland 40 T: O'Kelly, O'Connell, Hickie, Hayes, Duffy; C: O'Gara (2), Humphreys; PG: O'Gara (3)
Scotland 13 T: Southwell, Petrie; PG: Paterson

11 March 2006, Lansdowne Road, Dublin
Ireland 15 PG: O'Gara (5)
Scotland 9 PG: Paterson (3)

IRELAND

10 March 2007, Murrayfield, Edinburgh
Ireland   19   T: O'Gara; C: O'Gara; PG: O'Gara (4)
Scotland   18   PG: Paterson (6)

11 August 2007, Murrayfield, Edinburgh
Scotland   31   T: Henderson (3), Hogg, Murray; C: Paterson (3)
Ireland   21   T: Boss, Trimble; C: P Wallace; PG: P Wallace (2), Murphy

23 February 2008, Croke Park, Dublin
Ireland   34   T: Bowe (2), Wallace, Kearney, Horan; C: O'Gara (3); PG: O'Gara
Scotland   13   T: Webster; C: Paterson; PG: Paterson (2)

14 March 2009, Murrayfield, Edinburgh
Ireland   22   T: Heaslip; C: O'Gara; PG: O'Gara (4); DG: O'Gara
Scotland   15   PG: Paterson (5)

Centenary Quaich			Current holder: Ireland			Number of titles: Scotland 12, Ireland 9	
No	Date	Venue		Result			Holder
1	04/03/1989	Murrayfield, Edinburgh	Scotland	37–21	Ireland		Scotland
2	03/02/1990	Lansdowne Road, Dublin	Ireland	10–13	Scotland		Scotland
3	16/03/1991	Murrayfield, Edinburgh	Scotland	28–25	Ireland		Scotland
4	15/02/1992	Lansdowne Road, Dublin	Ireland	10–18	Scotland		Scotland
5	16/01/1993	Murrayfield, Edinburgh	Scotland	15–3	Ireland		Scotland
6	05/03/1994	Lansdowne Road, Dublin	Ireland	6–6	Scotland		Scotland
7	04/02/1995	Murrayfield, Edinburgh	Scotland	26–13	Ireland		Scotland
8	20/01/1996	Lansdowne Road, Dublin	Ireland	10–16	Scotland		Scotland
9	01/03/1997	Murrayfield, Edinburgh	Scotland	38–10	Ireland		Scotland
10	07/02/1998	Lansdowne Road, Dublin	Ireland	16–17	Scotland		Scotland
11	20/03/1999	Murrayfield, Edinburgh	Scotland	30–13	Ireland		Scotland
12	19/02/2000	Lansdowne Road, Dublin	Ireland	44–22	Scotland		Ireland
13	29/09/2001	Murrayfield, Edinburgh	Scotland	32–10	Ireland		Scotland
14	02/03/2002	Lansdowne Road, Dublin	Ireland	43–22	Scotland		Ireland
15	16/02/2003	Murrayfield, Edinburgh	Scotland	6–36	Ireland		Ireland
16	27/03/2004	Lansdowne Road, Dublin	Ireland	37–16	Scotland		Ireland
17	12/02/2005	Murrayfield, Edinburgh	Scotland	13–40	Ireland		Ireland
18	11/03/2006	Lansdowne Road, Dublin	Ireland	15–9	Scotland		Ireland
19	10/03/2007	Murrayfield, Edinburgh	Scotland	18–19	Ireland		Ireland
20	23/02/2008	Croke Park, Dublin	Ireland	34–13	Scotland		Ireland
21	14/03/2009	Murrayfield, Edinburgh	Scotland	15–22	Ireland		Ireland

IRELAND

Ireland vs South Africa

Ireland vs South Africa

Played: 18
Won: 3
Lost: 14
Drawn: 1
For: 200
Against: 368

Average score:
11.11–20.44

Ireland percentages:
Won: 16.66%
Lost: 77.78%
Drawn: 5.56%

South Africa and Ireland have been playing rugby against each other for more than a hundred years, albeit very intermittently, having met just 18 times. The series has been dominated by the Springboks who have lost just three times to the Irish, most recently in an unexpected record loss in Ireland. They first met in 1906 in a Belfast thriller which produced seven tries and was won by South Africa. Six years later the Boks stamped their authority over the Irish, winning by a scoreline of 38–0 which still stands today as a record. In 1965, Ireland beat the Springboks for the first time and in 1981 narrowly lost a two-test series in South Africa. The two sides were not to meet for the next 17 years until 1998 in a very physical and at times brutal series which was comprehensively won by South Africa. Another series win in 2004 by South Africa ensured that the Irish have never won on South African soil. However, the Irish have since won the last two encounters.

24 November 1906, Balmoral Showgrounds, Belfast
South Africa   15   T: Loubser (2), Krige, A Stegmann; PG: Joubert
Ireland   12   T: Maclear (2), Sugar; PG: Parke

30 November 1912, Lansdowne Road, Dublin
South Africa   38   T: J Stegmann (3), McHardy (3), J Morkel (2), Francis, Millar;
                        C: G Morkel (3), Luyt
Ireland   0

19 December 1931, Lansdowne Road, Dublin
South Africa   8   T: Zimmerman (2); C: Osler
Ireland   3   PG: Beamish

8 December 1951, Lansdowne Road, Dublin
South Africa   17   T: van Wyk (2), Ochse, van Schoor; C: Geffin; DG: Brewis
Ireland   5   T: Browne; C: Murphy

17 December 1960, Lansdowne Road, Dublin
South Africa   8   T: Gainsford, H van Zyl; C: Lockyear
Ireland   3   PG: Kiernan

13 May 1961, Newlands, Cape Town
South Africa   24   T: Greenwood (2), B van Zyl (2), Hopwood; C: Nimb (3); PG: Nimb
Ireland   8   T: Kiernan; C: Kiernan; PG: Kiernan

6 April 1965, Lansdowne Road, Dublin
Ireland   9   T: McGrath; PG: Kiernan (2)
South Africa   6   T: Mans; PG: Stewart

10 January 1970, Lansdowne Road, Dublin
Ireland   8   T: Duggan; C: Kiernan; PG: Kiernan
South Africa   8   T: Greyling; C: H de Villiers; PG: H de Villiers

30 May 1981, Newlands, Cape Town
South Africa   23   T: Gerber (2), Louw; C: Botha; PG: Botha (3)
Ireland   15   T: McGrath, McLennan; C: Campbell (2); PG: Cambell

6 June 1981, Kings Park, Durban
South Africa   12   PG: Botha ; DG: Botha (3)
Ireland   10   T: O'Brein; PG: Quinn (2)

13 June 1998, Free State Stadium, Bloemfontein
South Africa   37   T: Terblanche (4), Andrews; C: du Toit (3); PG: du Toit (2)
Ireland   13   T: Bishop; C: Elwood; PG: Elwood (2)

20 June 1998, Loftus Versfeld, Pretoria
South Africa   33   T: van der Westhuizen, Dalton, Erasmus, Rossouw, Teichmann;
                        C: Montgomery (4)
Ireland   0

28 November 1998, Lansdowne Road, Dublin
| South Africa | 27 | T: van der Westhuizen, Erasmus, Skinstad; C: Montgomery (3); PG: Montgomery (2) |
| Ireland | 13 | T: Wood; C: Elwood; PG: Elwood (2) |

19 November 2000, Lansdowne Road, Dublin
| South Africa | 28 | T: Krige, Venter, van der Westhuizen; C: Montgomery, van Straaten; PG: Montgomery (2), van Straaten |
| Ireland | 18 | T: Hickie, Howe; C: O'Gara; PG: O'Gara (2) |

12 June 2004, Vodacom Park, Bloemfontein
| South Africa | 31 | T: Botha (2), Wannenburg, Julies; C: du Toit; PG: du Toit (3) |
| Ireland | 17 | T: Horgan; PG: O'Gara (3); DG: O'Gara |

19 June 2004, Newlands, Cape Town
| South Africa | 26 | T: Paulse, Fourie; C: Montgomery (2); PG: Montgomery (4) |
| Ireland | 17 | T: O'Driscoll, Howe; C: O'Gara, Humphreys; DG: O'Gara |

13 November 2004, Lansdowne Road, Dublin
| Ireland | 17 | T: O'Gara; PG: O'Gara (3); DG: O'Gara |
| South Africa | 12 | PG: Montgomery (4) |

11 November 2006, Lansdowne Road, Dublin
| Ireland | 32 | T: Horan, Wallace, Horgan, Trimble; C: O'Gara (3); PG: O'Gara (2) |
| South Africa | 15 | T: Habana, Steyn; C: Pretorius; PG: Pretorius |

Ireland vs Tonga

3 June 1987, Ballymore, Brisbane (RWC, Pool 2)
| Ireland | 32 | T: McNeill (2), Mullin (3); C: Ward (3); PG: Ward (2) |
| Tonga | 9 | PG: Amone (3) |

14 June 2003 Teufaiva Sports Stadium, Nuku'alofa
| Ireland | 40 | T: Easterby (2), Kelly (2), McHugh, Bell; C: O'Gara (2); PG: O'Gara (2) |
| Tonga | 19 | T: Hola (2); PG: Hola (3) |

Ireland vs United States of America

Ireland vs USA	
Played:	6
Won:	6
Lost:	0
Drawn:	0
For:	269
Against:	60
Average score:	
44.83–10	
Ireland percentages:	
Won:	100%
Lost:	0%
Drawn:	0%

5 November 1994, Lansdowne Road, Dublin
| Ireland | 26 | T: Bradley, Geoghegan; C: McGowan (2); PG: McGowan (3); DG: O'Shea |
| USA | 15 | T: Anitoni, Bachelet; C: Williams; PG: Williams |

6 January 1996, Life College Stadium, Atlanta
| Ireland | 25 | T: Wallace; C: Elwood; PG: Elwood (3), Burke (3) |
| USA | 18 | T: Tardits, Walker; C: Alexander; PG: Alexander; DG: Alexander |

2 October 1999, Lansdowne Road, Dublin (RWC, Pool E)
| Ireland | 53 | T: Wood (4), Bishop, O'Driscoll, penalty try; C: Humphreys (4), Elwood (2) PG: Humphreys (2) |
| USA | 8 | T: Dalzell; PG: Dalzell |

10 June 2000, Manchester
| Ireland | 83 | T: Mullins (3), Murphy (2), O'Kelly, Topping, Wallace, G Easterby (2), S Easterby (2), Humphreys; C: O'Gara (8), Humphreys |
| USA | 3 | PG: Wells |

20 November 2004, Lansdowne Road, Dublin
| Ireland | 55 | T: Murphy (2), Bowe, Horan, Miller, Stringer, Sheahan; C: Humphreys (7); PG: Humphreys (2) |
| USA | 6 | PG: Hercus (2) |

31 May 2009 Santa Clara University, Santa Clara
| Ireland | 27 | T: Casey, Whitten, Best, penalty try; C: Keatley (2); PG: Keatley |
| United States | 10 | T: Suniula; C: Malifa; DG: Malifa |

Ireland vs Wales

Ireland vs Wales	
Played:	114
Won:	46
Lost:	62
Drawn:	6
For:	1,189
Against:	1,317

Average score:
10.43–11.55

Ireland percentages:
Won:	40.35%
Lost:	54.39%
Drawn:	5.26%

These two first met on 28 January 1882 at Lansdowne Road in Dublin. In the early years, the games were closely fought but often not taken too seriously; once, in 1884, the Irish arrived in Cardiff two players short of a team. The intensity and importance of these matches, however, soon grew with the game's popularity and by the beginning of the twentieth century the Welsh had improved to such a level that they lost to the Irish only three times in 18 internationals from 1900 to 1922 and often won by large margins. The Irish became strong competitors in the 1920s and 1930s and secured in 1948 their most famous victory over the Welsh when they pipped them to the post in Belfast during the final match of the Five Nations to secure their first Grand Slam triumph. The Welsh once again dominated the Irish in the 1950s. In the 1970s Wales posted regular and often large victories over the Irish. In the entertaining 1977 game, Geoff Wheel of Wales and Willie Duggan of Ireland were both given their marching orders by the Scottish referee Norman Sanson for punching. With both sides reduced to 14 men, Wales won by 25–9 with Irish centre Mike Gibson playing for a record 13th time against Wales; he went on to play once more. Through the 1980s and 1990s, each team won and lost regularly and, in a remarkable switch of form, both tended to win away from home and lose at home. From the mid-1990s to the present the Irish have had the better of the Welsh and have lost just four times in 16 tests, often by large scorelines, including a 2002 record 54–10 thrashing. A thrilling one-point victory by Ireland in the 1995 RWC sent Wales home for the second consecutive tournament without reaching the quarter-finals. In 2003, Ronan O'Gara snatched another exciting one-point victory with a last-minute drop goal, however, Wales upset Ireland at Croke Park in Dublin to set themselves up for their 2008 Grand Slam triumph.

28 January 1882, Lansdowne Road, Dublin
Wales 8 (2G 2T) T: Evans, Bridie, Jones, Clapp; C: Lewis (2)
Ireland 0

12 April 1884, Cardiff Arms Park, Cardiff
Wales 5 (2T 1DG) T: Norton, Clapp; DG: Stadden
Ireland 0

12 March 1887, Rodney Parade, Newport
Wales 4 (1T 1DG) T: Morgan; DG: Gould
Ireland 3 (3T) T: Montgomery (3)

3 March 1888, Lansdowne Road, Dublin
Ireland 7 (1G 1T 1DG) T: Warren, Shanahan; C: Rambaut; DG: Carpendale
Wales 0

2 March 1889, St Helen's, Swansea
Ireland 2 (2T) T: McDonnell, Cotton
Wales 0

1 March 1890, Lansdowne Road, Dublin
Ireland 3 (1G) T: Dunlop; C: Roche
Wales 3 (1G) T: C Thomas; C: Bancroft

7 March 1891, Stradey Park, Llanelli
Wales 6 T: D Samuel; C: Bancroft; DG: Bancroft
Ireland 4 T: Lee; DG: Walkingtony

5 March 1892, Lansdowne Road, Dublin
Ireland 9 T: Walsh (2), Davies; PG: Roche
Wales 0

11 March 1893, Stradey Park, Llanelli
Wales 2 T: Gould
Ireland 0

IRELAND

10 March 1894, Ballynafeigh, Belfast
Ireland 3   PG: J Lytle
Wales 0

16 March 1895, Cardiff Arms Park, Cardiff
Wales 5   T: Pearson; C: Bancroft
Ireland 3   T: Crean

14 March 1896, Lansdowne Road, Dublin
Ireland 8   T: Crean, Lytle; C: Bulger
Wales 4   DG: Gould

18 March 1898, Thomond Park, Limerick
Wales 11   T: Dobson, Huzzey; C: Bancroft; PG: Bancroft
Ireland 3   PG: Bulger

18 March 1899, Cardiff Arms Park, Cardiff
Ireland 3   T: Doran
Wales 0

17 March 1900, Balmoral Showgrounds, Belfast
Wales 3   T: Davies
Ireland 0

16 March 1901, St Helen's, Swansea
Wales 10   T: Alexander (2); C: Bancroft (2)
Ireland 9   T: J Ryan, Freear, Davidson

8 March 1902, Lansdowne Road, Dublin
Wales 15   T: Nicholls, Llewellyn, L Lloyd; C: Brice; DG: Nicholls
Ireland 0

14 March 1903, Cardiff Arms Park, Cardiff
Wales 18   T: Llewellyn (2), Gabe, Morgan (2), Brice
Ireland 0

12 March 1904, Balmoral Showgrounds, Belfast
Ireland 14   T: Tedford (2), J Wallace, Thrift; C: Parke
Wales 12   T: Morgan (2), Gabe, C Pritchard

11 March 1905, St Helen's, Swansea
Wales 10   T: W Jones, Morgan; C: Davies (2)
Ireland 3   T: Robinson

10 March 1906, Balmoral Showgrounds, Belfast
Ireland 11   T: Thrift, Wallace, Maclear; C: Gardiner
Wales 6   T: Morgan, Gabe

9 March 1907, Cardiff Arms Park, Cardiff
Wales 29   T: Williams (3), Jones, Gabe, Bush; C: Winfield (2); DG: Bush; PG: Winfield
Ireland 0

14 March 1908, Balmoral Showgrounds, Belfast
Wales 11   T: Williams (2), Gibbs; C: Winfield
Ireland 5   T: Aston; C: Parke

13 March 1909, St Helen's, Swansea
Wales 18   T: J Jones, Hopkins, Watts, Trew; C: Bancroft (3)
Ireland 5   T: Thompson; C: Parke

12 March 1910, Lansdowne Road, Dublin
Wales 19   T: Williams (3), Gibbs, Dyke; DG: Bush
Ireland 3   T: McIldowie

11 March 1911, Cardiff Arms Park, Cardiff
Wales 16   T: T Evans, Webb, Gibbs; C: Bancroft (2); PG: Bancroft
Ireland 0

9 March 1912, Balmoral Showgrounds, Belfast
Ireland	12	T: McIvor, Brown; C: Lloyd; DG: Lloyd
Wales	5	T: Davies; C: Bancroft

8 March 1913, St Helen's, Swansea
Wales	16	T: B Lewis (2), Jones; C: Bancroft (2); PG: Bancroft
Ireland	13	T: Quinn, Stewart; C: Lloyd (2); PG: Lloyd

14 March 1914, Balmoral Showgrounds, Belfast
Wales	11	T: B Jones, Evans, Wetter; C: Lewis
Ireland	3	T: Foster

13 March 1920, Cardiff Arms Park, Cardiff
Wales	28	T: B Williams (3), Jenkins, Whitfield, Parker; C: Jenkins (2), Wetter; DG: Jenkins
Ireland	4	DG: McFarland

12 March 1921, Balmoral Showgrounds, Belfast
Wales	6	T: M Thomas; PG: Johnson
Ireland	0	

11 March 1922, St Helen's, Swansea
Wales	11	T: Whitfield (2), I Evans; C: Samuel
Ireland	5	T: Stokes; C: Wallis

10 March 1923, Lansdowne Road, Dublin
Ireland	5	T: Cussen; C: Crawford
Wales	4	DG: Powell

8 March 1924, Cardiff Arms Park, Cardiff
Ireland	13	T: T Hewitt, F Hewitt, G Stephenson; C: Crawford (2)
Wales	10	T: Richards, Pugh; DG: Watkins

14 March 1925, Ravenhill, Belfast
Ireland	19	T: Millin, G Stephenson, Browne, H Stephenson; C: G Stephenson (2); PG: G Stephenson
Wales	3	T: Turnbull

13 March 1926, St Helen's, Swansea
Wales	11	T: Harding, Hopkins, Herrera; C: Rees
Ireland	8	T: Hanrahan; C: Stephenson; PG: Stephenson

12 March 1927, Lansdowne Road, Dublin
Ireland	19	T: Stephenson (2), Ganly (2); C: Stephenson (2); PG: Stephenson
Wales	9	T: Morgan; C: Powell; DG: Lewis

10 March 1928, Cardiff Arms Park, Cardiff
Ireland	13	T: Arigho (2), Ganly; C: Stephenson (2)
Wales	10	T: D John, A Jenkins; C: I Johns (2)

9 March 1929, Ravenhill, Belfast
Ireland	5	T: Davy; C: Stephenson
Wales	5	T: Williams; C: Parker

8 March 1930, St Helen's, Swansea
Wales	12	T: Skym, A Jones, Peacock; PG: Bassett
Ireland	7	DG: Davy; PG: Murray

14 March 1931, Ravenhill, Belfast
Wales	15	T: Morley (2), Davey; C: Bassett; DG: Ralph
Ireland	3	T: Siggins

12 March 1932, Cardiff Arms Park, Cardiff
Ireland	12	T: Ross (2), Waide, Lightfoot
Wales	10	T: Davey, Ralph; DG: Ralph

11 March 1933, Ravenhill, Belfast
Ireland	10	T: Barnes; DG: Davy; PG: Siggins
Wales	5	T: Bowcott; C: Jenkins

IRELAND

10 March 1934, St Helen's, Swansea
Wales   13   T: Fear, Cowey, Jenkins; C: Jenkins (2)
Ireland   0

9 March 1935, Ravenhill, Belfast
Ireland   9   T: Doyle; PG: Siggins, Bailey
Wales   3   PG: James

14 March 1936, Cardiff Arms Park, Cardiff
Wales   3   PG: Jenkins
Ireland   0

3 April 1937, Ravenhill, Belfast
Ireland   5   T: Bailey; C: Walker
Wales   3   PG: Legge

12 March 1938, St Helen's, Swansea
Wales   11   T: Taylor, Clement; C: Legge; PG: Wooller
Ireland   5   T: Moran; C: McKibbin

11 March 1939, Ravenhill, Belfast
Wales   7   T: W Davies; DG: W Davies
Ireland   0

29 March 1947, St Helen's, Swansea
Wales   6   T: B Evans; PG: Tamplin
Ireland   0

13 March 1948, Ravenhill, Belfast
Ireland   6   T: Mullan, Daly
Wales   3   T: B Williams

12 March 1949, St Helen's, Swansea
Ireland   5   T: McCarthy; C: Norton
Wales   0

11 March 1950, Ravenhill, Belfast
Wales   6   T: K Jones, Thomas
Ireland   3   PG: Norton

10 March 1951, Cardiff Arms Park, Cardiff
Wales   3   PG: Edwards
Ireland   3   T: Kyle

8 March 1952, Lansdowne Road, Dublin
Wales   14   T: C Thomas, K Jones, Stephens; C: L Jones; PG: L Jones
Ireland   3   PG: Murphy

14 March 1953, St Helen's, Swansea
Wales   5   T: Griffiths; C: T Davies
Ireland   3   T: Pedlow

13 March 1954, Lansdowne Road, Dublin
Wales   12   DG: D Thomas; PG: Evans (3)
Ireland   9   T: Gaston; PG: Henderson, Kelly

12 March 1955, Cardiff Arms Park, Cardiff
Wales   21   T: Meredith, Griffiths, Morgan, Morris; C: Owen (3); PG: Owen
Ireland   3   PG: Henderson

10 March 1956, Lansdowne Road, Dublin
Ireland   11   T: Cunningham; C: Pedlow; DG: Kyle; PG: Pedlow
Wales   3   PG: Owen

9 March 1957, Cardiff Arms Park, Cardiff
Wales   6   PG: T Davies (2)
Ireland   5   T: Kavanagh; C: Pedlow

IRELAND

Most tests as captain: Ireland

No.	Player	Period
56	Brian O'Driscoll	2002–2009
36	Keith Wood	1996–2003
24	Tom Kiernan	1963–1973
19	Cirian Fitzgerald	1982–1986

Most points by a player in a career: Ireland

No.	Player	Tests	Career	Points			
				T	C	PG	DG
919	Ronan O'Gara	92	19/02/2000–21/03/2009	14	144	173	14
560	David Humphreys	72	17/02/1996–26/11/2005	6	88	110	8
308	Michael Kiernan	43	31/01/1982–02/02/1991	6	40	62	6
296	Eric Elwood	35	06/03/1993–15/10/1999	-	43	68	2
217	Ollie Campbell	22	17/01/1976–04/02/1984	1	15	54	7

Most tries by a player in a career: Ireland

No.	Player	Tests	Career
36	Brian O'Driscoll	93	12/06/1999–21/03/2009
29	Denis Hickie	62	01/02/1997–30/09/2007
20	Shane Horgan	64	19/02/2000–08/11/2008
19	Girvan Dempsey	82	14/11/1998–15/11/2008
18	Geordan Murphy	63	10/06/2000–21/03/2009

Most conversions by a player in a career: Ireland

No.	Player	Tests	Career
144	Ronan O'Gara	92	19/02/2000–21/03/2009
88	David Humphreys	72	17/02/1996–26/11/2005
43	Eric Elwood	35	06/03/1993–15/10/1999
40	Michael Kiernan	43	31/01/1982–02/02/1991
26	Tom Kiernan	59	13/02/1960–24/02/1973

Most penalties by a player in a career: Ireland

No.	Player	Tests	Career
173	Ronan O'Gara	92	19/02/2000–21/03/2009
110	David Humphreys	72	17/02/1996–26/11/2005
68	Eric Elwood	35	06/03/1993–15/10/1999
62	Michael Kiernan	43	31/01/1982–02/02/1991
54	Ollie Campbell	22	17/01/1976–04/02/1984

IRELAND

	Most drop goals by a player in a career: Ireland		
No.	Player	Tests	Career
14	Ronan O'Gara	92	19/02/2000–21/03/2009
8	David Humphreys	72	17/02/1996–26/11/2005
7	Ollie Campbell	22	17/01/1976–04/02/1984
7	Richard Lloyd	19	12/02/1910–03/04/1920
6	Michael Kiernan	43	31/01/1982–02/02/1991
6	Mike Gibson	69	08/02/1964–16/06/1979
6	Barry McGann	25	25/01/1969–05/06/1976

	Most points by a player in a match: Ireland							
No.	Player	Points				Versus	Venue	Date
		T	C	PG	DG			
32	Ronan O'Gara	2	2	5	1	Samoa	Apia Park, Apia	20/06/2003
30	Ronan O'Gara	-	6	6	-	Italy	Lansdowne Road, Dublin	04/03/2000
26	Paul Wallace	1	6	3	-	Pacific Islanders	Lansdowne Road, Dublin	26/11/2006
26	David Humphreys	1	6	3	-	Italy	Thomond Park, Limerick	30/08/2003
26	David Humphreys	1	3	5	-	Scotland	Murrayfield, Edinburgh	16/02/2003
24	David Humphreys	-	-	7	1	Argentina	Stade Felix Bollaert, Lens	20/10/1999
24	Paul Burke	-	-	8	-	Italy	Lansdowne Road, Dublin	04/01/1997

	Most tries by a player in a match: Ireland			
No.	Player	Versus	Venue	Date
4	Brian Robinson	Zimbabwe	Lansdowne Road, Dublin	06/10/1991
4	Keith Wood	United States	Lansdowne Road, Dublin	02/10/1999
4	Dennis Hickie	Italy	Thomond Park, Limerick	30/08/2003

	Most conversions by a player in a match: Ireland			
No	Player	Versus	Venue	Date
10	Eric Elwood	Georgia	Lansdowne Road, Dublin	14/11/1998
10	Ronan O'Gara	Japan	Lansdowne Road, Dublin	11/11/2000
8	Ronan O'Gara	United States	Manchester, United States	10/06/2000
7	Michael Kiernan	Romania	Lansdowne Road, Dublin	01/11/1986
7	Ronan O'Gara	Namibia	Aussie Stadium, Sydney	19/10/2003
7	David Humphreys	United States	Lansdowne Road, Dublin	20/11/2004

Most penalties by a player in a match: Ireland

No.	Player	Versus	Venue	Date
8	Paul Burke	Italy	Lansdowne Road, Dublin	04/01/1997
7	David Humphreys	Argentina	Stade Felix Bollaert, Lens	20/10/1999
6	Ollie Campbell	Scotland	Lansdowne Road, Dublin	20/02/1982
6	Eric Elwood	Romania	Lansdowne Road, Dublin	13/11/1993
6	Simon Mason	Western Samoa	Lansdowne Road, Dublin	12/11/1996
6	Ronan O'Gara	Italy	Lansdowne Road, Dublin	04/03/2000
6	David Humphreys	Wales	Lansdowne Road, Dublin	03/02/2002
6	Ronan O'Gara	Australia	Lansdowne Road, Dublin	09/11/2002

Most drop goals by a player in a match: Ireland

No	Player	Versus	Venue	Date
2	Mike Gibson	Australia	Lansdowne Road, Dublin	21/01/1967
2	Billy McCombe	France	Lansdowne Road, Dublin	01/03/1975
2	Ollie Campbell	Australia	Sydney Cricket Ground, Sydney	16/06/1979
2	Eric Elwood	England	Lansdowne Road, Dublin	20/03/1993
2	David Humphreys	Wales	Wembley, London	20/02/1999
2	David Humphreys	New Zealand	Lansdowne Road, Dublin	17/11/2001
2	Ronan O'Gara	Argentina	Lansdowne Road, Dublin	27/11/2004
2	Ronan O'Gara	England	Lansdowne Road, Dublin	27/02/2005

Most points in a match by Ireland

No.	Result	Points				Versus	Venue	Date
		T	C	PG	DG			
83	83–3	13	9	-	-	United States	Manchester, New Hampshire	10/06/2000
78	78–9	11	10	1	-	Japan	Lansdowne Road, Dublin	11/11/2000
70	70–0	10	10	-	-	Georgia	Lansdowne Road, Dublin	14/11/1998
64	64–17	9	5	3	-	Fiji	Lansdowne Road, Dublin	17/11/2002
64	64–7	10	7	-	-	Namibia	Aussie Stadium, Sydney	19/10/2003

Most consecutive test wins by Ireland

No.	Period	Details
10	07/09/2002–22/03/2003	Romania (H), Russia (A), Georgia (H), Australia (H), Fiji (H), Argentina (H), Scotland (A), Italy (A), France (H), Wales (A)

Milestones

Longest test career	Tony O'Reilly	22/01/1955–14/02/1970 (15 years & 24 days)
Youngest test player	Frank Hewitt	17 years 157 days on 08/03/1924 vs Wales in Cardiff
Oldest test player	Mike Gibson	36 years & 95 days on 16/06/1979 vs Australia in Sydney

Flanker Ian Kirkpatrick launches over the top of Irish flyhalf Barry McGann to score a crucial try in the test against Ireland in Wellington, 1976, won 11-3 by New Zealand.
Photo: New Zealand Rugby Museum

Top: Action from the Ireland vs New Zealand international in Dublin, 1924. New Zealand won by 6-0. *Photo*: New Zealand Rugby Museum

Above: Lock forward Moss Keane secures lineout possession for Ireland's scrumhalf John Moloney during the 1974 Ireland vs New Zealand international in Dublin, won 15-6 by New Zealand. *Photo*: New Zealand Rugby Museum

Italy

Italy vs Argentina *see* page 192

Italy vs Australia *see* page 221

Italy vs Australia XV

21 November 1973, Stadio Tommaso Fattori, L'Aquila
Australia XV	59	T: Shaw (2), McLean (2), Freney (2), Monaghan, Rowles, Fay, McCurrach; C: McGill (8); PG: L'Estrange
Italy	21	T: Visentin, Salsi; C: Lazzarini, Ponzi; PG: Ponzi (3)

4 November 1976, Arena Civca, Milan
Australia XV	16	T: Crowe, Loane, Batch; C: McLean (2)
Italy	15	T: Manni; C: Ponzi; PG: Ponzi (3)

Italy vs Belgium

10 October 1937, Stade Charlety, Paris
Italy	45	T: Cova (4), D'Alessio (2), Vigliano (2), re Garbagnati, Visentin; C: Vigliano (3), Visentin (3); PG: Vigliano
Belgium	0	

10 May 1969, King Baudouin Stadium, Brussels
Italy	31	T: Michelon (3), Rista (2), Pignotti, Boccaletto, Bollesan; C: Boccaletto, Bollesan; PG: di Zitti
Belgium	0	

Italy vs Border

23 June 1973 Basil Kenyon Stadium, East London
Border	25	T: Stephenson (3), Wilson, Coats; C: Brereton; PG: Brereton
Italy	12	PG: Lazzarini (3), Mattarolo

Italy vs Bulgaria

2 March 1969 Sofia
Italy	17	T: Cioni (2), Ambron, Pignotti; C: Pacifici; PG: di Zitti
Bulgaria	0	

Italy vs Canada	
Played:	6
Won:	4
Lost:	2
Drawn:	0
For:	178
Against:	76
Average score:	
29.67–12.67	
Italy percentages:	
Won:	66.67%
Lost:	0%
Drawn:	33.33%

Italy vs Canada

25 June 1983, Vancouver
Canada	19	T: Donaldson; PG: Wyatt (4), McLean
Italy	13	T: Ghizzoni; PG: Torresan (2); DG: Torresan

1 July 1983, Stanley Park, Toronto
Italy	37	T: Mascioletti, Bettarello, Zanon; C: Bettarello (2); PG: Bettarello (5); DG: Bettarello (2)
Canada	9	PG: Wyatt (3)

11 November 2000, Stadio Mario Battaglini, Rovigo
Canada	22	T: Wirachowski; C: Barker; PG: Barker (4); DG: Barker
Italy	17	T: M Dallan; PG: Mazzariol (3), Pez

21 October 2003, Bruce Stadium, Canberra (RWC, Pool D)
Italy	19	T: Parisse; C: Wakarua; PG: Wakarua (4)
Canada	14	T: Fyffe; PG: Barker (3)

6 November 2004, Stadio Tommaso Fattori, L'Aquila
Italy	51	T: Masi (2), Ongaro (2), Bergamasco, Travagli; C: Wakarua (6); PG: Wakarua (3)
Canada	6	PG: Barker (2)

25 November 2006, Stadio Comprensorial, Rome
Italy	41	T: Stanojevic (2), Bortolami, Castrogiavani, Zanni; C: Bortolussi (5); PG: Bortolussi (2)
Canada	6	PG: Monro (2)

ITALY

Italy vs Catalonia

14 April 1934, Barcelona
Catalonia	5*	T: (1); C: (1)
Italy	5	T: Cazzini; C: Aloisio

24 March 1935, Stadio Marassi, Genoa
Italy	5	T: Aloisio; C: Visentin
Catalonia	3*	T: (1)

Italy vs Cook Islands

6 July 1980, Tupapa Rugby Field, Avarua
Cook Islands	15	T: Tereora; C: Mamanu; PG: Mamanu (3)
Italy	6	PG: Bettarello; DG: Ghizzoni

Italy vs Croatia

17 June 1993, Stade Aime Giral, Perpignon
Italy	76	T: Dotto (2), Bonomi (2), Giovanelli (2), Barba (2), Tommasi, Favaro, Properzi-Curti; C: Troiani (9); PG: Troiani
Croatia	11*	T: (1); PG: (2)

Italy vs Czech Republic / Czechoslovakia

Italy vs Czech Republic	
Played:	12
Won:	10
Lost:	1
Drawn:	1
For:	266
Against:	62

Average score:
22.17–5.17

Italy percentages:
Won:	83.33%
Lost:	8.33%
Drawn:	8.34%

12 February 1933, Arena Civica, Milan
Italy	7	T: Maffioli; DG: Maffioli
Czechoslovakia	3*	T: (1)

16 April 1933, Great Strahov Stadium, Prague
Italy	12	T: Aymonod (2), Campagna, Maffioli
Czechoslovakia	3*	T: (1)

23 May 1948, Stade Comunale, Parma
Italy	17	T: Rossini, Rosi, Pitorri; C: Fava, Battagion; DG: Parmiggiani
Czechoslovakia	0	

22 May 1949, Great Strahov Stadium, Prague
Czechoslovakia	14*	T: (3); C: (1); PG: (1)
Italy	6	T: Rossini, Marini

11 December 1955, Stadio Flaminio, Rome
Italy	17	T: Barbini, Pisaneschi; C: Comin; PG: Perrini (2), Comin
Czechoslovakia	6*	PG: (2)

29 April 1956, Great Strahov Stadium, Prague
Italy	19	T: Pescetto (3), Lanfranchi, Simonelli; C: Perrini (2)
Czechoslovakia	9*	T: (1); PG: (2)

8 December 1965, Stadio Carlo Montano, Livorno
Italy	11	T: Ambron (2), Armellin; C: Speziali
Czechoslovakia	0	

26 April 1970, Krc Stadium, Prague
Italy	11	T: Pacifici; C: Michelon; PG: Michelon; DG: Cecchin
Czechoslovakia	3	T: (1)

4 November 1973, Stadio Mario Battaglini, Rovigo
Italy	3	PG: Ponzi
Czechoslovakia	3	DG: (1)

10 May 1975, Stadio Oreste Granillo, Reggio Calabria
Italy	49	T: de Anna (3), Vezzani (2), Marchetto, Rossi, Visentin; C: Ponzi (7); PG: Ponzi
Czechoslovakia	9*	T: (1); C: (1); PG: (1)

29 October 1977, Krc Stadium, Prague
Italy	10	T: Ghizzoni(2); C: Zuin
Czechoslovakia	4*	T: (1)

18 May 1994, Stadio Zaffanella, Viadana
Italy	104	T: Gerosa (3), Aldrovandi (3), Vaccari (2), Grespan, Filizzola (2), Ravazzolo (2), Troncon (2), Castellani; C: Troiani (12)
Czech Republic	8*	T: (1); PG: (1)

Italy vs Denmark

1 November 1997, Stadio Mompiano, Brescia

Italy	102	T: Rotilio (5), Gardner (2), Sanavacca (2), Barattin, Caione, Dallan, Gumeiro, Martin, Ravazzolo; C: Sanavacca (6), Mazzariol (5)
Denmark	3*	PG: (1)

Italy vs England *see page 267*

Italy vs England B

17 April 1985, Twickenham, London

England B	21	T: Clough, Harrison; C: Johnson (2); PG: Johnson (3)
Italy	9	T: Venturi; C: Bettarello; PG: Bettarello

Italy vs England u23

13 September 1975, County Ground, Gosforth

England u23	29*	T: (4); C: (2); PG: (3)
Italy	13	T: Marchetto; PG: Ponzi (3)

16 May 1979, Stadio Mompiano, Brescia

Italy	6	PG: Bettarello (2)
England u23	6*	T: (1); C: (1)

22 May 1982, Stadio Plebiscito, Padova

Italy	12	PG: Bettarello (2); DG: Bettarello (2)
England u23	7*	T: (1); PG: (1)

Italy vs England XV

10 May 1986 Stadio Olympio, Rome

Italy	15	T: Mascioletti; C: Bettarello; PG: Bettarello (3)
England XV	15	T: (1); C: (1); PG: (3)

Italy vs Fiji

Italy vs Fiji	
Played:	7
Won:	3
Lost:	4
Drawn:	0
For:	169
Against:	171
Average score:	
24.14–24.43	
Italy percentages:	
Won:	42.86%
Lost:	57.14%
Drawn:	0%

Italy vs Fiji

14 June 1980, National Stadium, Suva

Fiji	16	T: Lutumailagi (2), Racika; C: Vuetaki (2)
Italy	3	DG: Ghizzoni

31 May 1987, Carisbrook, Dunedin (RWC, Pool 3)

Italy	18	T: Mascioletti, Cuttitta, Cucchiella; PG: Collodo; DG: Collodo
Fiji	15	T: Naiviliwasa; C: Koroduadua; PG: Koroduadua (2); DG: Qoro

28 August 1999, Stadio Tommaso Fattori, L'Aquila

Fiji	50	T: Satala (2), Tikomaimakogia (2), Serevi; C: Little (5); PG: Little (5)
Italy	32	T: Martin, Pucciariello, Checchinato; C: Dominguez; PG: Dominquez (5)

15 July 2000, Churchill Park, Lautoka

Fiji	43	T: Vunibaka, Satala, Little, Raiwalui, Ligairi; C: Little (3); PG: Little (4)
Italy	9	PG: Queirolo (2), Mazzariol

10 November 2001, Stadio di Monigo, Treviso

Italy	66	T: Vaccari, Stoica, Dallan, Moscardi, Checchinato, Persico, Martin; C: Dominguez (4), Mazzariol; PG: Dominguez (7)
Fiji	10	T: Serevi; C: Serevi; PG: Serevi

26 November 2005, Stadio Brianteo, Milan

Italy	23	T: Mi Bergamasco, Ongaro; C: Pez (2); PG: Pez (3)
Fiji	8	T: Yabakitini; PG: Bai

17 June 2006, Churchill Park, Suva

Fiji	29	T: Ligairi, Caucaunibuca, Domolailai, Salabogi; C: Bai (3); PG: Bai
Italy	18	T: lo Cicero, Sole; C: Pez; PG: Pez (2)

Italy vs France *see page 307*

ITALY

Italy vs France XV

22 April 1935, Stadio Flaminio, Rome
France XV   44*
Italy   6   T: Vinci III, Maresccalchi

28 March 1948, Stadio Mario Battaglini, Rovigo
France XV   39*   T: (9); C: (4); DG: (1)
Italy   6   T: Rosi; PG: Fava

27 March 1949, Stade Velodrome, Marseille
France XV   27*   T: (6); PG: (3)
Italy   0

21 July 1955, Barcelona
France XV   16*   T: (4); C: (2)
Italy   8   T: Percudani; C: Perrini; PG: Perrini

9 November 1969, Stadio Santa Maria Goretti, Catania
France XV   22*   T: (4); C: (2); PG: (1); DG: (1)
Italy   8   T: Conforto; C: Pacifici; PG: Michelon

28 February 1971, Stade du Ray, Nice
France XV   37*   T: (7); C: (5); PG: (2)
Italy   13   T: Abbiati, Puglisi; C: Lazzarini (2); PG: Lazzarini

15 February 1975, Stadio Flaminio, Rome
France XV   16*   T: (3); C: (2)
Italy   9   T: Marchetto; C: Ponzi; PG: Ponzi

7 February 1976, Arena Civica, Milan
France XV   23*   T: (4); C: (2); PG: (1)
Italy   11   T: Blessano, de Anna; PG: Ponzi

6 February 1977, Stade Lesdiguieres, Grenoble
France XV   10*   T: (1); PG: (1); DG: (1)
Italy   3   PG: Ponzi

4 February 1978, Stadio Tomasso Fattori, L'Aquila
France XV   31*   T: (6); C: (2); PG: (1)
Italy   9   T: Blessano; C: Collodo; PG: Collodo

18 February 1979, Stadio Plebiscito, Padua
France XV   15*   T: (1); C: (1); PG: (3)
Italy   9   T: Marchetto; C: Zuin; PG: Zuin

22 September 1979, Makarska Stadium, Makarska
France XV   38   T: Malquier (2), Mesny (2), Blanco, Codorniou; C: Blanco (4); PG: Blanco (2)
Italy   12   PG: Trentin (2), Bettarello; DG: Bettarello

17 February 1980, Stade Marcel Michelin, Clermont-Ferrand
France XV   46*   T: (9); C: (5)
Italy   9   T: Mascioletti; C: Bettarello; DG: Bettarello

8 March 1981, Stadio Mario Battaglini, Rovigo
France XV   17*   T: (3); C: (1); PG: (1)
Italy   9   PG: Bettarello (2); DG: Bettarello

21 February 1982, Stade Albert Domecq, Carcassonne
France XV   25*   T: (4); C: (3); PG: (1)
Italy   19   T: Gaetaniello, Azzali, Morelli; C: Bettarello (2); DG: Bettarello

6 February 1983, Stadio Mario Battaglini, Rovigo
Italy   6   T: Zanon; C: Bettarello
France XV   6*   T: (1); C: (1)

13 September 1983, COC Stadium, Casablanca
France XV   26   T: Blanco, Belascain, Camberabero, Berbizier; C: Blanco (2); PG: Blanco;
                                      DG: Camberabero
Italy   12   PG: Bettarello (4)

19 February 1984, Stade Municipal, Chalon
France XV   38*   T: (6); C: (4); PG: (2)
Italy   16   T: Ghizzoni, Azzali; C: Bettarello; PG: Bettarello (2)

3 March 1985, Stadio di Monigo, Treviso
France XV   22*   T: (3); C: (2); PG: (1); DG: (1)
Italy   9   PG: Bettarello (3)

15 February 1986, Union Sportive Annecy Rugby, Annecy
France XV   18*   T: (3); C: (3)
Italy   0

22 February 1987, Stadio Plebiscito, Padova
France XV   22*   T: (3); C: (2); PG: (2)
Italy   6   PG: Troiani; DG: Collodo

7 February 1988, Stade Louis II, Monaco
France XV   19*   T: (4); DG: (1)
Italy   9   PG: Ambrosio (3)

19 February 1989, Stadio Mompiano, Brescia
France XV   40*   T: (7); C: (3); PG: (2)
Italy   12   PG: Capitani (3); DG: Tebaldi

18 February 1990, Stade Municipal, Albi
France XV   22*   T: (2); C: (1); PG: (4)
Italy   12   PG: Troiani (4)

2 March 1991, Stadio Flaminio, Rome
France XV   15*   T: (2); C: (2); PG: (1)
Italy   9   T: Marcello Cuttitta; C: Troiani; PG: Troiani

16 February 1992, Stade Maurice Trelut, Tarbes
France XV   21*   T: (2); C: (2); PG: (3)
Italy   18   T: Barba, Bottacchiari; C: Dominguez (2); PG: Dominguez (2)

20 February 1993, Stadio di Monigo, Treviso
France XV   14*   T: (1); PG: (2); DG: (1)
Italy   12   PG: Dominguez (4)

25 June 1993, Stade Méditerranée, Beziers
France XV   31*   T: (3); C: (2); PG: (4)
Italy   6   PG: Filizzola (2)

11 November 1993, Stadio di Monigo, Treviso
Italy   16   T: penalty try; C: Dominguez; PG: Dominguez (3)
France XV   9   PG: (3)

4 December 1994, Digione
France XV   14*   T: (1); PG: (1); DG: (2)
Italy   9   PG: Troiani (3)

30 January 1999, Stadio Luigi Ferraris, Genoa
France XV   49*   T: (7); C: (4); PG: (2)
Italy   24   T: Troncon (2), Moscardi; C: Dominguez (3); PG: Dominguez

Italy vs Georgia

6 September 2003, del Parco Tanaro, Asti
Italy   31   T: Troncon, lo Cicero, Castrogiavanni, Checchinato; C: Pez; PG: Pez (3)
Georgia   22   T: Urjukashvili; C: Jimsheladze; PG: Jimsheladze (4), Urjukashvili

Italy vs Germany
Played: 20
Won: 15
Lost: 4
Drawn: 1
For: 253
Against: 123

Average score:
12.65–6.15

Italy percentages:
Won: 75%
Lost: 20%
Drawn: 5%

Italy vs Germany

14 May 1936, Berlin
Germany 19* T: (5); DG: (1)
Italy 8 T: Cazzini, Vinci III; C: Rizzoli

1 January 1937, Arena Civica, Milan
Germany 6* T: (2)
Italy 3 T: Vinci III

14 October 1937, Stade Charlety, Paris
Italy 9 T: Vinci III, Visentin; PG: Vigliano
Germany 7* T: (1); DG: (1)

6 March 1938, Stuttgart
Germany 10* T: (2); C: (2)
Italy 0

11 February 1939, Arena Civica, Milan
Germany 12* T: (2); C: (1); DG: (1)
Italy 3 PG: Bottonelli

5 May 1940, Stuttgart
Italy 4 DG: Vinci III
Germany 0

27 April 1952, Stadio Plebiscito, Padua
Italy 14 T: Gerosa (2), Rosi, Masci; C: Cecchetto-Milani
West Germany 6* PG: (1); DG: (1)

17 May 1953, Hanover
Italy 21 T: Dari (3), Rosi, Lanfranchi; C: Marini (3)
West Germany 3* T: (1)

13 March 1955, Arena Civica, Milan
Italy 24 T: Barbini, Stievano, Taveggia, Aiolfi; C: Comin (2), Taveggia; PG: Taveggia (2)
West Germany 8* T: (2); C: (1)

25 March 1956, Fritz Grunebaum Stadium, Heidelberg
Italy 12 T: Cantoni, Mancini; PG: Lanfranchi; DG: Perrini
West Germany 3* PG: (1)

7 December 1957, Arena Civica, Milan
Italy 8 T: Navarrini; C: Barbini; PG: Barbini
West Germany 0

10 April 1960, Hanover
Italy 11 T: Fusco; C: Busson; PG: Busson, Martini
West Germany 5* T: (1); C: (1)

15 January 1961, Stadio Beltrametti, Piacenza
Italy 19 T: Bellinazzo, Luise, del Bono, Sguario; C: Busson, Martini; PG: Martini
West Germany 0

27 May 1962, Berlin
Italy 13 T: Ambron, Troncon, Angioli; C: Lanfranchi (2)
West Germany 11* T: (2); C: (1); PG: (1)

22 March 1964, Camp Arcoveggio, Bologna
Italy 17 T: Ambron, Fusco, Lanfranchi; C: Martini; PG: Martini; DG: Martini
West Germany 3* T: (1)

30 October 1966, Berlin
West Germany 3* PG: (1)
Italy 3 PG: di Zitti

ITALY

3 November 1968, Stadio Pierluigi Penzo, Venice
Italy   22   T: Ambron (2), Modonesi; C: Autore, Martini; PG: Martini (2); DG: Valle
West Germany   14*   T: (1); C: (1); PG: (2); DG: (1)

5 May 1974, Stadio Rho, Rho
Italy   16   T: Aio, Fedrigo; C: Lazzarini; PG: Lazzarini (2)
West Germany   10*   T: (1); PG: (2)

29 November 1981, Stadio Mario Battaglini, Rovigo
Italy   23   T: Mascioletti (2), Azzali; C: Bettarello; PG: Battarello (3)
West Germany   0

7 November 1982, Hanover
Italy   23   T: Gaetaniello, Francescato, Azzali, Zanon; C: Bettarello (2); PG: Bettarello
West Germany   3*   PG: (1)

Italy vs Ireland *see* page 338

Italy vs Ireland *see* page 338

Italy vs Japan	
Played:	4
Won:	4
Lost:	0
Drawn:	0
For:	145
Against:	40
Average score:	
36.25–10	
Italy percentages:	
Won:	100%
Lost:	0%
Drawn:	0%

Italy vs Japan

21 October 1976, Stadio Plebiscito, Padua
Italy   25   T: Marchetto, Blessano, Francescato, Rossi, Bonetti; C: Ponzi; PG: Ponzi
Japan   3   PG: Ueyama

4 July 2004, Chichibunomiya Stadium, Tokyo
Italy   32   T: Castrogiavanni (3), Canale; C: Wakarua (3); PG: Wakarua (2)
Japan   19   T: Onozawa; C: Ikeda; PG: Ikeda (3); DG: Morita

11 June 2006, Chichibunomiya Stadium, Tokyo
Italy   52   T: Mi Bergamasco (2), Bortolussi, de Jager, Dallan, Dellape, Sole; C: Pez (4), Marcato (3); PG: Pez
Japan   6   PG: Ikeda (2)

18 August 2007, Stadio Rugby, Saint Vincent
Italy   36   T: Stanojevic (2), Robertson, lo Cicero, Ma Bergamasco; C: Bortolussi (4); PG: Bortolussi
Japan   12   T: Nishiura, Makiri; C: Ando

Italy vs Madagascar

24 May 1970, Municipal Stadium, Antananarivo
Italy   17   T: Finocchi, Cioni, Bollesan; C: Michelon; PG: Michelon; DG: Pacifici
Madagascar   9*   T: (1); PG: (2)

31 May 1970, Municipal Stadium, Antananarivo
Italy   9   T: Michelon (2); DG: Pacifici
Madagascar   6*   PG: (2)

Italy vs Middlesex

15 March 1974, Stoop Memorial Ground, London
Middlesex   28*   T: (4); C: (3); PG: (2)
Italy   12   T: Marchetto; C: Lazzarini; PG: Lari (2)

Italy vs Morocco	
Played:	8
Won:	6
Lost:	2
Drawn:	0
For:	184
Against:	52
Average score:	
23–6.5	
Italy percentages:	
Won:	75%
Lost:	25%
Drawn:	0%

Italy vs Morocco

21 February 1971, Stadio San Paolo, Naples
Morocco   8*   T: (2); C: (1)
Italy   6   T: Dotto; PG: Ambron

6 March 1977, COC Stadium, Casablanca
Morocco   10*   T: (1); PG: (2)
Italy   9   PG: Ponzi (2); DG: Ponzi

20 September 1979, Makarska Stadium, Makarska
Italy   10   T: Ghizzoni, Angrisani; C: Trentin
Morocco   7*   T: (1); PG: (1)

ITALY

22 December 1979, Stadio Santa Colomba, Benevento
Italy   34   T: Gaetaniello (2), Mascioletti (2), Limone, Basei, Bettarello; C: Bettarello (3)
Morocco   6*   PG: (2)

19 December 1982, COC Stadium, Casablanca
Italy   13   T: Zanon; PG: Bettarello (3)
Morocco   3*   PG: (1)

10 September 1983, COC Stadium, Casablanca
Italy   15   PG: Bettarello (5)
Morocco   9*   PG: (3)

18 March 1984, Stadio Beltrametti, Piacenza
Italy   27   T: Ghizzoni, Screnci, Zanon; C: Bettarello (3); PG: Bettarello (3)
Morocco   0

19 June 1993, Stade Albert Domecq, Carcassone
Italy   70   T: Francescato (4), Mar Cuttitta (3), Bonomi, Mas Cuttitta, Orlandi; C: Filizzola (10)
Morocco   9*   PG: (1); DG: (2)

Italy vs Namibia

15 June 1991, South West Stadium, Windhoek
Namibia   17   T: Stoop, Mans, Deysel; C: Coetzee; PG: Cotzee
Italy   7   T: Vaccari; PG: Dominguez

22 June 1991, South West Stadium, Windhoek
Namibia   33   T: Mans, Meyer, Alberts; C: Coetzee (3); PG: Coetzee (5)
Italy   19   T: Vaccari, Barba, Pietrosanti, Croci; PG: Troiani

23 June 2001, South West Stadium, Windhoek
Italy   49   T: Checchinato (2), Pozzebon (2), Mazzucato, Perziano, Troncon; C: Mazzariol (7)
Namibia   24   T: Powell, Blaauw, Furter; C: Kotze (3); PG: Kotze

Italy vs Natal

30 June 1973, Kings Park, Durban
Natal   23   T: Thoresson (4); C: Thoresson, Swanby; PG: Swanby
Italy   3   PG: Mattarolo

Italy vs Netherlands	
Played:	4
Won:	4
Lost:	0
Drawn:	0
For:	178
Against:	27

Average score:
44.5– 6.75

Italy percentages:

Won:	100%
Lost:	0%
Drawn:	0%

Italy vs Netherlands

23 November 1975, Sportpark Berg & Bos, Apeldoorn
Italy   24   T: Blessano, de Anna, Cossara, Gaetaniello; C: Caligiuri;
                                         PG: Caligiuri, Ponzi
Netherlands   0

3 October 1990, Stadio di Monigo, Treviso
Italy   24   T: Barba; C: Troiani; PG: Troiani (5); DG: Bonomi
Netherlands   11*   T: (2); PG: (1)

21 May 1994, Centro San Michele, Calvisano
Italy   63   T: Mar Cuttitta (2), Aldrovandi, Bonomi, Pedroni, Dominguez, Mas
                                         Cuttitta, Troncon; C: Dominguez (7); PG: Dominguez (3)
Netherlands   9*   PG: (3)

18 November 1998, McAlpine Stadium, Huddersfield
Italy   67   T: Checchinato (2), Bergamasco (2), Caione, Pini, Stoica, Dallan,
                                         Dominguez, Giovanelli, de Carli; C: Dominguez (4), Mazzariol (2)
Netherlands   7   T: Elisara; C: Everts

Italy vs New Zealand

Italy vs New Zealand
Played: 10
Won: 0
Lost: 10
Drawn: 0
For: 102
Against: 624

Average score:
10.2–62.4

Italy percentages:
Won: 0%
Lost: 100%
Drawn: 0%

22 May 1987, Eden Park, Auckland (RWC, Pool 3)

New Zealand	70	T: Kirk (2), McDowell, penalty try, Jones, Taylor, Green (2), Kirwan (2), Stanley, A Whetton; C: Fox (8); PG: Fox (2)
Italy	6	PG: Collodo; DG: Collodo

13 October 1991, Welford Road, Leicester (RWC, Pool 1)

New Zealand	31	T: Z Brooke, Tuigamala, Hewitt, Innes; C: Fox (3); PG: Fox (3)
Italy	21	T: M Cuttitta, Bonomi; C: Troiani (2); PG: Troiani (3)

28 October 1995, Stadio Renato Dall'Ara, Bologna

New Zealand	70	T: Little (2), Lomu (2), Rush, I Jones, M Jones, Fitzpatrick, Z Brooke, Wilson; C: Culhane (7); PG: Culhane (2)
Italy	6	PG: Dominguez (2)

14 October 1999, McAlpine Stadium, Huddersfield (RWC, Pool B)

New Zealand	101	T: Wilson (3), Lomu (2), Osborne (2), Brown, Mika, Randell, Robertson, Gibson, Cullen, Hammett; C: Brown (11); PG: Brown (3)
Italy	3	PG: Dominguez

25 November 2000, Stadio Luigi Ferraris, Genova

New Zealand	56	T: Reihana (2), Tiatia, Howlett, Spencer, Marshall, Cribb (2); C: Spencer (5); PG: Spencer (2)
Italy	19	T: lo Cicero, Saviozzi; PG: Pez (3)

8 June 2002, Waikato Stadium, Hamilton

New Zealand	64	T: Ralph (3), McDonnell, Meeuws, Kelleher, Lomu, Cullen, Hewett; C: Mehrtens (8); PG: Mehrtens
Italy	10	T: Bortolami; C: Peens; PG: Peens

11 October 2003, Telstra Dome, Melbourne (RW, Pool D)

New Zealand	70	T: Howlett (2), Spencer (2), Rokocoko (2), Thorne, Thorn, Marshall, Carter, MacDonald; C: Carter (6); PG: Spencer
Italy	7	T: Phillips; C: Peens

13 November 2004, Stadio Flaminio, Rome

New Zealand	59	T: Muliaina (2), Umaga (2), McCaw (2), Taumoepeau, Smith, Carter; C: Carter (7)
Italy	10	T: Bergamasco; C: Wakarua; PG: Wakarua

8 September 2007, Stade Velodrome, Marseille (RWC, Pool C)

New Zealand	76	T: Howlett (3), McCaw (2), Sivivatu (2), Collins (2), Jack, Muliaina; C: Carter (7), McAlister (2); PG: Carter
Italy	14	T: Stanojevic, Mi Bergamasco; C: Bortolussi, de Marigny

27 June 2009, AMI Stadium, Christchurch

New Zealand	27	T: Rokocoko, Ross, Whitelock; C: McAlister (3); PG: McAlister (2)
Italy	6	PG: McLean (2)

Italy vs New Zealand Juniors

5 July 1980, Eden Park, Auckland

NZ Juniors	30	T: McLean (2), Hollander, Taylor, Mills; C: McLean, Halligan; PG: McLean, Halligan
Italy	13	T: de Anna, Tinari; C: Bettarello; PG: Bettarello

Italy vs New Zealand XV

28 November 1979, Stadio Mario Battaglini, Rovigo

New Zealand XV	18	T: Fraser, Mexted; C: Hewson (2); PG: Hewson, R Wilson
Italy	12	T: N Francescato; C: Bettarello; PG: Bettarello (2)

Italy vs North Eastern Cape

27 June 1973, Cradock Rugby Club, Cradock
North Eastern Cape   31   T: Francis (2), Norval (2), D Nel, K Nel; C: van Vuuren (2); PG: van Vuuren
Italy   12   T: Francescato; C: Lazzarini; PG: Lazzarini, Caligiuri

Italy vs Northern Orange Free State

9 July 1973, North West Stadium, Welkom
Northern Orange Free State   12*   T: (2); C: (2)
Italy   11   T: Mattarolo, Caligiuri; PG: Mattarolo

Italy vs Oxfordshire

20 March 1974, Iffley Road, Oxford
Oxfordshire   30*   T: (4); C: (4); PG: (2)
Italy   6   PG: Lazzarini, Lari

Italy vs Pacific Islanders

22 November 2008, Stadio Giglio, Reggio Emilia
Pacific Islanders   25   T: Delasau (2), Ratuvou; C: Bai (2); PG: Bai (2)
Italy   17   T: Ghiraldini, Ma Bergamasco; C: Marcato (2); PG: Marcato

Italy vs Poland

Italy vs Poland

Played:	7
Won:	6
Lost:	1
Drawn:	0
For:	165
Against:	49

Average score:
23.57–7

Italy percentages:

Won:	85.71%
Lost:	14.29%
Drawn:	0%

25 October 1975, Stadio di Monigo, Treviso
Italy   28   T: Marchetto (3), Mazzucchelli (2); C: Caligiuri (3), Ponzi
Poland   13*   T: (2); C: (1); PG: (1)

2 April 1977, Stadio Santa Maria Goretti, Catania
Italy   29   T: Mariani (3), Ghizzoni; C: Ponzi (2); PG: Ponzi (3)
Poland   3*   PG: (1)

23 October 1977, Skra Stadium, Warsaw
Poland   12*   T: (1); C: (1); DG: (2)
Italy   6   T: Franceschini; C: Collodo

14 April 1979, Stadio Tamosso Fattori, L'Aquila
Italy   18   T: Marchetto (2), Mascioletti, Mariani; C: Bettarello
Poland   3*   PG: (1)

30 September 1979, Sochacewz
Italy   13   T: Marchetto; PG: Trentin (3)
Poland   3*   PG: (1)

5 October 1980, Stadio Mario Battaglini, Rovigo
Italy   37   T: Ghizzoni (2), R Francescato, Bettarello, Robazza; C: Bettarello (4); PG: Bettarello (3)
Poland   12*   T: (1); C: (1); PG: (2)

7 April 1990, Naples
Italy   34   T: Mar Cuttitta (2), Venturi, Pietrosanti, Zanon; C: Troiani (4); PG: Troiani (2)
Poland   3*   DG: (1)

Italy vs Portugal

Italy vs Portugal

Played:	12
Won:	10
Lost:	1
Drawn:	1
For:	333
Against:	71

Average score:
27.75–5.92

Italy percentages:

Won:	83.33%
Lost:	8.33%
Drawn:	8.34%

7 May 1967, Stadio Marassi, Genoa
Italy   6   PG: di Zitti (2)
Portugal   3   PG: Faria

12 May 1968, Universitario Lisboa, Lisbon
Italy   17   T: Ambron (3), Modonesi; C: Autore; PG: Autore
Portugal   3   PG: Branco

20 February 1972, Stadio Plebiscito, Padua
Italy   0
Portugal   0

2 April 1972, Universitario Lisboa, Lisbon
Italy 15 T: Dotto (2), Puppo; DG: Caluzzi
Portugal 7 T: Faria; PG: Faria

25 February 1973, Sergio Conceicao, Coimbra
Portugal 9 T: Pinto; C: Pinto; PG: Pinto
Italy 6 PG: Lazzarini, Caluzzi

10 February 1974, Universitario Lisboa, Lisbon
Italy 11 T: Marchetto, Bollesan; PG: Lari
Portugal 3 PG: Faria

13 April 1986, Stadio Jesi Arriva, Jesi
Italy 26 T: Mascioletti, Gaetaniello, Venturi, Lorigiola; C: Bettarello (2); PG: Bettarello (2)
Portugal 24 T: Ferreira, Malo; C: Queimado (2); PG: Queimado (4)

18 January 1987, Universitario Lisboa, Lisbon
Italy 41 T: Ghizzoni, Cuttitta, Collodo, Gardin, Colella, penalty try; C: Troiani (4); PG: Troiani (2); DG: Collodo
Portugal 3 PG: Queimado

17 April 1993, Sergio Conceicao, Coimbra
Italy 33 T: Tommasi, Perziano, Casellato, Rigo, Coppo; C: Filizzola; PG: Filizzola (2)
Portugal 11 T: Morais; PG: Queimado (2)

2 March 1996, Universitario Lisboa, Lisbon
Italy 64 T: Francescato (2), Platania (2), Babbo (2), Orlandi, Mazzucato, Dominguez, Properzi-Curti; C: Dominguez (7)
Portugal 3 PG: Vilar-Gomes

7 October 2006, Stadio Tamosso Fattori, L'Aquila
Italy 83 T: Robertson (3), Stanojevic (3), Masi (2), Dellape, Mi Bergamasco, Bortolami, Festuccia, Canavosio;
C: Bortolussi (8), Peens
Portugal 0

19 September 2007, Parc des Princes, Paris (RWC, Pool C)
Italy 31 T: Masi (2), Bergamasco; C: Bortolussi (2); PG: Bortolussi (4)
Portugal 5 T: Penalva

Italy vs Romania

Italy vs Romania	
Played:	41
Won:	22
Lost:	16
Drew:	3
For:	577
Against:	612
Average score:	
14.07–14.93	
Italy percentages:	
Won:	53.66%
Lost:	39.02%
Draw:	7.32%

26 December 1934, Arena Civica, Milan
Italy 7 T: Cazzini; DG: Vinci III
Romania 0

17 May 1936, Berlin
Italy 8 T: Cazzini, Aloisio; C: Rizzoli
Romania 7 T: Barsan; DG: Crissoveloni

25 April 1937, Dinamo Stadion, Bucharest
Romania 0
Italy 0

29 April 1939, Stadio Testaccio, Rome
Italy 3 T: Vigliano
Romania 0

14 April 1940, Dinamo Stadion, Bucharest
Romania 3 T: Marculescu
Italy 0

2 May 1942, Arena Civica, Milan
Italy 22 T: Cova, Costa, Romano, Stenta, Figari; C: Vigliano (2); PG: Vigliano
Romania 3 T: Calistrat

24 May 1953, Dinamo Stadion, Bucharest
Italy 16 T: Rosi, Fornari; C: Battaglini (2); PG: Battaglini; DG: Pisaneschi
Romania 14 T: Buda, Nanu, Mehedinti, Dumitrescu; C: Buda

ITALY

7 December 1958, Stadio Santa Maria Goretti, Catania
Italy	6	PG: Barbini (2)
Romania	3	PG: Ionescu

10 June 1962, Dinamo Stadion, Buchrest
Romania	14	T: Irimescu, Wusek, Rusu; C: Chiriac; PG: Penciu
Italy	6	PG: Lanfranchi (2)

6 November 1966, Stadio Tomasso Fattori, L'Aquila
Italy	3	PG: Ambron
Romania	0	

14 May 1967, Dinamo Stadion, Bucharest
Romania	24	T: Wusek (2), Irimescu, Baciu, Rascanu; C: Irimescu (3); PG: Irimescu
Italy	3	PG: di Zitti

25 October 1970, Stadio Mario Battaglini, Rovigo
Romania	14	T: Nica, Irimescu; C: Irimescu; DG: Nica, Irimescu
Italy	3	T: Bollesan

11 April 1971, Dinamo Stadion, Bucharest
Romania	32	T: Teleasa (3), Suciu (2), Rascanu, Demian; C: Durbac (4); DG: Durbac
Italy	6	PG: Michelon (2)

27 April 1975, Dinamo Stadion, Bucharest
Romania	3	PG: Nica
Italy	3	DG: Ponzi

24 April 1976, Stade Comunale, Parma
Italy	13	T: Marchetto; PG: Ponzi (3)
Romania	12	T: Constantin; C: Bucos; PG: Bucos; DG: Bucos

1 May 1977, Dinamo Stadion, Bucharest
Romania	69	T: Motrescu (4), Stoica (2), Constantin, Alexandru, Nica, Ortelecan, Murariu, Daraban; C: Bucos (5), Nica (4); DG: Alexandru
Italy	0	

26 November 1977, Reggio
Italy	10	T: Ghizzoni; PG: Gaetaniello, Collodo
Romania	10	T: Motrescu; DG: Bucos (2)

22 April 1979, Dinamo Stadion, Bucharest
Romania	44	T: Dinu (2), Murariu (2), Dumitru (2), Beches, Constantin, Stoica; C: Constantin (3), Tudose
Italy	0	

13 April 1980, Stadio Tomasso Fattori, L'Aquila
Italy	24	T: N Francescato, Mascioletti, de Anna, Bargelli; C: Bettarello; PG: Bettarello (2)
Romania	17	T: Stoica, Aldea; PG: Constantin (3)

12 April 1981, Brailia
Romania	35	T: Fuicu (2), Munteanu (2), Paraschiv, Lungu, Aldea; C: Constantin (2); PG: Constantin
Italy	9	T: Bettarello; C: Bettarello; PG: Bettarello

11 April 1982, Stadio Maria Battaglini, Rovigo
Italy	21	T: Ghizzoni, Azzali; C: Bettarello (2); PG: Bettarello (3)
Romania	15	T: Mot (2); C: Podarascu (2); PG: Podarascu

10 April 1983 Buzau
Romania	13	T: Varzaru; PG: Ion (2), Alexandru
Italy	6	PG: Bettarello; DG: Bettarello

22 April 1984, Stadio Tomassao Fattori, L'Aquila
Italy	12	PG: Bettarello (3); DG: Bettarello
Romania	6	PG: Alexandru; DG: Podarescu

14 April 1985, Brasov
Romania	7	T: Toader; PG: Ion
Italy	6	PG: Bettarello (2)

7 December 1985, Stadio Tomasso Fattori, L'Aquilla
Italy	19	T: Bettarello, Morelli, Appiani; C: Bettarello (2); PG: Bettarello
Romania	3	PG: Ion

12 April 1987, Stade 1 Mai, Constanza
Romania	9	PG: Alexandru (3)
Italy	3	PG: Bettarello

2 April 1988, Stadio San Siro, Milan
Romania	12	T: Radulescu; C: Ignat; DG: Ignat (2)
Italy	3	PG: Bonomi

15 April 1989, Dinamo Stadion, Bucharest
Romania	28	T: Boldor, Ignat, Murariu, Coman; C: Ignat (3); PG: Ignat; DG: Ignat
Italy	4	T: Ceselin

14 April 1990, Frascati
Romania	16	T: Ion; PG: Ignat (4)
Italy	9	PG: Troiani (3)

7 October 1990, Stadio Plebiscito, Padua
Italy	29	T: Brunello, Francescato, Saetti; C: Troiani; PG: Troiani (2); DG: Bonomi (2), Brunello
Romania	21	T: Radulescu; C: Nichitean; PG: Nichitean (4); DG: Nichitean

21 April 1991, Dinamo Stadion, Bucharest
Italy	21	T: Venturi, Pivetta; C: Troiani (2); PG: Troiani (3)
Romania	18	T: Sasu; C: Ignat; PG: Ignat (2); DG: Nichitean (2)

18 April 1992, Stadio Mario Battaglini, Rovigo
Italy	39	T: Mar Cuttitta (2), Pietrosanti (2); C: Dominguez (4); PG: Dominguez (4); DG: Dominguez
Romania	13	T: Serban; PG: Ignat (3)

1 October 1992, Stadio Flaminio, Rome
Italy	22	T: Mar Cuttitta, Checchinato, Bottacchiar; C: Bonomi, Troiani; PG: Bonomi
Romania	3	PG: Nichitean

14 May 1994, Dinamo Stadion, Bucharest
Romania	26	T: Leonte; PG: Nichitean (6); DG: Nichitean
Italy	12	PG: Dominguez (4)

1 October 1994, Stadio Angelo Massimino, Catania
Italy	24	PG: Dominguez (8)
Romania	6	PG: Nichitean (2)

21 October 1995, Ferro Carril Oeste Stadium, Buenos Aires
Italy	40	T: Checchinato (2), Roselli, Mazzariol, Moscardi; C: Bonomi (3); PG: Bonomi (3)
Romania	3	PG: Besarau

26 October 1997, Stade Maurice Trelut, Tarbes
Italy	55	T: Francescato (2), Vaccari, Dallan, de Carli, Sgorlon; C: Dominguez (5); PG: Dominguez (5)
Romania	32	T: Radoi (2), Girbu, Solomie; C: Tofan (3); PG: Tofan (2)

18 November 2000, Benevento
Italy	37	T: Caione (2), Martin, Raineri, Pez, Troncon, lo Cicero; C: Preo
Romania	17	T: Ghioc, Septar; C: Mitu (2); PG: Mitu

28 September 2002, Stade Comunale, Parma
Italy	25	T: lo Cicero; C: Peens; PG: Peens (6)
Romania	17	T: Sirbu, Corodeanu; C: Tofan (2); PG: Tofan

26 June 2004, Dinamo Stadion, Bucharest
Romania	25	T: Tofan, Mersoiu, Tonita; C: Tofan (2); PG: Tofan, Dumbrava
Italy	24	T: Canale, Mazzucato, Robertson, Griffen; C: Mazzariol, Griffen

12 September 2007, Stade Velodrome, Marseille (RW, Pool C)
Italy	24	T: Dellape, penalty try; C: Pez PG: Pez (3), Bortolussi
Romania	18	T: Tincu, Manta; C: Dimofte; PG: Dimofte (2)

ITALY

Italy vs Russia/USSR

Played: 17
Won: 7
Lost: 9
Drawn: 1
For: 316
Against: 209

Average score:
18.71–12.18

Italy percentages:
Won: 41.17%
Lost: 52.94%
Drawn: 5.88%

Italy vs Russia / USSR

18 November 1978, Stadio Flaminio, Rome
USSR   11*   T: (2); PG: (1)
Italy   9   T: Caligiuri; C: Zuin; PG: Zuin

28 October 1979, Sparta Stadium, Moscow
USSR   9*   T: (1); C: (1); PG: (1)
Italy   0

2 November 1980, Stadio Mario Battaglini, Rovigo
USSR   4*   T: (1)
Italy   3   PG: Bettarello

25 October 1981, Sparta Stadium, Moscow
USSR   12*   T: (1); C: (1); PG: (2)
Italy   12   PG: Bettarello (4)

22 May 1983, Stadio Santa Maria Goretti, Catania
Italy   12   T: Ghizzoni; C: Bettarello; PG: Bettarello; DG: Bettarello
USSR   10*   T: (1); PG: (2)

30 October 1983, La Vila Stadium, Kiev
USSR   16*   T: (3); C: (2)
Italy   7   T: Zanon; DG: Torresan

18 November 1984, Stadio Tomasso Fattori, L'Aquila
Italy   13   T: Bettarello; PG: Bettarello (3)
USSR   12*   T: (1); C: (1); PG: (2)

10 November 1985, Sparta Stadium, Moscow
USSR   15*   T: (1); C: (1); PG: (2); DG: (1)
Italy   13   T: Ghizzoni; PG: Bettarello (2); DG: Bettarello

16 November 1986, Stadio Marassi, Genoa
USSR   16   T: (1); PG: (3); DG: (1)
Italy   14*   T: Collodo, Ghizzoni, Innocenti; C: Bettarello

7 November 1987, Republican Stadium, Kishinev
USSR   12*   PG: (3); DG: (1)
Italy   9   PG: Bettarello (3)

5 November 1988, Stadio di Monigo, Treviso
USSR   18*   T: (1); C: (1); PG: (2); DG: (2)
Italy   12   PG: Bettarello (4)

5 November 1989, Sparta Stadium, Moscow
USSR   15*   T: (1); C: (1); PG: (3)
Italy   12   T: Mascioletti; C: Troiani; PG: Troiani (2)

24 November 1990, Stadio Mario Battaglini, Rovigo
Italy   34   T: Brunello, Francescato, Cuttitta, Croci; C: Troiani (3); PG: Troiani (4)
USSR   12*   T: (2); C: (2)

3 November 1991, Sparta Stadium, Moscow
Italy   21   T: Cuttitta (2), Venturi, Pivetta; C: Dominguez; PG: Dominguez
Russia   3*   PG: (1)

6 November 1993, Sparta Stadium, Moscow
Italy   30   T: Checchinato (2), Filizzola; C: Dominguez (3); PG: Dominguez (3)
Russia   19*   T: (1); C: (1); PG: (4)

18 April 1998, Central Stadium, Krasnoyarsk
Italy   48   T: Pertile, Roselli, Stoica, Martin, Cuttitta; C: Dominguez (4); PG: Dominguez (5)
Russia   18*   T: (2); C: (1); PG: (2)

14 October 2006, Sparta Stadium, Moscow
Italy   67   T: Robertson (2), Mi Bergamasco (2), Canavosio (2), Masi, Castrogiovanni, Bortolami; C: Bortolussi (8); PG: Bortolussi (2)
Russia   7   T: Khrokin; C: Motorin

Italy vs South Africa Africans

7 July 1973, Boet Erasmus Stadium, Port Elizabeth
Italy 24   T: Bollesan, Bonetti; C: Lazzarini (2); PG: Lazzarini (3); DG: Lazzarini
South Africa Africans 4   T: Cushe

15 May 1974, Stadio Mompiano, Brescia
Italy 25   T: Marchetti, Rossi, Abbiati, Bonetti; C: Lari (3); PG: Lari
South Africa Africans 10   T: Cushe, Mgweba; C: Swartz

Italy vs Samoa

27 May 1995, Basil Kenyon Stadium, East London (RWC, Pool B)
Western Samoa 42   T: Lima (2), Harder (2), Kellett, Tatupu; C: Kellett (3); PG: Kellett (2)
Italy 18   T: Vaccari, Mar Cuttitta; C: Dominguez; PG: Dominguez; DG: Dominguez

8 July 2000, Apia Park, Apia
Samoa 43   T: Samania, So'oalo, Vaega, Lima, Vili; C: Samania (3); PG: Samania (4)
Italy 24   T: Stoica, Gritti, Checchinato; C: Pez (3); PG: Pez

24 November 2001, Stadio Tommaso Fattori, L'Aquila
Samoa 17   T: Fa'atau; PG: Leaega (2), Vili (2)
Italy 9   PG: Dominguez (3)

Italy vs Scotland

Italy vs Scotland	
Played:	15
Won:	5
Lost:	10
Drawn:	0
For:	286
Against:	358
Average score:	
19.07–23.87	
Italy percentages:	
Won:	33.33%
Lost:	66.67%
Drawn:	0%

Scotland and Italy did not play officially until as recently as the 1996 season. They are closely fought affairs with Italy being somewhat of a bogey side for the Scots, having won five of their 15 clashes. Their best win was in their first Six Nations showing on 5 February 2000 in Rome, thanks to a slick hat-trick of drops from magnificent flyhalf Diego Dominguez. Italy also won their first-ever away game in the Six Nations when they stunned Scotland 37–17 in Edinburgh after racing to 21–0 after just eight minutes.

14 December 1996, Murrayfield, Edinburgh
Scotland 29   T: Logan (2), Stark, Stanger; C: Chalmers (3); PG: Shepherd
Italy 22   T: penalty try; C: Dominguez; PG: Dominguez (4); DG: Dominguez

24 January 1998, Stadio di Monigo, Trevaiso
Italy 25   T: Vaccari; C: Dominguez; PG: Dominguez (6)
Scotland 21   T: Shepherd, Tait; C: Shepherd; PG: Shepherd (3)

6 March 1999, Murrayfield, Edinburgh
Scotland 30   T: Logan, Murray, Townsend; C: Logan (3); PG: Logan (3)
Italy 12   T: Martin (2); C: Dominguez

5 February 2000, Stadio Flaminio, Rome
Italy 34   T: de Carli; C: Dominguez; PG: Dominguez (6); DG: Dominguez (3)
Scotland 20   T: Bulloch, M Leslie; C: Logan (2); PG: Logan (2)

17 March 2001, Murrayfield, Edinburgh
Scotland 23   T: Smith; PG: Hodge (5); DG: Hodge
Italy 19   T: Bergamasco; C: Dominguez; PG: Dominguez (4)

16 February 2002, Stadio Flaminio, Rome
Scotland 29   T: Townsend, Laney; C: Laney (2); PG: Laney (5)
Italy 12   PG: Dominguez (4)

29 March 2003, Murrayfield, Edinburgh
Scotland 33   T: White, McLaren, Logan, Paterson; C: Paterson (2); PG: Paterson (3)
Italy 25   T: Bergamasco, Pez, Palmer; C: Pez (2); PG: Pez (2)

23 August 2003, Murrayfield, Edinburgh
Scotland 47   T: Blair, Laney, Ross, McLaren, White, Danielli; C: Ross (2), Paterson (2); PG: Ross (3)
Italy 15   T: Palmer, Mazzucato; C: Pez; PG: Pez

6 March 2004, Stadio Flaminio, Rome
Italy	20	T: Ongaro; PG: de Marigny (5)
Scotland	14	T: Webster; PG: Paterson (3)

26 February 2005, Murrayfield, Edinburgh
Scotland	18	PG: Paterson (6)
Italy	10	T: Masi; C: de Marigny; PG: de Marigny

18 March 2006, Stadio Flaminio, Rome
Scotland	13	T: Paterson; C: Paterson; PG: Paterson; DG: Ross
Italy	10	T: Bergamasco; C: Pez; PG: Pez

24 February 2007, Murrayfield, Edinburgh
Italy	37	T: Ma Bergamasco, Scanavacca, Robertson, Troncon; C: Scanavacca (4); PG: Scanavacca (3)
Scotland	17	T: Dewey, Paterson; C: Paterson (2); PG: Paterson

29 September 2007, Stade Geoffroy Guichard, Saint Etienne (RWC, Pool C)
Scotland	18	PG: Paterson (6)
Italy	16	T: Troncon; C: Bortolussi; PG: Bortolussi (3)

15 March 2008, Stadio Flaminio, Rome
Italy	23	T: penalty try, Canale; C: Marcato (2); PG: Marcato (2); DG: Marcato
Scotland	20	T: Hogg, Blair; C: Paterson (2); PG: Paterson, Parks

28 February 2009, Murrayfield, Edinburgh
Scotland	26	T: Danielli, Gray; C: Godman, Paterson; PG: Paterson (3), Godman
Italy	6	PG: McLean; DG: Parisse

Italy vs Scotland A

19 December 1992, The Greenyards, Melrose
Scotland A	22	T: Townsend, S Hastings; PG: Chalmers (4)
Italy	17	T: Checchinato; PG: Dominguez (3); DG: Dominguez

18 December 1993, Stadio Mario Battaglini, Rovigo
Italy	18	PG: Dominguez (6)
Scotland A	15	PG: Dods (5)

7 January 1995, McDiarmid Park, Perth
Scotland A	18	T: Redpath, Peters; C: Glasgow; PG: Glasgow, Shepherd
Italy	16	T: Troiani; C: Dominguez; PG: Dominguez (3)

Italy vs South Africa

Italy vs South Africa	
Played:	7
Won:	0
Lost:	7
Drawn:	0
For:	95
Against:	417
Average score:	
13.57–59.57	
Italy percentages:	
Won:	0%
Lost:	100%
Drawn:	0%

12 November 1995, Stadio Olympico, Rome
South Africa	40	T: Pienaar, penalty try, le Roux, Mulder; C: Stransky (4); PG: Stransky (4)
Italy	21	T: Orlandi, Arancio; C: Dominguez; PG: Dominguez (3)

9 November 1997, Stadio Renato Dall'Ara, Bologna
South Africa	62	T: Rossouw (2), Erasmus (2), Small (2), du Randt, Muir, Swart; C: Honiball (7); PG: Honiball
Italy	31	T: Gardner, Vaccari, Francesco; C: Dominguez (2); PG: Dominguez (4)

12 June 1999 Telkom Park, Port Elizabeth
South Africa	74	T: Boome, Teichmann, du Toit (2), Paulse (3), Fleck, Montgomery, Terblanche, penalty try; C: du Toit (8); PG: du Toit
Italy	3	PG: Mazzaroil

19 June 1999, Kings Park, Durban
South Africa	101	T: Terblanche (5), Kayser (3), Drotske, Vos, Fleck, von Hoesslin (2), Marais, Montgomery; C: du Toit (8), van Straaten (5)
Italy	0	

30 June 2001, Telkom Park, Port Elizabeth
South Africa	60	T: Andrews, Venter, Montgomery, Paulse (2), Delport, van der Westhuizen (2); C: Montgomery (3), Jantjes; PG: Montgomery (4)
Italy	14	T: Troncon; PG: Mazzariol (3)

17 November 2001, Stadio Luigi Ferraris, Genoa
South Africa	54	T: Smit, Meyer, Matfield, Skinstad, Hall, Halstead (2), van der Westhuizen; C: van Straaten (5), Koen (2)
Italy	26	T: Dominguez, Barteluchi; C: Dominguez, Mazzariol; PG: Dominguez (3); DG: Dominguez

21 June 2008, Newlands, Cape Town
South Africa	26	T: du Plessis (2), Mtawarira, Steyn; C: Steyn (3)
Italy	0	

Italy vs South Eastern Transvaal

4 July 1973, Witbank Stadium, Witbank
South Eastern Transvaal	39*	T: (8), C: (2), PG: (1)
Italy	12	PG: Mattarolo (3); DG: Visentin

Italy vs Spain

Italy vs Spain	
Played:	27
Won:	23
Lost:	3
Drawn:	1
For:	581
Against:	182
Average score:	
21.15–6.74	
Italy percentages:	
Won:	85.19%
Lost:	11.11%
Drawn:	3.7%

20 May 1929, Barcelona
Spain	9	T: Aguilar, Facios, Climent
Italy	0	

29 May 1930, Arena Civica, Milan
Italy	3	T: Vinci
Spain	0	

6 May 1951, Stadio Flaminio, Rome
Italy	12	T: Rosi, Battaglini, Cherubini; PG: Battaglini
Spain	0	

13 April 1952, Barcelona
Italy	6	T: Gerosa; PG: Cecchetto-Milani
Spain	0	

19 April 1954, Stadio San Paolo, Naples
Italy	16	T: Stievano, Rosi, Gerosa, Masci; C: Dari (2)
Spain	3	DG: Atienza

18 July 1955, Barcelona
Italy	8	T: Luise, Percudani; C: Barbini
Spain	0	

4 May 1969, Stadio Tomasso Fattori, L'Aquila
Italy	12	T: Pacifici; PG: di Zitti; DG: Pacifici, Ricci
Spain	3	T: Vitoria

14 May 1972, Campo Central de la Ciudad Universitaria, Madrid
Spain	10	T: Sinovas; PG: Cabezas (2)
Italy	0	

21 May 1972, Ivrea
Italy	6	PG: Ambron (2)
Spain	6	T: López; C: Mostajo

6 April 1975, Campo Central de la Ciudad Universitaria, Madrid
Italy	19	T: Marchetto, de Anna; C: Ponzi; PG: Ponzi (3)
Spain	3	PG: Cienfuegos

20 December 1975, Campo Central de la Ciudad Universitaria, Madrid
Italy	19	T: Marchetto (2), di Carlo; C: Ponzi (2); PG: Ponzi
Spain	6	T: penalty try; C: Mattern

27 November 1976, Stadio Flaminio, Rome
Italy	17	T: Marchetto, Manni; PG: Ponzi (3)
Spain	4	T: Moreno

17 December 1977, Campo Central de la Ciudad Universitaria, Madrid
Spain	10	T: Cabeza, Roca; C: Mostajo
Italy	3	DG: Collodo

17 December 1978, Stadio di Monigo, Treviso
| Italy | 35 | T: Mascioletti, Francescato, Gaetaniello, Bona, Marchetto; C: Zuin (3); PG: Zuin (3) |
| Spain | 3 | PG: Godas |

18 September 1979, Makarska Stadium, Makarska
| Italy | 16 | T: penalty try, Mascioletti; C: Bettarello; PG: Bettarello; DG: Bettarello |
| Spain | 9 | PG: Mostajo (2), Martínez |

21 December 1980, Campo Central de la Ciudad Universitaria, Madrid
| Italy | 18 | T: Francescato, Limone, Bargelli; PG: Bettarello (2) |
| Spain | 13 | T: Canosa, García; C: Sánchez; PG: Sánchez |

7 September 1983, COC Stadium, Casablanca
| Italy | 27 | T: Mascioletti (2), Morelli; C: Bettarello (3); PG: Bettarello; DG: Bettarello, Ghizzoni |
| Spain | 9 | T: Palmero; C: Mostajo; DG: Mostajo |

18 May 1985, Stadio Danilo Martelli, Mantova
| Italy | 22 | T: Vittadello, Venturi, Gaetaniello, Pivetta; C: Bettarello (3) |
| Spain | 13 | T: Aretxabaleta, de la Torre; C: Doval; PG: Doval |

5 December 1987, Barcelona
| Italy | 13 | T: de Baise, Gaetaniello; C: Bettarello; PG: Bettarello |
| Spain | 0 | |

2 June 1989, Stadio Tomasso Fattori, L'Aquila
| Italy | 33 | T: Venturi, Ambrosio, Pietrosanti, Covi, Pivetta; C: Troiani (2); PG: Troiani (3) |
| Spain | 19 | T: Malo, Soto; C: Paternain; PG: Chacón (3) |

30 September 1990, Stadio Mario Battaglini, Rovigo
| Italy | 30 | T: Giovanelli, Venturi; C: Troiani (2); PG: Troiani (5); DG: Bonomi |
| Spain | 6 | PG: Paternain, Soto |

9 February 1992, Campo Central de la Ciudad Universitaria, Madrid
| Italy | 22 | T: Venturi, Mar Cuttitta, Troiani; C: Dominguez (2); PG: Dominguez; DG: Dominguez |
| Spain | 21 | T: Izaguirre, Landazabal; C: Bermudo (2); PG: Simón (2), Bermudo |

14 February 1993, Campo Central de la Ciudad Universitaria, Madrid
| Italy | 52 | T: Venturi (2), Rigo (2), Mar Cuttitta, Dotto; C: Dominguez (5); PG: Dominguez (4) |
| Spain | 0 | |

21 June 1993, Stade Aime Giral, Perpignon
| Italy | 38 | T: Filizzola (2), Checchinato (2), Mas Cuttita; C: Filizzola (5); PG: Filizzola |
| Spain | 6 | PG: Paternain, Soto |

7 May 1994, Stade Comunale, Parma
| Italy | 62 | T: Vacarri (2), Aldrovandi, Mar Cuttita, Pedroni, Francescato, Gardner, Ravazzolo; C: Troiani (8); PG: Troiani (2) |
| Spain | 15 | T: Puertas-Soto, Ventura-Miranda; C: Pueras-Soto; PG: Puertas-Soto |

26 August 1999, Stadio Tomasso Fattori, L'Aquila
| Italy | 42 | T: Masi, Stoica, Ceppolino, Troncon, Caione, Mazzi; C: Dominguez (5), Mazzariol |
| Spain | 11 | T: Gutierrez; PG: de la Rosa (2) |

22 September 2002, Estadio Pepe Rojo, Valladolid
| Italy | 50 | T: Stoica, Barbini, Dallan, Troncon, de Rossi, Bergamasco, Pozzebon; C: Peens (5), Scanavacca; PG: Peens |
| Spain | 3 | PG: Molina |

Italy vs Sussex

17 March 1974, Withdean Stadium, Brighton
| Sussex | 16 | T: Endacott, Scott, Pope; C: Yorke (2) |
| Italy | 7 | T: Scalzotto; PG: Lazzarini |

Italy vs Tonga

10 October 1999, Welford Road, Leicester (RWC, Pool B)
Tonga	28	T: Taufahema, S Tu'ipulotu, Fatani; C: S Tu'ipulotu (2) PG: S Tu'ipulotu (2); DG: S Tu'ipulotu
Italy	25	T: Moscardi; C: Dominguez; PG: Dominguez (6)

15 October 2003, Bruce Stadium, Canberra (RWC, Pool D)
Italy	36	T: D Dallan (2), M Dallan; C: Wakarua (3); PG: Wakarua (5)
Tonga	12	T: Payne, Tu'ifua; C: Tu'ipulotu

12 November 2005, Stadio Lungobisenzio, Rome
Italy	48	T: Bergamasco (2), Bortolami (2), Sole (2), Canale; C: Pez (5); PG: Pez
Tonga	0	

Italy vs Transvaal B

11 July 1973, Ellis Park, Johannesburg
Transvaal B	28	T: Claassen (2), Bothma (2), Burgers; C: (4)*
Italy	24	T: Visentin; C: Lazzarini; PG: Mattarolo (3); DG: Caligiuri (3)

Italy vs Tunisia

Italy vs Tunisia	
Played:	4
Won:	4
Lost:	0
Drawn:	0
For:	111
Against:	27

Average score:
27.75–6.75

Italy percentages:
Won:	100%
Lost:	0%
Drawn:	0%

20 October 1984, Stade Moustapha Benn Jenat, Monastir
Italy	20	T: Lorigiola, Colella; PG: Bettarello (4)
Tunisia	6*	PG: (2)

8 February 1986, Stadio Mario Battaglini, Rovigo
Italy	18	T: Bettarello; C: Bettarello; PG: Bettarello (4)
Tunisia	4*	T: (1)

18 October 1986, Stade Africain de Menzel Bourghiba, Menzel Bourghiba
Italy	22	T: Osti, Artuso; C: Bettarello; PG: Bettarello (3); DG: Bettarello
Tunisia	9*	T: (1); C: (1); PG: (1)

27 March 1993, Leno
Italy	51*
Tunisia	8*

Italy vs United States of America

5 October 1991, Cross Green, Otley (RWC, Pool 1)
Italy	30	T: Vaccari, Gaetaniello, Barba, Francescato; C: Dominguez (4); PG: Dominguez (2)
USA	9	T: Swords; C: Williams; PG: Williams

27 November 2004, Stadio Lamarmora, Biella
Italy	43	T: Robertson (2), Pozzebon, Stoica, Orquera; C: Orquera (3); PG: Orquera (3), Scanavacca
USA	25	T: Emerick (2), Wyatt; C: Hercus (2); PG: Hercus (2)

Italy vs Uruguay

22 August 1999, Stadio Tomasso Fattori, L'Aquila
Italy	49	T: Vaccari (2), Roselli (2), Pini, Stoica, Saviozzi; C: Dominguez (4); PG: Dominguez (2)
Uruguay	17	T: Ormaechea (2), Berruti; C: Cardoso

7 July 2001, Parque Federico Omar Saroldi, Montevideo
Italy	14	T: Perziano; PG: Mazzariol (3)
Uruguay	3	PG: Aguirre

2 June 2007, Parque Federico Omar Saroldi, Montevideo
Italy	29	T: Pratichetti (3), Aguero; C: Burton (3); PG: Burton
Uruguay	5	T: Arocena

ITALY

Italy vs Wales

Played:	16
Won:	2
Lost:	13
Drawn:	1
For:	294
Against:	534

Average score:
18.38–33.38

Italy percentages:

Won:	12.5%
Lost:	81.25%
Drawn:	6.25%

Italy vs Wales

12 October 1994, National Stadium, Cardiff
Wales	29	T: Davies; PG: Jenkins (7); DG: Jenkins
Italy	19	T: Francescato; C: Dominguez; PG: Dominguez (4)

16 January 1996, National Stadium, Cardiff
Wales	31	T: J Thomas, Evans (2); C: A Thomas (2); PG: A Thomas (4)
Italy	26	T: Gardner, Curti; C: Dominguez (2); PG: Dominguez (4)

5 October 1996, Stadio Olympio, Rome
Wales	31	T: G Thomas (2), James; C: Jenkins (2); PG: Jenkins (4)
Italy	22	T: Francescato; C: Dominguez; PG: Dominguez (5)

7 February 1998, Stradey Park, Llanelli
Wales	23	T: penalty try, G Thomas; C: Jenkins (2); PG: Jenkins (3)
Italy	20	T: Stoica, Sgorlon; C: Dominguez (2); PG: Dominguez (2)

20 March 1999, Stadio di Monigo, Treviso
Wales	60	T: Thomas (4), Howley, N Jenkins, Quinnell; C: N Jenkins (5); PG: N Jenkins (5)
Italy	21	T: Martin, Saviozzi; C: Dominguez; PG: Dominguez (3)

19 February 2000, Millennium Stadium, Cardiff
Wales	47	T: S Quinnell, Williams, Bateman, Howarth; C: Jenkins (3); PG: Jenkins (7)
Italy	16	T: Visser; C: Dominguez; PG: Dominguez (2); DG: Dominguez

8 April 2001, Stadio Flaminio, Rome
Wales	33	T: Gibbs (2), Cooper; C: Jenkins (3); PG: Jenkins (4)
Italy	23	T: Checchinato; PG: Dominguez (5); DG: Dominguez

2 March 2002, Millennium Stadium, Cardiff
Wales	44	T: C Morgan, James, R Williams, Quinnell, Marinos; C: Jones (5); PG: Jones (3)
Italy	20	T: Checchinato, Mazzariol; C: Pez, Peens; PG: Pez, Peens

15 February 2003, Stadio Flaminio, Rome
Italy	30	T: de Carli, Festuccia, Phillips; C: Dominguez (3); PG: Dominguez; DG: Dominguez (2)
Wales	22	T: S Williams, Shanklin, Peel; C: Harris (2); PG: Harris

25 October 2003, Canberra Stadium, Canberra (RWC, Pool D)
Wales	27	T: M Jones, Parker, D Jones; C: Harris (3); PG: Harris (2)
Italy	15	PG: Wakarua (5)

27 March 2004, Millennium Stadium, Cardiff
Wales	44	T: S Williams (2), R Williams (2), Thomas, Shanklin; C: S Jones (4); PG: S Jones (2)
Italy	10	T: Masi; C: Wakarua; PG: de Marigny

12 February 2005, Stadio Flaminio, Rome
Wales	38	T: Jonathan Thomas, Shanklin, M Williams, Sidoli, Cockbain, S Williams; C: S Jones (4)
Italy	8	T: Orquera; PG: de Marigny

11 March 2006, Millennium Stadium, Cardiff
Wales	18	T: M Jones, S Jones; C: S Jones; PG: S Jones (2)
Italy	18	T: Galon, Canavosio; C: Pez; PG: Pez (2)

10 March 2007, Stadio Flaminio, Rome
Italy	23	T: Robertson, Mauro Bergamasco; C: Pez (2); PG: Pez (3)
Wales	20	T: S Williams, Rees; C: Hook, S Jones; PG: Hook (2)

23 February 2008, Millennium Stadium, Cardiff
Wales	47	T: Byrne (2), S Williams (2), Shanklin; C: S Jones (3), Hook (2); PG: S Jones (4)
Italy	8	T: Castrogiavani; PG: Marcato

14 March 2009, Stadio Flaminio, Rome
Wales	20	T: S Williams, Shanklin; C: Hook (2); PG: Hook (2)
Italy	15	PG: Marcato (5)

Italy vs Western Transvaal

20 June 1973, Olen Park, Potchefstroom
Western Transvaal   32   T: Schaap (3), Koorts (2); C: Strydom (2), du Randt; PG: Strydom (2)
Italy   6   PG: Lazzarini (2)

Italy vs Yugoslavia

29 December 1968, Stadio Rugby San Dona, San Dona di Piave
Italy   22   T: Rista, Autore, Pignotti, Conforto, Gini, Bollesan; C: Martini (2)
Yugoslavia   3   T: Kesic

26 November 1972, Stadio Mario Puchoz, Aosta
Italy   13   T: Fedrigo; PG: Vialetto (3)
Yugoslavia   12   T: Arambasic, S Radic; C: Bartolic, Staglicic

11 November 1973, Maksimir Stadium, Zagreb
Italy   25   T: Marchetto, Salvan, Vezzani; C: Lazzarini (2); PG: Lari; DG: Salvan, Visentin
Yugoslavia   7   T: Ivanisevic; PG: Bojovic

Italy vs Zimbabwe / Rhodesia

Italy vs Zimbabwe / Rhodesia	
Played:	4
Won:	3
Lost:	1
Drawn:	0
For:	74
Against:	67
Average score:	
18.5–16.75	
Italy percentages:	
Won:	75%
Lost:	25%
Drawn:	0%

16 June 1973, Old Hararians Rugby Club, Salisbury
Rhodesia   42   T: Youngelson (2), Barrett (2), Murphy, Loodts, Stewart; C: Robertson (4); PG: Robertson; DG: Roberton
Italy   4   T: Bollesan

22 June 1985, Hartsfield, Bulawayo
Italy   25   T: Mascioletti, Tebaldi, Pivetta, Zanon; C: Torresan (3); PG: Torresan
Zimbabwe   6*   PG: (1); DG: (1)

30 June 1985, Police Grounds, Harare
Italy   12   PG: Bettarello (2); DG: Bettarello (2)
Zimbabwe   10*   T: (2); C: (1)

30 September 1989, Stadio di Monigo, Treviso
Italy   33   T: Cuttitta (2), Capitani, de Bernardo, Reale, penalty try; C: Troiani (3); PG: Troiani
Zimbabwe   9*   T: (1); C: (1); PG: (1)

Italy: summaries and records

Home matches	
Played	170
Won	86
Lost	77
Drawn	7
Points for	3,336
Points against	3,176
Average score	19.62/18.68
Win %	50.59
Lose %	45.29
Draw %	4.12

Away matches	
Played	190
Won	57
Lost	127
Drawn	6
Points for	2,760
Points against	4,343
Average score	14.53/22.86
Win %	30
Lose %	66.84
Draw %	3.16

Neutral venues	
Played	35
Won	19
Lost	15
Drawn	1
Points for	886
Points against	801
Average score	25.31/22.89
Win %	54.29
Lose %	42.86
Draw %	2.86

Total matches	
Played	395
Won	162
Lost	219
Drawn	14
Points for	6,982
Points against	8,320
Average score	17.68/21.06
Win %	41.01
Lose %	55.44
Draw %	3.54

ITALY

Most capped players: Italy

Player	Caps	Career	T	C	PG	DG	Total
					Points		
Alessandro Troncon	101	07/05/1994–29/09/2007	19	-	-	-	95
Carlo Checchinato	83	30/09/1990–20/03/2004	21	-	-	-	105
Andrea lo Cicero	78	18/03/2000–15/11/2008	7	-	-	-	35
Mauro Bergamasco	76	18/11/1998–27/06/2009	14	-	-	-	70
Marco Bortalami	76	23/06/2001–27/06/2009	7	-	-	-	35

Most tests as captain: Italy

No.	Player	Period
37	Marco Bortolami	2002–2007
37	Massimo Giovanelli	1992–1999
37	Marco Bollesan	1968–1975
22	Massimo Cuttitta	1993–1999
21	Alessandro Troncon	2000–2007

Most points by a player in a career: Italy

No.	Player	Tests	Career	T	C	PG	DG
					Points		
983	Diego Dominguez	74	02/03/1991–22/02/2003	9	127	208	20
483	Stefano Bettarello	55	14/04/1979–03/12/1988	7	46	104	17
294	Luigi Troiani	46	07/12/1985–04/06/1995	2	57	57	-
254	Ramiro Pez	40	08/07/2000–29/09/2007	4	33	50	6
147	David Bortolussi	16	11/06/2006–10/02/2008	1	32	25	1

Most tries by a player in a career: Italy

No.	Player	Tests	Career
25	Marcello Cuttitta	53	18/01/1987–20/01/1999
22	Paolo Vaccari	64	15/06/1991–29/03/2003
21	Carlo Checchinato	83	30/09/1990–20/03/2004
21	Manrico Marchetto	43	26/11/1972–21/10/1981
19	Alessandro Troncon	101	07/05/1994–29/09/2007

Most conversions by a player in a career: Italy

No.	Player	Tests	Career
127	Diego Dominguez	74	02/03/1991–22/02/2003
57	Luigi Troiani	46	07/12/1985–04/06/1995
46	Stefano Bettarello	55	14/04/1979–03/12/1988
33	Ramiro Pez	40	08/07/2000–29/09/2007
32	David Bortolussi	16	11/06/2006–10/02/2008

Most penalties by a player in a career: Italy

No	Player	Tests	Career
208	Diego Dominguez	74	02/03/1991–22/02/2003
104	Stefano Bettarello	55	14/04/1979–03/12/1988
57	Luigi Troiani	46	07/12/1985–04/06/1995
50	Ramiro Pez	40	08/07/2000–29/09/2007
31	Enrico Ponzi	20	04/11/1973–01/05/1977

Most drop goals by a player in a career: Italy

No.	Player	Tests	Career
20	Diego Dominguez	74	02/03/1991–22/02/2003
17	Stefano Bettarello	55	14/04/1979–03/12/1988
6	Ramiro Pez	40	08/07/2000–29/09/2007
5	Massimo Bonomi	34	07/02/1988–16/01/1996
5	Oscar Collodo	15	23/10/1977–31/05/1987

Most points by a player in a match: Italy

No.	Player	T	C	PG	DG	Versus	Venue	Date
29	Diego Dominguez	-	4	7	-	Fiji	Stadio di Monigo, Treviso	10/11/2001
29	Diego Dominguez	-	1	6	3	Scotland	Stadio Flaminio, Rome	05/02/2000
29	Stefano Bettarello	1	2	5	2	Canada	Stanley Park, Toronto	01/07/1983
28	Diego Dominguez	1	7	3	-	Netherlands	Centro San Michele, Calvisano	21/05/1994

Most tries by a player in a match: Italy

No.	Player	Versus	Venue	Date
5	Pierpaolo Rotillo	Denmark	Stadio Mompiano, Brescia	01/11/1997
4	Ivan Francescato	Morocco	Stade Albert Domecq, Carcassone	19/06/1993
4	Renzo Cova	Belgium	Stade Charlety, Paris	10/10/1937

Most conversions by a player in a match: Italy

No.	Player	Versus	Venue	Date
12	Luigi Troiani	Czech Republic	Stadio Zaffanella, Viadana	18/05/1994
10	Gabriel Filizzola	Morocco	Stade Albert Domecq, Carcassone	19/06/1993
9	Luigi Troiani	Croatia	Stade Aime Giral, Perpignon	17/06/1993
8	David Bortolussi	Russia	Sparta Stadium, Moscow	14/10/2006
8	David Bortolussi	Portugal	Stadio Tomasso Fattori, L'Aquila	07/10/2006
8	Luigi Troiani	Spain	Stade Comunale, Parma	07/05/1994

ITALY

Most penalties by a player in a match: Italy

No.	Player	Versus	Venue	Date
8	Diego Dominguez	Romania	Stadio Angelo Massimino, Catania	01/10/1994
7	Diego Dominguez	Fiji	Stadio di Monigo, Treviso	10/11/2001
6	Ramiro Pez	Australia	Stadio Flaminio, Rome	11/11/2006
6	Gert Peens	Argentina	Estadio Padre Maltearena, Salta	11/06/2005
6	Gert Peens	Romania	Stade Comunale, Parma	28/09/2002
6	Diego Dominguez	Ireland	Stadio Renato Dall'Ara, Bologna	20/12/1997
6	Diego Dominguez	Argentina	Stade Antoine Beguere, Lourdes	22/10/1997
6	Diego Dominguez	Ireland	Lansdowne Road, Dublin	04/01/1997
6	Diego Dominguez	Scotland 'A'	Stadio Mario Battaglini, Rovigo	18/12/1993

Most drop goals by a player in a match: Italy

No.	Player	Versus	Venue	Date
3	Diego Dominguez	Scotland	Stadio Flaminio, Rome	05/02/2000
3	Rocco Caligiuri	Transvaal B	Ellis Park, Johannesburg	11/07/1973
2	Ramiro Pez	Ireland	Stadio Flaminio, Rome	17/03/2007
2	Ramiro Pez	England	Stadio Flaminio, Rome	11/02/2006
2	Diego Dominguez	Wales	Stadio Flaminio, Rome	15/02/2003
2	Diego Dominguez	Ireland	Lansdowne Road, Dublin	10/04/1999
2	Massimo Bonomi	Romania	Stadio Plebiscito, Padua	07/10/1990
2	Stefano Bettarello	Zimbabwe	Police Ground, Harare	30/06/1985
2	Stefano Bettarello	Canada	Stanley Park, Toronto	01/07/1983
2	Stefano Bettarello	England u23	Stadio Plebiscito, Padova	22/05/1982

Most points in a match by Italy

No.	Result	Points				Versus	Venue	Date
		T	C	PG	DG			
104	104–8	16	12	-	-	Czech Republic	Stadio Zaffanella, Viadana	18/05/1994
102	102–3	16	11	-	-	Denmark	Stadio Mompiano, Brescia	01/11/1997
83	83–0	13	9	-	-	Portugal	Stadio Tomasso Fattori, L'Aquila	07/10/2006
76	76–11	11	9	1	-	Croatia	Stade Aime Giral, Perpignon	17/06/1993
70	70 –9	10	10	-	-	Morocco	Stade Albert Domecq, Carcassone	19/06/1993

Most consecutive test wins by Italy

No.	Period	Details
6	12/05/1968–10/05/1969	Portugal (A), Germany (H), Yugoslavia (H), Bulgaria (A), Spain (H), Belgium (A)
5	27/03/1993–21/06/1993	Tunisia (H), Portugal (A), Croatia (N), Morocco (N), Spain (N)

New Zealand

ALL BLACKS®

New Zealand vs Argentina *see* page 194

New Zealand vs Australia *see* page 222

New Zealand vs British and Irish Lions

This is one of the most hotly anticipated fixtures in the international calendar. Any New Zealand vs British and Irish Lions game is sure to entertain at the highest level. The two sides met for the first time in 1904 when the Lions tacked an 'extra' test onto their tour to Australia, to play New Zealand in Dunedin. The New Zealanders so impressed the tourists, and on their tour to the UK in 1905/1906, that in 1908 an Anglo-Welsh side toured New Zealand for a full three-test series, bypassing Australia for the first time. The series was comprehensively won by New Zealand who set the trend for the series as the British Isles failed to win a series until 1971. Their first test win came in 1930 but they had to wait until 1959 for a second. In 1971 the Lions won their first and only series against New Zealand and have since managed to win a test just twice: in 1977 and 1993. In 2005 the Lions were inflicted with the heaviest series defeat in their history, losing by a aggregate points scoreline of 40–107.

New Zealand vs British Lions	
Played:	38
Won:	29
Lost:	6
Drawn:	3
For:	634
Against:	345

Average score:
16.68–9.07

New Zealand percentages:

Won:	76.32%
Lost:	15.79%
Drawn:	7.89%

13 August 1904, Athletic Park, Wellington
| New Zealand | 9 | T: D McGregor (2); PG: Wallace |
| British Lions | 3 | PG: Harding |

6 June 1908, Carisbrook, Dunedin
| New Zealand | 32 | T: Mitchinson (2), Roberts (2), Cameron, Hunter, Thomson; C: Gillett (2), Roberts, Francis; PG: Roberts |
| British Lions | 5 | T: Gibbs; C: Jackson |

27 June 1908, Athletic Park, Wellington
| New Zealand | 3 | PG: Francis |
| British Lions | 3 | T: Jones |

25 July 1908, Potters Park, Auckland
| New Zealand | 29 | T: Mitchinson (3), Deans, Hunter, Gillett, Glasgow, Francis, Hayward; C: Colman |
| British Lions | 0 | |

21 June 1930, Carisbrook, Dunedin
| British Lions | 6 | T: Reeve, Morley |
| New Zealand | 3 | T: Hart |

5 July 1930, Lancaster Park, Christchurch
| New Zealand | 13 | T: Hart, Oliver; C: Nicholls (2); GM: Nicholls |
| British Lions | 10 | T: Aarvold (2); C: Prentice (2) |

26 July 1930, Eden Park, Auckland
| New Zealand | 15 | T: McLean (2), Lucas; C: Strang; DG: Nicholls |
| British Lions | 10 | T: Bowcott, Aarvold; C: Jones, Black |

9 August 1930, Athletic Park, Wellington
| New Zealand | 22 | T: Porter (2), Cooke (2), Strang, Batty; C: Strang (2) |
| British Lions | 8 | T: Novis; C: Black; PG: Parker |

27 May 1950, Carisbrook, Dunedin
| New Zealand | 9 | T: Roper, Elvidge; PG: Scott |
| British Lions | 9 | T: Kyle, Jones; PG: Robins |

10 June 1950, Lancaster Park, Christchurch
| New Zealand | 8 | T: Crowley, Roper; C: Haigh |
| British Lions | 0 | |

NEW ZEALAND

1 July 1950, Athletic Park, Wellington
New Zealand 6   T: Elvidge; PG: Scott
British Lions 3   PG: Robins

29 July 1950, Eden Park, Auckland
New Zealand 11   T: Wilson, Henderson; C: Scott; DG: Scott
British Lions 8   T: K Jones; C: B Jones; PG: B Jones

18 July 1959, Carisbrook, Dunedin
New Zealand 18   PG: D Clarke (6)
British Lions 17   T: Price (2), O'Reilly, Jackson; C: Risman; PG: Hewitt

15 August 1959, Athletic Park, Wellington
New Zealand 11   T: Caulton (2), D Clarke; C: D Clarke
British Lions 8   T: Young; C: Davies; PG: Davies

29 August 1959, Lancaster Park, Christchurch
New Zealand 22   T: Caulton (2), Meads, Urbahn; C: D Clarke (2); PG: D Clarke; DG: D Clarke
British Lions 8   T: Hewitt; C: Faull; PG: Faull

19 September 1959, Eden Park, Auckland
British Lions 9   T: O'Reilly, Jackson, Risman
New Zealand 6   PG: D Clarke (2)

16 July 1966, Carisbrook, Dunedin
New Zealand 20   T: McLeod, Williment, Lochore; C: Williment; PG: Williment (2); DG: Herewini
British Lions 3   PG: Wilson

6 August 1966, Athletic Park, Wellington
New Zealand 16   T: Tremain, C Meads, Steel; C: Williment (2); PG: Williment
British Lions 12   PG: Wilson (3); DG: Watkins

27 August 1966, Lancaster Park, Christchurch
New Zealand 19   T: Nathan (2), Steel; C: Williment (2); PG: Williment (2)
British Lions 6   T: Lamont, D Watkins

10 September 1966, Eden Park, Auckland
New Zealand 24   T: Nathan, Dick, MacRae, Steel; C: Williment (3); PG: Williment; DG: Herewini
British Lions 11   T: Hinshelwood, McFadyean; C: Wilson; PG: Wilson

26 June 1971, Carisbrook, Dunedin
British Lions 9   T: McLauchlan; PG: John (2)
New Zealand 3   PG: McCormick

10 July 1971, Lancaster Park, Christchurch
New Zealand 22   T: Burgess (2), Going, penalty try, Kirkpatrick; C: Mains (2); PG: Mains
British Lions 12   T: G Davies (2); PG: John; DG: John

31 July 1971, Athletic Park, Wellington
British Lions 13   T: G Davies, John; C: John (2); DG: John
New Zealand 3   T: Mains

14 August 1971, Eden Park, Auckland
New Zealand 14   T: Cottrell, Lister; C: Mains; PG: Mains (2)
British Lions 14   T: Dixon; C: John; PG: John (2); DG: J Williams

18 June 1977, Athletic Park, Wellington
New Zealand 16   T: Going, Johnstone, Batty; C: Williams (2)
British Lions 12   PG: Bennett (3), Irvine

9 July 1977, Lancaster Park, Christchurch
British Lions 13   T: JJ Williams; PG: Bennett (3)
New Zealand 9   PG: Williams (3)

30 July 1977, Carisbrook, Dunedin
New Zealand 19   T: Kirkpatrick, Haden C: Wilson PG: Wilson (2); DG: Robertson
British Lions 7   T: Duggan; PG: Irvine

13 August 1977, Eden Park, Auckland
New Zealand 10   T: Knight; PG: Wilson (2)
British Lions 9   T: Morgan; C: Morgan; PG: Morgan

4 June 1983, Lancaster Park, Christchurch
New Zealand 16 T: M Shaw; PG: Hewson (3); DG: Hewson
British Lions 12 PG: Campbell (3); DG: Campbell

18 June 1983, Athletic Park, Wellington
New Zealand 9 T: Loveridge; C: Hewson; PG: Hewson
British Lions 0

2 July 1983, Carisbrook, Dunedin
New Zealand 15 T: S Wilson; C: Hewson; PG: Hewson (3)
British Lions 8 T: Baird, Rutherford

16 July 1983, Eden Park, Auckland
New Zealand 38 T: S Wilson (3), Hewson, Hobbs, Haden; C: Hewson (4); PG: Hewson (2)
British Lions 6 PG: G Evans (2)

12 June 1993, Lancaster Park, Christchurch
New Zealand 20 T: Bunce; PG: Fox (5)
British Lions 18 PG: Hastings (6)

26 June 1993, Athletic Park, Wellington
British Lions 20 T: Underwood; PG: Hastings (4); DG: Andrew
New Zealand 7 T: Clarke; C: Fox

3 July 1993, Eden Park, Auckland
New Zealand 30 T: Bunce, Preston, Fitzpatrick; C: Fox (3); PG: Fox (3)
British Lions 13 T: Gibbs; C: Hastings; PG: Hastings (2)

25 June 2005, Jade Stadium, Christchurch
New Zealand 21 T: Williams, Sivivatu; C: Carter; PG: Carter (3)
British Lions 3 PG: Wilkinson

2 July 2005, Westpac Stadium, Wellington
New Zealand 48 T: Carter (2), Umaga, Sivivatu, McCaw; C: Carter (4); PG: Carter (5)
British Lions 18 T: Thomas, Easterby; C: Wilkinson; PG: Wilkinson (2)

9 July 2005, Eden Park, Auckland
New Zealand 38 T: Umaga (2), Smith, Williams, Gear; C: McAlister (5); PG: McAlister
British Lions 19 T: Moody; C: Jones; PG: Jones (4)

New Zealand vs Canada

New Zealand vs Canada	
Played:	4
Won:	4
Lost:	0
Drawn:	0
For:	234
Against:	39
Average score:	58.5–9.75
New Zealand percentages:	
Won:	100%
Lost:	0%
Drawn:	0%

20 October 1991 Stade du Nord, Lille (RWC, Q/F)
New Zealand 29 T: Timu (2), Z Brooke, Kirwan, McCahill; C: Fox (3); PG: Fox
Canada 13 T: Charron, Tynan; C: Wyatt; PG: Wyatt

22 April 1995 Eden Park, Auckland
New Zealand 73 T: Osborne (2), Ellis (2), Bunce (2), Bachop, Brown, Mehrtens, Wilson; C: Mehrtens (7); PG: Mehrtens (3)
Canada 7 T: Stewart; C: Ross

17 October 2003 Telstra Dome, Melbourne (RWC, Pool D)
New Zealand 68 T: Muliaina (4), Ralph (2), So'oialo (2), Meeuws, Nonu; C: Carter (9)
Canada 6 PG: Baker (2)

16 June 2007 Waikato Stadium, Hamilton
New Zealand 64 T: Carter (3), Sivivatu, McAlister, Schwalger, Hore, Masoe, Howlett, Gear; C: Carter (7)
Canada 13 T: Pyke; C: Pritchard; PG: Pritchard (2)

New Zealand vs England (Hillary Shield) *see* page 268

New Zealand vs Fiji	
Played:	4
Won:	4
Lost:	0
Drawn:	0
For:	304
Against:	36

Average score:
76–9

New Zealand percentages:

Won:	100%
Lost:	0%
Drawn:	0%

New Zealand vs Fiji

27 May 1987, Lancaster Park, Christchurch (RWC, Pool 3)

New Zealand	74	T: Green (4), Gallagher (4), Kirk, Kirwan, A Whetton, penalty try; C: Fox (10); PG: Fox (2)
Fiji	13	T: Savai; PG: Koroduadua (3)

14 June 1997, North Harbour Stadium, Albany

New Zealand	71	T: Wilson (5), Cullen (2), Marshall, Umaga, Jones, Reichelmann; C: Mehrtens (8)
Fiji	5	T: Lasagavibau

9 June 2002, Westpac Trust Stadium, Wellington

New Zealand	68	T: Cullen (3), Meeuws (2), Maxwell (2), Howlett, MacDonald, A Mauger, Robertson; C: A Mauger (5); PG:A Mauger
Fiji	18	T: Ligairi (2); C: Little; PG: Little (2)

10 June 2005, North Harbour Stadium, Albany

New Zealand	91	T: Sivivatu (4), Umaga (2), Howlett (2), Carter, Mauger, Somerville, Williams, So'oialo, Mealamu, Muliaina; C: Carter (5), Mauger (3)
Fiji	0	

New Zealand vs France (Dave Gallaher Cup) *see page 310*

New Zealand vs Ireland *see page 340*

New Zealand vs Italy *see page 373*

New Zealand vs Japan

4 June 1995, Free State Stadium, Bloemfontein (RWC, Pool C)

New Zealand	145	T: Ellis (6), Wilson (3), Rush (3), R Brooke (2), Loe, Osborne (2), Ieremia, Dowd, Henderson, Culhane; C: Culhane (20)
Japan	17	T: Kajihara (2); C: Hirose (2); PG: Hirose

New Zealand vs Pacific Islanders

10 July 2004, North Harbour Stadium, Albany

New Zealand	41	T: Rokocoko (2), Marshall, Gear, Meeuws, Umaga; C: Carter (4); PG: Carter
Pacific Islanders	26	T: Sivivatu (2), Rabeni, Lauaki; C: Baikeinuku (3)

New Zealand vs Portugal

15 September 2007, Stade Gerland, Lyon (RWC, Pool C)

New Zealand	108	T: Rokocoko (2), Mauger (2), Smith (2), Toeava, Williams, Collins, Masoe, Leonard, Evans, Ellis, Hore, MacDonald, Hayman; C: Evans (14)
Portugal	13	T: Cordeiro; C: Pinto; PG: Pinto; DG: Malheiro

New Zealand vs Romania

24 October 1981, Dinamo Stadion, Bucharest

New Zealand	14	T: Salmon, Dalton; PG: Hewson; DG: Rollerson
Romania	6	PG: Constantin; DG: Alexandru

29 September 2007, Stade Municipal, Toulouse (RWC, Pool C)

New Zealand	85	T: Rokocoko (3), Sivivatu (2), Toeava (2), Howlett, Evans, Hore, Masoe, Smith, Mauger; C: Evans (6), McAlister (4)
Romania	8	T: Tincu; PG: Viaicu

New Zealand vs Samoa

New Zealand vs Samoa	
Played:	5
Won:	5
Lost:	0
Drawn:	0
For:	308
Against:	56

Average score:
61.6–11.2

New Zealand percentages:
Won:	100%
Lost:	0%
Drawn:	0%

31 July 1993, Eden Park, Auckland
New Zealand 35 T: Stensness, Z Brooke; C: Fox (2); PG: Fox (7)
Western Samoa 13 T: Aiolupo; C: Kellett; PG: Kellett (2)

7 June 1996, McLean Park, Napier
New Zealand 51 T: Cullen (3), Wilson, Marshall, McLeod, Brown; C: Mehrtens (5); PG: Mehrtens (2)
Western Samoa 10 T: Telea; C: Fa'amasino; PG: Fa'amasino

18 June 1999, North Harbour Stadium, Albany
New Zealand 71 T: Wilson (4), Umaga (2), Lomu, Maxwell, Randall; C: Brown (7); PG: Brown (4)
Samoa 13 T: Fuga; C: Va'a; PG: Va'a, Bachop

16 June 2001, North Harbour Stadium, Albany
New Zealand 50 T: Brown (3), Maxwell, Howlett, Flavell, Wilson; C: Brown (3); PG: Brown (3)
Samoa 6 PG: Leaega (2)

3 September 2008, Yarrow Stadium, New Plymouth
New Zealand 101 T: Muliaina (3), Smith (2), Kahui (2), Cowan, Weepu, Thomson, Donald, Williams, Kaino, Toeava, penalty try; C: Donald (7), Carter (6)
Samoa 14 T: Mai, Faosiliva; C: Mai, Warren

New Zealand vs Scotland

New Zealand vs Scotland	
Played:	27
Won:	25
Lost:	0
Drawn:	2
For:	776
Against:	291

Average score:
28.74–10.78

New Zealand percentages:
Won:	92.59%
Lost:	0%
Drawn:	7.41%

Like Ireland, Scotland have been unable to register a victory over New Zealand in more than a century. In recent years the outcome of this fixture has proved a foregone conclusion but during the earlier years matches were much tighter with Scotland often unlucky to lose or draw on many occasions. In the 1925 New Zealand tour of the United Kingdom, the opportunity for 'The Invincibles' to post a Grand Slam was denied when the game against Scotland was cancelled because of allegations of professionalism levelled against the New Zealanders. Scotland have twice held the All Blacks to a draw: in 1964 and 1983, latterly when the two sides shared an unbelievable 50 points, a then world-record scoreline for a draw. Since this encounter, however, matches have been extremely one-sided with New Zealand regularly clocking up wins of 40 points or more. They have met in just about every RWC (except in 2003), the most recent game ending in a thumping 40–0 win for New Zealand in 2007 in Edinburgh.

18 November 1905, Inverleith, Edinburgh
New Zealand 12 T: Smith (2), Glasgow, Cunningham
Scotland 7 T: MacCallum; DG: E Simson

23 November 1935, Murrayfield, Edinburgh
New Zealand 18 T: Caughey (3), Hadley; C: Gilbert (3)
Scotland 8 T: Fyfe, Dick; C: Murdoch

13 February 1954, Murrayfield, Edinburgh
New Zealand 3 PG: Scott
Scotland 0

18 January 1964, Murrayfield, Edinburgh
Scotland 0
New Zealand 0

2 December 1967, Murrayfield, Ediburgh
New Zealand 14 T: MacRae, Davis; C: McCormick; PG: McCormick (2)
Scotland 3 DG: Chisholm

16 December 1972, Murrayfield, Edinburgh
New Zealand 14 T: Wyllie, Batty, Going; C: Karam
Scotland 9 PG: P Brown, Irvine; DG: McGeechan

NEW ZEALAND

14 June 1975, Eden Park, Auckland
New Zealand   24   T: Williams (2), Macdonald, Robertson; C: Karam (4)
Scotland   0

9 December 1978, Murrayfield, Edinburgh
New Zealand   18   T: Seear, Robertson; C: McKechnie (2); PG: McKechnie (2)
Scotland   9   T: Hay; C: Irvine; DG: Irvine

10 November 1979, Murrayfield, Edinburgh
New Zealand   20   T: S Wilson, Dunn, Loveridge, Mexted; C: R Wilson (2)
Scotland   6   PG: Irvine (2)

13 June 1981, Carisbrook, Dunedin
New Zealand   11   T: Wilson, Loveridge; PG: Hewson
Scotland   4   T: Deans

20 June 1981, Eden Park, Auckland
New Zealand   40   T: Wilson (3), Hewson (2), Robertson, Mourie; C: Hewson (6)
Scotland   15   T: Hay; C: Irvine; PG: Irvine (2); DG: Renwick

12 November 1983, Murrayfield, Edinburgh
Scotland   25   T: Pollock; PG: Dods (5); DG: Rutherford (2)
New Zealand   25   T: Hobbs, Fraser (2); C: Deans (2); PG: Deans (3)

6 June 1987, Lancaster Park, Christchurch (RWC, Q/F)
New Zealand   30   T: A Whetton, Gallagher; C: Fox (2); PG: Fox (6)
Scotland   3   PG: G Hastings

16 June 1990, Carisbrook, Dunedin
New Zealand   31   T: Kirwan (2), Crowley, I Jones, Fox; C: Fox (4); PG: Fox
Scotland   16   T: Lineen, Gray, Sole; C: G Hastings (2)

23 June 1990, Eden Park, Auckland
New Zealand   21   T: Loe; C: Fox; PG: Fox (5)
Scotland   18   T: Stanger, Moore; C: G Hastings (2); PG: G Hastings (2)

30 October 1991, National Stadium, Cardiff (RWC, 3/4 play-off)
New Zealand   13   T: Little; PG: Preston (3)
Scotland   6   PG: G Hastings (2)

20 November 1993, Murrayfield, Edinburgh
New Zealand   51   T: Wilson (3), Ellis (2), Bunce, Z Brooke; C: Cooper (4), Wilson; PG: Cooper (2)
Scotland   15   PG: G Hastings (4), Chalmers

11 June 1995, Loftus Versfeld, Pretoria (RWC, Q/F)
New Zealand   48   T: Little (2), Lomu, Mehrtens, Bunce, Fitzpatrick; C: Mehrtens (6); PG: Mehrtens (2)
Scotland   30   T: Weir (2), S Hastings; C: G Hastings (3); PG: G Hastings (3)

15 June 1996, Carisbrook, Dunedin
New Zealand   62   T: Cullen (4), Lomu, I Jones, Marshall, Z Brooke, Mehrtens; C: Mehrtens (7); PG: Mehrtens
Scotland   31   T: Peters, Joiner, Townsend; C: Shepherd (2); PG: Shepherd (3); DG: Shepherd

22 June 1996, Eden Park, Auckland
New Zealand   36   T: Kronfeld (2), Z Brooke, M Jones, penalty try; C: Mehrtens (4); PG: Mehrtens
Scotland   12   T: Shepherd, Peters; C: Shepherd

24 October 1999, Murrayfield, Edinburgh (RWC, Q/F)
New Zealand   30   T: Umaga (2), Wilson, Lomu; C: Mehrtens (2); PG: Mehrtens (2)
Scotland   18   T: Pountney, C Murray; C: Logan; PG: Logan DG: Townsend

24 June 2000, Carisbrook, Dunedin
New Zealand   69   T: Lomu (3), Oliver (2), Umaga (2), Cribb, Cullen, Alatini, Flavell; C: Mehrtens (7)
Scotland   20   T: Metcalfe, Simpson; C: Hodge (2); PG: Hodge (2)

1 July 2000, Eden Park, Auckland
New Zealand   48   T: Umaga (2), Kronfeld, Cribb, Ieremia, Robinson, Marshall, Cullen; C: Mehrtens (3), Brown
Scotland   14   T: Paterson, Murray; C: Hodge (2)

24 November 2001, Murrayfield, Edinburgh
New Zealand   37   T: Lomu, Robinson, Umaga; C: Mehrtens (2); PG: Mehrtens (6)
Scotland   6   PG: Paterson (2)

26 November 2005, Murrayfield, Edinburgh
New Zealand   29   T: Gear (2), Evans, Lauaki; C: Evans (2), MacDonald; PG: Evans
Scotland   10   T: Webster; C: Paterson; PG: Paterson

23 September 2007, Murrayfield, Edinburgh (RWC, Pool C)
New Zealand   40   T: Howlett (2), McCaw, Kelleher, Williams, Carter; C: Carter (2); PG: Carter (2)
Scotland   0

8 November 2008, Murrayfield, Edinburgh
New Zealand   32   T: Tuitavake, Weepu, Kahui, Boric; C: Donald (2), Carter; PG: Donald (2)
Scotland   6   PG: Paterson (2)

New Zealand vs South Africa (Freedom Cup)

New Zealand vs South Africa	
Played:	75
Won:	42
Lost:	30
Drawn:	3
For:	1,355
Against:	1,119

Average score:
18.06–14.92

New Zealand percentages:

Won:	56%
Lost:	40%
Drawn:	4%

This is perhaps the fiercest rivalry that exists today in the world of rugby, with a long history both on and off the field. New Zealand's and South Africa's early form on tours to the United Kingdom suggested that they were the two strongest countries in world rugby. However, it was not until 1921 that the two officially met when South Africa toured New Zealand to compete for the mythical title of world champions. It was on this tour that Maori culture clashed with South African racism when the New Zealand Maoris played the Springboks, losing 8–9 in a dirty game. Following the match, a report in the South African press was widely published in New Zealand which recorded 'Springbok disgust' at having to play a non-white team:

'This was the most unfortunate match ever played. Only great pressure brought to bear on the manager induced the Springboks to meet the Maoris, who had assisted largely in the entertainment of the Springboks. It was bad enough having to play a team officially designated "New Zealand Natives" but the spectacle of Europeans frantically cheering on a band of coloured men to defeat members of their own race was too much for the Springboks, who were frankly disgusted.'

Nevertheless, Maori teams continued to play touring South African sides but, shamefully, the NZRFU agreed not to select any Maori players for the 1928, 1949 and 1960 tours to South Africa. In 1967, the NZRFU finally refused an invitation by South Africa to tour when it was again stated that no Maoris were allowed. When the 1970 tour to South Africa was undertaken, Maori players were permitted under the title of 'honorary whites' for the duration of the tour. The first showdown in 1921 between South Africa and New Zealand came to be known as The World Championship: a drawn series as was the following in 1928. It was not until 1937 that the world was indeed finally given a champion when Phillip Nel's Springboks beat New Zealand in New Zealand by 2–1. In the final test South Africa inflicted a massive 17–6 defeat on New Zealand, including five tries to one. A further seven series were played between the two sides – each won by the home team – until South Africa was eventually banned from international sport. The most famous was the 1949 series when New Zealand were defeated 4–0 thanks to Springbok prop Okey Geffin's accurate goal kicking in the first test when Hennie 'Windhond' Müller won penalty after penalty for Geffin to convert. The series defeat was hard for New Zealand to swallow, singling out over-generous home refereeing decisions as a reason for their defeat as well as not being allowed to play their top scrumhalf: a Maori by the name of Vince Bevan. In 1956 New Zealand won their first series against South Africa 3–1, with South Africa winning the 1960 series and losing the 1965 one. After refusing to tour in 1967, New Zealand next found themselves in South Africa in 1970 with the first Maori tourist, winger Bryan Williams, allowed in. South Africa won the series 3–1. In 1976 New Zealand bravely toured again, this time to a country in the throes of civil unrest. New Zealand lost the series and incredibly extended an invitation to South Africa to tour in 1981, knowing full well the strife this would cause following earlier Springbok tours to the UK in 1969/1970 and Australia in 1971. Five years previously, in 1976, the field at Lancaster Park in Christchurch was splattered with graffiti, 'Welcome to a racist

NEW ZEALAND

game', in protest against the presence of two South African rugby players in the city: John Williams and Johan Oosthuizen. This was a precursor of what lay ahead for the 1981 touring South Africans. Tight security, sometimes brutal, ensured that the tour went ahead. But games were delayed because of threats of nails and glass being sprinkled on the field; protestors invaded the pitch at Hamilton, causing the cancellation of the Waikato and Timaru games; a vicar slipped onto the field in Auckland dressed as a referee and stole the ball; and flour bombs that were dropped from a Cessna aircraft that overflew Eden Park 67 times during the third test. The series was won 2–1 by New Zealand and the two did not to meet again until 1992 when South Africa was readmitted into international rugby. In 1994 the Springboks lost the three-test series, most remembered for the Springbok prop Johan le Roux's moment of madness when he bit Sean Fitzpatrick's ear. After the epic RWC final of 1995 Sean Fitzpatrick's side of 1996 became the first New Zealand team to win a series in South Africa. At of the end of the 1996 series, South Africa and New Zealand were locked at 22 wins apiece with three draws but since then the All Blacks have dominated in the Tri-Nations. Today, the Freedom Cup is competed for between South Africa and New Zealand, aptly named considering the rugby history that exists between the two nations and how racism cruelly affected the game. Appropriately, South Africa's first test after readmission was against New Zealand in 1992. The Freedom Cup was introduced in 2004 to commemorate the tenth anniversary of South Africa's first democratic election. It was initially contested every second year, alternating on a home-and-away basis. The Freedom Cup is played for in those matches under the Tri-Nations umbrella. At Ellis Park, South Africa was the first to win the trophy with a convincing 40–26 victory. The trophy was contested in a three-test series in 2006 due to the expanded format of the Tri-Nations, and won 2–1 by New Zealand. The following year, the structure was again changed to an annual basis involving all Tri-Nations games. New Zealand retained the trophy in 2007, winning the series 2–0. In the event of the series being drawn, the cup is retained by the current holder. The non-holder has to win the following series outright to regain the cup.

13 August 1921, Carisbrook, Dunedin
New Zealand   13   T: Belliss, Steel, Storey; C: M.F. Nicholls (2)
South Africa   5   T: van Heerden; C: PG Morkel

27 August 1921, Eden Park, Auckland
South Africa   9   T: Sendin; PG Morkel; DG: PG Morkel
New Zealand   5   T: McLean; C: Nicholls

17 September 1921, Athletic Park, Wellington
New Zealand   0
South Africa   0

30 June 1928, Kingsmead, Durban
South Africa   17   T: Slater; PG: Osler (2); DG: Osler (2)
New Zealand   0

21 July 1928, Ellis Park, Johannedburg
New Zealand   7   PG: Lindsay; DG: Strang
South Africa   6   PG: Osler; GM: Mostert

18 August 1928, Crusaders Ground, Port Elizabeth
South Africa   11   T: Nel, de Jongh, Daneel; C: Osler
New Zealand   6   T: Stewart, Grenside

1 September 1928, Newlands, Cape Town
New Zealand   13   T: Swain; PG: Nicholls (2); DG: Nicholls
South Africa   5   T: van der Westhuizen; C: Osler

14 August 1937, Athletic Park, Wellington
New Zealand   13   T: Dick; PG: Trevathan (2); DG: Trevathan
South Africa   7   T: Williams; DG: White

4 September 1937, Lancaster Park, Christchurch
South Africa   13   T: Turner, Bastard; C: Brand (2); PG: Brand
New Zealand   6   T: Sullivan (2)

25 September 1937, Eden Park, Auckland
South Africa   17   T: Babrow (2), Bergh, Williams, Turner; C: Brand
New Zealand   6   PG: Trevathan (2)

16 July 1949, Newlands, Cape Town
South Africa 15 PG: Geffin (5)
New Zealand 11 T: Henderson; C: Scott; DG: Kearney; PG: Scott

13 August 1949, Ellis Park, Johannesburg
South Africa 12 T: Brewis, Lategan; DG: Brewis; PG: Geffin
New Zealand 6 DG: Kearney; PG: Scott

3 September 1949, Kingsmead, Durban
South Africa 9 PG: Geffin (3)
New Zealand 3 T: Goddard

17 September 1949, Crusaders Ground, Port Elizabeth
South Africa 11 T: du Toit; C: Geffin; PG: Geffin; DG: Brewis
New Zealand 8 T: Johnstone, Elvidge; C: Scott

14 July 1956, Carisbrook, Dunedin
New Zealand 10 T: White, Jarden; C: Jarden (2)
South Africa 6 T: Howe; PG: Dryburgh

4 August 1956, Athletic Park, Wellington
South Africa 8 T: Retief, du Rand; C: Viviers
New Zealand 3 T: Brown

18 August 1956, Lancaster Park, Christchurch
New Zealand 17 T: Dixon, Jarden, White; C: Clarke; PG: Clarke (2)
South Africa 10 T: Lochner, Rosenberg; C: Viviers (2)

1 September 1956, Eden Park, Auckland
New Zealand 11 T: Jones; C: Clarke; PG: Clarke (2)
South Africa 5 T: Dryburgh; C: Viviers

21 June 1960, Ellis Park, Johannesburg
South Africa 13 T: H van Zyl (2); C: Dryburgh, Lockyear; PG: Lockyear
New Zealand 0

23 July 1960, Newlands, Cape Town
New Zealand 11 T: Meads; C: Clarke; PG: Clarke; DG: Clarke
South Africa 3 T: Oxlee

13 August 1960, Free State Stadium, Bloemfontein
South Africa 11 T: Oxlee; C: Lockyear; PG: Lockyear (2)
New Zealand 11 T: McMullen; C: Clarke; PG: Clarke (2)

27 August 1960, Boet Erasmus Stadium, Port Elizabeth
South Africa 8 T: Pelser; C: Lockyear; PG: Lockyear
New Zealand 3 PG: Clarke

31 July 1965, Athletic Park, Wellington
New Zealand 6 T: Birtwistle, Tremain
South Africa 3 DG: Oxlee

21 August 1965, Carisbrook, Dunedin
New Zealand 13 T: Tremain, McLeod, Rangi; C: Williment (2)
South Africa 0

4 September 1965, Lancaster Park, Christchurch
South Africa 19 T: Gainsford (2), Brynard (2); C: Naudé (2); PG: Naudé
New Zealand 16 T: Tremain, Rangi, Moreton; C: Williment (2); PG: Williment

18 September 1965, Eden Park, Auckland
New Zealand 20 T: Smith (2), Conway, Birtwistle, Gray; C: McCormick; DG: Herewini
South Africa 3 PG: Naudé

25 July 1970, Loftus Versfeld, Pretoria
South Africa 17 T: de Villiers, Nomis; C: McCallum; PG: McCallum (2); DG: Visagie
New Zealand 6 T: Williams; PG: McCormick

Did you know: On South Africa's 1921 tour to New Zealand there were five members of the Morkel family in the Springboks: fullback P. G. (Gerhard) Morkel, captain and prop W. H. (Boy) Morkel, giant forward J. A. (Royal) Morkel, lock forward H. J. (Harry) Morkel and wing H. W. (Henry) Morkel?

NEW ZEALAND

8 August 1970, Newlands, Cape Town
New Zealand 9 T: Laidlaw, Kirkpatrick; PG: McCormick
South Africa 8 T: Jansen; C: McCallum; PG: McCallum

29 August 1970, Boet Erasmus Stadium, Port Elizabeth
South Africa 14 T: Muller (2); C: McCallum; PG: McCallum (2)
New Zealand 3 PG: Williams

12 September 1970, Ellis Park, Johannesburg
South Africa 20 T: Visagie, Muller; C: McCallum; PG: McCallum (4)
New Zealand 17 T: Williams; C: Kember; PG: Kember (4)

24 July 1976, Kings Park, Durban
South Africa 16 T: Germishuys, Krantz; C: Bosch; PG: Bosch; DG: Robertson
New Zealand 7 T: Jaffray; PG: Williams

14 August 1976, Free State Stadium, Bloemfontein
New Zealand 15 T: Morgan; C: Going; PG: Going (2); DG: Bruce
South Africa 9 PG: Bosch (3)

4 September 1976, Newlands, Cape Town
South Africa 15 T: Oosthuizen; C: Bosch; PG: Bosch (2); DG: Snyman
New Zealand 10 T: B Robertson; PG: Williams (2)

18 September 1976, Ellis Park, Johannesburg
South Africa 15 T: Kritzinger; C: Bosch; PG: Bosch (2); DG: Bosch
New Zealand 14 T: Kirkpatrick, Going; PG: Williams; DG: Bruce

15 August 1981, Lancaster Park, Christchurch
New Zealand 14 T: Rollerson, Wilson, Shaw; C: Rollerson
South Africa 9 T: Bekker; C: Botha; DG: Botha

29 August 1981, Athletic Park, Wellington
South Africa 24 T: Germishuys; C: Botha; PG: Botha (5); DG: Botha
New Zealand 12 PG: Hewson (4)

12 September 1981, Eden Park, Auckland
New Zealand 25 T: Wilson, Knight; C: Rollerson; PG: Hewson (4), Rollerson
South Africa 22 T: Mordt (3); C: Botha (2); PG: Botha (2)

15 August 1992, Ellis Park, Johannesburg
New Zealand 27 T: Z Brooke, Kirwin, Timu; C: Fox (3); PG: Fox (2)
South Africa 24 T: Gerber (2), Muller; C: Botha (3); PG: Botha

9 July 1994, Carisbrook, Dunedin
New Zealand 22 T: Kirwan; C: Howarth; PG: Howarth (5)
South Africa 14 T: Straeuli; PG: Joubert (3)

23 July 1994, Athletic Park, Wellington
New Zealand 13 T: Timu, Z Brooke; PG: Howarth
South Africa 9 PG: van Rensburg (3)

6 August 1994, Eden Park, Auckland
New Zealand 18 PG: Howarth (6)
South Africa 18 T: Venter, Johnson; C: Johnson; PG: Johnson (2)

24 June 1995, Ellis Park, Johannesburg (RWC, Final)
South Africa 15 PG: Stransky (3); DG: Stransky (2)
New Zealand 12 PG: Mehrtens (3); DG: Mehrtens

20 July 1996, Lancaster Park, Christchurch
New Zealand 15 PG: Mehrtens (5)
South Africa 11 T: Joubert; PG: Stransky (2)

10 August 1996, Norwich Park Newlands, Cape Town
New Zealand 29 T: Osborne, Dowd; C: Mehrtens (2); PG: Mehrtens (5)
South Africa 18 T: Mulder, du Randt; C: Stransky; PG: Stransky (2)

17 August 1996, Kings Park, Durban
New Zealand 23 T: Wilson, Cullen, Z Brooke; C: Culhane; PG: Culhane (2)
South Africa 19 T: van Schalkwyk; C: Stransky; PG: Stransky (4)

24 August 1996, Loftus Versfeld, Pretoria
New Zealand 33 T: Wilson (2), Z Brooke; C: Culhane (3); PG: Culhane, Preston (2); DG: Z Brooke
South Africa 26 T: Strydom, Kruger, van der Westhuizen; C: Stransky; PG: Stransky (3)

31 August 1996, Ellis Park, Johannesburg
South Africa 32 T: van der Westhuizen (2), Joubert; C: Honiball; PG: Honiball (2), Joubert (3)
New Zealand 22 T: Fitzpatrick, Little, Marshall; C: Mehrtens (2); PG: Mehrtens

19 July 1997, Ellis Park, Johannesburg
New Zealand 35 T: Wilson, Bunce (2), Spencer; C: Spencer (3); PG: Spencer (3)
South Africa 32 T: Drotske, Bennett; C: de Beer (2); PG: de Beer (4); DG: de Beer (2)

9 August 1997, Eden Park, Auckland
New Zealand 55 T: Cullen (2), Randell, Marshall, Spencer, Ieremia, Umaga; C: Spencer (4); PG: Spencer (4)
South Africa 35 T: Kruger, Montgomery, Teichmann, Rossouw, van der Westhuizen; C: de Beer (3), Honiball (2)

25 July 1998, Athletic Park, Wellington
South Africa 13 T: Rossouw; C: Montgomery; PG: Montgomery (2)
New Zealand 3 PG: Mehrtens

15 August 1998, Kings Park, Durban
South Africa 24 T: Terblanche, Skinstad, van der Westhuizen, Dalton; C: Montgomery (2)
New Zealand 23 T: Marshall, Randell; C: Mehrtens (2); PG: Mehrtens (3)

10 July 1999, Carisbrook, Dunedin
New Zealand 28 T: Marshall, Cullen, Wilson; C: Mehrtens, Brown; PG: Mehrtens (3)
South Africa 0

7 August 1999, Minolta Loftus, Pretoria
New Zealand 34 T: Cullen (2); PG: Mehrtens (7); DG: Wilson
South Africa 18 T: van der Westhuizen, Snyman; C: du Toit; PG: du Toit (2)

4 November 1999, Millenium Stadium, Cardiff (RWC, 3/4 play-off)
South Africa 22 T: Paulse; C: Honiball; PG: Honiball (3); DG: Montgomery (2)
New Zealand 18 PG: Mehrtens (6)

22 July 2000, Lancaster Park, Christchurch
New Zealand 25 T: Cullen (2); PG: Mehrtens (3), Brown; DG: Mehrtens
South Africa 12 PG: van Straaten (3); DG: Montgomery

19 August 2000, Ellis Park, Johannesburg
South Africa 46 T: Swanepoel (2), Fleck (2), Williams, Delport; C: van Straaten (5); PG: van Straaten (2)
New Zealand 40 T: Umaga (2), Cullen (2); C: Mehrtens (4); PG: Mehrtens (3); DG: Mehrtens

21 July 2001, Fedsure Park Newlands, Cape Town
New Zealand 12 PG: Brown (4)
South Africa 3 PG: Montgomery

25 August 2001, Eden Park, Auckland
New Zealand 26 T: Alatini, penalty try; C: Mehrtens (2); PG: Mehrtens (4)
South Africa 15 PG: van Straaten (5)

20 July 2002, Westpac Trust Stadium, Wellington
New Zealand 41 T: Hammett, Thorne, Robertson, Marshall, Howlett; C: Mehrtens (2); PG: Mehrtens (3); DG: Mehrtens
South Africa 20 T: Joubert, Greeff; C: Pretorius (2); PG: Pretorius; DG: Greeff

10 August 2002, ABSA Stadium, Durban
New Zealand 30 T: Howlett, Mauger, MacDonald, penalty try; C: Mehrtens (2); PG: Mehrtens (2)
South Africa 23 T: de Kock, Pretorius; C: Pretorius (2); PG: Pretorius (2); DG: Pretorius

19 July 2003, Securicor Loftus , Pretoria
New Zealand 52 T: Howlett (2), Rokocoko (2), Spencer, Mauger, Meeuws; C: Spencer (4); PG: Spencer (3)
South Africa 16 T: Willemse; C: Koen; PG: Koen (2); DG: Koen

9 August 2003, Carisbrook, Dunedin
New Zealand 19 T: Rokocoko; C: Spencer; PG: Spencer (4)
South Africa 11 T: Bands; PG: Koen (2)

8 November 2003, Colonial Stadium, Melbourne (RWC, Q/F)
New Zealand 29 T: Mealamu, MacDonald, Rokocoko; C: MacDonald; PG: MacDonald (3); DG: Muager
South Africa 9 PG: Hougaard (3)

NEW ZEALAND

24 July 2004, Jade Stadium, Christchurch
New Zealand   23   T: Howlett; PG: Carter (5), Spencer
South Africa   21   T: Cronje, du Preez, de Villiers; C: Montgomery (3)

14 August 2004, Ellis Park, Johannesburg
South Africa   40   T: Joubert (3), Paulse, de Villiers; C: Montgomery (3); PG: Montgomery (3)
New Zealand   26   T: Muliaina, Rokocoko; C: Mehrtens (2); PG: Mehrtens (4)

6 August 2005, Newlands, Cape Town
South Africa   22   T: de Villiers; C: Montgomery; PG: Montgomery (4); DG: Pretorius
New Zealand   16   T: Gear; C: Carter; PG: Carter (3)

27 August 2005, Carisbrook, Dunedin
New Zealand   31   T: Rokocoko (2), MacDonald, Mealamu; C: MacDonald (3), McAlister; PG: MacDonald
South Africa   27   T: Januarie, Fourie, Habana; C: Montgomery (3); PG: Montgomery (2)

22 July 2006, Westpac Stadium, Wellington
New Zealand   35   T: McCaw, Weepu; C: Carter (2); PG: Carter (7)
South Africa   17   T: du Preez, Paulse; C: Montgomery (2); PG: Montgomery

26 August 2006, Loftus Versfeld, Pretoria
New Zealand   45   T: Tialata, McAlister, Sivivatu, Muliaina, Gear; C: Carter (4); PG: Carter (4)
South Africa   26   T: Fourie (2), du Preez; C: Pretorius; PG: Montgomery (2), James

2 August 2006, Royal Bafokeng Sports Palace, Rustenburg
South Africa   21   T: Habana, Wannenburg; C: Pretorius; PG: Pretorius (3)
New Zealand   20   T: Carter, Rokocoko; C: Carter (2); PG: Carter (2)

23 June 2007, The ABSA Stadium, Durban
New Zealand   26   T: McCaw, Rokocoko; C: Carter (2); PG: Carter (3); DG: Mauger
South Africa   21   T: Burger, James; C: Montgomery; PG: Montgomery (2), Pienaar

14 July 2007 Jade Stadium, Christchurch
New Zealand   33   T: Carter, Leonard, Evans; C: Carter (3); PG: Carter (4)
South Africa   6   PG: Hougaard (2)

5 July 2008, Westpac Stadium, Wellington
New Zealand   19   T: Kaino; C: Carter; PG: Carter (4)
South Africa   8   T: Habana; PG: James

12 July 2008, Carisbrook, Dunedin
South Africa   30   T: Januarie, Pietersen; C: Steyn; PG: Montgomery (3), James (2); DG: James
New Zealand   28   T: Lauaki; C: Carter; PG: Carter (6); DG: Carter

16 August 2008, Newlands, Cape Town
New Zealand   19   T: Smith, Carter, Mealamu; C: Carter (2)
South Africa   0

Freedom Cup		Current holder: New Zealand			Number of titles: New Zealand 3, South Africa 1			
No.	Date	Venue	Result			Series	Holder
1	14/08/2004	Ellis Park, Johannesburg	South Africa	40–26	New Zealand	1–0	South Africa
2	22/07/2006	Westpac Trust Stadium, Wellington	New Zealand	35–17	South Africa	1–2	New Zealand
3	26/08/2006	Loftus Versfeld, Pretoria	South Africa	26–45	New Zealand		
4	02/09/2006	Royal Bafokeng Sports Palace, Rustenburg	South Africa	21–20	New Zealand		
5	23/06/2007	The ABSA Stadium, Durban	South Africa	21–26	New Zealand	2–0	New Zealand
6	14/07/2007	Jade Stadium, Christchurch	New Zealand	33–6	South Africa		
7	05/07/2008	Westpac Stadium, Wellington	New Zealand	19–8	South Africa	2–1	New Zealand
8	12/07/2008	Carisbrook, Dunedin	New Zealand	28–30	South Africa		
9	16/08/2008	Newlands, Cape Town	South Africa	0–19	New Zealand		

New Zealand vs Tonga

3 October 1999, Ashton Gate, Bristol (RWC, Pool B)
New Zealand   45   T: Lomu (2), Kronfeld, Maxwell, Kellaher; C: Mehrtens (4); PG: Mehrtens (4)
Tonga   9   PG: Taumalolo (3)

16 June 2000, North Harbour Stadium, Albany
New Zealand   102   T: Flavell (3), Howlett (2), Umaga (2), Ieremia, Cullen, Hammett, Blackadder, Kronfeld, Tiatia, Marshall, Brown;
    C: Brown (12); PG: Brown
Tonga   0

24 October 2003, Suncorp Stadium, Brisbane (RWC, Pool D)
New Zealand   91   T: Muliaina (2), Ralph (2), Howlett (2), Carter, Flynn, Braid, Spencer, Meeuws, penalty try, MacDonald;
    C: MacDonald (12), Spencer
Tonga   7   T: Hola C: Tu'ipulotu

New Zealand vs United States of America

15 November 1913, California Field, Berkeley
New Zealand   51   T: Roberts (3), Gray (2), McKenzie (2), Murray (2), McDonald (2), Wylie, McGregor; C: Graham (4),
    McDonald, Mitchinson
USA   3   PG: Jones

8 October 1991, Kingsholm, Gloucester (RWC, Pool 1)
New Zealand   46   T: Wright (3), Timu, Earl, Purvis, Tuigamala, Innes; C: Preston (4); PG: Preston (2)
USA   6   PG: Williams (2)

New Zealand vs Wales

New Zealand vs Wales	
Played:	24
Won:	21
Lost:	3
Drew:	0
For:	722
Against:	225

Average score:
30.08–9.38

New Zealand percentages:

Won:	87.5%
Lost:	12.5%
Drawn:	0%

Ever since the first controversial clash between Wales and New Zealand in 1905, this encounter has become one of the most anticipated in any rugby calendar. During the early years, matches were tight, often dominated by the Welsh who at one stage led the series 3–1, following their record 13–8 win in 1953. That, however, was the last time Wales beat New Zealand, with narrow 12–13 and 25–26 losses in 1978 and 2004 respectively bringing any credibility to their efforts. Games have now become one-sided with heavy defeats regularly imposed on the Welsh. Yet, despite the likely outcome of their encounters with the All Blacks, the Welsh are always bullish of their chances. The two sides did produce the match of the 2003 RWC when, at one stage and against all odds, Wales led New Zealand 37–36 in the 51st minute in a thrilling display of free-flowing rugby; New Zealand eventually won 53–37. In 2005, much was expected of Wales when they met the All Blacks in the 1905 centenary game. Instead, however, they suffered a record 3–41 defeat at home. Once again, much hype was built up around the 2008 clash. After confronting the *haka* like no other team had done before, the Welsh refused to take their positions once the *haka* was over, with the two teams staring each other down until referee Jonathan Kaplan and New Zealand skipper Riche McCaw intervened to get the game started. Wales led 9–6 at the break but ended up losing 9–29.

16 December 1905, Cardiff Arms Park, Cardiff
Wales   3   T: Morgan
New Zealand   0

29 November 1924, St Helen's, Swansea
New Zealand   19   T: Irvine (2), Svenson, M Brownlie; C: Nicholls (2); PG: Nicholls
Wales   0

21 December 1935, Cardiff Arms Park, Cardiff
Wales   13   T: Rees-Jones (2), Davey; C: Jenkins (2)
New Zealand   12   T: Ball (2); C: Gilbert; DG: Gilbert

NEW ZEALAND

19 December 1953, Cardiff Arms Park, Cardiff
Wales   13   T: Judd, K Jones; C: Rowlands (2); PG: Rowlands
New Zealand   8   T: Clark; C: Jarden; PG: Jarden

21 December 1963, Cardiff Arms Park, Cardiff
New Zealand   6   PG: Clarke; DG: Watt
Wales   0

11 November 1967, Cardiff Arms Park, Cardiff
New Zealand   13   T: Birtwistle, Davis; C: McCormick (2); PG: McCormick
Wales   6   PG: Gale; DG: John

31 May 1969, Lancaster Park, Christchurch
New Zealand   19   T: Dick, McLeod, Gray, Lochore; C: McCormick (2);
                               PG: McCormick
Wales   0

14 June 1969, Eden Park, Auckland
New Zealand   33   T: Skudder, MacRae, Kirkpatrick; C: McCormick (3);
                               PG: McCormick (5); DG: McCormick
Wales   12   T: M Richards, Jarrett; PG: Jarrett (2)

2 December 1972, National Stadium, Cardiff
New Zealand   19   T: Murdoch; PG: Karam (5)
Wales   16   T: J Bevan; PG: Bennett (4)

11 November 1978, National Stadium, Cardiff
New Zealand   13   T: S Wilson; PG: McKechnie (3)
Wales   12   PG: W Davies (3), Fenwick

1 November 1980, National Stadium, Cardiff
New Zealand   23   T: Mourie, Fraser, Allen, Reid; C: Rollerson (2); PG: Rollerson
Wales   3   PG: Fenwick

14 June 1987, Ballymore, Brisbane (RWC, S/F)
New Zealand   49   T: Shelford (2), Kirwan (2), Drake, A Whetton, Stanley, Brooke-Cowden; C: Fox (7); PG: Fox
Wales   6   T: Devereux; C: Thorburn

28 May 1988, Lancaster Park, Christchurch
New Zealand   52   T: Kirwan (4), Wright (2), Gallagher, Deans, Shelford, G Whetton; C: Fox (6)
Wales   3   PG: Ring

11 June 1988, Eden Park, Auckland
New Zealand   54   T: Kirwan (2), Wright (2), Taylor, Deans, M Jones, McDowell; C: Fox (8); PG: Fox (2)
Wales   9   T: J Davies; C: Ring; PG: Ring

4 November 1989, National Stadium, Cardiff
New Zealand   34   T: Innes (2), Bachop, Wright; C: Fox (3); PG: Fox (4)
Wales   9   PG: Thorburn (3)

31 May 1995, Ellis Park, Johannesburg (RWC, Pool C)
New Zealand   34   T: Little, Ellis, Kronfeld; C: Mehrtens (2); PG: Mehrtens (4); DG: Mehrtens
Wales   9   PG: Jenkins (2); DG: Jenkins

29 November 1997, Wembley, London
New Zealand   42   T: Cullen (3), Randell, Marshall; C: Mehrtens (4); PG: Mehrtens (2); DG: Z Brooke
Wales   7   T: Walker; C: Jenkins

23 November 2002, Millennium Stadium, Cardiff
New Zealand   43   T: Howlett (2), Meeuws, King; C: Mehrtens (4); PG: Mehrtens (5)
Wales   17   T: Robinson, penalty try; C: S Jones, I Harris; PG: S Jones

21 June 2003, Waikato Stadium, Hamilton
New Zealand   55   T: Rokocoko (2), Howlett, Spencer, Carter, Umaga, Meeuws, Mealamu; C: Carter (6); PG: Carter
Wales   3   PG: S Jones

2 November 2003, Stadium Australia, Sydney (RWC, Pool D)
New Zealand   53   T: Rokocoko (2), Howlett (2), MacDonald, Williams, Spencer, Mauger; C: MacDonald (5); PG: MacDonald
Wales   37   T: Taylor, Parker, Charvis, Williams; C: S Jones (4); PG: S Jones (3)

> **Did you know**: The first time a national anthem was sung before a rugby international was on 16 December 1905 when Wales responded to the New Zealand haka by singing their national anthem with great gusto. The singing of the anthem lifted the spirits of the Welsh who memorably defeated the All Blacks 3–0.

20 November 2004, Millennium Stadium, Cardiff
New Zealand 26 T: Rokocoko (2), Muliaina; C: Carter; PG: Carter (3)
Wales 25 T: Shanklin, Davies; PG: S Jones (3), Henson (2)

5 November 2005, Millennium Stadium, Cardiff
New Zealand 41 T: Gear (3), Carter (2); C: Carter (5); PG: Carter (2)
Wales 3 PG: S Jones

25 November 2006, Millennium Stadium, Cardiff
New Zealand 45 T: Sivivatu (3), McAlister, penalty try; C: Carter (2), Evans (2) PG: Carter (4)
Wales 10 T: M Williams; C: Hook; PG: S Jones

22 November 2008, Millennium Stadium, Cardiff
New Zealand 29 T: Nonu, Kaino; C: Carter (2); PG: Carter (5)
Wales 9 PG: S Jones (3)

New Zealand vs World XV

18 April 1992, Lancaster Park, Christchurch
World XV 28 T: Hendriks (2), Knoetze; C: Camberabero (2); PG: Camberabero, Hastings; DG: Camberabero (2)
New Zealand 14 T: Turner, Tuigamala; PG: Fox (2)

22 April 1992, Athletic Park, Wellington
New Zealand 54 T: G Cooper (2), Loe (2), Clarke (2), Pene, Larsen, Tuigamala, Strachan; C: G Cooper (6), Fox
World XV 26 T: Yoshida, Hendriks, Eales, Cecillon, Hastings; C: Botha (3)

25 April 1992, Eden Park, Auckland
New Zealand 26 T: Pene, Kirwan, Loe, Clarke; C: G Cooper (2); PG: G Cooper (2)
World XV 15 T: Fatialofa; C: Botha; PG: Botha (3)

New Zealand: summaries and records

Home matches	
Played	217
Won	175
Lost	36
Drawn	6
Points for	5,792
Points against	2,529
Average score	26.69/11.65
Win %	80.65
Lose %	16.59
Draw %	2.76

Away matches	
Played	203
Won	135
Lost	57
Drawn	11
Points for	4,172
Points against	2,613
Average score	20.55/12.87
Win %	66.5
Lose %	28.08
Draw %	5.42

Neutral venues	
Played	27
Won	23
Lost	4
Drawn	0
Points for	1,383
Points against	404
Average score	51.22/14.96
Win %	85.19
Lose %	14.81
Draw %	0

Total matches	
Played	447
Won	333
Lost	97
Drawn	17
Points for	11,347
Points against	5,546
Average score	25.38/12.41
Win %	74.5
Lose %	21.7
Draw %	3.8

Most capped players: New Zealand			Points				
Player	Caps	Career	T	C	PG	DG	Total
Sean Fitzpatrick	92	28/06/1986–29/11/1997	12	-	-	-	55
Justin Marshall	81	18/11/1995–09/07/2005	24	-	-	-	120
Ian Jones	79	16/06/1990–24/10/1999	9	-	-	-	42
Tana Umaga	74	14/06/1997–26/11/2005	36	-	-	-	180
Mils Muliaina	71	14/06/2003–27/06/2009	24	-	-	-	120
Richie McCaw	70	17/11/2001–29/11/2008	14	-	-	-	70
Andrew Mehrtens	70	22/04/1995–14/08/2004	7	169	188	10	967

NEW ZEALAND

Most tests as captain: New Zealand

No.	Player	Period
51	Sean Fitzpatrick	1992–1997
33	Richie McCaw	2004–2008
30	Wilson Whineray	1958–1965
23	Reuben Thorne	2002–2007
22	Taine Randell	1998–2002

Most points by a player in a career: New Zealand

No.	Player	Tests	Career	Points			
				T	C	PG	DG
967	Andrew Mehrtens	70	22/04/1995–14/08/2004	7	169	188	10
879	Daniel Carter	59	21/06/2003–29/11/2008	25	155	146	2
645	Grant Fox	46	26/10/1985–31/07/1993	1	118	128	7
291	Carlos Spencer	35	21/06/1997–07/08/2004	14	49	41	-
245	Doug Howlett	62	16/06/2000–29/09/2007	49	-	-	-

Most tries by a player in a career: New Zealand

No.	Player	Tests	Career
49	Doug Howlett	62	16/06/2000–29/09/2007
46	Christian Cullen	58	07/06/1996–16/11/2002
44	Jeff Wilson	60	20/11/1993–25/08/2001
44	Joe Rokocoko	55	14/06/2003–27/06/2009
37	Jonah Lomu	63	26/06/1994–23/11/2002

Most conversions by a player in a career: New Zealand

No.	Player	Tests	Career
169	Andrew Mehrtens	70	22/04/1995–14/08/2004
155	Daniel Carter	59	21/06/2003–29/11/2008
118	Grant Fox	46	26/10/1985–31/07/1993
49	Carlos Spencer	35	21/06/1997–07/08/2004
43	Tony Brown	18	18/06/1999–11/08/2001

Most penalties by a player in a career: New Zealand

No.	Player	Tests	Career
188	Andrew Mehrtens	70	22/04/1995–14/08/2004
146	Daniel Carter	59	21/06/2003–29/11/2008
128	Grant Fox	46	26/10/1985–31/07/1993
43	Alan Hewson	19	13/06/1981–21/07/1984
41	Carlos Spencer	35	21/06/1997–07/08/2004

Most drop goals by a player in a career: New Zealand

No.	Player	Tests	Career
10	Andrew Mehrtens	70	22/04/1995–14/08/2004
7	Grant Fox	46	26/10/1985–31/07/1993
5	Doug Bruce	14	24/07/1976–09/12/1978
5	Don Clarke	31	18/08/1956–29/08/1964
5	Macfarlane Herewini	10	22/09/1962–19/08/1967

Most points by a player in a match: New Zealand

No.	Player	Points				Versus	Venue	Date
		T	C	PG	DG			
45	Simon Culhane	1	20	-	-	Japan	Free State Stadium, Bloemfontein	04/06/1995
36	Tony Brown	1	11	3	-	Italy	McAlpine Stadium, Huddersfield	14/10/1999
33	Nick Evans	1	14	-	-	Portugal	Stade Gerland, Lyon	15/09/2007
33	Dan Carter	2	4	5	-	British & Irish Lions	Westpac Trust Stadium, Wellington	02/07/2005
33	Andrew Mehrtens	1	5	6	-	Ireland	Lansdowne Road, Dublin	15/11/1997
33	Carlos Spencer	2	10	1	-	Argentina	Athletic Park, Wellington	21/06/1997

Most tries by a player in a match: New Zealand

No.	Player	Versus	Venue	Date
6	Marc Ellis	Japan	Free State Stadium, Bloemfontein	04/06/1995
5	Jeff Wilson	Fiji	North Harbour Stadium, Albany	14/06/1997
4	Sitiveni Sivivatu	Fiji	North Harbour Stadium, Albany	10/06/2005
4	Mils Muliaina	Canada	Telstra Dome, Melbourne	17/10/2003
4	Jeff Wilson	Samoa	North Harbour Stadium, Albany	18/06/1999
4	Christian Cullen	Scotland	Carisbrook, Dunedin	15/06/1996
4	Jonah Lomu	England	Newlands, Cape Town	18/06/1995
4	John Kirwan	Wales	Lancaster Park, Christchurch	28/05/1988
4	John Gallagher	Fiji	Lancaster Park, Christchurch	27/05/1987
4	Craig Green	Fiji	Lancaster Park, Christchurch	27/05/1987
4	Duncan McGregor	England	Crystal Palace, London	02/12/1905

Most conversions by a player in a match: New Zealand

No.	Player	Versus	Venue	Date
20	Simon Culhane	Japan	Free State Stadium, Bloemfontein	04/06/1995
14	Nick Evans	Portugal	Stade Gerland, Lyon	15/09/2007
12	Leon MacDonald	Tonga	Suncorp Stadium, Brisbane	24/10/2003
12	Tony Brown	Tonga	North Harbour Stadium, Albany	16/06/2000
11	Tony Brown	Italy	McAlpine Stadium, Hudddersfield	14/10/1999

NEW ZEALAND

Most penalties by a player in a match: New Zealand

No.	Player	Versus	Venue	Date
9	Andrew Mehrtens	France	Stade de France, Paris	11/11/2000
9	Andrew Mehrtens	Australia	Eden Park, Auckland	24/07/1999
7	Daniel Carter	Australia	Eden Park, Auckland	21/07/2007
7	Daniel Carter	South Africa	Westpac Stadium, Wellington	22/07/2006
7	Andrew Mehrtens	South Africa	Minolta Loftus, Pretoria	07/08/1999
7	Grant Fox	Western Samoa	Eden Park, Auckland	31/07/1993

Most drop goals by a player in a match: New Zealand

No.	Player	Versus	Venue	Date
2	Andrew Mehrtens	Australia	Eden Park, Auckland	22/07/1995
2	Frano Botica	France	Lancaster Park, Christchurch	28/06/1986
2	Doug Bruce	Ireland	Lansdowne Road, Dublin	04/11/1978

Most points in a match by New Zealand

No.	Result	Points				Versus	Venue	Date
		T	C	PG	DG			
145	145–17	21	20	-	-	Japan	Free State Stadium, Bloemfontein	04/06/1995
108	108–13	16	14	-	-	Portugal	Stade Gerland, Lyon	15/09/2007
102	102–0	15	12	1	-	Tonga	North Harbour Stadium, Albany	16/06/2000
101	101–14	15	13	-	-	Samoa	Yarrow Stadium, New Plymouth	03/09/2008
101	101–3	14	11	3	-	Italy	McAlpine Stadium, Huddersfield	14/10/1999

Most consecutive test wins by New Zealand

No.	Period	Details
17	18/09/1965–14/06/1969	South Africa (H), British Isles (H), British Isles (H), British Isles (H), British Isles (H), Australia (H), England (A), Wales (A), France (A), Scotland (A), Australia (A), Australia (A), France (H), France (H), France (H), Wales (H), Wales (H)
15	13/08/2005–26/08/2006	Australia (A), South Africa (H), Australia (H), Wales (A), Ireland (A), England (A), Scotland (A), Ireland (H), Ireland (H), Argentina (A), Australia (H), South Africa (H), Australia (A), Australia (H), South Africa (A)
12	30/07/1988–04/08/1990	Australia (A), France (H), France (H), Argentina (H), Argentina (H), Australia (H), Wales (A), Ireland (A), Scotland (H), Scotland (H), Australia (H), Australia (H)

Milestones

Longest test career	Colin Meads	25/05/1957–14/08/1971 (14 years, 2 months & 21 days)
Youngest test player	Jonah Lomu	19 years & 45 days on 26/06/1994 vs France in Christchurch
Oldest test player	Ned Hughes	40 years & 123 days on 27/08/1921 vs South Africa in Auckland

Top left: All Black Swin Hadley secures lineout possession against the Springboks during the first test of the 1928 series in Durban. South Africa went on to win by 17-0, a record-winning margin which remains the All Blacks heaviest ever loss to South Africa. *Photo*: New Zealand Rugby Museum

Above: Centre Pat Walsh dives to force the ball in the in-goal area to score a hotly contested try against England during the second test of the 1963 series in Christchurch. The score proved crucial as New Zealand won the match 9-6 and the series 2-0. *Photo*: New Zealand Rugby Museum

Left: The 1926 New Zealand Maoris staying warm on a bed of hay during halftime against France in Paris. The match was won 12-3 by the Maoris. *Photo*: FrédéricHumbert/www.flickr.com/photos/rugby_pioneers/creative commons license

Action from the third test between New Zealand and the British Lions in Auckland, 1930. Welsh Lions winger Jack Morley leads the chase (left) after the loose ball with Fred Lucas (right) the closest New Zealander to the ball. *Photo*: New Zealand Rugby Museum

Above left: Action from the third test of the 1964 Bledisloe Cup series in Wellington. Scrumhalf Des Connor is seen passing as captain and flank John Graham (right) and lock Allan Stewart (left) look on. With the series already won by New Zealand, Australia recorded a famous 20-5 victory but lost the series 1-2.
Photo: New Zealand Rugby Museum

Above right: Flanker Kelvin Tremain scores a crucial try in the first test of the 1965 series against South Africa in the mud of Wellington. His score ensured New Zealand won the international by 6-3 and ultimately the test series by 3-1. *Photo*: New Zealand Rugby Museum

Flyhalf Earle Kirton crashes over in the corner for one of his two tries at Twickenham, against England in 1967, won comfortably by the All Blacks, 23-11. Winger Bill Birtwhistle is in support. *Photo*: New Zealand Rugby Museum

Centre: Flank and captain Graham Mourie looks to pass the ball during the first test of the 1982 Bledisloe Cup series in Christchurch. Moving in to tackle him is Wallaby centre Glen Ella. New Zealand won the match 23-16 and the series 2-1.
Photo: New Zealand Rugby Museum

Above: Winger Bert Greenside leads the haka in the fourth and deciding match of the 1928 series in Cape Town. New Zealand went on to win this infamous 'Umbrella Test' to draw the series 2-2. *Photo*: New Zealand Rugby Museum

Above: Dynamic flanker Ian Kirkpatrick busts through a Lions tackle during the second test of the 1971 series in Christchurch. He scored a brilliant individual try in the match to ensure New Zealand won the match by 22-12.
Photo: New Zealand Rugby Museum

Below: Scrumhalf Ginger Nicholls makes a break from a scrum during the first-ever test match between New Zealand and South Africa on 13 August 1921 in Dunedin. Springbok winger Attie van Heerden (3) moves up in defence.
Photo: New Zealand Rugby Museum

Winger George Hart meets the Governor-General of New Zealand, Lord Bledisloe, prior to the opening match of the 1935/36 All Black tour to the United Kingdom. It was Lord Bledisloe who donated the famous Bledisloe Cup to the transTasman clash between Australia and New Zealand and which has been competed for since 1931.
Photo: New Zealand Rugby Museum

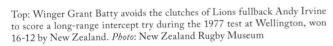

Top: Winger Grant Batty avoids the clutches of Lions fullback Andy Irvine to score a long-range intercept try during the 1977 test at Wellington, won 16-12 by New Zealand. *Photo*: New Zealand Rugby Museum

Above: Colin Meads raking the ball during the third test of the 1964 Bledisloe Cup series in Wellington. *Photo*: New Zealand Rugby Museum

Right: Eighthman Laurie Knight dives over for the series-winning try to the delight of the Eden Park fans in the last seconds of the fourth test of the 1977 series to win the match 10-9 and the series 3-1 for New Zealand. Unable to stop him is Lions captain Phil Bennett. *Photo*: New Zealand Rugby Museum

New Zealand flyhalf Thomas Wolfe kicks ahead on the run during the first test of the 1962 Bledisloe series in Wellington. Chasing his kick are teammates (from left) Dennis Young (hooker), Colin Meads (lock), Wilson Whineray (captain and prop), Ian Clarke (prop) and Kelvin Tremain (flank). The match was drawn 9-9 with New Zealand winning the series 2-0. *Photo*: New Zealand Rugby Museum

Flying winger Bryan Williams shrugs off the attentions of Irish centre Mike Gibson during the 1976 test at Wellington, won 11-3 by New Zealand. *Photo*: New Zealand Rugby Museum

Centre Stu Wilson rides the tackle of an unidentified Springbok defender to score in the first test of the 1981 series in Christchurch, won 14-9 by New Zealand. Bok lock Hennie Bekker looks on forlornly in the background. *Photo*: New Zealand Rugby Museum

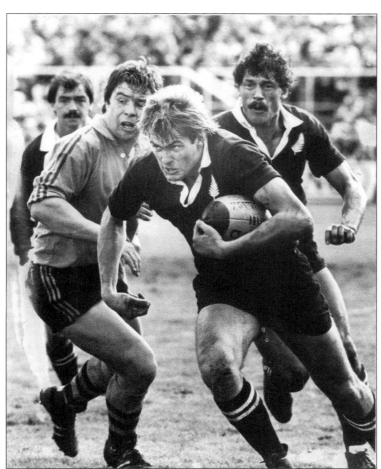

Left: Flanker Mark Shaw ranges forward during the third Bledisloe test of 1982 in Auckland, a match won 33-18 by New Zealand, with Shaw himself scoring a great try. Close up in support is eighthman Murray Mexted.
Photo: New Zealand Rugby Museum

Above: New Zealand winger Bernie Fraser scores a scintillating try in the first test of the 1982 Bledisloe Cup series, won 23-16 by New Zealand in Christchurch.
Photo: New Zealand Rugby Museum

Below: Fullback Laurie Mains dives over for a spectacular try during the third test of the infamous 1971 series against the British Lions in Wellington. His try would prove to be New Zealand's only points of the match as the Lions won by 13-3 and ultimately the series by 2-1. *Photo*: New Zealand Rugby Museum

Scotland

Scotland vs Argentina *see page 198*

Scotland vs Australia (Hopetoun Cup) *see page 237*

Scotland vs Canada

21 January 1995, Murrayfield, Edinburgh

Scotland	22	T: Cronin; C: Hastings; PG: Hastings (5)
Canada	6	PG: Rees (2)

15 June 2002, Thunderbird Stadium, Vancouver

Canada	26	T: Thiel, Murphy; C: Barker (2); PG: Barker (4)
Scotland	23	T: Paterson, Blair, Taylor; C: Laney; PG: Laney (2)

November 2008, Pittodrie Stadium, Aberdeen

Scotland	41	T: Walker (2), Cairns, Barclay, Strokosch, Lamont; C: Godman (3), Park; PG: Godman
Canada	0	

Scotland vs Côte d'Ivoire

26 May 1995, Olympia Park, Rustenburg (RWC, Pool D)

Scotland	89	T: Hastings (4), Logan (2), Walton (2), Burnell, Wright, Chalmers, Stanger, Shiel; C: Hastings (9); PG: Hastings (2)
Côte d'Ivoire	0	

Scotland vs England (Calcutta Cup) *see page 271*

Scotland vs Fiji

Scotland vs Fiji	
Played:	4
Won:	3
Lost:	1
Drawn:	0
For:	122
Against:	110

Average score:
30.5–27.5

Scotland percentages:

Won:	75%
Lost:	25%
Drawn:	0%

28 October 1989 Murrayfield, Edinburgh

Scotland	38	T: Stanger (2), K Milne, Gray, Tukalo, G Hastings; C: G Hastings (4); PG: G Hastings (2)
Fiji	17	T: Lovo, Rasari; PG: Serevi (2), Koroduadua

26 May 1998 National Stadium, Suva

Fiji	51	T: Lasagavibau (3), Tuilevu, Naevo, Vetayaki, Waqa; C: Serevi (4), Little; PG: Serevi, Little
Scotland	26	T: Bulloch, Gilmour; C: Lee (2); PG: Lee (4)

24 November 2002 Murrayfield, Edinburgh

Scotland	36	T: Craig (3), Laney, Grimes; C: Laney; PG: Laney (3)
Fiji	22	T: Niavu, Lingeri; PG: Narruhn (4)

1 November 2003 Aussie Stadium, Sydney (RWC, Pool B)

Scotland	22	T: Smith; C: Paterson; PG: Paterson (5)
Fiji	20	T: Caucaunibuca (2); C: Little (2); PG: Little (2)

Scotland vs France *see page 317*

Scotland vs Ireland (Centenary Quaich) *see page 342*

Scotland vs Italy *see page 379*

SCOTLAND

Scotland vs Japan

5 October 1991, Murrayfield, Edinburgh (RWC, Pool 2)
Scotland 47 T: S Hastings, Stanger, Chalmers, penalty try, White, Tukalo, G Hastings; C: G Hastings (5); PG: G Hastings (2), Chalmers
Japan 9 T: Hosokawa; C: Hosokawa; DG: Hosokawa

12 October 2003, Dairy Farmers Stadium, Townsville (RWC, Pool B)
Scotland 32 T: Paterson (2), Grimes, Taylor, Danielli; C: Paterson, Townsend; PG: Paterson
Japan 11 T: Onozawa; PG: Hirose (2)

13 November 2004, McDiarmid Park, Perth
Scotland 100 T: Paterson (3), Russell (2), Southwell (2), Petrie, Hogg, MacFadyen, Lamont, Parks, Morrison, Henderson, Blair; C: Paterson (11); PG: Paterson
Japan 8 T: Daiman; PG: Ikeda

Scotland vs New Zealand *see* page 393

Scotland vs Pacific Islanders

18 November 2006, Murrayfield, Edinburgh
Scotland 34 T: di Rollo, Callam, Brown, Henderson; C: Paterson (3), Parks; PG: Paterson; DG: di Rollo
Pacific Islanders 22 T: Ratuvou (2), Leo, Caucaunibuca; C: Pisi

Scotland vs Portugal

9 September 2007, Stade Geoffroy-Guichard, Saint-Etienne (RWC, Pool C)
Scotland 56 T: R Lamont (2), Lawson, Dewey, Southwell, Brown, Parks, Ford; C: Parks (4), Paterson (4)
Portugal 10 T: Carvalho; C: Pinto; PG: Pinto

Scotland vs Romania

Scotland vs Romania	
Played:	12
Won:	10
Lost:	2
Drawn:	0
For:	441
Against:	168
Average score:	
36.75–14	
Scotland percentages:	
Won:	83.33%
Lost:	16.67%
Drawn:	0%

26 September 1981, Murrayfield, Edinburgh
Scotland 12 PG: Irvine (4)
Romania 6 PG: Constantin (2)

12 May 1984, Dinamo Stadion, Bucharest
Romania 28 T: Dumitru, Parachiv, Radulescu; C: Alexandru (2); PG: Alexandru (3); DG: Alexandru
Scotland 22 T: Leslie, Dods; C: Dods; PG: Dods (3); DG: Robertson

29 March 1986, Dinamo Stadion, Bucharest
Scotland 33 T: Jeffrey, S Hastings, Deans; C: G Hastings (3); PG: G Hastings (5)
Romania 18 PG: Ignat (5); DG: Ignat

2 June 1987, Carisbrook, Dunedin (RWC, Pool 4)
Scotland 55 T: Tait (2), Jeffrey (3), G Hastings (2), Duncan, Tukalo; C: G Hastings (8); PG: G Hastings
Romania 28 T: Murariu (2), Toader; C: Alexandru, Ion; PG: Alexandru (4)

9 December 1989, Murrayfield, Edinburgh
Scotland 32 T: Stanger (3), White, Sole; C: G Hastings (3); PG: G Hastings (2)
Romania 0

31 August 1991, Dinamo Stadium, Bucharest
Romania 18 T: Ciorascu, Sasu C: Ion (2); PG: Ion (2)
Scotland 12 T: Tukalo; C: Dods; PG: Dods (2)

22 April 1995 Murrayfield, Edinburgh
Scotland 49 T: Stanger (2), Joiner, Shiel, G Hastings, Logan, Peters; C: G Hastings (4); PG: G Hatsings (2)
Romania 16 T: Racean; C: Nichitean; PG: Nichitean (3)

28 August 1999 Hampden Park, Glasgow
Scotland   60   T: Logan (2), Tait, Grimes, Smith, McLaren, M Leslie, penalty try; C: Logan (5), Hodge (2); PG: Logan (2)
Romania   19   T: Mitu; C: Mitu; PG: Mitu (4)

9 November 2002, Murrayfield, Edinburgh
Scotland   37   T: Grimes, Paterson, Leslie, Pountney, Moffat; C: Laney (3); PG: Laney (2)
Romania   10   T: Tofan; C: Tofan; PG: Tofan

5 June 2005, Dinamo Arena, Bucharest
Romania   19   T: Sauan; C: Dumbrava; PG: Dumbrava (4)
Scotland   39   T: Henderson, Brown, Paterson, E Murray, Lawson, Parks; C: Paterson (3); PG: Paterson

11 November 2006, Murrayfield, Edinburgh
Scotland   48   T: Southwell (2), Beattie, Dewey, Godman, Hall, Cusiter; C: Godman (5); PG: Godman
Romania   6   PG: Vlaicu (2)

18 September 2007, Murrayfield, Edinburgh (RWC, Pool C)
Scotland   42   T: Hogg (3), R Lamont (2), Paterson; C: Paterson (6)
Romania   0

Scotland vs Samoa

Scotland vs Samoa	
Played:	6
Won:	5
Lost:	0
Drawn:	1
For:	165
Against:	63
Average score:	
27.5–10.5	
Scotland percentages:	
Won:	83.33%
Lost:	0%
Drawn:	16.67%

19 October 1991, Murrayfield, Edinburgh (RWC, Q/F)
Scotland   28   T: Jeffrey (2), Stanger; C: G Hastings (2); PG: G Hastings (4)
Western Samoa   6   PG: Vaea (2)

18 November 1995, Murrayfield, Edinburgh
Scotland   15   PG: Dods (5)
Western Samoa   15   T: Kaleta, Leaupepe; C: Kellet; PG: Kellet

20 October 1999, Murrayfield, Edinburgh (RWC, Q/F PO)
Scotland   35   T: penalty try, Leslie, C Murray; C: Logan; PG: Logan (5); DG: Townsend
Samoa   20   T: Setiti, Lima; C: Leaege (2); PG: Leaege (2)

18 November 2000, Murrayfield, Edinburgh
Scotland   31   T: Petrie, Logan, Smith, Bulloch; C: Townsend; PG: Townsend (3)
Samoa   8   T: Patu; PG: Sanft

4 June 2004, Westpac Trust Stadium, Wellington
Scotland   38   T: Ross, Hinshelwood, Hogg, Webster, Blair; C: Paterson (2); PG: Paterson (3)
Samoa   3   PG: Warren

20 November 2005, Murrayfield, Edinburgh
Scotland   18   T: Hogg, di Rollo; C: Paterson; PG: Paterson (2)
Samoa   11   T: Al Tuilagi; PG: Warren (2)

Scotland vs South Africa

Scotland vs South Africa	
Played:	20
Won:	4
Lost:	16
Drawn:	0
For:	216
Against:	501
Average score:	
10.8–25.05	
Scotland percentages:	
Won:	20%
Lost:	80%
Drawn:	0%

Like the Scotland–Ireland fixture, South Africa and Scotland have been playing against each another for more than a century yet have only met 20 times. They first played in 1906, with Scotland victors in Glasgow but following this South Africa were not to lose again until 1965, in the interim posting a world-record margin of victory when they beat Scotland 44–0 in Edinburgh in a near perfect display of rugby. A narrow loss for South Africa in 1969 was to be the last game between the two for the next 25 years before they finally met in Edinburgh in 1994 when Scottish captain Gavin Hastings rashly stated that he wanted to 'shove the 44–0 defeat down the Springboks' throat!' It was not to be: South Africa won well and followed this with another victory in 1997 when they downed the Scots by a record margin of 68–10 in an exquisite display of running rugby, scoring ten tries in the process. Barring the unexpected Scottish win over a depleted Springbok squad in 2002, South Africa have continued to dominate the series, most recently by 14–10 in a closely fought, scrappy Edinburgh encounter in 2008.

SCOTLAND

17 November 1906, Hampden Park, Glasgow
Scotland	6	T: MacLeod, Purves
South Africa	0	

23 November 1912, Inverleith, Edinburgh
South Africa	16	T: McHardy, J Stegmann (2), W Morkel; C: P Morkel, D Morkel
Scotland	0	

16 January 1932, Murrayfield, Edinburgh
South Africa	6	T: Osler, Craven
Scotland	3	T: Lind

24 November 1951, Murrayfield, Edinburgh
South Africa	44	T: du Rand, van Schoor, Koch (2), Delport, van Wyk, Muller, Dinkelmann, Lategan; C: Geffin (7); DG: Brewis
Scotland	0	

30 April 1960, Boet Erasmus Stadium, Port Elizabeth
South Africa	18	T: van Zyl (2), van Jaarsveldt, Gericke; C: Gerber (3)
Scotland	10	T: Bruce, Smith; C: Smith (2)

21 January 1961, Murrayfield, Edinburgh
South Africa	12	T: Hopwood, Claassen; PG: du Preez (2)
Scotland	5	T: Smith; C: Scotland

17 April 1965, Murrayfield, Edinburgh
Scotland	8	T: Shackleton; C: Wilson; DG: Chisholm
South Africa	5	T: Engelbrecht; C: Mans

6 December 1969, Murrayfield, Edinburgh
Scotland	6	T: I Smith; PG: I Smith
South Africa	3	PG: Visagie

19 November 1994, Murrayfield, Edinburgh
South Africa	34	T: Mulder, Williams, van der Westhuizen (2), Straeuli; C: Joubert (3); PG: Joubert
Scotland	10	T: Stanger; C: Hastings; PG: Hastings

6 December 1997, Murrayfield, Edinburgh
South Africa	68	T: Montgomery (2), Small (2), Snyman, Venter, Rossouw, Teichmann, Erasmus, Smith; C: Montgomery (8), de Beer
Scotland	10	T: Stark; C: Shepherd; PG: Shepherd

21 November 1998, Murrayfield, Edinburgh
South Africa	35	T: van der Westhuizen, Snyman, Skinstad, Terblanche, Rossouw; C: Montgomery (2); PG: Montgomery (2)
Scotland	10	T: Hodge; C: Hodge; PG: Hodge

3 October 1999, Murrayfield, Edinburgh (RWC, Pool A)
South Africa	46	T: van der Westhuizen, le Roux, Kayser, Fleck, B Venter, A Venter; C: de Beer (5); PG: de Beer (2)
Scotland	29	T: Tait, M Leslie; C: Logan (2); PG: Logan (4); DG: Townsend

16 November 2002, Murrayfield, Edinburgh
Scotland	21	T: Pountney, Walker; C: Laney; PG: Laney (3)
South Africa	6	PG: James (2)

7 June 2003, ABSA Stadium, Durban
South Africa	29	T: Terblanche, Halstead; C: Koen (2); PG: Koen (5)
Scotland	25	T: White, Paterson, Craig; C: Paterson (2); PG: Paterson (2)

14 June 2003, Ellis Park, Johannesburg
South Africa	28	T: Terblanche; C: Koen; PG: Koen (6); DG: Koen
Scotland	19	T: Craig; C: Paterson; PG: Paterson (4)

29 November 2004, Murrayfield, Edinburgh
South Africa	45	T: Habana (2), Tyibilika, Fourie, van der Westhuyzen; C: Montgomery (4); PG: Montgomery; DG: van der Westhuyzen (3)
Scotland	10	T: penalty try; C: Paterson; PG: Paterson

10 June 2006, The ABSA Stadium, Durban

South Africa	36	T: Burger, Paulse, Snyman, Montgomery; C: Montgomery (2); PG: Montgomery (4)
Scotland	16	T: Webster; C: Paterson; PG: Paterson (3)

17 June 2006, EPRFU Stadium, Port Elizabeth

South Africa	29	T: du Preez; PG: Montgomery (7), van der Westhuyzen
Scotland	15	T: Webster, MacFadyen; C: Paterson; PG: Paterson

25 August 2007, Murrayfield, Edinburgh

South Africa	27	T: du Preez, Fourie, Habana; C: Montgomery (3); PG: Montgomery (2)
Scotland	3	PG: Paterson

15 November 2008, Murrayfield, Edinburgh

South Africa	14	T: Fourie; PG: Pienaar (3)
Scotland	10	T: Hines; C: Godman; PG: Godman

Scotland vs Spain

16 October 1999, Murrayfield, Edinburgh (RWC, Pool A)

Scotland	48	T: Mather (2), penalty try, Hodge, Murray, McLaren, Longstaff; C: Hodge (5); PG: Hodge
Spain	0	

Scotland vs Tonga

30 May 1995, Loftus Versfeld, Pretoria (RWC, Pool D)

Scotland	41	T: G Hastings, Peters, S Hastings; C: G Hastings; PG: G Hastings (8)
Tonga	5	T: Fenukitau

10 November 2001, Murrayfield, Edinburgh

Scotland	43	T: McLaren, Metcalfe, Reid, Simpson; C: Ross (4); PG: Ross (5)
Tonga	20	T: Vaki; PG: Tuipulotu (4), Taumalolo

Scotland vs United States of America

4 November 2000, Murrayfield, Edinburgh

Scotland	53	T: Pountney, Paterson, Townsend, Leslie (2); C: Townsend (5); PG: Townsend (6)
USA	6	PG: Wells (2)

22 June 2002, Boxer Stadium, San Francisco

Scotland	65	T: Paterson (2), Hodge (2), Kerr, Craig, Laney, Hines, White, Henderson; C: Laney (6); PG: Laney
USA	23	T: Timoteo, Keyter; C: Wilfley (2); PG: Wilfley (3)

20 October 2003, Suncorp Stadium, Brisbane (RWC, Pool B)

Scotland	39	T: Danielli (2), Kerr, Townsend, Paterson; C: Paterson (4); PG: Paterson (2)
USA	15	PG: Hercus (5)

Scotland vs Uruguay

8 October 1999, Murrayfield, Edinburgh (RWC, Pool A)

Scotland	43	T: Leslie, Armstrong, Simpson, Metcalfe, Townsend, Russell; C: Logan (5); PG: Logan
Uruguay	12	PG: Aguirre (3), Sciarra

SCOTLAND

Scotland vs Wales	
Played:	114
Won:	48
Lost:	63
Drawn:	3
For:	1,169
Against:	1,402

Average score:
10.25–12.3

Scotland percentages:

Won:	42.11%
Lost:	55.26%
Drawn:	2.63%

Scotland vs Wales

The last of the home-union fixtures to get going was Scotland vs Wales. In their first game on 8 January 1883 Scotland won 9 (3G)–3 (1G) at Raeburn Place in Edinburgh. Wales struggled during the early years and only started winning on a more regular basis ten years after the first encounter. By 1900 however, and until World War I, Wales were virtually invincible as they racked up record victories over Scotland on their march to securing their trio of Grand Slams. Along with England, Scotland emerged after World War I as one the dominant European nations, reflected in their results against Wales who failed to win again until 1928. Following this, matches became tighter with lower scorelines, with the inclement British weather in February tending to dictate the quality and style of play. In the mid-1960s Welsh rugby was on the wax as they dominated the Scots for the next two decades. However, Scotland proved to be a bogey side for the Welsh, especially in Edinburgh where, more than once, they rattled the Welsh. So great was the anticipation of these Edinburgh games that the 1975 clash attracted a world-record rugby attendance of an estimated 104,000 – all within the confines of the old Murrayfield stadium. Aside from these rare Scottish wins however, Wales regularly won by large margins. But by the 1980s Scottish rugby was on the ascendancy which the Scots proved in spectacular fashion by destroying Wales in a record 34–18 (five tries to one) walloping in Cardiff – an unheard-of feat in those days at fortress Cardiff. Through the 1980s and until now neither side has dominated, with typically the home side winning. In 1996 Scotland avoided a draw in Cardiff, following a missed Arwel Thomas conversion. Remarkably, in a series that has produced 114 matches, there have been only three draws: none more memorable than the 28–28 thriller that took place in 2001. In 2005 Wales produced some of the most scintillating rugby the Six Nations has witnessed when they ran rings around Scotland at Murrayfield to win by a record 46–22, scoring six magnificent tries in the process.

8 January 1883, Raeburn Place, Edinburgh
Scotland 9 (3G)
Wales 3 (1G)

T: MacFarlan (2), Donn Wauchope; C: MacLagan (3)
T: Judson; C: Lewis

12 January 1884, Rodney Parade, Newport
Scotland 4 (1T 1DG)
Wales 0

T: Ainslie; DG: Asher

10 January 1885, Hamilton Crescent, Glasgow
Scotland 0
Wales 0

9 January 1886, Cardiff Arms Park, Cardiff
Scotland 7 (2G 1T)
Wales 0

T: Clay, Todd, Donn Wauchope; C: MacLeod (2)

26 February 1887, Raeburn Place, Edinburgh
Scotland 20 (4G 8T)

Wales 0

T: Lindsay (5), Reid, Don Wauchope, Orr, Morton, MacMillan, McEwan, MacLagan; C: Berry (2), Woodrow (2)

4 February 1888, Rodney Parade, Newport
Wales 1 (1T)
Scotland 0

T: Pryce-Jenkins

2 February 1889, Raeburn Place, Edinburgh
Scotland 2 (2T)
Wales 0

T: Orr, Ker

1 February 1890, Cardiff Arms Park, Cardiff
Scotland 8 (1G 2T)
Wales 2 (1T)

T: Anderson, Boswell, MacLagan; C: McEwan
T: Gould

7 February 1891, Raeburn Place, Edinburgh
Scotland 15 T: C Orr, J Orr, Goodhue, Clauss (2), Leggatt, Boswell; C: McEwan; DG: W Nielson, Stevenson
Wales 0

6 February 1892, St Helen's, Swansea
Scotland 8 T: Boswell, Campbell; C: Boswell
Wales 2 T: Hannan

4 February 1893, Raeburn Place, Edinburgh
Wales 9 T: Biggs, Gould, McCutcheon; PG: Bancroft
Scotland 0

3 February 1894, Rodney Parade, Newport
Wales 7 T: Fitzgerald; DG: Fitzgerald
Scotland 0

26 January 1895, Raeburn Place, Edinburgh
Scotland 5 T: Gowans; C: H Smith
Wales 4 GM: Bancroft

25 January 1896, Cardiff Arms Park, Cardiff
Wales 6 T: Bowen, Gould
Scotland 0

4 March 1899, Inverleith, Edinburgh
Scotland 21 T: Gedge, Smith, Monypenny; DG: Lamond, Gedge; GM: Thomson
Wales 10 T: L Lloyd, Llewellyn; C: Bancroft (2)

27 January 1900, St Helen's, Swansea
Wales 12 T: Llewellyn (2), Nicholls, Williams
Scotland 3 T: Dykes

9 February 1901, Inverleith, Edinburgh
Scotland 18 T: Gillespie (2), Turnbull, Flett; C: Gillespie (2), Flett
Wales 8 T: L Lloyd, Boots; C: Bancroft

1 February 1902, Cardiff Arms Park, Cardiff
Wales 14 T: Llewellyn (2), Gabe (2); C: Strand-Jones
Scotland 5 T: Welsh; C: Gillespie

7 February 1903, Inverleith, Edinburgh
Scotland 6 T: Kyle; PG: Timms
Wales 0

6 February 1904, St Helen's, Swansea
Wales 21 T: Gabe, Jones, Morgan, Brice; C: Winfield (3); PG: Winfield
Scotland 3 T: Orr

4 February 1905, Inverleith, Edinburgh
Wales 6 T: Llewellyn (2)
Scotland 3 T: Little

3 February 1906, Cardiff Arms Park, Cardiff
Wales 9 T: Hodges, C Pritchard, Maddocks
Scotland 3 PG: MacLeod

2 February 1907, Inverleith, Edinburgh
Scotland 6 T: Purves, Monteith
Wales 3 PG: Winfield

1 February 1908, St Helen's, Swansea
Wales 6 T: Trew, Williams
Scotland 5 T: Purves; C: Geddes

6 February 1909, Inverleith, Edinburgh
Wales 5 T: Trew; C: Bancroft
Scotland 3 PG: Cunningham

SCOTLAND

5 February 1910, Cardiff Arms Park, Cardiff
Wales 14   T: Pugsley, Spiller, Baker, I Morgan; C: Bancroft
Scotland 0

4 February 1911, Inverleith, Edinburgh
Wales 32   T: Gibbs (3), Spiller (2), Williams (2), R Thomas; C: Dyke (2); DG: Spiller
Scotland 10   T: Turner, Scott; DG: Munro

3 February 1912, St Helen's, Swansea
Wales 21   T: Hirst, Morgan, Plummer; C: Bancroft (2); DG: Trew, Birt
Scotland 6   T: Will, Milroy

1 February 1913, Inverleith, Edinburgh
Wales 8   T: C Lewis, T Jones; C: C Lewis
Scotland 0

7 February 1914, Cardiff Arms Park, Cardiff
Wales 24   T: I Davies, Wetter, Hirst; C: Bancroft (2); DG: Hirst, Lewis; PG: Bancroft
Scotland 5   T: Stewart; C: Laing

7 February 1920, Inverleith, Edinburgh
Scotland 9   T: Sloan; PG: Kennedy (2)
Wales 5   T: Jenkins; C: Jenkins

5 February 1921, St Helen's, Swansea
Scotland 14   T: Thomson, Sloan, Buchanan; C: Maxwell; PG: Maxwell
Wales 8   DG: Jenkins (2)

4 February 1922, Inverleith, Edinburgh
Scotland 9   T: Browning (2); PG: Browning
Wales 9   T: Bowen; C: Samuel; DG: I Evans

3 February 1923, Cardiff Arms Park, Cardiff
Scotland 11   T: Liddell, Stuart, Gracie; C: Drysdale
Wales 8   T: Lewis; C: A Jenkins; PG: A Jenkins

2 February 1924, Inverleith, Edinburgh
Scotland 35   T: Smith (3), Bryce, Bertram, Wallace, Waddell, Macpherson; C: Drysdale (4); PG: Drysdale
Wales 10   T: Griffiths, I Jones; C: Male (2)

7 February 1925, St Helen's, Swansea
Scotland 24   T: Smith (4), Wallace (2); C: Drysdale (3)
Wales 14   T: Hopkins, Jones, Cornish; C: Parker; PG: Parker

6 February 1926, Murrayfield, Edinburgh
Scotland 8   T: Waddell; C: Drysdale; PG: Gillies
Wales 5   T: Herrera; C: Everson

5 February 1927, Cardiff Arms Park, Cardiff
Scotland 5   T: Kerr; C: Gillies
Wales 0

4 February 1928, Murrayfield, Edinburgh
Wales 13   T: A Jenkins, D John, Roberts; C: Male (2)
Scotland 0

2 February 1929, St Helen's, Swansea
Wales 14   T: Roberts (2), Morgan, Peacock; C: I Jones
Scotland 7   DG: Dykes; PG: Brown

1 February 1930, Murrayfield, Edinburgh
Scotland 12   T: Simmers (2); C: Waters; DG: Waddell
Wales 9   T: G Jones; C: I Jones; DG: G Jones

7 February 1931, Cardiff Arms Park, Cardiff
Wales 13   T: Morley, Thomas, Boon; C: Bassett (2)
Scotland 8   T: Crichton-Miller (2); C: Allan

6 February 1932, Murrayfield, Edinburgh
Wales	6	T: Boon; PG: Bassett
Scotland	0	

4 February 1933, St Helen's, Swansea
Scotland	11	T: Smith, Jackson; C: Fyfe; PG: Fyfe
Wales	3	T: Arthur

3 February 1934, Murrayfield, Edinburgh
Wales	13	T: Cowey (2), Rees; C: Jenkins (2)
Scotland	6	T: Logan; PG: Ritchie

2 February 1935, Cardiff Arms Park, Cardiff
Wales	10	T: Jones, Wooller; DG: Jenkins
Scotland	6	T: Thom, Shaw

1 February 1936, Murrayfield, Edinburgh
Wales	13	T: Wooller, Davey, Jones; C: Jenkins (2)
Scotland	3	T: Murray

6 February 1937, St Helen's, Swansea
Scotland	13	T: W Shaw, Dick (2); C: D Shaw (2)
Wales	6	T: Wooller (2)

5 February 1938, Murrayfield, Edinburgh
Scotland	8	T: Crawford; C: Crawford; PG: Crawford
Wales	6	T: McCarley (2)

4 February 1939, Cardiff Arms Park, Cardiff
Wales	11	T: M Davies, Travers; C: Wooller; PG: Wooller
Scotland	3	PG: Crawford

1 February 1947, Murrayfield, Edinburgh
Wales	22	T: K Jones (2), B Williams, Cleaver, L Williams; C: Tamplin (2); PG: Tamplin
Scotland	8	T: Elliot; C: Geddes; PG: Geddes

7 February 1948, Cardiff Arms Park, Cardiff
Wales	14	T: B Williams, Matthews, K Jones; C: Tamplin; PG: Tamplin
Scotland	0	

5 February 1949, Murrayfield, Edinburgh
Scotland	6	T: Gloag, Smith
Wales	5	T: Williams; C: Trott

4 February 1950, St Helen's, Swansea
Wales	12	T: Thomas, K Jones; DG: Cleaver; PG: L Jones
Scotland	0	

3 February 1951, Murrayfield, Edinburgh
Scotland	19	T: Gordon (2), Dawson; C: Inglis, Thomson; DG: Kinninmonth; PG: Thomson
Wales	0	

2 February 1952, Cardiff Arms Park, Cardiff
Wales	11	T: K Jones; C: M Thomas; PG: M Thomas (2)
Scotland	0	

7 February 1953, Murrayfield, Edinburgh
Wales	12	T: B Williams (2), Jones; PG: Davies
Scotland	0	

10 April 1954, St Helen's, Swansea
Wales	15	T: Rhys Williams, Meredith, Morgan, Ray Williams; PG: Evans
Scotland	3	T: Henderson

5 February 1955, Murrayfield, Edinburgh
Scotland	14	T: Smith, Nichol; C: Elgie; DG: Docherty; PG: Elgie
Wales	8	T: Brewer (2); C: Stephens

Did you know: The farthest successful penalty ever kicked was by Welsh fullback Paul Thorburn who kicked a goal a staggering 64.22 metres against Scotland in 1988.

SCOTLAND

4 February 1956, Cardiff Arms Park, Cardiff
Wales	9	T: H Morgan, C Morgan, Davies
Scotland	3	PG: Cameron

2 February 1957, Murrayfield, Edinburgh
Scotland	9	T: Smith; DG: Dorward; PG: Scotland
Wales	6	T: R Davies; PG: T Davies

1 February 1958, Cardiff Arms Park, Cardiff
Wales	8	T: Wells, Collins; C: T Davies
Scotland	3	PG: A Smith

7 February 1959, Murrayfield, Edinburgh
Scotland	6	T: Bruce; PG: Scotland
Wales	5	T: Price; C: T Davies

6 February 1960, Cardiff Arms Park, Cardiff
Wales	8	T: Bebb; C: Morgan; PG: Morgan
Scotland	0	

11 February 1961, Murrayfield, Edinburgh
Scotland	3	T: A Smith
Wales	0	

3 February 1962, Cardiff Arms Park, Cardiff
Scotland	8	T: Glasgow, ten Bos; C: Scotland
Wales	3	PG: Rees

2 February 1963, Murrayfield, Edinburgh
Wales	6	DG: Rowlands; PG: Hodgson
Scotland	0	

1 February 1964, Cardiff Arms Park, Cardiff
Wales	11	T: Bradshaw, Thomas; C: Bradshaw; PG: Bradshaw
Scotland	3	T: Laughland

6 February 1965, Murrayfield, Edinburgh
Wales	14	T: S Watkins, Gale; C: T Price; PG: T Price (2)
Scotland	12	DG: Simmers (2); PG: Simmers (2)

5 February 1966, Cardiff Arms Park, Cardiff
Wales	8	T: K Jones (2); C: Bradshaw
Scotland	3	PG: Wilson

4 February 1967, Murrayfield, Edinburgh
Scotland	11	T: Hinshelwood, Telfer; C: Wilson; DG: Chisholm
Wales	5	T: Watkins; C: T Price

3 February 1968, Cardiff Arms Park, Cardiff
Wales	5	T: K Jones; C: Jarrett
Scotland	0	

1 February 1969, Murrayfield, Edinburgh
Wales	17	T: John, Edwards, M Richards; C: Jarrett; PG: Jarrett (2)
Scotland	3	PG: Blaikie

7 February 1970, National Stadium, Cardiff
Wales	18	T: Daniel, Llewelyn, Dawes, Morris; C: Edwards (2), Daniel
Scotland	9	T: Robertson; DG: Robertson; PG: Lauder

6 February 1971, Murrayfield, Edinburgh
Wales	19	T: Taylor, Edwards, John, T Davies; C: John, Taylor; PG: John
Scotland	18	T: Carmichael, Rea; PG: P Brown (4)

5 February 1972, National Stadium, Cardiff
Wales	35	T: Edwards (2), Bergiers, T Davies, Taylor; C: John (3); PG: John (3)
Scotland	12	T: Clark; C: P Brown; PG: Renwick, P Brown

3 February 1973, Murrayfield, Edinburgh
Scotland 10   T: Telfer, Steele; C: Morgan
Wales 9   PG: Bennett (2), Taylor

19 January 1974, National Stadium, Cardiff
Wales 6   T: Cobner; C: Bennett
Scotland 0

1 March 1975, Murrayfield, Edinburgh
Scotland 12   DG: McGeechan; PG: Morgan (3)
Wales 10   T: T Evans; PG: Fenwick (2)

7 February 1976, National Stadium, Cardiff
Wales 28   T: JJ Williams, Edwards, T Evans; C: Bennett (2); DG: Fenwick; PG: Bennett (3)
Scotland 6   T: Irvine; C: Morgan

19 March 1977, Murrayfield, Edinburgh
Wales 18   T: JJ Williams, Bennett; C: Bennett (2); PG: Bennett (2)
Scotland 9   T: Irvine; C: Irvine; DG: McGeechan

18 February 1978, National Stadium, Cardiff
Wales 22   T: Edwards, Gravell, Fenwick, Quinnell; DG: Bennett; PG: Bennett
Scotland 14   T: Renwick, Tomes; PG: Morgan (2)

20 January 1979, Murrayfield, Edinburgh
Wales 19   T: E Rees, Holmes; C: Fenwick; PG: Fenwick (3)
Scotland 13   T: Irvine; PG: Irvine (3)

1 March 1980, National Stadium, Cardiff
Wales 17   T: Holmes, Keen, D Richards; C: Blyth; PG: Fenwick
Scotland 6   T: Renwick; C: Irvine

7 February 1981, Murrayfield, Edinburgh
Scotland 15   T: Tomes, penalty try; C: Renwick (2); PG: Renwick
Wales 6   DG: Fenwick (2)

20 March 1982, National Stadium, Cardiff
Scotland 34   T: Calder, Renwick, Pollock, White, Johnstone; C: Irvine (4); DG: Renwick, Rutherford
Wales 18   T: Butler; C: G Evans; PG: G Evans (4)

19 February 1983, Murrayfield, Edinburgh
Wales 19   T: S Jones, E Rees; C: Wyatt; PG: Wyatt (3)
Scotland 15   T: Renwick; C: Dods; PG: Dods (3)

21 January 1984, National Stadium, Cardiff
Scotland 15   T: Paxton, Aitken; C: Dods (2); PG: Dods
Wales 9   T: Titley; C: H Davies; PG: H Davies

2 March 1985, Murrayfield, Edinburgh
Wales 25   T: Pickering (2); C: Wyatt; PG: Wyatt (4); DG: W Davies
Scotland 21   T: Paxton (2); C: Dods (2); PG: Dods; DG: Rutherford (2)

1 February 1986, National Stadium, Cardiff
Wales 22   T: Hadley; PG: Thorburn (5); DG: J Davies
Scotland 15   T: Duncan, Jeffrey, G Hastings; PG: G Hastings

21 March 1987, Murrayfield, Edinburgh
Scotland 21   T: Beattie, Jeffrey; C: G Hastings (2); PG: G Hastings (2); DG: Rutherford
Wales 15   T: M Jones; C: Wyatt; PG: Wyatt (2); DG: J Davies

20 February 1988, National Stadium, Cardiff
Wales 25   T: J Davies, I Evans, Watkins; C: Thorburn (2); PG: Thorburn; DG: J Davies (2)
Scotland 20   T: F Calder, Duncan; PG: G Hastings (4)

21 January 1989, Murrayfield, Edinburgh
Scotland 23   T: White, Chalmers, Armstrong; C: Dods; PG: Dods (2); DG: Chalmers
Wales 7   T: Hall; PG: Bowen

SCOTLAND

3 March 1990, National Stadium, Cardiff
Scotland 13   T: Cronin; PG: Chalmers (3)
Wales 9   T: Emyr; C: Thorburn; PG: Thorburn

2 February 1991, Murrayfield, Edinburgh
Scotland 32   T: Chalmers, White (2), Armstrong; C: Chalmers, G Hastings; PG: Chalmers, G Hastings (2); DG: Chalmers
Wales 12   T: Ford; C: Thorburn; PG: Thorburn (2)

21 March 1992, National Stadium, Cardiff
Wales 15   T: Webster; C: Jenkins; PG: N Jenkins (3)
Scotland 12   PG: G Hastings, Chalmers (2); DG: Chalmers

20 February 1993, Murrayfield, Edinburgh
Scotland 20   T: Turnbull; PG: G Hastings (5)
Wales 0

15 January 1994, National Stadium, Cardiff
Wales 29   T: Rayer (2), I Evans; C: N Jenkins; PG: N Jenkins (4)
Scotland 6   PG: Hastings (2)

4 March 1995, Murrayfield, Edinburgh
Scotland 26   T: Peters, Hilton; C: G Hastings (2); PG: G Hastings (4)
Wales 13   T: Jones; C: Jenkins; PG: Jenkins (2)

17 February 1996, National Stadium, Cardiff
Scotland 16   T: Townsend; C: Dods; PG: Dods (3)
Wales 14   T: Proctor; PG: A Thomas (3)

18 January 1997, Murrayfield, Edinburgh
Wales 34   T: S Quinnell, I Evans, Jenkins, Thomas; C: Jenkins (4); PG: Jenkins (2)
Scotland 19   T: Hastings; C: Shepherd; PG: Shepherd (3); DG: Chalmers

7 March 1998, Wembley, London
Wales 19   T: Proctor; C: A Thomas; PG: A Thomas (3), Jenkins
Scotland 13   T: Townsend, Cronin; PG: Chalmers

6 February 1999, Murrayfield, Edinburgh
Scotland 33   T: Townsend, J Leslie, Murray, Tait; C: Logan (2); PG: Hodge, Logan (2)
Wales 20   T: James, Gibbs; C: Jenkins (2); PG: Jenkins (2)

18 March 2000, Millennium Stadium, Cardiff
Wales 26   T: Williams (2); C: Jones (2); PG: Jones (4)
Scotland 18   T: M Leslie, Townsend; C: Hodge; PG: Hodge (2)

17 February 2001, Murrayfield, Edinburgh
Scotland 28   T: Patterson, McLaren, Smith; C: Logan, Hodge; PG: Logan (3)
Wales 28   T: Taylor; C: Jenkins; PG: Jenkins (4); DG: Jenkins (3)

6 April 2002, Millennium Stadium, Cardiff
Scotland 27   T: Bulloch (2); C: Laney; PG: Laney (4), Hodge
Wales 22   T: R Williams; C: S Jones; PG: S Jones (5)

8 March 2003, Murrayfield, Edinburgh
Scotland 30   T: Douglas, Taylor, Paterson; C: Paterson (3); PG: Paterson (3)
Wales 22   T: Cooper, Taylor, R Williams; C: Jones, Harris; PG: Jones

30 August 2003, Millennium Stadium, Cardiff
Wales 23   T: Owen; PG: Harris (5); DG: Sweeney
Scotland 9   PG: Laney (3)

14 February 2004, Millennium Stadium, Cardiff
Wales 23   T: R Williams (2), A Jones; C: S Jones; PG: S Jones (2)
Scotland 10   T: Taylor; C: Paterson; DG: Paterson

13 March 2005, Murrayfield, Edinburgh
Wales 46   T: R Williams (2), Morgan (2), R Jones, S Williams; C: S Jones (5); PG: S Jones (2)
Scotland 22   T: Craig, R Lamont, Paterson; C: Paterson (2); PG: Paterson

12 February 2006, Millennium Stadium, Cardiff
Wales   28   T: G Thomas (2), Sidoli, penalty try; C: S Jones (4)
Scotland   18   T: Southwell, Paterson; C: Paterson; PG: Paterson (2)

10 February 2007, Murrayfield, Edinburgh
Scotland   21   PG Paterson (7)
Wales   9   PG: S Jones (3)

9 February 2008, Millennium Stadium, Cardiff
Wales   30   T: S Williams (2), Hook; C: Hook (2), S Jones; PG: S Jones (2), Hook
Scotland   15   PG: Paterson (5)

8 February 2009, Murrayfield, Edinburgh
Wales   26   T: Halfpenney, Wyn Jones, Shanklin, S Williams; PG: S Jones (2)
Scotland   13   T: Evans; C: Paterson; PG: Paterson (2)

Scotland vs World XV

31 March 1973, Murrayfield, Edinburgh
Scotland   27   T: Gill (2), Shedden, Telfer, McHarg; C: Irvine (2); PG: Irvine
World XV   16   T: McLean, Hales, Burnet; C: McLean (2)

Scotland vs Zimbabwe

30 May 1987, Athletic Park, Wellington (RWC, Pool 4)
Scotland   60   T: Tait (2), Duncan (2), Oliver, G Hastings, Jeffrey, Paxton (2), Tukalo (2); C: G Hastings (8)
Zimbabwe   21   T: D Buitendag; C: Grobler; PG: Grobler (5)

9 October 1991, Murrayfield, Edinburgh (RWC, Pool 2)
Scotland   51   T: Tukalo (3), Turnbull, Stanger, S Hastings, Weir, White; C: Dods (5); PG: Dods (2); DG: Wyllie
Zimbabwe   12   T: Garvey (2); C: Currin (2)

Scotland: summaries and records

Home matches	
Played	305
Won	162
Lost	125
Drawn	18
Points for	4,339
Points against	3,878
Average score	14.23/12.71
Win %	53.11
Lose %	40.98
Draw %	5.9

Away matches	
Played	260
Won	74
Lost	174
Drawn	12
Points for	2,640
Points against	3,944
Average score	10.15/15.17
Win %	28.46
Lose %	66.92
Draw %	4.62

Neutral venues	
Played	17
Won	10
Lost	6
Drawn	1
Points for	560
Points against	321
Average score	32.94/18.88
Win %	58.82
Lose %	35.29
Draw %	5.88

Total matches	
Played	582
Won	246
Lost	305
Drawn	31
Points for	7,539
Points against	8,143
Average score	12.95/13.99
Win %	42.27
Lose %	52.41
Draw %	5.33

Most capped players: Scotland							
Player	Caps	Career	Points				
			T	C	PG	DG	Total
Chris Paterson	95	16/10/1999–21/03/2009	22	86	150	2	738
Scott Murray	87	22/11/1997–23/09/2007	3	-	-	-	15
Gregor Townsend	82	06/03/1993–08/11/2003	17	8	14	7	164
Gordon Bulloch	75	06/12/1997–19/03/2005	4	-	-	-	20
Jason White	74	02/04/2000–21/03/2009	4	-	-	-	20

SCOTLAND

Most tests as captain: Scotland

No.	Player	Period
25	David Sole	1989–1992
21	Bryan Redpath	1998–2003
20	Gavin Hastings	1993–1995
19	Ian McLauchlan	1973–1979
19	Jason White	2005–2008

Most points by a player in a career: Scotland

No.	Player	Tests	Career	Points			
				T	C	PG	DG
738	Chris Paterson	95	16/10/1999–21/03/2009	22	86	150	2
667	Gavin Hastings	61	17/01/1986–11/06/1995	17	86	140	-
273	Andy Irvine	51	16/12/1972–11/07/1982	10	25	61	-
220	Kenny Logan	70	20/06/1992–08/11/2003	13	34	29	-
210	Peter Dods	23	15/01/1983–30/10/1991	2	26	50	-

Most tries by a player in a career: Scotland

No.	Player	Tests	Career
24	Tony Stanger	52	28/10/1989–22/03/1998
24	Ian Smith	32	02/02/1924–01/04/1933
22	Chris Paterson	95	16/10/1999–21/03/2009
17	Gregor Townsend	82	06/03/1993–08/11/2003
17	Alan Tait	27	23/05/1987–24/10/1999
17	Gavin Hastings	61	17/01/1986–11/06/1995

Most conversions by a player in a career: Scotland

No.	Player	Tests	Career
86	Chris Paterson	95	16/10/1999–21/03/2009
86	Gavin Hastings	61	17/01/1986–11/06/1995
34	Kenny Logan	70	20/06/1992–08/11/2003
26	Peter Dods	23	15/01/1983–30/10/1991
25	Andy Irvine	51	16/12/1972–11/07/1982

Most penalties by a player in a career: Scotland

No.	Player	Tests	Career
150	Chris Paterson	95	16/10/1999–21/03/2009
140	Gavin Hastings	61	17/01/1986–11/06/1995
61	Andy Irvine	51	16/12/1972–11/07/1982
50	Peter Dods	23	15/01/1983–30/10/1991
32	Craig Chalmers	60	21/01/1989–28/08/1999

Most drop goals by a player in a career: Scotland

No.	Player	Tests	Career
12	John Rutherford	42	20/01/1979–23/05/1987
9	Craig Chalmers	60	21/01/1989–21/08/1999
7	Gregor Townsend	82	06/03/1993–08/11/2003
7	Ian McGeechan	32	16/12/1972–17/03/1979
6	Doug Morgan	21	03/02/1973–04/03/1978

Most points by a player in a match: Scotland

No.	Player	Points				Versus	Venue	Date
		T	C	PG	DG			
44	Gavin Hastings	4	9	2	-	Côte d'Ivoire	Olympia Park, Rustenburg	26/05/1995
40	Chris Paterson	3	11	1	-	Japan	McDiarmid Park, Perth	13/11/2004
33	Gregor Townsend	1	5	6	-	United States	Murrayfield, Edinburgh	04/11/2000
31	Gavin Hastings	1	1	8	-	Tonga	Loftus Versfeld, Pretoria	30/05/1995
27	Gavin Hastings	2	8	1	-	Romania	Carisbrook, Dunedin	02/06/1987

Most tries by a player in a match: Scotland

No.	Player	Versus	Venue	Date
5	George Lindsay	Wales	Raeburn Place, Edinburgh	26/02/1887
4	Gavin Hastings	Côte d'Ivoire	Olympia Park, Rustenburg	26/05/1995
4	Ian Smith	Wales	St Helen's, Swansea	07/02/1925
4	Ian Smith	France	Inverleith, Edinburgh	24/01/1925
4	William Stewart	Ireland	Inverleith, Edinburgh	22/02/1913

Most conversions by a player in a match: Scotland

No.	Player	Versus	Venue	Date
11	Chris Paterson	Japan	McDiarmid Park, Perth	13/11/2004
9	Gavin Hastings	Côte d'Ivoire	Olympia Park, Rustenburg	26/05/1995
8	Gavin Hastings	Romania	Carisbrook, Dunedin	02/06/1987
8	Gavin Hastings	Zimbabwe	Athletic Park, Wellington	30/05/1987
6	Chris Paterson	Romania	Murrayfield, Edinburgh	18/09/2007
6	Brendan Laney	United States	Boxer Stadium, San Francisco	22/06/2002

Most penalties by a player in a match: Scotland

No	Player	Versus	Venue	Date
8	Gavin Hastings	Tonga	Loftus Versfeld, Pretoria	30/05/1995
7	Chris Paterson	Wales	Murrayfield, Edinburgh	10/02/2007
6	Chris Paterson	Italy	Stade Geoffroy-Guichard, Saint Etienne	29/09/2007
6	Chris Paterson	Ireland	Murrayfield, Edinburgh	10/03/2007
6	Chris Paterson	Italy	Murrayfield, Edinburgh	26/02/2005
6	Gavin Hastings	France	Murrayfield, Edinburgh	18/01/1986

Most drop goals by a player in a match: Scotland

No.	Player	Versus	Venue	Date
2	Craig Chalmers	England	Twickenham, London	18/03/1995
2	John Rutherford	Ireland	Murrayfield, Edinburgh	21/02/1987
2	John Rutherford	Wales	Murrayfield, Edinburgh	02/03/1985
2	John Rutherford	New Zealand	Murrayfield, Edinburgh	12/11/1983
2	Bryan Gossman	France	Parc des Princes, Paris	05/02/1983
2	Doug Morgan	Ireland	Murrayfield, Edinburgh	24/02/1973
2	Brian Simmers	Wales	Murrayfield, Edinburgh	06/02/1965
2	Ninian Finlay	Ireland	Hamilton Crescent, Glasgow	14/02/1880
2	Robert MacKenzie	Ireland	Ormeau, Belfast	19/02/1877

Most points in a match by Scotland

No.	Result	Points				Versus	Venue	Date
		T	C	PG	DG			
100	100–8	15	11	1	-	Japan	McDiarmid Park, Perth	13/11/2004
89	89–0	13	9	2	-	Côte d'Ivoire	Olympia Park, Rustenburg	26/05/1995
65	65–23	10	6	1	-	United States	Boxer Stadium, San Francisco	22/06/2002
60	60–19	8	7	2	-	Romania	Hampden Park, Glasgow	28/08/1999
60	60–21	11	8	-	-	Zimbabwe	Athletic Park, Wellington	30/05/1987

Most consecutive test wins by Scotland

No.	Period	Details
6	28/10/1989–17/03/1990	Fiji (H), Romania (H), Ireland (A), France (H), Wales (A), England (H)
6	24/01/1925–06/02/1926	France (H), Wales (A), Ireland (A), England (H), France (A), Wales (H)

Milestones

Longest test career	William Murdoch	16/03/1935–20/03/1948 (13 years & 5 days)
Youngest test player	Ninian Finlay	17 years & 36 days on 19/02/1875 vs England in Edinburgh
Oldest test player	John McLauchlan	37 years & 210 days on 10/11/1979 vs New Zealand in Edinburgh

Did you know: The lowest official attendance at a recognised test match was on 25 September 1981 when 35 people watched South Africa beat the United States at the Owl Creek Polo Field in New York, an American football field where the goalposts are positioned behind the dead-ball line. Because of the threat of violent anti-apartheid demonstrations, the match was played in secret, originally scheduled at the Bleeker Stadium the following day. The game was so suddenly rescheduled that the referee could not be found and had to be replaced by a Dr D. Morrison. Only the team reserves, match officials, 20 policemen, a television crew and one reporter attended. Amazingly, the USA Rugby Union President and the rest of the Springbok party only found out about the game after the players had returned to their hotel. This bizarre test was played on an unlevel field, with the players literally having to run uphill, depending on whether they were attacking or defending. So unprecedented was the occasion that Springbok reserve Thys Burger had the most unusual day: first he helped the officials erect the goalposts, then acted as a touch judge and then came on as a substitute loose forward, finishing his day by scoring a try!

Top left and right: Action from the first-ever international between Scotland and New Zealand at Inverleith in Edinburgh, 1905. The match was won 12-7 by New Zealand. *Photo*: New Zealand Rugby Museum

Above: Eighthman Alex Wyllie dives over for a try against Scotland at Murrayfield, Edinburgh in 1972, won 14-9 by New Zealand. *Photo*: New Zealand Rugby Museum

Top left: Andy Irvine. *Photo*: Scottish Rugby/PAI

Top centre: David Sole. *Photo*: Scottish Rugby/PAI

Top right: John Rutherford. *Photo*: Scottish Rugby/PAI

Above left: Gordon Brown. *Photo*: Scottish Rugby/PAI

Above right: Wilson Shaw. *Photo*: Scottish Rugby/PAI

South Africa

SA RUGBY.

South Africa vs Argentina (Danie Craven Cup) *see* page 199

South Africa vs Australia (Nelson Mandela Challenge Plate) *see* page 239

South Africa vs British and irish Lions

South Africa vs British and Irish Lions	
Played:	46
Won:	23
Lost:	17
Drew:	6
For:	600
Against:	516

Average score:
13.04–11.22

South Africa percentages:

Won:	50%
Lost:	36.96%
Drawn:	13.04%

This is South Africa's oldest international rugby fixture: the two sides first met more than a century ago in 1891. The British and Irish Lions have since toured South Africa 12 times and won four of these, the last tour being in 2009. In the early years of this encounter, the Lions dominated, winning both the 1891 and 1896 test series with ease. During the 1896 tour, however, the South Africans won their first test match, announcing their arrival on the international scene. From the 1903 series on, the South Africans did not lose a test series to the Lions until 1974. The 1955 series was drawn, the only draw in the history of this encounter. The South Africans dominated completely through the post-war period, with a record 34–14 win over the 1962 Lions, yet such encounters are inevitably remembered by the away team's triumphs such as the great Lions side of 1974, captained by Irishman Willie-John McBride. Welsh flanker John Taylor refused to take part in the tour for political reasons; other players repeated this boycott in 1980, but their actions had little effect as McBride and his soldiers became the first Lions side to emulate the team of 1891, marching through South Africa unbeaten with just a single draw in the final test match in Johannesburg. In 1980 Morné du Plessis' Springboks gained revenge by downing Bill Beaumont's 1980 side 3–1, a series clinched by Naas Botha's touchline conversion in Port Elizabeth. In 1986, the British Isles were scheduled to tour South Africa but the tour was cancelled because of the sports boycott. It was another 17 years before the British Lions toured South Africa again, when they arrived in 1997 as the first-ever professional Lions outfit. It was a series that the world-champion Springboks should never have lost, but the record books show that they did. The Lions won the first test with a powerful performance; in the second in Durban the Springboks scored three tries to zero, but were unable to convert a single kick at goal, despite utilising three kickers during the game. To South Africa's dismay, a late Jeremy Guscott drop goal sunk the Springboks and the series was lost. However, Morné Steyn's spectacular last-second goal in the second test to win the 2009 series was sweet revenge.

July 1891, Port Elizabeth Cricket Ground, Port Elizabeth
British Lions	4	T: Aston, Whittaker; C: Rotherham
South Africa	0	

28 August 1891, Eclectic Cricket Ground, Kimberley
British Lions	3	DG: Mitchell
South Africa	0	

5 September 1891, Newlands, Cape Town
British Lions	4	T: Aston, MacLagan; C: Rotherham
South Africa	0	

30 July 1896, Port Elizabeth Cricket Ground, Port Elizabeth
British Lions	8	T: Carey, Bulger; C: Byrne
South Africa	0	

22 August 1896, The Wanderers, Johannesburg
British Lions	17	T: Todd, Crean, Hancock; C: Byrne (2); DG: Mackie
South Africa	8	T: Samuels (2); C: Cope

29 August 1896, The Kimberley Athletics Club, Kimberley
British Lions	9	T: Mackie; C: Byrne; DG: Byrne
South Africa	3	T: Jones

SOUTH AFRICA

5 September 1896, Newlands, Cape Town
South Africa   5   T: Larard; C: Hepburn
British Lions   0

26 August 1903, The Wanderers, Johannesburg
South Africa   10   T: Dobbin, Frew; C: Heatlie (2)
British Lions   10   T: Skrimshire, Cave; C: Gillespie (2)

5 September 1903, The Kimberley Athletics Club, Kimberley
South Africa   0
British Lions   0

12 September 1903, Newlands, Cape Town
South Africa   8   T: Barry, Reid; C: Heatlie
British Lions   0

6 August 1910, The Wanderers, Johannesburg
South Africa   14   T: de Villiers, D Morkel, F Luyt, Hahn; C: D Morkel
British Lions   10   T: Foster, Spoors; DG: Jones

27 August 1910, Crusaders Ground, Port Elizabeth
British Lions   8   T: Spoors, Neale; C: Pillman
South Africa   3   T: Mills

3 September 1910, Newlands, Cape Town
South Africa   21   T: Roos, F Luyt, Allport, Reyneke; C: D Morkel (3); PG: D Morkel
British Lions   5   T: Spoors; C: Pillman

16 August 1924, Kingsmead, Durban
South Africa   7   T: Aucamp; DG: Osler
British Lions   3   T: Whitley

23 August 1924, The Wanderers, Johannesburg
South Africa   17   T: Starke, Mostert, van Druten, Albertyn; C: Osler; PG: Osler
British Lions   0

13 September 1924, Crusaders Ground, Port Elizabeth
South Africa   3   T: van Druten
British Lions   3   T: Cunningham

20 September 1924, Newlands, Cape Town
South Africa   16   T: Starke (2), Bester, Slater; DG: Starke
British Lions   9   T: Boyce, Harris; PG: Boyce

6 August 1938, The Wanderers, Johannesburg
South Africa   26   T: Williams (2), S Louw, Harris; C: Brand (4); PG: Brand (2)
British Lions   12   PG: Jenkins (3), Taylor

3 September 1938, Crusaders Ground, Port Elizabeth
South Africa   19   T: du Toit, Lochner, Bester; C: Turner (2); PG: Turner (2)
British Lions   3   T: Duff

10 September 1938, Newlands, Cape Town
British Lions   21   T: Jones, Dancer, Alexander, Duff; C: McKibbin; PG: McKibbon; DG: Grieve
South Africa   16   T: Turner, Bester, Lotz; C: Turner (2); PG: Turner

6 August 1955, Ellis Park, Johannesburg
British Lions   23   T: Pedlow, Butterfield, Morgan, Greenwood, O'Reilly; C: Cameron (4)
South Africa   22   T: Briers (2), Swart, Koch; C: van der Schyff (2); PG: van der Schyff (2)

20 August 1955, Newlands, Cape Town
South Africa   25   T: van Vollenhoven (3), Rosenberg, Dryburgh, Briers, Ackermann; C: Dryburgh (2)
British Lions   9   T: Butterfield, B Meredith; PG: Cameron

3 September 1955, Loftus Versfeld, Pretoria
British Lions   9   T: Butterfield; PG: Baker; DG: Butterfield
South Africa   6   PG: Dryburgh (2)

24 September 1955, Crusaders Ground, Port Elizabeth
South Africa   22   T: Briers (2), Ulyate, Retief, van Vollenhoven; C: Dryburgh (2); DG: Ulyate
British Lions   8   T: Greenwood, O'Reilly; C: Pedlow

23 June 1962, Ellis Park, Johannesburg
South Africa   3   T: Gainsford
British Lions   3   T: D Jones

21 July 1962, Kingsmead, Durban
South Africa   3   PG: Oxlee
British Lions   0

4 August 1962, Newlands, Cape Town
South Africa   8   T: Oxlee; C: Oxlee; PG: Oxlee
British Lions   3   DG: Sharp

25 August 1962, Free State Stadium, Bloemfontein
South Africa   34   T: Roux (2), Wyness, G van Zyl, Gainsford, Claassen; C: Oxlee (5); PG: Oxlee (2)
British Lions   14   T: Cowan, Campbell-Lamerton, Rowlands; C: Willcox; PG: Willcox

8 June 1968, Loftus Versfeld, Pretoria
South Africa   25   T: Naudé, de Villiers, du Preez C: Visagie (2); PG: Visagie (2), Naudé (2)
British Lions   20   T: McBride; C: Kiernan; PG: Kiernan (5)

22 June 1968, Boet Erasmus Stadium, Port Elizabeth
South Africa   6   PG: Naudé, Visagie
British Lions   6   PG: Kiernan (2)

13 July 1968, Newlands, Cape Town
South Africa   11   T: Lourens; C: Visagie; PG: Visagie, Naudé
British Lions   6   PG: Kiernan (2)

27 July 1968, Ellis Park, Johannesburg
South Africa   19   T: Roux, Ellis, Olivier, Nomis; C: Visagie (2); DG: Gould
British Lions   6   PG: Kiernan (2)

8 June 1974, Newlands, Cape Town
British Lions   12   PG: Bennett (3); DG: Edwards
South Africa   3   DG: Snyman

22 June 1974, Loftus Versfeld, Pretoria
British Lions   28   T: JJ Williams (2), Bennett, Brown, Milliken; C: Bennett; PG: Bennett; DG: McGeechan
South Africa   9   PG: Bosch (2); DG: Bosch

13 July 1974, Boet Erasmus Stadium, Port Elizabeth
British Lions   26   T: Brown, JJ Williams (2); C: Irvine; PG: Irvine (2); DG: Bennett (2)
South Africa   9   PG: Snyman (3)

27 July 1974, Ellis Park, Johannesburg
South Africa   13   T: Cronje; PG: Snyman (3)
British Lions   13   T: Uttley, Irvine; C: Bennett; PG: Irvine

31 May 1980, Newlands, Cape Town
South Africa   26   T: Louw, W du Plessis, van Heerden, Serfontein, Germishuys; C: Botha (3)
British Lions   22   T: Price; PG: Ward (5); DG: Ward

14 June 1980, Free State Stadium, Bloemfontein
South Africa   26   T: Louw, Stofberg, Germishuys, Pienaar; C: Botha (2); PG: Botha (2)
British Lions   19   T: O'Driscoll, Gravell; C: G Davies; PG: G Davies (2), Irvine

28 June 1980, Boet Erasmus Stadium, Port Elizabeth
South Africa   12   T: Germishuys; C: Botha; PG: Botha; DG: Botha
British Lions   10   T: Hay; PG: Campbell (2)

12 July 1980, Loftus Versfeld, Pretoria
South Africa   13   T: W du Plessis; PG: Pienaar (2), Botha
British Lions   17   T: C Williams, Irvine, O'Driscoll; C: Ward; PG: Ward

SOUTH AFRICA

21 June 1997, Norwich Park Newlands, Cape Town
British Lions   25   T: Dawson, Tait; PG: Jenkins (5)
South Africa   16   T: du Randt, Bennett; PG: Honiball, Lubbe

28 June 1997, Kings Park, Durban
British Lions   18   PG: Jenkins (5); DG: Guscott
South Africa   15   T: van der Westhuizen, Montgomery, Joubert

5 July 1997, Ellis Park, Johannesburg
South Africa   35   T: Montgomery, Snyman, van der Westhuizen, Rossouw; C: de Beer (2), Honiball; PG: de Beer (3)
British Lions   16   T: Dawson; C: Jenkins; PG: Jenkins (3)

20 June 2009, The ABSA Stadium, Durban
South Africa   26   T: Smit, Brüssow; C: Pienaar (2); PG: Pienaar (3), F Steyn
British Lions   21   T: Croft (2), Phillips; C: S Jones (3)

27 June 2009, Loftus Versfeld, Pretoria
South Africa   28   T: Pietersen, Habana, Fourie; C: M Steyn (2); PG: M Steyn (2), F Steyn
British Lions   25   T: Kearney; C: S Jones; PG: S Jones (5); DG: S Jones

4 July 2009 Coca-Cola Park, Johannesburg
British Lions   28   T: S Williams (2), Monye; C: S Jones (2); PG: S Jones (3)
South Africa   9   PG: M Steyn (3)

South Africa vs Canada

3 June 1995, Boet Erasmus Stadium, Port Elizabeth (RWC, Pool A)
South Africa   20   T: Richter (2); C: Stransky (2); PG: Stransky (2)
Canada   0

10 June 2000, Basil Kenyon Stadium, East London
South Africa   51   T: Paulse (2), Fleck (2), Kempson, Vos, Barry, Montgomery; C: van Straaten (4); PG: van Straaten
Canada   18   T: Charron, Stanley; C: Stewart; PG: Stewart (2)

South Africa vs England *see page 283*

South Africa vs Fiji

2 July 1996, Loftus Versfeld, Pretoria
South Africa   43   T: penalty try, Andrews, Mulder, Joubert, van Schalkwyk; C: Joubert, Honiball (2); PG: Honiball (2), Joubert (2)
Fiji   18   T: Rauluni, Veitayaki; C: Little; PG: Little (2)

7 October 2007, Stade Velodrome, Marseille (RWC, S/F)
South Africa   37   T: Smit, Smith, James, Pietersen, Fourie; C: Montgomery (3); PG: Montgomery, Steyn
Fiji   20   T: Delasau, Bobo; C: Bai (2); PG: Bai (2)

South Africa vs France *see page 322*

South Africa vs Georgia

24 October 2003 Aussie Stadium Sydney (RW, Pool C)
South Africa   46   T: Rossouw (2), Botha, van Niekerk, Fourie, Burger, Hougaard; C: Hougaard (4); PG: Hougaard
Georgia   19   T: Dadunashvili; C: Jimsheladze; PG: Jimsheladze (3), Kvirikashvili

South Africa vs Ireland *see page 351*

South Africa vs Italy *see page 379*

South Africa vs Namibia

15 August 2007, Newlands, Cape Town
South Africa   105   T: Burger (3), Smith (3), du Randt, van der Linde, Willemse, de Villiers, Fourie, Pietersen, Pienaar, Montgomery, du Plessis; C: Montgomery (12); PG: Montgomery (2)
Namibia   13   T: Langenhoven; C: Wessels; PG: Wessels (2)

South Africa vs New Zealand (Freedom Cup) *see page 395*

South Africa vs New Zealand Cavaliers

South Africa vs New Zealand Cavaliers	
Played:	4
Won:	3
Lost:	1
Drew:	0
For:	96
Against:	62

Average score:
24–15.5

South Africa percentages:

Won:	75%
Lost:	25%
Drawn:	0%

In 1985 New Zealand were scheduled to tour South Africa but at late notice the tour was cancelled in July due to a legal ruling in New Zealand that it would be incompatible with and in conflict with the NZRFU's legally stated purpose of the 'fostering and encouragement of the game of rugby'. This was at a time when everyone was banned from playing South Africa because of that country's racial discrimination. Despite the ban however, the lure to South Africa remained too strong for the players and 28 of the original 30 defected from the NZRFU to tour as the New Zealand Cavaliers: the official name for this unofficial side: essentially an All Blacks team in everything but name. The IRFB officially expressed its disapproval, yet it is widely believed that the tourists and the Springboks were paid to play – a serious allegation during the amateur era. What's more, Toyota paid ZAR57,000 to have its logo on the right breast of the South African jersey, the first such advertising in rugby which has become so commonplace today. However, the tour did underline the need to overhaul rugby's commercial status, with the Cavaliers' jersey sporting various sponsor logos, a springbok and a silver fern. The New Zealand side was coached by Colin Meads and captained by Andy Dalton but was comprehensively beaten by South Africa in the four-test series. On their return to New Zealand the players had a two-test ban imposed by the NZRFU, an extremely lenient punishment considering the severity of their actions, political and financial. In days gone by such actions would have warranted a life ban but the commercial floodgates were creaking open and never again would rugby be the same amateur game.

10 May 1986, Newlands, Cape Town
South Africa 21 T: C du Plessis; C: Botha; PG: Botha (3); DG: Botha (2)
NZ Cavaliers 15 T: penalty try; C: Fox; PG: Fox (3)

17 May 1986, Kings Park, Durban
South Africa 18 T: Reinach; C: Botha; PG: Botha (4)
NZ Cavaliers 19 T: Taylor, Mexted; C: Fox; PG: Fox (3)

24 May 1986, Loftus Versfeld, Pretoria
South Africa 33 T: Gerber, Reinach, Schmidt, Botha; C: Botha (4); PG: Botha (3)
NZ Cavaliers 18 T: Crowley; C: Fox; PG: Fox (3); DG: Fox

31 May 1986, Ellis Park, Johannesburg
South Africa 24 T: Wright; C: Botha; PG: Botha (5); DG: M du Plessis
NZ Cavaliers 10 T: Donald; PG: Deans (2)

South Africa vs Pacific Islanders

17 July 2004, Express Advocate Stadium, Gosford
South Africa 38 T: Paulse (2), Cronje, de Villiers; C: Montgomery (3); PG: Montgomery (4)
Pacific Islanders 24 T: Sivivatu (2), Bobo, Lauaki; C: Rabeni (2)

South Africa vs Romania

29 May 1995, Newlands, Cape Town (RWC, Pool A)
South Africa 21 T: Richter (2); C: Johnson; PG: Johnson (3)
Romania 8 T: Guranescu; PG: Ivanciuc

SOUTH AFRICA

South Africa vs Samoa

13 April 1995, Ellis Park, Johannesburg

| South Africa | 60 | T: Johnson (3), Williams (2), Small, Stransky, Andrews, Rossouw; C: Johnson (5), Stransky; PG: Johnson |
| Western Samoa | 8 | T: Lima; PG: Umaga |

10 June 1995, Ellis Park, Johannesburg (RWC, Q/F)

| South Africa | 42 | T: Williams (4), Andrews, Rossouw; C: Johnson (3); PG: Johnson (2) |
| Western Samoa | 14 | T: Falaniko, Nu'uali'itia; C: Fa'amasino (2) |

6 July 2002, Minolta Loftus, Pretoria

| South Africa | 60 | T: Barry (2), Hall (2), Matfield, van Niekerk, Greeff, du Preez; C: Pretorius (7); PG: Pretorius (2) |
| Samoa | 18 | T: Viliamu, Sititi, Tuilagi; C: Va'a |

1 November 2003, Suncorp Stadium, Brisbane (RWC, Pool C)

| South Africa | 60 | T: van Niekerk, Smith, Hougaard, Willemse, Muller, van der Westhuyzen, de Kock, Fourie; C: Hougaard (5), Koen (2); PG: Hougaard; DG: Hougaard |
| Samoa | 10 | T: Palepoi; C: Va'a; PG: Va'a |

9 June 2007, Ellis Park, Johannesburg

| South Africa | 35 | T: Smit, Pietersen, Steyn, Wannenburg, Montgomery; C: Hougaard, Montgomery; PG: Hougaard (2) |
| Samoa | 8 | T: Anitelela Tuilaga; PG: Williams |

9 September 2007 Parc des Prince, Paris (RWC, Pool A)

| South Africa | 59 | T: Habana (4), Montgomery (2), Fourie, Pietersen; C: Montgomery (5); PG: Montgomery (3) |
| Samoa | 7 | T: Williams; C: Williams |

South Africa vs Scotland *see* page 415

South Africa vs South America

To keep the pariah Springboks in the game, the president of the SARB, Dr Danie Craven, conjured up the Jaguars: a composite South American team to tour South Africa in 1980 and 1982, plus a few Spaniards thrown in for the 1984 tour. This outfit was essentially Argentina in disguise with the legendary Hugo Porta as captain. The SARB financed every aspect of the tour from the South Americans' kit to the gifts for the players after the games. Six tests were played in all with the Springboks expected to dominate, which they duly did. Following a massive 50–18 win in Pretoria in the first test of 1982, the Springboks were expected to annihilate the Jaguars a week later in Bloemfontein, but in fact lost by an unimpressive nine points, one of the great upsets in world rugby.

26 April 1980, The Wanderers, Johannesburg

| South Africa | 24 | T: T du Plessis, Mordt, Germishuys; C: Botha (3); PG: Botha; DG: Botha |
| South America | 9 | T: Travaglini; C: Porta; PG: Porta |

3 May 1980, Kings Park, Durban

| South Africa | 18 | T: M du Plessis; C: Botha; PG: Botha; DG: Botha (3) |
| South America | 9 | PG: Piccardo (3) |

18 October 1980, Wanderers Club, Montevideo

| South Africa | 22 | T: Stofberg, Gerber, Burger; C: Botha (2); PG: Botha; DG: Botha |
| South America | 13 | T: Cubelli, Madero; C: Porta; DG: Landejo |

25 October 1980, Prince of Wales Country Club, Santiago

| South Africa | 30 | T: Mordt (2), Germishuys (2), Gerber, M du Plessis; C: Botha (3) |
| South America | 16 | T: Campo, Iachetti; C: Porta; PG: Porta; DG: Porta |

27 March 1982, Loftus Versfeld, Pretoria
South Africa   50   T: Gerber (3), Mordt (2), Oosthuizen, C du Plessis, W du Plessis; C: Botha (6); PG: Heunis; DG: Botha
South America   18   T: Puccio; C: Porta; PG: Porta (4)

3 April 1982, Free State Stadium, Bloemfontein
South America   21   T: Porta; C: Porta; PG: Porta (4); DG: Porta
South Africa   12   T: Gerber; C: Botha; PG: Botha (2)

South Africa vs South America and Spain

20 October 1984, Loftus Versfeld, Pretoria
South Africa   32   T: Louw, Gerber, Mallett, Heunis, Serfontein; C: Tobias (2), Gerber; PG: Tobias (2)
SA & Spain   15   T: Palma, de Vedia; C: Porta (2); PG: Porta

27 October 1984, Newlands, Cape Town
South Africa   22   T: C du Plessis, Ferreira, Mordt, Gerber; PG: Tobias (2)
SA & Spain   13   T: Sansot; PG: Porta (3)

South Africa vs Spain

10 October 1999, Murrayfield, Edinburgh (RWC, Pool A)
South Africa   47   T: Vos (2), Leonard, Swanepoel, Muller, Skinstad, penalty try; C: de Beer (6)
Spain   3   PG: Velasco

South Africa vs Tonga

10 June 1997, Norwich Park Newlands, Cape Town
South Africa   74   T: Drotske, Garvey (2), Kruger (2), van Heerden, van der Westhuizen, Small (2), Snyman (3); C: Lubbe (7)
Tonga   10   T: Ta'u; C: Taumalolo; PG: Tonga

22 September 2007, Stade Felix Bollaert, Lens (RWC, Pool A)
South Africa   30   T: Pienaar (2), Skinstad, Smith; C: Pretorius, Montgomery; PG: Steyn, Montgomery
Tonga   25   T: Pulu, Vaki, Hufanga; C: Hola (2); PG: Hola (2)

South Africa vs United States of America

25 September 1981, Owl Creek Polo Field, New York
South Africa   38   T: Mordt (3), Geldenhuys, Burger, Beck, Germishuys (2); C: Botha (3)
USA   7   T: Walton; PG: Smith

1 December 2001, Robertson Stadium, Houston
South Africa   43   T: Jantjes (2), Hall, Rossouw, van Biljon, Vos; C: Koen (5); PG: Koen
USA   20   T: McDonald; PG: Wilfley (4); DG: Keyter

30 September 2007, Stade de la Mosson, Montpellier (RWC, Pool A)
South Africa   64   T: Habana (2), Fourie (2), Burger, Steyn, Smith, van der Linde, du Preez; C: Montgomery (6), James (2);
         PG: Montomery
USA   15   T: Ngwenya, Wyles; C: Hercus; PG: Hercus

South Africa vs Uruguay

15 October 1999, Hampden Park, Glasgow (RWC, Pool A)
South Africa   39   T: van den Berg (2), Kayser, Fleck, van der Westhuizen; C: de Beer (4); PG: de Beer (2)
Uruguay   3   PG: Aguirre

11 October 2003, Subiaco Oval, Perth (RWC, Pool C)
South Africa   72   T: van der Westhuizen (3), Botha (2), Bands, Greeff, Fourie, van Niekerk, Rossouw, Delport, Scholtz;
         C: Koen (5), Hougaard
Uruguay   6   PG: D Aguirre (2)

11 June 2005, ABSA Stadium, East London
South Africa   134   T: Chavhanga (6), Tyibilika (2), Habana (2), Fourie, de Villiers (2), van den Berg (2), Steenkamp, Cronje,
         Rossouw, Januarie, Joubert, van der Westhuyzen; C: van der Westhuyzen (7), Montgomery (6); PG: Montgomery
Uruguay   3   PG: del Castillo

SOUTH AFRICA

South Africa vs Wales	
Played:	23
Won:	21
Lost:	1
Drawn:	1
For:	635
Against:	295

Average score:
27.61–12.83

South Africa percentages:

Won:	91.3%
Lost:	4.35%
Drawn:	4.35%

South Africa vs Wales (Prince William Cup)

During the early years of the series, this was one of the most anticipated international fixtures when Welsh rugby was at its sublime best. Matches were tight affairs, often played in atrocious weather conditions, yet with many games going down in the annals of rugby history. So it is surprising to read that the Springboks went undefeated against the Welsh until 1999 when they were beaten before a crowd of fewer than 20,000 in a half-built Millennium Stadium. This loss aside, South Africa have dominated the Welsh in recent times, including record hauls, none more so than the 96–13 drubbing in 1998. Today, the Prince William Cup is contested by South Africa and Wales in all test matches, excluding the RWC. The cup was introduced in November 2007 to mark a century of test-match rugby between the two, with Prince William, the Vice Royal Patron of the WRU, in attendance and who presented the cup to the winning captain John Smit. A series of events were staged in and around the Millennium Stadium to celebrate the launch of the cup, including the arrival of HMS *Kent* in Cardiff. Prince William was involved in the design of the silver cup, which has a Welsh oak base and the maps of Wales and South Africa etched onto its surface. The hammered edges spiralling around the trophy represent the landscape of Wales; inscribed on it is one of Nelson Mandela's most stirring quotes: 'The greatest glory in living lies not in never falling, but in rising every time we fall.'

1 December 1906, St Helen's, Swansea
South Africa   11   T: Joubert, Loubser, Raaff C: Joubert
Wales   0

14 December 1912, Cardiff Arms Park, Cardiff
South Africa   3   PG: D Morkel
Wales   0

5 December 1931, St Helen's, Swansea
South Africa   8   T: Daneel, Bergh; C: Osler
Wales   3   T: W Davies

22 December 1951, Cardiff Arms Park, Cardiff
South Africa   6   T: Ochse; DG: Brewis
Wales   3   T: B Williams

3 December 1960, Cardiff Arms Park, Cardiff
South Africa   3   PG: Oxlee
Wales   0

23 May 1964, Kings Park, Durban
South Africa   24   T: Marais, Hopwood, Smith; C: Oxlee (3); PG: Oxlee (2); DG: Wilson
Wales   3   PG: Bradshaw

24 January 1970, National Stadium, Cardiff
Wales   6   T: Edwards; PG: Edwards
South Africa   6   T: Nomis; PG: H de Villiers

26 November 1994, National Stadium, Cardiff
South Africa   20   T: Straeuli, Joubert, Williams; C: le Roux; PG: le Roux
Wales   12   PG: Jenkins (4)

2 September 1995, Ellis Park, Johannesburg
South Africa   40   T: Pienaar, Wiese, Small, Teichmann, Mulder; C: Stransky (3); PG: Stransky (3)
Wales   11   T: Bennett; PG: Jenkins (2)

15 December 1996, National Stadium, Cardiff
South Africa   37   T: van der Westhuizen (3), Joubert, Olivier; C: Honiball (2), Joubert; PG: Honiball (2)
Wales   20   T: A Thomas; PG: Jenkins (5)

27 June 1998, Minolta Loftus, Pretoria
| South Africa | 96 | T: Rossouw (3), Montgomery (2), Venter (2), Otto, Terblanche (2), Erasmus, van der Westhuizen, Smith, Hendriks, Skinstad; C: Montgomery (9); PG: Montgomery |
| Wales | 13 | T: A Thomas; C: A Thomas; PG: A Thomas (2) |

14 November 1998, Wembley, London
| South Africa | 28 | T: penalty try, Venter, van der Westhuizen; C: Smith (2); PG: Smith (3) |
| Wales | 20 | T: Thomas; PG: Jenkins (5) |

26 June 1999, Millennium Stadium, Cardiff
| Wales | 29 | T: Taylor, Thomas; C: Jenkins (2); PG: Jenkins (5) |
| South Africa | 19 | T: Swanepoel, Montgomery; PG: van Straaten (2), du Toit |

26 November 2000, Millennium Stadium, Cardiff
| South Africa | 23 | T: van der Westhuizen, Paulse; C: van Straaten (2); PG: van Straaten (3) |
| Wales | 13 | T: Gibbs; C: Jenkins; PG: Jenkins, A Thomas |

8 June 2002, Vodacom Park, Bloemfontein
| South Africa | 34 | T: Matfield, Skinstad, Joubert, Rautenbach, penalty try; C: Pretorius (3); PG: Pretorius |
| Wales | 19 | T: R Williams, C Morgan; PG: Jones (2); DG: Jones |

15 June 2002, Newlands, Cape Town
| South Africa | 19 | T: Russell, Davidson; PG: Pretorius (3) |
| Wales | 8 | T: Charvis; PG: Jones |

26 June 2004, Securicor Loftus, Pretoria
| South Africa | 53 | T: Russell (2), Smit, Burger, Paulse, Julies, Conradie; C: Montgomery (6); PG: Montgomery (2) |
| Wales | 18 | T: Peel, Williams; C: Henson; PG: Henson (2) |

6 November 2004, Millennium Stadium, Cardiff
| South Africa | 38 | T: van Niekerk, van der Westhuyzen, de Villiers, Montgomery; C: Montgomery (3); PG: Montgomery (4) |
| Wales | 36 | T: Henson (2), Peel; C: S Jones (3); PG: S Jones (5) |

19 November 2005, Millennium Stadium, Cardiff
| South Africa | 33 | T: Habana (2), Jantjes, Rossouw; C: Bosman (2); PG: Montgomery (3) |
| Wales | 16 | T: Sweeney; C: S Jones; PG: S Jones (3) |

24 November 2007, Millennium Stadium, Cardiff
| South Africa | 34 | T: Fourie (2), Smith, Kankowski, Pietersen; C: Pretorius (3); PG: Steyn |
| Wales | 12 | T: Charvis, Stoddart; C: Hook |

7 June 2008, Vodacom Park, Bloemfontein
| South Africa | 43 | T: Spies, de Villiers, Jantjes, Montgomery; C: James (4); PG: James (5) |
| Wales | 17 | T: Williams, Roberts C: S Jones, Hook; PG: S Jones |

14 June 2008, Loftus Versfeld, Pretoria
| South Africa | 37 | T: de Villiers (2), Januarie, du Plessis; C: James (4); PG: James (3) |
| Wales | 21 | T: Cooper, Williams; C: S Jones; PG: S Jones (3) |

8 November 2008, Millennium Stadium, Cardiff
| South Africa | 20 | T: Jacobs, de Villiers; C: Pienaar (2); PG: Pienaar (2) |
| Wales | 15 | PG: Hook (4), Halfpenny |

Prince of Wales Cup		Current holder: South Africa			Number of titles: South Africa 3, Wales 0		
No.	Date	Venue	Result				Holder
1	24/11/2007	Millennium Stadium, Cardiff	Wales	12–34	South Africa		South Africa
2	07/06/2008	Vodacom Park, Bloemfontein	South Africa	43–17	Wales	South Africa	
3	14/06/2008	Loftus Versfeld, Pretoria	South Africa	37–21	Wales		
4	08/11/2008	Millennium Stadium, Cardiff	Wales	15–20	South Africa		South Africa

South Africa vs World XV

In 1989 the SARB celebrated its centenary by hosting a tour of a combination World XV with IRFB approval, and including players from Australia, England, France, Ireland, Scotland and Wales. New Zealand was not represented owing to the ill feeling that still existed following the 1986 New Zealand Cavaliers' tour.

27 August 1977, Loftus Verfeld, Pretoria
South Africa   45   T: Snyman, Potgieter, Germishuys, Stofberg (2), Wolmarans; C: Blair (3); PG: Blair (5)
World XV   24   T: Averous (2), McLean, Haden; C: McLean (4)

26 August 1989, Newlands, Cape Town
South Africa   20   T: Knoetze, Botha, Smal; C: Botha; PG: Botha (2)
World XV   19   T: Rodriguez, Sella, Williams; C: Charvet (2); PG: Charvet

2 September 1989, Ellis Park, Johannesburg
South Africa   22   T: Heunis, M du Plessis; C: Botha; PG: Botha (3); DG: Botha
World XV   16   T: Berbizier, Rendall; C: Martin; PG: Charvet, Martin

South Africa: summaries and records

Home matches	
Played	204
Won	139
Lost	53
Drawn	12
Points for	4,842
Points against	2,862
Average score	23.74/14.03
Win %	68.14
Lose %	25.98
Draw %	5.88

Away matches	
Played	149
Won	81
Lost	61
Drawn	7
Points for	2,776
Points against	2 ,93
Average score	18.63/16.06
Win %	54.36
Lose %	40.94
Draw %	4.7

Neutral venues	
Played	19
Won	16
Lost	3
Drawn	0
Points for	710
Points against	291
Average score	37.37/15.32
Win %	84.21
Lose %	15.79
Draw %	0

Total matches	
Played	372
Won	236
Lost	117
Drawn	19
Points for	8,328
Points against	5,546
Average score	22.39/14.91
Win %	63.44
Lose %	31.45
Draw %	5.11

Most capped players: South Africa							
Player	Caps	Career	T	C	PG	DG	Total
Percy Montgomery	102	28/06/1997–30/08/2008	25	153	148	6	893
Joost van der Westhuizen	89	06/11/1993–08/11/2003	38	-	-	-	190
John Smit	84	10/06/2000–04/07/2009	5	-	-	-	20
Victor Matfield	83	30/06/2001–04/07/2009	5	-	-	-	25
Pieter du Randt	80	08/10/1994–20/10/2007	5	-	-	-	25

Most tests as captain: South Africa			
No.	Player		Period
58	John Smit		2003–2009
36	Gary Teichmann		1996–1999
29	François Pienaar		1993–1996
22	Dawie de Villiers		1965–1969
18	Corné Krige		1999–2003

Most points by a player in a career: South Africa

No.	Player	Tests	Career	Points			
				T	C	PG	DG
893	Percy Montgomery	102	28/06/1997–30/08/2008	25	153	148	6
312	Naas Botha	28	26/04/1980–14/11/1992	2	50	50	18
240	Joel Stransky	22	31/07/1993–31/08/1996	6	30	47	3
221	Braam van Straaten	21	19/06/1999–24/11/2001	2	23	55	-
190	Joost van der Westhuizen	89	06/11/1993–08/11/2003	38	-	-	-

Most tries by a player in a career: South Africa

No.	Player	Tests	Career
38	Joost van der Westhuizen	89	06/11/1993–08/11/2003
33	Bryan Habana	46	20/11/2004–27/06/2008
26	Breyton Paulse	64	12/06/1999–14/07/2007
25	Jaque Fourie	45	11/10/2003–04/07/2009
25	Percy Montgomery	102	28/06/1997–30/08/2008

Most conversions by a player in a career: South Africa

No.	Player	Tests	Career
153	Percy Montgomery	102	28/06/1997–30/08/2008
50	Naas Botha	28	26/04/1980–14/11/1992
38	Henry Honiball	35	21/08/1993–04/11/1999
33	Jannie de Beer	13	05/07/1997–30/10/1999
31	André Pretorius	31	08/06/2002–24/11/2007

Most penalties by a player in a career: South Africa

No.	Player	Tests	Career
148	Percy Montgomery	102	28/06/1997–30/08/2008
55	Braam van Straaten	21	19/06/1999–24/11/2001
50	Naas Botha	28	26/04/1980–14/11/1992
47	Joel Stransky	22	31/07/1993–31/08/1996
31	Louis Koen	15	08/07/2000–08/11/2003

Most drop goals by a player in a career: South Africa

No.	Player	Tests	Career
18	Naas Botha	28	26/04/1980–14/11/1992
8	André Pretorius	31	08/06/2002–24/11/2007
8	Jannie de Beer	13	05/07/1997–30/10/1999
6	Percy Montgomery	102	28/06/1997–30/08/2008
5	Piet Visagie	25	15/07/1967–07/08/1971
5	Hansie Brewis	10	16/07/1949–22/08/1953

SOUTH AFRICA

No.	Player	T	C	PG	DG	Versus	Venue	Date
35	Percy Montgomery	1	12	2	-	Namibia	Newlands, Cape Town	15/08/2007
34	Jannie de Beer	-	2	5	5	England	Stade de France, Paris	24/10/1999
31	Percy Montgomery	2	9	1	-	Wales	Minolta Loftus, Pretoria	27/06/1998
30	Tonderai Chavhanga	6	-	-	-	Uruguay	ABSA Stadium, East London	11/06/2005
29	Percy Montgomery	2	5	3	-	Samoa	Parc des Princes, Paris	09/09/2007
29	Gaffie du Toit	2	8	1	-	Italy	Telkom Park, Port Elizabeth	12/06/1999

Most points by a player in a match: South Africa (Points columns: T, C, PG, DG)

Most tries by a player in a match: South Africa

No.	Player	Versus	Venue	Date
6	Tonderai Chavhanga	Uruguay	ABSA Stadium, East London	11/06/2005
5	Stefan Terblanche	Italy	Kings Park, Durban	19/06/1999
4	Jongi Nokwe	Australia	Coca-Cola Park, Johannesburg	30/08/2008
4	Bryan Habana	Samoa	Parc des Princes, Paris	09/09/2007
4	Stefan Terblanche	Ireland	Free State Stadium, Bloemfontein	13/06/1998
4	Pieter Rossouw	France	Parc des Princes, Paris	22/11/1997
4	Chester Williams	Western Samoa	Ellis Park, Johannesburg	10/06/1995

Most conversions by a player in a match: South Africa

No.	Player	Versus	Venue	Date
12	Percy Montgomery	Namibia	Newlands, Cape Town	15/08/2007
9	Butch James	Argentina	Coca-Cola Park, Johannesburg	09/08/2008
9	Percy Montgomery	Wales	Minolta Loftus, Pretoria	27/06/1998
8	Gaffie du Toit	Italy	Kings Park, Durban	16/06/1999
8	Gaffie du Toit	Italy	Telkom Park, Port Elizabeth	12/06/1999
8	Percy Montgomery	Scotland	Murrayfield, Edinburgh	06/12/1997

Most penalties by a player in a match: South Africa

No.	Player	Versus	Venue	Date
7	Percy Montgomery	France	Newlands, Cape Town	24/06/2006
7	Percy Montgomery	Scotland	EPRFU Stadium, Port Elizabeth	17/06/2006
6	Louis Koen	Scotland	Ellis Park, Johannesburg	14/06/2003
6	Percy Montgomery	France	Ellis Park, Johannesburg	16/06/2001
6	Braam van Straaten	Australia	ABSA Stadium, Durban	26/08/2000
6	Braam van Straaten	England	Minolta Loftus, Pretoria	17/06/2000
6	Jannie de Beer	Australia	Twickenham, London	30/10/1999
6	Joel Stransky	Australia	Free State Stadium, Bloemfontein	03/08/1996
6	Gerald Bosch	France	Loftus Versfeld, Pretoria	28/06/1975

Most drop goals by a player in a match: South Africa

No.	Player	Versus	Venue	Date
5	Jannie de Beer	England	Stade de France, Paris	24/10/1999
4	Andre Pretorius	England	Twickenham, London	25/11/2006
3	Jaco van der Westhuyzen	Scotland	Murrayfield, Edinburgh	27/11/2004
3	Naas Botha	Ireland	Kings Park, Durban	06/06/1981
3	Naas Botha	South America	Kings Park, Durban	03/05/1980

Most points in a match by South Africa

No.	Result	Points				Versus	Venue	Date
		T	C	PG	DG			
134	134–3	21	13	1	-	Uruguay	ABSA Stadium, East London	11/06/2005
105	105–13	15	12	2	-	Nambia	Newlands, Cape Town	15/08/2007
101	101–0	15	13	-	-	Italy	Kings Park, Durban	09/06/1999
96	96–13	15	9	1	-	Wales	Minolta Loftus, Pretoria	27/06/1998
74	74–3	11	8	1	-	Italy	Telkom Park, Port Elizabeth	12/06/1999
74	74–10	12	7	-	-	Tonga	Norwich Park Newlands, Cape Town	10/06/1997

Most consecutive test wins by South Africa

No.	Period	Details
17	23/08/1997–28/11/1998	Australia (H), Italy (A), France (A), France (A), England (A), Scotland (A), Ireland (H), Ireland (H), Wales (H), England (H), Australia (A), New Zealand (A), New Zealand (H), Australia (H), Wales (N), Scotland (A), Ireland (A)
15	08/10/1994–02/07/1996	Argentina (H), Argentina (H), Scotland (A), Wales (A), Western Samoa (H), Australia (H), Romania (H), Canada (H), Western Samoa (H), France (H), New Zealand (H), Wales (H), Italy (A), England (A), Fiji (H)
13	15/08/2007–21/06/2008	Namibia (H), Scotland (A), Samoa (N), England (N), Tonga (N), United States (N), Fiji (N), Argentina (N), England (N), Wales (A), Wales (H), Wales (H), Italy (H)

Milestones

Longest test career	Pieter 'Os' du Randt	08/10/1994–20/10/2007 (13 years & 13 days)
Youngest test player	Jack Hartley	18 years & 18 days on 05/09/1891 vs British Isles in Cape Town
Oldest test player	Johann Ackermann	37 years & 34 days on 07/07/2007 vs Australia in Sydney

Top: Dribbling action from the second test in Auckland during the 1921 'World Championship' series between New Zealand and South Africa. South Africa won by 9-5.
Photo: New Zealand Rugby Museum

Above: Springbok flyhalf Terrence Harris cuts inside All Black winger Jack Sullivan as Bok legend Danie Craven moves up in support during the third and crucial test of the 1937 series in Auckland. South Africa comprehensively outplayed New Zealand to win 17-6 to ensure they returned home as the 'World Champions'.
Photo: New Zealand Rugby Museum

Left: Springbok wing Mike Antelme makes a break during the second test of the 1960 series against New Zealand in Cape Town. In hot pursuit is All Black hooker Dennis Young (left) and lock Ron Horsley (with scrumcap). The test was won 11-3 by New Zealand. *Photo*: New Zealand Rugby Museum

Below left: Legendary Springbok centre John Gainsford scores the first of his two tries against the All Blacks in the third test of the 1965 series in Christchurch. His tries helped South Africa turn around a 5-16 halftime deficit into a famous 19-16 triumph. *Photo*: New Zealand Rugby Museum

Below: All Black scrumhalf Kevin Briscoe is harassed by one-eyed Springbok flanker Martin Pelser during the Cape Town test of the 1960 series. New Zealand won the test 11-3 but lost the series 1-2. *Photo*: New Zealand Rugby Museum

Bottom right: All Black centre Joe Morgan outpaces Springbok captain Morné du Plessis to score during the second test of the 1976 series in Bloemfontein. New Zealand won the match 15-9 but lost the series 1-3. *Photo*: New Zealand Rugby Museum

A typically ferocious South African ruck as All Black lock Peter Whiting is unceremoniously cleared out during the 1976 series won 3-1 by South Africa. *Photo*: New Zealand Rugby Museum

Below: Springbok scrumhalf Divan Serfontein makes a break down the blindside during the second test of the 1981 series against New Zealand in Wellington, a match won 24-12 by South Africa. Ranging up in support in the background is Bok flyhalf Naas Botha.
Photo: New Zealand Rugby Museum

Left: Springbok scrumhalf Divan Serfontein clears from a ruck during the third test of the 1981 series against New Zealand, with an impenetrable wall of Springbok forwards protecting him. *Photo*: New Zealand Rugby Museum

Above: Springbok flanker Daan Retief evades the attention of defending All Black winger Ron Jarden (left), captain and scrumhalf Pat Vincent (centre) and fullback Pat Walsh (right) to score a crucial try in the second test of the 1956 series in Wellington. The match was won 8-3 by South Africa but the series 3-1 by New Zealand.
Photo: New Zealand Rugby Museum

South Africa's legendary flyhalf Naas Botha in customary pose.
Photo: New Zealand Rugby Museum

447

Wales

WRU™©

Wales vs Argentina *see page 203*

Wales vs Australia (James Bevan Trophy) *see page 245*

Wales vs British Barbarians

6 October 1990, National Stadium, Cardiff
British Barbarians	31	T: Stanley, Guscott, Farr-Jones, Rush; C: Barnes (3); PG: Barnes (3)
Wales	24	T: Thorburn; C: Thorburn; PG: Thorburn (5); DG: Evans

24 August 1996, National Stadium, Cardiff
Wales	31	T: Davies (2), Proctor, Howley, Humphreys; C: Jenkins (3)
British Barbarians	10	T: Pene, Corkery

Wales vs Canada

<table>
<tr><td>Wales vs Canada</td></tr>
<tr><td>Played:</td><td>12</td></tr>
<tr><td>Won:</td><td>11</td></tr>
<tr><td>Lost:</td><td>1</td></tr>
<tr><td>Drew:</td><td>0</td></tr>
<tr><td>For:</td><td>460</td></tr>
<tr><td>Against:</td><td>207</td></tr>
<tr><td colspan="2">Average score:</td></tr>
<tr><td colspan="2">38.33–17.25</td></tr>
<tr><td colspan="2">Wales percentages:</td></tr>
<tr><td>Won:</td><td>91.67%</td></tr>
<tr><td>Lost:</td><td>8.33%</td></tr>
<tr><td>Drawn:</td><td>0%</td></tr>
</table>

3 June 1987, Rugby Park, Invercargill (RWC, Pool 2)
Wales	40	T: I Evans (4), Bowen, Devereux, A Phillips, Hadley C: Thorburn (4)
Canada	9	PG: Rees (3)

10 November 1993, National Stadium, Cardiff
Canada	26	T: Charon, Stuart; C: Rees (2); PG: Rees (4)
Wales	24	PG: Jenkins (8)

11 June 1994, Fletcher's Field, Toronto
Wales	33	T: Hall (2), I Evans; C: Jenkins (3); PG: Jenkins (4)
Canada	15	PG: Rees (5)

19 July 1997, Fletcher's Field, Toronto
Wales	28	T: Davies, Proctor, G Thomas; C: Thomas (2); PG: Thomas (3)
Canada	25	T: Schmid (2), Ross; C: Rees (2); PG: Rees; DG: Ross

21 August 1999, Millennium Stadium, Cardiff
Wales	33	T: Walne, Jenkins; C: Jenkins; PG: Jenkins (7)
Canada	19	T: Lougheed; C: Rees; PG: Rees (3); DG: Rees

16 November 2002, Millennium Stadium, Cardiff
Wales	32	T: McBryde, Robinson; C: S Jones (2); PG: S Jones (6)
Canada	21	PG: Barker (6); DG: Williams

12 October 2003, Colonial Stadium, Melbourne (RWC, Pool D)
Wales	41	T: Parker, Cooper, M Jones, Charvis, Thomas; C: Harris (5); PG: Harris (2)
Canada	10	T: Tkachuk; C: Pritchard; DG: Ross

11 June 2005, York Stadium, Toronto
Wales	60	T: J Thomas (2), Taylor, Charvis, Broster, Morgan, Czekaj, R Williams, Popham; C: Sweeney (6); PG: Sweeney
Canada	3	PG: Daypuck

17 November 2006, Millennium Stadium, Cardiff
Wales	61	T: J Thomas (2), G Thomas, S Williams, Rees, Peel, penalty try, Sweeney, Shanklin; C: Hook (8)
Canada	26	T: Pike, D Fletch; C: Pritchard (2); PG: Pritchard (3); DG: Pritchard

9 September 2007, Stade de la Beaujoire, Nantes (RWC, Pool B)
Wales	42	T: S Williams (2), AW Jones, Parker, Charvis; C: S Jones (4); PG: Hook (3)
Canada	17	T: Cudmore, Culpan, Williams; C: Pritchard

14 November 2008, Millennium Stadium, Cardiff
Wales	34	T: Halfpenny (2), penalty try (2), Stoddart; C: Biggar (3); PG: Biggar
Canada	13	T: Smith; C: Pritchard; PG: Pritchard (2)

30 May 2009, York University Stadium, Totonto
Wales	32	T: Czekaj, James; C: Biggar (2); PG: Biggar (6)
Canada	23	T: Duke, Fairhurst; C: Pritchard (2); PG: Pritchard (3)

Wales vs Fiji

Played:	7
Won:	6
Lost:	1
Drawn:	0
For:	207
Against:	103

Average score:
29.57-14.71

Wales percentages:

Won:	85.71%
Lost:	14.29%
Drawn:	0%

Wales vs England *see page 286*

Wales vs Fiji

9 November 1985, National Stadium, Cardiff

Wales	40	T: P Davies (2), Titley, Holmes, Hadley, James, Pickering; C: Thorburn (3) PG: Thorburn (2)
Fiji	3	PG: Damu

31 May 1986, National Stadium, Suva

Wales	22	T: J Davies, Bowen; C: Bowen; PG: Dacey (3); DG: J Davies
Fiji	15	T: Niuqila, Tuvula; C: Kubu (2); PG: Lovokuru

18 June 1994, National Stadium, Suva

Wales	23	T: Rayer, Collins; C: A Davies (2); PG: A Davies (3)
Fiji	8	T: Veitayaki; PG: Little

11 November 1995, National Stadium, Cardiff

Wales	19	T: Moore, Jenkins; PG: Jenkins (3)
Fiji	15	T: Bari, Rayasi; C: Waqa; PG: Waqa

9 November 2002, Millennium Stadium, Cardiff

Wales	58	T: R Williams, M Jones (2), Charvis, Parker, penalty try, G Thomas; C: S Jones (3), Harris; PG: S Jones (5)
Fiji	14	T: Ligairi, Serevi; C: Little, Serevi

11 November 2005, Millennium Stadium, Cardiff

Wales	11	T: Owen; PG: Robinson; DG: Robinson
Fiji	10	T: Rawaqa; C: Vulakoro; DG: Bai

29 September 2007, Stade de la Beaujoire, Nantes (RWC, Pool B)

Fiji	38	T: Delasau, Leawere, Qera, Dewes; C: Little (3); PG: Little (4)
Wales	34	T: M Jones, Popham, G Thomas, S Williams, M Williams; C: S Jones (2), Hook; PG: S Jones

Wales vs France *see page 325*

Wales vs Ireland *see page 353*

Wales vs Italy *see page 384*

Wales vs Japan

Played:	7
Won:	7
Lost:	0
Drawn:	0
For:	463
Against:	88

Average score:
66.14-12.57

Wales percentages:

Won:	100%
Lost:	0%
Drawn:	0%

Wales vs Japan

16 October 1993, National Stadium, Cardiff

Wales	55	T: I Evans (2), Gibbs (2), Moon, Clement, Lewis, Rayer, N Jenkins; C: Jenkins (5)
Japan	5	T: Williams

27 May 1995, Free State Stadium, Bloemfontein (RWC, Pool C)

Wales	57	T: Thomas (3), I Evans (2), Moore, Taylor; C: Jenkins (5); PG: Jenkins (4)
Japan	10	T: Oto (2)

9 October 1999, Millennium Stadium, Cardiff (RWC, Pool D)

Wales	64	T: Taylor (2), Bateman, penalty try, Howley, Gibbs, Howarth, Llewellyn, Thomas; C: Jenkins (8); PG: Jenkins
Japan	15	T: Ohata, Tuidraki; C: Hirose; PG: Hirose

10 June 2001, Hanazono Stadium, Osaka

Wales	64	T: Williams (4), Morgan (2), M Jones, Durston, Lloyd, Thomas; C: S Jones (7)
Japan	10	T: Vatuvei, Ito

17 June 2001, Chichibu Stadium, Tokyo

Wales	53	T: Gareth Thomas (3), Shanklin (2), Robinson, Gavin Thomas (2), Williams; C: S Jones (4)
Japan	30	T: Kubo, Masuho, Onojowa; C: Kuirhara (3); PG: Kurihara (3)

WALES

26 November 2004, Millennium Stadium, Cardiff
Wales	98	T: Charvis (4), Shanklin (3), R Williams (2), Cooper, S Williams (2), Davies, Jenkins; C: Henson (14)
Japan	0	

20 September 2007, Millennium Stadium, Cardiff (RWC, Pool B)
Wales	72	T: S Williams (2), M Williams (2), A Jones, Hook, James, R Thomas, Morgan, Phillips, Cooper; C: S Jones (5), Sweeney (2); PG: S Jones
Japan	18	T: Endo, Onozawa; C: Robins; PG: Onishi (2)

Wales vs Namibia

2 June 1990, South West Stadium, Windhoek
Wales	18	T: Thorburn, Bridges; C: Thorburn (2); PG: Thorburn (2)
Namibia	9	T: Mans; C: McCulley; PG: McCulley

9 June 1990, South West Stadium, Windhoek
Wales	34	T: E Jones (2), O Williams, penalty try; C: Thorburn (3); PG: Thorburn (3); DG: Clement
Namibia	30	T: Swartz (2), Coetzee (2), Mans; C: McCulley (2); PG: Coetzee; DG: Coetzee

5 June 1993, South West Stadium, Windhoek
Wales	38	T: Lewis (2), Proctor, Hill, Moon; C: Jenkins (2); PG: Jenkins (3)
Namibia	23	T: Coetzee, Kotze; C: Coetzee (2); PG: Coetzee (3)

Wales vs New Zealand *see* page 401

Wales vs New Zealand Maoris

22 December 1888, St Helen's, Swansea
Wales	5 (1G 12T)	T: Thomas, Hannan, Towers; C: Webb
NZ Maoris	0	

Wales vs New Zealand Services

21 April 1919, St Helen's, Swansea
NZ Services	6	PG: Stohr (2)
Wales	3	PG: Shea

Wales vs Pacific Islanders

11 November 2006, Millennium Stadium, Cardiff
Wales	38	T: M Jones, Hook, Morgan, Byrne, Sweeney; C: Sweeney (5); PG: Sweeney
Pacific Islanders	20	T: Va'a, Mapusua, Ratuvou; C: Pisi; PG: Pisi

---

Wales vs Romania

Played:	8
Won:	6
Lost:	2
Drew:	0
For:	342
Against:	96

Average score:
42.75–12

Wales percentages:
Won:	75%
Lost:	25%
Drawn:	0%

Wales vs Portugal

18 May 1994, Universitario Lisboa Field, Lisbon
Wales	102	T: Walker (4), I Evans (3), Hall (3), R Jones (2), Taylor, Quinnell, Llewellyn, penalty try; C: Jenkins (11)
Portugal	11	T: Murinello; PG: Vilar-Gomes (2)

Wales vs Romania

12 November 1983, Dinamo Stadion, Bucharest
Romania	24	T: Caraguea, Muriaru, Aldea, Lungu; C: Alexandru; PG: Alexandru (2)
Wales	6	PG: G Evans (2)

10 December 1988, National Stadium, Cardiff
Romania	15	T: Ion; C: Ignat; PG: Ignat (3)
Wales	9	T: I Evans; C: Thorburn; PG: Thorburn

17 September 1994, Dinamo Stadion, Bucharest
Wales	16	T: Evans; C: Jenkins; PG: Jenkins (3)
Romania	9	PG: Nichitean (3)

30 August 1997, Racecourse Ground, Wrexham
Wales	70	T: Bateman (2), Davies (2), A Thomas (2), John, Walker, Morgan, S Williams, B Williams; C: A Thomas (5), Jarvis; PG: A Thomas
Romania	21	T: Draguceanu, Rotaru; C: Guranescu; PG: Guranescu (3)

19 September 2001, Millennium Stadium, Cardiff
Wales   81   T: Charvis (3), James (3), B Williams (2), Wyatt, Bateman, S Quinnell; C: Jones (10); PG: Jones (2)
Romania   9   PG: Tofan (3)

1 November 2002, Racecourse Ground, Wrexham
Wales   40   T: Quinnell, M Jones, G Thomas, penalty try; C: N Jenkins (4); PG: N Jenkins (4)
Romania   3   PG: Tofan

27 August 2003, Racecourse Ground, Wrexham
Wales   54   T: S Williams (2), Philips, Popham, Brew, G Thomas; C: Henson (6); PG: Henson (4)
Romania   8   T: Balan; PG: Dumbrava

12 November 2004, Millennium Stadium, Cardiff
Wales   66   T: Shanklin (4), R Williams, Jenkins, Cooper, Henson, D Jones, S Jones; C: S Jones (8)
Romania   7   T: Sirbu; C: Tofan

Wales vs Samoa

Wales vs Samoa	
Played:	6
Won:	3
Lost:	3
Drawn:	0
For:	159
Against:	114
Average score:	
26.5–19	
Wales percentages:	
Won:	50%
Lost:	50%
Drawn:	0%

14 June 1986, Apia Park, Apia
Wales   32   T: Titley (2), Bowen, R Moriarty; C: Dacey (2); PG: Dacey (3); DG: J Davies
Western Samoa   14   T: Tafua, Palamo; PG: Aialupo (2)

12 November 1988, National Stadium, Cardiff
Wales   24   T: N Davies (2), J Davies, C Davies; C: Thorburn (4)
Western Samoa   6   T: Lemamea; C: Aiolupo

6 October 1991, National Stadium, Cardiff (RWC, Pool 3)
Western Samoa   16   T: Vaega, Viafale; C: Vaea; PG: Vaea (2)
Wales   13   T: Emyr, I Evans; C: Ring; PG: Ring

25 June 1994, Apia Park, Apia
Western Samoa   34   T: Lima (2), Lam; C: Kellett (2); PG: Kellett (5)
Wales   9   PG: Jenkins (3)

14 October 1999, Millennium Stadium, Cardiff (RWC, Pool D)
Samoa   38   T: Bachop (2), Falaniko, Lam, Leaega; C: Leaega (5); PG: Leaega
Wales   31   T: penalty try (2), Thomas; C: Jenkins (2); PG: Jenkins (4)

11 November 2000, Millennium Stadium, Cardiff
Wales   50   T: S Williams (2), Taylor, Gough, Bateman, penalty try; C: Thomas (4); PG: Thomas (4)
Samoa   6   PG: Velipatu, Sanft

Wales vs Scotland see page 418

Wales vs South Africa (Prince William Cup) see page 438

Wales vs Spain

21 May 1994, Campo Universitaria, Madrid
Wales   54   T: I Evans (3), Quinnell, Walker, G Jenkins, penalty try; C: N Jenkins (5); PG: N Jenkins (3)
Spain   0

Wales vs Tonga

Wales vs Tonga	
Played:	6
Won:	6
Lost:	0
Drawn:	0
For:	186
Against:	71
Average score:	
31–11.83	
Wales percentages:	
Won:	100%
Lost:	0%
Drawn:	0%

7 June 1986, Teufaiva Stadium, Nuku'alofa
Wales   15   T: P Moriarty; C: Dacey; PG: Bowen (2), Dacey
Tonga   7   T: Fifita; PG: Lovo

29 May 1987, Showgrounds Oval, Palmerston North (RWC, Pool 2)
Wales   29   T: Webb (3), Hadley; C: Thorburn (2); PG: Thorburn (2); DG: J Davies
Tonga   16   T: Fiela, Etaiki; C: Liava'a; PG: Amone, Liava'a

22 June 1994, National Stadium, Nuku'alofa
Wales   18   PG: N Jenkins (6)
Tonga   9   PG: Tu'ipulotu (3)

16 November 1997, St Helen's, Swansea
Wales	46	T: G Thomas (2), Davies, Walker, Anthony, Wyatt; C: Jenkins (2); PG: Jenkins (4)
Tonga	12	T: Tatafu, Tai; C: Tonga

17 November 2001, Millennium Stadium, Cardiff
Wales	51	T: G Thomas, Howley, Quinnell, Robinson, R Williams, B Williams; C: Harris (3); PG: Harris (5)
Tonga	7	T: Afeaki; C: Hola

19 October 2003, Canberra Stadium, Canberra (RWC, Pool D)
Wales	27	T: Cooper, M Williams; C: S Jones; PG: S Jones (4); DG: M Williams
Tonga	20	T: Hola, Kivalu, Lavaka; C: Hola; PG: Hol

Wales vs USA	
Played:	7
Won:	7
Lost:	0
Drawn:	0
For:	305
Against:	86
Average score:	
43.57–12.29	
Wales percentages:	
Won:	100%
Lost:	0%
Drawn:	0%

Wales vs United States of America

7 November 1987, National Stadium, Cardiff
Wales	46	T: Bowen (2), Clement (2), Webbe, Young, Norster, P Moriarty; C: Thorburn (4); PG: Thorburn (2)
USA	0	

11 January 1997, National Stadium, Cardiff
Wales	34	T: Evans (2), Gibbs, penalty try; C: Thomas (4); PG: Thomas (2)
USA	14	T: Bachelet; PG: Alexander (3)

5 July 1997, Wilmington
Wales	30	T: Thomas (2), Jones, Walker; C: Thomas (2); PG: Thomas (2)
USA	20	T: Takau, Anitoni; C: Alexander (2); PG: Alexander (2)

12 July 1997, Boxer Stadium, San Francisco
Wales	28	T: Proctor (3), Thomas; C: Thomas; PG: Thomas (2)
USA	23	T: Walker, Anitoni; C: Alexander (2); PG: Alexander (3)

18 November 2000, Millennium Stadium, Cardiff
Wales	42	T: James (2), Williams, H Taylor, N Jenkins, A Thomas; C: A Thomas (2), Jenkins; PG: A Thomas (2)
USA	11	T: Delai; PG: Wells (2)

4 June 2005, Rentschler Stadium, Hartford
Wales	77	T: Sweeney, C Morgan, Robinson, K Morgan, Charvis (2), J Thomas, Phillips, Selly, Pugh, Williams; C: Sweeney (11)
USA	3	PG: Hercus

6 June 2009, Toyota Park, Chicago
Wales	48	T: Davies (2), James, M Jones, Cooper, penalty try; C: Robinson (3), Biggar (2), James; PG: Robinson (2)
USA	15	T: Tuilevuka, Gagiani; C; de Bartalo; PG: de Bartalo

Wales vs Zimbabwe

22 May 1993, Hartsfield Ground, Bulawayo
Wales	35	T: Moon, Hill, Proctor, P Davies; C: N Jenkins (3); PG: N Jenkins (2); DG: A Davies
Zimbabwe	14	T: Olonga; PG: Walters (3)

29 May 1993, Police Grounds, Harare
Wales	42	T: G Llewellyn (2), Bidgood, J Davies, N Jenkins, S Davies; C: N Jenkins (3); PG: N Jenkins (2)
Zimbabwe	13	T: Olonga; C: Noble; PG: Noble (2)

6 June 1998, Police Grounds, Harare
Wales	49	T: Haywood (3), A Thomas (2), Rees (2), Proctor; C: A Thomas (3); PG: A Thomas
Zimbabwe	11	T: Bekker; PG: Tsimba (2)

Wales: summaries and records

Home matches	
Played	305
Won	185
Lost	109
Drawn	11
Points for	5,275
Points against	3,711
Average score	17.30/12.17
Win %	60.66
Lose %	35.74
Draw %	3.61

Away matches	
Played	274
Won	116
Lost	142
Drawn	16
Points for	3,875
Points against	4,400
Average score	14.14/16.66
Win %	42.34
Lose %	51.82
Draw %	5.84

Neutral venues	
Played	21
Won	11
Lost	10
Drawn	0
Points for	509
Points against	516
Average score	24.24/24.57
Win %	52.38
Lose %	47.62
Draw %	0

Total matches	
Played	600
Won	312
Lost	261
Drawn	27
Points for	9,659
Points against	8,627
Average score	16.1/14.38
Win %	52
Lose %	43.5
Draw %	4.5

Most capped players: Wales							
Player	Caps	Career	T	C	PG	DG	Total
Gareth Thomas	100	27/05/1995–29/09/2007	40	-	-	-	200
Colin Charvis	94	01/12/1996–24/11/2007	22	-	-	-	110
Gareth Llewellyn	92	04/11/1989–20/11/2004	5	-	-	-	24
Martyn Williams	88	24/08/1996–21/03/2009	14	-	-	1	73
Neil Jenkins	87	19/01/1991–01/11/2002	11	130	235	10	1049

Most tests as captain: Wales		
No.	Player	Period
28	Ieuan Evans	1991–1995
22	Colin Charvis	2002–2004
22	Rob Howley	1998–1999
21	Gareth Thomas	2003–2007
19	Jonathan Humphreys	1995–2003

Most points by a player in a career: Wales							
No.	Player	Tests	Career	T	C	PG	DG
1 049	Neil Jenkins	87	19/01/1991–01/11/2002	11	130	235	10
693	Stephen Jones	80	27/06/1998–21/03/2009	6	117	138	5
304	Paul Thorburn	37	30/03/1985–22/07/1991	2	43	70	-
230	Shane Williams	65	05/02/2000–21/03/2009	46	-	-	-
211	Arwel Thomas	23	05/10/1996–26/11/2000	11	30	32	-

Most tries by a player in a career: Wales

No.	Player	Tests	Career
46	Shane Williams	65	05/02/2000–21/03/2009
40	Gareth Thomas	100	27/05/1995–29/09/2007
33	Ieuan Evans	72	07/02/1987–07/02/1998
22	Colin Charvis	94	01/12/1996–24/11/2007
20	Gareth Edwards	53	01/04/1967–18/03/1978
20	Gerald Davies	46	03/12/1966–17/06/1978
20	Tom Shanklin	63	17/06/2001–21/03/2009

Most conversions by a player in a career: Wales

No.	Player	Tests	Career
130	Neil Jenkins	87	19/01/1991–01/11/2002
117	Stephen Jones	80	27/06/1998–21/03/2009
43	Paul Thorburn	37	30/03/1985–22/07/1991
38	Jack Bancroft	18	16/01/1909–02/03/1914
34	James Hook	33	11/06/2006–14/03/2009

Most penalties by a player in a career: Wales

No.	Player	Tests	Career
235	Neil Jenkins	87	19/01/1991–01/11/2002
138	Stephen Jones	80	27/06/1998–21/03/2009
70	Paul Thorburn	37	30/03/1985–22/07/1991
36	Phil Bennett	29	22/03/1969–18/03/1978
35	Steve Fenwick	30	18/01/1975–07/02/1981
35	James Hook	33	11/06/2006–14/03/2009

Most drop goals by a player in a career: Wales

No.	Player	Tests	Career
13	Jonathan Davies	32	20/04/1985–15/03/1997
10	Neil Jenkins	87	19/01/1991–01/11/2002
8	Barry John	25	03/12/1966–25/03/1972
7	Gareth Davies	21	11/06/1978–30/03/1985
5	Stephen Jones	80	27/06/1998–21/03/2009

Most points by a player in a match: Wales

No.	Player	T	C	PG	DG	Versus	Venue	Date
30	Neil Jenkins	1	5	5	–	Italy	Stadio di Monigo, Treviso	20/03/1999
29	Neil Jenkins	–	1	9	–	France	Millennium Stadium, Cardiff	28/08/1999
28	Gavin Henson	–	14	–	–	Japan	Millennium Stadium, Cardiff	26/11/2004
28	Neil Jenkins	1	4	3	2	France	Stade de France, Paris	17/03/2001
28	Neil Jenkins	1	1	7	–	Canada	Millennium Stadium, Cardiff	21/08/1999

\multicolumn{5}{c}{Most tries by a player in a match: Wales}
No.	Player	Versus	Venue	Date
4	Colin Charvis	Japan	Millennium Stadium, Cardiff	26/11/2004
4	Tom Shanklin	Romania	Millennium Stadium, Cardiff	12/11/2004
4	Shane Williams	Japan	Hanazono Stadium, Osaka	10/06/2001
4	Gareth Thomas	Italy	Stadio di Monigo, Treviso	20/03/1999
4	Nigel Walker	Portugal	Universitario Lisboa, Lisbon	19/05/1994
4	Ieuan Evans	Canada	Rugby Park, Invercargill	03/06/1987
4	Maurice Richards	England	National Stadium, Cardiff	12/04/1969
4	Reggie Gibbs	France	National Stadium, Cardiff	02/03/1908
4	Willie Llewellyn	England	St Helen's, Swansea	07/01/1899

\multicolumn{5}{c}{Most conversions by a player in a match: Wales}
No.	Player	Versus	Venue	Date
14	Gavin Henson	Japan	Millennium Stadium, Cardiff	26/11/2004
11	Ceri Sweeney	United States	Rentschler Stadium, Hartford	04/06/2005
11	Neil Jenkins	Portugal	Universitario Lisboa, Lisbon	19/05/1994
10	Stephen Jones	Romania	Millennium Stadium, Cardiff	19/09/2001
8	James Hook	Canada	Millennium Stadium, Cardiff	17/11/2006
8	Neil Jenkins	Japan	Millennium Stadium, Cardiff	09/10/1999
8	Jack Bancroft	France	St Helen's, Swansea	01/01/1910

\multicolumn{5}{c}{Most penalties by a player in a match: Wales}
No.	Player	Versus	Venue	Date
9	Neil Jenkins	France	Millennium Stadium, Cardiff	28/08/1999
8	Neil Jenkins	Canada	National Stadium, Cardiff	10/11/1993
7	Neil Jenkins	Italy	Millennium Stadium, Cardiff	19/02/2000
7	Neil Jenkins	Canada	Millennium Stadium, Cardiff	21/08/1999
7	Neil Jenkins	Italy	National Stadium, Cardiff	12/10/1994

\multicolumn{5}{c}{Most drop goals by a player in a match: Wales}
No.	Player	Versus	Venue	Date
3	Neil Jenkins	Scotland	Murrayfield, Edinburgh	17/02/2001
2	Neil Jenkins	France	Stade de France, Paris	17/03/2001
2	Jonathan Davies	Scotland	National Stadium, Cardiff	20/02/1988
2	Jonathan Davies	Ireland	Athletic Park, Wellington	25/05/1987
2	Malcolm Dacey	England	Twickenham, London	17/03/1984
2	Barry John	England	National Stadium, Cardiff	1971/01/16
2	Albert Jenkins	Scotland	St Helen's, Swansea	1921/02/05
2	Jerry Shea	England	St Helen's, Swansea	1920/01/17

WALES

No.	Result	T	C	PG	DG	Versus	Venue	Date
		Points						
102	102–11	16	11	-	-	Portugal	Universitario Lisboa, Lisbon	18/05/1994
98	98–0	14	14	-	-	Japan	Millennium Stadium, Cardiff	26/11/2004
81	81–9	11	10	2	-	Romania	Millennium Stadium, Cardiff	19/09/2001
77	77–3	11	11	-	-	United States	Rentschler Stadium, Hartford	04/06/2005
72	72–18	11	7	1	-	Japan	Millennium Stadium, Cardiff	20/09/2007

Most points in a match by Wales

No.	Period	Details
11	09/03/1907 - 01/01/1910	Ireland (H), England (A), Scotland (H), France (H), Ireland (A), Australia (H), England (H), Scotland (A), France (A), Ireland (H), France (H)
10	06/03/1999 - 09/10/1999	France (A), Italy (A), England (A), Argentina (A), Argentina (A), South Africa (H), Canada (H), France (H), Argentina (H), Japan (H)

Most consecutive test wins by Wales

Milestones		
Longest test career	Gareth Llewellyn	04/11/1989–20/11/2004 (15 years & 17 days)
Youngest test player	Norman Biggs	18 years & 49 days on 22/12/ 1888 vs New Zealand Maoris in Swansea
Oldest test player	Tommy Vile	38 years & 152 days on 05/02/1921 vs Scotland in Swansea

Action photo from the 1905 international between Wales and New Zealand in Cardiff, won so famously by Wales. *Photo*: New Zealand Rugby Museum

Top left: Welsh Lions legend Barry John scores his crucial try against the All Blacks during the third test of 1971 in Wellington, won 13-3 by the Lions.
Photo: New Zealand Rugby Museum

Above: Welsh winger Gerald Davies evades his opposite number Bryan Williams during the second test of the 1971 British Lions vs New Zealand series. Davies went on to score two tries in the match and was a star performer in the Lions famous 2-1 series victory. *Photo*: New Zealand Rugby Museum

New Zealand prop Ken Gray crashes over Welsh fullback J.P.R. Williams to score in the first test of the 1969 series in Christchurch. Colin Meads (left) moves up in support as Mervyn Davies watches in despair in the background. New Zealand won by 19-0.
Photo: New Zealand Rugby Museum

International summaries and records

In international rugby there is an elite 'club' of players who have reached the impressive milestone of having played over 100 internationals in their career: a feat that has only become possible with the advent of the jet age and the resultant increase in fixtures. In 1994 slick French centre Philippe Sella became the first player to reach 100 tests. George Gregan of Australia tops the list, having played more internationals than any other player in the world with a total of 139: a record hardly likely to be broken, certainly not in the foreseeable future. South African fullback Percy Montgomery became the most recent player to join the Hundred Club during the 2008 Tri-Nations tournament

Spare a thought though for those players in the early years of rugby, many of whom played in a dozen seasons and more, but who were only able to appear in a few test matches. A prime example is South African Barry 'Fairy' Heatlie who captained South Africa in their first test victory and played for 13 seasons from 1891 to 1903 but won just six caps. More recently, legendary South Africans Naas Botha and Danie Gerber both played 13 seasons from 1980 to 1992 but only played in 28 and 24 internationals respectively because of South Africa's internatiional pariah status.

Listed in the following pages are tables of international records, both player and country. These records are being broken more and more frequently as rugby becomes a more global game, with top sides racking up records in what were once rare games against emerging nations. In 1951 South Africa beat Scotland by a then world-record margin of 44–0 which was considered a stupendous performance never to be eclipsed, but just 50 years later victory margins of 150 points or more are not considered unusual, neither is a player scoring 40 points or more in a match. A mere two decades ago it was considered a near-impossible achievement for a player to score over 1,000 points in a career, but as the game has evolved to yield bigger scores, coupled with the busier fixture lists of today's professional era, players have more opportunities to write their names into the record books than yesteryear's counterparts.

Most capped players

Caps	Player	Team	Career	Points T	C	PG	DG	Total
139	George Gregan	Australia	18/06/1994–06/10/2007	18	-	-	3	99
114 / 5 — 119	Jason Leonard	England	28/07/1990–15/02/2004	1	1	-	-	-	5	5
		British & Irish Lions	26/06/1993–07/07/2001	-		-	-	-	-
118	Fabien Pelous	France	17/10/1995–13/10/2007	8	-	-	-	40
111	Philippe Sela	France	31/10/1982–22/06/1995	36	-	-	-	125
100 / 3 — 103	Gareth Thomas	Wales	27/05/1995–29/09/2007	40	41	-	-	-	200	205
		British & Irish Lions	25/06/2005–09/07/2005	1		-	-	-	5
102	Percy Montgomery	South Africa	28/06/1997–30/08/2008	25	153	148	6	893
102	Stephen Larkham	Australia	22/06/1996–08/09/2007	25	2	-	2	135
101	Alessandro Trocon	Italy	07/05/1994–29/09/2007	19	-	-	-	95
101	David Campese	Australia	14/08/1982–01/012/1996	84	8	7	2	315
99	George Smith	Australia	04/11/2000–27/06/2009	9	-	-	-	45
93 / 6 — 99	Brian O'Driscoll	Ireland	12/06/1999–21/03/2009	36	37	-	-	5	195	200
		British & Irish Lions	30/06/2001–27/06/2009	1		-	-	-	5

Most tests as captain

Tests	Player	Teams	Period
59	Will Carling	England	05/11/19–17/03/1996
59	George Gregan	Australia	01/11/20–23/09/2007
58	John Smit	South Africa	24/10/2003–04/07/2009
56 / 1 — 57	Brian O'Driscoll	Ireland	09/11/2002–21/03/2009
		British & Irish Lions	25/06/2005
55	John Eales	Australia	06/07/1996–01/09/2001
51	Sean Fitzpatrick	New Zealand	18/04/1992–16/08/1997
48	Lisandro Arbizu	Argentina	1992–2003
39 / 6 — 45	Martin Johnson	England	26/06/1999–22/11/2003
		British & Irish Lions	21/06/1997–14/07/2001
42	Takura Miuchi	Japan	2002–2008
42	Fabien Pelous	France	1997–19/010/2007

Most points by a player in a career

Total points		Player	Team	Tests		Career	Points split							
							T		C		PG		DG	
1,032	1,099	Jonny Wilkinson	England	70	76	04/04/1998–15/03/2008	6	7	144	151	209	225	29	29
67			British & Irish Lions	6		30/06/2001–02/07/2005	1		7		16		-	
1049	1,090	Neil Jenkins	Wales	87	91	19/01/1991–01/11/2002	11	11	130	131	235	248	10	10
41			British & Irish Lions	4		21/06/1997–07/07/2001	-		1		13		-	
983	1,010	Diego Dominguez	Italy	74	76	02/03/1991–22/02/2003	9	9	127	133	208	213	20	20
27			Argentina	2		10/10/1989–12/10/1989	-		6		5		-	
	967	Andrew Mehrtens	New Zealand		70	22/04/1995–14/08/2004		7		169		188		10
919	919	Ronan O'Gara	Ireland	92	94	19/02/2000–21/03/2009	14	14	144	144	173	173	14	14
-			British & Irish Lions	2		09/07/2005–27/06/2009	-		-		-		-	
	911	Michael Lynagh	Australia		72	09/06/1984–11/06/1995		17		140		177		9
	893	Percy Montgomery	South Africa		102	28/06/1997–30/08/2008		25		153		148		6
	879	Daniel Carter	New Zealand		59	21/06/2003–29/11/2008		25		155		146		2
	878	Matthew Burke	Australia		81	21/08/1993–21/08/2004		29		104		174		1
693	746	Stephen Jones	Wales	80	86	27/06/1998–21/03/2009	6	6	117	124	138	150	5	6
53			British & Irish Lions	6		25/06/2005–04/07/2009	-		7		12		1	
	738	Chris Paterson	Scotland		95	16/10/1999–21/03/2009		22		86		150		2
667	733	Gavin Hastings	Scotland	61	67	17/01/21986–11/06/1995	17	18	86	87	140	160	-	-
66			British & Irish Lions	6		01/07/1989–03/07/1993	1		1		20		-	

Most tries by a player in a career

Tries		Player	Team	Tests		Career
	69	Daisuke Ohata	Japan		58	09/11/1996–25/11/2006
	64	David Campese	Australia		101	14/08/1982–01/12/199
49	50	Rory Underwood	England	85	91	18/02/1984–17/03/1996
1			British & Irish Lions	6		01/07/1989–03/07/1993
	49	Doug Howlett	New Zealand		62	16/06/2000–29/09/2007
46	48	Shane Williams	Wales	65	69	05/02/2000–21/03/2009
2			British & Irish Lions	4		23/05/2005–04/07/2009
	46	Christian Cullen	New Zealand		58	07/06/1996–16/11/2002
	44	Joe Rokocoko	New Zealand		55	14/06/2003–27/06/2009
	44	Jeff Wilson	New Zealand		60	21/11/1993–25/08/2001
40	41	Gareth Thomas	Wales	100	103	27/05/1995–09/07/2005
1			British & Irish Lions	3		25/06/2005–16/11/2002
	40	Chris Latham	Australia		78	21/11/1999–06/10/2007

Conversions		Player	Team	Tests		Career
169		Andrew Mehrtens	New Zealand		70	22/04/1995–14/08/2004
155		Daniel Carter	New Zealand		59	21/06/2003–29/11/2008
153		Percy Montgomery	South Africa		102	28/06/1997–30/08/2008
144	151	Johnny Wilkinson	England	70	76	04/04/1998–15/03/2008
7			British & Irish Lions	6		30/06/2001–02/07/2005
144	144	Ronan O'Gara	Ireland	92	94	19/02/2000–21/03/2009
-			British & Irish Lions	2		09/07/2005–27/06/2009
140		Michael Lynagh	Australia		72	09/06/1984–11/06/1995
127	133	Diego Domiguez	Italy	74	76	02/03/1991–22/02/2003
6			Argentina	2		10/10/1989–12/010/1989
130	131	Neil Jenkins	Wales	87	91	19/01/1991–01/11/2002
1			British & Irish Lions	4		21/06/1997–07/07/2001
117	124	Stephen Jones	Wales	80	86	27/06/1998–21/03/2009
7			British & Irish Lions	6		25/06/2005–04/07/2009
118		Grant Fox	New Zealand		46	26/10/1985–31/07/1993

Most conversions by a player in a career

PGs		Player	Team	Tests		Career
235	248	Neil Jenkins	Wales	87	91	19/01/1991–01/11/2002
13			British & Irish Lions	4		21/06/1997–07/07/2001
209	225	Johnny Wilkinson	England	70	76	04/04/1998–15/03/2008
16			British & Irish Lions	6		30/06/2001–02/07/2005
208	213	Diego Dominguez	Italy	74	76	02/03/1991–22/02/2003
5			Argentina	2		10/10/1989–12/10/1989
	188	Andrew Mehrtens	New Zealand		70	22/04/1995–14/08/2004
	177	Michael Lynagh	Australia		72	09/06/1984–11/06/1995
	174	Matthew Burke	Australia		81	21/08/1993–21/08/2004
173	173	Ronan O'Gara	Ireland	92	94	19/02/2000–21/03/2009
-			British & Irish Lions	2		09/07/2005–27/06/2009
140	160	Gavin Hastings	Scotland	61	67	17/01/21986–11/06/1995
20			British & Irish Lions	6		01/07/1989–03/07/1993
138	150	Stephen Jones	Wales	80	86	27/06/1998–21/03/2009
12			British & Irish Lions	6		25/06/2005–04/07/2009
	150	Chris Paterson	Scotland		95	16/10/1999–21/03/2009

Most penalties by a player in a career

461

Most drop goals by a player in a career					
DGs		Player	Team	Tests	Career
29	29	Johnny Wilkinson	England	70	76	04/04/1998–15/03/2008
-			British & Irish Lions	6		30/06/2001–02/07/2005
	28	Hugo Porta	Argentina	58	10/10/1971–10/11/1990
21	23	Rob Andrew	England	71	76	05/01/1985–15/03/1997
2			British & Irish Lions	5		08/07/1989–03/07/1993
20	20	Diego Dominguez	Italy	74	76	02/03/1991–22/02/2003
-			Argentina	2		10/10/1989–12/10/1989
	18	Naas Botha	South Africa	28	26/04/1980–14/11/1992
	17	Stefano Bettarello	Italy	55	14/04/1979–03/12/1988
	15	Jean-Patrick Lescarboura	France	28	06/02/1982–24/05/1990
14	14	Ronan O'Gara	Ireland	92	94	19/02/2000–21/03/2009
-			British & Irish Lions	2		09/07/2005–27/06/2009
	14	Goncalo Malheiro	Portugal	37	30/05/1998–01/12/2007
	13	Jonathan Davies	Wales	32	20/04/1985–15/03/1997
	13	Dumitru Alexandru	Romania	47	14/03/1974–20/09/1988

Most points by a player in a match								
No.	Player	Points				Country	Versus	Venue	Date
		T	C	PG	DG				
60	Toru Kurihara	6	15	-	-	Japan	Chinese Taipei	Taipei Municipal Stadium, Taipei	21/07/2002
50	Ashley Billington	10	-	-	-	Hong Kong	Singapore	Hoki Petaling Jaya Staidum, Kuala Lumpur	27/10/1994
50	Eduardo Morgan	6	13	-	-	Argentina	Paraguay	Clube Atlético, São Paulo	14/10/1973
45	José-Mariá Nuñez-Piossek	9	-	-	-	Argentina	Paraguay	Luis Franzini Stadium, Montevideo	27/04/2003
45	Simon Culhane	1	20	-	-	New Zealand	Japan	Free State Stadium Bloemfontein	04/06/1995
44	Pierre Hola	2	17	-	-	Tonga	Korea	Teufaiva Sports Park, Nuku'alofa	21/03/2001
44	Charlie Hodgson	2	14	2	-	England	Romania	Twickenham, London	17/11/2001
42	Gavin Hastings	4	9	2	-	Scotland	Cote d'Ivoire	Olympia Park, Rustenburg	26/05/1995
40	Mat Rogers	2	16	-	-	Australia	Namibia	Adelaide Oval, Adelaide	25/10/2003
40	Chris Paterson	3	11	1	-	Scotland	Japan	McDiarmid Park, Perth	13/11/2004
40	Daisuke Ohata	8	-	-	-	Japan	Chinese Taipei	Chichubunomiya Stadium, Tokyo	07/07/2002
40	Gustavo Jorge	8	-	-	-	Argentina	Brazil	Clube Atletico, Sao Paulo	02/10/1993

Most tries by a player in a match

No.	Player	Country	Versus	Venue	Date
11	Uriel O'Farrell	Argentina	Brazil	GEBA, Buenos Aires	13/09/1951
10	Ashley Billington	Hong Kong	Singapore	Hoki Petaling Jaya Staidum, Kuala Lumpur	27/10/1994
9	José-Maria Nunez-Piossek	Argentina	Paraguay	Luis Franzini Stadium, Montevideo	27/04/2003
8	Daisuke Ohata	Japan	Chinese Taipei	Chichubunomiya Stadium, Tokyo	07/07/2002
8	Gustavo Jorge	Argentina	Brazil	Clube Atlético, São Paulo	02/10/1993

Most conversions by a player in a match

No.	Player	Country	Versus	Venue	Date
20	Simon Culhane	New Zealand	Japan	Free State Stadium, Bloemfontein	04/06/1995
18	Severo Koroduadua	Fiji	Papua New Guinea	National Stadium, Suva	10/09/1983
17	Pierre Hola	Tonga	Korea	Teufaiva Sports Park, Nuku'alofa	21/03/2003
17	John McKee	Hong Kong	Singapore	Hoki Petaling Jaya Staidum, Kuala Lumpur	27/10/1994
16	Mat Rogers	Australia	Namibia	Adelaide Oval, Adelaide	25/10/2003
16	Jose Cilley	Argentina	Paraguay	Mendoza Rugby Club Stadium, Mendoza	01/05/2002

Most penalties by a player in a match

No.	Player	Country	Versus	Venue	Date
9	Andrew Mehrtens	New Zealand	France	Stade de France, Paris	11/11/2000
9	Thierry Teixeira	Portugal	Georgia	Universitario Lisboa Field, Lisbon	08/02/2000
9	Neil Jenkins	Wales	France	Millennium Stadium, Cardiff	28/08/1999
9	Andrew Mehrtens	New Zealand	Australia	Eden Park, Auckland	24/07/1999
9	Keiji Hirose	Japan	Tonga	Chichibunomiya Stadium, Tokyo	08/05/1999

Most drop goals by a player in a match

No.	Player	Country	Versus	Venue	Date
5	Jannie de Beer	South Africa	England	Stade de France, Paris	24/10/1999
4	André Pretorius	South Africa	England	Twickenham, London	25/11/2006
4	Juan Menchaca	Uruguay	Chile	Carrasco Polo Club, Montevideo	07/09/2002

No.	Result	Points				Country	Versus	Venue	Date
		T	C	PG	DG				
						Most points in a match by a team			
164	164–13	26	17	-	-	Hong Kong	Singapore	Hoki Petaling Jaya Staidum, Kuala Lumpur	27/10/1994
155	155–3	23	20	-	-	Japan	Chinese Taipei	Chichubunomiya Stadium, Tokyo	07/07/2002
152	152–0	24	16	-	-	Argentina	Paraguay	Mendoza Rugby Club Ground, Mendoza	01/05/2002
147	147–7	23	16	-	-	Argentina	Venezuela	Prince of Wales Country Club, Santiago	01/05/2004
145	145–17	21	20	-	-	New Zealand	Japan	Free State Stadium, Bloemfontein	04/06/1995

No.	Country	Period	Details
			Most consecutive test wins by a team
17	South Africa	23/08/1997–28/11/1998	Australia (H), Italy (A), France (A), France (A), England (A), Scotland (A), Ireland (H), Ireland (H), Wales (H), England (H), Australia (A), New Zealand (A), New Zealand (H), Australia (H), Wales (A), Scotland (A), Ireland (A)
17	New Zealand	18/09/1965–14/06/1969	South Africa (H), British Isles (H), British Isles (H), British Isles (H), British Isles (H), Australia (H), England (A), Wales (A), France (A), Scotland (A), Australia (A), Australia (A), France (H), France (H), France (H), Wales (H), Wales (H)
15	South Africa	08/10/1994–02/07/1996	Argentina (H), Argentina (H), Scotland (A), Wales (A), Western Samoa (H), Australia (H), Romania (H), Canada (H), Western Samoa (H), France (H), New Zealand (H), Wales (H), Italy (A), England (A), Fiji (H)
15	New Zealand	13/08/2005–26/08/2006	Australia (A), South Africa (H), Australia (H), Wales (A), Ireland (A), England (A), Scotland (A), Ireland (H), Ireland (H), Argentina (A), Australia (H), South Africa (H), Australia (A), Australia (H), South Africa (A)

Teddy Morgan of Wales (partially obscured bottom left) crosses for probably the most hotly debated try in rugby history, that against the 1905 touring All Blacks, which won the game 3-0 for Wales. *Photo*: Frédéric Humbert/www.flickr.com/photos/rugby_pioneers/creative commons license

Chapter Eight
Great players

This chapter provides a snapshot introduction to some of the greatest players from each of the top rugby nations, those magical people who have helped make the game what it is today. Through their skills and achievements each of these players has become a legend. There is no definitive, comprehensive or agreed list of the game's greatest stars; a separate volume would be required for all the greats.

Argentina

Agustín Pichot

Full name:	Agustín Pichot
Born:	22 August 1974 (Buenos Aires, Argentina)
Tests:	73 (31 as captain)
Debut:	30 April 1995 vs Australia, Brisbane
Position:	scrumhalf
Career:	30/04/1995–19/10/2007
Points:	60 (12 Ts)

Photo: Unión Argentina de Rugby

One of Argentina's greatest captains and surely their greatest-ever scrumhalf, Agustín Pichot made his debut in 1995 against then world champions, Australia, scoring a try in the process. Pichot went on to secure the number 9 Puma jersey as his own until the end of the 2007 RWC, being a permanent threat to the opposition with his sniping breaks from the rucks and mauls, which rewarded him with 12 tries in his career. Pichot's ability to influence and talk to the referee was also a real skill and won his team many tight decisions. In 1997, Pichot played a pivotal part in the side that beat Australia 18–16 in Buenos Aires to tie the two-test series, again scoring a try. At the 1999 RWC, he was a senior member of the side. Argentina had high expectations, which were met by reaching the quarter-finals for the first time, with Pichot scoring a try in the match against France. On 3 June 2000, Pichot was made captain for the first time in a tough encounter against Ireland where he led by example as Argentina won convincingly 34–23. His appointment as captain was at first temporary, but by 2003 he had become the regular national skipper, finishing his career in triumphant style as he led his side to third place in the 2007 RWC, after which he retired. Forever, a Puma legend, Pichot was also a great ambassador for the game off the field in Argentina, speaking out against amateurism and the need for Argentina to be included in annual global tournaments. As such, he has often been likened to Hugo Porta in his efforts to bring worldwide recognition to Argentinian rugby.

Hugo Porta

Full name:	Hugo Porta
Born:	11 September 1951 (Buenos Aires, Argentina)
Tests:	58 (38 as captain)
Debut:	10 October 1971 vs Chile, Montevideo
Position(s):	flyhalf, centre
Career:	10/10/1971–17/04/1999
Points:	595 (10 Ts, 84 Cs, 102 PGs, 26 DGs)

Photo: Unión Argentina de Rugby

No player from any country in the world has had as long an international career as Hugo Porta, who played top-flight rugby for Argentina for an incredible 19 years and 32 days. And if one takes into account Porta's 'celebrity' replacement appearance against a World XV in 1999 in a celebratory centenary match, officially recognised as a test match by the UAR, he can technically boast an international playing career of 27 years and 188 days to the time when he last took the field at the age of 47 years and 217 days, a record that will unlikely ever be broken. He made his debut as a 20-year-old against Chile in the 1971 South American Championship in Montevideo. He scored three tries in that tournament as well as three drop goals, illustrating his drop-goal-kicking prowess for which he became so famous. He went on to become arguably the greatest flyhalf of all time, able to influence and leave his mark on the game, all the while playing for a side that more often than not struggled against the top sides. He scored a massive 595 points for Argentina (a national record) which is all the more impressive when once considers he was often not the side's premier goal kicker. At the age of 25, Porta was given the captaincy thanks to his leadership qualities, ability to make clean breaks, amazing tactical awareness and skills as a kicker with ball in hand. His first game as captain was against France on 25 June 1977, and in just his second game at the helm he produced one of his finest performances, leading from the front and kicking all Argentina's points in an 18–18 draw. In 1979, he put together one of the finest performances of his career, leading Argentina to a 24–13 victory over Australia and kicking 16 points, including three drop goals. The victory became a landmark for Argentinian rugby and by 1985, Porta had written himself into the history books when he scored all 21 of his side's points, with three drop goals and four penalties, to draw with the All Blacks. Following the 1987 RWC, Porta retired at the age of 36, only to be called out of retirement in 1990 for the Pumas' tour to the British Isles. His final match, which turned out to be his penultimate because of his unique later appearance against the World XV in 1999, was against Scotland in Edinburgh on 10 November 1990. In addition to his 58 Argentinian caps, Porta also played and captained the South American Jaguars eight times, a side that took on South Africa during their isolation in the 1980s. Without doubt, his finest performance came on 3 April 1982 in Bloemfontein when he turned around an 18–50 drubbing the week before into a 21–12 victory for South America, scoring all 21 of his side's points with a complete 'full house': a try, a conversion, four penalties and the inevitable drop goal. Following his retirement, Porta was appointed Argentinian ambassador to South Africa and in 1994 he became Argentina's Minister of Sport. Such is his status in Argentina that in 2000, Porta was highjacked in Buenos Aires – only for the thieves to return his vehicle once they'd learned whose car they had stolen!

Australia

Matt Burke

Full name:	Matthew Burke
Born:	26 March 1973 (Sydney, Australia)
Tests:	81
Debut:	21 August 1993 vs South Africa, Sydney
Position(s):	fullback, centre, wing
Career:	21/08/1993–21/08/2004
Points:	878 (29 Ts, 104 Cs, 174 PGs, 1 DG)

Photo: Thys Lombard

Matt Burke progressed through the ranks of Australian rugby from the Australian Schoolboys side in 1990 to his international debut in the third test against South Africa in 1993, and went on to become one of the greatest Australian players of all time, notching up record individual scores time and again. In 1998, he scored all Australia's 24 points against New Zealand: a record against New Zealand by any player. The following year, he scored 24 points against South Africa in the RWC semi-final and 25 against France in the final to win the 1999 RWC. In addition, he holds individual Australian records against the Lions and Scotland, with 25 in a match. Primarily a fullback, Burke switched position later in his career to centre and wing to accommodate the young Chris Latham at fullback. He was a powerful runner and made a significant contribution to the adventurous game that brought so many rewards for Australian rugby in the 1990s. He is best remembered for his remarkable 70-metre individual try against New Zealand in 1996, when he beat nearly half the All Blacks side. For the final years of his career, Burke was relegated to the bench and on 21 August 2004 made his final appearance for Australia for just a few minutes as a replacement, against South Africa – the team he had made his debut against exactly 11 years earlier to the day. During his career, he played in three RWCs, winning one in 1999; he also won two Tri-Nations titles. He became the first player in the history of New South Wales rugby to play more than 100 games for the side and due to this legacy the New South Wales Waratahs player of the year wins the trophy named in his honour: the Matt Burke Trophy. He is currently the all-time second-highest points scorer in Australian international rugby, behind Michael Lynagh, and is one of Australia's most capped players of all time.

David Campese

Full name:	David Ian Campese
Born:	21 October 1962 (Queanbeyan, Australia)
Tests:	101
Debut:	14 August 1982 vs New Zealand, Christchurch
Position(s):	wing, fullback
Career:	14/08/1982–01/12/1996
Points:	315 (64 Ts, 8 Cs, 7 PGs, 2 DGs)

Considered by many to be the greatest winger of all time, David Campese held the world record for international tries until Daisuke Ohata of Japan overtook his tally in 2006. It was the way in which he scored his tries that makes Campese a legend. He was a gifted player with the panache and daring to attempt brilliant rugby while often walking a fine line between success and failure. His captain for many years, Nick Farr-Jones, summed up Campese as 'one of those instinctive players that just have pure genius'. Terry McLean added that 'he could side-step his way through a sealed paper bag'. However, he is most remembered for those famous goose-step tries that unravelled his opponents – a hitch-kick-type motion that left defenders eating his dust. Aside from his brilliant attacking skills, he was also shrewd in defence, often playing at fullback where his booming boot solved many awkward defensive situations. He made his debut against New Zealand as a teenager on 14 August 1982, when he notoriously replied, 'Stu who?' when asked about facing the legendary Stu Wilson of New Zealand. Despite genuinely not knowing who Stu Wilson was, Campese quickly featured in the press as a young upstart. He had a good series, scoring a try in each of the first two tests and beating Wilson not a few times. Wilson was later quoted as calling Campese 'a prick [who] made life hell for me for three tests'. Campese became a star for the Wallabies throughout the 1980s and it was during the Wallaby Grand Slam tour of 1984 that he really caught the world's attention by playing crucial roles in all the tests, setting up several tries and scoring one of his own from far out, against Scotland. He had a magnificent year in 1986, which included a Bledisloe series win, with coach Alan Jones describing him as the 'the Bradman of rugby'. His unorthodox play led to some of the best rugby ever seen but could also work against him, as it did in a 1989 match when he gifted Lions winger Ieuen Evans with the series-winning try – a moment still considered his career low and for which he was shredded in the Australian press. He bounced back in 1991 when he was voted the player of the RWC in which he was greatly influential in Australia's triumphant campaign. During the semi-final, New Zealand lined up to perform the *haka*, with Australia confronting them – bar one Campese, who snubbed the All Blacks by staying in the in-goal area, practising his kicking. He went on to score a try and create another to ensure victory for Australia. In the run-up to the final, Campese was quoted as saying 'I wouldn't play for England if you paid me', criticising their ten-man style of play. Many believe this is why England changed their game plan and, upon losing, Campese quipped: 'If England actually played ten-man rugby they probably would've beaten us.' In 1992, he was voted the international player of the year. As the years wore on, he lost his pace, but not his flair, and after the disappointment of the 1995 RWC and an ordinary 1996 season, he retired on 1 December 1996 after 14 years of international rugby.

Ken Catchpole

Full name:	Kenneth William Catchpole
Born:	21 June 1939 (Paddington, Australia)
Tests:	27 (13 as captain)
Debut:	10 June 1961 vs Fiji, Brisbane
Position:	scrumhalf
Career:	10/06/1961–15/06/1968
Points:	9 (3 Ts)

One of the best passers of the ball, Ken Catchpole ranks among the world's greatest scrumhalfs. He was a very small man for a rugby player, or even for a man, standing just over 1.5m tall, or slightly under 5 feet, but made up for this with his strength and his speed off the mark, which led to many of his sniping breaks wherever he sniffed, ferret-like, the opportunity. He captained Australia in 13 of his 27 internationals, being just 21 when he first led Australia, against the touring Fijians in 1961. He led Australia to their startling 20–5 win over New Zealand in 1964 as well as the 1966 victories over England and Wales. On 15 June 1968, his career was abruptly ended by All Black Colin Meads in the first test of the 1968 series. With New Zealand leading 19–3, Catchpole found himself in the unenviable position of lying over a New Zealand ball in a ruck, but couldn't move due to the weight of the players on top of him. Legendary lock Colin Meads, unaware of Catchpole's predicament, grabbed his outstretched leg and yanked it sideways to make the ball available. Such was the force of the tug that Catchpole's hamstring was torn completely free of the bone, severely rupturing his groin muscles. Catchpole himself held no animosity toward Meads, but some commentators condemned Meads for what they considered a deliberate action. Catchpole has since laid the issue to rest, stating it was merely a silly accident. In 2005, Catchpole was inducted into the Wallaby Hall of Fame.

John Eales

Full name:	John Anthony Eales AM
Born:	27 June 1970 (Brisbane, Australia)
Tests:	86 (55 as captain)
Debut:	22 July 1991 vs Wales, Brisbane
Position(s):	lock, eighthman
Career:	22/07/1991–01/09/2001
Points:	173 (2 Ts, 31 Cs, 34 PGs)

One of the few players in the game's history to have won two RWC gold medals, John Eales made his debut as a 21-year-old in a thumping win over Wales in 1991 and went on to become one of the most successful Australian rugby captains of all time. He achieved every accolade possible, beating all opponents and winning every available trophy, domestic and international. Eales was one of the first truly all-round professional athletes, the epitome of the modern rugby forward. He was such a brilliant sportsman and all-rounder that he was given the nickname Nobody ('nobody's perfect'), an apt acknowledgment of his skill and talent, but also for his innate sense of fairness and diplomacy. Remarkably, and rarely for a lock forward, Eales was very often the team's number-one goal kicker and his haul of 173 points for Australia is a world record for a forward in international rugby. A career-threatening shoulder injury sidelined Eales, but he was back in action to win the Bledisloe Cup in 1994. After the disappointment of the 1995 RWC, he was appointed captain for the 1996 Tri-Nations series – a daunting challenge which started with a 6–43 humiliation against New Zealand. He was eventually to lead Australia to World Cup glory, defeating France in the 1999 final in Cardiff. In 2000, he kicked the crucial penalty from the sideline against New Zealand in Wellington to ensure a 24–23 victory, which led to Australia winning their first Tri-Nations title. In 2001, he led Australia to their first series win over the British and Irish Lions, finishing his career by winning the 2001 Tri-Nations. His 86 caps make him the second-most capped Australian forward of all time after George Smith. In 2007, his services to rugby were honoured when he was inducted into the IRB Hall of Fame. He was also appointed a Member of the Order of Australia (AM).

Mark Ella

Full name:	Mark Gordon Ella
Born:	5 June 1959 (Sydney, Australia)
Tests:	25 (10 as captain)
Debut:	21 June 1980 vs New Zealand, Sydney
Position:	flyhalf
Career:	21/06/1980–08/12/1984
Points:	78 (6 Ts, 3 Cs, 8 PGs, 8 DGs)

Mark Ella first appeared on the international arena in the 1979 tour to Argentina, but was not to feature in an international until the following year, against New Zealand in a spectacular Bledisloe Cup series, when he played an integral part in Australia's series triumph.

In 1982 and 1983, he was given the Australian captaincy, with modest success, but it was on the Wallaby Grand Slam tour of 1984 that he wrote his name into the history books. With Andrew Slack relieving him of the captaincy, he was freed from the associated pressures and together with rookie scrumhalf Nick Farr-Jones was able to play his characteristic free-flowing game. Ella became the first tourist to score a try in every single test against the home unions. Despite this remarkable achievement, Ella stunned the rugby world by retiring after the tour at the age of just 25 due to a sour relationship with coach Alan Jones. The game, and Australia, undoubtedly lost many years of Ella dominance, but his twin brother Glen and younger brother Gary were both destined to represent Australia, although never together in the same test. Ella is regarded by many, including David Campese, as the greatest rugby player ever seen. A proficient exponent of the flat attack style, Ella had a unique approach to playing the flyhalf position, different to that of any other flyhalf of the time.

Nick Farr-Jones

Full name:	Nicholas Campbell Farr-Jones
Born:	18 April 1962 (Carringbah, Australia)
Tests:	63 (36 as captain)
Debut:	3 November 1984 vs England, London
Position:	scrumhalf
Career:	03/11/1984–21/08/1993
Points:	36 (9 Ts)

Along with great Australian scrumhalfs such as Ken Catchpole, John Hipwell and George Gregan, Farr-Jones undoubtedly remains one of the finest, leading his nation to 1991 World Cup glory. He formed a formidable long-time partnership with flyhalf Michael Lynagh, playing together 47 times. Farr-Jones was such an influential player in Australia's attacking game plan that it was calculated he had a hand in 46 of David Campese's 64 tries. He made his debut during Australia's Grand Slam tour of 1984, playing behind a dominant pack and thriving on attack. He played a crucial role in the Wallabies' famous Bledisloe triumph in New Zealand in 1986. With the failure of the 1987 RWC campaign, skipper Andrew Slack was sacked and Farr-Jones took over as captain at the age of 25, against England on 5 June 1988. His early years as captain were difficult, as his side lost heavily to New Zealand and a series to the British Lions in 1989. However, by 1991, fortunes had shifted, with victories over New Zealand; by the 1991 RWC, Australia were considered strong candidates. Farr-Jones led the team magnificently despite suffering an ongoing shoulder injury, which removed him from the field against Ireland, and played crucial roles in the Lansdowne Road semi-final triumph over New Zealand and again in the final against England. The 1992 season was extremely successful, as the team lost just once in the process of regaining the Bledisloe Cup and also beating South Africa. Farr-Jones retired after the 1992 season, but was persuaded to return for one last series when South Africa toured in 1993. He relinquished the captaincy for the series, but his experience saw the Australians through to a 2–1 series win.

George Gregan

Full name:	George Musarurwa Gregan AM
Born:	19 April 1973 (Lusaka, Zambia)
Tests:	139 (59 as captain)
Debut:	18 June 1994 vs Italy, Brisbane
Position:	scrumhalf
Career:	18/06/1994–06/10/2007
Points:	99 (18 Ts, 3 DGs)

Few have had as long and distinguished a career as George Gregan. A World Cup winner in 1999 and Tri-Nations winner in 2000 and 2001, Gregan holds the world record for the most international appearances: an astounding 139. With the retirement of John Eales in 2001, Gregan was the natural successor, taking them to the final of the 2003 RWC. He went on to captain Australia a world-record 59 times and with this and his other rugby achievements, was appointed a Member of the Order of Australia (AM). Gregan was born in

Lusaka, Zambia, to a Zimbabwean mother and an Australian father, moving to Australia at a young age. He made his debut in 1994 against Italy. That same year, he made one of the most famous tackles in the game's history against New Zealand when he dislodged the ball mid-air from a diving Jeff Wilson, a try that, had it been scored, would have sealed the Bledisloe Cup for New Zealand. It would be a full year before Gregan was to taste test defeat, in the dramatic 1995 RWC quarter-final against England in Cape Town. He missed the 1995 Bledisloe matches but in 1996, cemented his place as first-choice scrumhalf, and in 1997 was appointed vice captain. He helped the team convert mixed success into world triumph when Australia won the RWC for the first time in 1999, and with the retirement of John Eales in 2001, became captain. He led Australia to the 2003 RWC final, only to lose narrowly in extra-time. In 2004, he made his 100th test appearance when Australia beat South Africa in Perth. He appeared in a record 79 tests with flyhalf Stephen Larkham, a world-beating partnership. In the match against France in November 2005, he surpassed Englishman Jason Leonard's record of 114 test caps for one team. On 17 June 2006, he became the most capped player in history when he donned his 120th cap against England, surpassing Leonard's 119 caps for England and the Lions. In 2007, Gregan was dropped as captain, but remained the starting scrumhalf through to the 2007 RWC. His illustrious career came to an abrupt end after the quarter-final against England when he announced his retirement.

Tim Horan

Full name:	Timothy James Horan
Born:	18 May 1970 (Darlinghurst, Australia)
Tests:	80 (1 as captain)
Debut:	5 August 1989 vs New Zealand, Auckland
Position(s):	centre, flyhalf, wing
Career:	05/08/1989–17/06/2000
Points:	140 (30 Ts)

Nicknamed 'Helmet' for his immaculate hairstyle, Tim Horan was one of the best centres in the world during the 1990s, earning himself two RWC winners' medals. Renowned for his attacking prowess, with a nose for the try line, rock-solid defence, and a playmaker supreme, Horan played 11 seasons of international rugby, scoring 30 tries. He was one half of the formidable centre pairing with long-time teammate Jason Little, whom he had met when he was 13. He made his debut in 1989 against New Zealand and scored one of the great tries of the 1991 RWC in the semi-final against New Zealand when Campese put him magically into space. The highlight of 1992 was his performance against South Africa in rainy weather in Cape Town where his playmaking put Campese in for a brilliant try. His career was nearly cut short in 1994 by a knee injury that sidelined him for a year. On recovery, he was selected to play flyhalf and was given the captaincy for the first (and only) time for the test against Wales. In 1999, he reverted to centre, a position where he was to reach the peak of his career in the RWC that year, named player of the tournament and also winning a year's supply of Guinness by scoring the quickest try of the tournament! He retired the following year due to ongoing injury problems, with his last appearance against Argentina.

Stephen Larkham

Full name:	Stephen James Larkham
Born:	29 May 1974 (Canberra, Australia)
Tests:	102
Debut:	22 June 1996 vs Wales, Sydney (as a replacement)
Position(s):	flyhalf, fullback, wing, centre
Career:	22/06/1996–08/09/2007
Points:	135 (25 Ts, 2 Cs, 2 DGs)

Larkham made his debut for Australia in 1996 as a fullback, but from 1997 through to 2007 was Australia's first-choice flyhalf after taking over the reins from David Knox. It was this move from fullback to flyhalf that is today hailed as coach Rod Macqueen's masterstroke which ultimately led to the Wallabies winning the 1999 RWC. Not in the typical mould of a flyhalf, Larkham became one of the finest in the game's history, with his intelligent play revolving around his elusive and incisive running which led to many great tries for both him and his backline. Ironically, Larkham is not remembered as a kicking flyhalf; yet arguably the greatest moment of his career was 'that kick' against South Africa in the 1999 RWC semi-final when he fluff-kicked a wobbly 48-metre drop goal against the defending champions to give Australia victory. Despite his slight build, Larkham was a solid defender, but inevitably suffered a rash of injuries. Nevertheless, he still managed to amass 100 international caps, thereby becoming the sixth man to do so when he ran out against South Africa in Sydney in 2007. Larkham and his scrumhalf George Gregan set a world record of 79 appearances together as a halfback combination. He finished his international career against Japan in the 2007 RWC.

Michael Lynagh

Full name:	Michael Patrick Thomas Lynagh
Born:	25 October 1963 (Brisbane, Australia)
Tests:	72 (15 as captain)
Debut:	9 June 1984 vs Fiji, Suva
Position(s):	flyhalf, centre, fullback
Career:	09/06/1984–11/06/1995
Points:	911 (17 Ts, 140 Cs, 177 PGs, 9 DGs)

Michael Lynagh played for Australia over 11 seasons and captained the side for the final three from 1993 to 1995. His personal haul of 911 international points, with an astonishing average of 13 points per match, was a world record only bettered by Welshman Neil Jenkins in 1999. During his career, he won against every rugby-playing nation, including an RWC in 1991, a Grand Slam in 1984 and several Bledisloe Cups. He made his debut against Fiji in 1984 at centre, as the flyhalf berth was securely held by Mark Ella. Upon Ella's retirement at the end of the season, Lynagh switched to flyhalf where the skills he'd learned at centre went a long way in unleashing the lethal Australian backs. Noddy, as was his nickname, was a prolific scorer, notching up several Australian individual records. He struck gold in his partnership with captain and scrumhalf Nick Farr-Jones, playing together in a staggering 47 tests. Despite this, Lynagh and Farr-Jones were unable to ensure victory in the 1987 RWC. During the 1990 series against France, Lynagh scored his 500th international point – the first player to reach this milestone. He was instrumental in the Australian RWC triumph of 1991, scoring the vital try against Ireland in Dublin after he had taken the captain's armband when Farr-Jones went off injured. In 1993, he was given the captaincy, but due to injury could not take it at that stage. His career ended as captain of the reigning world champions but unable to defend the title, bowing out to England in the quarter-finals.

John Thornett

Full name:	John Edward Thornett MBE
Born:	30 March 1935 (Sydney, Australia)
Tests:	37 (16 as captain)
Debut:	29 August 1955 vs New Zealand, Wellington
Position(s):	flanker, lock, prop
Career:	29/08/1955–11/02/1967
Points:	3 (1 T)

Photo: ARU

Thornett was one of Australia's finest captains in an era when Australian rugby was in a trough. He captained the country from 1962 to 1967, leading his side on four of his eight tours with Australia. He played 37 internationals and more than a 100 games for Australia. He was a firm believer that rugby union was a means of building character and supported the fundamental ideals of the game wherever he could. An incredibly versatile player, Thornett represented Australia in three different positions during his career. In 1964, he was honoured by Danie Craven to captain Craven's team of internationals at the SARB's 75th anniversary and in the same year was one of New Zealand Rugby Almanac's five international players of the year. He was an inspirational leader who advocated hard but fair play.

Under his leadership, Australia posted memorable victories over all the top nations. He became a Member of the Order of the British Empire (MBE) for his services to rugby union in New South Wales.

Johnny Wallace

Full name:	Arthur Cooper Wallace
Born:	5 September 1900 (Macksville, Australia)
Died:	3 November 1975
Tests:	8 for Australia, 9 for Scotland
Debut:	Australia: 3 September 1921 vs New Zealand XV, Christchurch Scotland: 20 January 1923 vs France, Edinburgh
Position:	wing
Career:	Australia: 03/09/1921–22/01/1928, Scotland: 20/01/1923–02/01/1926
Points:	Total 48: 15 for Australia (5 Ts), 33 for Scotland (11 Ts)

Photo: ARU

One of the dual-national rugby internationals, Johnny Wallace played 17 internationals: eight for Australia and nine for Scotland. He first wore the famous New South Wales jersey on tour to New Zealand in 1921. The following year, he went to study law at Oxford in England where he gained rugby blues for the university from 1922 to 1925. Because of his ancestry, Wallace was chosen to represent Scotland in the 1925 Five Nations, along with two of his Oxford backline teammates, helping Scotland win their first Grand Slam in spectacular style. Wallace returned to Australia in 1926 and was selected as captain for the 1927/1928 Waratahs' tour of Britain, France and Canada. Wallace's team was an immediate hit with him a very popular captain. Of the five internationals, his team won three and the tour was considered a great success. Wallace retired from international rugby in 1928, but stayed in the game, coaching Australia against the 1937 Springboks, and again on their tour of South Africa in 1953. He died on 3 November 1975, in small part due to his well-established smoking and drinking habits but will always be remembered as one of Australia's greatest players, captains, coaches and rugby administrators.

England

Bill Beaumont

Full name:	William Blackledge Beaumont
Born:	9 March 1952 (Lancashire, England)
Tests:	34 for England (21 as captain), 7 for Lions (4 as captain)
Debut:	England: 18 January 1975 vs Ireland, Dublin Lions: 9 July 1977 vs New Zealand, Christchurch
Position:	lock
Career:	England: 18/01/1975–16/01/1982 Lions: 09/07/1977–12/07/1980
Points:	0

Had it not been for a career curtailed by injury, Bill Beaumont may well have gone on to become the first player to captain the Lions on two tours. He was an inspirational captain, who, during the lean years of the 1970s and 1980s, captained England to a famous Grand Slam triumph in 1980. He made his debut in 1975 against Ireland as a late replacement for Roger Uttley, a match in which he had to play for 75 minutes as a prop after the starting prop Mike Burton left the field. He survived the ordeal, illustrating just how versatile he was. It was on the 1977 Lions tour to New Zealand that he first made a name for himself as a part of the strong Lions scrum. Having only joined the tour as a replacement, he went on to play in the final three tests. He first took on the English captaincy in 1978 against France. After his impressive season in 1980, which included captaining the North of England to a 21–9 win over New Zealand, he was chosen to lead the Lions tour to South Africa that year. Although the series was lost 1–3, he remained a popular captain on a tough tour, dealing diplomatically with the ugly politcal issues of the time. One of the best scrummagers in the game, Beaumont had to retire prematurely in 1982 after a series of head injuries. He represented England 34 times, a record for a lock in those days, and played seven tests for the Lions. He never scored any international points for England or the Lions, but claims his finest moment came in 1980 when he scored in the England/Wales–Scotland/Ireland international, stating 'I was always lethal from one yard out!' Today he is a popular commentator and has represented England on the IRB panel since 1999. He was the team manager for the 2005 British and Irish Lions tour to New Zealand. He is the Honorary President of the Wooden Spoon rugby charity. The winner of the English County Championship is awarded the Bill Beaumont Cup.

Will Carling

Full name:	William David Charles Carling OBE
Born:	12 December 1965 (Bradford-on-Avon, England)
Tests:	72 for England (59 as captain), 1 for Lions
Debut:	England: 16 January 1988 vs France, Paris Lions: 12 June 1993 vs New Zealand, Christchurch
Position:	centre
Career:	England: 16/01/1988–15/03/1997, Lions: 12/06/1993
Points:	54 for England (12 Ts)

England's longest-serving captain and the most capped captain of all time in international rugby, Will Carling was made England captain as a 22-year-old, having only played a few internationals. He was extremely committed to his team, which led to his – unheard of then – resignation from the army to concentrate on rugby; a bold move considering rugby was an amateur sport at the time. Carling was highly instrumental in raising the profile of rugby in the UK due to his clean-cut image and media-friendly persona. By the time he retired in 1997, rugby had progressed from its traditional image of a game played by beer-guzzling louts to an international sport watched by chic PR girls and discussed in trendy London restaurants. He was a part of England's record 8–28 loss against Australia in 1988 and was highly critical of the captaincy style of incumbent John Orwin, believing he could do better. Coach Geoff Cooke believed in the whippersnapper, giving him the captaincy later that year in the one-off test against Australia in London where England fired on all cylinders to defeat Australia 28–19. The rest is history. Of his 59 tests as captain, he led England to an incredible 44 victories: this after the slump of the 1980s. He led England to three Grand Slams in 1991, 1992 and 1995; a Five Nations title in 1996, which included a Triple Crown; as well as an RWC final in 1991, not to mention regular triumphs over southern-hemisphere opponents. Unluckily, Carling only played one test as a Lion, in 1993, when his tour to New Zealand was adversely affected by injury. He was England's first rugby player to gain celebrity status, but at a price: the media intruded into his personal life, with allegations of an affair with Princess Diana levelled against him. But it was his celebrity appeal that went a long way in increasing the popularity of the game. The RFU owes him a great debt, despite the fact that he called the RFU committee '57 old farts' in 1995, a comment that got him fired as captain and as a player. He was, however, reinstated, following a public outcry, coupled with the team's refusal to play under another skipper. A public apology from Carling had him reinstated in the 1995 RWC squad. He stood down as captain at the end of the 1996 Five Nations, but was still regarded highly enough to keep his position in the team above the dynamic Jeremy Guscott. His last test was against Wales in 1997 and he retired completely from rugby in 1999/2000.

David Duckham

Full name:	David John Duckham MBE
Born:	28 June 1946, (Coventry, England)
Tests:	36 for England, 3 for Lions
Debut:	England: 8 February 1969 vs Ireland, Dublin Lions 10 July 1971 vs New Zealand, Christchurch
Position(s):	centre, wing
Career:	England: 08/02/1969–21/02/1976, Lions: 10/07/1971–14/08/1971
Points:	36 for England (10 Ts)

One of the finest runners with a rugby ball in hand, David Duckham was perhaps born before his time, when running with the ball wasn't as important as it is today. His swerving runs and wonderful sidesteps were a feature of his game that brought him ten tries in an English jersey: in context an impressive record, considering he was on the winning side of only 11 of the 36 internationals he played. He was the star in an English team that struggled to compete in the 1970s and was very often the rare shining light. He was the only Englishman to feature in the famous 1973 Barbarians victory over New Zealand where he had a fine game, with the Cardiff fans nicknaming him Dai, as one of their own. He was an integral part of the British Lions team that beat New Zealand in 1971, with coach Carwyn James encouraging Duckham to play his natural game: an instruction that led to 11 tries in 16 matches for Duckham, more than in his entire career with England. He made his debut for England in 1969 against Ireland, scoring a try in the process. His ability to wrong-foot defenders with his trademark outside swerves, inside cuts and aggressive handoffs became the feature of his game. He specialised in scoring tries from open play and earned a call-up to the 1971 Lions tour of New Zealand, playing a crucial role in the tour's success. Duckham played his last match against Scotland in 1976; he was awarded an MBE for services to rugby in 1977. His autobiography is fittingly entitled *Dai for England*.

Eric Evans

Full name:	Eric Evans MBE
Born:	1 February 1921 (Droylsden, England)
Died:	13 January 1991
Tests:	30 (13 as captain)
Debut:	3 January 1948 vs Australia, London
Position(s):	hooker, prop
Career:	03/01/1948–15/03/1958
Points:	15 (5 Ts)

One of England's great captains, Eric Evans finished his career with England undefeated as captain across two seasons (1957 and 1958) and having led England to their 1957 Grand Slam victory, their first since 1928. A versatile front-row player, Evans made his debut against the touring 1948 Wallabies as a prop, but was not selected again until 1950. By 1951, Evans had established himself as England's first-choice hooker, representing his country in all internationals for the next four seasons. In 1956, he was made captain and went on to lead England 13 times over the next three seasons, his infectious vigour and enthusiasm rubbing off on his teammates for whom he set high standards of personal fitness. As a result, England won the Grand Slam in 1957 in front of a young Queen Elizabeth at Twickenham, followed by an outright championship win in 1958. In all, he played 30 tests over ten seasons and retired in 1958 at 37. On 15 June 1982, he was honoured by Her Majesty with an MBE for his inspirational rugby career and his charitable work for the disabled. He died on 13 January 1991 and, fittingly, his ashes were scattered over the Twickenham turf. He is today remembered by the ERIC room at Twickenham, an acronym for the England Rugby Internationals Club, of which he was a founder.

Dusty Hare

Full name:	William Henry Hare MBE
Born:	29 November 1952 (Newark, England)
Tests:	25
Debut:	16 March 1974 vs Wales, London
Position:	fullback
Career:	16/03/1974–09/06/1984
Points:	240 (2 Ts, 14 Cs, 67 PGs, 1 DG)

A long-serving player for England through some challenging years, Dusty Hare became an England legend, amassing 240 points, a record until 1992. He scored a world-record 7,337 points in first-class rugby from 1971 through to 1989. He was awarded an MBE in 1989 for his achievements and his services to English rugby. As if his rugby talents were not enough, Hare also played cricket for Nottinghamshire. At 21, he made his debut in the famous 1974 win against Wales but, incredibly, was dropped and did not to play again for England until 1978. It was his points-scoring feast of the 1980 Five Nations that wrote him into the record books and secured England's Grand Slam win against all odds, including his scoring all England's points in the 9–8 win over Wales, kicking the winning penalty deep into injury time. Times were lean for both Hare and England following this, as he had to fight not only for his position at fullback, but also to win matches. He toured New Zealand in 1983 with the British Lions, but did not play in any of the internationals. His final season ended in disappointment, with England managing just one win in the Five Nations, before losing uncompromisingly to South Africa, upon which Hare retired.

Martin Johnson

Full name:	Martin Osborne Johnson CBE
Born:	9 March 1970 (Solihull, England)
Tests:	84 for England (39 as captain), 8 for Lions (6 as captain)
Debut:	England: 16 January 1993 vs France, London Lions: 26 June 1993 vs New Zealand, Wellington
Position:	lock
Career:	England: 16/01/1993–22/11/2003, Lions: 26/06/1993–14/07/2001
Points:	10 for England (2 Ts)

Photo: TalkingEnglish/commons.wikimedia.org/creative commons license

Martin Johnson is regarded as one of the greatest lock forwards of all time and one of England's greatest-ever captains. He led them to Grand Slam and World Cup glory in 2003 and toured three times with the Lions, in the process becoming the only man in British and Irish Lions' history to captain them on two tours. Oddly enough, Johnson began his first-class rugby career in New Zealand when All Black Colin Meads persuaded him to play for King Country. Johnson did for two seasons and in 1990 was selected to tour Australia with the New Zealand under-21 side alongside Va'aiga Tuigamala, John Timu and Blair Larsen. Fortuitously, for England at any rate, he was persuaded by his wife to return to UK and by 1992 had earned his England under-21 colours. In 1993, he was selected for the senior side to play France in the Five Nations. It was a dramatic start to his career: his debut was as a last-minute emergency replacement for the injured Wade Dooley. In similar circumstances, Johnson was again summoned as a replacement for Wade Dooley for the Lions tour to New Zealand later that year, playing in the final two test matches. In 1994, Johnson played in his first full Five Nations campaign and became an integral member of the pack that dominated in the English 1995 Grand Slam. In 1997, he was selected to captain the British and Irish Lions tour to South Africa despite having never captained England. He led the Lions to a memorable victory and in 1999 was finally chosen to lead England against Australia on 26 June 1999 in Sydney. He again led the Lions in 2001, this time to Australia, but was unable to reach the peaks of 1997. In 2003, he led England to the elusive Grand Slam title. That same year he captained England to victories over New Zealand and Australia and reached a career high when he lifted the William Webb Ellis trophy in Sydney. Johnson was an inspirational leader and retired after the success of the 2003 RWC, although many believed he had several more years of international rugby in him. Since his retirement, he has stayed in the game, initially as a critic and analyst. However, in July 2008, he was appointed the England team coach, despite having no coaching experience, in an attempt to resurrect English rugby to the heights it had reached under his captaincy.

Jason Leonard

Full name:	Jason Leonard OBE
Born:	14 August 1968 (Barking, England)
Tests:	114 for England (1 as captain), 5 for Lions
Debut:	England: 28 July 1990 vs Argentina, Buenos Aires Lions: 26 June 1993 vs New Zealand, Wellington
Position:	prop
Career:	England: 28/07/1990–15/02/2004, Lions: 26/06/1993–07/07/2001
Points:	5 for England (1 T)

At the tender age of 21, Jason Leonard became the youngest prop to play for England when he made his 1990 debut against Argentina in Buenos Aires. On 15 November 2003, he won his 112th cap for England against France, becoming the most capped international player of all time, breaking Philippe Sella's record of 111. Today, Leonard remains the most capped forward in the game after scrumhalf George Gregan broke his initial record. He notched up an impressive four Grand Slams in 1991, 1992, 1995 and 2003 and a World Cup gold medal in 2003, a dozen years after receiving a silver against the same opposition in London. He was the rock of the English pack during these years and had it not been for a career-threatening injury to his neck in 1992, which required a piece of his hip bone to repair two damaged vertebrae, he would have appeared in many more tests. He was selected to tour New Zealand with the Lions, making his Lions debut in Wellington on 26 June 1993 in that famous victory. On 14 December 1996, he captained England for his first and only time and, fittingly, scored his one and only international try when he crashed over against Argentina at Twickenham. He was again selected for the Lions in 1997, featuring as a replacement in the first international. In 2001, he was selected for a third Lions tour, to Australia, where he came on as a replacement in the first two internationals of the series. He featured in every single match of the 2003 RWC, and in 2004 was awarded his 114th and final cap for England, against Italy before his retirement in March that year.

Brian Moore

Full name:	Brian Christopher Moore
Born:	11 January 1962 (Birmingham, England)
Tests:	64 for England, 5 for Lions
Debut:	England: 4 April 1987 vs Scotland, London Lions: 1 July 1989 vs Australia, Sydney
Position:	hooker
Career:	England: 04/04/1987–22/06/1995, Lions: 01/07/1989–03/07/1993
Points:	4 for England (1 T)

There are few players to have worn the English jersey as proudly as Brian Moore and who would do literally anything to ensure victory. Not a particularly large man for a hooker, Moore made up for this with sheer strength and commitment, earning him the nickname Pitbull, given to him by teammate Wade Dooley. He played in three RWCs in 1987, 1991 and 1995 and went on to play in all three tests of the successful 1989 Lions tour to Australia, where he was infamously caught celebrating the morning after the third test on Sydney Harbour Bridge doing aeroplane impressions. In the Five Nations of 1989, Moore scored his only international try, against Ireland, from close range: a memory he cherishes. In 1990, when England lost their Grand Slam decider to Scotland it broke Moore's heart and he vowed never again to lose to the men from the north. He kept his vow, by beating them on their way to a Grand Slam in 1991 and then by beating them again in the nail-biting 1991 RWC semi-final in Edinburgh. England went on to lose that final and Moore publicly blamed his own teammates, criticising them for opting for a running game when it was clear that the English pack was better. He was incensed by Campese's deliberate knock-down and was quoted as saying, 'Campese sets himself up as the saviour of rugby yet when it comes down to it he's as cynical as anyone.' Despite these disappointments, Moore was named the Rugby World Player of the Year. In 1993, he was selected for the British Lions tour to New Zealand. He played in second test when he and props Jason Leonard and Nick Popplewell dominated the All Blacks front row, with Moore completely overshadowing his opposite number Sean Fitzpatrick. In 1995, his final year of international rugby, Moore won a third Grand Slam title and gleefully sent Australia packing in a tightly fought RWC quarter-final in the same year. His final two tests were disappointing affairs with England losing to New Zealand in the semis and then to France in 3rd place play-off, thereby ending his career as England's most capped forward at the time. He is today a qualified manicurist and a respected international rugby critic and commentator.

Adrian Stoop

Full name:	Adrian Dura Stoop
Born:	27 March 1883 (London, England)
Died:	27 November 1957
Tests:	15 (2 as captain)
Debut:	18 March 1905 vs Scotland, Richmond
Position:	flyhalf
Career:	18/03/1905–16/03/1912
Points:	6 (2 Ts)

Photo: Frédéric Humbert/www.flickr.com/photos/rugby_pioneers/ creative commons license

With a Dutch father and an Irish-Scottish mother, Stoop became an English-naturalised rugby union player. He attended Rugby School in 1898 and played an amazing 182 times for the London-based Harlequins, 143 times as captain, over no fewer than 39 seasons from 1901 to 1939, playing his last game for the club at the age of 56! Stoop Memorial Ground at Harlequins is named after him. He made his debut for England in the 1905 Calcutta Cup match and ended his international career after the same fixture in 1912, with a total of 15 tests. Had he not broken his collarbone in 1907, he would undoubtedly have added a lot more to his cap tally. He twice captained his country, including the first English international played at Twickenham in 1910 when Wales were beaten 11–6. Stoop introduced the idea of playing a scrumhalf and flyhalf instead of a left and right halfback, a tactic which heralded a massively successful era for the English, which came to be known as the Stoop Era. He is credited with revolutionising back play, developing it into the style that we recognise today. In his retirement, he stayed involved in the game: as president of the RFU in 1932 and as a selector for both Harlequins and England.

Rory Underwood

Full name:	Rory Underwood MBE
Born:	19 June 1963 (Middlesbrough, England)
Tests:	85 for England, 6 for Lions
Debut:	England: 18 February 1984 vs Ireland, London Lions: 1 July 1989 vs Australia, Sydney
Position:	wing
Career:	England: 18/02/1984–17/03/1996, Lions: 01/07/1989–03/07/1993
Points:	Total 215: 210 for England (49 Ts), 5 for Lions (1 T)

For many years, Rory Underwood was England's most capped player (a record today held by Jason Leonard) and is still today England's most prolific try scorer, notching up 49 tries in his career, including a haul of five in a match against Fiji in 1989. Not a particularly big man, Underwood made up for his slightness with an ability to score tries from far out and to force his way through the smallest of gaps using his balance, strength and determination. He became the first Englishman to play in 50 internationals when he appeared against Scotland in the 1991 RWC semi-final. However, in the earlier part of his career his talent was stifled by an ailing side, but when Carling took over the captaincy and Geoff Cooke the coaching, Underwood began to thrive. His try-scoring feats earned him a place on the Lions tour to Australia in 1989 when he played in all three tests. He was part of the 1991 Grand Slam side and an integral member of the 1991 RWC squad, which came very close to winning the tournament. In 1992, he switched from right wing to left wing to accommodate his younger brother Tony the first pair of brothers since 1937 to represent England in a match. Rory formed a formidable partnership with Tony for many years, with the Underwood brothers proving excellent finishers on either wing. In 1993, he was again selected to tour with the Lions, this time to New Zealand where he played in all three tests, scoring a magnificent solo try in the second test to seal victory. Despite the disappointment of losing the series, Underwood played on to win his third Grand Slam medal in 1995, retiring at the end of the 1996 Five Nations when England won the Triple Crown.

Wavell Wakefield

Full name:	Baron William Wavell Wakefield of Kendal
Born:	10 March 1898 (Beckenham, England)
Died:	12 August 1983
Tests:	31 (13 as captain)
Debut:	17 January 1920 vs Wales, Swansea
Position:	flank
Career:	17/01/1920–02/04/1927
Points:	18 (6 Ts)

Photo: Frédéric Humbert/www. flickr.com/photos/rugby_pioneers/

Wakefield was an astonishing talent who played his rugby for Harlequins, but after World War I was hastily made captain of the Royal Air Force rugby team He was best suited as a flanker but was adept in any of the back-five positions. Many credit him with changing the forward role to focus more on loose-forward play, such as applying pressure to the opposition flyhalf. Essentially, he shaped forward play as we know it today, recognising the limitations of a scrum when forwards scrummed down according to whatever order they'd haphazardly arrived on the scene. Wakefield decided that specialist positions for the forwards would improve the game, assigning each member of the pack a specific position and function. He played 136 times for Harlequins, 82 as captain, over 12 seasons, scoring 51 tries: a lethal strike rate for a loose forward. He made his debut against Wales in Swansea in 1920 and played an astonishing 31 internationals, 13 as captain – two English records that stood unbroken until Bill Beaumont superseded them in the 1980s. He was one of England's most successful captains, leading his side to back-to-back Grand Slams in 1923 and 1924. He retired after playing against France in 1927. He changed his focus to politics in 1935 and became a Conservative MP and knighted in 1944. In 1963, he became the first Baron Wakefield of Kendal. In 1950, he served as RFU president and was president of Harlequins from 1950 to 1980. He died in 1983, but his name goes down in rugby legend, having been inducted into the International Rugby Hall of Fame.

Jonny Wilkinson

Full name:	Jonathan Peter Wilkinson MBE, OBE
Born:	25 May 1979 (Frimley, England)
Tests:	70 for England (2 as captain), 6 for Lions
Debut:	England: 4 April 1998 vs Ireland, London Lions: 30 June 2001 vs Australia, Brisbane
Position(s):	flyhalf, centre
Career:	England: 04/04/1998–present, Lions: 30/06/2001–09/07/2005
Points:	Total 1,099: 1,032 for England (6 Ts, 144 Cs, 209 PGs, 29 DGs) 67 for Lions (1 T, 7 Cs, 16 PGs)

Without doubt, Jonny Wilkinson has been the world's best flyhalf for a large chunk of his career and will always be remembered for scoring 'that' last-minute, extra-time drop goal to clinch the 2003 RWC for England. He twice toured with the British and Irish Lions, with a record haul of 67 points in his six appearances. His career has been plagued with injuries and having won the 2003 RWC for England, was prevented because of injury from any further appearances for England until the 2007 Six Nations. One can only imagine the effect this had on his career and yet, despite a four-year absence, Wilkinson remains the highest points scorer, not only in the world, but in RWC, Six Nations, Lions and English rugby. He made his debut at the age of 18 as a replacement against Ireland on 4 April 1998 in London. His introduction to international rugby was tough, with England losing by record scores, including a 76–0 drubbing by Australia on their 1998 southern-hemisphere tour. By 1999, he had begun to establish himself as England's premier flyhalf and by 2000 had finally claimed the number 10 jersey as his own, playing the entire Six Nations and kicking a record 27 points against South Africa in Bloemfontein. In 2001, he set an individual Six Nations record of 35 points against Italy and was selected to tour with the Lions to Australia later that year where he played in all three tests. In 2003, he was key to England's amazing season, playing a crucial role in their Grand Slam Six Nations triumph, as well as in their successful tour down under. His part in England's RWC triumph is legendary as he sank South Africa, Samoa, Wales, France and Australia with his left boot. He was named the 2003 IRB World Player of the Year, with an MBE and an OBE under his belt, to boot. In 2005, he toured with the Lions to New Zealand, playing in two of the three tests. More injuries again set him back and it was not until 29 January 2007 that he was again to play for England – his first national appearance since the RWC final on 22 November 2003. He made a remarkable comeback, scoring 27 points against the Scots, but was unable to complete the tournament due to injury. He represented England at the 2007 RWC where he was instrumental in turning England's campaign around to make the final in a tournament where he became the leading points scorer in the cup's history. During the 2008 Six Nations, Wilkinson notched up his 1,000th point for England against Italy and became the leading drop-goal kicker in the game's history, against France when he dropped his 29th goal.

France

Abdel Benazzi

Full name:	Abdelatif Benazzi
Born:	20 August 1968 (Oujda, Morocco)
Tests:	78 (10 as captain)
Debut:	9 June 1990 vs Australia, Sydney
Position(s):	flank, lock
Career:	09/06/1990–07/04/2001
Points:	45 (9 Ts)

Born in Morocco, Abdelatif Benazzi first played international rugby for Morocco before moving to France, where he went on to represent France in 78 internationals. He started his sporting career as a soccer goalkeeper, but by the age of 16 had taken to rugby and soon after represented his native country. Equally adept at either lock or as a back-row forward, his skill on the rugby field was quickly picked up by French selectors and in 1990 he made his debut against Australia. Benazzi played through some magical years with the French national rugby team, winning a series in New Zealand in 1994, back-to-back Grand Slams in 1997 and 1998 (he was captain in 1997) and reaching the final of the 1999 RWC when he was denied a decisive try, which may well have swung the match had he not tiptoed onto the touchline. In 1995, he very nearly scored the winning try in the semi-final against South Africa when he fell just inches short of the try line. He later stated: 'We were crying because we should have been there, but at least I made Nelson Mandela happy!' Benazzi retired from international rugby on 7 April 2001 after France were humiliated 48–19 by England in London.

Serge Blanco

Full name:	Serge Blanco
Born:	31 August 1958 (Caracas, Venezuela)
Tests:	93 (4 as captain)
Debut:	8 November 1980 vs South Africa, Pretoria
Position(s):	fullback, wing
Career:	08/11/1980–19/10/1991
Points:	233 (38 Ts, 6 Cs, 21 PGs, 2 DGs)

Born in Venezuela to a local father and a French mother, Blanco was brought up in Biarritz in the Basque country of France. He came to epitomise French flair with his elegant running style, creativity and inventive spirit. His nickname was '*le Superman du rugby*', coined by the French sports daily *L'Equipe*. It is not an exaggeration to say he is considered one of the greatest fullbacks in the game's history. Pivotal in so many of France's great tries, many of which he finished off himself, he was a threat from anywhere on the field as he so forcefully illustrated in the 1991 game against England in London, starting a move from behind his own goal line that ended with winger Philippe Saint-André scoring under the poles. He holds the current record for most tries by a Frenchman (38) and, for many years, held the French record for international appearances. The greatest moment of his career was his famous match-winning, injury-time try against Australia in the 1987 RWC semi-final in Sydney: with the scores poised at 24–24, he sprinted from 30 metres out, outpacing four defenders in the process to win the game 30–24. He ended his career captaining France in the 1991 RWC when they were knocked out by England in a fiery encounter in Paris. Difficult though it is to comprehend, Blanco was a heavy smoker, known to smoke as many as 75 cigarettes (Gauloises of course) a day but this did not impact on a memorable career that included two Grand Slams in 1981 and 1987. In 1997, he was inducted into the International Rugby Hall of Fame. He a now a successful businessman and is still involved in rugby, serving as president of France's National Professional League.

André Boniface

Full name:	André Boniface
Born:	14 August 1934 (Monfort-en-Chalosse, France)
Tests:	48
Debut:	23 January 1954 vs Ireland, Paris
Position(s):	centre, wing
Career:	23/01/1954–26/03/1966
Points:	44 (11 Ts, 1 C, 1 PG, 2 DGs)

André Boniface was one of the first great French backs to typify the style of French rugby with his silky skills at centre and on the wing. Over 13 seasons he scored 11 tries, but made many more with his abrupt change of pace and ability to put fellow players into space. He was quoted as saying, 'If defence is my primary role, I would have given up the game long ago,' and indeed it was the attacking component of the game that he so loved that made him such a great player. One of his most memorable tries came during the then record 13–0 win over England in 1966 when he ran the length of the field to score in the final minute of the match. He made his debut against Ireland in 1954 as a 19-year-old and in just his second international was part of only the second French team to beat New Zealand when they won 3–0. He played alongside his brother Guy in the French midfield in 18 of his 48 tests, in one of the most renowned brother combinations in international rugby. Guy went on to notch up 15 tries in his 35 tests for France, many of which he could thank his older brother André for creating. A member of the French team that won three Five Nations titles during his career, André retired at the end of the 1966 Five Nations tournament.

Benoit Dauga

Full name:	Benoit Dauga
Born:	8 May 1942 (Montgaillard, France)
Tests:	63 (9 as captain)
Debut:	4 January 1964 vs Scotland, Edinburgh
Position(s):	lock, eighthman
Career:	04/01/1964–25/03/1972
Points:	34 (11 T)

Benoit Dauga was one of the most determined and focused French players of all time, described as mean and menacing by his opponents due to the fact that he rarely smiled in his quest for victory, all the while oozing an aura of intense, brooding power. He was a completely rounded player with amazing stamina and commitment, versatile enough to play in all of the back-five forward positions. He was most effective at lock and could jump anywhere in the lineout, more often than not dominating his opposite jumpers with apparent ease. His lineout skills led to his nickname, the Control Tower. This coupled with his role in the powerful French pack was in no small measure the reason for the French successes of the 1960s and 1970s. He made his debut against Scotland in Edinburgh in 1964 and went on to captain his country nine times. He was a key member of the side that won France's first-ever Grand Slam in 1968 and has been described by many who watched him or played against him as the greatest forward of all time. His final international was against Wales in 1972; shortly afterwards the rugby world was stunned when he suffered a serious neck injury in a national championship game that paralysed him. He fought back, however, with great determination to near full recovery and is still an avid rugby fan today.

Jo Maso

Full name:	Joseph Maso
Born:	27 December 1944 (Toulouse, France)
Tests:	25
Debut:	9 April 1966 vs Italy, Naples
Position(s):	centre, flyhalf
Career:	09/04/1966–11/11/1973
Points:	15 (4 Ts)

The son of a former French rugby league international, Maso started playing league before switching to union, making his French debut soon afterwards against Italy, which he celebrated by scoring a try. From his debut he remained an integral part of the successful French sides of the late 1960s and was a member of the first French side to record a Grand Slam title, in 1968. He was a versatile player who preferred the centre berth, but also represented France at flyhalf in 1968 on two occasions. His most memorable performance in a French jersey came against England in Paris in 1972, when his elusive running split the English defence, creating several tries for his teammates and taking them to a record 37–12 victory. His last appearance was against Romania in Valence on 11 November 1973. Despite his retirement from the international game, he is still involved with the French national side as the team manager. In 2003 he was elected to the International Rugby Hall of Fame.

Lucien Mias

Full name:	Lucien Mias
Born:	28 September 1930 (Saint-Germain-de-Calberte, France)
Tests:	29 (2 as captain)
Debut:	13 January 1951 vs Scotland, Paris
Position(s):	lock, prop
Career:	13/01/1951–18/04/1959
Points:	3 (1 T)

It is no coincidence that the first glorious era of French rugby happened at the same time as the career of one Lucien Mias. This period included France's first win against New Zealand, a 1958 series victory over South Africa in South Africa and France's first outright Five Nations tournament victory in 1959. He was known as the father of French forward play, memorably described by Chris Hewett in the the *Independent* as a 'bulldozer with a brain' and nicknamed Doctor Pack because of his intimate knowledge of forward play – and he'd studied medicine. He introduced the concept of the advantage line in rugby tactics, revolutionising French forward play to the extent that his lineout calls and moves are still practised by the French national side today. He was a powerful driving forward, an inspirational organiser, pack leader and captain. After a brief stint away from rugby to concentrate on his medical studies, Mias returned for the 1958 Five Nations and took over as captain to lead France to an unthinkable series victory over South Africa in South Africa: the first team to do so since the British Lions of 1896. He will be most remembered for his antics before the decisive test against South Africa when he drank a bottle of rum on the eve of the game to calm his nerves and, despite waking up with a massive hangover, went on to play a blinder. His teammate Roger Vigier recalls his epic performance: 'I was so full of admiration for what Lucien was doing that I stopped playing myself that day.' Mias led his nation to France's first outright Five Nations title in 1959 and was thus able to retire on a crest that same year.

Robert Paparemborde

Full name:	Robert Paparemborde
Born:	5 July 1948 (Laruns, France)
Died:	18 April 2001, Paris
Tests:	55
Debut:	21 June 1975 vs South Africa, Bloemfontein
Position:	prop
Career:	21/06/1975–19/03/1983
Points:	32 (8 Ts)

One of the most powerful tighthead prop forwards of all time, Robert Paparemborde was often the base on which the French built their tough, effective teams of the late 1970s and early 1980s. He is one of the all-time greats of the game and is regularly named in dream teams across the world. For a prop forward, he was excellent with the ball in hand and an immensely strong scummager. He was quite simply the best of his generation and a man who wore the French shirt with immense pride. With a judo black belt, he was nicknamed the Bear of the Pyrenees. He made his debut as a 27-year-old on the French tour to South Africa in 1975, playing in both tests – one of the toughest debuts for any player. Neverthless, Paparemborde scored a try in each of the internationals and went on to become a regular feature in the French side until his retirement in 1983. He was a pillar of strength in the 1977 and 1981 Grand Slam sides which based their strategy around the powerful French pack with Paparemborde leading from the front. He formed a devastating front row with Gerard Cholley and Philippe Dintrans, which laid the foundation for the team's success. He retired from international rugby after winning the 1983 Five Nations championship. He kept himself involved in the game, managing the national side from 1984 to 1992 as well as coaching the Racing Club.

Fabien Pelous

Full name:	Fabien Pelous
Born:	7 December 1973 (Toulouse, France)
Tests:	118 (42 as captain)
Debut:	17 October 1995 vs Romania, Tucuman
Position:	lock
Career:	17/10/1995–13/10/2007
Points:	40 (8 Ts)

The third-most capped player in the history of rugby and the most capped Frenchman of all time, Fabien Pelous is regarded as one of the best French lock forwards and captains of any era. He was captain in 42 of his 118 appearances and made his debut at Tucuman in Argentina against Romania during the 1995 Latin Cup. From this moment on, he became a permanent feature of the French side, winning five Six Nations titles – four as Grand Slams – in his career and playing in the RWC final in 1999. Pelous is one of the great professional-era lock forwards, a giant in the lineout and physically dominating in the loose. After the 2003 RWC, he succeeded Fabien Galthié as national captain and enjoyed immediate success, leading his side to a Six Nations Grand Slam in 2004, second place in 2005 and the Six Nations title in 2006. He lost the captaincy due to a spate of injuries in 2007, but managed to regain his form and was selected for the 2007 RWC squad. Following defeat against England in the semi-final, Pelous called it quits and in 2008 retired from all rugby, after his beloved Toulouse's defeat in the Heineken Cup final.

Jean Prat

Full name:	Jean Prat
Born:	1 August 1923 (Lourdes, France)
Died:	25 February 2005 (Tarbes, France)
Tests:	51 (16 as captain)
Debut:	1 January 1945 vs British Army, Paris
Position:	flank
Career:	01/01/1945–10/04/1955
Points:	139 (9 Ts, 26 Cs, 15 PGs, 5 DGs)

Prat won his first French international cap during World War II when France took on the British Army in Paris on New Year's Day 1945. He kicked two conversions to help France win and from then on remained an integral member of the side for the next decade. He was a magnificent leader and took over the French captaincy in 1948, promptly leading his side to historic victories over Wales in Wales that year, England in England in 1951 and New Zealand in 1954. It was in the New Zealand game that probably the greatest moment of his career occurred when he scored a magnificent solo try to win the game 3–0. That year he also captained France to their first Five Nations title, shared with England and Wales. He was incredibly skilled for a flanker and was dubbed 'Monsieur Rugby' by the Daily Express. He had it all: a fierce tackle, exceptionally quick hands, a great rugby brain, an uncanny ability to read a game and a deadly accurate boot – all this from a flanker. During the 1955 clash at Twickenham against England, France were leading deep into the game with England fighting desperately for a draw. Captain Prat drew his troops together – in what is accepted as the game's first captain's huddle – and berated them: 'For centuries you have put up with the bloody English annoying you. Surely you can hold them off for another ten minutes!' The team duly did to set up a Grand Slam showdown with Wales, Prat's 50th appearance for France. However, it was not to be: the French lost by five points as the Welsh dashed French hopes and Prat's final moment of glory eluded him. He retired two weeks later after playing against Italy in Grenoble. With his leadership and commitment, he had laid the foundations for France to begin to dominate on the world rugby stage. During his career he played several times alongside his younger brother Maurice, a magnificent centre in his own right. In 2001, Prat was inducted into the International Rugby Hall of Fame.

Jean-Pierre Rives

Full name:	Jean-Pierre Rives
Born:	31 December 1952 (Toulouse, France)
Tests:	59 (34 as captain)
Debut:	1 February 1975 vs England, London
Position:	flank
Career:	01/02/1975–17/03/1984
Points:	20 (5 Ts)

One of the legends of French, and world, rugby, Jean-Pierre Rives, nicknamed *Casque d'or* (golden helmet) or Asterix, played 59 tests for his country across an illustrious career, despite many predicting he would go nowhere because of his diminutive size. Of his 59 appearances, he captained 34 times, which at the time of his retirement was a world record for captaincy appearances. He was instated as captain in 1978, leading France to a shared series in New Zealand and a Grand Slam in 1981. Renowned for his passionate commitment, as well as for his personal fearlessness, he won his opponents' respect in every instance. This was illustrated in the so-called 'summer test' when France took on South Africa in November 1980. During the match, Rives sustained a serious gash to the head with a massive loss of blood ensuing. He played on, bandages sodden, but the bleeding would not stop which so alarmed the Springbok captain Morné du Plessis that he had a serious word with Rives, asking that he leave the field to get urgent medical attention. Rives would have none of it and finished the match covered in blood. He was a key component of the French Grand Slam sides of 1977 and 1981, and rewarded by being voted French rugby player of the year for both seasons. He retired at the end of the 1984 Five Nations season, hoping to end his career on a high against Scotland in the deciding Grand Slam match of the tournament. Unfortunately for Rives, Scotland won and his stellar career came to a disappointing end. He has turned his attention to art and is today an internationally renowned sculptor. However, he is still involved in rugby, having played a major role in France's bid to host the 2007 RWC.

Philippe Sella

Full name:	Philippe Jean-Paul Sella
Born:	14 February 1962 (Tonneins, France)
Tests:	111
Debut:	31 October 1982 vs Romania, Bucharest
Position(s):	centre, wing, fullback
Career:	31/10/1982–22/06/1995
Points:	125 (30 Ts)

One of the most remarkable centres of all time, Philippe Sella was the first player to break the 100-test-appearances record. He based his game on a solid defence and a lethal finish. His eye to spot a gap and the pace to take it earned him 30 test tries. He made his debut at 20 against Romania but France lost and Sella woke up in hospital concussed to hear the result. But in his very next test he scored a brace of tries against Argentina. He played a large part in France's successful 1983 Five Nations season and came within a whisker of winning the 1984 Grand Slam. In 1986, he enjoyed his best Five Nations season when he achieved the rare feat of scoring a try in every match, rounding off the season by beating the All Blacks in Nantes. The 1987 season was even better, as the French lost just once: in the RWC final against New Zealand. Sella won his first Grand Slam that season and played a critical role in the RWC, scoring a crucial try in the semi-final against Australia. The 1991 RWC was a disappointment for the French and Sella, with mediocre Five Nations performances making for lean times. Sella reached a low in his career in 1994 when he was sent off against Canada, with the French losing the game. Considering this, little was expected of France against New Zealand but, remarkably, the French were to win the 1994 series in New Zealand, with Sella and notching up his 100th test match on 26 June 1994 in the win over New Zealand in Christchurch. He finished his career at the 1995 RWC, with France finishing third, upon which Sella retired with a record 111 internationals behind him.

Pierre Villepreux

Full name:	Pierre Villepreux
Born:	5 July 1943 (Pompadour, France)
Tests:	34
Debut:	26 March 1967 vs Italy, Toulon
Position:	fullback
Career:	26/03/1967–24/06/1972
Points:	163 (2 Ts, 29 Cs, 32 PGs, 1 DG)

Pierre Villepreux was one of the most powerful kickers of the ball the game has ever witnessed, a talent he illustrated perfectly during the French tour of New Zealand in 1968 when, from more than 60 metres out, he lined up for a kick at goal on the sodden Athletic Park turf in Wellington. The crowd sniggered in disbelief, but with exquisite timing he astounded everyone by converting the goal with room to spare. He made his debut against Italy in 1967 and became one of the first great attacking fullbacks, revelling in the wide spread of the ball in attack. His play was often risky and always audacious, marshalling the most magnificent counter-attacks through his superb balance and loping running style. Opposite fullbacks desperately needed to find touch if Villepreux was on the prowl. His instinctive, attacking style of play ensured that he was the first Frenchman to be selected to play for the Barbarians and, deservedly, was labelled the greatest fullback of his era. He retired following the successful series victory over Australia in Australia but kept himself involved in rugby, first coaching Italy and Tahiti; then serving as assistant French coach to Jean-Claude Skrela.

Ireland

Willie Duggan

Full name:	William Patrick Duggan
Born:	12 March 1950 (Kilkenny, Ireland)
Tests:	41 for Ireland (2 as captain), 4 for Lions
Debut:	Ireland: 18 January 1975 vs England, Dublin Lions: 18 June 1977 vs New Zealand, Wellington
Position:	eighthman
Career:	Ireland: 18/01/1975–03/03/1984, Lions: 18/06/1977–13/08/1977
Points:	Total 8: 4 for Ireland (1 T), 4 for Lions (1 T)

Like Serge Blanco of France, Willie Duggan of Ireland was a heavy smoker, but this in no way affected his characteristic style of play. He was once informed that were he to give up smoking he would be much faster around the pitch and, in true Duggan style, he replied, 'But then I would spend most of the match offside!' He loathed training but on the field was regarded as the best eighthman in the British Isles, reflected with his selection to tour with the British Lions to New Zealand in 1977. He made his debut in a winning Irish team against England in the 1975 Five Nations and went on to represent Ireland a total of 41 times. He played no small part in the 1982 Irish team that won their first Triple Crown since 1949, as well as being on the only Irish side ever to win a test series in the southern hemisphere, when they defeated Australia in 1979. His rock-solid defence, ever-reliable support play and barnstorming runs were characteristic of his game. He was selected for all four Lions tests in New Zealand in 1977 and scored the only Lions try in the third test. In 1984, he was given the captaincy of Ireland and retired at the end of a disappointing Five Nations campaign after the match with eventual Grand Slam champions Scotland. He remains today one of the most loved and remembered Irish rugby players.

Mike Gibson

Full name:	Cameron Michael Henderson Gibson MBE
Born:	3 December 1942 (Belfast, Northern Ireland)
Tests:	69 for Ireland, 12 for Lions
Debut:	Ireland: 8 February 1964 vs England, London Lions: 16 July 1966 vs New Zealand, Dunedin
Position(s):	centre, flyhalf, wing
Career:	Ireland: 08/02/1964–16/06/1979, Lions: 16/07/1966–14/08/1971
Points:	112 for Ireland (9 Ts, 7 Cs, 16 PGs, 6 DGs)

Few players in the game have had as long a career as Mike Gibson, who played across 16 seasons for Ireland and the British Lions. He went on no fewer than five British Lions tours, a record he shares with compatriot Willie-John McBride; he played in 12 Lions internationals and was instrumental in the victory on the 1971 tour to New Zealand. Gibson became the first-ever replacement in a Lions international when he replaced Barry John during the Pretoria test against South Africa in 1968. Fresh out of Oxford, he made his Ireland debut against England in 1964 as flyhalf, and helped ensure an 18–5 victory for the Irish. He is a player who will go down in rugby folklore as one of the finest backline players of all time. He was incredibly versatile, playing in three different positions for his country and often called up as the team kicker. He had great hands, streetwise mischievousness, physical durability, sound defence, a good kick and the instinct to run a great line with perfect time. But it was perhaps his rugby brain and calmness under pressure that set him apart. He could dog it out or set the stadium alight and his technical ability was devastatingly simple. He finished his career in style at the age of 36 – the oldest player ever to represent Ireland – when Ireland toured Australia and memorably won the two-test series: the first and only Irish side to date to win a series against southern-hemisphere opposition. His 69 Irish caps stood as a record for 26 years until broken by Malcolm O'Kelly. Gibson continued playing first-class rugby until the age of 42 and was awarded an MBE. He was one of the first to be elected to the International Rugby Hall of Fame when it was established in 1997.

Tom Kiernan

Full name:	Thomas Joseph Kiernan
Born:	7 January 1939 (Cork, Ireland)
Tests:	54 for Ireland (24 as captain), 5 for Lions (4 as captain)
Debut:	Ireland: 13 February 1960 vs England, London Lions: 4 August 1962 vs South Africa, Cape Town
Position:	fullback
Career:	Ireland: 13/01/1960–24/02/1973, Lions: 04/08/1962–27/07/1968
Points:	Total 193: 158 for Ireland (2 Ts, 26 Cs, 31 PGs, 2 DGs) 35 for Lions (1 C, 11 PGs)

One of the best fullbacks of all time, Kiernan started his career as a centre, however, his first senior game at fullback happened to be his first game for Ireland. He was a solid last line of defence for Ireland, extremely dependable under the high ball and strong in both field kicking and goal kicking. He made his debut against England in London in 1960 in a match the Irish lost. Two years later he was selected to tour with the 1962 British Lions to South Africa where he played in one of the internationals. He returned to the Lions in 1968, this time as captain. But the team struggled, failing to win a single international despite Kiernan's best efforts: he remarkably scored 35 of the team's 38 points in the series. When he retired, Kiernan took up coaching and led Munster to their illustrious victory over the 1978 New Zealanders and coached Ireland to their 1982 Triple Crown and Five Nations triumphs.

Jackie Kyle

Full name:	John Wilson Kyle
Born:	10 January 1926 (Belfast, Northern Ireland)
Tests:	46 for Ireland (6 as captain), 6 for Lions
Debut:	Ireland: 25 January 1947 vs France, Dublin Lions: 19 August 1950 vs Australia, Brisbane
Position:	flyhalf
Career:	Ireland: 25/01/1947–01/03/1958, Lions: 27/05/1950–26/08/1950
Points:	Total 30: 24 for Ireland (7 Ts, 1 DG), 6 for Lions (2 Ts)

Few rugby players can claim to have written their name across a particular period of the game so emphatically: the post-war period came to be known as the Jack Kyle era. Kyle made his debut against France and led Ireland to their first Grand Slam triumph the following year in 1948, scoring the vital try against the English to triumph 11–10 in London. He was one of rugby's first and greatest stars in the decade following World War II. He played in seven successive seasons until 1955 when injury temporarily sidelined him, but he eventually went on to play a then Irish record of 46 tests. He first represented his nation during the 'Victory' internationals of 1945 and 1946, but got his first official Irish cap on 25 January 1947 against France in Dublin. In 1950, he was selected to tour Australia and New Zealand with the British Lions and played in all six internationals. This tour was a highlight of his career and he proved himself the complete flyhalf of the time with his handling, temperament, solid defence and exceptional link work: a skill set which had him named as one of New Zealand Rugby Almanac's six players of that year. He was one of those deceptive runners who, seemingly closely marked, could ghost past the would-be tacklers to score. In 1953, Kyle scored an amazing solo try against France in Belfast, which inspired a newspaper scribe to parody *The Scarlet Pimpernel* with the following verse:

> They seek him here, they seek him there
> Those Frenchies seek him everywhere
> That paragon of pace and guile
> That damned elusive Jackie Kyle.

He retired in 1958, and not surprisingly, the Scots were the happiest to see the back of him: he played against Scotland ten times and was on the winning side in all ten. A qualified doctor, Kyle moved to Chingola, Zambia where he worked as a surgeon until 2000 when he returned to Ireland. He was voted Ireland's best player of all time and in 1999 was inducted into rugby's Hall of Fame.

Willie-John McBride

Full name:	William James McBride MBE
Born:	6 June 1940 (Toomebridge, Ireland)
Tests:	63 for Ireland (12 as captain), 17 for Lions (4 as captain)
Debut:	Ireland: 10 February 1962 vs England, London Lions: 4 August 1962 vs South Africa, Cape Town
Position:	lock
Career:	Ireland: 10/02/1962–15/03/1975, Lions: 04/08/1962–27/07/1974
Points:	4 for Ireland (1 T)

No matter which team he played for or against, Willie-John McBride automatically commanded the respect of his teammates and opponents almost from the start of his career. It was this that made McBride one of the greatest Irish and Lions captains of all time. In the eyes of Irish supporters no single man better personifies the spirit and pride of Ireland. He played a remarkable 14 international seasons and today holds the record for the most international appearances by any player for the Lions: 17 in total, a record that is unlikely to be broken even in this day and age. As a child, he spent most of his spare time working on the family farm and as such only took up rugby at the relatively late age of 17, immediately making his school's 1st XV. He made his debut in 1962 at the age of 21 against England in London and such was his impact that by the end of his first season he was selected to tour with the Lions to South Africa, the first of his five Lions tours. His last two were the most famous in Lions history. In 1971, McBride was pack leader of the successful side in New Zealand and captain of the unbeaten 1974 Lions in South Africa: a series that is regarded as the most physical in the game's history. His memorable catchphrase was: 'We take no prisoners'. This uncompromising approach, along with his fire and commitment, made him the inspirational leader that he was during the brutal tour. This series has become synonymous with Willie-John and his '99' call: essentially a call to arms for the Lions to retaliate against the dirty Springbok tactics, when each Lion would aassault the Bok nearest him. He was the perfect leader for the tour, deftly managing the sensitive political issues so prevalent at the time. He played in a number of successful Irish treams which registered victories over South Africa in 1965 and Australia in 1967 as well being an integral part of the Five Nations 1974 championship side. In his second-last appearance for his beloved Ireland and his last appearance on home soil, Willie-John succeeded in scoring his only international try when he crashed over against France in Dublin to steer Ireland to an emphatic 25–6 victory, with the ecstatic crowd enveloping him, draping the Irish flag over his shoulders. Two weeks later, his career ended against Wales in Cardiff, with Ireland succumbing 4–32 to the powerful Welsh. He is still active in rugby, and coached the 1983 Lions to New Zealand. In 1997, he was one of the first to be inducted into the International Rugby Hall of Fame.

Syd Millar

Full name:	John Sydney Millar CBE, MBE
Born:	23 May 1934 (Ballymena, Northern Ireland)
Tests:	37 for Ireland, 9 for Lions
Debut:	Ireland: 19 April 1958 vs Fance, Paris Lions: 6 June 1959 vs Australia, Brisbane
Position:	prop
Career:	Ireland: 19/04/1958–14/03/1970, Lions: 06/06/1959– 22/06/1968
Points:	0

Syd Millar was one of the great prop forwards of his era. Highly technical, he was capable of packing down on either side of the scrum. His versatility and power in the Irish front row earned him 37 national caps as well as nine for the British and Irish Lions. He made his debut in the final Irish match of the 1958 Five Nations on 19 April against France in Paris. By the following year he had sufficiently impressed the Lions selectors to tour New Zealand, the first of his three tours. He made his test debut for the Lions against Australia in Brisbane and was again selected to tour South Africa in 1962 where he played in all four tests. His final Lions tour was in 1968 to South Africa where he played in two of the four tests. He retired from international rugby after Ireland defeated Wales on 14 March 1970, but continued to play club rugby for Ballymena until the age of 44. He became a successful businessman and stayed very involved in the game. Not even the great Willie-John McBride can compare to Millar's involvement with the Lions: in addition to his three tours as a player, Miller coached the famous 1974 Lions to success in South Africa and again managed them in 1980 in South Africa. He became a Lions selector in 1977 and a committee member in 1993 and 1997, and chairman in 2001. He coached the Irish national side in 1987. He also served as president of the IRFB and in November 2003 was elected IRB chairman, a position he relinquished after the 2007 RWC final. In 2005, he was awarded the CBE in the Queen's Birthday Honours List for his 55-year involvement in the game as a player, coach and administrator. Millar is a true servant and legend of the game.

Brian O'Driscoll

Full name:	Brian Gerald O'Driscoll
Born:	21 January 1979 (Contarf, Ireland)
Tests:	93 for Ireland (56 as captain), 6 for Lions (1 as captain)
Debut:	Ireland: 12 June 1999 vs Australia, Brisbane Lions: 30 June 2001 vs Australia, Brisbane
Position:	centre
Career:	Ireland: 12/06/1999–present, Lions: 30/06/2001–04/07/2009
Points:	Total 200: 195 for Ireland (36 Ts, 5 DGs) 5 for Lions (1 T)

Photo: Paul Walsh/commons.wikimedia.org/ creative commons license

Arguably the greatest centre, and even backline player that Ireland has ever produced, O'Driscoll, through his presence and leadership qualities, has brought Ireland much success in the first decade of 2000. His power, flair, ability to step off both feet at pace and solid defence caused opponents and fans worldwide to take notice. He made his debut against Australia as a 20-year-old in Brisbane before he had even played senior club rugby in Ireland. From that point on, O'Driscoll cemented his spot in the Irish team and has undoubtedly become a rugby great. He is the second-most capped Irishman of all time (93), the leading Irish try scorer (36) and the most capped Irish skipper, with 56 tests as captain. In 2001, he was selected to tour with the Lions to Australia where he appeared in all three tests and scored one of the finest individual Lions tries of all time with a solo effort from well inside his own half. Following captain Keith's Wood retirement in 2003, he was the obvious choice to take over. He led Ireland to second spot in the 2004 Six Nations and their first Triple Crown since 1985. In 2005, he became the ninth Irishman to lead a Lions tour, to New Zealand, but his tour was cruelly ended in the very first minute of the first test when a dreadful off-the-ball combination spear tackle from opposition captain Tana Umaga and Keven Mealamu went unpunished as O'Driscoll limped off with a dislocated shoulder. Controversy still rages with no official verdict ever reached. The New Zealanders claim, naturally, it was an accident and their apology was accepted at face value by O'Driscoll. However, little doubt remains that New Zealand recognised the threat of O'Driscoll and had him surgically removed from the game as they went on to comfortably win the series, sans O'Driscoll. He has led Ireland to four Triple Crowns in 2004, 2006, 2007 and 2009, and was inspirational in taking them to their second only Grand Slam in 2009.

Tony O'Reilly

Full name:	Sir Anthony Joseph Francis O'Reilly
Born:	7 May 1936 (Dublin, Ireland)
Tests:	29 for Ireland, 10 for Lions
Debut:	Ireland: 22 January 1955 vs France, Dublin Lions: 6 August 1955 vs South Africa, Johannesburg
Position:	wing
Career:	Ireland: 22/01/1955–14/02/1970, Lions: 06/08/1955–19/09/1959
Points:	Total 33: 15 for Ireland (5 Ts), 18 for Lions (6 Ts)

At just 18, Tony O'Reilly made his debut for Ireland in the 1955 Five Nations against France and that year became a touring Lion in South Africa. He became the youngest player to earn a Lions cap in the most daunting of matches: against South Africa in Johannesburg before a crowd of 95,000. Unfazed, O'Reilly scored a crucial try in the Lions' dramatic 23–22 victory over the Boks. He played in all four tests, helping the Lions draw the series 2–2 and scoring a record 16 tries on tour. He had a remarkable try-scoring rate and still holds the record for the most tries in a Lions career: 38 in just two tours, including a record hall of 22 on the 1959 tour. He played in all six tests of that tour down under, scoring tries in both tests against Australia and twice against New Zealand. From his Irish debut through to 1963, he was a regular in the side, but a surprise recall at 33 in 1970 gave him his 29th and final cap for Ireland against England at Twickenham, capping a career of 16 seasons. Today he holds the record for the highest number of appearances (30) for the glamorous British Barbarians. Sir Anthony became a successful businessman, heading up the Dublin-based Independent News & Media Group.

Fergus Slattery

Full name:	John Fergus Slattery
Born:	12 February 1949 (Dublin, Ireland)
Tests:	61 for Ireland (17 as captain), 4 for Lions
Debut:	Ireland: 10 January 1970 vs South Africa, Dublin Lions: 8 June 1974 vs South Africa, Cape Town
Position:	flank
Career:	Ireland: 10/01/1970–21/01/1984, Lions: 08/06/1974–27/07/1974
Points:	12 for Ireland (3 Ts)

Fergus Slattery played a phenomenal 14 international seasons and was the most capped flanker in the game's history. It is no coincidence that his time in the emerald-green jersey resulted in some of Ireland's golden rugby years. He made his debut against the ill-fated touring Springboks on 10 January 1970 while still an undergraduate at University College Dublin. Quite remarkably, the following season he was selected to tour New Zealand with the Lions, but did not play in any of the tests. In 1973, he played in Ireland's well-publicised 10–10 draw with New Zealand, followed by playing in the legendary Barbarians match against New Zealand in which he scored a try and had a hand in two others. In 1974, Slattery became an outright Five Nations champion for the first time and was duly rewarded with a spot in the 1974 British Lions tour to South Africa when he played in all four internationals. He had a controversial try disallowed in the final test that would have given the touring side a 100-percent winning record; instead the match was drawn 13 apiece. After 28 consecutive tests for Ireland he missed the entire 1976 Five Nations due to injury. In 1979, he was made captain of Ireland, a position he retained until 1981. He captained the most successful Irish touring side of all time, defeating Australia by two tests to nil. In 1982, relieved of the captaincy, Slattery played an instrumental role in securing Ireland's first Triple Crown since 1949. He bowed out of international rugby with his final appearance against France, in his 33rd consecutive international since 1977.

Keith Wood

Full name:	Keith Gerald Mallinson Wood
Born:	27 January 1972 (Limerick, Ireland)
Tests:	58 for Ireland (36 as captain), 5 for Lions
Debut:	Ireland: 5 June 1994 vs Australia, Brisbane Lions: 21 June 1997 vs South Africa, Cape Town
Position:	hooker
Career:	Ireland: 05/06/1994–09/11/2003, Lions: 21/06/1997–14/07/2001
Points:	75 for Ireland (15 Ts)

Nicknamed 'The Raging Potato' owing to his shiny pate, there are few players more committed to the game than was Irish hooker Keith Wood. In 2001, the Lions team doctor James Robson summed him up: 'Keith Wood has just got everything [injuries] because he just tries so hard and lays his body on the line and always needs total body therapy [after each game].' Rugby runs in the Wood family: Father Gordon was capped 29 times for Ireland and toured with the 1959 Lions. Keith made his debut on the Irish tour of Australia in 1994 and played in three RWCs. Two years after his debut, he was elected as Irish captain and in 1997 was a key part of the Lions' triumphant tour of South Africa, playing in two of the three tests. During the 1999 RWC, he became the first hooker in international rugby to score four tries in a test and in 2001 was named the IRB Rugby Player of the Year. He was again selected to tour with the 2001 Lions to Australia, tipped to lead the team but losing out to Martin Johnson. Throughout his career Wood was blighted by injury, starting at the 1995 RWC; he would surely have played well more than his final tally of 58 appearances. During the lean Irish years of the 1990s, Wood stood out in many a losing test, and was a prolific try scorer for a front-row forward. He currently holds the record for most tries by an international hooker together with All Black Sean Fitzpatrick, who played nearly twice as many tests as Wood. Following the Irish defeat to the French in the 2003 RWC quarter-final, Wood retired, stating: 'The head is willing, the heart is willing, but the body has had enough'.

Italy

Stefano Bettarello

Full name:	Stefano Bettarello
Born:	2 April 1958 (Rovigo, Italy)
Tests:	55
Debut:	14 April 1979 vs Poland, L'Aquila
Position:	flyhalf
Career:	14/04/1979–03/12/1988
Points:	483 (7 Ts, 46 Cs, 104 PGs, 17 DGs)

The son of Romano Bettarello, a former Italian rugby international himself, Stefano was always destined to play rugby and excel at national level. During his illustrious career, Bettarello junior became the first player in the world to score 400 points in full internationals. His performances on the rugby field are in no small part thanks to the tutorage he received from the great British Lions coach Carwyn James at his club Rovigo, which honed Bettarello's natural attacking skills and perfected his legendary sidestep which brought him 18 tries in international rugby. He was also blessed with superb kicking skills, both at goal and in open play. Such was his quality that Bettarello became the first Italian to be selected for the Barbarians. In 1983, in his finest performance, he scored a full house against Canada in Toronto with a try, two conversions, five penalties and two drop goals for a personal match haul of 29 points, posting for underdog Italy an emphatic 37–9 victory. His Italian records were unbroken for many years until Diego Dominguez came onto the scene. Bettarello's final international was against Australia in 1988.

Carlo Checchinato

Full name:	Carlo Checchinato
Born:	30 August 1970 (Adria, Italy)
Tests:	83
Debut:	30 September 1990 vs Spain, Rovigo
Position(s):	eighthman, flank
Career:	30/09/1990–20/03/2004
Points:	105 (21 Ts)

Photo: Federazione Italiana Rugby

Checchinato was born into a rugby family: his father Giancarlo represented Italy in the 1970s as a lock. In his fine career, Carlo scored 21 tries, a record for a forward which has only recently been overtaken by Colin Charvis of Wales with 22. For a short while, Checchinato was Italy's most capped player of all time, until surpassed by Alessandro Troncon. However, he is still Italy's most capped forward. Checchinato was a very physical player which, coupled with his tremendous experience, made him seem to grow in stature in every game, undoubtedly inspiring those around him. His mobility as a loose forward and his commitment were unmatched in the Italian team where his sheer presence provided the perfect platform for Italy's younger players in the early 2000s. Checchinato played in four RWCs and currently holds the national record for having played in 242 matches in the Italian division, a record which clearly illustrates his commitment, fitness and love for the game. He retired in 2004 after playing Ireland. He is currently the Italian team manager.

Diego Dominguez

Full name:	Diego Dominguez
Born:	25 April 1966 (Córdoba, Argentina)
Tests:	74 for Italy, 2 for Argentina
Debut:	Italy: 2 March 1991 vs France XV, Rome Argentina: 10 October 1989 vs Chile, Montevideo
Position:	flyhalf
Career:	Italy: 02/03/1991–22/02/2003, Argentina: 10/10/1989–12/10/1989
Points:	Total 1,010: 983 for Italy (9 Ts, 127 Cs, 208 PGs, 20 DGs) 27 for Argentina (6 Cs, 5 PGs)

Photo: Federazione Italiana Rugby

Born in Argentina, Dominguez was chosen to represent Argentina when he toured with the national side to France in 1986 as an understudy to incumbent legend Hugo Porta. Following Porta's retirement, Dominguez forced his way into the Argentinian side for the 16th South American Championship in Montevideo where he played in two of the four tests. He realised, however, that his best chances of playing regular top-flight rugby would be in Italy where he qualified for Italian citizenship through his grandmother. He moved to Milan and on 2 March 1991 made his Italian debut against a French XV in Rome. He featured in the RWC later that year, with his form in the mid-to-late 1990s ultimately seeing the Italians included in the new Six Nations tournament in 2000. He announced his retirement from international rugby at the end of the 2000 season, but a dearth of quality flyhalfs in Italy persuaded him to come out of retirement to play against Ireland on 22 February 2003, in what was his final match for Italy. Without doubt, Dominguez's greatest match was Italy's first Six Nations test, played against Scotland in 2000 when Italy were expected to be thumped. Instead, Dominguez turned in one of the greatest kicking displays witnessed in international rugby, kicking 29 points from a conversion, six penalties and three drop goals to steer Italy to an astonishing 34–20 victory. This was closely matched by his 20-point haul against France (won 40–32 by Italy) and 27 points against Ireland (won 37–22) in 1997. He amassed a massive 983 points for Italy which, in conjunction with the 27 points for Argentina, has ensured that Dominguez is one of only three players to have scored 1,000 international points, behind only Neil Jenkins of Wales (1,049) and Jonny Wilkinson of England (1,099). Dominguez is also the sixth-most capped Italian player of all time and holds just about all Italian rugby-scoring records possible.

Alessandro Troncon

Full name:	Alessandro Troncon
Born:	6 September 1973 (Treviso, Italy)
Tests:	101 (21 as captain)
Debut:	7 May 1994 vs Spain, Parma
Position:	scrumhalf
Career:	07/05/1994–29/09/2007
Points:	95 (19 Ts)

Photo: Federazione Italiana Rugby

Any player who appears more than a hundred times for his country is unquestionably a rugby legend, and few deserve this honour more than scrumhalf Alessandro Troncon. Today, Troncon is revered as the most notable Italian rugby player of all time. He made his debut on 7 May 1994 against Spain and partnered his outside half Diego Dominguez 53 times, a national record. Troncon's feisty temperament, precision and pace at box kicks from the base of a scrum or ruck and his skill in sniffing the elusive gap made him a world-class performer. These skills saw Troncon selected as Italian captain in 2002 but, unluckily, he lost the captaincy following a knee injury and missed the entire 2004 Six Nations. In 2007, he played arguably the greatest match of his career as he scored a try to help Italy secure their first Six Nations away win when they beat Scotland in Edinburgh. He notched up his 100th cap against Portugal in the 2007 RWC, his fourth RWC, but his dreams of progressing into the quarter-finals of an RWC for the first time were shattered after Italy's narrow loss to Scotland in his 101st and final international, despite scoring a try. He is today an integral member of the Italian coaching staff.

New Zealand

Don Clarke

Full name:	Donald Barry Clarke
Born:	10 November 1933 (Pihama New Zealand)
Died:	29 December 2002 (Johannesburg, South Africa)
Tests:	31
Debut:	18 August 1956 vs South Africa, Christchurch
Position:	fullback
Career:	18/08/1956–29/08/1964
Points:	207 (2 Ts, 33 Cs, 38 PGs, 5 DGs, 2 GMs)

Photo: New Zealand Rugby Museum

Don Clarke was an extremely versatile sportsman. He opened the bowling for Auckland at the age of just 17. As fate would have it – and thankfully for New Zealand rugby – Clarke chose to pursue a career in rugby. He was an amazing talent and during his nine-year international career, his goal-kicking skills set records atumbling, earning him the simple nickname of The Boot. He played 89 times for New Zealand, amassing 781 points for his country, a record that stood for 24 years until Grant Fox cropped up. In addition to his goal kicking, Clarke was one of the best last lines of defence and seldom missed a tackle. He was a very large man with many coaches trying to convince him as a youngster to play in the forwards but his father's encouragement to stay at fullback saw him become one of the greatest All Blacks of all time. Had it not been for a series of injuries incurred between 1952 and 1955, Clarke would no doubt have made his debut earlier and clocked up dozens more points and records. By 1956, he was back to his best and selected to take on the might of the Springboks in the third test of the series. He did not relinquish the fullback jersey for the next eight years. He piled on the points against Australia in 1957 and 1958, and in 1959 made headlines across the world as he posted a world-record individual haul of 18 points (six penalties) to sink the British Lions by 18–17. The tourists were furious as they had scored four tries to none, yet still lost the game. Clarke went on to score 39 points in the series, including the winning try in the second test. The Lions never forgot him. His final test was on 29 August 1964 against Australia, with his troublesome knee preventing him from playing the Springboks the following year. Following his retirement, Clarke immigrated to South Africa and seldom returned home. He was seriously injured in a car accident in 1997; in 2001 he was diagnosed with melanoma and died the next year.

Sean Fitzpatrick

Full name:	Sean Brian Thomas Fitzpatrick MNZM
Born:	4 June 1963 (Auckland, New Zealand)
Tests:	92 (51 as captain)
Debut:	28 June 1986 vs France, Christchurch
Position:	hooker
Career:	08/11/1986–29/11/1997
Points:	55 (12 Ts)

Photo: New Zealand Rugby Museum

Son of an All Blacks centre Brian Fitzpatrick who played three internationals, Sean Fitzpatrick became the most capped New Zealander and hooker of all time, while also holding the world record for the most consecutive international appearances: 63 tests from his third appearance in 1986 to the 1995 RWC Japan match when he was rested. Respected throughout the rugby-playing world, Fitzpatrick was, however, someone that everyone outside of New Zealand loved to hate. An accurate lineout thrower, he was also expert in influencing referees, a skill which generally won him favourbale decisions. He made his debut against France in 1986, filling the void of suspended Cavaliers players. As understudy to the legendary Andy Dalton, Fitzpatrick however grabbed the opportunity with both hands and became a regular member of the team that won the 1987 RWC. In April 1992, he was awarded the captaincy of New Zealand to play a

World XV outfit. He initially had a tough time as captain: first losing the Bledisloe to Australia in 1992, very nearly losing to the British Lions the following year, losing to England in 1993 and then suffering a shock home-series defeat at the hands of the French. But it was during the 1995 RWC that Fitzpatrick and his young team began to sparkle, just losing the final to an inspired South African side. Fitzpatrick's revenge was to take the 1996 Tri-Nations title undefeated and then, in 1996, become the first New Zealand captain to win a series in South Africa. He made his final All Blacks appearance as a substitute against Wales at Wembley on 29 November 1997 with a then world-record for a forward of 92 caps. He is a member of the Sports Laureus Academy.

Grant Fox

Full name:	Grant James Fox
Born:	6 June 1962 (New Plymouth, New Zealand)
Tests:	46
Debut:	26 October 1985 vs Argentina, Buenos Aires
Position:	flyhalf
Career:	26/10/1985–31/07/1993
Points:	645 (1 T, 118 Cs, 128 PGs, 7 DGs)

Photo: New Zealand Rugby Museum

For many years New Zealand's record points scorer Grant Fox was one of the most effective flyhalfs and most reliable goal kickers ever to don the black jersey. A true kicking flyhalf, Fox wasn't overly effective in releasing his backline, nor was he capable of long-range kicking, but his precision within range was surgical. He was the first of the modern-day kicking automatons, as espoused by the likes of Jonny Wilkinson. He made his debut on the 1985 New Zealand tour to Argentina. Surprisingly, he was not the first-choice goal kicker, with that role filled by fullback Kieran Crowley. Fox did, however, drop a trademark goal on debut but had to wait out his Cavaliers ban until the 1987 RWC opening match against Italy for his second appearance. He cemented his position at flyhalf and was instrumental in New Zealand's triumphant campaign, featuring in all six internationals and grabbing a tournament record of 126 points, a record which still stands today. Following this, the automaton gathered momentum with Fox hauling in point after point both home and away, breaking Don Clarke's record in the process. He retained the number 10 jersey after the All Blacks disappointing 1991 RWC but retired after the 1993 clash with Samoa, and after helping New Zealand defeat the British Lions with his decisive kicking – especially in the first test when he converted a hotly debated, last-minute penalty. His record haul of 645 test points stood for almost ten years until it was broken by another automaton: Andrew Mehrtens.

Michael Jones

Full name:	Michael Niko Jones
Born:	8 April 1965 (Auckland, New Zealand)
Tests:	55 for New Zealand, 1 for Western Samoa
Debut:	New Zealand: 22 May 1987 vs Italy, Auckland Western Samoa: 14 June 1986 vs Wales, Apia
Position:	flank
Career:	New Zealand: 22/05/1987–01/08/1998, Western Samoa: 14/06/1986
Points:	56 for New Zealand (13 Ts)

Photo: New Zealand Rugby Museum

Nicknamed 'The Iceman' because of his characteristic cool demeanour, Michael Jones is ranked the third-greatest All Black of all time after Colin Meads and Sean Fitzpatrick. Later in his career, his nickname was abridged to Ice because of the large number of ice packs he continually had to call for to soothe the endless injuries he incurred. He made his international debut for Western Samoa against Wales in 1986, qualifying through one of his parents. He played just this one match for Western Samoa before he caught the attention of the New Zealand selectors, being hastily included in the 1987 RWC squad, a move which would be impossible today because of the laws on representing two nations in a career. Jones scored a try in his first All Blacks international in the RWC opener against Italy, and became the first player to score a try in an RWC. He consolidated his place in the side, scoring the opening try of the final against France. Devoutly religious, Jones refused to play on Sundays, which led to his unavailability for selection in some games of the 1991 RWC, including the vital semi-final against Australia. As such, he was not considered for selection for the 1995 RWC due to New Zealand's Sunday fixtures. His religious beliefs and recurring injuries certainly curtailed a stellar career. A player with remarkable pace (until a knee injury slowed him down), devastating defence, slick handling, superior fitness and an uncanny instinct to be wherever the ball was, Jones defined the role of the modern loose forward. Injury-plagued yet again, he was dropped from the All Blacks at the age of 33, playing his last international against Australia in 1998. Still involved in the game, he coached Samoa from 2003 to 2007 and was inducted into the International Rugby Hall of Fame in 2003.

Ian Kirkpatrick

Full name:	Ian Andrew Kirkpatrick
Born:	24 May 1946 (Gisborne, New Zealand)
Tests:	39 (9 as captain)
Debut:	25 November 1967 vs France, Paris
Position:	flank
Career:	25/11/1967–13/08/1977
Points:	57 (16 Ts)

Photo: New Zealand Rugby Museum

Probably the first specialist blind-side flanker, Kirkpatrick became one of the most prolific try-scoring flankers in the game's history. He was picked by coach Fred Allen from relative obscurity for the All Blacks tour to Europe in 1967 where he made his debut as a 21-year-old against France. His try-scoring feats began with this first game. His most stunning performance was as a substitute on 15 June 1968 against Australia in Sydney, when he came on to replace Brian Lochore and scored a famous hat-trick of tries. From then on he started every game. In 1972, he was made captain of New Zealand and was for two years until Andy Leslie took over in 1974. His final appearance was in the fourth test against the British Lions in 1977, after which he was astonishingly and unexpectedly dropped from the side to tour France later that year, with no official reason given. He scored 16 tries in his international career, which remained an All Blacks record until broken by Stu Wilson in 1983. On his retirement from all rugby in 1979, Kirkpatrick had scored an incredible 115 tries in his first-class career: a remarkable record for a forward. He has remained involved in rugby, most notably as manager of the 1986 New Zealand Cavaliers tour to South Africa. He is regularly consulted by the media for comments on the game and often used as a mentor to current All Blacks sides. In 2003, he was inducted in the International Rugby Hall of Fame.

John Kirwan

Full name:	John James Kirwan ONZM, MBE
Born:	16 December 1964 (Auckland, New Zealand)
Tests:	63
Debut:	16 June 1984 vs France, Christchurch
Position:	wing
Career:	16/06/1984–06/08/1994
Points:	143 (35 Ts)

Photo: New Zealand Rugby Museum

At more than 1.9 metres, over 6 feet 2, tall, Kirwan was a large man for a wing. His strong build belied his extreme pace and single-minded determination to reach the try line. He made his debut at 19 against France in 1984; despite his youth many felt his All Blacks appearance was long overdue. However, injuries were to plague Kirwan's career; uninterrupted, he would undoubtedly have scored many more tries than his final tally. A fit Kirwan meant his automatic selection throughout his career, a then record of 63 internationals. His glory years were from 1986 to 1988. He played a crucial role in New Zealand's win at the inaugural 1987 RWC in which he scored the greatest individual try in the tournament's history with a length-of-the-field effort against Italy, leaving half the Italian side sprawled in his dust. In his 1988 season, Kirwan scored ten tries in just five tests and by the time he retired had scored a then New Zealand record of 35 tries. His final game for New Zealand was against South Africa on 6 August 1994, after which he retired. However, he was persuaded to come out of retirement and play rugby league for two seasons with the Auckland Warriors before reverting to union and finishing his playing days in Japan. Since his retirement, Kirwan has coached the Italian national side from 2002 to 2005 and Japan in 2007. He was appointed an MBE in 1989 for his rugby achievements and in 2007 was made Officer of the New Zealand Order of Merit for his services to mental-health awareness in New Zealand.

Brian Lochore

Full name:	Sir Brian James Lochore ONZ, KNZM, OBE
Born:	3 September 1940 (Masterton, New Zealand)
Tests:	25 (18 as captain)
Debut:	4 January 1964 vs England, London
Position(s):	eighthman, lock
Career:	04/01/1964–31/07/1971
Points:	6 (2 Ts)

Photo: New Zealand Rugby Museum

In 1959, 18-year-old Lochore caught the attention of rugby fans with a sterling display against the 1959 Lions in a midweek game. Five years later, he made his All Blacks debut against England in London and played in all the tests against the 1965 Springboks. Following his mercurial performances in this series at number 8, Lochore became a permanent All Black and after just six internationals was selected by coach Fred Allen to lead the All Blacks against the mighty 1966 Lions. He was skipper for 18 tests until his retirement, with the All Blacks losing just three times under his captaincy, all three in South Africa in 1970. Lochore retired following the disappointment of the 1970 South African tour, but was persuaded to play one last time for the injury-plagued national side that desperately needed his experience against the great 1971 Lions. He stayed in rugby after his retirement and in 1983 became an All Blacks selector; then New Zealand coach from 1985 to 1987. He managed the 1995 RWC team and is still today an All Blacks selector. In 1999, he was honoured as Knight Companion of the New Zealand Order of Merit and in 2007, he was awarded the Order of New Zealand. In 1999, he was inducted into the International Rugby Hall of Fame.

Jonah Lomu

Full name:	Jonah Tali Lomu MNZM
Born:	12 May 1975 (Auckland, New Zealand)
Tests:	63
Debut:	26 June 1994 vs France, Christchurch
Position:	wing
Career:	26/06/1994–23/11/2002
Points:	185 (37 Ts)

Photo: New Zealand Rugby Museum

A giant of a man and the first true global rugby superstar of the professional era, Jonah Lomu remains a worldwide rugby phenomenon and a folk hero. Standing at 1.96 metres (over 6 feet 4) and weighing 120 kilos (265 pounds), Lomu was bigger than most lock forwards but played as a wing. Despite his size, he ran the 100 metres in 10.89 seconds. Tragically, Lomu was diagnosed with the kidney illness, nephritic syndrome, which hit him at the peak of his career and ultimately brought his playing days to a sad and premature end. Considering that for most of his career Lomu suffered such a severe handicap it makes his achievements all the more remarkable. He grew up in one of the poorer areas of Auckland, bursting onto the rugby scene as a brash 18-year-old. In 1994, aged 19, he became the youngest man to ever play test rugby for New Zealand when he made his debut against France on the wing. He had an inauspicious start: to be expected, as prior to playing for New Zealand he had been a flanker. He went on to a glittering career, forever remembered for his 1995 and 1999 RWC performances. As a relative unknown it was in the 1995 RWC that he hit the world stage like a meteor, scoring seven tries in the tournament, including four in the semi-final against England. One was possibly the most famous World Cup try ever scored, when he ran through and over the top of a flailing Mike Catt. After the game England captain Will Carling was quoted as saying, 'He is a freak and the sooner he goes away the better.' In 1996, the first signs of Lomu's health problems manifested themselves and confirmation of his kidney disorder saw him miss most of the 1997 season. By 1999, he had been relegated to the bench but returned to the All Blacks with a bang in the 1999 RWC, scoring eight tries in six appearances, an RWC record now shared with Springbok Bryan Habana. In 2000, he scored the winning try in the so-called 'game of the century' against Australia, brushing aside the desperate attempts of Stephen Larkham and sprinting down the side line to win the game. Lomu was in the All Blacks squad until 2002, with his final international against Wales on 23 November 2002 in Cardiff. By 2003, the worst was confirmed and he withdrew totally from rugby, never to play for New Zealand again despite his numerous brave attempts to make a comeback. He underwent a kidney transplant on 28 July 2004. Lomu still dreamed of reclaiming his black jersey for the 2007 RWC, but his hopes were dashed after not being selected for a New Zealand Super 14 team. He retired permanently from all rugby in 2007. He has since been appointed a Member of the New Zealand Order of Merit and was inducted into the International Rugby Hall of Fame in 2007.

Colin Meads

Full name:	Colin Earl Meads DCNZM MBE
Born:	3 June 1936 (Cambridge, New Zealand)
Tests:	55 (4 as captain)
Debut:	25 May 1957 vs Australia, Sydney
Position(s):	lock, flank, eighthman
Career:	25/05/1957–14/08/1971
Points:	21 (7 Ts)

Photo: New Zealand Rugby Museum

Colin 'Pinetree' Meads is perhaps more than any other player the symbol of the power and dominance of New Zealand rugby, with his rugged and uncompromising approach to the game. A New Zealand writer summed him up as playing with 'a total dislike of the opposition'. He was even referred to by his teammate Fergie McCormick as 'a terrible man with the silver fern on'. Legend has it that his training involved running over the hills on his farm with a ram under each arm. Nicknamed Pinetree due to his towering presence, he locked the All Blacks scrum with his brother Stanley 11 times in test matches. One of the finest rugby players of all time, Colin Meads is often remembered for the wrong reasons. He was only the second All Black in history to be sent off during a match, against Scotland on 2 December 1967, while most remember him for inflicting an horrific injury on Australian scrumhalf Ken Catchpole to end his career. This was by no means intentional, but sowed much bitterness between the two sides. These incidents aside, Meads was a player of immense talent who knew exactly how to use every rule in the book to his advantage in order to niggle and ultimately quell his opponents (nor was he the first New Zealander to do so). An incredibly versatile player, Meads played in four different positions for New Zealand, including a stint on the wing, even scoring a try. He is remembered for his lanky style of running with ball in one hand and for his high threshold for pain, so clearly illustrated in a match in South Africa when he broke his arm but played out the game. He made his debut against Australia in 1957, two days short of his 21st birthday and went on to play, amazingly, international rugby for 15 years, a New Zealand record that still stands today. He was the first New Zealander to reach 50 international appearances and in 1971, at the venerable age of 35, captained New Zealand against the conquering British Lions. Meads was gracious in defeat and heaped praise on the visitors. He stayed in the game as a selector and coach, but in 1986 was struck from the NZRFU for coaching the Cavaliers in South Africa, but was soon back in the fold as New Zealand manager. At the NZRFU Awards Dinner in 1999 he was named the New Zealand Player of the Century.

Andrew Mehrtens

Full name:	Andrew Philip Mehrtens
Born:	28 April 1973 (Durban, South Africa)
Tests:	70
Debut:	22 April 1995 vs Canada, Auckland
Position:	flyhalf
Career:	22/04/1995–14/08/2004
Points:	967 (7 Ts, 169 Cs, 188 PGs, 10 DGs)

Photo: New Zealand Rugby Museum

Many feel that Andrew Mehrtens is the greatest-ever All Blacks flyhalf. Grant Fox's record of 645 points at the time appeared unbreakable, but just two years after Fox's retirement a youthful Mehrtens began amassing points in the same number 10 jersey, calling it a day nine years later with a New Zealand record of 967 points. Lacking in physique and weak in defence, Mehrtens made up for this with his immense skill, vision, precision kicking and ability to release his backs. He was born in Durban, South Africa into a sporting family, with both his grandfather and father having represented New Zealand at rugby. He made a startling debut for New Zealand in 1995 against Canada, scoring 28 points; he became the fastest player in the history of the game to amass 100 test points – in just five tests! He had an excellent tournament in the 1995 RWC and would have won the final for New Zealand had he not missed a close-range drop goal. However, he remained a permanent fixture in the All Blacks squad, but injuries and strong competition from Carlos Spencer saw him miss a number of tests. By 1999, he had reasserted his dominance and clocked up numerous New Zealand and world records, including a record 328 points in Tri-Nations tournaments. However, by 2003 his form had dipped and he was left out of the RWC squad only to regain his position the following season. He made his 70th and final appearance against South Africa on 14 August 2004 and remains to this day one of the greatest New Zealand flyhalfs of all time.

Graham Mourie

Full name:	Graham Neil Kenneth Mourie
Born:	8 September 1952 (Opunake, New Zealand)
Tests:	21 (19 as captain)
Debut:	30 July 1977 vs British Isles, Dunedin
Position:	flank
Career:	30/07/1977–11/09/1982
Points:	16 (4 Ts)

Photo: New Zealand Rugby Museum

One of the finest All Blacks captains ever, Graham Mourie knew he was destined for the job after he was chosen to lead the All Blacks to Argentina in 1976, where they remained unbeaten. He made his international debut in the third international against the British Lions in 1977. Following this series he was instated as captain for the All Blacks tour to France. He skippered the team for the rest of his career, the pinnacle being when he led the All Blacks to their first-ever Grand Slam tour of the United Kingdom in 1978. His performance on tour led to his being named Player of the Year by the UK publication *Rothmans Rugby Yearbook*. He may have been a small man for a flanker, but he made up for it with his ever-reliable support play, tight defence and scavenging ability which yielded four tries during his career. He was a fast, constructive flanker who led by example, making him the perfect captain. In 1981, he stuck by his principles and refused to play against the touring Springboks. With this decision, he temporarily lost the All Blacks captaincy but returned later that year to close off his All Blacks career by beating Australia in a tightly fought three-test series to reclaim the Bledisloe Cup. Mourie has since dabbled in coaching the Hurricanes in the Super 12 and today serves on the NZRFU board.

George Nepia

Full name:	George Nepia
Born:	25 April 1905 (Wairoa, New Zealand)
Died:	27 June 1986 (Ruatoria, New Zealand)
Tests:	9
Debut:	1 November 1924 vs Ireland, Dublin
Position:	fullback
Career:	01/11/1924–09/08/1930
Points:	5 (1 C, 1 PG)

Photo: New Zealand Rugby Museum

One of the most famous Maori players of all time, George Nepia was also one of the greatest New Zealand fullbacks, always to be remembered for his feats of the 1924/1925 All Blacks tour of Britain, France and Canada, a team which came to be known as 'The Invincibles'. The team played 32 matches and Nepia appeared in every one at fullback, a staggering feat of endurance which led to his description as the face of the tour, an image largely derived from the fact that he led the *haka* which had been specially composed for the tour. Amazingly, Nepia was only formally introduced to rugby in the early 1920s, yet by the end of 1924 he was the first-choice national fullback. He could kick powerfully, defend fiercely and was an excellent runner. He made his debut at 19 against Ireland in Dublin in 1924, but only made sporadic appearances for the All Blacks following this tour. He was refused entry to South Africa for the 1928 tour because of his skin colour and missed several opportunities to play for the All Blacks because of the isolated location of his farm on the east coast of New Zealand. Injury also took its toll on his career and his last appearance came in the final test of the 1930 British Isles series. He suffered extreme financial hardship during the Depression years and so in 1935 accepted an offer to play rugby league in Britain for a fee of £500 to support his family who stayed behind in New Zealand. He returned to union (with permission of course) after World War II and continued to play well into his 40s, before taking up refereeing. Nepia holds the unusual records of being the oldest New Zealander to play in a first-class game and the only father to have played against his son in a first-class game.

Buck Shelford

Full name:	Wayne Thomas Shelford
Born:	13 December 1957 (Rotorua, New Zealand)
Tests:	22 (14 as captain)
Debut:	8 November 1986 vs France, Toulouse
Position:	eighthman
Career:	08/11/1986–23/06/1990
Points:	20 (5 Ts)

Photo: New Zealand Rugby Museum

Wayne Thomas Shelford, otherwise known as Buck, played in 22 test matches for New Zealand, captaining 14 times from 1987 to 1990 and scoring 20 points from five tries. He made his first All Blacks appearance on the 1985 tour of Argentina. After serving a ban following his involvement in the 1986 Cavaliers' tour to South Africa, he played his first international in the first test of the 1986 French series. The infamous second test against the French in 1986, dubbed the 'Battle of Nantes' by the press, was the only international he lost. In one of the most brutal games ever played, Shelford found himself at the bottom of a very physical, aggressive ruck when an errant French boot found its way to his groin, inflicting probably the most painful injury possible for a sportsman. His scrotum was torn open by the studs, leaving one testicle hanging out. But Shelford was not the type to let this put a dampner on the game and calmly instructed the medic to stitch him up; the pitch-side camera recorded the incident. He returned to the fracas to later leave the field knocked out cold with four missing teeth. An integral part of the triumphant 1987 New Zealand RWC side, Shelford took over the captaincy from David Kirk soon after the World Cup, leading the All Blacks through one of their great periods of domination. They were unbeaten under his captaincy from 1987 to 1990. Frustrated with the way in which the All Blacks had been performing the *haka*, with players clueless as to its meaning or significance, he took the squad to a Maori college in Hawkes Bay to witness the students perform a traditional *haka*, taking it upon himself to teach the All Blacks the proper way to perform the *Ka Mare*. Remarkably, following a rare lapse in form, Shelford was later dropped and replaced by a young Zinzan Brooke after the 2–0 home series win over Scotland in 1990. Despite public calls to 'bring back Buck', he was not selected again.

Billy Wallace

Full name:	William Joseph Wallace
Born:	2 August 1878 (Wellington, New Zealand)
Died:	2 March 1972 (Wellington, New Zealand)
Tests:	11
Debut:	15 August 1903 vs Australia, Sydney
Position(s):	wing, fullback
Career:	15/08/1903–27/06/1908
Points:	50 (4 Ts, 12 Cs, 2 PGs, 2GMs)

Photo: New Zealand Rugby Museum

Billy Wallace is certainly one of the early legends of New Zealand rugby, making his debut in the first New Zealand international against Australia on 15 August 1903 in Sydney. He was an outstanding member of the 1905/1906 'Originals' who rampaged through Britain and France. A gifted player capable of playing anywhere in the backline (his favourite position was wing), he became the first New Zealander to notch up 50 appearances in the black jersey and the first to top 500 first-class points: 379 for New Zealand, a record which stood for over 50 years until Don Clarke broke it. His 246 tour points on the Originals tour is a record that still stands today and one never likely to be broken. Most famously, Wallace was the central figure in the much-disputed disallowed New Zealand try against Wales in 1905: it was he who put Bob Deans into space for the try. Till his dying day in 1972, Wallace insisted it was a try and no man was closer to the incident than he. He was manager of the New Zealand side to Australia in 1932.

Wilson Whineray

Full name:	Sir Wilson James Whineray KNZM OBE
Born:	10 July 1935 (Auckland, New Zealand)
Tests:	32 (30 as captain)
Debut:	25 May 1957 vs Australia, Sydney
Position:	prop
Career:	25/05/1957–18/09/1965
Points:	6 (2 Ts)

Photo: New Zealand Rugby Museum

Regarded by many as one of the greatest All Blacks captains of all time, Whineray was a towering figure in the game and an extremely mobile man for a prop forward. He was not a destructive scrummager, but powerful enough to hold his own, His true gift was how he could read a game. He made his debut on the 1957 New Zealand tour to Australia as a 21-year-old and the following year, he was appointed All Blacks captain against Australia. He was to skipper New Zealand in every test he played in, including tours to South Africa in 1960 and the United Kingdom and France in 1963/1964. Of his 30 internationals as captain, a record until 1997, he won 23, drew three and lost just four, three of which were against South Africa. Whineray played his final international on 18 September 1965 in Auckland against South Africa in a then record 20–3 victory over the old enemy, ensuring a series victory for New Zealand. After retiring, Whineray gained an MBA, became a successful businessman and even ran for Governor General in 2006. On 21 October 2007, Whineray was inducted into the IRB's Hall of Fame.

Scotland

Gordon Brown

Full name:	Gordon Lamont Brown
Born:	1 November 1947 (Troon, Scotland)
Died:	19 March 2001
Tests:	30 for Scotland, 8 for Lions
Debut:	Scotland: 6 December 1969 vs South Africa, Edinburgh Lions: 31 July 1971 vs New Zealand, Wellington
Position:	lock
Career:	Scotland: 06/12/1969–20/03/1976, Lions: 31/07/1971–13/08/1977
Points:	8 for Lions (2 Ts)

Photo: Scottish Rugby / PAI

Of good Scottish sporting stock, Brown's father Jock played goalkeeper for Scotland and Gordon's older brother Peter played for and captained the Scotland rugby side. Affectionately known as *Broon frae Troon* or simply 'Troonie' because of his birthplace, Gordon Brown made a daunting debut against the 1969 touring Springboks in Edinburgh, but finished on top as Scotland won the day. With this performance he retained his place for the opening match of the 1970 Five Nations against France. He was dropped for the next game against Wales and replaced, interestingly, by brother Peter who was the first to break the news to Gordon so subtly over the phone: 'Ah'm in, you're out.' As it happened, Gordon replaced Peter at half-time when the Scottish physio (their father Jock) diagnosed Peter with a serious calf injury. Gordon thus became the first brother to replace a sibling in an international. The two played together many times through the 1970s and were key figures in an awesome pack that brought Scotland much success. Gordon impressed sufficiently to be selected for the 1971 Lions tour to New Zealand, playing in the final two tests. Alongside Willie-John McBride, he was the cornerstone of the pack that so soldidly sealed the series. He was again selected to tour South Africa with the 1974 Lions, partnering captain McBride in the second row. He refused to bow to the physicality of the Springboks and took a stance against their bullying tactics. The Lions pack, with McBride and Brown a formidable second row, dominated their South African counterparts and won the series. He went on his third Lions tour in 1977 to New Zealand, partnering Bill Beaumont, but the Lions were unable to win the series and Brown retired from international rugby. He was described by the 1971 Lions coach Carwyn James as 'the ideal all-round lock forward', as proved by his try-scoring exploits, posting eight tries in 12 appearances with the 1974 Lions. Sadly, he died of cancer in 2001 and was inducted into the International Rugby Hall of Fame that same year.

Gavin Hastings

Full name:	Andrew Gavin Hastings OBE
Born:	3 January 1962 (Edinburgh, Scotland)
Tests:	61 for Scotland (20 as captain), 6 for Lions (3 as captain)
Debut:	Scotland: 17 January 1986 vs France, Edinburgh Lions: 1 July 1989 vs Australia, Sydney
Position:	fullback
Career:	Scotland: 17/01/1986–11/06/1995, Lions: 01/07/1989–03/07/1993
Points:	Total 733: 667 for Scotland (17 Ts, 86 Cs, 140 PGs) 66 for Lions (1 T, 1 C, 20 PGs)

Photo: Scottish Rugby / PAI

Gavin Hastings is regarded as one of the strongest-running and hardest-tackling fullbacks of all time and without doubt the most outstanding fullback of his era. He was one of the most prolific goal kickers Scotland has ever produced, but unfortunately will be remembered by some as being unreliable, capable of missing some of the simplest and most critical kicks, as in the 1991 RWC semi-final against England. Brave, resolute and adventurous, Hastings had all the qualities of a world-class fullback: secure under the high ball, an excellent touch kicker, willing to turn defence into attack, devastating on the crash ball and solid in defence. He was destined for rugby greatness when he kicked 18 points on debut against France to see Scotland win by 18–17 and another 21 against England a month later to win by a record 33–6. He made his debut alongside his brother Scott, with whom he played his entire career. The two brothers earned their 50th caps together in the same match eight years later against France on 19 March 1994 in Edinburgh. Scotland lost 12–20. In 1989, he toured Australia with the British Lions and his goal kicking ensured a series win. He was a member of the last Scottish Grand Slam team in 1990; in 1993 he was selected to captain the British Lions team to New Zealand ahead of Will Carling. One of his finest performances came in the 1995 Five Nations when he sank France in the Paris snow to ensure a rare Scottish win in Paris, following a magnificent individual try after latching onto a Gregor Townsend pass. His record 44 individual points in the 1995 RWC against Côte d'Ivoire was broken by Simon with 45 against Japan nine days later. He retired at the end of the 1995 RWC Scottish campaign with a record 227 points in three World Cups (since bettered by Jonny Wilkinson) and was piped off the field in Pretoria. His 667 points for Scotland stood as a national record until beaten by Chris Paterson in 2008, as did his 66 points for the British Lions and 227 points scored in RWCs, both subsequently bettered by Wilkinson. Following his retirement from rugby union, Hastings switched, incredible though it may seem, to American football as a kicker for the Scottish Claymores who went on to win that year's World Bowl. He is regularly referred to as the greatest Scottish player of all time and in 2003 was inducted into the International Rugby Hall of Fame.

Scott Hastings

Full name:	Scott Hastings
Born:	4 December 1964
Tests:	65 for Scotland, 2 for Lions
Debut:	Scotland: 17 January 1986 vs France, Edinburgh Lions: 8 July 1989 vs Australia, Brisbane
Position:	centre
Career:	Scotland: 17/01/1986–01/02/1997, Lions: 08/07/1989–15/07/1989
Points:	43 for Scotland (10 Ts)

Photo: Scottish Rugby / PAI

Scott made his debut on 17 January 1986 at 21 with his older brother Gavin and played with Gavin in 51 games, a world record for a brother combination. He retired with 65 caps, a Scottish record until bettered by Gregor Townsend, but still a Scottish record for a centre. In 1989, he was selected to tour with the Lions to Australia and played alongside Jeremy Guscott in the two final tests following the loss of the first. He played with Gavin in both matches, the only brothers to have played together in the same British Lions test. It came as little surprise to many that he was selected for the final two tests, which yielded a series victory for the Lions. The following year, he was a member of the victorious Scottish Grand Slam side and was again selected to tour with the Lions to New Zealand in 1993, but a shattered cheekbone in a midweek game ruled him out for the tests. He featured in three RWCs, playing in ten of Scotland's 14 games in 1987, 1991 and 1995. He retired from international rugby in 1997 and professional rugby in 1999, but played on until 2002 for his club Watsonians for which he played 227 times.

Andy Irvine

Full name:	Andrew Robertson Irvine
Born:	16 October 1951 (Edinburgh, Scotland)
Tests:	51 for Scotland (15 as captain), 9 for Lions
Debut:	Scotland: 16 December 1972 vs New Zealand, Edinburgh Lions: 13 July 1974 vs South Africa, Port Elizabeth
Position(s):	fullback, wing
Career:	Scotland: 16/12/1972–11/07/1982, Lions: 13/07/1974–12/07/1980
Points:	Total 301: 273 for Scotland (10 Ts, 25 Cs, 61 PGs) 28 for Lions (2 Ts, 1 C, 6 PGs)

Photo: Scottish Rugby / PAI

One of the first true attacking fullbacks, Andy Irvine revolutionised the position, with running skills that took one's breath away. One of the great counter-attacking fullbacks of his era, he was capable of scoring or setting up opportunities from anywhere on the field. Perhaps only Christian Cullen in the modern game can compete for the fullback crown. Irvine's defensive capabilities were known to let him down from time to time, but it was his genius with ball in hand for which he is remembered. He spent most of his career at fullback, with occasional appearances on the wing. He made his debut against the 1972 All Blacks in Edinburgh and over his 11 international seasons was to score a then world record of 301 international points: 273 for Scotland and 28 for the Lions. His elusive running skills, made so distinctive by his skipping stride, his swerve, balance and grace had him on three Lions tours in 1974, 1977 and 1980. Few players of his era played and loved the game the way Irvine did. He thrilled crowds across the world, but most frequently at Murrayfield where he was known as an unusually spontaneous rugby entertainer. There is much debate among Scottish fans as to who holds the position of the greatest Scottish fullback: Hastings or Irvine. An impossibly difficult question, but Irvine's incisive running, blistering pace and mere presence in the backline created rampant confusion for defenders and certainly made him a crowd favourite. Retiring in 1982, Irvine stayed in the game as president of the SRU. He was inducted into the International Rugby Hall of Fame in 1999.

Ian McGeechan

Full name:	Ian Robert McGeechan OBE
Born:	30 October 1946 (Leeds, England)
Tests:	32 for Scotland (9 as captain);, 8 for Lions
Debut:	Scotland: 16 December 1972 vs New Zealand, Edinburgh Lions: 8 June 1974 vs South Africa, Cape Town
Position(s):	centre, flyhalf, wing
Career:	Scotland: 16/12/1972–17/03/1979, Lions: 08/06/1974–13/08/1977
Points:	Total 24: 21 for Scotland (7 DGs), 3 for Lions (1 DG)

Photo: Scottish Rugby / PAI

One of the most balanced runners of his day, McGeechan's jinking style of running, positional awareness and solid defence made him a great player. He couldn't have asked for a more difficult debut international – against New Zealand in 1972 – but he performed well and retained his place for the 1973 Five Nations. He impressed the Lions selectors and in 1974 was selected to tour to South Africa where he played in all four tests and was an integral part of the famous winning side. He again toured with the Lions to New Zealand in 1977, playing in all four tests, with the Lions coming within a whisker of sharing the series. Incredibly, McGeechan failed to score a single try in any of his appearances, but his support play and ability to release his outside backs into space created dozens. He retired from international rugby after playing against France in the final match of the 1979 Five Nations at the age of 33, with a recurring knee injury hampering his game. He remained highly involved in rugby and became the Lions coach to Australia in 1989, with success down under earning him promotion as Scotland coach in 1990 when he promptly took them to the Grand Slam. He is one of the greatest Lions legends, having not only played and won a series as a Lion but also coaching the Lions to two series victories. In total, he coached the Lions as head coach four times: victory against Australia in 1989, a narrow defeat against New Zealand in 1993, victory over South Africa in 1997 and a tight loss in South Africa in 2009. He was inducted into the International Rugby Hall of Fame in 2005.

Chris Paterson

Full name:	Christopher Douglas Paterson
Born:	30 March 1978 (Edinburgh, Scotland)
Tests:	95 (13 as captain)
Debut:	16 October 1999 vs Spain, Edinburgh
Position(s):	fullback, wing, flyhalf
Career:	16/10/1999–present
Points:	738 (22 Ts, 86 Cs, 150 PGs, 2 DGs)

Photo: Scottish Rugby / PAI

Chris Paterson holds just about every Scottish record possible, having so far amassed a record haul of 738 points for his country in a record 95 appearances, overtaking Gavin Hastings during his tour of Argentina in 2008. He became the youngest-ever player to earn 50 caps for Scotland at the age of just 26 and is statistically the best goal kicker in the world, having kicked a record 36 consecutive goals for Scotland between 11 August 2007 (vs Ireland) and 7 June 2008 (vs Argentina) and not missing a single attempt during the 2007 RWC: a remarkable record unlikely to be broken. Paterson is also currently third on the all-time try-scoring list for Scotland with 22, just two behind the record of 24 held by Tony Stanger and Ian Smith, another record he surely will break in the forthcoming season. He made his debut against Spain in the 1999 RWC and went on to feature in the 2000 Six Nations for Scotland. He is an extremely versatile player, having represented Scotland at fullback, wing and flyhalf. He has spent most of his career at fullback, although many believe he is best suited for the flyhalf berth. A small man for international rugby at just over 80 kilograms, or 175 pounds, Paterson makes up for this with his pace, tactical kicking, security under the high ball, prodigious goal kicking and reliability in the last line in defence. He quotes Gregor Townsend and Christian Cullen as his rugby heroes and in many ways has emulated these two greats with his attacking prowess and try-scoring feats in a Scottish team that has underperformed throughout his career and in which he is consistently a beacon of light.

John Rutherford

Full name:	John Young Rutherford
Born:	4 October 1955 (Selkirk, Scotland)
Tests:	42 for Scotland, 1 for Lions
Debut:	Scotland: 20 January 1979 vs Wales, Edinburgh Lions: 2 July 1983 vs New Zealand, Dunedin
Position(s):	flyhalf, centre
Career:	Scotland: 20/01/1979–23/05/1987, Lions: 02/07/1983
Points:	Total 68: 64 for Scotland (7 Ts 12 DGs), 4 for Lions (1 T)

Photo: Scottish Rugby / PAI

One of the finest Scottish flyhalfs of all time, Rutherford played an elegant game and possessed a deceptively lazy style of running that made him extremely difficult to pin down. Rutherford's pace, balance, swerve and intelligent boot brought much success to the Scots during the 1980s. He still holds today the Scottish record for the most drop goals ever scored: 12. He made his debut in 1979 against Wales and remained the number-one Scottish flyhalf for his career, when at one time he was the second-most capped flyhalf in the game's history behind Jackie Kyle. In 1983, he earned a call-up to the British Lions tour of New Zealand where he played just a single test: the third, at centre, surprisingly, and scored a try. He was a pivotal member of the 1984 Scottish Grand Slam side and made the 1987 Scottish RWC squad, but featured in just one international, against France, where he aggravated an old leg injury, which ultimately led to his retirement.

Wilson Shaw

Full name:	Robert Wilson Shaw CBE
Born:	11 April 1913 (Glasgow, Scotland)
Died:	1979
Tests:	19 (9 as captain)
Debut:	3 February 1934 vs Wales, Edinburgh
Position(s):	wing, centre, flyhalf
Career:	03/02/1934–18/03/1939
Points:	28 (8 Ts, 2 Cs)

Photo: Scottish Rugby / PAI

No other Scot in the history of Scottish rugby can lay claim to scoring tries against England at Twickenham in three consecutive games as did Wilson Shaw in 1934, 1936 and twice in 1938 . His performance in 1938 is still admired today on grainy film in DVD collections of great tries. It was a performance that secured Scotland the Triple Crown and only their second victory at Twickenham to date. The match came to be known as 'Shaw's match' for he was also captain, seeing his team through to a 21–16 victory and feted off the Twickenham pitch on his teammates' shoulders. He was an exceptionally talented player, blessed with the ability to lead and prepared to run the ball which, with his pace, ensuring he could squeeze through the tightest of gaps. Following Scotland's Triple Crown in 1938, he was hailed by the British press as 'the greatest rugby player of his generation'. He was adept at playing in just about every backline position; in 1937 against Ireland, he played on the wing with his brother Ian at centre. He regularly put in scintillating performances, with the one against the 1935 All Blacks going down in the annals as he released his teammates Ken Fyfe and Charles Dick into space to score crucial tries. Despite his efforts, Scotland lost 8–18. His last international was on 18 March 1939; World War II cut short his international career and he was forced to retire. He stayed involved in Scottish rugby and served as the president of the SRU in 1971.

Ian Smith

Full name:	Ian Scott Smith
Born:	31 October 1903 (Melbourne, Australia)
Died:	18 September 1972
Tests:	32 for Scotland (23 as captain), 2 for Lions
Debut:	Scotland: 2 February 1924 vs Wales, Edinburgh Lions: 16 August 1924 vs South Africa, Durban
Position:	wing
Career:	Scotland: 02/02/1924–01/04/1933, Lions: 16/08/1924–23/08/1924
Points:	72 for Scotland (24 Ts)

Photo: Scottish Rugby / PAI

One of the most prolific try scorers in rugby history, Ian Smith scored a try every 107 minutes while playing international rugby, an emphatic strike rate which, with his record of 24 tries earned him the nickname 'The Flying Scotsman'. This record stood for over 50 years until broken by David Campese in 1987. Although he was born in Melbourne and brought up in New Zealand, Smith attended Oxford University. While playing for Oxford he was selected to play for Scotland in 1924, eligible thanks to his Lowland relatives. On debut he scored a hat-trick of tries to help Scotland crush Wales 35–10 (equivalent to 51–14 today) and was selected to tour with the Lions to South Africa that same year. He played in the first two tests, but with both matches lost he faced the selectors' axe. He bounced back in 1925 and was a key player in Scotland's first-ever Grand Slam, during which he scored four tries in each of the matches against France and Wales, a feat which no Scottish player, or any other for that matter, has since emulated. Remarkably, Smith amassed his tries and played for the Lions while still an undergraduate. Indeed, the 1925 Scottish Grand Slam side's backline was composed of four Oxford students who all wreaked havoc on their opponents. Smith finished his career captaining Scotland to their Triple Crown success of 1933. His 24 tries by a Scotsman is a record that still stands today, shared with Tony Stanger.

David Sole

Full name:	David Michael Barclay Sole
Born:	8 May 1962 (Aylesbury, England)
Tests:	44 for Scotland (25 as captain), 3 for Lions
Debut:	Scotland: 17 January 1986 vs France, Edinburgh Lions: 1 July 1989 vs Australia, Sydney
Position:	prop
Career:	Scotland: 17/01/1986–21/06/1992, Lions: 01/07/1989–15/07/1989
Points:	12 for Scotland (3 Ts)

Photo: Scottish Rugby / PA)

David Sole is one of Scotland's great captains and one of only three Scottish captains who can lay claim to having led his nation to Grand Slam glory, in 1990. Despite being a relatively small man for a prop forward, Sole was nonetheless extremely powerful, technically sound and a very strong scrummager. He was the archetypal modern forward, possessing excellent handling ability; he was ferociously competitive in the loose and had a turn of pace that belied a traditional prop's attributes. He made his debut along with the Hastings brothers against France in 1986 and his consistently powerful performances earned him a deserved selection to tour Australia with the 1989 British Lions. He played in all three tests as first-choice loosehead prop and was a key part of the pack which laid the foundations for the Lions series victory. An inspirational leader and a dynamic forward, he was chosen to captain Scotland for the 1990 season. The highlight of his career, in his first season as captain, was leading Scotland to a Grand Slam over the old enemy England who themselves were attempting a Grand Slam. He will forever be remembered for leading the 'slow walk' out of the tunnel to face England at this decider, being roared on with approval by the partisan crowd. He took Scotland to fourth spot in the 1991 RWC where they could so easily have reached the final had it not been for Gavin Hastings's wayward kicking. He retired at the end of the 1992 Five Nations, having played 44 internationals and set a Scottish record of 25 tests as captain, a record which still stands.

South Africa

Naas Botha

Full name:	Hendrik Egnatius Botha
Born:	27 February 1958 (Breyton, South Africa)
Tests:	28 (9 as captain)
Debut:	26 April 1980 vs South America, Johannesburg
Position:	flyhalf
Career:	26/04/1980–14/11/1992
Points:	312 (2 Ts, 50 Cs, 50 PGs, 18 DGs)

Photo: New Zealand Rugby Museum

South Africa's leading points scorer in test rugby until Percy Montgomery overtook his record in 2004, Naas Botha was prolific and the most accurate kicker in South Africa's history. Nicknamed 'Nasty Booter', had he had the opportunity to play more than his 28 tests during South Africa's years of isolation he would undoubtedly have scored many, many more points. He was a teenage prodigy who became an international star par excellence. He was also a player that everyone had an opinion of: you either loved him or you hated him. Regardless, he was quite simply the greatest goal kicker the Springboks have ever produced. During his career he scored a staggering 51 percent of all of South African points in the matches he played. He made his debut in 1980 against the touring South Americans in Johannesburg and scored 12 points, to which he added a hat-trick of drop goals in the next. He followed this with 27 points against the Lions and famously sealed the series in the third test with the toughest kick imaginable: a 75th-minute touchline conversion into the teeth of a howling gale and driving rain. His conversion won the match 12–10 and the series 3–0 for the Boks. His finest performance was against the All Blacks in 1981 in Wellington where he scored a then South African record of 20 points against New Zealand with a conversion, five penalties and a drop goal. The tragedy was that South Africa's apartheid policies severely restricted his career. In 1984,

Botha defected from rugby union to play for the Dallas Cowboys as their goal kicker in the American Grid Iron League. On his return to South Africa in 1986, he captained South Africa to a comprehensive series victory over the touring rebel New Zealand Cavaliers and was in the team that beat the World XV in 1989. He went on to become South Africa's first post-isolation captain and performed credibly in a rusty team that struggled to adapt to the international scene. He was a master goal kicker, especially gifted in the art of drop goals, slotting over no fewer than 18 in his 28 tests. He twice kicked more than three in a test, which included single-handedly sinking the Irish in 1981. He is today a highly respected TV critic of the game in South Africa and is often called up to assist as a kicking coach for the Springboks.

Johan Claassen

Full name:	Johannes Theodorus Claassen
Born:	23 September 1929 (Prince Albert, South Africa)
Tests:	28 (9 as captain)
Debut:	6 August 1955 vs British Lions, Johannesburg
Position:	lock
Career:	06/08/1955–25/08/1962
Points:	10 (2 Ts, 2 Cs)

Johan Claassen was an immovable fixture with automatic selection for the Springboks in the late 1950s and early 1960s. He established himself as the best lineout specialist in the world at the time. One of the most legendary locks and captains in Springbok history, Claassen made his debut in the series cauldron against the 1955 British Lions. He played in all the tests and in every test of the 1956 tour to Australia and New Zealand where he made a name for himself as a rugged, hard-tackling forward. It was one of the roughest and toughest series in the history of rugby union, with Claassen establishing a reputation as the finest lock to have visited New Zealand. He was given the Springbok captaincy in 1958 against the French, but tarnished his reputation when the Springboks lost a home series for the first time since 1896. He was stripped of the captaincy, but went on to play critical roles in a revenge series victory over New Zealand in 1960 and the Grand Slam tour of the United Kingdom and France in 1960/1961. Following this success, he was again selected as captain in 1961 against Ireland and Australia. He retained the captaincy for the series against the British Lions, which South Africa won well and was thus undefeated in his second stint as captain. He retired at the end of the 1962, having lost just one test as captain. He remained an integral part of Springbok rugby, becoming a selector and coaching the team until 1974; then managing them on their tour to New Zealand in 1981.

Danie Craven

Full name:	Daniël Hartman Craven
Born:	11 October 1910 (Lindley, South Africa)
Died:	4 January 1993 (Stellenbosch, South Africa)
Tests:	16 (4 as captain)
Debut:	5 December 1931 vs Wales, Cardiff
Position(s):	scrumhalf, flyhalf, centre, fullback, eighthman
Career:	05/12/1931–10/09/1938
Points:	6 (2 Ts)

Born on 11 October 1910, Danie Craven was destined to become the most influential and important figure in South African rugby history, earning him the nickname 'Mr Rugby' and regarded by many as the greatest rugby player in the world at the time. He was spotted by legendary Springbok coach 'Ou Baas' Markotter who plucked him from the Stellenbosch 2nd XV to play scrumhalf for the Springboks on their United Kingdom tour. Craven was a dynamic and constructive player, once described as a ballet dancer on a rugby field, alluding to his silky, near-untouchable running style. At the age of just 20, he was selected for the 1930/1931 tour to the United Kingdom where he made his international debut against Wales in Cardiff, a tough debut at the best of times. It was on this tour that Craven put in one of his most commanding performances as a Springbok, against Scotland when, with the scores level at 3–3 and the match almost over, Craven dived over from a scrum for the winning try, scored so quickly that the Scottish defence were completely oblivious of it until it was indicated by the referee. With this, he secured the Grand Slam for the Springboks. His halfback partner Bennie Osler described the performance as 'one of the most perfect exhibitions of scrumhalf play I ever had the pleasure of seeing'. Craven was famous for inventing the dive pass which he unveiled on the 1937 Springbok tour to New Zealand. He also holds the record for playing in five different positions in five consecutive Springbok matches, moving from eighthman to fullback. Had it not been for the outbreak of World War II, Craven would have played many more internationals, but it was not to be and he was forced to retire at the tender age of 27. He became the Springbok coach from 1949 to 1956 and then took up the post of president of the SARB from 1956 until his death in 1993, the longest-serving president in South Africa's history. In 2007, Craven's service to rugby was honoured when he was inducted into the IRB Hall of Fame.

Morné du Plessis

Full name:	Morné du Plessis
Born:	21 October 1949 (Vereeniging, South Africa)
Tests:	22 (15 as captain)
Debut:	17 July 1971 vs Australia, Sydney
Position(s):	eighthman, flank
Career:	17/07/1971–08/11/1980
Points:	12 (3 Ts)

Morné du Plessis was one of South Africa's most successful captains of all time and half of the only father-son combination to captain South Africa: his father Felix captained South Africa to three successive victories over New Zealand in 1949. Du Plessis led the Boks to 13 victories in 15 matches he captained, including series victories over France in 1975, New Zealand in 1976 and the British Isles in 1980; an achievement that few captains in the world can boast. He was a massive man who put his imposing frame to great use intimidating his opponents, and thereby establishing himself as a brilliant eighthman as well as a world-renowned captain. He was everywhere in the loose and a tower of strength in the lineouts. He made his unexpected debut on the 1971 tour of Australia after Tommy Bedford suffered a broken cheekbone, and he never looked back. He missed just three South African tests until his retirement, two during the 1974 British Lions tour. The nation went into shock when du Plessis announced his retirement prior to the 1981 tour to New Zealand and despite heavy persuasion to return to the game and lead the Springboks, he stuck to his word and played his last game against France in the summer test of 1980. It was inconceivable that the Boks would tour New Zealand without his imposing presence, with many putting the series loss down to the fact he was not there to lead them. He is still very much involved in the game; in 1995, he was the inspirational manager for the Springbok side that won the RWC. He was once aptly described by ex-IRB president Syd Millar as 'a great man'.

Frik du Preez

Full name:	Frederik Christoffel Hendrik du Preez
Born:	28 November 1935 (Dwaalboom, South Africa)
Tests:	38
Debut:	7 January 1961 vs England, London
Position(s):	lock, flank
Career:	07/01/1961–07/08/1971
Points:	11 (1 T, 1 C, 2 PGs)

Photo: www.sarugby.org.uk

Regarded as possibly the greatest Springbok of all time and officially tagged as the South African Player of the Century, Frik du Preez was not only a brilliant Springbok forward, but also one of the great characters of the game. He was extremely mobile, equally at home at lock or flank, although he preferred the latter and, what's more, he could also kick at goal. A big man for his time, he routinely outjumped taller men in the lineout, once described by Danie Craven as 'a forward and a back rolled into one . . . who could have played anywhere on the field with equal brilliance'. He made his 1961 debut against England at Twickenham, following injuries to several senior players.

To add to the pressure he was trusted with the goal-kicking duties which he performed admirably, crucially converting Doug Hopwood's try, however, he never again kicked for goal following the end of the tour. To the surprise of many, he only scored one try in his career, but a try that is still spoken about today by those privileged enough to have witnessed it: a spectacular effort against the 1968 British Lions at his home stadium of Loftus Versfeld where he ran half the length of pitch, beating defenders along the touchline and bouncing Lions fullback Tom Kiernan out the way to score in the corner. He held the record as the most capped Springbok of all time, along with Jan Ellis, for nearly 30 years before it was broken in 1997 by winger James Small. He played an integral part in all the Springbok series victories of the 1960s. At 36, he fittingly retired at the end of the 1971 tour to Australia with the side undefeated, a team which became known as the 'Invincibles'. Du Preez was given the honour of leading the team onto the field, following which speeches were made by his teammates. Du Preez declined to reply, since described as 'the most eloquent non-speech ever heard'. The nation went into mourning following his retirement, with Danie Craven putting his contribution to rugby into perspective: 'I very much doubt whether we will ever again see the likes of Frik du Preez.'

Os du Randt

Full name:	Jacobus Petrus du Randt
Born:	8 September 1972 (Elliot, South Africa)
Tests:	80
Debut:	8 October 1994 vs Argentina, Port Elizabeth
Position:	prop
Career:	08/10/1994–20/10/2007
Points:	25 (5 Ts)

Photo: Thys Lombard

Pieter 'Os' du Randt is one of the greatest South African forwards of all time and one of the most popular Springboks, as testified by the crowd chanting, 'Os, Os, Os' (Afrikaans for ox), commonplace at home tests. Du Randt had one of the most unique and successful Springbok careers, which spanned a South African record of 13 years and 13 days. He was a genuine all-round forward with his powerful scrummaging, surprising mobility, extremely solid defence and good ball handling. As a 21-year-old he debuted against Argentina and just a few months later was a member of the side that won the 1995 RWC. He became a regular in the team until the end of the 1999 RWC when a series of injuries began to plague him, which ultimately led to his decision to retire altogether from rugby. In 2003, however, he was persuaded back to the game by the Free State coach 'Rassie' Erasmus and in 2004 new national coach Jake White selected du Randt for the Springboks after a four-year absence from the side. His return was eminently successful and by the end of the season, du Randt had played in every test that year. Once again, he became the cornerstone of the Springboks pack throughout White's tenure as coach. His career ended on a high as he helped guide the Springboks to their second RWC title in 2007, thereby becoming the only Springbok player in history to win two RWC titles. Os du Randt was one of the last remaining players of the amateur era. In addition to his brace of RWC medals, he won two Tri-Nations titles, in 1998 and 2004, as well as a Currie Cup medal in 2005.

Danie Gerber

Full name:	Daniel Mattheus Gerber
Born:	14 April 1958 (Port Elizabeth, South Africa)
Tests:	24
Debut:	18 October 1980 vs South America, Montevideo
Position:	centre
Career:	18/10/1980–14/11/1992
Points:	82 (19 Ts, 1 C)

Simply put, Danie Gerber is the greatest centre to have ever played. He requires no introduction to rugby fans across the globe. He consistently continues to make dream-team selections across the world. He scored tries at will but it was the way he scored them that made him so special. He had everything: speed; a strong build, an uncanny sense for the gap and the ability to rapidly step off either foot at will. His tries were things of beauty and had it not been for apartheid isolation he would have scored many more. However, he did make scratch appearances in Europe, scoring nine tries in just four appearances for various invitation sides, including four against Cardiff for the Barbarians. He made his 1980 debut against South America as a 22-year-old on a strange tour before just 3,000 people in Montevideo. He marked his entry onto the rugby stage with a try from his own 22 and scored another in the next test in Santiago. He twice posted hat-tricks, against South America in 1982 and England in 1984; his three against England were scored within 33 minutes, with the English simply having no answer to his power and pace. He was also a member of the 1986 side that defeated the Cavaliers. It seemed that his career was over given the stricter bans imposed on apartheid South Africa, but he defied all odds to appear six years later in South Africa's first post-isolation international, against New Zealand in Johannesburg. He was 34 years old and despite having lost some of his pace, he was still the king of centres as he crossed twice for South Africa to almost steal the match. He did not tour Europe until he was 34, when he was selected to play France and England. He finished his career by scoring a try in each of the tests against France, with his 19-try haul a South African record until broken by James Small. His final game for South Africa was, appropriately, at Twickenham, where he had been banned from playing for his entire career. Politicians have much to answer for.

Japie Krige

Full name:	Jacob Daniël Krige
Born:	5 July 1879 (Klein Drakenstein, Caledon, South Africa)
Died:	14 January 1961 (Cape Town, South Africa)
Tests:	5
Debut:	26 August 1903 vs British Isles, Johannesburg
Position:	centre
Career:	26/08/1903–01/12/1906
Points:	3 (1 T)

Born in the farmlands of the Orange Free State, Japie Krige was destined to become one of the greatest backline players to grace the South African game. Legend has it he could score a try on request. He started his career playing for Stellenbosch University and by the age of 17, had already won the Currie Cup title with Western Province. His form for club and province soon earned him a call-up to the national side to take on the might of the touring Lions, making his debut in the drawn first test on 26 August 1903 in Johannesburg. He missed the second, but a recall for the third saw the Springboks win the test and a series for the first time in their history. Krige's speed and elusive running kept the opposition backline busy throughout the game and the space he made for his teammates ultimately led to the victory. His performance in the two tests got him selected for South Africa's first tour abroad, to the United Kingdom in 1906/1907 when the South Africans acquired their name, the Springboks. Krige's tour was interrupted by injuries, but he still appeared in three of the four tests, scoring a crucially brilliant try against the Irish in Belfast and was an instrumental member in the classic victory over the 'invincible' Welsh who had beaten the All Blacks the year before.

Percy Montgomery

Full name:	Percival Colin Montgomery
Born:	15 March 1974 (Walvis Bay, Namibia)
Tests:	102
Debut:	28 June 1997 vs British Lions, Durban
Position(s):	fullback, centre, flyhalf
Career:	28/06/199–30/08/2008
Points:	893 (25 Ts, 153 Cs, 148 PGs, 6 DGs)

Photo: Thys Lombard

Think of any South African record and, more than likely Percy Montgomery will hold it or feature somewhere in that record. He played a record 102 times for the Springboks, scoring a record 893 points during his career. He is the fourth-most prolific try scorer in South African history, South Africa's most-capped fullback and holds the individual record for the most points scored in an international: 35 against Namibia in 2007. During his 12-year career, Montomgery played under five different coaches (a remarkable statistic), won two Tri-Nations titles and an RWC, playing an instrumental role in each of these successes. He was the leading points scorer at the 2007 tournament with 105 points, which saw South Africa win the title for a second time. After donning his 50th cap, against Italy in 2001, Montgomery left South Africa to further his career in Wales, only to return to South Africa in 2004 to feature in coach Jake White's four-year campaign which ultimately led to the 2007 RWC crown. South African crowds loved to hate Monty in his earlier career, but by the end he was loved by all and became known as Mr Reliable, the points-scoring machine. With his miserly two-step run-up to a place kick, his achievements are all the more remarkable considering he was not the starting goal kicker in 42 of his 102 tests.

Hennie Müller

Full name:	Hendrik Scholtz Vosloo Müller
Born:	26 March 1922 (Witbank, South Africa)
Died:	26 April 1977 (Cape Town, South Africa)
Tests:	13 (9 as captain)
Debut:	16 June 1949 vs New Zealand, Cape Town
Position:	eighthman
Career:	16/06/1949–26/09/1953
Points:	16 (3 Ts, 2 Cs, 1 PG)

Nicknamed *Windhond* (Afrikaans for greyhound) by the great Danie Craven, Müller was one of the most versatile players to have been produced by the Springboks. He possessed great pace (at 14, he ran the 100 metres in just 10.5 seconds), could kick with either foot, handle like a flyhalf and was resolute in defence. He was a complete player, one of the fastest back-rowers the game has known and was once described 'as fast as a track sprinter and as alert and hungry as a hawk'. Müller was also a magnificent leader and captained the Springboks in nine of his 13 internationals, including the momentous 1951/1952 Grand Slam tour to the United Kingdom when he took over the captaincy from an injured Basil Kenyon. The team was undefeated in all the internationals under his leadership, including the 44–0 drubbing of the luckless Scots who cheered Müller off the field at the final whistle. He then led South Africa to a 3–1 series win over Australia, capping his career with only one lost test. Such was his passion that in preparation for a big game Müller was reputed to have stopped talking to his wife three days before a match. Injury prevented him from playing more than his 13 games, but he stayed in the game after his retirement as a Springbok coach and selector. He died in Cape Town in 1977.

Bennie Osler

Full name:	Benjamin Louwrens Osler
Born:	23 November 1901 (Aliwal North, South Africa)
Died:	28 April 1962 (Cape Town, South Africa)
Tests:	17 (5 as captain)
Debut:	16 August 1924 vs British Lions, Durban
Position:	flyhalf
Career:	16/08/1924–02/09/1933
Points:	46 (2 Ts, 6 Cs, 4 PGs, 4 DGs)

One of the first great South African kicking flyhalfs, Bennie Osler was to dominate in one of the most successful eras in South African rugby: the Springboks did not lose a single series during his career. All 17 of his internationals were consecutive. He made his debut against the 1924 Lions in Durban where he kicked the vital drop goal to win the test by 7–3. His form in the series saw the Springboks go unbeaten against the tourists, drawing only the third, in part because Osler was knocked out cold and played most of the game in a daze. He was a tactical, kicking flyhalf – the best of his era – and resented running for territory, preferring to kick for it which resulted in the forward-dominated game plan that was a characteristic of Springbok play for decades. He was the ulimate general for South Africa and was in no small part the architect of the classic Springbok style: tough up front and marshalled by great kickers at the back. The performance of his career came during the highly anticipated series against the 1928 All Blacks. In the first test Osler scored a then world-record 14 points as New Zealand were defeated 17–0, a record margin for South Africa over New Zealand. It was a monumental series that eventually ended in a draw, but his masterly play and ability to control the game with his boot saw him selected as captain of the Springboks to tour the United Kingdom in 1931/1932. He was an inspirational leader and led his side to a Grand Slam triumph, losing just once on the entire tour. He was criticised by the British press for not playing a more entertaining brand of rugby, a criticism that was taken seriously by the administrators at home, and following a resounding 17–3 win over the touring 1933 Australians which was again dominated by his boot, the selectors forced him and the Springboks to run the ball in the second half. Osler objected vociferously, stating that the Springboks would lose, but his protest fell on deaf ears and after 80 minutes of rugby, the Springboks were humiliated in a record 6–21 defeat. Osler was stripped of the captaincy, but played the remainder of the series, which was won by South Africa as they reverted to their successful kicking game. He retired at the end of the series and died in 1962. He was inducted into the International Rugby Hall of Fame in 2007.

François Pienaar

Full name:	Jacobus François Pienaar
Born:	2 January 1967 (Vereeniging, South Africa)
Tests:	29 (all as captain)
Debut:	26 June 1993 vs France, Durban
Position(s):	flank, eighthman
Career:	26/06/1993–10/08/1996
Points:	15 (3 Ts)

Photo: www.sarugby.org.uk

One of the greatest leaders South Africa has ever had, François Pienaar managed to take one of the most inexperienced teams in the history of Springbok rugby and win the 1995 RWC. He was an inspirational captain and during the world cup campaign became a superb ambassador for the 'new South Africa' and a major influence in developing the changing values of the post-apartheid era. The image of Pienaar lifting the William Webb Ellis trophy with a beaming Nelson Mandela beside him is an iconic image of South African rugby and the 'rainbow nation'. Pienaar played in 29 internationals and captained them all from his debut at the drawn test against France on 26 June 1993 in Durban. He lost just eight of his 29 tests in a nervous era of Springbok rugby, the country only recently returned from international isolation. This was a remarkable achievement considering that Sprinbok rugby was at least a decade behind the times. There was public outcry when he was controversially dropped as captain by new coach André Markgraaff, after Pienaar had left the field concussed in the final 1996 Tri-Nations match against New Zealand. Sour relations between the two resulted in Pienaar never again playing for South Africa, with him moving to UK to further his career with Saracens. In his retirement, Pienaar has remained active in South African rugby ... and crisp adverts. He is is a well-known public figure and ambassador for his country, leading South Africa's abortive campaign to host the 2011 RWC.

Joost van der Westhuizen

Full name:	Joost Heystek van der Westhuizen
Born:	20 February 1971 (Pretoria, South Africa)
Tests:	89 (10 as captain)
Debut:	6 November 1993 vs Argentina, Buenos Aires
Position(s):	scrumhalf, wing
Career:	06/11/1993–08/11/2003
Points:	190 (38 Ts)

Photo: www.sarugby.org.uk

In a glittering career that lasted ten years and two days, Joost van der Westhuizen featured in 89 internationals, amassing a Springbok record of 38 tries: an astounding tally and a world record for a scrumhalf, including a magnificent hat-trick against Wales in Cardiff in 1996. During his career, he became one of only five Springboks to win a Currie Cup, Tri-Nations and World Cup medal and had it not been for the injuries that plagued his career, he would have featured in dozens more records. He was tall for a scrumhalf, yet in spite of his size, needed only the slightest of gaps to score a try. With an asutue rugby brain, he was a master around the fringe of a scrum, scoring many of his tries from close range in the blink of an eye. Of his 89 appearances, he featured as Bok captain ten times and had the honour of captaining South Africa at the 1999 RWC when he courageously led his team to third place. He is fondly remembered by all Bok supporters for the tries he started or scored, but specifically for his defence, which is best remembered in the 1995 RWC final when he flattened the 'unstoppable' Jonah Lomu (who never scored a try against the Springboks) several times to see his side through to their famous victory. He retired after South Africa's disappointing campaign at the 2003 RWC during which he posted his second hat-trick, this time against Uruguay.

Wales

Phil Bennett

Full name:	Phillip Bennett OBE
Born:	24 October 1948 (Felinfoel, Wales)
Tests:	29 for Wales (8 as captain), 8 for Lions (4 as captain)
Debut:	Wales: 22 March 1969 vs France, Paris Lions: 8 June 1974 vs South Africa, Cape Town
Position(s):	flyhalf, fullback, wing, centre
Career:	Wales: 22/03/1969–18/03/1978, Lions: 08/06/1974–13/08/1977
Points:	Total 210: 166 for Wales (4 Ts, 18 Cs, 36 PGs, 2 DGs) 44 for Lions (1 T, 2 Cs, 10 PGs, 2 DGs)

Photo: New Zealand Rugby Museum

Phil Bennett made his debut as a 20-year-old when he replaced Gerald Davies against France in Paris and from that moment he was a firm crowd favourite, thanks to his ability to entertain with his brilliant sidestep and swerve that left many a defender flailing in his wake. In the earlier part of his career he appeared in several positions for Wales, but finally settled in the flyhalf berth, following the retirement of Barry John in 1972. He played his greatest rugby in this position. He was so impressive in the brilliant Welsh side of the 1970s that he was selected to tour with the 1974 Lions to South Africa where he showed tremendous form to help secure the series. He sank the Boks in Cape Town with his goal kicking and in the second test produced the game of his life, scoring an astonishing 50-metre individual try and, had it not been for a deep gash to his ankle, he would likely have kicked more than the single conversion and penalty in the game. He continued this form into the Five Nations and in 1977 was chosen to lead the Lions to New Zealand. It was a difficult tour, one he described as 'the worst time of my rugby life'. To emulate the success of 1974 was near impossible as the Lions played through the coldest and wettest of New Zealand winters and, with his teammates demotivated and homesick, Bennett struggled to lift the side. Nonetheless, he still finished the tour as top scorer with 112 points. He retired from the international game following the Welsh Grand Slam success of 1978 and is today a respected critic and commentator. He was inducted into the International Rugby Hall of Fame.

Gerald Davies

Full name:	Thomas Gerald Reames Davies CBE
Born:	7 February 1945 (Llansaint, Wales)
Tests:	46 for Wales, 5 for Lions
Debut:	Wales: 3 December 1966 vs Australia, Cardiff Lions: 13 July 1968 vs South Africa, Cape Town
Position(s):	wing, centre
Career:	Wales: 03/12/1966–17/06/1978, Lions: 13/07/1968–14/08/1971
Points:	Total 81: 72 for Wales (20 Ts), 9 for Lions (3 Ts)

Photo: New Zealand Rugby Museum

Gerald Davies was one of the finest runners the game has seen, showcasing his amazing skills in the great Welsh sides of the 1970s. He is, and will always be, one of the greats of Welsh rugby. He made his debut in the winter of 1966 as a 21-year-old and went on to represent Wales for a dozen seasons. He was equally adept playing at centre, where he started his career, or on the wing, but it was the latter where he is best remembered for his try-scoring wizardry, with his magical swerve and brilliant sidestep that complemented his speed. His try-scoring feats earned him selection on Lions tours to South Africa in 1968 and New Zealand in 1971. He played in just one test against South Africa, but in 1971 played in all four tests, scoring three superb tries to see the Lions clinch a series in New Zealand for the first time. He declined to tour with the 1974 Lions to South Africa and again to New Zealand in 1977: had he not he would surely have become the most capped British Lions winger. He retired at the end of the disappointing Welsh tour to Australia in 1978 as joint leading try scorer (20) for Wales, along with Gareth Edwards. He became a rugby journalist, and in 2007 was appointed the Lions manager for the 2009 tour to South Africa.

Mervyn Davies

Full name:	Thomas Mervyn Davies OBE
Born:	9 December 1946 (Swansea, Wales)
Tests:	38 for Wales (9 as captain), 8 for Lions
Debut:	Wales: 1 February 1969 vs Scotland, Edinburgh Lions: 26 June 1971 vs New Zealand, Dunedin
Position:	eighthman
Career:	Wales: 01/02/1969–06/03/1976, Lions: 26/06/1971–27/07/1974
Points:	7 for Wales (2 Ts)

Photo: New Zealand Rugby Museum

Mervyn Davies proved that he was the best eighthman of his generation. He quickly assumed the nickname of 'Merve the Swerve' as his superb athleticism made him capable of the most amazing breaks and sidesteps, swerving with apparent ease around opponents, with his mobility and tactical awareness making him a vital playmaker coming off the back of the scrum. He made his debut in the 1969 Triple Crown season, against Scotland, and never looked backed, garnering 38 consecutive caps for Wales. He assumed the Welsh captaincy for the 1975 Five Nations tournament, leading the team to Grand Slam success the following season and was widely tipped to lead the Lions to New Zealand in 1977. However, it was never to be: he suffered a career-ending brain haemorrhage while playing for Swansea; undoubtedly the prompt pitchside medical attention saved his life. He spent several months in hospital before fully recovering. Aged 29, his playing days were done, yet he still finished his career as the game's most capped eighthman of all time. In a 2002 Welsh rugby poll, Davies was voted the all-time-greatest Welsh captain and eighthman. In 2001, he was inducted into the International Rugby Hall of Fame.

Gareth Edwards

Full name:	Gareth Owen Edwards CBE
Born:	12 July 1947 (Glanaman, Wales)
Tests:	53 for Wales (13 as captain), 10 for Lions
Debut:	Wales: 1 April 1967 vs France, Paris Lions: 8 June 1968 vs South Africa, Pretoria
Position:	scrumhalf
Career:	Wales: 01/04/1967–18/03/1978, Lions: 08/06/1968–27/07/1974
Points:	Total 91: 88 for Wales (20 Ts, 2 Cs, 1 PG, 3 DGs), 3 for Lions (1 DG)

Photo: New Zealand Rugby Museum

Gareth Edwards is recognised as not only the best scrumhalf to have played the game, but probably the best rugby player of all time. Voted Rugby Player of the Century, Edwards makes every dream-team World XV with ease. Born the son of a miner in 1947, he went on to play 53 internationals, all consecutively, for Wales over 11 years. He was never dropped and never missed a game. His record of 20 tries for Wales was a record held together with Gerald Davies for many years. He made his debut as a 19-year-old against France in 1967 and became Wales's youngest-ever skipper at 20 years and seven months when he captained his side against Scotland in 1968. He never had a dip in form and his extreme pace, clinical finishing, strength, agility and guile made him the great player he was. His form cemented him as first-choice Lions scrumhalf on three tours, including the 1968 tour to South Africa and the successful tours to New Zealand in 1971 and South Africa in 1974. His rugby CV is impeccable: he won seven Five-Nations championships, five Triple Crowns and three Grand Slams. With a masterful boot and an accurate pass, he could also score tries from anywhere on the field, as he did against Scotland in 1972 when he scored a magnificent solo effort from within his own half. It was Gareth Edwards who scored 'that try', possibly the greatest try ever scored in a rugby union match when the Barbarians defeated New Zealand in Cardiff in 1973. The success of the 1970s' Welsh team is in no small part due to the rugby skills of Gareth Edwards, but also to the relationships that he struck with his flyhalfs: Barry John and then Phil Bennett. He retired following the 1978 Grand Slam success, but when he published his autobiography he was branded a 'professional' by the IRFB and banned from further involvement in the game. Ludicrous but true. The ban was lifted 1997, with Edwards one of the first to be inducted into the International Rugby Hall of Fame. In a poll conducted by *Rugby World* magazine in 2003, Edwards was declared the greatest player of all time. In 2007, he was made a CBE for his services to sport.

Ieuan Evans

Full name:	Ieuan Cennydd Evans MBE
Born:	21 March 1964 (Capel Dewi, Wales)
Tests:	72 for Wales (28 as captain), 7 for Lions
Debut:	Wales: 7 February 1987 vs France, Paris Lions: 1 July 1989 vs Australia, Sydney
Position:	wing
Career:	Wales: 07/02/1987–07/02/1998, Lions: 01/07/1989–21/06/1997
Points:	Total 161: 157 for Wales (33 Ts), 4 for Lions (1 T)

For many years, Ieuan Evans held the Welsh record for the most tries and most appearances and was one of the best wingers to have graced the game in an era when Wales struggled to perform and in a career plagued by injury. A player who possessed true pace and strength, Evans was renowned for scoring tries from anywhere on the pitch. He was once described by legendary commentator Bill McLaren as 'Merlin the Magician' in reference to his uncanny ability to score the most amazing tries out of nothing. His ability earned him deserved selection for Lions tours to Australia in 1989, New Zealand in 1993 and South Africa in 1997. He was also a true opportunist, as the Wallabies know only too well when Evans pounced on a Campese fumble to score his only Lions try, a vital one at that, to clinch the 1989 series. He scored many mesmeric tries for Wales but is probably best remembered for his try against England in 1993 at the National Stadium when he sped past Rory Underwood to dot down a bouncing ball and secure Wales a 10–9 win over the old enemy. In 1994, he captained Wales to their first outright Five Nations win since 1979 and featured in three RWCs. He played in all three tests of each of the 1989 and 1993 Lions tours, but in 1997 a groin injury cut short his tour and he only played in the first test in Cape Town, his last for the Lions. During his career, he set Welsh records for most caps, most tries and most tests and his record tally of 28 tests as captain still stands. He retired after the 1998 Italy game and in 2007 was inducted into the International Rugby Hall of Fame.

Reggie Gibbs

Full name:	Reginald Arthur Gibbs
Born:	7 May 1882 (Cardiff, Wales)
Died:	28 November 1938 (Cardiff, Wales)
Tests:	16 for Wales, 2 for Lions
Debut:	Wales: 3 February 1906 vs Scotland, Cardiff Lions: 6 June 1908 vs New Zealand, Dunedin
Position(s):	wing, centre
Career:	Wales: 03/02/1906–11/03/1911, Lions: 06/06/1908–27/06/1908
Points:	Total 60: 57 for Wales (17 Ts, 3 Cs), 3 for Lions (1 T)

Photo: Frédéric Hubert/commons.wikimedia.org/ creative commons license

Reggie Gibbs was a successful Cardiff businessman and shipowner, but was more widely known for his heroic feats on the rugby field. He was a central figure in the successful Welsh sides at the turn of twentieth century when they won three Grand Slams in four seasons. In Wales's first-ever Grand Slam success in 1908, although France hadn't yet been formally admitted into the competition, Gibbs equalled Willie Llewellyn's feat of scoring four tries in an international, against the French. He went on to score a total of six that season: a Welsh season record that still stands today. His achievement of scoring four tries in a test has subsequently been equalled by eight other Welshmen. His form in the 1908 season saw him selected to tour with the Lions, though more of an Anglo-Welsh outfit, to New Zealand where he played in the first two tests and scored a try in the first. He was a member of the side that won the 1909 Grand Slam, even though he failed to score that season. However, a hat-trick against France in 1910 propelled him to his try-scoring best for the 1911 Grand Slam season, with brilliant tries against England and Ireland and yet another superb hat-trick against Scotland. Following this triumph, Gibbs retired from the game. It came as little surprise that Welsh form slumped after Gibbs was gone; they had to wait until 1950 to win another Grand Slam. Gibbs's tally of 17 tries in 16 appearances for Wales is a remarkable strike rate, a record that will be tough to better.

Barry John

Full name:	Barry John
Born:	6 June 1945 (Cefneithin, Wales)
Tests:	25 for Wales, 5 for Lions
Debut:	Wales: 3 December 1966 vs Australia, Cardiff Lions: 8 June 1968 vs South Africa, Pretoria
Position:	flyhalf
Career:	Wales: 03/12/1966–25/03/1972, Lions: 08/06/1968–14/08/1971
Points:	Total 120: 90 for Wales (5 Ts, 13 PGs, 6 Cs, 8 DGs) 30 for Lions (1 T, 3 Cs, 5 PGs, 2 DGs)

There are few players whose image conjures up the sense of awe as Barry John with ball in hand. His elusive running, superb decision-making, unshakeable confidence and tactical kicking made him the legend he is. He was nicknamed 'The King' in New Zealand in 1971, scoring 30 of the Lions' 48 points in that memorable series, with his famous try scored in the third test. In total, he played five times for the Lions, his first against South Africa when a broken collarbone prematurely removed him from the series. His combination with Gareth Edwards brought out the best in him: with 23 tests together, it was was one of the most effective halfback pairings of all time. The entertainment value he brought to the game was immense and the crowds revered him, conferring on him an almost godlike celebrity status. He wasn't a big man by any means, but it was his ability to release his backs into space that made him so dangerous and such a marked man. Such was his performance on the 1971 Lions tour to New Zealand that he permanently changed the way New Zealand looked at back play. It has been said of John that he dominated British rugby at a time when British rugby dominated the world. He made his Welsh debut against Australia in 1966; his last appearance was the Grand Slam clincher against France in which he scored the crucial winning try, as well as kicking a penalty. Despite his confident exterior, Barry John found it difficult to cope with his status and to the disappointment of an entire nation, decided to retire at the age of just 27, simply to escape the attention, finding fame more unnerving than any rugby opposition. He was inducted into the International Rugby Hall of Fame in 1997.

Cliff Morgan

Photo: Rugby Pioneers/commons.wikimedia.org/ creative commons license

Full name:	Clifford Isaac Morgan OBE, CVO
Born:	April 7 1930 (Trebanog, Wales)
Tests:	29 for Wales (13 as captain), 4 for Lions (1 as captain)
Debut:	Wales: 10 March 1951 vs Ireland, Cardiff Lions: 6 August 1955 vs South Africa, Johannesburg
Position:	flyhalf
Career:	Wales: 10/03/1951–29/03/1958, Lions: 06/08/1955–24/09/1955
Points:	Total 12: 9 for Wales (3 Ts), 3 for Lions (1 T)

One of many great Welsh flyhalfs, Cliff Morgan was blessed with a superb all-round game, characterised by his speed off the mark and elusive running which resulted in numerous memorable Welsh tries. He had the gift of deception that enabled him to operate brilliantly in close quarters, confusing opponents. He made his 1951 debut against Ireland and the following year made the flyhalf position his own. He was instrumental in securing Wales a Triple Crown and a Grand Slam. Morgan had a magnificent 1955 British Lions series in New Zealand, drawn 2–2, and captaining the side in the third test. He scored a mesmeric try from a tight scrum in the first international in Johannesburg, beating all three Springbok loose forwards, in the days when loose forwards didn't have to stay bound. He excelled on the hard fields of the Highveld which were conducive to running rugby and where his mastery of backline play saw his outside backs Tony O'Reilly and Jeff Butterfield scoring try after try. Affectionately know as Cliffie, he was dubbed 'Morgan the Magnificent' by the South African press. Returning to Wales for the 1956 Five Nations, he was appointed captain following his success in South Africa. He retired at the end of the 1958 Five Nations and stayed involved in the game as a BBC television commentator. A highlight of his commentating career was describing with such feeling Gareth Edwards's famous try for the Barbarians against the 1973 All Blacks. He quit commentating in 1987, but still talks on radio and contributes to a number of rugby publications. He was inducted into the International Rugby Hall of Fame in 1997.

Teddy Morgan

Photo: Rugby Pioneers/commons.wikimedia.org/ creative commons license

Full name:	Edward Theodore Morgan
Born:	22 May 1880 (Aberdare, Wales)
Died:	1 September 1949, North Walsham (England)
Tests:	16 for Wales, 4 for Lions (2 as captain)
Debut:	Wales: 11 January 1902 vs England, Blackheath Lions: 2 July 1904 vs Australia, Sydney
Position:	wing
Career:	Wales: 11/01/1902–01/12/1906, Lions: 02/07/1904–13/08/1904
Points:	Total 45: 42 for Wales (14 Ts), 3 for Lions (1 T)

Based in London from 1902 onward, Morgan played his rugby with the Welsh exiles, his talent and skills earning him his first international test cap against England that year in Blackheath. Throughout his career for Wales he scored 14 tries in 16 tests; this in the day when scorelines were regularly single figures. He was selected to tour with the British Isles in 1904 to Australia and New Zealand where he played in all four tests, scoring a try in the third against Australia. He captained the last test against Australia and the one against New Zealand. It was his try against the first All Blacks side in 1905 for which he will forever be remembered. It was a much-anticipated contest as the undefeated New Zealanders readied themselves for their final game of the tour against the Welsh, the 1905 Triple Crown champions, to claim the Grand Slam and remain invincible. But it was not the tourists' day as Morgan led his team, and the Cardiff crowd, as answer to the New Zealand *haka*, in singing the Welsh national anthem: the first time a national anthem was sung at a rugby match. It was an extremely tight game, decided by just a single score: Teddy Morgan's brilliant 25th-minute backline try in the corner. He was also involved in the notoriously controversial decision late in the match when New Zealand's Bob Deans scored what seemed like a perfectly good try only for it to be disallowed. Morgan later described the try as perfectly legitimate in his opinion, which further fuelled New Zealand's claims of having been robbed of a Grand Slam and their invincibility status. He finished his playing days against South Africa in 1906 in Swansea.

Gwyn Nicholls

Full name:	Erith Gwyn Nicholls
Born:	15 July 1874 (Westbury-on-Severn, England)
Died:	24 March 1939 (Cardiff, Wales)
Tests:	24 for Wales (10 as captain), 4 for Lions
Debut:	Wales: 25 January 1896 vs Scotland, Cardiff Lions: 24 June 1899 vs Australia, Sydney
Position:	centre
Career:	Wales: 25/01/1896–01/12/1906, Lions: 24/06/1899–12/08/1899
Points:	Total 19: 13 for Wales (3 Ts, 1 DG), 6 for Lions (2 Ts)

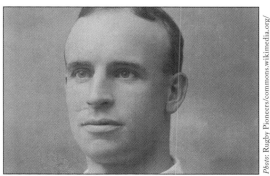

Photo: Rugby Pioneers/commons.wikimedia.org/ creative commons license

One of the greatest Welsh centres of all time, Gywn Nicholls played 18 seasons for his beloved Cardiff and ten for Wales. He won 24 caps for Wales, ten as captain, famously leading the Welsh to their Triple Crown victory of 1902. He was nicknamed 'The Prince of Threequarters' because of his lightning pace and perfect passing, being one of the great Welsh backline players to shine during the first golden era of Welsh rugby in the early 1900s, winning three Triple Crowns in five years. He made his debut against Scotland in Cardiff on 25 January 1896, with his early form earning him selection for the 1899 Lions tour to Australia; he was the only Welsh player on the tour. His form on tour was brilliant: he scored twice in the test series and finished top try scorer with 12 tries. He formally announced his retirement from the international game at the end of the 1905 season, but such was his influence and impact on the Welsh game that he was persuaded to return as skipper against the 1905 All Blacks, leading his side to a classic victory. He played a final season following the match against New Zealand and retired fully after a disappointing loss to the touring 1906 Springboks in Swansea. He became an international referee, taking charge of the 1909 Calcutta Cup match, as well as a Welsh selector for seven years. In 1949, the Gywn Nicholls Memorial Gate was opened in his honour at the old National Stadium in Cardiff. In 2005, he was inducted into the International Rugby Hall of Fame.

Gareth Thomas

Full name:	Gareth Thomas
Born:	25 July 1974 (Sarn, Wales)
Tests:	100 for Wales (21 as captain), 3 for Lions (2 as captain)
Debut:	Wales: 27 May 1995 vs Japan, Bloemfontein Lions: 25 June 2005 vs New Zealand, Christchurch
Position(s):	wing, centre, fullback
Career:	Wales: 27/05/1995–29/09/2007, Lions: 25/06/2005–09/07/2005
Points:	Total 205: 200 for Wales (40 Ts), 5 for Lions (1 T)

Photo: Manuel/commons.wikimedia.org/ creative commons license

Any man who plays 100 times for his country is *ipso facto* a legend of the game. He surpassed Gareth Llewellyn as Wales's most capped player on 26 May 2007 against Australia and gained his 100th cap against Fiji in the 2007 RWC, an international he would rather forget as Wales were stunned by Fiji who won a thrilling encounter to knock the Welsh out of the tournament. Thomas made his debut as a 21-year-old in the 1995 RWC against Japan, which he celebrated by a scoring a hat-trick of tries. Today, he jointly holds the Welsh try-scoring record of four tries in a match, against Italy in 1999. A powerful force at fullback, wing or centre, Thomas was one of the finest runners in the game thanks to his size, pace and power, which brought him one of the most important tries in Welsh history when he dotted down against South Africa in 1999 to see Wales through to their historic first-ever win over the Springboks. He held the Welsh individual try-scoring record for three years when he broke Ieuan Evans's record in 2004 with his tally of 40, which stood until 2008 when it was broken by speedster Shane Williams. His form as captain of the 2005 Grand Slam Welsh side saw him selected to tour New Zealand with the Lions, where he played in all three tests. He was captain for the last two tests, following the injury to Brian O'Driscoll and scored an early try in the second test. He was selected as Welsh captain for the 2007 RWC, which turned out to be a disastrous tournament for Wales. He announced his retirement from international rugby after his 100th test.

J.P.R. Williams

Full name:	John Peter Rhys Williams
Born:	2 March 1949 (Cardiff, Wales)
Tests:	55 for Wales, 8 for Lions
Debut:	Wales: 1 February 1969 vs Scotland, Edinburgh Lions: 26 June 1971 vs New Zealand, Dunedin
Position(s):	fullback, flank
Career:	Wales: 01/02/1969–07/02/1981, Lions: 26/06/1971–27/07/1974
Points:	Total 39: 36 for Wales (6 Ts, 2 Cs, 3 PGs), 3 for Lions (1 DG)

John Williams was known simply as JPR because of the confusion that abounded when he played in the same back three with another famous John Williams, 'JJ', a frequent teammate on the wing during his career for both Wales and the Lions. Thankfully for the game and fans across the world, Williams chose rugby over tennis after winning the Junior Wimbledon title in 1966, which illustrates his remarkable versatility as a sportsman. To this day, JPR remains the finest fullback to have graced the game. He epitomised the perfect fullback: he seldom missed touch, he was a solid last line of defence and extremely reliable under the high ball. Not as quick off the mark as Christian Cullen, for example, his formidable physical presence nevertheless powered him through gap after gap, with his blistering pace over 50 metres ensuring his name went down in history as the greatest attacking fullback of all time. His versatility, size and strength saw him, bizarrely, represent Wales at flank on their tour to Australia in 1978 when injuries had decimated the side, in the only game of his 55 internationals when he did not play at fullback. He was a big man and at fullback often bigger than some of the forwards. He made his debut on 1 February 1969 against Scotland in Edinburgh and became a central figure in 1970s' Welsh rugby, enjoying a glittering career during this golden era. He was a pivotal Lions member in two of their greatest tours: to New Zealand in 1971 and South Africa in 1974, playing in all the tests. Images of a heavy sideburned JPR responding to his captain's call of '99' on that 1974 tour are legendary, tearing into the fray to attack the biggest of the Bok forwards. From the halfway line he kicked the most audacious series-winning drop goal for the Lions in the final test. He retired after the Scotland game in 1981 to continue his career as an orthopaedic surgeon.

IRB Player of the Year

In 2001 the IRB first instigated the prestigious 'IRB Player of the Year' award – an honour awarded to a player who is adjudged to have been the finest player of the preceding season. The winner is chosen from a shortlist of five players who are nominated by an IRB judging panel of administrators, coaches and peers. To date no player has won the award twice. Australia, Argentina, Scotland and Italy have yet to have one of their players win the award.

Year	IRB Player of the Year	Nominees
2001	Keith Wood (Ireland)	George Gregan (Australia)
		George Smith (Australia)
		Brian O'Driscoll (Ireland)
		Jonny Wilkinson (England)
2002	Fabien Galthié (France)	Richie McCaw (New Zealand)
		Joe van Niekerk (South Africa)
		Brian O'Driscoll (Ireland)
		Jason Robinson (England)
2003	Jonny Wilkinson (England)	Imanol Harinordoquy (France)
		Richie McCaw (New Zealand)
		Steve Thompson (England)
		Phil Waugh (Australia)
2004	Schalk Burger (South Africa)	Serge Betsen (France)
		Gordon D'Arcy (Ireland)
		Matt Giteau (Australia)
		Marius Joubert (South Africa)
2005	Daniel Carter (New Zealand)	Bryan Habana (South Africa)
		Victor Matfield (South Africa)
		Richie McCaw (New Zealand)
		Tana Umaga (New Zealand)
2006	Richie McCaw (New Zealand)	Daniel Carter (New Zealand)
		Chris Latham (Australia)
		Paul O'Connell (Ireland)
		Fourie du Preez (South Africa)
2007	Bryan Habana (South Africa)	Felipe Contepomi (Argentina)
		Juan Martín Hernández (Argentina)
		Yannick Jauzion (France)
		Richie McCaw (New Zealand)
2008	Shane Williams (Wales)	Mike Blair (Scotland)
		Daniel Carter (New Zealand)
		Ryan Jones (Wales)
		Sergio Parisse (Italy)

IRB Hall of Fame

In 2006 the IRB launched the 'IRB Hall of Fame' to honour those people – players, teams, clubs, coaches, administrators, commentators, match officials, institutions etc. – that have had a profound impact on the game of rugby through achievement, contribution or service. An annual induction ceremony is held; not only to induct new nominees but to remember those historically already in the Hall of Fame. Nominations are made through public online-voting and deliberations by the Hall of Fame Induction Panel, usually chaired by the IRB President. The IRB Hall of Fame is not to be confused with the International Rugby Hall of Fame (next page) which is a separate Hall of Fame for rugby union.

Year	Inductee	Country	Details
2006	William Webb Ellis	England	In recognition of the history and tradition that rugby owes to these two icons of the game
	Rugby School	England	
2007	Danie Craven	South Africa	Player (16 tests), coach and president of SA Rugby until his death in 1993
	Pierre de Coubertin	France	Founder of the modern Olympic Games who included rugby in the programme
	John Eales	Australia	86 tests (55 as captain) and world-record points scorer for a forward in test rugby
	Gareth Edwards	Wales	63 tests (53 for Wales, 10 for Lions) ; voted Rugby Player of the Century
	Wilson Whineray	New Zealand	32 tests (30 as captain); one of most successful NZ captains of all time
2008	1888 New Zealand Maoris	New Zealand	First rugby union touring side to UK, NZ & Australia; played 107 matches
	Joe Warbrick	New Zealand	1888 NZ Maoris' tour manager and organiser
	Jack Kyle	Ireland	52 tests (46 for Ireland, 6 for Lions); voted greatest Irish player of all time
	Melrose Rugby Club	Scotland	One of oldest clubs in the world; hosted first-ever sevens tournament
	Ned Haig	Scotland	Founder of rugby sevens
	Hugo Porta	Argentina	58 tests for Argentina (34 as captain); later Argentinian Minister of Sport.
	Philippe Sella	France	111 tests for France; first player to exceed 100 internationals

International Rugby Hall of Fame

Started in 1997 as a charitable trust based out of London, the International Rugby Hall of Fame was conceptualised in New Zealand by a group of Kiwi rugby enthusiasts who appreciated the critical importance of preserving and presenting rugby's heritage before it got lost. The function of the trust – the majority of the trustees are inductees – is simply to acknowledge those players, coaches, administrators and anyone else who has had a major impact on the game since 1900. New inductees are accepted biennially.

Year	Inductee	Country
1997	Serge Blanco	France
	Danie Craven	South Africa
	Gareth Edwards	Wales
	Mark Ella	Australia
	Mike Gibson	Ireland
	Barry John	Wales
	Willie John McBride	Ireland
	Colin Meads	New Zealand
	Cliff Morgan	Wales
	George Nepia	New Zealand
	Frik du Preez	South Africa
	Tony O'Reilly	Ireland
	Hugo Porta	Argentina
	Jean-Pierre Rives	France
	JPR Williams	Wales
1999	Gerald Davies	Wales
	Morné du Plessis	South Africa
	Nick Farr-Jones	Australia
	Andy Irvine	Scotland
	Carwyn James	Wales
	Jack Kyle	Ireland
	Brian Lochore	New Zealand
	Philippe Sella	France
	Wavell Wakefield	England
	Wilson Whineray	New Zealand
2001	Gordon Brown	Scotland
	David Campese	Australia
	Ken Catchpole	Australia
	Don Clarke	New Zealand
	Mervyn Davies	Wales
	Sean Fitzpatrick	New Zealand
	Michael Lynagh	Australia
	Bill McLaren	Scotland
	Hennie Muller	South Africa
	Jean Prat	France

Year	Inductee	Country
2003	Bill Beaumont	England
	Gavin Hastings	Scotland
	Tim Horan	Australia
	Michael Jones	New Zealand
	Ian Kirkpatrick	New Zealand
	John Kirwan	New Zealand
	Jo Maso	France
	Syd Millar	Ireland
2005	Fred Allen	New Zealand
	Phil Bennett	Wales
	André Boniface	France
	Naas Botha	South Africa
	John Eales	Australia
	Grant Fox	New Zealand
	Dave Gallaher	New Zealand
	Martin Johnson	England
	Ian McGeechan	Scotland
	Gwyn Nicholls	Wales
	Francois Pienaar	South Africa
	Keith Wood	Ireland
2007	Ieuan Evans	Wales
	Danie Gerber	South Africa
	Tom Kiernan	Ireland
	Jason Leonard	England
	Jonah Lomu	New Zealand
	Terry McLean	New Zealand
	Graham Mourie	New Zealand
	Bennie Osler	South Africa
	Fergus Slattery	Ireland
	Joost van der Westhuizen	South Africa

Chapter Nine
Stadia

From the crusty 19th century bastions of old to the hypermodern arenas of the 21st century, the world's famous international rugby grounds are true sporting cathedrals in every sense. Some of these stadiums are very old and some no longer exist today, but nonetheless still have a great deal of venerable significance in the history of rugby, such as the old National Stadium in Cardiff.

Argentina

Argentina has no official rugby stadium, although the national team play the majority of their home internationals at the Estadio José Amalfitani, more commonly known as the Vélez Sársfield Stadium, in Buenos Aires. Through Argentina's rugby history most home internationals have been played in Buenos Aires at various venues, but of late, matches have been played in other cities, most recently at the Estadio Olimpico in Córdoba. Commonly used alternative venues include:

- Estadio Brigadier General Estanislao López, Sante Fe (capacity 32,500)
- Estadio Malvinas Argentinas, Mendoza (capacity 48,000)
- Estadio Raúl Conti, Puerto Madryn (capacity 15,000)
- Estadio Gigante de Arroyito, Rosario (capacity 41,500)
- Estadio Padre Ernesto Martearena, Salta (capacity 20,500)

Estadio José Amalfitani, Buenos Aires

Established:	c.1947
First test:	31 May 1986 (Argentina vs France)
No. of tests:	27
Capacity:	49,540
Record attendance:	49,450

Argentina's record at Estadio José Amalfitani						
Opponent	Played	Won	Lost	Drawn	For	Against
France	11	5	6	0	179	256
Australia	2	1	0	1	46	38
Italy	1	1	0	0	21	16
England	3	1	2	0	45	64
New Zealand	3	0	3	0	39	89
Spain	1	1	0	0	38	10
Wales	2	1	1	0	65	62
South Africa	2	0	2	0	30	73
Ireland	1	1	0	0	16	0
Scotland	1	0	1	0	14	26
Totals	27	11	15	1	493	634

Photo: Unión Argentina de Rugby

Home to the Vélez Sársfield football side, the Estadio José Amalfitani is fondly known as *El Fortín* (the fort) by local soccer fans or simply the Vélez Sársfield Stadium by foreigners. Primarily used for soccer matches, the stadium is today effectively the national rugby stadium (though not officially recognised as such), with almost all Argentina's high-profile internationals being played here since 1986. Their first was a memorable occasion, as they beat France and the following year sealed a series victory over 1987 RWC semi-finalists Australia. In 2003 Vélez Sársfield Stadium hosted a thrilling two-test series win over France – Argentina's first against France – and in 2007 they kept Ireland scoreless. Because Argentina only play top opposition teams at the venue due to its capacity, their record at the stadium is not particularly worrying to touring sides, despite the fact that Argentina have regularly recorded victories against most top sides at this stadium.

Estadio Arquitecto Ricardo Etcheverri (Ferro Carril Oeste), Buenos Aires

Established:	2 January 1905
First test:	16 July 1932 (Argentina vs Junior Springboks)
No. of tests:	53
Capacity:	24,500
Record attendance:	24,500
Former names:	Estadio El Templo de Madera, Estadio El Monumental de Madera

Argentina's record at Estadio Arquitecto Ricardo Etchevedrri						
Opponent	Played	Won	Lost	Drawn	For	Against
France	9	1	7	1	156	249
South Africa	4	0	4	0	85	171
Australia	4	2	2	0	69	69
England	4	1	2	1	78	90
Romania	3	3	0	0	90	28
Wales	2	0	2	0	42	59
Scotland	2	2	0	0	35	32
Junior Springboks	2	0	2	0	3	76
Ireland XV	2	2	0	0	14	6
Oxbridge	2	2	0	0	17	6
SA Gazelles	2	1	1	0	24	30
New Zealand XV	2	0	2	0	15	47
World XV	1	1	0	0	36	22
Fiji	2	2	0	0	72	38
New Zealand	2	0	1	1	41	54
United States	2	2	0	0	39	17
Canada	2	1	1	0	44	45
Japan	1	1	0	0	45	20
Chile	1	1	0	0	70	7
Paraguay	1	1	0	0	51	3
Uruguay	1	1	0	0	44	3
Ireland	1	1	0	0	34	23
Italy	1	1	0	0	38	17
Totals	53	26	24	3	1,142	1,112

Photo: Unión Argentina de Rugby

The Estadio Arquitecto Ricardo Etcheverri is more commonly known as the Ferro Carril Oeste Stadium because of its principal occupant's club name: the Ferro Carril Oeste Soccer Club. The venue has staged more rugby internationals than any other stadium in the country, but stopped hosting major tests from 2001, as the Estadio José Amalfitani is now preferred because of its greater capacity. Argentina enjoyed much success at the Ferro Carril Oeste Stadium, despite a poor start in a two-test series against the touring Junior Springboks in 1932 when they were heavily beaten. They did not play here for another 42 years until they beat an Irish XV in 1971 when, from here on, the stadium became Argentina's premier rugby venue until the UAR switched to the Estadio José Amalfitani.

GEBA, Buenos Aires

Established:	c.1924
First test:	12 June 1910 (Argentina vs British Isles XV)
No. of tests:	31
Capacity:	31,400
Record attendance:	31,400
Former name:	Estadio del Bosque

Argentina's record at GEBA						
Opponent	Played	Won	Lost	Drawn	For	Against
France	7	0	7	0	26	146
British Lions XV	5	0	5	0	6	168
Oxbridge XV	4	0	4	0	9	92
Ireland XV	2	0	1	1	3	9
Junior Springboks	2	0	2	0	12	34
SA Gazelles	2	0	2	0	18	29
Wales XV	2	1	0	1	18	14
Scotland XV	2	1	1	0	23	9
Chile	2	2	0	0	46	6
Brazil	1	1	0	0	72	0
Uruguay	1	1	0	0	62	0
Canada	1	1	0	0	35	0
Totals	31	7	22	2	330	507

The first test match played by Argentina in 1910 took place at the Club de Gimnasia y Esgrima La Plata's stadium. Founded in 1887, this is the oldest sports club in Argentina; in the early twentieth century it boasted some of the best sporting facilities in the country, including the club's stadium, the Estadio Juan Carlos Zerillo. The club is more commonly referred to by its acronym GELP which, in English archives, was always referred to as GEBA (Gimnasia Esgrima Buenos Aires, or the Gymnastics and Fencing Club of Buenos Aires). It was at GEBA's stadium where Argentina played all their early internationals; today it is simply referred to as GEBA. Historical records are sketchy as regards the exact venue of Argentina's early matches, but it is clear that at least 31 internationals were played at GEBA: a time when Argentinian rugby was nowhere near as strong as it is today, and consequently, their record at GEBA is not impressive. In 1981, GEBA hosted its final rugby test when Argentina beat Canada. The stadium was closed in 2006 by the government due to security issues, but has since been reopened and is used primarily for soccer.

The Estadio José Amalfitani is fondly known as *El Fortín* (the fort) by local soccer fans, or simply the Vélez Sársfield Stadium.

Photo: Unión Argentina de Rugby

Australia

ANZ Stadium, Sydney

Established:	June 1999 (broke ground September 1996)
First test:	26 June 1999 (Australia vs England)
No. of tests:	28 (24 Australian, 4 neutral RWC)
Capacity:	83,500
Record attendance:	109,874
Former names:	Stadium Australia, Telstra Stadium

<table>
<tr><td colspan="7" align="center">Australia's record at ANZ Stadium</td></tr>
<tr><th>Opponent</th><th>Played</th><th>Won</th><th>Lost</th><th>Drawn</th><th>For</th><th>Against</th></tr>
<tr><td>New Zealand</td><td>9</td><td>6</td><td>3</td><td>-</td><td>221</td><td>213</td></tr>
<tr><td>England</td><td>3</td><td>2</td><td>1</td><td>-</td><td>73</td><td>38</td></tr>
<tr><td>South Africa</td><td>4</td><td>4</td><td>-</td><td>-</td><td>101</td><td>53</td></tr>
<tr><td>France</td><td>3</td><td>3</td><td>-</td><td>-</td><td>87</td><td>44</td></tr>
<tr><td>Wales</td><td>2</td><td>2</td><td>-</td><td>-</td><td>59</td><td>33</td></tr>
<tr><td>Scotland</td><td>1</td><td>1</td><td>-</td><td>-</td><td>34</td><td>13</td></tr>
<tr><td>Argentina</td><td>1</td><td>1</td><td>-</td><td>-</td><td>24</td><td>8</td></tr>
<tr><td>Samoa</td><td>1</td><td>1</td><td>-</td><td>-</td><td>74</td><td>7</td></tr>
<tr><td>British Lions</td><td>1</td><td>1</td><td>-</td><td>-</td><td>29</td><td>23</td></tr>
<tr><td>Totals</td><td>25</td><td>21</td><td>4</td><td>-</td><td>702</td><td>432</td></tr>
</table>

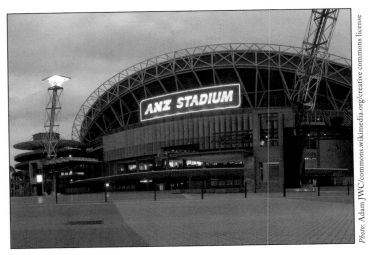

Established in the heart of the Sydney Olympic Park, the stadium was officially opened in 1999 as Stadium Australia more than a year ahead of the 2000 Sydney Olympic Games, for which it was primarily designed. It was initially built with a capacity of 110,000, making it the largest Olympic stadium in history, capable of holding four Boeing 747s side by side under the span of the main arches of the grandstands. It recorded the largest crowd in the history of the Olympics when 114,714 filled the stadium for the closing ceremony. It also lays claim to hosting the largest crowd in history for a rugby match: 109,874 watched the thrilling 2000 Bledisloe clash, won 39–35 by New Zealand, a game which came to be known as the 'match of the century'. In 2002 the stadium was renamed the Telstra Stadium and redesigned so the stands could be moved nearer the field, according to the type of event being hosted, allowing it to be reconfigured from rectangular to oval mode in just 12 hours. This reduced the seating capacity to 83,500 but was completed in time for the 2003 RWC when it hosted seven matches, including the opening game, both semi-finals and the epic final which was lost narrowly in extra-time by Australia to England. From 1 January 2008, the stadium became known as the ANZ Stadium after the Australia and New Zealand (ANZ) Banking Group bought the naming rights. It annually hosts at least two Australian internationals and is Australia's most successful venue, as the Wallabies have lost there just four times.

Ballymore, Brisbane

Established:	acquired by the QRU in 1966
First test:	22 June 1968 (Australia vs New Zealand)
No. of tests:	44 (40 Australian, 4 neutral RWC)
Capacity:	24,000
Record attendance:	24,000

Australia's record at Ballymore						
Opponent	Played	Won	Lost	Drawn	For	Against
New Zealand	6	1	3	2	96	102
France	4	3	1	-	106	81
Argentina	4	3	1	-	148	50
Wales	3	3	-	-	137	39
Ireland	3	2	1	-	91	50
Scotland	3	2	1	-	77	36
Canada	2	2	-	-	117	24
Italy	2	2	-	-	62	38
USA	2	2	-	-	114	21
Fiji	2	2	-	-	73	37
England	2	2	-	-	52	37
Tonga	2	1	1	-	63	30
South Africa	1	1	-	-	28	20
Japan	1	1	-	-	50	25
Korea	1	1	-	-	65	18
British Lions	1	-	1	-	12	19
Samoa	1	1	-	-	25	13
Totals	40	29	9	2	1,316	640

Ballymore was the first stadium constructed in Australia used exclusively for rugby union matches. It was acquired by the QRU in 1966, with the first test played against New Zealand on 22 June 1968 – a cracker won 19–18 by New Zealand. In 1974, the stadium was badly damaged during heavy flooding, with the pitch two metres under water. The stadium was repaired and the nearby river re-routed. In 1987 Ballymore hosted five internationals during the inaugural RWC, including the semi-final between New Zealand and Wales. On 17 June 2000, Ballymore hosted its final Australian international, when the Wallabies defeated Argentina 53–6. The stadium remained the home of Queensland rugby until 2007 when fixtures were switched to Suncorp Stadium. Today, Brisbane tests are played at the Suncorp Stadium and occasionally at the GABBA, both of which boast moderner facilities and more seats: the downfall of Ballymore.

ANZ Stadium, Sydney.

Etihad Stadium, Melbourne

Established:	9 March 2000 (broke ground 1996)
First test:	8 July 2000 (Australia vs South Africa)
No. of tests:	16 (10 Australian, 6 neutral RWC)
Capacity:	56,359
Record attendance:	56,605 (Australia vs British and Irish Lions, 7 August 2001)
Former names:	Telstra Dome, Colonial Stadium, Victoria Stadium, Docklands Stadium

Australia's record at Etihad Stadium						
Opponent	Played	Won	Lost	Drawn	For	Against
South Africa	1	1	-	-	44	23
British Isles	1	1	-	-	35	14
France	1	1	-	-	29	17
England	2	1	1	-	57	43
Ireland	2	2	-	-	35	28
Scotland	1	1	-	-	35	15
Italy	2	2	-	-	103	33
Totals	10	9	1	-	338	173

Photo: Plattopus/commons.wikimedia.org/ creative commons license

Situated in the dockland precinct of Melbourne, the stadium was originally named the Colonial Stadium after the Colonial State Bank until 1 October 2002 when it changed to Telstra Dome, and recently again to Etihad Stadium. It was built specifically for Australian Rules football, but has also played host to soccer, cricket, rugby league and rugby union games. Noted for its Colosseum-type architecture and retractable roof 38 metres above the pitch, it is the only stadium of its kind in the southern hemisphere with a fully retractable roof. It has now become a regular venue for the Wallabies. In recognition of the historic importance of the nearby Melbourne Cricket Ground, Etihad has agreed not to compete with the MCG in terms of hosting rights, so Melbourne-based tests are frequently alternated between the two. The first test at the stadium was against South Africa in 2000: the inaugural Nelson Mandela Challenge Plate match, with the crowd being addressed by Nelson Mandela via satellite on the big screen. To date, Australia have lost just once here; against England in June 2003. That same year, the stadium hosted six internationals during the 2003 RWC, including the two quarter-finals between New Zealand and South Africa and France and Ireland.

Subiaco Oval, Perth

Established:	9 May 1908
First test:	18 July 1998 (Australia vs South Africa)
No. of tests:	14 (9 Australian and 5 neutral RWC)
Capacity:	43,500
Record attendance:	44,142 (Australian Rules football match, 1991)
Former name:	Mueller Park

Australia's record at Subiaco Oval						
Opponent	Played	Won	Lost	Drawn	For	Against
South Africa	5	2	2	1	92	85
Ireland	3	3	-	-	114	57
Fiji	1	1	-	-	49	0
Totals	9	6	2	1	255	142

Photo: Scruffy/

Subiaco Oval is the largest sports stadium in Western Australia, mainly used for Australian Rules football matches, although the ground has been increasingly utilised for rugby union and, as of 2006, is home to the newest Super 14 franchise, the Western Force. The venue hosted five internationals during the 2003 RWC and has since become a regular venue for the Wallabies who play here on an annual basis. The ground was opened on 9 May 1908 as Mueller Park and has since undergone extensive refurbishment. Despite its capacity, the stadium is often unable to accommodate the volumes of home-team fans with plans currently underway to either upgrade the existing venue or build another one. The first test was played on 18 July 1998 as the ARU attempted to spread the game into Western Australia. On that occasion, South Africa beat Australia 14–13 on a rainy night, with many arguing that playing in Perth was more like an away game for the home side, taking into account the vast continental distances. However, the Wallabies continue to play here and have only lost two from nine.

Suncorp Stadium, Brisbane

Established:	c.1891, officially opened c.1914
First test:	26 June 1965 (Australia vs South Africa)
No. of tests:	23 (16 Australian, 7 neutral RWC)
Capacity:	52,500
Record attendance:	52,498 (Australia vs New Zealand, 29 July 2006)
Former names:	John Brown Oval, Lang Park, Suncorp Metway Stadium

Australia's record at Suncorp Stadium						
Opponent	Played	Won	Lost	Drawn	For	Against
South Africa	5	5	-	-	154	43
England	2	2	-	-	127	15
New Zealand	3	-	3	-	58	73
Scotland	1	1	-	-	33	16
British Isles	1	-	1	-	0	31
Romania	1	1	-	-	90	8
France	2	2	-	-	77	41
Wales	1	1	-		31	0
Totals	16	12	4	-	570	227

Photo: Mdmanser/commons.wikimedia.org/ creative commons license

Interestingly, the Suncorp Stadium is situated on top of the old North Brisbane Cemetery, the city's primary cemetery of the day which was closed in 1875 because of hygiene concerns. In 1891 the rancid area was rehabilitated and set aside as a recreational sports area, and later fenced off for football and cricket matches. The site slowly grew as adjacent fields were incorporated. In 1914 it became known as the John Brown Oval when it was officially opened by the city council. The site grew to more than 6 hectares and its name changed to Lang Park after Reverend John Lang who had established the earlier resting place for the dead. The park soon evolved into a sporting precinct with tennis courts, an athletics track and a pitch for football and cricket. In 1957 Lang Park become the headquarters of Queensland Rugby League (QRL) which began a process of improvements to the ground. Increasingly used by the QRL, it was no longer viable as a public recreational facility, unable to cope with the massive crowds attracted to the matches. This resulted in the formation of the Lang Park Trust with the sports ground transformed into the stadium it is today. It was renamed Suncorp Stadium in 1994 when naming rights were attained by the Queensland financial institution, Suncorp-Metway Ltd. Through its history, the stadium has been used primarily for rugby league but increasingly for rugby union. It hosted its first rugby union test match on 26 June 1965 when Australia beat South Africa 12–8 and is now home to the The Reds, Queensland's Super 14 side, and annually hosts Wallaby internationals. The stadium is now rectangular in shape after a complete refurbishment in 2003 to allow spectators to sit nearer the field, and in time for the RWC when the stadium hosted nine matches, including two quarter-finals. The venue has proved a happy hunting ground for the Wallabie who have lost just four of 16 matches, most recently a nailbiter against New Zealand at the end of the 2008 Tri-Nations. They inflicted a record 76–0 defeat here on a young English side in 1998 and thrashed South Africa 49–0 in 2006.

Sydney Cricket Ground, Sydney

Established:	c.1851
First test:	24 June 1899 (Australia vs British Isles)
No. of tests:	80
Capacity:	44,000
Record attendance:	49,327 (New South Wales vs New Zealand, 13 July 1907)
Former name:	Moore Park

Australia's record at Sydney Cricket Ground						
Opponent	Played	Won	Lost	Drawn	For	Against
New Zealand	33	9	22	2	344	511
South Africa	9	1	8	-	87	161
British Isles	9	2	7	-	43	124
Fiji	7	5	2	-	146	90
France	5	3	1	1	84	67
NZ Maoris	3	1	1	1	24	18
England	2	2	-	-	34	18
Scotland	2	2	-	-	56	12
Ireland	2	-	2	-	8	20
Argentina	2	2	-	-	55	13
Wales	2	1	1	-	35	36
Tonga	1	1	-	-	30	12
Japan	1	1	-	-	37	7
USA	1	1	-	-	49	3
Canada	1	1	-	-	59	3
Totals	80	32	44	4	1,091	1,095

Photo: One Salient Oversight/commons.wikimedia.org/creative commons license

Although it is no longer used for rugby, the Sydney Cricket Ground has hosted more Australian internationals than any other venue in the country. In 1851, a piece of land south of the Victoria Barracks was granted to the British Army for use as a garden and a cricket ground by the New South Wales government. The patch came to be known as Moore Park and quickly became the primary venue for the city's cricket matches. By 1875, cricket in New South Wales had become increasingly popular so an upgrade of Moore Park was needed. The snazzy new ground was described by Governor Sir Hercules Robinson as the 'first Sydney cricket ground', with the first match being played in 1877. It was not until 1894, however, that the ground officially received its famous name. It hosted Australia's first rugby international when the British Isles were beaten 13–3 on 24 June 1899. As Sydney's premier sporting venue, it regularly hosted rugby internationals until the 1980s, the last against Argentina on 12 July 1986. Today, the Sydney Cricket Ground is owned and operated by the SCG Trust which also manages the neighbouring Sydney Football Stadium. With the opening of the latter in 1988, the Sydney Cricket Ground became surplus to rugby union needs and is now used primarily for cricket.

Sydney Football Stadium, Sydney

Established: 1988 (broke ground in 1986)
First test: 1 July 1989 (Australia vs British Lions)
No. of tests: 27 (22 Australian, 5 neutral RWC)
Capacity: 45,500
Record attendance: 41,917 (Australia vs New Zealand, 17 August 1994)
Former name: Aussie Stadium

Australia's record at Sydney Football Stadium						
Opponent	Played	Won	Lost	Drawn	For	Against
New Zealand	6	4	2	-	122	117
France	3	2	1	-	69	52
South Africa	3	2	1	-	52	47
England	2	2	-	-	65	21
British Isles	2	1	1	-	48	31
Scotland	2	2	-	-	72	15
Ireland	1	1	-	-	32	18
Wales	1	1	-	-	42	3
Samoa	1	1	-	-	73	3
Argentina	1	1	-	-	30	13
Totals	22	17	5	-	605	320

Photo: Commons.wikimedia.org/creative commons license

Formerly known as the Aussie Stadium, after Aussie Home Loans purchased the naming rights in 2002, the ground reverted to its original name of Sydney Football Stadium in 2007. Today, the stadium hosts rugby league, rugby union, soccer and music concerts and is home to the New South Wales Waratahs rugby union team. It was built in 1988 because the oval field of the Sydney Cricket Ground was no longer deemed suitable for rectangular-field games. It received much acclaim for its wave-like structure at the 1988 opening when it was launched as the premier Australian rugby league venue but also hosted all the Sydney-based rugby union internationals for the next decade. It has witnessed many sublime moments of Australian rugby – none more magical than George Gregan's memorable tackle on Kiwi winger Jeff Wilson in the 1994 test to prevent a match-winning try to regain the Bledisloe Cup. It has proved an extremely successful venue for the Wallabies, including record victories over England in 1991, Wales in 1996 and Scotland in 1998. They have lost just five of their 22 internationals here. Appropriately, the last Wallaby international here was played against New Zealand on 29 August 1998 with Australia triumphing by 19–14. With the construction of ANZ Stadium in 1999, this larger, more modern stadium relegated the Sydney Football Stadium to a second-tier venue. Nevertheless, the Sydney Football Stadium played host to several high-profile events during the 2000 Sydney Olympics and five games in the 2003 RWC.

England

Since Twickenham was established in 1909 the majority of England's home internationals have been played at this famous venue with the exceptions to this being in 1923 when they played Ireland in Leicester; in 1992 when they played Canada at Wembley in London; in 1997 when they played New Zealand at Old Trafford in Manchester; in 1998 when they played a small RWC qualifying tournament against Italy and Netherlands at the McAlpine Stadium in Huddersfield and in 1999 when they played Wales at Wembley – a venue that acted as Wales's 'home' ground for the 1999 Five Nations and in 2009 when they played Argentina in Manchester.

Twickenham, London

Established:	October 1909
First test:	15 January 1910 (England vs Wales)
No. of tests:	254 (252 England, 2 neutral RWC)
Capacity:	82,000
Record attendance:	82,000 (often)

England's record at Twickenham						
Opponent	Played	Won	Lost	Drawn	For	Against
Wales	45	26	12	7	696	414
Scotland	44	35	4	5	760	382
Ireland	43	27	12	4	692	374
France	42	26	11	5	677	429
Australia	18	10	7	1	293	278
New Zealand	17	4	12	1	210	310
South Africa	16	8	6	-	270	246
Italy	8	8	-	-	372	87
Argentina	4	3	1	-	108	43
Romania	3	3	-	-	210	18
Canada	3	3	-	-	166	30
Fiji	2	2	-	-	103	47
USA	2	2	-	-	143	17
Samoa	2	2	-	-	67	12
Pacific Islanders	1	1	-	-	39	13
Tonga	1	1	-	-	101	10
World XV	1	1	-	-	11	28
Totals	252	162	65	23	4,918	2,738

Photo: Rugby Football Union

Photo: Andrew de Klerk

Before the Twickenham stadium was established, England played their home test matches at a variety of venues, including the Kennington Cricket Oval, or 'The Oval' in London, Whalley Range in Manchester, Rectory Field in Blackheath, Athletic Ground in Richmond and occasional games in Leeds, Bristol, Leicester and Gloucester. At the start of the twentieth century, the RFU deemed the situation unsatisfactory and followed Scotland's lead by seeking a permanent venue of their own, following sell-out games against the touring 1905 New Zealanders and 1906 South Africans at Crystal Palace in London. RFU committee member William Williams, an all-round sportsman and property entrepreneur, was charged by the RFU in 1906 to find a ground. The next year he settled on a ten-acre market garden used for growing cabbages in the suburb of Twickenham, at a cost of £5,572 12s 6d, which is the origin of the ground's nickname:

'The Cabbage Patch' or the 'Billy Williams' Cabbage Patch'. Construction began in 1907 with two covered stands erected on the east and west sides of the pitch. The first game was played on 9 October 1909 before 2,000 spectators when Harlequins beat Richmond. The first test match was played on 15 January 1910 when England beat Wales 11–6 before 20,000 spectators. Since then, the venue has proved a tough spot for opponents to win at. England lost here for the first time on 4 January 1913 against the touring South Africans; it would take Wales until 1933 to register their first win and France until 1951. In 44 internationals at Twickenham Scotland have managed just four victories. It was not until 20 March 1926 that England lost their first Five Nations game here. More recently, from 15 October 1999 to 6 September 2003, England remained unbeaten for 22 consecutive internationals. During World War I Twickenham was used for grazing livestock, with horse stables constructed around the pitch. During World War II it became a Civil Defence Depot with special responsibilities as a decontamination centre in the event of a chemical attack on London; the car park was used for storing coal. Although the stadium never received a direct hit, the house directly opposite the West Gate was flattened by a V1. Since 1945, the stadium has been rebuilt and refurbished several times, with the latest 2005 additions upping the capacity to 82,000. The venue is used almost exclusively for rugby union fixtures, with the national team playing all their internationals exclusively at Twickenham. Known as 'The Vacuum' because of its lack of atmosphere, the stadium vibe finally changed in 1988 after England turned a 0–3 half-time deficit against Ireland into a 35–3 win. It was during this match that 'Swing Low, Sweet Chariot' was first sung, bringing some much-needed atmosphere to the ground. Today the song is synonymous with Twickenham and an integral part of a full experience in the stands. In 1991, the stadium hosted both opening games of the 1991 RWC as well as the final; in 1999 it hosted both semi-finals. Twickenham is home to the world-famous Museum of Rugby which covers the global game and not just English rugby. The museum has a series of special exhibitions with some unique artefacts, including an English jersey worn in the first test of 1871. Over the years, Twickenham has established an aura of its own; it is variously referred to as the home of English rugby, the RFU's headquarters and even the home of rugby: inaccurately considering the location of the IRB's offices in Dublin and the age of older stadiums such as Lansdowne Road and Newlands.

France

France have played their international rugby fixtures at a variety of venues across the country, the majority in Paris. Aside from the main Paris-based venues, they have frequently played at other French grounds, more often than not against weaker sides such as Romania and Italy. Other venues include the larger city of Bordeaux through to the smaller towns of Strasbourg, le Havre and Tarbes.

Parc des Princes, Paris

Established:	18 July 1897
First test:	1 January 1906 (France vs New Zealand)
No. of tests:	89 (85 France, 4 neutral RWC)
Capacity:	48,257
Record attendance:	48,713

France's record at Parc des Princes						
Opponent	Played	Won	Lost	Drawn	For	Against
England	16	6	9	1	234	278
Ireland	15	12	3	-	335	148
Wales	15	12	3	-	266	168
Scotland	15	12	3	-	260	175
New Zealand	6	1	5	-	54	144
South Africa	4	1	3	-	59	91
British Isles XV	1	-	1	-	27	29
Australia	3	2	1	-	52	36
Great Britain XV	1	-	1	-	3	36
British Army	1	1	-	-	21	9
British Empire	1	1	-	-	10	0
Germany	3	3	-	-	83	26
Argentina	3	2	1	-	59	61
Italy	1	1	-	-	43	5
Totals	85	54	30	1	1,506	1,206

Photo: Frédéric Hubert/www.flickr.com/ photos/rugby_pioneers/ creative commons license

Photo: El Mostrito/commons.wikimedia.org/ creative commons license

The Parc des Princes (the princes' park) was originally used for royal recreational activities: 18th century hunting grounds until Emperor Napoleon III decided to place this enormous area under the city's authority. The stadium was originally built as a velodrome, hosting the finish of the Tour de France since its inception in 1903 until the cyle track was demolished. The stadium was first built in 1897 but so hurriedly and so poorly that spectators were denied access at the officially opening on 18 July 1897 for fears that the stands might collapse. During its early years it was solely used as a cycling track but was later redesigned to accommodate a modern sports field in the middle, capable of hosting all track and field events and ball sports, which meant it could host the 1924 Olympic Games with an increased capacity of 40,000. Shortly thereafter, it was demolished and rebuilt with a moderner track. In 1967 the track and stadium were once again demolished to make way for a purpose-built soccer and rugby stadium which opened in June 1972 and remained France's national stadium until the Stade de France was built for the 1998 FIFA World Cup. The first rugby international was played on 1 January 1906 against the touring All Blacks before a crowd of 3,000. During the early years of French rugby until the end of World War I, home internationals were played intermittently at the Parc des Princes without a single victory. It was not until the end of France's IRFB ban that France again played here. Sundry games were played against the British Army in World War II, but it was not until the French national team officially relocated from the Stade Colombes in 1973 to the newly refurbished Parc des Princes that international rugby was again played here when France beat Scotland 16–13 on 13 January 1973. For 24 years, France played all their Five Nations games at the stadium but since 1998 have played all their Paris-based games at the new Stade de France. During the 2007 RWC, the Parc des Princes once again hosted international rugby with five matches at the stadium, including the 3rd and 4th play-off between France and Argentina. This was France's first test at the Parc des Princes in more than a decade and which ended in a crushing defeat by Argentina, reminiscent of France's previous match at Parc des Princes on 22 November 1997 when they bade a forgettable farewell to the beloved stadium as South Africa demolished them 10–52. The South Africans were cheered off the field while the French were booed into their dressing room. The future of Parc des Princes is unclear but unconfirmed plans to upgrade the current stadium to a capacity of 114,000 are being mooted.

Stade de France, Paris

Established: January 1998
First test: 7 February 1998 (France vs England)
No. of tests: 49 (44 France, 5 neutral RWC)
Capacity: 80,000
Record attendance: 82,500 (2007 RWC)

France's record at Stade de France						
Opponent	Played	Won	Lost	Drawn	For	Against
England	7	4	3	-	130	112
Ireland	7	6	1	-	216	120
Wales	6	3	3	-	172	143
Scotland	6	5	1	-	160	86
Italy	5	5	-	-	162	68
Australia	4	1	3	-	74	82
New Zealand	4	-	3	1	63	127
South Africa	2	2	-	-	46	30
Argentina	2	1	1	-	39	43
Canada	1	1	-	-	35	3
Totals	44	28	15	1	1,097	814

Photo: Scott Allen

Situated in Saint Denis on the outskirts of Paris, the Stade de France is the current French national stadium, replacing the Parc des Princes. It hosts rugby union, soccer, track and field events and music concerts and has no permanent tenant. The word 'France' in the stadium's name does not refer to the country, but rather to the historical province of Île de France, or *Pays de France*, a fertile plain north of Paris with the town of Saint Denis as its administrative centre. Today, Saint Denis is part of the Paris metropolis. The Stade de France was built for the 1998 FIFA World Cup and hosted the final, as well as the 2007 RWC final: the first stadium in the world to host two such finals. For the 2007 RWC it hosted seven matches, including the opening game, a quarter-final, both semi-finals and the final. It also hosted the dramatic 1999 RWC quarter-final between South Africa and England. The first rugby international was held at the stadium on 7 February 1998 when France beat England 24–17 during the Five Nations. The Stade de France has since hosted 49 internationals, 45 of them involving France. The French have had mixed success here; they began by winning the 1998 Grand Slam but suffered five successive defeats from 1998 through to 2000. They have reached incredible highs at the Stade de France where they rounded off their 2002 and 2004 Grand Slams but have also plumbed the depths, with record defeats to New Zealand in 2004 and 2006, and to England who stunned them with a semi-final defeat in the 2007 RWC.

Stade Municipal, Toulouse

Established: c.1937

First test: 16 December 1956 (France vs Czechoslovakia)

No. of tests: 17 (13 France, 4 neutral RWC)

Capacity: 37,000

Record attendance: 37,000 (often)

France's record at Stade Municipal						
Opponent	Played	Won	Lost	Drawn	For	Against
New Zealand	4	2	2	-	56	60
Romania	2	1	-	1	32	21
South Africa	1	-	1	-	4	13
Australia	1	-	1	-	11	13
Argentina	1	1	-	-	25	12
Fiji	1	1	-	-	28	19
Namibia	1	1	-	-	87	10
Czechoslovakia	1	1	-	-	28	3
Tonga	1	1	-	-	43	8
Totals	13	8	4	1	314	159

Photo: AlphaTangoBravo/Adam Baker/commons.wikimedia.org/ creative commons license

Stade Municipal, sometimes referred to as Stade Toulouse, is a multi-purpose sports stadium in one of the most famous rugby towns of Europe. It first hosted an international in 1956 when France took on Czechoslovakia and has since staged a total of 17 rugby test, 13 of which have involved the French. The stadium was upgraded for the 1998 FIFA World Cup and was an automatic venue choice for four 2007 RWC pool matches. The venue has returned mixed success for the French: they recorded famous victories over New Zealand in 1977 and 1995 and have won eight of their 13 internationals here.

Photo: Jonathan Smith/commons.wikimedia.org/creative commons license

Stade Olympique Yves-du-Manoir, Paris

Established:	c.1907
First test:	1 January 1908 (France vs England)
No. of tests:	99
Capacity:	30,000
Record attendance:	70,000

France's record at Stade Olympique Yves-du-Manoir						
Opponent	Played	Won	Lost	Drawn	For	Against
England	21	12	8	1	213	161
Wales	21	9	11	1	163	201
Scotland	19	11	7	1	164	142
Ireland	18	11	6	1	195	120
Australia	5	4	1	-	78	40
New Zealand	4	1	3	-	30	47
South Africa	3	-	2	1	14	41
Germany	3	3	-	-	88	5
USA	2	1	1	-	17	22
Romania	1	1	-	-	59	3
NZ Maoris	1	-	1	-	3	12
Fiji	1	1	-	-	24	3
Totals	99	54	40	5	1,048	797

Photo: Frédéric Hubert/www.flickr.com/photos/rugby_pioneers/creative commons license

The Stade Olympique Yves-du-Manoir, commonly known as Stade Colombes because of its location in the Colombes area of northwest Paris, was the main stadium for the 1924 Paris Olympic Games, with an original capacity of 45,000. This made it the largest stadium in the country and the obvious choice to host many of France's early rugby internationals. The capacity was later expanded to 60,000 to host the 1938 soccer World Cup final, but its capacity has since decreased due to more stringent safety regulations now law. The Stade Olympique Yves-du-Manor was the national rugby stadium for many years, hosting crowds of up to 70,000; from 1914 to 1972 it was the home of French rugby, hosting its first test on 1 January 1908 when France played England and was France's largest stadium until the Parc des Princes was renovated in 1972. Plans are now afoot to have it rejigged into a smaller 15,000 all-seater stadium; a far cry from its former glory. It yielded mixed success for the French who struggled in the early years, but from the 1950s they turned the stadium into a formidably difficult venue for opposition teams, beating allcomers except the Springboks and the New Zealand Maoris. It was France's home venue for their first outright Five Nations championship title in 1959 and their 1968 Grand Slam. It is currently home to Racing Metro 92 Rugby Club.

Stade Vélodrome, Marseille

Established:	3 June 1937
First test:	18 November 2000 (France vs New Zealand)
No. of tests:	14 (9 French, 5 neutral RWC)
Capacity:	60,000
Record attendance:	60,000

France's record at Stade Velodrome						
Opponent	Played	Won	Lost	Drawn	For	Against
New Zealand	1	1	-	-	42	33
Australia	2	2	-	-	40	29
South Africa	1	1	-	-	30	10
England	2	2	-	-	39	25
Argentina	2	1	1	-	26	30
Georgia	1	1	-	-	64	7
Totals	9	8	1	-	241	134

Photo: Scott Allen

One of the newest rugby stadiums in the country, the Stade Vélodrome was to the fore during the 1938 and 1998 Football World Cups. It was opened in June 1937 and has since been used primarily for soccer matches. It was not until 18 November 2000 that France played their first rugby international here when they outstripped the All Blacks in a thrilling 42–33 victory. With this the French now play here on an annual basis and are tough to beat in Marseille, having beaten all the top rugby-playing nations and losing just one of their nine tests: a surprising loss to Argentina in 2004. In 2007 the venue hosted six RWC games, including the two spectacular quarter-finals where England narrowly edged out Australia and Fiji and came close to upsetting soon-to-be champions South Africa. Plans are afoot to upgrade the stadium to accommodate 80,000 spectators.

Photo: Dkhgdnh/commons.wikimedia.org/creative commons license

Ireland

Most of Ireland's international home games – 244 of 298 – have been played at Lansdowne Road in Dublin. However, until 1954, matches were regularly held at Belfast's Ravenhill Stadium, where most recently a lone international was played against Italy in 2007. Other venues include Leinster which has hosted just one test (uniquely, Ireland's first home game in 1875), Cork which has hosted three, Limerick four and, as a temporary solution while Lansdowne Road is being rebuilt, Croke Park in Dublin with nine.

Croke Park, Dublin

Established:	c.1884
First test:	11 February 2007 (Ireland vs France)
No. of tests:	9
Capacity:	82,500
Record attendance:	90,556 (All-Ireland Senior Football Final, 1961)
Former names:	City and Suburban Racecourse, Jones Road Sports Ground

Irelands's record at Croke Park						
Opponent	Played	Won	Lost	Drawn	For	Against
France	2	1	1	1	47	41
England	2	2	-	-	57	26
Italy	1	1	-	-	16	11
Scotland	1	1	-	-	34	13
Wales	1	-	1	-	12	16
New Zealand	1	-	1	-	3	22
Argentina	1	1	-	-	17	3
Totals	9	6	3	1	186	132

Photo: Commons.wikimedia.org/creative commons license

Croke Park is the home of the Gaelic games, the headquarters of the Gaelic Athletic Association (GAA) and has been at the heart of Irish sporting life for over a century. In 2007, history was made when the first rugby and soccer internationals were played here with Lansdowne Road closed for rebuilding. It is the largest sports facility in Ireland and the sixth-largest in Europe. On 21 November 1920, Croke Park was the scene of a dreadful massacre perpetrated by the British Army's Auxiliary Division, a day of infamy which came to be known as Bloody Sunday. In retaliation for the assassination of 14 British intelligence officers earlier that day by the Irish Republican Army, the Auxiliaries stormed into the ground during a Dublin–Tipperary Gaelic football match, randomly shooting into the crowd and killing 31 people, including a player. Debate still rages regarding the use of Croke Park for sports other than those of Irish heritage. The GAA was founded as a nationalist organisation to maintain and promote indigenous sport, culture and language. It emphasises Ireland's independence of Britain, disapproving of most things British and honourbound throughout its history to oppose 'foreign' sports. It was not until January 2006 that this moratorium was lifted and the first rugby international held at Croke Park on 11 February 2007 when Ireland were defeated by France. The second rugby game was between Ireland and England on 24 February 2007 and for or obvious reasons, it was a highly symbolic occasion; it was joked that the English wouldn't have the advantage of rifles and armoured cars when taking to the field. But there were real concerns as to how the crowd would react to the English national anthem and the Union Jack fluttering above. With emotions running wild, it was a highly charged atmosphere that proved too much for England: the Irish were ruthless, posting a record 43–13 victory over the old invaders. To date, Ireland have played nine times at the stadium, recording mixed success.

Lansdowne Road, Dublin

Established:	c.1872
First test:	11 March 1878 (Ireland vs England)
No. of tests:	247 (244 Ireland, 3 neutral RWC)
Capacity:	49,500
Record attendance:	49,500 (often)

Ireland's record at Lansdowne Road						
Opponent	Played	Won	Lost	Drawn	For	Against
England	57	25	28	4	459	551
Scotland	46	26	17	3	541	467
Wales	37	17	17	3	508	424
France	34	13	17	4	392	454
Australia	15	5	10	-	174	237
New Zealand	12	-	11	1	96	264
South Africa	10	3	6	1	108	167
Italy	7	6	1	-	236	131
Romania	5	5	-	-	225	64
Argentina	4	4	-	-	89	68
Samoa	3	2	1	-	109	70
USA	3	3	-	-	134	29
Japan	2	2	-	-	110	25
Fiji	2	2	-	-	108	25
Georgia	2	2	-	-	133	14
Canada	1	1	-	-	33	11
Pacific Islanders	1	1	-	-	61	17
World XV	1	-	-	1	18	18
Zimbabwe	1	1	-	-	55	11
NZ Maoris	1	-	1	-	4	13
Totals	244	118	109	17	3,593	3,060

Photo: Newlands Rugby Museum

Photo: Adrian van de Vyver

Lansdowne Road is the oldest international rugby stadium in the world and has a long and proud sporting history synonymous with the Irish rugby team. The creation of a multi-purpose stadium in Dublin was the vision of Henry Dunlop who found his efforts frustrated by the Dublin City Council until 1872 when he was allowed to take a 69-year, £60-a-year lease from the Pembroke Estate. In 1872 the stadium was opened for athletics and named The Royal Irish Parks Stadium. This name was dropped in the early twentieth century in favour of Lansdowne Road, from the address. (The street is named after the Marquess of Lansdowne from the English county of Somerset.) This original stadium was a multi-sports venue accommodating athletics, cricket, croquet, association football, archery and tennis. The first representative rugby match played at Lansdowne Road was a 20-a-side game between Leinster and Munster in December 1876. Six years after construction, Lansdowne Road hosted its first rugby test when Ireland met England on 11 March 1878. For the use of his stadium Dunlop charged the Irish RFU £5 and half of any profits over £50 after expenses. Ireland's first victory at Lansdowne Road was on 5 February 1887 against England by 6 $^{(2G)}$–0. Harry Sheppard, treasurer of the IRFU, then acquired the lease from Dunlop, and only upon Sheppard's death in 1906 did the IRFU secure the lease of Lansdowne Road from the Pembroke Estate for £200. The first covered stand was built in 1908 while an uncovered stand was erected over the Lansdowne Road club pavilion in the northwest corner. The IRFU purchased the freehold of the land in 1974 and today the plot is worth approximately £600 million. Over time, Lansdowne Road ceased to be a multi-purpose sports ground, being used almost exclusively for Irish rugby. Prior to 1954, Irish games were shared between Lansdowne Road and Ravenhill in Belfast, an arrangement that was cancelled that year when Lansdowne Road was expanded by 8,000 seats, making it subeconomic to hold games at the smaller Ravenhill. Ireland were not to play another test match at Ravenhill until 2007. Since 1955, Ireland have played all their home games at Lansdowne Road, with the exception of three in 2002, 2003 and 2008 at Thomond Park in Limerick, a single match at Ravenhill in 2007, and with current fixtures being held at Croke Park, while Lansdowne Road is being upgraded.

Being the oldest rugby ground in the world, the stadium has seen numerous developments and alterations over its 130-year history, the most recent when Ireland's planning appeals board, *An Bord Pleanala*, gave the go-ahead for its redevelopment in March 2007 into a state-of-the-art €365 million 50,000-seater stadium, the culmination of much hard work by the Lansdowne Road Development Company. It had been acknowledged for some time that the stadium was no longer suitable for international sport and simply wasn't up to scratch. A number of traditionalists wishing to preserve the stadium's heritage protested the development but to no avail. The new stadium is due for completion in 2009. The last international here was on 26 November 2006 when Ireland met the Pacific Islanders for the first time, winning 61–17.

Ravenhill Stadium, Belfast

Established:	c.1921
First test:	9 February 1924 (Ireland vs England)
No. of tests:	18 (16 Ireland, 2 neutral RWC)
Capacity:	12,300 (up to 19,000 with extra seating)
Record attendance:	23,000

Ireland's record at Ravenhill						
Opponent	Played	Won	Lost	Drawn	For	Against
Wales	9	5	3	1	60	50
France	4	3	1	-	39	16
Scotland	1	1	-	-	6	0
England	1	-	1	-	3	14
Italy	1	1	-	-	23	20
Totals	16	10	5	1	131	100

Photo: Commons.wikimedia.org/ creative commons license

Irish internationals have been played in Belfast, close to the site of the current Ravenhill Stadium, since 1877 when matches were played in the Ormeau and Ballynafeigh districts until 1894. Subsequently, Belfast internationals were played at the Balmoral Showgrounds until 1921 when the Ravenhill Stadium was officially opened for the 1923/1924 season. The first test played at the Ravenhill Stadium was on 9 February 1924 when Ireland were beaten 5–14 by the English. Agreement was then reached with Lansdowne Road whereby Ravenhill would host an Irish Five Nations game every year. This deal stayed in place until 1954 when Lansdowne Road was upgraded, making it unfeasible to host internationals at the smaller Ravenhill Stadium which hosted its last game for the next 53 years when Ireland beat Scotland 6–0 on 27 February 1954. Ravenhill has, however, hosted two RWC pool encounters: one each in 1991 and 1999. With Lansdowne Road again being upgraded in 2007, Ravenhill was chosen by the IRFU to host its first test since 1954, against Italy on 24 August 2007 in an RWC warm-up game, narrowly won 23–20 by Ireland thanks to a late Ronan O'Gara drop goal. The future of internationals at Ravenhill, the home of Ulster rugby, is still uncertain, considering the glittering future of a new Lansdowne Road.

Italy

Since their first home game in Milan, Italy have played their home internationals in no fewer than 31 different centres, from the small town of San Doná di Piave to the bustling capital Rome. They have recently settled with the Stadio Flaminio in Rome as their primary base. The national side's most regular alternative venues have included:

- Arena Civica, Milan (capacity 20,000, no longer used)
- Stadio Tommaso Fattori, L'Aquila (capacity 10,000)
- Stadio Mario Battaglini, Rovigo (capacity 7,000)
- Stadio Plebiscito, Padova (capacity 10,000)
- Stadio Comunale di Monigo, Treviso (capacity 9,000)
- Stadio Comunale Luigi Ferraris, Genoa (capacity 35,000)

Stadio Flaminio, Rome

Established:	c.1927 (rebuilt 12 July 1957, officially opened March 1959)
First test:	22 April 1935 (Italy vs France XV)
No. of tests:	37
Capacity:	30,000 (up to 42,000 with extra seating)
Record attendance:	30,000

<table>
<tr><th colspan="7">Italy's record at Stadio Flaminio</th></tr>
<tr><th>Opponent</th><th>Played</th><th>Won</th><th>Lost</th><th>Drawn</th><th>For</th><th>Against</th></tr>
<tr><td>Scotland</td><td>5</td><td>3</td><td>2</td><td>0</td><td>99</td><td>96</td></tr>
<tr><td>Wales</td><td>5</td><td>2</td><td>3</td><td>0</td><td>99</td><td>133</td></tr>
<tr><td>Ireland</td><td>5</td><td>0</td><td>5</td><td>0</td><td>84</td><td>198</td></tr>
<tr><td>England</td><td>4</td><td>0</td><td>4</td><td>0</td><td>53</td><td>149</td></tr>
<tr><td>France</td><td>5</td><td>0</td><td>5</td><td>0</td><td>70</td><td>228</td></tr>
<tr><td>France XV</td><td>3</td><td>0</td><td>3</td><td>0</td><td>24</td><td>75</td></tr>
<tr><td>Australia</td><td>2</td><td>0</td><td>2</td><td>0</td><td>24</td><td>80</td></tr>
<tr><td>Spain</td><td>2</td><td>2</td><td>0</td><td>0</td><td>29</td><td>6</td></tr>
<tr><td>Argentina</td><td>2</td><td>0</td><td>2</td><td>0</td><td>22</td><td>59</td></tr>
<tr><td>New Zealand</td><td>1</td><td>0</td><td>1</td><td>0</td><td>10</td><td>59</td></tr>
<tr><td>Czechoslovakia</td><td>1</td><td>1</td><td>0</td><td>0</td><td>17</td><td>6</td></tr>
<tr><td>Romania</td><td>1</td><td>1</td><td>0</td><td>0</td><td>22</td><td>3</td></tr>
<tr><td>Russia</td><td>1</td><td>0</td><td>1</td><td>0</td><td>9</td><td>11</td></tr>
<tr><td>Totals</td><td>37</td><td>9</td><td>28</td><td>0</td><td>562</td><td>1,103</td></tr>
</table>

Photo: Federazione Italiana Rugby

The Stadio Flaminio, opened by the National Fascist Party, was built in 1927 on the site of an older 1911 stadium that needed upgrading. To date, the biggest sporting event to be held here was the 1934 FIFA World Cup final. The stadium as we know it today was rebuilt in 1957 for the 1960 Rome Olympics. It is located along the Via Flaminia: an ancient Roman road that led to the north of Italy. Usually devoted to football matches, Stadio Flaminio is today the premier Italian rugby stadium, with all Six Nations home games being held here. Yet it remains modest in size compared with other Six Nations venues, with a capacity of only 30,000 which, with temporary mobile stands, can be increased to 42,000. The venue was, however, chosen strategically in preference to Rome's enormous Olympic Stadium which seldom gets sold out even for the highest-profile soccer matches, let alone for a rugby match. The Stadio Flaminio therefore offers sell-out home games in a unique atmosphere within Rome's historic Olympic village, a much sought-after destination for visiting fans. However, with the increase in popularity of rugby in Italy, it is a concern that the stadium is inadequate. Rumours point to the Stadio Luigi Ferraris in Genoa, the heart of Italian rugby, as the new home of rugby; the downside would be the loss of Rome as a tourist trap. Italy have had limited success at the stadium but look set to build on their nine victories as they improve exponentially.

New Zealand

AMI Stadium, Christchurch

Established:	c.1880, officially opened 15 October 1881
First test:	20 September 1913 (New Zealand vs Australia)
No. of tests:	49 (47 New Zealand, 2 neutral RWC)
Capacity:	36,500
Record attendance:	38,500
Former names:	Lancaster Park, Jade Stadium

NZ's record at AMI Stadium						
Opponent	Played	Won	Lost	Drawn	For	Against
Australia	12	8	4	-	228	142
British Lions	9	8	1	-	150	82
France	8	7	1	-	159	101
South Africa	8	6	2	-	149	101
England	3	3	-	-	71	31
Wales	2	2	-	-	71	3
Scotland	1	1	-	-	30	3
Argentina	1	1	-	-	67	19
Fiji	1	1	-	-	74	13
Italy	1	1	-	-	27	6
World XV	1	-	1	-	14	28
Totals	47	38	9	-	1,040	529

Photo: New Zealand Rugby Museum

The AMI Stadium, named after the insurance company but previously known as Lancaster Park until 1998 and Jade Stadium (after Jade Software Corporation) until 2007, is home to the Canterbury Crusaders rugby team. The stadium was founded in 1880 after the Hagley Oval in Canterbury could no longer cope with hosting all the town's sporting events. Consequently, the Canterbury Cricket and Athletics Sports Company purchased 10 acres, 3 rods and 30 perches from Lancaster Estate for £2,841. Simply referred to as 'the new ground down Ferry Road', the area became known as Lancaster Park a year later, after the previous owner Benjamin Lancaster of Bournemouth, England. By the end of 1881, the ground was ready for business and was officially opened on 15 October 1881 when the Canterbury Athletics Association held a sporting meet. The first significant rugby game played at the stadium was in 1882 between the touring Southern Rugby Union of New South Wales and Canterbury, although a poorly organised England–Colonies match was played earlier that year. Such was the demand for sporting turf in Christchurch that rugby and cricket games often overlapped and clashed on the same field so in 1883 agreement was reached whereby a cricket match would stop for two hours to allow a rugby game to be played. During World War I the main field was ploughed up for the cultivatation of potatoes; during World War II the ground was used as a military base accommodating 800 troops. Since then the stadium has been developed considerably. By 1957, it had been extended to a capacity of 33,000; in 1996 floodlights were installed with a further capacity upgrade to 43,000 on the cards for the 2011 RWC, which will make it the second-largest stadium in the country. On 20 September 1913, the first rugby international was played when Australia surprisingly and convincingly beat New Zealand 16–5. The venue has proved extremely successful for New Zealand who have lost here just nine times in 47 internationals. New Zealand have not lost at the AMI Stadium since 1998.

Athletic Park, Wellington

Established:	6 April 1896
Date of closure:	10 October 1999
First test:	13 August 1904 (New Zealand vs British Isles)
No. of tests:	45 (42 New Zealand, 3 neutral RWC)
Capacity:	39,000
Record attendance:	39,000

New Zealand's record at Athletic Park						
Opponent	Played	Won	Lost	Drawn	For	Against
Australia	15	9	5	1	268	156
British Lions	10	7	2	1	102	82
South Africa	7	3	3	1	50	64
France	3	3	-	-	68	13
Argentina	3	3	-	-	188	35
Ireland	2	2	-	-	70	9
England	1	1	-	-	42	15
World XV	1	1	-	-	54	26
Totals	42	29	10	3	842	400

Photos: New Zealand Rugby Museum

Rugby in Wellington first made an appearance in the 1870s and quickly became popular with the locals. In the early years of the Wellington Union's growth, development was hampered by the fact that Wellington lacked a dedicated rugby ground. In those days rugby tended to be confined to the boggy terrain of Newtown Park, with cricket claiming the better site of Basin Reserve. In 1894 a site was selected in the suburb of Newtown and on 6 April 1896, the site now sufficiently developed to host sport, was officially opened as Athletic Park. Since then Athletic Park was Wellington's foremost rugby stadium until 1999 when the decision was made to demolish the old stadium upon completion of the new Westpac Trust Stadium. The ground was renowned for its Victorian architecture which was never upgraded; the steep Millard Stand tended to sway in the gale-force winds so common in a wintry Wellington. Before Athletic Park was finally demolished, more than a decade of investigations and planning went into maintaining and upgrading 'the home of New Zealand rugby', which had become astronomically expensive to maintain. In 1994, just five days before the international against the Springboks, a large slab of concrete fell from the Millard Stand and destroyed the seats below. It was declared a one-off accident and the test went ahead as planned but the incident called for decisive action on the future of the stadium. Engineers reported that the Millard Stand was deteriorating so fast that it would need a minimum of $NZ2 million in repairs within ten years or it would totally collapse. In 1995 Wellington City Council therefore approved a $NZ15 million loan to begin construction of the Westpac Trust Stadium. Athletic Park was demolished a few years later and a retirement village now exists over the hallowed turf where the All Blacks once racked up victory after victory. Athletic Park hosted its first test on 13 August 1904 when New Zealand defeated the British Isles, while the last test also finished on a winning note when on 26 June 1999 the All Blacks obliterated France by 54–7. The ground hosted four RWC internationals during the 1987 tournament, but perhaps the greatest international ever played at the old ground was the first-ever Tri-Nations clash: New Zealand vs Australia on 6 July 1996 in torrential rain and howling winds, when New Zealand put on the greatest display of controlled rugby ever seen in wet weather to run out 43–6 victors, by six tries to zero.

Carisbrook, Dunedin

Established:	c.1883
First test:	6 August 1908 (New Zealand vs British Isles)
No. of tests:	39 (36 New Zealand, 3 neutral RWC)
Capacity:	35,000
Record attendance:	42,000

New Zealand's record at Carisbrook						
Opponent	Played	Won	Lost	Drawn	For	Against
Australia	10	9	1	-	208	112
British Lions	8	5	2	1	119	64
South Africa	8	7	1	-	164	93
Scotland	4	4	-	-	173	71
Ireland	2	2	-	-	64	29
England	2	2	-	-	100	25
Argentina	1	1	-	-	60	9
France	1	-	1	-	22	27
Totals	36	30	5	1	910	430

Photo: New Zealand Rugby Museum

Carisbrook, home to the Otago Rugby Football Union, is known as 'The House of Pain' to visiting sides because it is virtually impossibile for them to win here, mainly due to geography. At a latitude of 45°53', Carisbrook is the most southerly international rugby stadium in the world, which greatly assists the home team in beating touring sides unaccustomed to extreme winter weather and lengthy travel itineraries. The stadium is named after Carisbrook Estate which was owned by an early settler James MacAndrew; the estate in turn being named after Carisbrook Castle on the Isle of Wight. The site was first developed for sport in the 1870s and hosted its first test on 6 August 1908 when New Zealand comprehensively beat the British Isles by 32–5. The ground hosted three games during the 1987 RWC and is the scene of many famous New Zealand victories, most notably a 28–0 whitewash over world champions South Africa. The state of the ground has been deteriorating and is due for an urgent upgrade to ensure its survival in the modern era; there are unconfirmed plans to demolish the old Carisbrook and build an entirely new modern indoor stadium in time for the 2011 RWC. With this in the offing, the NZRFU announced that a one-off 2008 Tri-Nations game would be played here between New Zealand and South Africa. In seven attempts dating back to 1921 the Springboks had yet to win at Carisbrook but in one of the most remarkable matches ever witnessed, South Africa came from behind in the dying minutes to win by 30–28 and record their first victory in Dunedin. Carisbrook is by far and away New Zealand's most successful stadium: the All Blacks have lost just five of 36 outings, most recently against France in 2009.

Eden Park, Auckland

Established:	c.1903 by the Eden Cricket Club
First test:	27 August 1921 (New Zealand vs South Africa)
No. of tests:	66 (63 New Zealand, 3 neutral RWC)
Capacity:	48,000
Record attendance:	65,000 (1956 New Zealand vs South Africa)

New Zealand's record at Eden Park						
Opponent	Played	Won	Lost	Drawn	For	Against
Australia	20	16	4	-	441	290
South Africa	8	5	2	1	166	124
British Lions	9	7	1	1	186	99
France	8	6	2	-	207	123
England	5	4	1	-	144	69
Scotland	5	5	-	-	169	59
Wales	2	2	-	-	87	21
Italy	1	1	-	-	70	6
Ireland	2	2	-	-	67	25
Samoa	1	1	-	-	35	13
Canada	1	1	-	-	73	7
World XV	1	1	-	-	26	15
Totals	63	51	10	2	1,671	851

Photo: New Zealand Rugby Museum

Currently New Zealand's largest stadium, Eden Park was founded in 1903 when the Eden Cricket Club bought 15 acres of swamp. In 1909 the ground was sold to the Auckland Cricket Association and by 1914 had been drained and converted into two oval fields with two grandstands on the main oval. Since then the stadium has been steadily developed over the years. The government has committed $NZ320 million to the refurbishment of the stadium in time for the 2011 RWC when it will accommodate 60,000 people. It has been home to Auckland Cricket since 1910, with the Auckland Rugby Union first leasing the ground in 1914 and officially making it their home in 1925. It still hosts cricket and rugby with the cricket block, or square, now being removable. The first rugby international played at the ground was on 27 August 1921 against the first touring Springboks. To date, Eden Park has hosted more New Zealand test matches than any other ground. Eden Park has witnessed some of the finest moments in rugby history, not least those involving matches against the Springboks. In 1921 the All Blacks lost 5–9 to South Africa and in 1937 the Springboks became the 'greatest team to ever leave New Zealand's shores' after they crushed New Zealand 17–6 at Eden Park. Nineteen years later the All Blacks had their revenge, defeating the Boks on 1 September 1956 by 11–5, thereby inflicting on the South Africans their first series defeat in more than half a century, with this match holding the record crowd attendance at the stadium to this day. On 18 September 1965, New Zealand comprehensively outplayed the Springboks, winning 20–3 and wrapping up the series. The most infamous of tests is remembered for all the wrong reasons. During South Africa's 1981 tour, the match played at Eden Park was marred by anti-apartheid demonstrations which culminated in a Cessna light aircraft dropping multitudes of anti-apartheid pamphlets and 50kg bags of flour onto the pitch: it hence became known as the 'flour bomb test'. The tour split the country but was capped off in a dramatic climax with Bok winger Ray Mordt scoring a hat-trick to level the scores at 22 apiece, only for Alan Hewson to win the game for New Zealand. In 1997, New Zealand achieved a record score against South Africa, winning 55–35 in a dozen-try match. Aside from clashes with the Springboks, the stadium has also witnessed the only British Lions' triumph in New Zealand when J. P. R. Williams dropped a cheeky goal from the halfway to secure a 14–14 draw and a 2–1 series victory for the Lions. Additionally, the only player in history to score four tries against

New Zealand did so at Eden Park: Wallaby flanker Greg Cornelsen in Australia's 1978 victory. British Lions fans wept when All Blacks eighthman Laurie Knight scored the 1977 series-winning try in the dying seconds of the final test, won 10–9 by New Zealand. In 1994 the Eden Park crowd witnessed quite possibly the greatest try in the history of the game, by Frenchman, Jean-Luc Sadourney and which came to be known as 'the try from the end of the Earth' that saw no fewer than nine different French players handle the ball to score a 90-metre try at the end of the match to secure a French series win. Eden Park also hosted five RWC internationals in 1987, including the final when New Zealand won. Eden Park will be the first stadium in the world to host two RWC finals, with the announcement that it will host the 2011 finale.

Westpac Stadium, Wellington

Established:	3 January 2000
First test:	5 August 2000 (New Zealand vs Australia)
No. of tests:	13 (12 New Zealand, 1 neutral)
Capacity:	36,000 (up to 40,000 with extra seating)
Record attendance:	37,693 (20 July 2002, New Zealand vs South Africa)
Former name:	Westpac Trust Stadium

New Zealand's record at Westpac Stadium						
Opponent	Played	Won	Lost	Drawn	For	Against
Australia	2	1	1	-	39	31
South Africa	3	3	-	-	95	45
England	1	-	1	-	13	15
France	3	3	-	-	112	32
Ireland	1	1	-	-	21	11
British Isles	1	1	-	-	48	18
Fiji	1	1	-	-	68	18
Totals	12	10	2	-	382	160

Nicknamed 'The Cake Tin' or 'Ring of Fire' owing to its shape, the stadium was built on reclaimed railway land to replace the derelict Athletic Park as the premier stadium in Wellington. A far cry from the old Athletic Park, it is today New Zealand's newest sporting arena and a multi-purpose modern facility, used mainly for rugby union and cricket fixtures. It is home to the Hurricanes Super 14 team. It hosted its first test on 5 August 2000 when John Eales inflicted a last-second defeat on New Zealand with a pinpoint penalty kick. The venue has proved a strong ground for New Zealand, who have lost just two of their 12 internationals played here.

Scotland

Inverleith

Established:	purchased c.1897, building completed 1899
First test:	18 February 1899 (Scotland vs Ireland)
No. of tests:	39

Scotland's record at Inverleith						
Opponent	Played	Won	Lost	Drawn	For	Against
Ireland	11	8	3	-	121	72
Wales	11	6	4	1	120	96
England	10	3	6	1	62	87
France	5	4	1	-	99	13
New Zealand	1	-	1	-	7	12
South Africa	1	-	1	-	0	16
Totals	39	21	16	2	409	296

Photo: Frédéric Humbert/www.flickr.com/photos/rugby_pioneers/ creative commons license

With the option of renting Raeburn Place from Edinburgh Academy scrapped in 1895, the SFU purchased a ground at Inverleith in Edinburgh for £3,800 in 1897. With this acquisition, Scotland became the first country to own its own rugby ground (complete with a stand) to be used exclusively by the SFU. Immediate construction and upgrading of the stadium commenced, with matches being played at Powderhall Stadium in Edinburgh for the next two years. It was planned to open the new stadium for the international against Wales in 1899, however inclement weather forced the game to be abandoned, so the first test was against Ireland a month later, on 18 February. Inverleith hosted all Scottish internationals bar one until World War I, whereupon the ground fell into a state of disrepair from wartime neglect. After the war, it became clear that owing to the poor state of the ground and the increased popularity of rugby the stadium could no longer cope with the increased demand for seats. It became necessary to consider purchasing a larger piece of land on which to build a larger stadium. In 1922 the SFU successfully completed negotiations with the Edinburgh Polo Club to purchase 19 acres of land at Murrayfield and so Inverleith hosted its final Scottish international, against France, and fittingly on Burns Day, 25 January 1925.

Murrayfield, Edinburgh

Established:	c.1922
First test:	21 March 1925 (Scotland vs England)
No. of tests:	232 (231 Scotland, 1 neutral RWC)
Capacity:	67,500
Record attendance:	104,000 (Scotland vs Wales, 1 March 1975)

<table>
<tr><th colspan="7">Scotland's record at Murrayfield</th></tr>
<tr><th>Opponent</th><th>Played</th><th>Won</th><th>Lost</th><th>Drawn</th><th>For</th><th>Against</th></tr>
<tr><td>Ireland</td><td>42</td><td>19</td><td>22</td><td>1</td><td>582</td><td>596</td></tr>
<tr><td>England</td><td>41</td><td>21</td><td>17</td><td>3</td><td>495</td><td>499</td></tr>
<tr><td>Wales</td><td>39</td><td>21</td><td>17</td><td>1</td><td>529</td><td>522</td></tr>
<tr><td>France</td><td>34</td><td>19</td><td>14</td><td>1</td><td>419</td><td>421</td></tr>
<tr><td>Australia</td><td>14</td><td>6</td><td>8</td><td>-</td><td>173</td><td>288</td></tr>
<tr><td>New Zealand</td><td>14</td><td>-</td><td>12</td><td>2</td><td>115</td><td>331</td></tr>
<tr><td>South Africa</td><td>13</td><td>3</td><td>10</td><td>-</td><td>125</td><td>345</td></tr>
<tr><td>Italy</td><td>8</td><td>7</td><td>1</td><td>-</td><td>223</td><td>146</td></tr>
<tr><td>Romania</td><td>6</td><td>6</td><td>-</td><td>-</td><td>220</td><td>38</td></tr>
<tr><td>Samoa</td><td>5</td><td>4</td><td>-</td><td>1</td><td>127</td><td>60</td></tr>
<tr><td>Argentina</td><td>4</td><td>1</td><td>3</td><td>-</td><td>106</td><td>82</td></tr>
<tr><td>Fiji</td><td>2</td><td>2</td><td>-</td><td>-</td><td>74</td><td>39</td></tr>
<tr><td>Japan</td><td>1</td><td>1</td><td>-</td><td>-</td><td>47</td><td>9</td></tr>
<tr><td>Canada</td><td>1</td><td>1</td><td>-</td><td>-</td><td>22</td><td>6</td></tr>
<tr><td>USA</td><td>1</td><td>1</td><td>-</td><td>-</td><td>53</td><td>6</td></tr>
<tr><td>Tonga</td><td>1</td><td>1</td><td>-</td><td>-</td><td>43</td><td>20</td></tr>
<tr><td>Uruguay</td><td>1</td><td>1</td><td>-</td><td>-</td><td>43</td><td>12</td></tr>
<tr><td>Pacific Islanders</td><td>1</td><td>1</td><td>-</td><td>-</td><td>34</td><td>22</td></tr>
<tr><td>Spain</td><td>1</td><td>1</td><td>-</td><td>-</td><td>48</td><td>0</td></tr>
<tr><td>World XV</td><td>1</td><td>1</td><td>-</td><td>-</td><td>27</td><td>16</td></tr>
<tr><td>Zimbabwe</td><td>1</td><td>1</td><td>-</td><td>-</td><td>51</td><td>12</td></tr>
<tr><td>Totals</td><td>231</td><td>118</td><td>104</td><td>9</td><td>3,556</td><td>3,470</td></tr>
</table>

Photo: Adrian van de Vyver

In 1922, the SFU purchased 19 acres at Murrayfield from the Edinburgh Polo Club. Funds were raised by way of debentures; with this cash inflow construction work on the new stadium commenced and was completed in March 1925. The first test was played a few days later on 21 March when the stadium was officially opened with an international against England. During that season, Scotland had already enjoyed victories over France at Inverleith (25–4), Wales (24–14) and Ireland (14–8) and stood to win their first Five Nations Grand Slam. In front of 70,000 spectators an exhilerating game was played out, with Scotland securing a 14–11 victory, their first Grand Slam and their first match at Murrayfield. Moving to the more spacious Murrayfield was fully justified and in 1936 two wing extensions were added, increasing the seating capacity to 15,228. During the early years, numerous upgrades and extensions were undertaken, but at the outbreak of World War II in 1939, Murrayfield was offered to the nation and taken over by the Royal Army Service Corps and used as a supply depot. Full international rugby resumed on 1 February 1947. However, five years of wartime neglect had taken their toll on the stadium and so the entire structure was slowly overhauled and repaired over the next two decades. Extra rows of seats were added, changing rooms upgraded, ladies' tearooms built and in 1964 the SFU's offices were moved to the stadium. In the early 1950s, investigations were made as to the possibility of installing undersoil heating on the pitch, as winter conditions posed a constant threat to games when the pitch froze. It proved costly but in 1959 a Dr C. A. Hepburn donated £10,000 toward the cause, making Murrayfield the first stadium in the UK to have undersoil heating. On 1 March 1975, in a match against Wales, Murrayfield witnessed a world-record crowd for a rugby match with over 104,000 spectators; and all in the stadium. Memorably, Scotland went on to record a rare 12–10 victory over the star-studded Welsh side. Following this record attendance, it was decided that all future matches would be all-ticket attendances restricted to 70,000. By 1983, a new covered stand had been erected and in 1994 a revamped Murrayfield, complete with electronic scoreboard and floodlights, was opened by the Princess Royal. Murrayfield is now the exclusive venue for all Scottish internationals. Since that first test against England 84 years ago, Scotland have played every home game at Murrayfield apart from just four: two at Hampden Park in Glasgow and one apiece at Pittodrie Stadium in Aberdeen and McDiarmid Park in Perth.

Raeburn Place, Edinburgh

Established: unknown
First test: 27 March 1871 (Scotland vs England)
No. of tests: 23

Scotland's record at Raeburn Place						
Opponent	Played	Won	Lost	Drawn	For	Against
England	10	3	3	4	21	19
Ireland	7	7	-	-	43	1
Wales	6	5	1	-	51	16
Totals	23	15	4	4	115	36

Photo: Frédéric Hubert/www.flickr.com/photos/rugby_pioneers/creative commons license

Before the existence of Inverleith and Murrayfield, Scottish rugby was played predominantly at Raeburn Place in Edinburgh. It was here on Monday 27 March 1871 that the very first rugby international was played on the Raeburn Place cricket field belonging to the Edinburgh Academy. Following this, a few matches were played on another established cricket field: Hamilton Crescent in Glasgow. These fields had to be rented by the SFU at a cost of £25 per game in 1875, which rose to £30 in 1881 as the popularity of the game and gate-takings increased. The SFU became increasingly frustrated with the arrangement of renting the field, as it was in constant use by pupils of the Royal High School in Edinburgh, Saturdays included. This left little time to prepare the ground for an international, which in those days were played on Monday afternoons and very often the field had been used by the pupils on the Monday morning. In 1890, the SFU began their search for a new ground, as the cricket clubs from which the SFU rented fields complained about the unruly crowds damaging their pitches, the erection of temporary stands and the SFU's insistence that cricket club members should pay for entry to watch the games. These matters reached a head in October 1895 when the Edinburgh Academicals Club decided not to lease Raeburn Place to the SFU. With this, hurried arrangements were made to have the 1896 home match against England played at Old Hampden Park in Glasgow and the following year's against Ireland at Powderhall Stadium in Edinburgh.

South Africa

The ABSA Stadium, Durban

Established:	c.1958
First test:	21 July 1962 (South Africa vs British Lions)
No. of tests:	29 (25 South Africa , 4 neutral RWC)
Capacity:	52,000
Record attendance:	52,000 (often)
Former name:	Kings Park

South Africa's record at the ABSA Stadium						
Opponent	Played	Won	Lost	Drawn	For	Against
France	6	3	-	3	123	91
New Zealand	5	2	3	-	103	109
Australia	4	2	2	-	72	74
British Lions	3	2	1	-	44	39
Scotland	2	2	-	-	65	41
Wales	1	1	-	-	24	3
Italy	1	1	-	-	101	0
Ireland	1	1	-	-	12	10
South America	1	1	-	-	18	9
NZ Cavaliers	1	-	1	-	18	19
Totals	25	15	7	3	580	395

Photo: Newlands Rugby Museum

In 1890, the Natal Rugby Union (NRU) was formed, constructing a small stadium for its own use the following year. So small was the stadium that Durban games were held at the Kingsmead cricket ground. Despite the NRU's formation, the management of the game in Natal was shoddy and several other so-called sub-unions sprung up, including the Durban Rugby Sub-Union (DRSU). In the 1950s, the DRSU acquired the plot where the NRU's ground was situated and immediately arranged for the construction of a brand-new bigger stadium that would one day become Kings Park. The NRU management slowly got their act together to become the leading regional union and as such inherited the stadium under construction from the DRSU, which now fell under their jurisdiction. In 1953 the first stand was completed and in 1958 the stadium was officially opened by the President of the SA Rugby Board, Danie Craven, and named Kings Park Rugby Ground, with a capacity of 12,000. During the 1960s the stadium underwent extensive reconstruction to increase its capacity and by 1976 it held 44,000, in time for the New Zealand test. By 1995, the stadium's capacity had increased to 52,000 for the RWC after extensive construction during the 1980s and 1990s. The stadium was renamed ABSA Stadium in 2000 when ABSA Bank bought the naming rights; in 2005 the definite article 'The' was officially added as a prefix. The first test at Kings Park was played on 21 July 1962 when South Africa beat the British Lions 3–0. Since then, South Africa have played and beaten every major rugby-playing nation at The ABSA Stadium, with the exception of the English who have never played the Boks here. The stadium hosted the 1995 RWC semi-final between hosts South Africa and France in torrential rain with the field under several inches of water in places. Nevertheless, a capacity crowd witnessed the Boks win by 19–15 and winger James Small miraculously stop a rampant Abdelatif Bennazzi from scoring what would have been a winning try in the dying moments of the game. It was also the successful venue for the triumphant 1997 British Lions, courtesy of a late Jeremy Guscott drop goal. On 15 August 1998, the stadium hosted the finest comeback in a South African match when South Africa beat New Zealand 24–23 after trailing 5–23 in the 68th minute. On 18 June 2005, South Africa drew 30 all with France, their third draw at the stadium, for a world-record shared tally of 60 points in a match. Plans were in place to refurbish the stadium for the 2010 FIFA World Cup but these were ditched to make way for a completely new stadium. The future of The ABSA Stadium is therefore somewhat uncertain as it will have to compete with the space-age 75,000-capacity stadium next door for hosting rights.

Coca-Cola Park, Johannesburg

Established:	10 October 1927, completed 1928
First test:	21 July 1928 (South Africa vs New Zealand)
No. of tests:	45 (42 South Africa, 3 neutral RWC)
Capacity:	62,000
Record attendance:	95,000 (South Africa vs British Lions, 6 August 1955)
Former name:	Ellis Park

South Africa's record at Coca-Cola Park						
Opponent	Played	Won	Lost	Drawn	For	Against
New Zealand	11	8	3	-	255	206
Australia	10	9	1	-	276	121
British Lions	6	2	2	2	101	89
France	4	-	4	-	59	78
England	2	1	1	-	44	27
Samoa	3	3	-	-	137	30
Wales	1	1	-	-	40	11
Scotland	1	1	-	-	28	19
Argentina	2	2	-	-	109	35
World XV	1	1	-	-	22	16
NZ Cavaliers	1	1	-	-	24	10
Totals	42	29	11	2	1,095	642

Photo: New Zealand Rugby Museum

Situated in Johannesburg, Ellis Park as the stadium was known for over three generations, has become synonymous with Springbok rugby but also hosts soccer matches and other events: and cricket was played here until 1956. In 2001, a crowd stampede occurred at Ellis Park during a local soccer derby between Orlando Pirates and Kaiser Chiefs, killing 42 people and injuring more than 250: the largest stadium disaster of its kind in South Africa, with reports suggesting that some 120,000 fans were admitted into the 60,000-capacity ground. During the early years of the Transvaal Rugby Football Union (TRFU) – today the Golden Lions Rugby Union – rugby matches were played at the old Wanderers Cricket Club stadium, but wrangles between different rugby clubs and the Wanderers as to who got to play on the field eventually forced the TRFU to search for a ground of their own. In 1927, a quarry area in Doornfontein was identified and the TRFU negotiated with J. D. Ellis of the Johannesburg City Council to purchase the site. On 10 October 1927, final agreement was reached and 13 acres were leased for £600. The city granted a loan of £5,000 to the TRFU to build the new stadium and named it after Ellis who'd facilitated the deal. The stadium was officially opened in 1928 and hosted its first test against the All Blacks. However, by the 1970s, the stadium was proving inadequate and on 31 March 1979 the old stadium hosted its last match, between Transvaal and the World XV, before being demolished and rebuilt at a cost of R53 million. In the interim rugby was again played at the Wanderers. Upon its completion the stadium was put under the management of a trust and listed on the local stock exchange, today making the union the wealthiest in South Africa. In June 2008, Coca-Cola bought the naming rights and it was renamed Coca-Cola Park. Ellis Park has hosted many memorable games and is regarded as a fortress of South African rugby, much in the same way as Twickenham is to England or Eden Park to New Zealand. On 6 August 1955, it held a record crowd of 95,000 (some reports suggest over 100,000) who witnessed Springbok Jack van der Schyff miss a match-winning conversion in the last seconds of the game to lose 22–23 to the British Lions. On 15 August 1992, South Africa was readmitted to international rugby when they took on Sean Fitzpatrick's All Blacks at Ellis Park, going down 24–27. In 1995 the stadium saw the triumphant home team beat New Zealand 15–12 in a pulsating RWC climax, with Nelson Mandela donning the famous green and gold to hand the trophy to François Pienaar, an image that is embedded in the hearts of all South Africans. In 2000, South Africa ran up a record 46–40 tally against New Zealand at Ellis Park in a try-ridden game. Incredibly, despite the aura of invincibility surrounding the Springboks at Ellis Park, they have never managed to beat the French, in four outings, losing most recently in 2001 by 21–32.

EPRFU Stadium, Port Elizabeth

Established: 30 April 1960
First test: 30 April 1960 (South Africa vs Scotland)
No. of tests: 18 (16 South Africa, 2 neutral RWC)
Capacity: 33,852
Record attendance: 60,000 (South Africa vs New Zealand, 27 August 1960)
Former names: Boet Erasmus Stadium, Telkom Park

South Africa's record at EPRFU Stadium						
Opponent	Played	Won	Lost	Drawn	For	Against
British Lions	3	1	1	1	27	42
Argentina	2	2	-	-	68	47
Italy	2	2	-	-	134	17
Australia	2	2	-	-	45	17
New Zealand	2	2	-	-	22	6
France	1	1	-	-	27	13
Scotland	2	2	-	-	47	25
England	1	1	-	-	33	15
Canada	1	1	-	-	20	0
Totals	16	14	1	1	423	182

Photo: Newlands Rugby Museum

The Eastern Province Rugby Football Union (EPRFU) Stadium is more commonly known by its original name, the Boet Erasmus Stadium and affectionately as 'The Boet'. Politician Boet Erasmus was a dedicated rugby administrator in the region and did outstanding work for the EPRFU for many years. He served the rugby community with distinction and his bubbly outlook on life and sport won him many friends and admirers. The stadium was also known as Telkom Park for a brief period in the late 1990s and early years of the new millennium. It was officially opened on 30 April 1960 with a game against the first Scottish tour team to South Africa. The stadium is currently in a poor state, is badly designed, badly placed and grey and ugly. It was nicknamed *Berchtesgaden* by sportswriter A. C. Parker in reference to Hitler's Alpine retreat as, coupled with the SS-style architecture, the press box was so elevated that players looked like ants. It was also described by another as 'unlovely', while South Africa's most famous referee André Watson called it 'a hole in the ground'. It is notoriously remembered for the power failure before the 1995 RWC Pool A match between South Africa and Canada, which led to the filthy 'Battle of the Boet', with three players sent off and two cited for foul play. Yet despite its bleakness, 'The Boet' is South Africa's most successful venue: the Springboks have lost only one of 16 internationals here and that to the great 1974 British Lions team. The Springboks have beaten all the major rugby-playing nations at the ground with the exception of Ireland and Wales. The stadium continues to host test matches every two years or so due to its geographical and political position: the Eastern Cape is the Xhosa stronghold and rugby happens to be popular among the black population here. The future of the EPRFU Stadium is currently uncertain. Following the construction of a brand-new stadium for the 2010 FIFA World Cup, 'The Boet' will surely take a back seat and like the Nazi moutain lair, might end it days as pile of rubble. Few would mourn its demise.

Loftus Versfeld, Pretoria

Established: c. 1903–1906
First test: 3 September 1955 (South Africa vs British Lions)
No. of tests: 34 (29 South Africa, 5 neutral RWC)
Capacity: 45,000
Former names: Eastern Sports Ground, Minolta Loftus, Securicor Loftus

South Africa's record at Loftus Versfeld						
Opponent	Played	Won	Lost	Drawn	For	Against
New Zealand	5	1	4	-	103	170
British Lions	5	2	3	-	81	99
Australia	4	4	-	-	117	56
England	3	2	1	-	88	67
France	2	2	-	-	70	33
Wales	3	3	-	-	186	52
South America	2	2	-	-	82	33
Ireland	1	1	-	-	33	0
Samoa	1	1	-	-	60	18
Fiji	1	1	-	-	43	18
World XV	1	1	-	-	45	24
NZ Cavaliers	1	1	-	-	33	18
Totals	29	21	8	-	941	588

Photo: Newlands Rugby Museum

First used as a sports venue in 1906, in its early days Loftus Versfeld was known as the Eastern Sports Ground. It is possible that organised sport was played here from as early as 1903, with reports of rugby being played at the ground as early as 1908. The first concrete structure was erected by the Pretoria City Council in 1923 to accommodate 2,000 people. The stadium was renamed Loftus Versfeld in May 1932 when Robert Owen Loftus Versfeld died, apparently keeling over in the east stand. Loftus was the founder of organised sports in Pretoria. He was one of four rugby-playing Versfeld brothers, two of whom represented South Africa. Interestingly, Loftus Versfeld played against the first British touring side to South Africa in 1891 in the only game in which the tourists conceded any points: a try scored by his brother Charles 'Hasie' Versfeld. The name of the stadium has changed in recent times: Minolta bought the naming rights and changed the name to Minolta Loftus in 1998; in 2003 the name was changed to Securicor Loftus, reverting to Loftus Versfeld once again on 1 September 2005 when Vodacom took over the stadium sponsorship. The stadium has seen numerous upgrades, turning it into the magnificent arena it is today: the fortress where so many visiting teams struggle to win. The stadium has undergone minor upgrades in preparation for the 2010 FIFA World Cup but long-term plans are to turn it into a modern sports complex. Throughout its existence Loftus Versfeld has been home to Northern Transvaal, now the Blue Bulls, and the stadium has become synonymous with the Bulls', and the Springboks', near invincibility . South Africa have recorded world-record victories at Loftus Versfeld: 61–22 over Australia in 1997 and 96–13 against Wales in 1998. It has, however, also been the site of some of South Africa's most humiliating defeats. In 1974 the all-conquering British Lions trounced South Africa 28–9, with five tries to zero. Then in 1994, the English surprised the Springboks by winning 32–15, with Rob Andrew scoring a 'full house'. And in 2003 the All Blacks handed South Africa their heaviest home defeat in their history: 16–52. These defeats aside, the stadium has proved to be a happy hunting ground for South Africa who have beaten all major rugby-playing nations, with the exception of Scotland who have yet to play here.

Newlands, Cape Town

Established:	purchased 1888, first game 31 May 1890
First test:	5 September 1891 (South Africa vs British Isles)
No. of tests:	48 (46 South Africa, 2 neutral RWC)
Capacity:	51,100
Record attendance:	55,000 (South Africa vs British Isles, 4 August 1962)
Former names:	Norwich Park Newlands, Fedsure Park Newlands

South Africa's record at Newlands						
Opponent	Played	Won	Lost	Drawn	For	Against
British Lions	12	8	4	-	155	116
New Zealand	9	3	6	-	89	130
Australia	9	6	3	-	135	127
Ireland	3	3	-	-	73	40
England	2	2	-	-	45	9
France	3	-	1	2	35	45
Wales	1	1	-	-	19	8
Italy	1	1	-	-	26	0
World XV	1	1	-	-	20	19
Romania	1	1	-	-	21	8
Tonga	1	1	-	-	74	10
Namibia	1	1	-	-	105	13
South America	1	1	-	-	22	13
NZ Cavaliers	1	1	-	-	21	15
Totals	46	30	14	2	840	553

Photo: Newlands Rugby Museum

In 1888, the Western Province Rugby Football Union (WPRFU) decided to purchase 'a wooded site' in the leafy Cape Town suburb of Newlands for £2,500. A playing field was developed and the first rugby match was held on 31 May 1890 between Villagers and Stellenbosch. A year later on 5 September 1891 the fledgling stadium hosted its first test, against the British Isles before a crowd of 3,000 people. Given the date of this game and the demolition of the old National Stadium in Cardiff, Newlands is now the second-oldest international rugby ground in the world after Lansdowne Road in Dublin and the oldest rugby stadium in South Africa. In 1919 the first concrete stands were erected which significantly increased the stadium's capacity. In the 1970s SARB permanently moved its headquarters to Newlands. Regular stadium reconstruction programmes throughout the 1970s, 1980s and 1990s were undertaken. The stadium has hosted more internationals than any other stadium in the country, with every major rugby-playing nation having been beaten here by the Springboks, except for the French. Newlands has hosted some memorable games, not least on 5 September 1896 when Alf Richards led a Springbok team that wore the green jersey for the first time and recorded their first test victory. Some 53 years later, prop forward Okey Geffin set a world record for individual points scored in a match when he kicked 15 to single-handedly defeat the All Blacks 15–11 on 16 July 1949. In 1980, South Africa won a scintillating encounter against Bill Beaumont's British Lions, scoring five tries to one, and in 2005 South Africa beat a classy New Zealand act for the first time in Cape Town since 1976. The stadium hosted four RWC games during the 1995 RWC, including the opening game of the tournament between South Africa and reigning champions Australia, plus the unforgettable semi-final between New Zealand and England when Jonah Lomu scored the most sublime quartet of tries of all time. Newlands has changed its name in recent times due to various sponsorships: in 1996 it became Norwich Park Newlands; in 2000, Fedsure Park Newlands and then back to Newlands in 2002. As with many stadiums in South Africa, the future of Newlands is unclear with the construction of the ultra-modern Green Point Stadium for the 2010 FIFA World Cup.

Vodacom Park, Bloemfontein

Established:	c.1960
First test:	13 August 1960 (South Africa vs New Zealand)
No. of tests:	19 (16 South Africa, 3 neutral RWC)
Capacity:	37,076
Record attendance:	73,000 (South Africa vs New Zealand, 14 August 1976)
Former names:	Orange Free State Stadium, Free State Stadium

South Africa's record at Vodacom Park						
Opponent	Played	Won	Lost	Drawn	For	Against
France	3	3	-	-	76	37
Australia	2	2	-	-	44	27
New Zealand	2	-	1	1	20	26
British Isles	2	2	-	-	60	33
Ireland	2	2	-	-	68	30
England	2	1	1	-	80	37
Wales	2	2	-	-	77	36
South America	1	-	1	-	12	21
Totals	16	12	3	1	437	247

Photo: Newlands Rugby Museum

The stadium was built in 1960 in time to host its first test when New Zealand came from behind to draw 11–11 with South Africa on 13 August that year. The early stadium was a large multi-purpose sports arena with an athletics track around the oval pitch and large creaky stands built on permanent scaffolding. It was capable of hosting crowds in excess of 70,000 but safety was a major concern. With South Africa granted the 1995 RWC hosting rights, the old Orange Free State Stadium was rebuilt into the modern Vodacom Park to stage three RWC games. Vodacom Park is currently due to undergo significant alteration in time for the 2010 FIFA World Cup which will increase its capacity to 52,000. The stadium has proved a successful venue for the Springboks: they have lost just three of their 16 internationals here: one was the greatest upset in the history of South African rugby when they lost to Hugo Porta's South American team which South Africa had beaten by more than 50 points the week before.

Photo: Andrew de Klerk

Wales

The Millennium Stadium, Cardiff

Established: 1999
First test: 26 June 1999 (Wales vs South Africa)
No. of tests: 70 (65 Wales, 1 Lions, 4 neutral RWC)
Capacity: 74,500
Record attendance: 74,500 (often)

Wales's record at Millennium Stadium						
Opponent	Played	Won	Lost	Drawn	For	Against
Scotland	6	5	1	-	152	97
France	7	2	5	-	144	192
England	6	3	3	-	94	155
Italy	5	4	-	1	200	72
South Africa	6	1	5	-	121	167
Ireland	5	1	4	-	86	117
Australia	6	2	3	1	116	146
Argentina	3	2	1	-	66	68
Samoa	2	1	1	-	81	44
Canada	4	4	-	-	160	79
New Zealand	5	-	5	-	64	184
Japan	3	3	-	-	234	33
Romania	2	2	-	-	147	16
Fiji	2	2	-	-	69	24
USA	1	1	-	-	42	10
Tonga	1	1	-	-	51	7
Pacific Islanders	1	1	-	-	38	20
Totals	65	35	28	2	1,865	1,431

Photo: Adrian van de Vyver

Photo: al_green/Alan/ commons.wikimedia.org/

In 1994, a redevelopment committee was established to consider rebuilding the old National Stadium but when Wales was chosen to host the 1999 RWC, it was decided to build a completely new, modern facility to replace the National Stadium. The Millennium Stadium is the result and is today the Welsh national stadium. Wales will always remember the first test match played at the stadium, on the 26 June 1999 when they recorded their first, and to date only, victory over South Africa, with the game played before 29,000 fans in a partially built stadium. Today, the stadium features a state-of-the-art retractable roof, the second-biggest of its kind in the world, with the option of additional seating for special events. Since completion of the stadium, Wales have played all their home games here, barring two against Romania which were played in Wrexham in 2002 and 2003. The Millennium Stadium has staged matches in two RWCs: the 1999 3rd and 4th play-off and final, as well as the infamous 2007 'forward pass' quarter-final between France and New Zealand when the All Blacks got knocked out at the quarter-final stage for the first time in their history. The Millennium Stadium was the venue of the brilliant 2005 and 2008 Welsh Grand Slam games, as well as the spectacular showpiece when Wales lost 25–26 to New Zealand in 2004. And here, in 2005, Wales recorded their first victory over Australia in 18 years with a thrilling 26–24 win.